UNIX® Shells
by Example
Third Edition

Ellie Quigley

Prentice Hall PTR
Upper Saddle River, NJ 07458
www.phptr.com

ISBN 0-13-066538-X

90000

9 780130 665386

Library of Congress Cataloging-in-Publication Data
Quigley, Ellie.
 UNIX shells by example / Ellie Quigley. -- 3rd ed.
  p. cm.
 ISBN 0-13-066538-X
   1. UNIX (Computer file)   2. UNIX Shells.   I. Title.

QA76.76.O63 Q54 2001
005.4'32--dc21

                                    2001050075

Production editor/compositor: *Vanessa Moore*
Acquisitions editor: *Mark Taub*
Marketing manager: *Bryan Gambrel*
Manufacturing manager: *Maura Zaldivar*
Editorial assistant: *Sarah Hand*
Cover design director: *Jerry Votta*
Cover designer: *Anthony Gemmellaro*
Project coordinator: *Anne R. Garcia*

© 2002 by Prentice Hall PTR
Prentice-Hall, Inc.
Upper Saddle River, NJ 07458

Prentice Hall books are widely used by corporations and government agencies
for training, marketing, and resale.

The publisher offers discounts on this book when ordered in bulk quantities.
For more information, contact: Corporate Sales Department, Phone: 800-382-3419;
Fax: 201-236-7141; E-mail: corpsales@prenhall.com; or write: Prentice Hall PTR,
Corp. Sales Dept., One Lake Street, Upper Saddle River, NJ 07458.

All products or services mentioned in this book are the trademarks or service marks of their
respective companies or organizations.

Printed in the United States of America
10 9 8 7 6 5 4 3 2 1

ISBN   0-13-066538-X

Pearson Education Ltd.
Pearson Education Australia PTY, Limited
Pearson Education Singapore, Pte. Ltd
Pearson Education North Asia Ltd.
Pearson Education Canada, Ltd.
Pearson Educación de Mexico, S.A. de C.V.
Pearson Education — Japan
Pearson Education Malaysia, Pte. Ltd.
Pearson Education, Upper Saddle River, New Jersey

This book is dedicated to my papa,
Archibald MacNichol Main, Jr.,
the best father in the world.

Contents

2   The UNIX Toolbox   29

3   The *grep* Family   43

4   *sed*, the Streamlined Editor   65

8   The Interactive Bourne Shell   213

Preface

Playing the "shell" game is a lot of fun. This book was written to make your learning experience both fun and profitable. Since the first edition was published, I have heard from many of you who have been helped by my book to realize that shell programming doesn't need to be difficult at all! Learning by example makes it easy and fun. In fact, due to such positive feedback, I have been asked by Prentice Hall to produce this new, updated version to include two additional and popular shells, the Bash and TC shells. Although often associated with Linux systems, the Bash and TC shells are freely available to anyone using UNIX as well. In fact, today many UNIX users prefer these shells to the traditional UNIX shells because they offer an enhanced and flexible interactive environment, as well as improved programming capabilities.

Writing *UNIX Shells by Example* is the culmination of 19 years of teaching and developing classes for the various shells and those UNIX utilities most heavily used by shell programmers. The course notes I developed for teaching classes have been used by the University of California Santa Cruz and University of California Davis UNIX programs, Sun Microsystems Education, Apple Computer, DeAnza College, and numerous vendors throughout the world. Depending on the requirements of my client, I normally teach one shell at a time rather than all of them. To accommodate the needs of so many clients, I developed separate materials for each of the respective UNIX shells and tools.

Whether I am teaching "Grep, Sed, and Awk," "Bourne Shell for the System Administrator," or "The Interactive Korn Shell," one student always asks, "What book can I get that covers all the shells and the important utilities such as *grep*, *sed*, and *awk*? Should I get the *awk* book, or should I get a book on *grep* and *sed*? Is there one book that really covers it all? I don't want to buy three or four books in order to become a shell programmer."

In response, I can recommend a number of excellent books covering these topics separately, and some UNIX books that attempt to do it all, but the students want one book with everything and not just a quick survey. They want the UNIX tools, regular expressions, all three shells, quoting rules, a comparison of the shells, exercises, and so forth, all in one book. *This is that book.* As I wrote it, I thought about how I teach the classes and organized the chapters in the same format. In the shell programming classes, the first topic is always an introduction to what the shell is and how it works. Then we talk about the UNIX utilities such as *grep*, *sed*, and *awk*, the most important tools in the shell programmer's toolbox. When learning about the shell, it is presented first as an interactive program where everything can be accomplished at the command line, and then as a programming language where the programming constructs are described and demonstrated in shell scripts. (Since the C and TC shells are almost identical as programming languages, there are separate chapters describing interactive use, but only one chapter discussing programming constructs.) When shell programming classes are over, whether they last two days or a week or even a semester, the students are proficient and excited about writing scripts. They have learned how to play the shell game. This book will teach how to play the same game whether you take a class or just play by yourself.

Having always found that simple examples are easier for quick comprehension, each concept is captured in a small example followed by the output and an explanation of each line of the program. This method has proven to be very popular with those who learned Perl programming from my first book, *Perl by Example*, and *UNIX Shells by Example* now has been well-received for those who needed to write, read, and maintain shell programs.

The five shells are presented in parallel so that if, for example, you want to know how redirection is performed in one shell, there is a parallel discussion of that topic in each of the other shell chapters. For a quick comparison chart, see Appendix B of this book.

It is a nuisance to have to go to another book or the UNIX man pages when all you want is enough information about a particular command to jog your memory on how the command works. To save you time, Appendix A contains a list of useful commands, their syntax and definitions. Examples and explanations are provided for the more robust and often-used commands.

The comparison chart in Appendix B will help you keep the different shells straight, especially when you port scripts from one shell to another, and serve as a quick syntax check when all you need is a reminder of how the construct works.

One of the biggest hurdles for shell programmers is using quotes properly. The section on quoting rules in Appendix C presents a step-by-step process for successful quoting in some of the most complex command lines. This procedure has dramatically reduced the amount of time programmers waste when debugging scripts with futile attempts at matching quotes properly.

I think you'll find this book a valuable tutorial and reference. The objective is to explain through example and keep things simple so that you have fun learning and save time. Since the book replicates what I say in my classes, I am confident that you will be a productive shell programmer in a short amount of time. Everything you need is right here at your fingertips. Playing the shell game is fun. You'll see!

Ellie Quigley (ellieq@ellieq.com)

ACKNOWLEDGMENTS

I would like to thank and acknowledge the following people, without whose help this book would not have been published:

Mark Taub, my acquisitions editor, and Vanessa Moore, my production editor at Prentice Hall; Beth Gerra, Roberta Harvey, and Gary Wilson for reviewing the original material; Steve Hansen for hardware and software support. Finally, I would like to thank all my students at UC Santa Cruz, UC Davis, and Sun Microsystems for their feedback.

chapter

1

Introduction to UNIX Shells

1.1   Definition and Function

The shell is a special program used as an interface between the user and the heart of the UNIX operating system, a program called the *kernel*, as shown in Figure 1.1. The kernel is loaded into memory at boot-up time and manages the system until shutdown. It creates and controls processes, and manages memory, file systems, communications, and so forth. All other programs, including shell programs, reside out on the disk. The kernel loads those programs into memory, executes them, and cleans up the system when they terminate. The shell is a utility program that starts up when you log on. It allows users to interact with the kernel by interpreting commands that are typed either at the command line or in a script file.

When you log on, an interactive shell starts up and prompts you for input. After you type a command, it is the responsibility of the shell to (a) parse the command line; (b) handle wildcards, redirection, pipes, and job control; and (c) search for the command, and if found, execute that command. When you first learn UNIX, you spend most of your time executing commands from the prompt. You use the shell interactively.

If you type the same set of commands on a regular basis, you may want to automate those tasks. This can be done by putting the commands in a file, called a *script file*, and then executing the file. A shell script is much like a batch file: It is a list of UNIX commands typed into a file, and then the file is executed. More sophisticated scripts contain programming constructs for making decisions, looping, file testing, and so forth. Writing scripts not only requires learning programming constructs and techniques, but assumes that you have a good understanding of UNIX utilities and how they work. There are some utilities, such as *grep, sed*, and *awk,* that are extremely powerful tools used in scripts for the manipulation of command output and files. After you have become familiar with these tools and the programming constructs for your particular shell, you will be ready to start writing useful scripts. When executing commands from within a script, you are using the shell as a programming language.

1

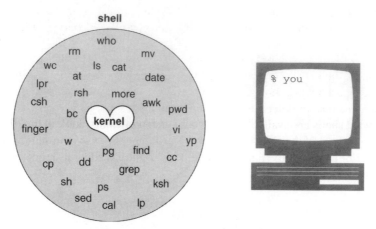

Figure 1.1   The kernel, the shell, and you.

1.1.1   The Three Major UNIX Shells

The three prominent and supported shells on most UNIX systems are the *Bourne* shell (AT&T shell), the *C* shell (Berkeley shell), and the *Korn* shell (superset of the Bourne shell). All three of these behave pretty much the same way when running interactively, but have some differences in syntax and efficiency when used as scripting languages.

The Bourne shell is the standard UNIX shell, and is used to administer the system. Most of the system administration scripts, such as the *rc start* and *stop* scripts and *shutdown* are Bourne shell scripts, and when in single user mode, this is the shell commonly used by the administrator when running as root. This shell was written at AT&T and is known for being concise, compact, and fast. The default Bourne shell prompt is the dollar sign ($).

The C shell was developed at Berkeley and added a number of features, such as command line history, aliasing, built-in arithmetic, filename completion, and job control. The C shell has been favored over the Bourne shell by users running the shell interactively, but administrators prefer the Bourne shell for scripting, because Bourne shell scripts are simpler and faster than the same scripts written in C shell. The default C shell prompt is the percent sign (%).

The Korn shell is a superset of the Bourne shell written by David Korn at AT&T. A number of features were added to this shell above and beyond the enhancements of the C shell. Korn shell features include an editable history, aliases, functions, regular expression wildcards, built-in arithmetic, job control, coprocessing, and special debugging features. The Bourne shell is almost completely upward-compatible with the Korn shell, so older Bourne shell programs will run fine in this shell. The default Korn shell prompt is the dollar sign ($).

1.1.2   The Linux Shells

Although often called "Linux" shells, Bash and TC shells are freely available and can be compiled on any UNIX system; in fact, the shells are now bundled with Solaris 8 and Sun's

UNIX operating system. But when you install Linux, you will have access to the GNU shells and tools, and not the standard UNIX shells and tools. Although Linux supports a number of shells, the Bourne Again shell (*bash*) and the TC shell (*tcsh*) are by far the most popular. The Z shell is another Linux shell that incorporates a number of features from the Bourne Again shell, the TC shell, and the Korn shell. The Public Domain Korn shell (*pdksh*) a Korn shell clone, is also available, and for a fee you can get AT&T's Korn shell, not to mention a host of other unknown smaller shells.

To see what shells are available under your version of Linux, look in the file, */etc/shell*.

To change to one of the shells listed in */etc/shell*, type the *chsh* command and the name of the shell. For example, to change permanently to the TC shell, use the *chsh* command. At the prompt, type:

```
chsh /bin/tcsh
```

1.1.3 History of the Shell

The first significant, standard UNIX shell was introduced in V7 (seventh edition of AT&T) UNIX in late 1979, and was named after its creator, Stephen Bourne. The Bourne shell as a programming language is based on a language called Algol, and was primarily used to automate system administration tasks. Although popular for its simplicity and speed, it lacks many of the features for interactive use, such as history, aliasing, and job control. Enter *bash*, the Bourne Again shell, which was developed by Brian Fox of the Free Software Foundation under the GNU copyright license and is the default shell for the very popular Linux operating system. It was intended to conform to the IEEE POSIX P1003.2/ISO 9945.2 Shell and Tools standard. Bash also offers a number of new features (both at the interactive and programming level) missing in the original Bourne shell (yet Bourne shell scripts will still run unmodified). It also incorporates the most useful features of both the C shell and Korn shell. It's big. The improvements over Bourne shell are: command line history and editing, directory stacks, job control, functions, aliases, arrays, integer arithmetic (in any base from 2 to 64), and Korn shell features, such as extended metacharacters, select loops for creating menus, the *let* command, etc.

The C shell, developed at the University of California at Berkeley in the late 1970s, was released as part of 2BSD UNIX. The shell, written primarily by Bill Joy, offered a number of additional features not provided in the standard Bourne shell. The C shell is based on the C programming language, and when used as a programming language, it shares a similar syntax. It also offers enhancements for interactive use, such as command line history, aliases, and job control. Because the shell was designed on a large machine and a number of additional features were added, the C shell has a tendency to be slow on small machines and sluggish even on large machines when compared to the Bourne shell.

The TC shell is an expanded version of the C shell. Some of the new features are: command line editing (*emacs* and *vi*), scrolling the history list, advanced filename, variable, and command completion, spelling correction, scheduling jobs, automatic locking and logout, time stamps in the history list, etc. It's also big.

With both the Bourne shell and the C shell available, the UNIX user now had a choice, and conflicts arose over which was the better shell. David Korn, from AT&T,

invented the Korn shell in the mid-1980s. It was released in 1986 and officially became part of the SVR4 distribution of UNIX in 1988. The Korn shell, really a superset of the Bourne shell, runs not only on UNIX systems, but also on OS/2, VMS, and DOS. It provides upward-compatibility with the Bourne shell, adds many of the popular features of the C shell, and is fast and efficient. The Korn shell has gone through a number of revisions. The most widely used version of the Korn shell is the 1988 version, although the 1993 version is gaining popularity. Linux users may find they are running the free version of the Korn shell, called The Public Domain Korn shell, or simply *pdksh*, a clone of David Korn's 1988 shell. It is free and portable and currently work is underway to make it fully compatible with its namesake, Korn shell, and to make it POSIX compliant. Also available is the Z shell (*zsh*), another Korn shell clone with TC shell features, written by Paul Falsted, and freely available at a number of Web sites.

1.1.4   Uses of the Shell

One of the major functions of a shell is to interpret commands entered at the command line prompt when running interactively. The shell parses the command line, breaking it into words (called *tokens*), separated by whitespace, which consists of tabs, spaces, or a newline. If the words contain special metacharacters, the shell evaluates them. The shell handles file I/O and background processing. After the command line has been processed, the shell searches for the command and starts its execution.

Another important function of the shell is to customize the user's environment, normally done in shell initialization files. These files contain definitions for setting terminal keys and window characteristics; setting variables that define the search path, permissions, prompts, and the terminal type; and setting variables that are required for specific applications such as windows, text-processing programs, and libraries for programming languages. The Korn shell and C shell also provide further customization with the addition of history and aliases, built-in variables set to protect the user from clobbering files or inadvertently logging out, and to notify the user when a job has completed.

The shell can also be used as an interpreted programming language. Shell programs, also called scripts, consist of commands listed in a file. The programs are created in an editor (although on-line scripting is permitted). They consist of UNIX commands interspersed with fundamental programming constructs such as variable assignment, conditional tests, and loops. You do not have to compile shell scripts. The shell interprets each line of the script as if it had been entered from the keyboard. Because the shell is responsible for interpreting commands, it is necessary for the user to have an understanding of what those commands are. See Appendix A for a list of useful commands.

1.1.5   Responsibilities of the Shell

The shell is ultimately responsible for making sure that any commands typed at the prompt get properly executed. Included in those responsibilities are:

1. Reading input and parsing the command line.
2. Evaluating special characters.

3. Setting up pipes, redirection, and background processing.
4. Handling signals.
5. Setting up programs for execution.

Each of these topics is discussed in detail as it pertains to a particular shell.

1.2 System Startup and the Login Shell

When you start up your system, the first process is called *init*. Each process has a process identification number associated with it, called the *PID*. Since *init* is the first process, its PID is 1. The *init* process initializes the system and then starts another process to open terminal lines and set up the standard input (*stdin*), standard output (*stdout*), and standard error (*stderr*), which are all associated with the terminal. The standard input normally comes from the keyboard; the standard output and standard error go to the screen. At this point, a login prompt would appear on your terminal.

After you type your login name, you will be prompted for a password. The */bin/login* program then verifies your identity by checking the first field in the *passwd* file. If your username is there, the next step is to run the password you typed through an encryption program to determine if it is indeed the correct password. Once your password is verified, the *login* program sets up an initial environment consisting of variables that define the working environment that will be passed on to the shell. The *HOME, SHELL, USER,* and *LOGNAME* variables are assigned values extracted from information in the *passwd* file. The *HOME* variable is assigned your home directory; the *SHELL* variable is assigned the name of the login shell, which is the last entry in the *passwd* file. The *USER* and/or *LOGNAME* variables are assigned your login name. A *search path* variable is set so that commonly used utilities may be found in specified directories When *login* has finished, it will execute the program found in the last entry of the *passwd* file. Normally, this program is a shell. If the last entry in the *passwd* file is */bin/csh*, the C shell program is executed. If the last entry in the *passwd* file is */bin/sh* or is null, the Bourne shell starts up. If the last entry is */bin/ksh*, the Korn shell is executed. This shell is called the *login shell*.

After the shell starts up, it checks for any systemwide initialization files set up by the system administrator and then checks your home directory to see if there are any shell-specific initialization files there. If any of these files exist, they are executed. The initialization files are used to further customize the user environment. After the commands in those files have been executed, a prompt appears on the screen. The shell is now waiting for your input.

1.2.1 Parsing the Command Line

When you type a command at the prompt, the shell reads a line of input and parses the command line, breaking the line into words, called tokens. Tokens are separated by spaces and tabs and the command line is terminated by a newline.[1] The shell then

---

1. The process of breaking the line up into tokens is called *lexical analysis*.

checks to see whether the first word is a built-in command or an executable program located somewhere out on disk. If it is built-in, the shell will execute the command internally. Otherwise, the shell will search the directories listed in the path variable to find out where the program resides. If the command is found, the shell will fork a new process and then execute the program. The shell will sleep (or wait) until the program finishes execution and then, if necessary, will report the status of the exiting program. A prompt will appear and the whole process will start again. The order of processing the command line is as follows:

1. History substitution is performed (if applicable).
2. Command line is broken up into tokens, or words.
3. History is updated (if applicable).
4. Quotes are processed.
5. Alias substitution and functions are defined (if applicable).
6. Redirection, background, and pipes are set up.
7. Variable substitution ($user, $name, etc.) is performed.
8. Command substitution (echo for *today is 'date'*) is performed.
9. Filename substitution, called *globbing* (*cat abc.??, rm *.c*, etc.) is performed.
10. Program execution.

1.2.2   Types of Commands

When a command is executed, it is an alias, a function, a built-in command, or an executable program on disk. Aliases are abbreviations (nicknames) for existing commands and apply to the C, TC, Bash, and Korn shells. Functions apply to the Bourne (introduced with AT&T System V, Release 2.0), Bash, and Korn shells. They are groups of commands organized as separate routines. Aliases and functions are defined within the shell's memory. Built-in commands are internal routines in the shell, and executable programs reside on disk. The shell uses the path variable to locate the executable programs on disk and forks a child process before the command can be executed. This takes time. When the shell is ready to execute the command, it evaluates command types in the following order:[2]

1. Aliases
2. Keywords
3. Functions (*bash*)
4. Built-in commands
5. Executable programs

If, for example, the command is *xyz* the shell will check to see if *xyz* is an alias. If not, is it a built-in command or a function? If neither of those, it must be an executable command residing on the disk. The shell then must search the path for the command.

---

2. Numbers 3 and 4 are reversed for Bourne and Korn(88) shells. Number 3 does not apply for C and TC shells.

1.3   Processes and the Shell

A process is a program in execution and can be identified by its unique PID (process identification) number. The kernel controls and manages processes. A process consists of the executable program, its data and stack, program and stack pointer, registers, and all the information needed for the program to run. When you start the shell, it is a process. The shell belongs to a process group identified by the group's PID. Only one process group has control of the terminal at a time and is said to be running in the foreground. When you log on, your shell is in control of the terminal and waits for you to type a command at the prompt.

The shell can spawn other processes. In fact, when you enter a command at the prompt or from a shell script, the shell has the responsibility of finding the command either in its internal code (built-in) or out on the disk and then arranging for the command to be executed. This is done with calls to the kernel, called *system calls*. A system call is a request for kernel services and is the only way a process can access the system's hardware. There are a number of system calls that allow processes to be created, executed, and terminated. (The shell provides other services from the kernel when it performs redirection and piping, command substitution, and the execution of user commands.)

The system calls used by the shell to cause new processes to run are discussed in the following sections. See Figure 1.2.

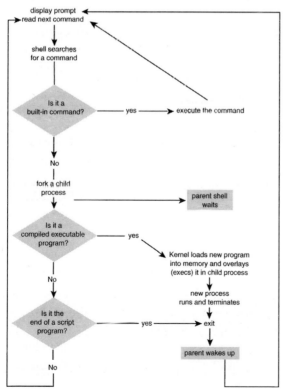

Figure 1.2   The shell and command execution.

1.3.1   What Processes Are Running?

The *ps* Command.   The *ps* command with its many options displays a list of the processes currently running in a number of formats. Example 1.1 shows all processes that are running by users on a Linux system. (See Appendix A for *ps* and its options.)

EXAMPLE   1.1

```
$ ps au   (BSD/Linux ps)   (use ps -ef for SVR4)
USER    PID %CPU %MEM   SIZE    RSS TTY STAT START   TIME COMMAND
ellie   456  0.0  1.3   1268    840   1 S    13:23   0:00 -bash
ellie   476  0.0  1.0   1200    648   1 S    13:23   0:00 sh /usr/X11R6/bin/sta
ellie   478  0.0  1.0   2028    676   1 S    13:23   0:00 xinit /home/ellie/.xi
ellie   480  0.0  1.6   1852   1068   1 S    13:23   0:00 fvwm2
ellie   483  0.0  1.3   1660    856   1 S    13:23   0:00 /usr/X11R6/lib/X11/fv
ellie   484  0.0  1.3   1696    868   1 S    13:23   0:00 /usr/X11R6/lib/X11/fv
ellie   487  0.0  2.0   2348   1304   1 S    13:23   0:00 xclock -bg #c0c0c0 -p
ellie   488  0.0  1.1   1620    724   1 S    13:23   0:00 /usr/X11R6/lib/X11/fv
ellie   489  0.0  2.0   2364   1344   1 S    13:23   0:00 xload -nolabel -bg gr
ellie   495  0.0  1.3   1272    848  p0 S    13:24   0:00 -bash
ellie   797  0.0  0.7    852    484  p0 R    14:03   0:00 ps au
root    457  0.0  0.4    724    296   2 S    13:23   0:00 /sbin/mingetty tty2
root    458  0.0  0.4    724    296   3 S    13:23   0:00 /sbin/mingetty tty3
root    459  0.0  0.4    724    296   4 S    13:23   0:00 /sbin/mingetty tty4
root    460  0.0  0.4    724    296   5 S    13:23   0:00 /sbin/mingetty tty5
root    461  0.0  0.4    724    296   6 S    13:23   0:00 /sbin/mingetty tty6
root    479  0.0  4.5  12092   2896   1 S    13:23   0:01 X :0
root    494  0.0  2.5   2768   1632   1 S    13:24   0:00 nxterm -ls -sb -fn
```

1.3.2   Creating Processes

The *fork* System Call.   A process is created in UNIX with the *fork* system call. The *fork* system call creates a duplicate of the calling process. The new process is called the *child* and the process that created it is called the *parent.* The child process starts running right after the call to *fork,* and both processes initially share the CPU. The child process has a copy of the parent's environment, open files, real and user identifications, *umask,* current working directory, and signals.

   When you type a command, the shell parses the command line and determines whether the first word is a built-in command or an executable command that resides out on the disk. If the command is built-in, the shell handles it, but if on the disk, the shell invokes the *fork* system call to make a copy of itself (Figure 1.3). Its child will search the path to find the command, as well as set up the file descriptors for redirection, pipes, command substitution, and background processing. While the child shell works, the parent normally sleeps. (See *wait,* below.)

Figure 1.3   The *fork* system call.

The *wait* System Call.   The parent shell is programmed to go to sleep (wait) while the child takes care of details such as handling redirection, pipes, and background processing. The *wait* system call causes the parent process to suspend until one of its children terminates. If *wait* is successful, it returns the PID of the child that died and the child's exit status. If the parent does not wait and the child exits, the child is put in a zombie state (suspended animation) and will stay in that state until either the parent calls *wait* or the parent dies.[3] If the parent dies before the child, the *init* process adopts any orphaned zombie process. The *wait* system call, then, is not just used to put a parent to sleep, but also to ensure that the process terminates properly.

The *exec* System Call.   After you enter a command at the terminal, the shell normally forks off a new shell process: the child process. As mentioned earlier, the child shell is responsible for causing the command you typed to be executed. It does this by calling the *exec* system call. Remember, the user command is really just an executable program. The shell searches the path for the new program. If it is found, the shell calls the *exec* system call with the name of the command as its argument. The kernel loads this new program into memory in place of the shell that called it. The child shell, then, is overlaid with the new program. The new program becomes the child process and starts executing. Although the new process has its own local variables, all environment variables, open files, signals, and the current working directory are passed to the new process. This process exits when it has finished, and the parent shell wakes up.

The *exit* System Call.   A new program can terminate at any time by executing the *exit* call. When a child process terminates, it sends a signal (*sigchild*) and waits for the parent to accept its exit status. The exit status is a number between 0 and 255. An exit status of zero indicates that the program executed successfully, and a nonzero exit status means that the program failed in some way.

For example, if the command *ls* had been typed at the command line, the parent shell would *fork* a child process and go to sleep. The child shell would then *exec* (overlay) the

---

3. To remove zombie processes, the system must be rebooted.

ls program in its place. The *ls* program would run in place of the child, inheriting all the environment variables, open files, user information, and state information. When the new process finished execution, it would exit and the parent shell would wake up. A prompt would appear on the screen, and the shell would wait for another command. If you are interested in knowing how a command exited, each shell has a special built-in variable that contains the exit status of the last command that terminated. (All of this will be explained in detail in the individual shell chapters.) See Figure 1.4 for an example of process creation and termination.

EXAMPLE 1.2

```
(C Shell)
1   % cp filex filey
    % echo $status
    0

2   % cp xyz
    Usage: cp [-ip] f1 f2; or: cp [-ipr] f1 ... fn d2
    % echo $status
    1


(Bourne and Korn Shells)
3   $ cp filex filey
    $ echo $?
    0
    $ cp xyz
    Usage: cp [-ip] f1 f2; or: cp [-ipr] f1 ... fn d2
    $ echo $?
    1
```

EXPLANATION

1   The *cp* (copy) command is entered at the C shell command line prompt. After the command has made a copy of *filex* called *filey*, the program exits and the prompt appears. The csh *status* variable contains the exit status of the last command that was executed. If the status is zero, the *cp* program exited with success. If the exit status is nonzero, the *cp* program failed in some way.

2   When entering the *cp* command, the user failed to provide two filenames: the source and destination files. The *cp* program sent an error message to the screen and exited with a status of one. That number is stored in the csh *status* variable. Any number other than zero indicates that the program failed.

3   The Bourne and Korn shells process the *cp* command as the C shell did in the first two examples. The only difference is that the Bourne and Korn shells store the exit status in the *?* variable, rather than the *status* variable.

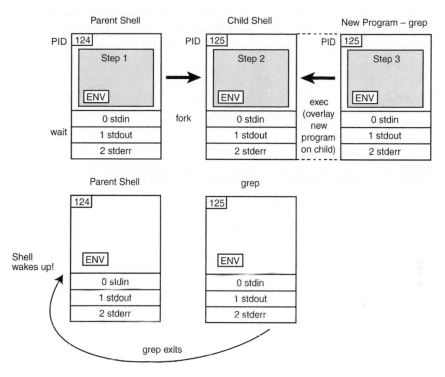

Figure 1.4 The *fork, exec, wait,* and *exit* system calls.

1   The parent shell creates a copy of itself with the *fork* system call. The copy is called the child shell.

2   The child shell has a new PID and is a copy of its parent. It will share the CPU with the parent.

3   The kernel loads the *grep* program into memory and executes (*exec*) it in place of the child shell. The *grep* program inherits the open files and environment from the child.

4   The *grep* program exits, the kernel cleans up, and the parent is awakened.

1.4 The Environment and Inheritance

When you log on, the shell starts up and inherits a number of variables, I/O streams, and process characteristics from the */bin/login* program that started it. In turn, if another shell is spawned (forked) from the login or parent shell, that child shell (*subshell*) will inherit certain characteristics from its parent. A subshell may be started for a number of reasons: for handling background processing, for handling groups of commands, or for executing scripts. The child shell inherits an environment from its parent. The environment consists of process permissions (who owns the process), the working directory, the file creation mask, special variables, open files, and signals.

1.4.1   Ownership

When you log on, the shell is given an identity. It has a real user identification (*UID*), one or more real group identifications (*GID*), and an effective user identification and effective group identification (*EUID* and *EGID*). The EUID and EGID are initially the same as the real UID and GID. These ID numbers are found in the *passwd* file and are used by the system to identify users and groups. The EUID and EGID determine what permissions a process has access to when reading, writing, or executing files. If the EUID of a process and the real UID of the owner of the file are the same, the process has the owner's access permissions for the file. If the EGID and real GID of a process are the same, the process has the owner's group privileges.

The real UID, from the */etc/passwd* file, is a positive integer associated with your login name. The real UID is the third field in the password file. When you log on, the login shell is assigned the real UID and all processes spawned from the login shell inherit its permissions. Any process running with a UID of zero belongs to root (the superuser) and has root privileges. The real group identification, the GID, associates a group with your login name. It is found in the fourth field of the password file.

The EUID and EGID can be changed to numbers assigned to a different owner. By changing the EUID (or EGID[4]) to another owner, you can become the owner of a process that belongs to someone else. Programs that change the EUID or EGID to another owner are called *setuid* or *setgid* programs. The */bin/passwd* program is an example of a *setuid* program that gives the user root privileges. *Setuid* programs are often sources for security holes. The shell allows you to create *setuid* scripts, and the shell itself may be a *setuid* program.

1.4.2   The File Creation Mask

When a file is created, it is given a set of default permissions. These permissions are determined by the program creating the file. Child processes inherit a default mask from their parents. The user can change the mask for the shell by issuing the *umask* command at the prompt or by setting it in the shell's initialization files. The *umask* command is used to remove permissions from the existing mask.

Initially, the *umask* is 000, giving a directory 777 (*rwxrwxrwx*) permissions and a file 666 (*rw–rw–rw–*) permissions as the default. On most systems, the *umask* is assigned a value of *022* by the */bin/login* program or the */etc/profile* initialization file.

The *umask* value is subtracted from the default settings for both the directory and file permissions as follows:

---

4. The *setgid* permission is system-dependent in its use. On some systems, a *setgid* on a directory may cause files created in that directory to belong to the same group that is owned by the directory. On others, the EGID of the process determines the group that can use the file.

```
 777 (Directory)         666 (File)
-022 (umask value)      -022 (umask value)
-------                  ---------
 755                     644
```

Result: **drwxr-xr-x**   **-rw-r--r--**

After the *umask* is set, all directories and files created by this process are assigned the new default permissions. In this example, directories will be given read, write, and execute for the owner; read and execute for the group; and read and execute for the rest of the world (others). Any files created will be assigned read and write for the owner, and read for the group and others. To change permissions on individual directories and permissions, the *chmod* command is used.

1.4.3   Changing Permissions with *chmod*

There is one owner for every UNIX file. Only the owner or the superuser can change the permissions on a file or directory by issuing the *chmod* command. The following example illustrates the permissions modes. A group may have a number of members, and the owner of the file may change the group permissions on a file so that the group can enjoy special privileges.

The *chown* command changes the owner and group on files and directories. Only the owner or superuser can invoke it. On BSD versions of UNIX, only the superuser, *root*, can change ownership.

Every UNIX file has a set of permissions associated with it to control who can read, write, or execute the file. A total of nine bits constitutes the permissions on a file. The first set of three bits controls the permissions of the owner of the file, the second set controls the permissions of the group, and the last set controls the permissions of everyone else. The permissions are stored in the *mode* field of the file's inode.

The *chmod* command changes permissions on files and directories. The user must own the files to change permissions on them.[5]

Table 1.1 illustrates the eight possible combinations of numbers used for changing permissions.

Table 1.1   Permission Modes

Decimal	Octal	Permissions
0	000	none
1	001	--x
2	010	-w-
3	011	-wx

---

5. The caller's EUID must match the owner's UID of the file, or the owner must be superuser.

Table 1.1　Permission Modes (continued)

4	100	r – –
5	101	r–x
6	110	rw–
7	111	rwx

The symbolic notation for *chmod* is as follows:
r = read; *w* = write; *x* = execute; *u* = user; *g* = group; *o* = others; *a* = all.

EXAMPLE 1.3

```
1   $ chmod 755 file
    $ ls -l file
    -rwxr-xr-x 1 ellie 0 Mar  7 12:52 file
2   $ chmod g+w file
    $ ls -l file
    -rwxrwxr-x  1 ellie 0 Mar 7 12:54 file
3   $ chmod go-rx file
    $ ls -l file
    -rwx-w---- 1 ellie0 Mar 7 12:56 file
4   $ chmod a=r file
    $ ls -l file
    -r--r--r-- 1 ellie 0 Mar 7 12:59 file
```

EXPLANATION

1　The first argument is the octal value *755*. It turns on *rwx* for the user, and *r* and *x* for the group and others for file.

2　In the symbolic form of *chmod*, write permission is added to the group.

3　In the symbolic form of *chmod*, read and execute permission are subtracted from the group and others.

4　In the symbolic form of *chmod*, all are given only read permission. The = sign causes all permissions to be reset to the new value.

EXAMPLE 1.4

```
(The Command Line)
1   $ chown steve filex
2   $ ls -l

(The Output)
-rwxrwxr-x 1 steve groupa 170 Jul 28:20 filex
```

EXPLANATION

1　The ownership of *filex* is changed to *steve*.

2　The *ls –l* command displays the owner *steve* in column 3.

1.4.4 Changing Ownership with the *chown* Command

The Working Directory.   When you log in, you are given a working directory within the file system, called the *home directory*. The working directory is inherited by processes spawned from this shell. Any child process of this shell can change its own working directory, but the change will have no effect on the parent shell.

The *cd* command, used to change the working directory, is a shell built-in command. Each shell has its own copy of *cd*. A built-in command is executed directly by the shell as part of the shell's code; the shell does not perform the *fork* and *exec* system calls when executing built-in commands. If another shell (script) is forked from the parent shell, and the *cd* command is issued in the child shell, the directory will be changed in the child shell. When the child exits, the parent shell will be in the same directory it was in before the child started.

EXAMPLE 1.5

```
1   % cd /

2   % pwd
    /

3   % sh

4   $ cd /home

5   $ pwd
    /home

6   $ exit

7   % pwd
    /

    %
```

EXPLANATION

1   The prompt is a C shell prompt. The *cd* command changes directory to /. The *cd* command is built into the shell's internal code.

2   The *pwd* command displays the present working directory, /.

3   The Bourne shell is started.

4   The *cd* command changes directories to /home.

5   The *pwd* command displays the present working directory, /home.

6   The Bourne shell is exited, returning back to the C shell.

7   In the C shell, the present working directory is still /. Each shell has its own copy of *cd*.

Variables.   The shell can define two types of variables: local and environment. The variables contain information used for customizing the shell, and information required by other processes so that they will function properly. Local variables are private to the shell in which they are created and not passed on to any processes spawned from that shell. Environment variables, on the other hand, are passed from parent to child process, from child to grandchild, and so on. Some of the environment variables are inherited by the login shell from the */bin/login* program. Others are created in the user initialization files, in scripts, or at the command line. If an environment variable is set in the child shell, it is not passed back to the parent.

File Descriptors.   All I/O, including files, pipes, and sockets, are handled by the kernel via a mechanism called the *file descriptor*. A file descriptor is a small unsigned integer, an index into a file-descriptor table maintained by the kernel and used by the kernel to reference open files and I/O streams. Each process inherits its own file-descriptor table from its parent. The first three file descriptors, 0, 1, and 2, are assigned to your terminal. File descriptor 0 is standard input (*stdin*), 1 is standard output (*stdout*), and 2 is standard error (*stderr*). When you open a file, the next available descriptor is 3, and it will be assigned to the new file. If all the available file descriptors are in use,[6] a new file cannot be opened.

Redirection.   When a file descriptor is assigned to something other than a terminal, it is called *I/O redirection*. The shell performs redirection of output to a file by closing the standard output file descriptor, 1 (the terminal), and then assigning that descriptor to the file (Figure 1.5).When redirecting standard input, the shell closes file descriptor 0 (the terminal) and assigns that descriptor to a file (Figure 1.6). The Bourne and Korn shells handle errors by assigning a file to file descriptor 2 (Figure 1.7). The C shell, on the other hand, goes through a more complicated process to do the same thing (Figure 1.8).

EXAMPLE 1.6

```
1   % who > file
2   % cat file1 file2 >> file3
3   % mail tom < file
4   % find / -name file -print 2> errors
5   % ( find / -name file -print > /dev/tty) >& errors
```

EXPLANATION

1   The output of the *who* command is redirected from the terminal to *file*. (All shells redirect output in this way.)

2   The output from the *cat* command (concatenate *file1* and *file2*) is appended to *file3*. (All shells redirect and append output in this way.)

3   The input of *file* is redirected to the *mail* program; that is, user *tom* will be sent the contents of *file*. (All shells redirect input in this way.)

---

6. See built-in commands, *limit* and *ulimit*.

EXPLANATION

4   Any errors from the *find* command are redirected to *errors*. Output goes to the terminal. (The Bourne and Korn shells redirect errors this way.)

5   Any errors from the *find* command are redirected to *errors*. Output is sent to the terminal. (The C shell redirects errors this way.)

Figure 1.5   Redirection of standard output.

Figure 1.6   Redirection of standard input.

find / -name filex 2> errors

Figure 1.7 Redirection of standard error (Bourne and Korn shells).

(find / -name filex > /dev/tty) >&errors

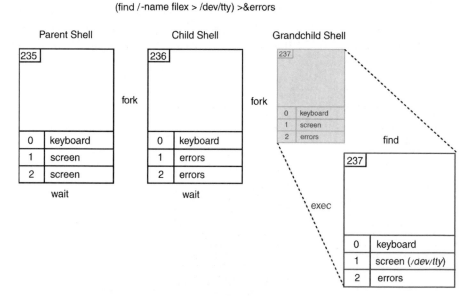

Figure 1.8 Redirection of standard error (C shell).

Pipes.   Pipes allow the output of one command to be sent to the input of another command. The shell implements pipes by closing and opening file descriptors; however, instead of assigning the descriptors to a file, it assigns them to a pipe descriptor created with the *pipe* system call. After the parent creates the pipe file descriptors, it forks a child process for each command in the pipeline. By having each process manipulate the pipe descriptors, one will write to the pipe and the other will read from it. The pipe is merely a kernel buffer from which both processes can share data, thus eliminating the need for intermediate temporary files. After the descriptors are set up, the commands are *exec*'ed concurrently. The output of one command is sent to the buffer, and when the buffer is full or the command has terminated, the command on the right-hand side of the pipe reads from the buffer. The kernel synchronizes the activities so that one process waits while the other reads from or writes from the buffer.

The syntax of the *pipe* command is

```
who | wc
```

The shell sends the output of the *who* command as input to the *wc* command. This is accomplished with the *pipe* system call. The parent shell calls the *pipe* system call, which creates two pipe descriptors, one for reading from the pipe and one for writing to it. The files associated with the pipe descriptors are kernel-managed I/O buffers used to temporarily store data, thus saving you the trouble of creating temporary files. Figures 1.9 through 1.13 illustrate the steps for implementing the pipe.

(1) The parent shell calls the *pipe* system call. Two file descriptors are returned: one for reading from the pipe and one for writing to the pipe. The file descriptors assigned are the next available descriptors in the file-descriptor (fd) table, *fd 3* and *fd 4*. See Figure 1.9.

Figure 1.9   The parent calls the *pipe* system call for setting up a pipeline.

(2) For each command, *who* and *wc*, the parent forks a child process. Both child processes get a copy of the parent's open file descriptors. See Figure 1.10.

Figure 1.10 The parent forks two child processes, one for each command in the pipeline.

(3) The first child closes its standard output. It then duplicates (the *dup* system call) file descriptor 4, the one associated with writing to the pipe. The *dup* system call copies *fd 4* and assigns the copy to the lowest available descriptor in the table, *fd 1*. After it makes the copy, the *dup* call closes *fd 4*. The child will now close *fd 3* because it does not need it. This child wants its standard *output* to go to the pipe. See Figure 1.11.

Child for who

436		436		
First Child Process		First Child Process		
ENV		ENV		After dup
0 stdin *terminal*		0 stdin *terminal*		
1 CLOSED		1 pipewriter *pipe*		
2 stderr *terminal*		2 stderr *terminal*		
3 pipereader *pipe*		3 CLOSED		
4 pipewriter *pipe*		4 CLOSED		

Figure 1.11 The first child is prepared to write to the pipe.

(4) Child 2 closes its standard input. It then duplicates (*dups*) *fd 3*, which is associated with reading from the pipe. By using *dup*, a copy of *fd 3* is created and assigned to the lowest available descriptor. Since *fd 0* was closed, it is the lowest available descriptor. *Dup* closes *fd 3*. The child closes *fd 4*. Its standard *input* will come from the pipe. See Figure 1.12.

Child for wc

Figure 1.12 The second child is prepared to read input from the pipe.

(5) The *who* command is executed in place of Child 1 and the *wc* command is executed to replace Child 2. The output of the *who* command goes into the pipe and is read by the *wc* command from the other end of the pipe. See Figure 1.13.

Figure 1.13 The output of *who* is sent to the input of *wc*.

1.4.5 The Shell and Signals

A *signal* sends a message to a process and normally causes the process to terminate, usually owing to some unexpected event such as a segmentation violation, bus error, or power failure. You can send signals to a process by pressing the Break, Delete, Quit, or Stop keys, and all processes sharing the terminal are affected by the signal sent. You can kill a process with the *kill* command. By default, most signals terminate the program. The shells allow you to handle signals coming into your program, either by ignoring them or by specifying some action to be taken when a specified signal arrives. The C shell is limited to handling ^C (Control-C).

1.5 Executing Commands from Scripts

When the shell is used as a programming language, commands and shell control constructs are typed in an editor and saved to a file, called a script. The lines from the file are read and executed one at a time by the shell. These programs are interpreted, not compiled. Compiled programs are converted into machine language before they are executed. Therefore, shell programs are usually slower than binary executables, but they are easier to write and are used mainly for automating simple tasks. Shell programs can also be written interactively at the command line, and for very simple tasks, this is the quickest way. However, for more complex scripting, it is easier to write scripts in an editor (unless you are a really great typist). The following script can be executed by any shell to output the same results. Figure 1.14 illustrates the creation of a script called *doit* and how it fits in with already existing UNIX programs/utilities/commands.

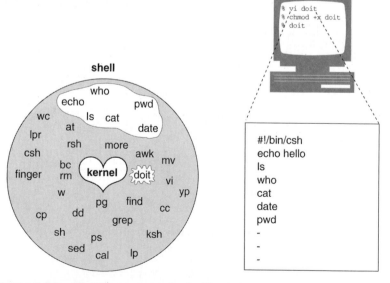

Figure 1.14 Creating a generic shell script.

EXPLANATION

1   Go into your favorite editor and type in a set of UNIX commands, one per line. Indicate what shell you want by placing the pathname of the shell after the *#!* on the first line. This program is being executed by the C shell and it is named *doit*.

2   Save your file and turn on the execute permissions so that you can run it.

3   Execute your program just as you would any other UNIX command.

1.5.1 Sample Scripts: Comparing Three Shells

At first glance, the following three programs look very similar. They are. And they all do the same thing. The main difference is the syntax. After you have worked with all three shells for some time, you will quickly adapt to the differences and start formulating your own opinions about which shell is your favorite. A detailed comparison of differences among the C, Bourne, and Korn shells is found in Appendix B.

The following scripts send a mail message to a list of users, inviting each of them to a party. The place and time of the party are set in variables. The people to be invited are selected from a file called *guests*. A list of foods is stored in a word list, and each person is asked to bring one of the foods from the list. If there are more users than food items, the list is reset so that each user is asked to bring a different food. The only user who is not invited is the user *root*.

1.5.2 The C Shell Script

EXAMPLE 1.7

```
1   #!/bin/csh -f
2   # The Party Program--Invitations to friends from the "guest" file
3   set guestfile = ~/shell/guests
4   if ( ! -e "$guestfile" ) then
        echo "$guestfile:t non-existent"
        exit 1
    endif
5   setenv PLACE "Sarotini's"
    @ Time = `date +%H` + 1
    set food = ( cheese crackers shrimp drinks "hot dogs" sandwiches )
6   foreach person ( `cat $guestfile` )
        if ( $person =~ root ) continue
```

EXAMPLE 1.7 (CONTINUED)

```
7      mail -v -s "Party" $person << FINIS    # Start of here document
       Hi ${person}! Please join me at $PLACE for a party!
       Meet me at $Time o'clock.
       I'll bring the ice cream. Would you please bring $food[1] and
       anything else you would like to eat? Let me know if you can't
       make it. Hope to see you soon.
           Your pal,
           ellie@`hostname`         # or `uname -n`
   FINIS
8      shift food
       if ( $#food ==  0 ) then
           set food = ( cheese crackers shrimp drinks "hot dogs"
                         sandwiches )
       endif
9  end

   echo "Bye..."
```

EXPLANATION

1   This line lets the kernel know that you are running a C shell script. The –*f* option is a fast startup. It says, "Do not execute the *.cshrc* file," an initialization file that is automatically executed every time a new csh program is started.

2   This is a comment. It is ignored by the shell, but important for anyone trying to understand what the script is doing.

3   The variable *guestfile* is set to the full pathname of a file called *guests*.

4   This line reads: If the file *guests* does not exist, then print to the screen "*guests nonexistent*" and exit from the script with an exit status of 1 to indicate that something went wrong in the program.

5   Set variables are assigned the values for the place, time, and list of foods to bring. The *PLACE* variable is an environment variable. The *Time* variable is a local variable. The @ symbol tells the C shell to perform its built-in arithmetic; that is, add 1 to the *Time* variable after extracting the hour from the *date* command. The *Time* variable is spelled with an uppercase *T* to prevent the C shell from confusing it with one of its reserved words, *time*.

6   For each person on the guest list, except the user *root*, a mail message will be created inviting the person to a party at a given place and time, and asking him or her to bring one of the foods on the list.

7   The mail message is created in what is called a *here document*. All text from the user-defined word *FINIS* to the final *FINIS* will be sent to the *mail* program. The *foreach* loop shifts through the list of names, performing all of the instructions from the *foreach* to the keyword *end*.

8   After a message has been sent, the food list is shifted so that the next person will get the next food item on the list. If there are more people than food items, the food list will be reset to ensure that each person is instructed to bring a food item.

9   This marks the end of the looping statements.

1.5.3 The Bourne Shell Script

EXAMPLE 1.8

```
1   #!/bin/sh
2   # The Party Program--Invitations to friends from the "guest" file
3   guestfile=/home/jody/ellie/shell/guests
4   if [ ! -f "$guestfile" ]
    then
        echo "`basename $guestfile` non-existent"
        exit 1
    fi
5   PLACE="Sarotini's"
    export PLACE
    Time=`date +%H`
    Time=`expr $Time + 1`
    set cheese crackers shrimp drinks "hot dogs" sandwiches
6   for person in `cat $guestfile`
    do
        if [ $person =~ root ]
        then
                continue
        else
7           mail -v -s "Party" $person <<- FINIS
            Hi ${person}! Please join me at $PLACE for a party!
            Meet me at $Time o'clock.
            I'll bring the ice cream. Would you please bring $1 and
            anything else you would like to eat? Let me know if you
            can't make it. Hope to see you soon.
                Your pal,
                ellie@`hostname`
            FINIS
8           shift
            if [ $# -eq 0 ]
            then
                set cheese crackers shrimp drinks "hot dogs" sandwiches
            fi
        fi
9   done
    echo "Bye..."
```

EXPLANATION

1   This line lets the kernel know that you are running a Bourne shell script.

2   This is a comment. It is ignored by the shell, but important for anyone trying to understand what the script is doing.

3   The variable *guestfile* is set to the full pathname of a file called *guests*.

4   This line reads: If the file *guests* does not exist, then print to the screen "*guests non-existent*" and exit from the script.

5   Variables are assigned the values for the place and time. The list of foods to bring is assigned to special variables (positional parameters) with the *set* command.

6   For each person on the guest list, except the user *root*, a mail message will be created inviting each person to a party at a given place and time, and asking each to bring a food from the list.

7   The mail message is sent when this line is uncommented. It is not a good idea to uncomment this line until the program has been thoroughly debugged, otherwise the e-mail will be sent to the same people every time the script is tested. The next statement, using the *cat* command with the *here document*, allows the script to be tested by sending output to the screen that would normally be sent through the mail when line 7 is uncommented.

8   After a message has been sent, the food list is shifted so that the next person will get the next food on the list. If there are more people than foods, the food list will be reset, insuring that each person is assigned a food.

9   This marks the end of the looping statements.

1.5.4 The Korn Shell Script

EXAMPLE 1.9

```
1   #!/bin/ksh
2   # The Party Program--Invitations to friends from the "guest" file
3   guestfile=~/shell/guests
4   if [[ ! -a "$guestfile" ]]
    then
        print "${guestfile##*/} non-existent"
        exit 1
    fi
5   export PLACE="Sarotini's"
    (( Time=$(date +%H) + 1 ))
    set cheese crackers shrimp drinks "hot dogs" sandwiches
6   for person in $(< $guestfile)
    do
        if  [[ $person = root ]]
        then
            continue
        else
```

EXAMPLE 1.9 (CONTINUED)

```
                    # Start of here document
7                   mail -v -s "Party" $person <<- FINIS
                    Hi ${person}! Please join me at $PLACE for a party!
                    Meet me at $Time o'clock.
                    I'll bring the ice cream. Would you please bring $1
                    and anything else you would like to eat? Let me know
                    if you can't make it.
                            Hope to see you soon.
                                    Your pal,
                                    ellie@`hostname`
                    FINIS
8                   shift
                    if (( $# == 0 ))
                    then
                       set cheese crackers shrimp drinks "hot dogs" sandwiches
                    fi
              fi
9         done
          print "Bye..."
```

EXPLANATION

1   This line lets the kernel know that you are running a Korn shell script.

2   This is a comment. It is ignored by the shell, but important for anyone trying to understand what the script is doing.

3   The variable *guestfile* is set to the full pathname of a file called *guests*.

4   This line reads: If the file *guests* does not exist, then print to the screen "*guests non-existent*" and exit from the script.

5   Variables are assigned the values for the place and time. The list of foods to bring is assigned to special variables (positional parameters) with the *set* command.

6   For each person on the guest list, except the user *root*, a mail message will be created inviting the person to a party at a given place and time, and assigning a food from the list to bring.

7   The mail message is sent. The body of the message is contained in a *here document*.

8   After a message has been sent, the food list is shifted so that the next person will get the next food on the list. If there are more people than foods, the food list will be reset, insuring that each person is assigned a food.

9   This marks the end of the looping statements.

chapter
2

The UNIX Toolbox

There are hundreds of UNIX utilities available, and many of them are everyday commands such as *ls, pwd, who,* and *vi*. Just as there are essential tools that a carpenter uses, there are also essential tools the shell programmer needs to write meaningful and efficient scripts. The three major utilities that will be discussed in detail here are *grep, sed,* and *awk*. These programs are the most important UNIX tools available for manipulating text, output from a pipe, or standard input. In fact, *sed* and *awk* are often used as scripting languages by themselves. Before you fully appreciate the power of *grep, sed,* and *awk,* you must have a good foundation on the use of regular expressions and regular expression metacharacters. A complete list of useful UNIX utilities is found in Appendix A of this book.

2.1 Regular Expressions

2.1.1 Definition and Example

For users already familiar with the concept of regular expression metacharacters, this section may be bypassed. However, this preliminary material is crucial to understanding the variety of ways in which *grep, sed,* and *awk* are used to display and manipulate data.

What is a regular expression? A regular expression[1] is just a pattern of characters used to match the same characters in a search. In most programs, a regular expression is enclosed in forward slashes; for example, */love/* is a regular expression delimited by forward slashes, and the pattern *love* will be matched any time the same pattern is found in the line being searched. What makes regular expressions interesting is that they can be controlled by special metacharacters. If you are new to the idea of regular expressions, let us look at an example that will help you understand what this whole concept

---

1. If you receive an error message that contains the string *RE*, there is a problem with the regular expression you are using in the program.

29

is about. Suppose that you are working in the vi editor on an e-mail message to your friend. It looks like this:

% **vi letter**

```
-------------------------------------------------------------
Hi tom,
I think I failed my anatomy test yesterday. I had a terrible
stomach ache. I ate too many fried green tomatoes.
Anyway, Tom, I need your help. I'd like to make the test up
tomorrow, but don't know where to begin studying. Do you
think you could help me? After work, about 7 PM, come to
my place and I'll treat you to pizza in return for your help. Thanks.
                                    Your pal,
                                    guy@phantom



~
~
~
~
-------------------------------------------------------------
```

Now, suppose you find out that Tom never took the test either, but David did. You also notice that in the greeting, you spelled *Tom* with a lowercase *t*. So you decide to make a global substitution to replace all occurrences of *tom* with *David*, as follows:

% **vi letter**

```
-------------------------------------------------------------
Hi David,
I think I failed my anaDavidy test yeserday. I had a terrible
sDavidachache. I think I ate too many fried green Davidatoes.
Anyway, Tom, I need your help. I'd like to make the test up
Davidorrow, but don't know where to begin studying. Do you
think you could help me? After work, about 7 PM, come to
my place and I'll treat you to pizza in return for your help. Thanks.
                                    Your pal,
                                    guy@phanDavid



~
~
~

-->   :1,$s/tom/David/g
-------------------------------------------------------------
```

The regular expression in the search string is *tom*. The replacement string is *David*. The *vi* command reads "for lines 1 to the end of the file ($), substitute *tom* everywhere it is found on each line and replace it with *David*." Hardly what you want! And one of the occurrences of *Tom* was untouched because you only asked for *tom*, not *Tom*, to be replaced with *David*. So what to do?

Regular expression metacharacters are special characters that allow you to delimit a pattern in some way so that you can control what substitutions will take place. There are metacharacters to anchor a word to the beginning or end of a line. There are metacharacters that allow you to specify any characters, or some number of characters, to find both upper- and lowercase characters, digits only, and so forth. For example, to change the name *tom* or *Tom* to *David*, the following *vi* command would have done the job:

```
:1,$s/\<[Tt]om\>/David/g
```

This command reads, "From the first line to the last line of the file (*1,$*), substitute (*s*) the word *Tom* or *tom* with *David*," and the g flag says to do this globally (i.e., make the substitution if it occurs more than once on the same line). The regular expression metacharacters are \< and \> for beginning and end of a word, and the pair of brackets, [*Tt*], match for one of the characters enclosed within them (in this case, for either *T* or *t*). There are five basic metacharacters that all UNIX pattern-matching utilities recognize, and then an extended set of metacharacters that vary from program to program.

2.1.2 Regular Expression Metacharacters

Table 2.1 presents regular expression metacharacters that can be used in all versions of *vi, ex, grep, egrep, sed,* and *awk*. Additional metacharacters are described for each of the utilities where applicable.

Table 2.1 Regular Expression Metacharacters

Metacharacter	Function	Example	What It Matches
^	Beginning-of-line anchor	/^love/	Matches all lines beginning with *love*.
$	End-of-line anchor	/love$/	Matches all lines ending with *love*.
.	Matches one character	/l..e/	Matches lines containing an *l*, followed by two characters, followed by an *e*.
*	Matches zero or more of the preceding characters	/ *love/	Match lines with zero or more spaces, followed by the pattern *love*.
[ ]	Matches one in the set	/[Ll]ove/	Matches lines containing *love* or *Love*.

Table 2.1 Regular Expression Metacharacters (continued)

Metacharacter	Function	Example	What It Matches
[x–y]	Matches one character within a range in the set	/[A–Z]ove/	Matches letters from A through Z followed by ove.
[^]	Matches one character not in the set	/[^A–Z]/	Matches any character not in the range between A and Z.
\	Used to escape a metacharacter	/love\./	Matches lines containing love, followed by a literal period. Normally the period matches one of any character.

Additional metacharacters are supported by many UNIX programs that use RE metacharacters:

\<	Beginning-of-word anchor	/\<love/	Matches lines containing a word that begins with love (supported by vi and grep).
\>	End-of-word anchor	/love\>/	Matches lines containing a word that ends with love (supported by vi and grep).
\(..\)	Tags match characters to be used later	/\(love\)able \1er/	May use up to nine tags, starting with the first tag at the left-most part of the pattern. For example, the pattern love is saved as tag 1, to be referenced later as \1; in this example, the search pattern consists of lovable followed by lover (supported by sed, vi, and grep).
x\{m\} or x\{m,\} or x\{m,n\}	Repetition of character x, m times, at least m times, at least m and not more than n times[a]	o\{5,10\}	Matches if line contains between 5 and 10 consecutive occurrences of the letter o (supported by vi and grep).

a. Not dependable on all versions of UNIX or all pattern-matching utilities; usually works with vi and grep.

Assuming that you know how the vi editor works, each metacharacter is described in terms of the vi search string. In the following examples, characters are highlighted to demonstrate what vi will find in its search.

EXAMPLE 2.1

```
(A Simple Regular Expression Search)
% vi picnic
------------------------------------------------------------
I had a lovely time on our little picnic.
Lovers were all around us. It is springtime. Oh
love, how much I adore you. Do you know
the extent of my love? Oh, by the way, I think
I lost my gloves somewhere out in that field of
clover. Did you see them?  I can only hope love
is forever. I live for you. It's hard to get back in the
groove.



~

~

~

/love/
------------------------------------------------------------
```

EXPLANATION

The regular expression is *love*. The pattern *love* is found by itself and as part of other words, such as *lovely, gloves,* and *clover.*

EXAMPLE 2.2

```
(The Beginning-of-Line Anchor (^))
% vi picnic
------------------------------------------------------------
I had a lovely time on our little picnic.
Lovers were all around us. It is springtime. Oh
love, how much I adore you. Do you know
the extent of my love? Oh, by the way, I think
I lost my gloves somewhere out in that field of
clover. Did you see them? I can only hope love
is forever. I live for you. It's hard to get back in the
groove.
~

~

~

/^love/
------------------------------------------------------------
```

EXPLANATION

The caret (^) is called the beginning-of-line anchor. *Vi* will find only those lines where the regular expression *love* is matched at the beginning of the line, i.e., *love* is the first set of characters on the line; it cannot be preceded by even one space.

EXAMPLE 2.3

```
(The End-of-Line Anchor ($))
% vi picnic
--------------------------------------------------------------
I had a lovely time on our little picnic.
Lovers were all around us. It is springtime. Oh
love, how much I adore you. Do you know
the extent of my love? Oh, by the way, I think
I lost my gloves somewhere out in that field of
clover. Did you see them? I can only hope love
is forever. I live for you. It's hard to get back in the
groove.


    ~
    ~
    ~

/love$/
--------------------------------------------------------------
```

EXPLANATION

The dollar sign ($) is called the end-of-line anchor. *Vi* will find only those lines where the regular expression *love* is matched at the end of the line, i.e., *love* is the last set of characters on the line and is directly followed by a newline.

EXAMPLE 2.4

```
(Any Single Character (.))
% vi picnic
--------------------------------------------------------------
I had a lovely time on our little picnic.
Lovers were all around us. It is springtime. Oh
love, how much I adore you. Do you know
the extent of my love? Oh, by the way, I think
I lost my gloves somewhere out in that field of
clover. Did you see them? I can only hope love
is forever. I live for you. It's hard to get back in the
groove.


    ~
    ~
    ~

/l.ve/
--------------------------------------------------------------
```

EXPLANATION

The dot (.) matches any one character, except the newline. *Vi* will find those lines where the regular expression consists of an *l*, followed by any single character, followed by a *v* and an *e*. It finds combinations of *love* and *live*.

EXAMPLE 2.5

```
(Zero or More of the Preceding Character (*))
% vi picnic
----------------------------------------------------------------
I had a lovely time on our little picnic.
Lovers were all around us. It is springtime. Oh
love, how much I adore you. Do you know
the extent of my love? Oh, by the way, I think
I lost my gloves somewhere out in that field of
clover. Did you see them? I can only hope love
is forever. I live for you. It's hard to get back in the
groove.


~

~

~

/o*ve/
---    -------------------------------------------     --------------------
```

EXPLANATION

The asterisk (*) matches zero or more of the preceding character.[2] It is as though the asterisk were glued to the character directly before it and controls only that character. In this case, the asterisk is glued to the letter *o*. It matches for only the letter *o* and as many consecutive occurrences of the letter *o* as there are in the pattern, even no occurrences of *o* at all. Vi searches for zero or more occurrences of the letter *o* followed by a *v* and an *e*, finding *love*, *loooove*, *lve*, and so forth.

EXAMPLE 2.6

```
(A Set of Characters ([]))
% vi picnic
---------  -------------------------------------------------------
I had a lovely time on our little picnic.
Lovers were all around us. It is springtime. Oh
love, how much I adore you. Do you know
the extent of my love? Oh, by the way, I think
I lost my gloves somewhere out in that field of
clover. Did you see them? I can only hope love
is forever. I live for you. It's hard to get back in the
```

---

2. Do not confuse this metacharacter with the shell wildcard (*). They are totally different. The shell asterisk matches for zero or more of any character, whereas the regular expression asterisk matches for zero or more of the preceding character.

```
groove.

~
~
~
/[Ll]ove/
```

EXPLANATION

The square brackets match for one of a set of characters. *Vi* will search for the regular expression containing either an uppercase or lowercase *l* followed by an *o*, *v*, and *e*.

EXAMPLE 2.7

```
(A Range of Characters ( [ - ] ))
% vi picnic
```

```
I had a lovely time on our little picnic.
Lovers were all around us. It is springtime. Oh
love, how much I adore you. Do you know
the extent of my love? Oh, by the way, I think
I lost my gloves somewhere out in that field of
clover. Did you see them? I can only hope love
is forever. I live for you. It's hard to get back in the
groove.

~
~
~
/ove[a-z]/
```

EXPLANATION

The dash between characters enclosed in square brackets matches one character in a range of characters. *Vi* will search for the regular expression containing an *o*, *v*, and *e*, followed by any character in the ASCII range between *a* and *z*. Since this is an ASCII range, the range cannot be represented as [*z–a*].

EXAMPLE 2.8

```
(Not One of the Characters in the Set ([^]))
% vi picnic
----------------------------------------------------------------
I had a lovely time on our little picnic.
Lovers were all around us. It is springtime. Oh
love, how much I adore you. Do you know
the extent of my love? Oh, by the way, I think
I lost my gloves somewhere out in that field of
clover. Did you see them? I can only hope love
is forever. I live for you. It's hard to get back in the
groove.


~

~

~

/ove[^a-zA-Z0-9]/
----------------------------------------------------------------
```

EXPLANATION

The caret inside square brackets is a negation metacharacter. *Vi* will search for the regular expression containing an *o*, *v*, and *e*, followed by any character *not* in the ASCII range between *a* and *z*, *not* in the range between *A* and *Z*, and *not* a digit between *0* and *9*. For example, it will find *ove* followed by a comma, a space, a period, and so on, because those characters are *not* in the set.

2.2   Combining Regular Expression Metacharacters

Now that basic regular expression metacharacters have been explained, they can be combined into more complex expressions. Each of the regular expression examples enclosed in forward slashes is the search string and is matched against each line in the text file.

EXAMPLE 2.9

```
Note: The line numbers are NOT part of the text file. The vertical
bars mark the left and right margins.
     ----------------------------------------------------------------
1    |Christian Scott lives here and will put on a Christmas party.|
2    |There are around 30 to 35 people invited.                    |
3    |They are:                                                    |
4    |                                                          Tom|
5    |Dan                                                          |
6    |    Rhonda Savage                                            |
7    |Nicky and Kimberly.                                          |
8    |Steve, Suzanne, Ginger and Larry,                            |
     ----------------------------------------------------------------
```

EXPLANATION

a */^[A–Z]..$/*
Will find all lines beginning with a capital letter, followed by two of any character, followed by a newline. Will find *Dan* on line 5.

b */^[A–Z][a–z]*3[0–5]/*
Will find all lines beginning with an uppercase letter, followed by zero or more lowercase letters or spaces, followed by the number 3 and another number between *0* and 5. Will find line 2.

c */[a–z]*\./*
Will find lines containing zero or more lowercase letters, followed by a literal period. Will find lines 1, 2, 7, and 8.

d */^ *[A–Z][a–z][a–z]$/*
Will find a line that begins with zero or more spaces (tabs do not count as spaces), followed by an uppercase letter, two lowercase letters, and a newline. Will find *Tom* on line 4 and *Dan* on line 5.

e */^[A–Za–z]*[^,][A–Za–z]*$/*
Will find a line that begins with zero or more uppercase and/or lowercase letters, followed by a noncomma, followed by zero or more upper- or lowercase letters and a newline. Will find line 5.

2.2.1 More Regular Expression Metacharacters

The following metacharacters are not necessarily portable across all utilities using regular expressions, but can be used in the *vi* editor and some versions of *sed* and *grep*. There is an extended set of metacharacters available with *egrep* and *awk*, which will be discussed in later sections.

EXAMPLE 2.10

```
(Beginning-of-Word (\<) and End-of-Word (\>) Anchors)
% vi textfile
------------------------------------------------------------
Unusual occurrences happened at the fair.
--> Patty won fourth place in the 50 yard dash square and fair.
Occurrences like this are rare.
The winning ticket is 55222.
The ticket I got is 54333 and Dee got 55544.
Guy fell down while running around the south bend in his last
event.
~
~
~
/\<fourth\>/
------------------------------------------------------------
```

EXPLANATION

Will find the word *fourth* on each line. The \< is the beginning-of-word anchor and the \> is the end-of-word anchor. A word can be separated by spaces, end in punctuation, start at the beginning of a line, end at the end of a line, and so forth.

EXAMPLE 2.11

```
    % vi textfile
    -------------------------------------------------------------
    Unusual occurrences happened at the fair.
--> Patty won fourth place in the 50 yard dash square and fair.
    Occurrences like this are rare.
    The winning ticket is 55222.
    The ticket I got is 54333 and Dee got 55544.
--> Guy fell down while running around the south bend in his last
    event.
    ~

    ~

    /\<f.*th\>/
    -------------------------------------------------------------
```

EXPLANATION

Will find any word (or group of words) beginning with an *f*, followed by zero or more of any character (.*), and a string ending with *th*.

EXAMPLE 2.12

```
    (Remembered Patterns \( and \))
       % vi textfile (Before Substitution)
    --------------------------     --------------------------------
    Unusual occurences happened at the fair.
    Patty won fourth place in the 50 yard dash square and fair.
    Occurences like this are rare.
    The winning ticket is 55222.
    The ticket I got is 54333 and Dee got 55544.
    Guy fell down while running around the south bend in his last
    event.
    ~
    ~
    ~
  1 :1,$s/\([Oo]ccur\)ence/\1rence/
    -------------------------------------------------------------
```

EXAMPLE 2.12 (CONTINUED)

```
        % vi textfile (After Substitution)
        -------------------------------------------------
--> Unusual occurrences happened at the fair.
    Patty won fourth place in the 50 yard dash square and fair.
--> Occurrences like this are rare.
    The winning ticket is 55222.
    The ticket I got is 54333 and Dee got 55544.
    Guy fell down while running around the south bend in his last
    event.
    ~
    ~
    ~
        -------------------------------------------------------------
```

EXPLANATION

1   The editor searches for the entire string *occurence* or *Occurrence* (note: the words
    are misspelled), and if found, the pattern portion enclosed in parentheses is
    tagged (i.e., either *occur* or *Occur* is tagged). Since this is the first pattern tagged,
    it is called tag 1. The pattern is stored in a memory register called register 1. On
    the replacement side, the contents of the register are replaced for *\1* and the rest
    of the word, *rence*, is appended to it. We started with *occurence* and ended up with
    occurrence.

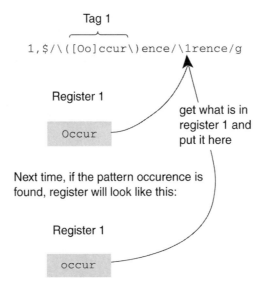

Figure 2.1   Remembered patterns and tags.

EXAMPLE 2.13

```
% vi textfile (Before Substitution)
------------------------------------------------------------
Unusual occurrences happened at the fair.
Patty won fourth place in the 50 yard dash square and fair.
Occurrences like this are rare.
The winning ticket is 55222.
The ticket I got is 54333 and Dee got 55544.
Guy fell down while running around the south bend in his last
event.
~
~
~
```

1   `:s/\(square\) and \(fair\)/\2 and \1/`
```
------------------------------------------------------------

% vi textfile (After Substitution)
------------------------------------------------------------
Unusual occurrences happened at the fair.
```
-->
```
Patty won fourth place in the 50 yard dash fair and square.
Occurrences like this are rare.
The winning ticket is 55222.
The ticket I got is 54333 and Dee got 55544.
Guy fell down while running around the south bend in his last
event.
~
~
~
------------------------------------------------------------
```

EXPLANATION

1   The editor searches for the regular expression *square and fair*, and tags *square* as 1
     and *fair* as 2. On the replacement side, the contents of register 2 are substituted
     for \2 and the contents of register 1 are substituted for \1. See Figure 2.2.

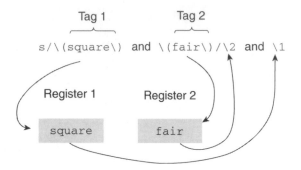

Figure 2.2   Using more than one tag.

```
(Repetition of Patterns ( \{n\} ))
    % vi textfile
    -------------------------------------------
    Unusual occurrences happened at the fair.
    Patty won fourth place in the 50 yard dash square and fair.
    Occurrences like this are rare.
--> The winning ticket is 55222.
    The ticket I got is 54333 and Dee got 55544.
    Guy fell down while running around the south bend in his last
    event.
    ~
    ~
    ~
    ~
1   /5\{2\}2\{3\}\./
    -----------------------------------------------------------------
```

1   Searches for lines containing two occurrences of the number 5, followed by three occurrences of the number 2, followed by a literal period.

chapter
3

The *grep* Family

The *grep* family consists of the commands *grep*, *egrep*, and *fgrep*. The *grep* command globally searches for regular expressions in files and prints all lines that contain the expression. The *egrep* and *fgrep* commands are simply variants of *grep*. The *egrep* command is an extended *grep*, supporting more regular expression metacharacters. The *fgrep* command, called *fixed grep*, and sometimes *fast grep*, treats all characters as literals; that is, regular expression metacharacters aren't special—they match themselves. The Free Software Foundation provides a free version of *grep*, called GNU *grep*. These versions of *grep* are the ones used on Linux systems, and can be found in */usr/xpg4/bin* on Sun's Solaris OS. The GNU version of *grep* has extended the basic regular expression metacharacter set, added POSIX compliancy, and included a number of new command line options. They also provide a recursive *grep* called *rgrep* for descending entire directory trees.

3.1   The *grep* Command

3.1.1   The Meaning of *grep*

The name *grep* can be traced back to the *ex* editor. If you invoked that editor and wanted to search for a string, you would type at the *ex* prompt:

```
: /pattern/p
```

The first line containing the string *pattern* would be printed as "*p*" by the *print* command. If you wanted all the lines that contained *pattern* to be printed, you would type:

```
: g/pattern/p
```

When g precedes *pattern*, it means "all lines in the file," or "perform a global substitution."

Because the search pattern is called a *regular expression*, we can substitute *RE* for *pattern* and the command reads:

```
: g/RE/p
```

And there you have it: the meaning of *grep* and the origin of its name. It means "globally search for the regular expression (*RE*) and print out the line." The nice part of using *grep* is that you do not have to invoke an editor to perform a search, and you do not need to enclose the regular expression in forward slashes. It is much faster than using *ex* or *vi*.

3.1.2 How *grep* Works

The *grep* command searches for a pattern of characters in a file or multiple files. If the pattern contains whitespace, it must be quoted. The pattern is either a quoted string or a single word[1], and all other words following it are treated as filenames. *Grep* sends its output to the screen and does not change or affect the input file in any way.

FORMAT

```
grep word filename filename
```

EXAMPLE 3.1

```
grep Tom /etc/passwd
```

EXPLANATION

Grep will search for the pattern *Tom* in a file called */etc/passwd*. If successful, the line from the file will appear on the screen; if the pattern is not found, there will be no output at all; and if the file is not a legitimate file, an error will be sent to the screen. If the pattern is found, *grep* returns an exit status of 0, indicating success; if the pattern is not found, the exit status returned is 1; and if the file is not found, the exit status is 2.

The *grep* program can get its input from a standard input or a pipe, as well as from files. If you forget to name a file, *grep* will assume it is getting input from standard input, the keyboard, and will stop until you type something. If coming from a pipe, the output of a command will be piped as input to the *grep* command, and if a desired pattern is matched, *grep* will print the output to the screen.

---

1. A word is also called a token.

EXAMPLE 3.2

```
% ps -ef | grep root
```

EXPLANATION

The output of the *ps* command (*ps –ef* displays all processes running on this system) is sent to *grep* and all lines containing *root* are printed.

The *grep* command supports a number of regular expression metacharacters (see Table 3.1) to help further define the search pattern. It also provides a number of options (see Table 3.2) to modify the way it does its search or displays lines. For example, you can provide options to turn off case sensitivity, display line numbers, display errors only, and so on.

EXAMPLE 3.3

```
% grep -n  '^jack:' /etc/passwd
```

EXPLANATION

Grep searches the */etc/passwd* file for *jack*; if *jack* is at the beginning of a line, *grep* prints out the number of the line on which *jack* was found and where in the line *jack* was found.

Table 3.1   *grep*'s Regular Expression Metacharacters

Metacharacter	Function	Example	What It Matches
^	Beginning-of-line anchor	'^love'	Matches all lines beginning with *love*.
$	End-of-line anchor	'love$'	Matches all lines ending with *love*.
.	Matches one character	'l..e'	Matches lines containing an *l*, followed by two characters, followed by an *e*.
*	Matches zero or more characters	' *love'	Matches lines with zero or more spaces, followed by the pattern *love*.
[ ]	Matches one character in the set	'[Ll]ove'	Matches lines containing *love* or *Love*.
[^]	Matches one character not in the set	'[^A–K]ove'	Matches lines not containing a character in the range *A* through *K*, followed by *ove*.
\<	Beginning-of-word anchor	'\<love'	Matches lines containing a word that begins with *love*.
\>	End-of-word anchor	'love\>'	Matches lines containing a word that ends with *love*.
\(..\)	Tags matched characters	'\(love\)ing'	Tags marked portion in a register to be remembered later as number 1. To reference later, use \1 to repeat the pattern. May use up to nine tags, starting with the first tag at the left-most part of the pattern. For example, the pattern *love* is saved in register 1 to be referenced later as \1.
x\{m\} x\{m,\} x\{m,n\}[a]	Repetition of character x: m times, at least m times, or between m and n times	'o\{5\}' 'o\{5,\}' 'o\{5,10\}'	Matches if line has 5 occurences of *o*, at least 5 occurences of *o*, or between 5 and 10 occurrences of *o*.

a.   The \{ \} metacharacters are not supported on all versions of UNIX or all pattern-matching utilities; they usually work with *vi* and *grep*.

Table 3.2 *grep*'s Options

Option	What It Does
–b	Precedes each line by the block number on which it was found. This is sometimes useful in locating disk block numbers by context.
–c	Displays a count of matching lines rather than displaying the lines that match.
–h	Does not display filenames.
–i	Ignores the case of letters in making comparisons (i.e., upper- and lowercase are considered identical).
–l	Lists only the names of files with matching lines (once), separated by newline characters.
–n	Precedes each line by its relative line number in the file.
–s	Works silently, that is, displays nothing except error messages. This is useful for checking the exit status.
–v	Inverts the search to display only lines that do not match.
–w	Searches for the expression as a word, as if surrounded by \< and \>. This applies to *grep* only. (Not all versions of *grep* support this feature; e.g., SCO UNIX does not.)

3.1.3 *grep* and Exit Status

The *grep* command is very useful in shell scripts, because it always returns an exit status to indicate whether it was able to locate the pattern or the file you were looking for. If the pattern is found, *grep* returns an exit status of 0, indicating success; if *grep* cannot find the pattern, it returns 1 as its exit status; and if the file cannot be found, *grep* returns an exit status of 2. (Other UNIX utilities that search for patterns, such as *sed* and *awk*, do not use the exit status to indicate the success or failure of locating a pattern; they report failure only if there is a syntax error in a command.)

In the following example, *john* is not found in the */etc/passwd* file.

EXAMPLE 3.4

```
1   % grep 'john' /etc/passwd
2   % echo $status (csh)
    1


    or


    $ echo $? (sh, ksh)
    1
```

EXPLANATION

1   *Grep* searches for *john* in the */etc/passwd* file, and if successful, *grep* exits with a status of 0. If *john* is not found in the file, *grep* exits with 1. If the file is not found, an exit status of 2 is returned.

2   The C shell variable, *status*, and the Bourne/Korn shell variable, *?*, are assigned the exit status of the last command that was executed.

3.2 *grep* Examples with Regular Expressions

The file being used for these examples is called *datafile*.

```
% cat datafile
northwest       NW    Charles Main        3.0    .98    3    34
western         WE    Sharon Gray         5.3    .97    5    23
southwest       SW    Lewis Dalsass       2.7    .8     2    18
southern        SO    Suan Chin           5.1    .95    4    15
southeast       SE    Patricia Hemenway   4.0    .7     4    17
eastern         EA    TB Savage           4.4    .84    5    20
northeast       NE    AM Main Jr.         5.1    .94    3    13
north           NO    Margot Weber        4.5    .89    5     9
central         CT    Ann Stephens        5.7    .94    5    13
```

EXAMPLE 3.5

```
grep NW datafile
northwest    NW    Charles Main    3.0    .98    3    34
```

EXPLANATION

Prints all lines containing the regular expression NW in a file called *datafile*.

EXAMPLE 3.6

```
grep NW d*
datafile: northwest   NW   Charles Main   3.0  .98  3    34
db:northwest          NW   Joel Craig     30   40   5    123
```

EXPLANATION

Prints all lines containing the regular expression NW in all files starting with a *d*. The shell expands *d** to all files that begin with a *d*, in this case the filenames are *db* and *datafile*.

EXAMPLE 3.7

```
grep '^n' datafile
```
northwest	NW	Charles Main	3.0	.98	3	34
northeast	NE	AM Main Jr.	5.1	.94	3	13
north	NO	Margot Weber	4.5	.89	5	9

EXPLANATION

Prints all lines beginning with an *n*. The caret (^) is the beginning-of-line anchor.

EXAMPLE 3.8

```
grep '4$' datafile
```
| northwest | NW | Charles Main | 3.0 | .98 | 3 | 34 |

EXPLANATION

Prints all lines ending with a *4*. The dollar sign ($) is the end of line anchor.

EXAMPLE 3.9

```
grep TB Savage datafile
grep: Savage: No such file or directory
datafile:eastern   EA TB Savage        4.4  .84  5  20
```

EXPLANATION

Since the first argument is the pattern and all of the remaining arguments are filenames, *grep* will search for *TB* in a file called *Savage* and a file called *datafile*. To search for *TB Savage*, see the next example.

EXAMPLE 3.10

```
grep 'TB Savage' datafile
```
| eastern | EA | TB Savage | 4.4 | .84 | 5 | 20 |

EXPLANATION

Prints all lines containing the pattern *TB Savage*. Without quotes (in this example, either single or double quotes will do), the whitespace between *TB* and *Savage* would cause *grep* to search for *TB* in a file called *Savage* and a file called *datafile*, as in the previous example.

```
% cat datafile
northwest         NW      Charles Main         3.0    .98    3    34
western           WE      Sharon Gray          53     .97    5    23
southwest         SW      Lewis Dalsass        2.7    .8     2    18
southern          SO      Suan Chin            5.1    .95    4    15
southeast         SE      Patricia Hemenway    4.0    .7     4    17
eastern           EA      TB Savage            4.4    .84    5    20
northeast         NE      AM Main Jr.          5.1    .94    3    13
north             NO      Margot Weber         4.5    .89    5    9
central           CT      Ann Stephens         5.7    .94    5    13
```

EXAMPLE 3.11

```
grep '5\..' datafile
western           WE      Sharon Gray          5.3    .97    5    23
southern          SO      Suan Chin            5.1    .95    4    15
northeast         NE      AM Main Jr.          5.1    .94    3    13
central           CT      Ann Stephens         5.7    .94    5    13
```

EXPLANATION

Prints a line containing the number 5, followed by a literal period and any single character. The "dot" metacharacter represents a single character, unless it is escaped with a backslash. When escaped, the character is no longer a special metacharacter, but represents itself, a literal period.

EXAMPLE 3.12

```
grep '\.5' datafile
north             NO      Margot Weber         4.5    .89    5    9
```

EXPLANATION

Prints any line containing the expression .5.

EXAMPLE 3.13

```
grep '^[we]' datafile
western           WE      Sharon Gray          5.3    .97    5    23
eastern           EA      TB Savage            4.4    .84    5    20
```

EXPLANATION

Prints lines beginning with either a *w* or an *e*. The caret (^) is the beginning-of-line anchor, and either one of the characters in the brackets will be matched.

EXAMPLE 3.14

```
grep '[^0-9]' datafile
```

northwest	NW	Charles Main	3.0	.98	3	34
western	WE	Sharon Gray	5.3	.97	5	23
southwest	SW	Lewis Dalsass	2.7	.8	2	18
southern	SO	Suan Chin	5.1	.95	4	15
southeast	SE	Patricia Hemenway	4.0	.7	4	17
eastern	EA	TB Savage	4.4	.84	5	20
northeast	NE	AM Main Jr.	5.1	.94	3	13
north	NO	Margot Weber	4.5	.89	5	9
central	CT	Ann Stephens	5.7	.94	5	13

EXPLANATION

Prints all lines containing one non-digit. Because all lines have at least one non-digit, all lines are printed. (See the –v option.)

EXAMPLE 3.15

```
grep '[A-Z][A-Z] [A-Z]' datafile
```

| eastern | EA | TB Savage | 4.4 | .84 | 5 | 20 |
| northeast | NE | AM Main Jr. | 5.1 | .94 | 3 | 13 |

EXPLANATION

Prints all lines containing two capital letters followed by a space and a capital letter, e.g., *TB Savage* and *AM Main*.

EXAMPLE 3.16

```
grep 'ss* ' datafile
```

| northwest | NW | Charles Main | 3.0 | .98 | 3 | 34 |
| southwest | SW | Lewis Dalsass | 2.7 | .8 | 2 | 18 |

EXPLANATION

Prints all lines containing an *s* followed by zero or more consecutive occurrences of the letter *s* and a space. Finds *Charles* and *Dalsass*.

```
% cat datafile
```

northwest	NW	Charles Main	3.0	.98	3	34
western	WE	Sharon Gray	53	.97	5	23
southwest	SW	Lewis Dalsass	2.7	.8	2	18
southern	SO	Suan Chin	5.1	.95	4	15
southeast	SE	Patricia Hemenway	4.0	.7	4	17
eastern	EA	TB Savage	4.4	.84	5	20
northeast	NE	AM Main Jr.	5.1	.94	3	13
north	NO	Margot Weber	4.5	.89	5	9
central	CT	Ann Stephens	5.7	.94	5	13

EXAMPLE 3.17

```
grep '[a-z]\{9\}' datafile
```

northwest	NW	Charles Main	3.0	.98	3	34
southwest	SW	Lewis Dalsass	2.7	.8	2	18
southeast	SE	Patricia Hemenway	4.0	.7	4	17
northeast	NE	AM Main Jr.	5.1	.94	3	13

EXPLANATION

Prints all lines where there are at least nine consecutive lowercase letters, for example, *northwest*, *southwest*, *southeast*, and *northeast*.

EXAMPLE 3.18

```
grep '\(3\)\.[0-9].*\1    *\1' datafile
```

| northwest | NW | Charles Main | 3.0 | .98 | 3 | 34 |

EXPLANATION

Prints the line if it contains a 3 followed by a period and another number, followed by any number of characters (.*), another 3 (originally tagged), any number of tabs, and another 3. Since the 3 was enclosed in parentheses, \(3\), it can be later referenced with \1. \1 means that this was the first expression to be tagged with the \(\) pair.

EXAMPLE 3.19

```
grep '\<north' datafile
```
northwest	NW	Charles Main	3.0	.98	3	34
northeast	NE	AM Main Jr.	5.1	.94	3	13
north	NO	Margot Weber	4.5	.89	5	9

EXPLANATION

Prints all lines containing a word starting with *north*. The \< is the beginning-of-word anchor.

EXAMPLE 3.20

```
grep '\<north\>' datafile
```
north	NO	Margot Weber	4.5	.89	5	9

EXPLANATION

Prints the line if it contains the word *north*. The \< is the beginning-of-word anchor, and the \> is the end-of-word anchor.

EXAMPLE 3.21

```
grep '\<[a-z].*n\>' datafile
```
northwest	NW	Charles Main	3.0	.98	3	34
western	WE	Sharon Gray	5.3	.97	5	23
southern	SO	Suan Chin	5.1	.95	4	15
eastern	EA	TB Savage	4.4	.84	5	20
northeast	NE	AM Main Jr.	5.1	.94	3	13
central	CT	Ann Stephens	5.7	.94	5	13

EXPLANATION

Prints all lines containing a word starting with a lowercase letter, followed by any number of characters, and a word ending in *n*. Watch the . * symbol. It means any character, including whitespace.

3.3 *grep* with Pipes

Instead of taking its input from a file, *grep* often gets its input from a pipe.

```
% ls -1
drwxrwxrwx  2   ellie      2441 Jan 6 12:34     dir1
-rw-r--r--  1   ellie      1538 Jan 2 15:50     file1
-rw-r--r--  1   ellie      1539 Jan 3 13:36     file2
drwxrwxrwx  2   ellie      2341 Jan 6 12:34     grades

% ls -1 | grep '^d'
drwxrwxrwx  2   ellie      2441 Jan 6 12:34     dir1
drwxrwxrwx  2   ellie      2341 Jan 6 12:34     grades
```

EXPLANATION

The output of the *ls* command is piped to *grep*. All lines of output that begin with a *d*
are printed; that is, all directories are printed.

3.4 *grep* with Options

The *grep* command has a number of options that control its behavior. Not all versions of
UNIX support exactly the same options, so be sure to check your man pages for a complete list.

% cat datafile						
northwest	NW	Charles Main	3.0	.98	3	34
western	WE	Sharon Gray	53	.97	5	23
southwest	SW	Lewis Dalsass	2.7	.8	2	18
southern	SO	Suan Chin	5.1	.95	4	15
southeast	SE	Patricia Hemenway	4.0	.7	4	17
eastern	EA	TB Savage	4.4	.84	5	20
northeast	NE	AM Main Jr.	5.1	.94	3	13
north	NO	Margot Weber	4.5	.89	5	9
central	CT	Ann Stephens	5.7	.94	5	13

EXAMPLE 3.23

```
grep -n '^south' datafile
```
```
3:southwest       SW      Lewis Dalsass        2.7   .8    2    18
4:southern        SO      Suan Chin            5.1   .95   4    15
5:southeast       SE      Patricia Hemenway    4.0   .7    4    17
```

EXPLANATION

The –*n* option precedes each line with the number of the line where the pattern was found, followed by the line.

EXAMPLE 3.24

```
grep -i 'pat' datafile
```
```
southeast         SE      Patricia Hemenway    4.0   .7    4    17
```

EXPLANATION

The –*i* option turns off case sensitivity. It does not matter if the expression *pat* contains any combination of upper- or lowercase letters.

EXAMPLE 3.25

```
grep -v 'Suan Chin' datafile
```
```
northwest         NW      Charles Main         3.0   .98   3    34
western           WE      Sharon Gray          5.3   .97   5    23
southwest         SW      Lewis Dalsass        2.7   .8    2    18
southeast         SE      Patricia Hemenway    4.0   .7    4    17
eastern           EA      TB Savage            4.4   .84   5    20
northeast         NE      AM Main Jr.          5.1   .94   3    13
north             NO      Margot Weber         4.5   .89   5    9
central           CT      Ann Stephens         5.7   .94   5    13
```

EXPLANATION

Here, the –*v* option prints all lines *not* containing the pattern *Suan Chin*. This option is used when deleting a specific entry from the input file. To really remove the entry, you would redirect the output of *grep* to a temporary file, and then change the name of the temporary file back to the name of the original file as shown here:

```
grep -v 'Suan Chin' datafile > temp
mv temp datafile
```

Remember that you must use a temporary file when redirecting the output from *datafile*. If you redirect from *datafile* to *datafile*, the shell will "clobber" the *datafile*. (See "Redirection" on page 16.)

```
% cat datafile
```

northwest	NW	Charles Main	3.0	.98	3	34
western	WE	Sharon Gray	53	.97	5	23
southwest	SW	Lewis Dalsass	2.7	.8	2	18
southern	SO	Suan Chin	5.1	.95	4	15
southeast	SE	Patricia Hemenway	4.0	.7	4	17
eastern	EA	TB Savage	4.4	.84	5	20
northeast	NE	AM Main Jr.	5.1	.94	3	13
north	NO	Margot Weber	4.5	.89	5	9
central	CT	Ann Stephens	5.7	.94	5	13

EXAMPLE 3.26

```
grep -l 'SE' *
datafile
datebook
```

EXPLANATION

The –*l* option causes *grep* to print out only the filenames where the pattern is found instead of the line of text.

EXAMPLE 3.27

```
grep -c 'west' datafile
3
```

EXPLANATION

The –*c* option causes *grep* to print the number of lines where the pattern was found. This does not mean the number of occurrences of the pattern. For example, if *west* is found three times on a line, it only counts the line once.

EXAMPLE 3.28

```
grep  -w 'north' datafile
north            NO      Margot Weber      4.5  .89   5   9
```

EXPLANATION

The –*w* option causes *grep* to find the pattern only if it is a word,[2] not part of a word. Only the line containing the word *north* is printed, not *northwest*, *northeast*, etc.

---

2. A word is a sequence of alphanumeric characters starting at the beginning of a line or preceded by whitespace and ending in whitespace, punctuation, or a newline.

EXAMPLE 3.29

```
echo $LOGNAME
lewis
grep -i "$LOGNAME" datafile
southwest        SW      Lewis Dalsass    2.7  .8   2    18
```

EXPLANATION

The value of the shell ENV variable, *LOGNAME*, is printed. It contains the user's login name. If the variable is enclosed in double quotes, it will still be expanded by the shell, and in case there is more than one word assigned to the variable, whitespace is shielded from shell interpretation. If single quotes are used, variable substitution does not take place; that is, $*LOGNAME* is printed.

3.4.1   *grep* Review

Table 3.3 contains examples of *grep* commands and what they do.

Table 3.3   Review of *grep*

grep *Command*	*What It Does*
grep '\<Tom\>' file	Prints lines containing the word *Tom*.
grep 'Tom Savage' file	Prints lines containing *Tom Savage*.
grep '^Tommy' file	Prints lines if *Tommy* is at the beginning of the line.
grep '\.bak$' file	Prints lines ending in .*bak*. Single quotes protect the dollar sign ($) from interpretation.
grep '[Pp]yramid' *	Prints lines from all files containing *pyramid* or *Pyramid* in the current working directory.
grep '[A–Z]' file	Prints lines containing at least one capital letter.
grep '[0–9]' file	Prints lines containing at least one number.
grep '[A–Z]...[0–9]' file	Prints lines containing five-character patterns starting with a capital letter and ending with a number.
grep –w '[tT]est' files	Prints lines with the word *Test* and/or *test*.
grep –s "Mark Todd" file	Finds lines containing *Mark Todd*, but does not print the line. Can be used when checking *grep's* exit status.
grep –v 'Mary' file	Prints all lines not containing *Mary*.
grep –i 'sam' file	Prints all lines containing *sam*, regardless of case (e.g., *SAM, sam, SaM, sAm*).

Table 3.3   Review of *grep* (continued)

grep *Command*	*What It Does*
grep –l 'Dear Boss' *	Lists all filenames containing *Dear Boss*.
grep –n 'Tom' file	Precedes matching lines with line numbers.
grep "$name" file	Expands the value of variable *name* and prints lines containing that value. Must use double quotes.
grep '$5' file	Prints lines containing literal *$5*. Must use single quotes.
ps –ef| grep "^ *user1"	Pipes output of *ps –ef* to *grep*, searching for *user1* at the beginning of a line, even if it is preceded by zero or more spaces.

3.5   *egrep* (Extended *grep*)

The main advantage of using *egrep* is that additional regular expression metacharacters (see Table 3.4) have been added to the set provided by *grep*. The \(\) and \{ \}, however, are not allowed. (See GNU *grep –E* if using Linux.)

Table 3.4   *egrep*'s Regular Expression Metacharacters

Metacharacter	Function	Example	What It Matches
^	Beginning-of-line anchor	'^love'	Matches all lines beginning with *love*.
$	End-of-line anchor	'love$'	Matches all lines ending with *love*.
.	Matches one character	'l..e'	Matches lines containing an *l*, followed by two characters, followed by an *e*.

Table 3.4 *egrep*'s Regular Expression Metacharacters (continued)

Metacharacter	Function	Example	What It Matches
*	Matches zero or more characters	'*love'	Matches lines with zero or more spaces of the preceding characters followed by the pattern *love*.
[ ]	Matches one character in the set	'[Ll]ove'	Matches lines containing *love* or *Love*.
[^]	Matches one character not in the set	'[^A–KM–Z]ove'	Matches lines not containing *A* through *K* or *M* through *Z*, followed by *ove*.
New with egrep:			
+	Matches one or more of the preceding characters	'[a–z]+ove'	Matches one or more lowercase letters, followed by *ove*. Would find *move*, *approve*, *love*, *behoove*, etc.
?	Matches zero or one of the preceding characters	'lo?ve'	Matches for an *l* followed by either one or not any occurrences of the letter *o*. Would find *love* or *lve*.
a|b	Matches either a or b	'love|hate'	Matches for either expression, *love* or *hate*.
()	Groups characters	'love(able|ly) (ov)+'	Matches for *lovable* or *lovely*. Matches for one or more occurrences of *ov*.

3.5.1 *egrep* Examples

The following example illustrates only the way the new extended set of regular expression metacharacters is used with *egrep*. The *grep* examples presented earlier illustrate the use of the standard metacharacters, which behave the same way with *egrep*. *Egrep* also uses the same options at the command line as *grep*.

```
% cat datafile
northwest          NW      Charles Main        3.0   .98   3   34
western            WE      Sharon Gray         53    .97   5   23
southwest          SW      Lewis Dalsass       2.7   .8    2   18
southern           SO      Suan Chin           5.1   .95   4   15
southeast          SE      Patricia Hemenway   4.0   .7    4   17
eastern            EA      TB Savage           4.4   .84   5   20
northeast          NE      AM Main Jr.         5.1   .94   3   13
north              NO      Margot Weber        4.5   .89   5   9
central            CT      Ann Stephens        5.7   .94   5   13
```

EXAMPLE 3.30

```
egrep 'NW|EA' datafile
northwest          NW      Charles Main        3.0   .98   3   34
eastern            EA      TB Savage           4.4   .84   5   20
```

EXPLANATION

Prints the line if it contains either the expression *NW* or the expression *EA*.

EXAMPLE 3.31

```
egrep '3+' datafile
northwest          NW      Charles Main        3.0   .98   3   34
western            WE      Sharon Gray         5.3   .97   5   23
northeast          NE      AM Main             5.1   .94   3   13
central            CT      Ann Stephens        5.7   .94   5   13
```

EXPLANATION

Prints all lines containing one or more occurrences of the number 3.

EXAMPLE 3.32

```
egrep '2\.?[0-9]' datafile
western            WE      Sharon Gray         5.3   .97   5   23
southwest          SW      Lewis Dalsass       2.7   .8    2   18
eastern            EA      TB Savage           4.4   .84   5   20
```

EXPLANATION

Prints all lines containing a 2, followed by zero or one period, followed by a number.

EXAMPLE 3.33

```
egrep '(no)+' datafile
northwest      NW     Charles Main    3.0  .98   3   34
northeast      NE     AM Main         5.1  .94   3   13
north          NO     Margot Weber    4.5  .89   5    9
```

EXPLANATION

Prints lines containing one or more consecutive occurrences of the pattern group *no*.

EXAMPLE 3.34

```
egrep 'S(h|u)' datafile
western        WE     Sharon Gray     5.3  .97   5   23
southern       SO     Suan Chin       5.1  .95   4   15
```

EXPLANATION

Prints all lines containing *S*, followed by either *h* or *u*.

EXAMPLE 3.35

```
egrep 'Sh|u' datafile
western        WE     Sharon Gray        5.3  .97   5   23
southern       SO     Suan Chin          5.1  .95   4   15
southwest      SW     Lewis Dalsass      2.7  .8    2   18
southeast      SE     Patricia Hemenway  4.0  .7    4   17
```

EXPLANATION

Prints all lines containing the expression *Sh* or *u*.

3.5.2 *egrep* Review

Table 3.5 contains examples of *egrep* commands and what they do.

Table 3.5 Review of *egrep*

egrep *Command*	*What It Does*
egrep '^ +' *file*	Prints lines beginning with one or more spaces.
egrep '^ *' *file*	Prints lines beginning with zero or more spaces.[a]
egrep '(Tom | Dan) Savage' *file*	Prints lines containing *Tom Savage* or *Dan Savage*.

Table 3.5   Review of *egrep* (continued)

egrep *Command*	*What It Does*
egrep '(ab)+' file	Prints lines with one or more occurrences of *ab*.
egrep '^X[0–9]?' file	Prints lines beginning with *X* followed by zero or one single digit.
egrep 'fun\.$' *	Prints lines ending in *fun.* from all files.[a]
egrep '[A–Z]+' file	Prints lines containing one or more capital letters.
egrep '[0–9]' file	Prints lines containing a number.[a]
egrep '[A–Z]...[0–9]' file	Prints lines containing five-character patterns starting with a capital letter, followed by three of any character, and ending with a number.[a]
egrep '[tT]est' files	Prints lines with *Test* and/or *test*.[a]
egrep "Susan Jean" file	Prints lines containing *Susan Jean*.[a]
egrep –v 'Mary' file	Prints all lines NOT containing *Mary*.[a]
egrep –i 'sam' file	Prints all lines containing *sam*, regardless of case (e.g., *SAM, sam, SaM, sAm,* etc.).[a]
egrep –l 'Dear Boss' *	Lists all filenames containing *Dear Boss*.[a]
egrep –n 'Tom' file	Precedes matching lines with line numbers.[a]
egrep –s "$name" file	Expands variable name, finds it, but prints nothing. Can be used to check the exit status of *egrep*.[a]

a. *egrep* and *grep* handle this pattern in the same way.

3.6   Fixed *grep* or Fast *grep*

The *fgrep* command behaves like *grep*, but does not recognize any regular expression metacharacters as being special. All characters represent only themselves. A caret is simply a caret, a dollar sign is a dollar sign, and so forth. (See GNU *grep –F* if using Linux.)

EXAMPLE 3.36

```
% fgrep '[A-Z]****[0-9]..$5.00'  file
```

EXPLANATION

Finds all lines in the file containing the literal string *[A–Z]****[0–9]..$5.00*. All characters are treated as themselves. There are no special characters.

UNIX TOOLS LAB EXERCISE

Lab 1: *grep* Exercise

Steve Blenheim:238-923-7366:95 Latham Lane, Easton, PA 83755:11/12/56:20300
Betty Boop:245-836-8357:635 Cutesy Lane, Hollywood, CA 91464:6/23/23:14500
Igor Chevsky:385-375-8395:3567 Populus Place, Caldwell, NJ 23875:6/18/68:23400
Norma Corder:397-857-2735:74 Pine Street, Dearborn, MI 23874:3/28/45:245700
Jennifer Cowan:548-834-2348:583 Laurel Ave., Kingsville, TX 83745:10/1/35:58900
Jon DeLoach:408-253-3122:123 Park St., San Jose, CA 04086:7/25/53:85100
Karen Evich:284-758-2857:23 Edgecliff Place, Lincoln, NB 92743:7/25/53:85100
Karen Evich:284-758-2867:23 Edgecliff Place, Lincoln, NB 92743:11/3/35:58200
Karen Evich:284-758-2867:23 Edgecliff Place, Lincoln, NB 92743:11/3/35:58200
Fred Fardbarkle:674-843-1385:20 Parak Lane, DeLuth, MN 23850:4/12/23:780900
Fred Fardbarkle:674-843-1385:20 Parak Lane, DeLuth, MN 23850:4/12/23:780900
Lori Gortz:327-832-5728:3465 Mirlo Street, Peabody, MA 34756:10/2/65:35200
Paco Gutierrez:835-365-1284:454 Easy Street, Decatur, IL 75732:2/28/53:123500
Ephram Hardy:293-259-5395:235 CarltonLane, Joliet, IL 73858:8/12/20:56700
James Ikeda:834-938-8376:23445 Aster Ave., Allentown, NJ 83715:12/1/38:45000
Barbara Kertz:385-573-8326:832 Ponce Drive, Gary, IN 83756:12/1/46:268500
Lesley Kirstin:408-456-1234:4 Harvard Square, Boston, MA 02133:4/22/62:52600
William Kopf:846-836-2837:6937 Ware Road, Milton, PA 93756:9/21/46:43500
Sir Lancelot:837-835-8257:474 Camelot Boulevard, Bath, WY 28356:5/13/69:24500
Jesse Neal:408-233-8971:45 Rose Terrace, San Francisco, CA 92303:2/3/36:25000
Zippy Pinhead:834-823-8319:2356 Bizarro Ave., Farmount, IL 84357:1/1/67:89500
Arthur Putie:923-835-8745:23 Wimp Lane, Kensington, DL 38758:8/31/69:126000
Popeye Sailor:156-454-3322:945 Bluto Street, Anywhere, USA 29358:3/19/35:22350
Jose Santiago:385-898-8357:38 Fife Way, Abilene, TX 39673:1/5/58:95600
Tommy Savage:408-724-0140:1222 Oxbow Court, Sunnyvale, CA 94087:5/19/66:34200
Yukio Takeshida:387-827-1095:13 Uno Lane, Ashville, NC 23556:7/1/29:57000
Vinh Tranh:438-910-7449:8235 Maple Street, Wilmington, VM 29085:9/23/63:68900

(Refer to the database called *datebook* on the CD.)

1   Print all lines containing the string *San*.

2. Print all lines where the person's first name starts with *J*.

3. Print all lines ending in *700*.

4. Print all lines that don't contain *834*.

5. Print all lines where birthdays are in *December*.

6. Print all lines where the phone number is in the *408* area code.

7. Print all lines containing an uppercase letter, followed by four lowercase letters, a comma, a space, and one uppercase letter.

8. Print lines where the last name begins with *K* or *k*.

9. Print lines preceded by a line number where the salary is a six-figure number.

10. Print lines containing *Lincoln* or *lincoln* (remember that *grep* is insensitive to case).

chapter

4

sed, the
Streamlined Editor

4.1   What Is *sed*?

Sed is a streamlined, noninteractive editor. It allows you to perform the same kind of editing tasks used in the vi and *ex* editors. Instead of working interactively with the editor, the *sed* program lets you type your editing commands at the command line, name the file, and then see the output of the editing command on the screen. The *sed* editor is nondestructive. It does not change your file unless you save the output with shell redirection. All lines are printed to the screen by default.

The *sed* editor is useful in shell scripts, where using interactive editors such as vi or *ex* would require the user of the script to have familiarity with the editor and would expose the user to making unwanted modifications to the open file. You can also put *sed* commands in a file called a *sed* script, if you need to perform multiple edits or do not like worrying about quoting the *sed* commands at the shell command line.[1]

4.2   How Does *sed* Work?

The *sed* editor processes a file (or input) one line at a time and sends its output to the screen. Its commands are those you may recognize from the vi and *ed/ex* editors. *Sed* stores the line it is currently processing in a temporary buffer called a *pattern space*. Once *sed* is finished processing the line in the pattern space (i.e., executing *sed* commands on that line), the line in the pattern space is sent to the screen (unless the command was to delete the line or suppress its printing). After the line has been processed, it is removed from the pattern space and the next line is then read into the pattern space, processed, and displayed. *Sed* ends when the last line of the input file has been pro-

---

1. Remember, the shell will try to evaluate any metacharacters or whitespace when a command is typed at the command line; any characters in the *sed* command that could be interpreted by the shell must be quoted.

cessed. By storing each line in a temporary buffer and performing edits on that line, the original file is never altered or destroyed.

4.3   Addressing

You can use addressing to decide which lines you want to edit. The addresses can be in the form of numbers or regular expressions, or a combination of both. Without specifying an address, *sed* processes all lines of the input file.

When an address consists of a number, the number represents a line number. A dollar sign can be used to represent the last line of the input file. If a comma separates two line numbers, the addresses that will be processed are within that range of lines, including the first and last line in the range. The range may be numbers, regular expressions, or a combination of numbers and regular expressions.

Sed commands tell *sed* what to do with the line: print it, remove it, change it, and so forth.

FORMAT

```
sed 'command' filename(s)
```

EXAMPLE 4.1

```
1  % sed '1,3p' myfile
2  % sed -n '/[Jj]ohn/p' datafile
```

EXPLANATION

1   Lines 1 through 3 of *myfile* are printed.
2   Only lines matching the pattern *John* or *john* in *myfile* are printed.

4.4   Commands and Options

Sed commands tell *sed* how to process each line of input specified by an address. If an address is not given, *sed* processes every line of input. (The % is the csh prompt.) See Table 4.1 for a list of *sed* commands and what they do, and see Table 4.2 for a list of options and how they control *sed*'s behavior.

EXAMPLE 4.2

```
% sed '1,3d' file
```

EXPLANATION

Sed will delete lines 1 through 3.

Table 4.1 *sed* Commands

Command	Function
a	Appends one or more lines of text to the current line.
c	Changes (replaces) text in the current line with new text.
d	Deletes lines.
i	Inserts text above the current line.
h	Copies the contents of the pattern space to a holding buffer.
H	Appends the contents of the pattern space to a holding buffer.
g	Gets what is in the holding buffer and copies it into the pattern buffer, overwriting what was there.
G	Gets what is in the holding buffer and copies it into the pattern buffer, appending to what was there.
l	Lists nonprinting characters.
p	Prints lines.
n	Reads the next input line and starts processing the newline with the next command rather than the first command.
q	Quits or exits *sed*.
r	Reads lines from a file.
!	Applies the command to all lines *except* the selected ones.
s	Substitutes one string for another.
Substitution Flags:	
g	Globally substitutes on a line.
p	Prints lines.
w	Writes lines out to a file.
x	Exchanges contents of the holding buffer with the pattern space.
y	Translates one character to another (cannot use regular expression metacharacters with *y*).

Table 4.2 *sed* Options

Options	Function
–e	Allows multiple edits.
–f	Precedes a *sed* script filename.
–n	Suppresses default output.

When multiple commands are used or addresses need to be nested within a range of addresses, the commands are enclosed in curly braces and each command is either on a separate line or terminated with semicolons.

The exclamation point (!) can be used to negate a command. For example,

```
% sed '/Tom/d' file
```

tells *sed* to delete all lines containing the pattern *Tom*, whereas

```
% sed '/Tom/!d' file
```

tells *sed* to delete lines not containing *Tom*.

The *sed* options are *–e*, *–f*, and, *–n*. The *–e* is used for multiple edits at the command line, the *–f* precedes a *sed* script filename, and the *–n* suppresses printing output.

4.5 Error Messages and Exit Status

When *sed* encounters a syntax error, it sends a pretty straightforward error message to standard error, but if it cannot figure out what you did wrong, *sed* gets "garbled," which we could guess means confused. The exit status that *sed* returns to the shell, if its syntax is error-free, is a zero for success and a nonzero integer for failure.[2]

EXAMPLE 4.3

```
1   % sed '1,3v ' file
    sed: Unrecognized command: 1,3v
    % echo $status (echo $?   if using Korn or Bourne shell)
    2

2   % sed '/^John' file
    sed: Illegal or missing delimiter: /^John
```

---

2. For a complete list of diagnostics, see the UNIX man page for *sed*.

EXAMPLE 4.3 (CONTINUED)

```
3    % sed 's/134345/g' file
     sed: Ending delimiter missing on substitution: s/134345/g
```

EXPLANATION

1 The v command is unrecognized by *sed*. The exit status was 2, indicating that *sed* exited with a syntax problem.

2 The pattern /^*John* is missing the closing forward slash.

3 The substitution command, *s*, contains the search string but not the replacement string.

4.5.1 Metacharacters

Like *grep*, *sed* supports a number of special metacharacters to control pattern searching See Table 4.3.

Table 4.3 *sed's* Regular Expression Metacharacters

Metacharacter	Function	Example	What It Matches
^	Beginning-of-line anchor	/^love/	Matches all lines beginning with *love*.
$	End-of-line anchor	/love$/	Matches all lines ending with *love*.
.	Matches one character, but not the newline character	/l..e/	Matches lines containing an *l*, followed by two characters, followed by an *e*.
*	Matches zero or more characters	/ *love/	Matches lines with zero or more spaces, followed by the pattern *love*.
[ ]	Matches one character in the set	/[Ll]ove/	Matches lines containing *love* or *Love*.
[^]	Matches one character not in the set	/[^A–KM–Z]ove/	Matches lines not containing *A* through *K* or *M* through *Z* followed by *ove*.

Table 4.3 *sed's* Regular Expression Metacharacters (continued)

Metacharacter	Function	Example	What It Matches
\(..\)	Saves matched characters	s\(love\)able\1er/	Tags marked portion and saves it as tag number 1. To reference later, use \1 to reference the pattern. May use up to nine tags, starting with the first tag at the leftmost part of the pattern. For example, *love* is saved in register 1 and remembered in the replacement string. *lovable* is replaced with *lover*.
&	Saves search string so it can be remembered in the replacement string	s/love/**&**/	The ampersand represents the search string. The string *love* will be replaced with itself surrounded by asterisks; i.e., *love* will become **love**.
\<	Beginning-of-word anchor	/\<love/	Matches lines containing a word that begins with *love*.
\>	End-of-word anchor	/love\>/	Matches lines containing a word that ends with *love*.
x\{m\}	Repetition of character x: m times	/o\{5\}/	Matches if line has 5 occurrences of *o*, at least 5 occurrences of *o*, or between 5 and 10 occurrences of *o*.
x\{m,\}	at least m times		
x\{m,n\} [a]	at least m and not more than n times		

a. Not dependable on all versions of UNIX or all pattern-matching utilities; usually works with *vi* and *grep*.

4.6 *sed* Examples

```
% cat datafile
northwest        NW    Charles Main       3.0   .98    3    34
western          WE    Sharon Gray        5.3   .97    5    23
southwest        SW    Lewis Dalsass      2.7   .8     2    18
southern         SO    Suan Chin          5.1   .95    4    15
southeast        SE    Patricia Hemenway  4.0   .7     4    17
eastern          EA    TB Savage          4.4   .84    5    20
northeast        NE    AM Main Jr.        5.1   .94    3    13
north            NO    Margot Weber       4.5   .89    5     9
central          CT    Ann Stephens       5.7   .94    5    13
```

4.6.1 Printing: The *p* Command

```
sed '/north/p' datafile
```

northwest	NW	Charles Main	3.0	.98	3	34
northwest	NW	Charles Main	3.0	.98	3	34
western	WE	Sharon Gray	5.3	.97	5	23
southwest	SW	Lewis Dalsass	2.7	.8	2	18
southern	SO	Suan Chin	5.1	.95	4	15
southeast	SE	Patricia Hemenway	4.0	.7	4	17
eastern	EA	TB Savage	4.4	.84	5	20
northeast	NE	AM Main Jr.	5.1	.94	3	13
northeast	NE	AM Main Jr.	5.1	.94	3	13
north	NO	Margot Weber	4.5	.89	5	9
north	NO	Margot Weber	4.5	.89	5	9
central	CT	Ann Stephens	5.7	.94	5	13

EXPLANATION

Prints all lines to standard output by default. If the pattern *north* is found, *sed* will print that line in addition to all the other lines.

```
sed -n '/north/p' datafile
```

northwest	NW	Charles Main	3.0	.98	3	34
northeast	NE	AM Main Jr.	5.1	.94	3	13
north	NO	Margot Weber	4.5	.89	5	9

EXPLANATION

The –*n* option suppresses the default behavior of *sed* when used with the *p* command. Without the –*n* option, *sed* will print duplicate lines of output as shown in the preceding example. Only the lines containing the pattern *north* are printed when –*n* is used.

```
% cat datafile
northwest        NW     Charles Main        3.0    .98    3    34
western          WE     Sharon Gray         5.3    .97    5    23
southwest        SW     Lewis Dalsass       2.7    .8     2    18
southern         SO     Suan Chin           5.1    .95    4    15
southeast        SE     Patricia Hemenway   4.0    .7     4    17
eastern          EA     TB Savage           4.4    .84    5    20
northeast        NE     AM Main Jr.         5.1    .94    3    13
north            NO     Margot Weber        4.5    .89    5     9
central          CT     Ann Stephens        5.7    .94    5    13
```

4.6.2   Deleting: The *d* Command

EXAMPLE 4.6

```
sed '3d' datafile
northwest        NW     Charles Main        3.0 .98    3    34
western          WE     Sharon Gray         5.3 .97    5    23
southern         SO     Suan Chin           5.1 .95    4    15
southeast        SE     Patricia Hemenway   4.0 .7     4    17
eastern          EA     TB Savage           4.4 .84    5    20
northeast        NE     AM Main Jr.         5.1 .94    3    13
north            NO     Margot Weber        4.5 .89    5     9
central          CT     Ann Stephens        5.7 .94    5    13
```

EXPLANATION

Deletes the third line. All other lines are printed to the screen by default.

EXAMPLE 4.7

```
sed '3,$d' datafile
northwest        NW     Charles Main        3.0 .98    3    34
western          WE     Sharon Gray         5.3 .97    5    23
```

EXPLANATION

The third line through the last line are deleted. The remaining lines are printed. The dollar sign ($) represents the last line of the file. The comma is called the *range operator*. In this example, the range of addresses starts at line 3 and ends at the last line, which is represented by the dollar sign ($).

EXAMPLE 4.8

```
sed '$d' datafile
```

northwest	NW	Charles Main	3.0	.98	3	34
western	WE	Sharon Gray	5.3	.97	5	23
southwest	SW	Lewis Dalsass	2.7	.8	2	18
southern	SO	Suan Chin	5.1	.95	4	15
southeast	SE	Patricia Hemenway	4.0	.7	4	17
eastern	EA	TB Savage	4.4	.84	5	20
northeast	NE	AM Main Jr.	5.1	.94	3	13
north	NO	Margot Weber	4.5	.89	5	9

EXPLANATION

Deletes the last line. The dollar sign ($) represents the last line. The default is to print all of the lines except those affected by the *d* command.

EXAMPLE 4.9

```
sed '/north/d' datafile
```

western	WE	Sharon Gray	5.3	.97	5	23
southwest	SW	Lewis Dalsass	2.7	.8	2	18
southern	SO	Suan Chin	5.1	.95	4	15
southeast	SE	Patricia Hemenway	4.0	.7	4	17
eastern	EA	TB Savage	4.4	.84	5	20
central	CT	Ann Stevens	5.7	.94	5	13

EXPLANATION

All lines containing the pattern *north* are deleted. The remaining lines are printed.

4.6.3 Substitution: The *s* Command

EXAMPLE 4.10

```
sed 's/west/north/g' datafile
```

northnorth	NW	Charles Main	3.0	.98	3	34
northern	WE	Sharon Gray	5.3	.97	5	23
southnorth	SW	Lewis Dalsass	2.7	.8	2	18
southern	SO	Suan Chin	5.1	.95	4	15
southeast	SE	Patricia Hemenway	4.0	.7	4	17
eastern	EA	TB Savage	4.4	.84	5	20
northeast	NE	AM Main Jr.	5.1	.94	3	13
north	NO	Margot Weber	4.5	89	5	9
central	CT	Ann Stephens	5.7	.94	5	13

EXPLANATION

The *s* command is for substitution. The *g* flag at the end of the command indicates that the substitution is global across the line; that is, if multiple occurrences of *west* are found, all of them will be replaced with *north*. Without the *g* command, only the first occurrence of *west* on each line would be replaced with *north*.

% **cat datafile**						
northwest	NW	Charles Main	3.0	.98	3	34
western	WE	Sharon Gray	5.3	.97	5	23
southwest	SW	Lewis Dalsass	2.7	.8	2	18
southern	SO	Suan Chin	5.1	.95	4	15
southeast	SE	Patricia Hemenway	4.0	.7	4	17
eastern	EA	TB Savage	4.4	.84	5	20
northeast	NE	AM Main Jr.	5.1	.94	3	13
north	NO	Margot Weber	4.5	.89	5	9
central	CT	Ann Stephens	5.7	.94	5	13

EXAMPLE 4.11

```
sed -n 's/^west/north/p' datafile
northern     WE     Sharon Gray          5.3  .97  5   23
```

EXPLANATION

The *s* command is for substitution. The *–n* option with the *p* flag at the end of the command tells *sed* to print only those lines where the substitution occurred; that is, if *west* is found at the beginning of the line and is replaced with *north,* just those lines are printed.

EXAMPLE 4.12

```
sed 's/[0-9][0-9]$/&.5/' datafile
northwest    NW    Charles Main       3.0  .98  3   34.5
western      WE    Sharon Gray        5.3  .97  5   23.5
southwest    SW    Lewis Dalsass      2.7  .8   2   18.5
southern     SO    Suan Chin          5.1  .95  4   15.5
southeast    SE    Patricia Hemenway  4.0  .7   4   17.5
eastern      EA    TB Savage          4.4  .84  5   20.5
northeast    NE    AM Main Jr.        5.1  .94  3   13.5
north        NO    Margot Weber       4.5  .89  5   9
central      CT    Ann Stephens       5.7  .94  5   13.5
```

EXPLANATION

The ampersand[3] (&) in the replacement string represents exactly what was found in the search string. Each line that ends in two digits will be replaced by itself, and .5 will be appended to it.

EXAMPLE 4.13

```
sed -n 's/Hemenway/Jones/gp' datafile
```
```
southeast     SE      Patricia Jones      4.0  .7   4    17
```

EXPLANATION

All occurrences of *Hemenway* are replaced with *Jones*, and only the lines that changed are printed. The *–n* option combined with the *p* command suppresses the default output. The *g* stands for global substitution across the line.

EXAMPLE 4.14

```
sed -n 's/\(Mar\)got/\1ianne/p' datafile
```
```
north         NO      Marianne Weber      4.5  .89  5    9
```

EXPLANATION

The pattern *Mar* is enclosed in parentheses and saved as tag 1 in a special register. It will be referenced in the replacement string as *\1*. *Margot* is then replaced with *Marianne*.

EXAMPLE 4.15

```
sed 's#3#88#g' datafile
```
```
northwest     NW      Charles Main        88.0  .98  88   884
western       WE      Sharon Gray         5.88  .97  5    288
southwest     SW      Lewis Dalsass       2.7   .8   2    18
southern      SO      Suan Chin           5.1   .95  4    15
southeast     SE      Patricia Hemenway   4.0   .7   4    17
eastern       EA      TB Savage           4.4   .84  5    20
northeast     NE      AM Main Jr.         5.1   .94  88   188
north         NO      Margot Weber        4.5   .89  5    9
central       CT      Ann Stephens        5.7   .94  5    188
```

---

3. To represent a literal ampersand in the replacement string, it must be escaped: \&.

EXPLANATION

The character after the s command is the delimiter between the search string and the replacement string. The delimiter character is a forward slash by default, but can be changed (only when the s command is used). Whatever character follows the s command is the new string delimiter. This technique can be useful when searching for patterns containing a forward slash, such as pathnames or birthdays.

```
% cat datafile
northwest       NW   Charles Main        3.0   .98   3   34
western         WE   Sharon Gray         5.3   .97   5   23
southwest       SW   Lewis Dalsass       2.7   .8    2   18
southern        SO   Suan Chin           5.1   .95   4   15
southeast       SE   Patricia Hemenway   4.0   .7    4   17
eastern         EA   TB Savage           4.4   .84   5   20
northeast       NE   AM Main Jr.         5.1   .94   3   13
north           NO   Margot Weber        4.5   .89   5    9
central         CT   Ann Stephens        5.7   .94   5   13
```

4.6.4 Range of Selected Lines: The Comma

EXAMPLE 4.16

```
sed -n '/west/,/east/p' datafile
▸northwest      NW   Charles Main        3.0  .98   3    34
 western        WE   Sharon Gray         5.3  .97   5    23
 southwest      SW   Lewis Dalsass       2.7  .8    2    18
 southern       SO   Suan Chin           5.1  .95   4    15
▸southeast      SE   Patricia Hemenway   4.0  .7    4    17
```

EXPLANATION

All lines in the range of patterns between *west* and *east* are printed. If *west* were to appear on a line after *east*, the lines from *west* to the next *east* or to the end of file, whichever comes first, would be printed. The arrows mark the range.

EXAMPLE 4.17

```
sed -n '5,/^northeast/p' datafile
```

southeast	SE	Patricia Hemenway	4.0	.7	4	17
eastern	EA	TB Savage	4.4	.84	5	20
northeast	NE	AM Main Jr.	5.1	.94	3	13

EXPLANATION

Prints the lines from line 5 through the first line that begins with *northeast*.

EXAMPLE 4.18

```
sed '/west/,/east/s/$/**VACA**/' datafile
```

►northwest	NW	Charles Main	3.0	.98	3	34**VACA**
western	WE	Sharon Gray	5.3	.97	5	23**VACA**
southwest	SW	Lewis Dalsass	2.7	.8	2	18**VACA**
southern	SO	Suan Chin	5.1	.95	4	15**VACA**
►southeast	SE	Patricia Hemenway	4.0	.7	4	17**VACA**
eastern	EA	TB Savage	4.4	.84	5	20
northeast	NE	AM Main Jr.	5.1	.94	3	13
north	NO	Margot Weber	4.5	.89	5	9
central	CT	Ann Stephens	5.7	.94	5	13

EXPLANATION

For lines in the range between the patterns *east* and *west*, the end of line ($) is replaced with the string ***VACA***. The newline is moved over to the end of the new string. The arrows mark the range.

4.6.5   Multiple Edits: The *e* Command

EXAMPLE 4.19

```
sed -e '1,3d' -e 's/Hemenway/Jones/' datafile
```

southern	SO	Suan Chin	5.1	.95	4	15
southeast	SE	Patricia Jones	4.0	.7	4	17
eastern	EA	TB Savage	4.4	.84	5	20
northeast	NE	AM Main	5.1	.94	3	13
north	NO	Margot Weber	4.5	.89	5	9
central	CT	Ann Stephens	5.7	.94	5	13

EXPLANATION

The *–e* option allows multiple edits. The first edit removes lines 1 through 3. The second edit substitutes *Hemenway* with *Jones*. Since both edits are done on a per-line basis (i.e., both commands are executed on the current line in the pattern space), the order of the edits may affect the outcome. For example, if both commands had performed substitutions on the line, the first substitution could affect the second substitution.

% **cat datafile**

northwest	NW	Charles Main	3.0	.98	3	34
western	WE	Sharon Gray	5.3	.97	5	23
southwest	SW	Lewis Dalsass	2.7	.8	2	18
southern	SO	Suan Chin	5.1	.95	4	15
southeast	SE	Patricia Hemenway	4.0	.7	4	17
eastern	EA	TB Savage	4.4	.84	5	20
northeast	NE	AM Main Jr.	5.1	.94	3	13
north	NO	Margot Weber	4.5	.89	5	9
central	CT	Ann Stephens	5.7	.94	5	13

4.6.6   Reading from Files: The *r* Command

EXAMPLE 4.20

```
% cat newfile
          ------------------------------------
          | ***SUAN HAS LEFT THE COMPANY*** |
          |_____|
% sed '/Suan/r newfile' datafile
northwest    NW     Charles Main      3.0  .98   3   34
western      WE     Sharon Gray       5.3  .97   5   23
southwest    SW     Lewis Dalsass     2.7  .8    2   18
southern     SO     Suan Chin         5.1  .95   4   15
          ------------------------------------
          | ***SUAN HAS LEFT THE COMPANY***  |
          |_____|
southeast    SE     Patricia Hemenway 4.0  .7    4   17
eastern      EA     TB Savage         4.4  .84   5   20
northeast    NE     AM Main           5.1  .94   3   13
north        NO     Margot Weber      4.5  .89   5   9
central      CT     Ann Stephens      5.7  .94   5   13
```

EXPLANATION

The *r* command reads specified lines from a file. The contents of *newfile* are read into the input file *datafile*, after the line where the pattern *Suan* is matched. If *Suan* had appeared on more than one line, the contents of *newfile* would have been read in under each occurrence.

4.6.7 Writing to Files: The *w* Command

EXAMPLE 4.21

```
sed -n '/north/w newfile' datafile
cat newfile
northwest     NW      Charles Main       3.0  .98   3    34
northeast     NE      AM Main Jr.        5.1  .94   3    13
north         NO      Margot Weber       4.5  .89   5     9
```

EXPLANATION

The *w* command writes specified lines to a file. All lines containing the pattern *north* are written to a file called *newfile*.

4.6.8 Appending: The *a* Command

EXAMPLE 4.22

```
sed '/^north /a\\
--->THE NORTH SALES DISTRICT HAS MOVED<---' datafile
northwest     NW      Charles Main       3.0  .98   3    34
western       WE      Sharon Gray        5.3  .97   5    23
southwest     SW      Lewis Dalsass      2.7  .8    2    18
southern      SO      Suan Chin          5.1  .95   4    15
southeast     SE      Patricia Hemenway  4.0  .7    4    17
eastern       EA      TB Savage          4.4  .84   5    20
northeast     NE      AM Main Jr.        5.1  .94   3    13
north         NO      Margot Weber       4.5  .89   5     9
--->THE NORTH SALES DISTRICT HAS MOVED<---
central       CT      Ann Stephens       5.7  .94   5    13
```

EXPLANATION

The *a* command is the append command. The string --->*THE NORTH SALES DISTRICT HAS MOVED*<--- is appended after lines beginning with the pattern *north*, when *north* is followed by a space. The text that will be appended must be on the line following the append command.

Sed requires a backslash after the *a* command. The second backslash is used by the C shell to escape the newline so that its closing quote can be on the next line.[4] If more than one line is appended, each line, except the last one, must also end in a backslash.

---

4. The Bourne and Korn shells do not require the second backslash to escape the newline because they do not require quotes to be matched on the same line, only that they match.

% **cat datafile**						
northwest	NW	Charles Main	3.0	.98	3	34
western	WE	Sharon Gray	5.3	.97	5	23
southwest	SW	Lewis Dalsass	2.7	.8	2	18
southern	SO	Suan Chin	5.1	.95	4	15
southeast	SE	Patricia Hemenway	4.0	.7	4	17
eastern	EA	TB Savage	4.4	.84	5	20
northeast	NE	AM Main Jr.	5.1	.94	3	13
north	NO	Margot Weber	4.5	.89	5	9
central	CT	Ann Stephens	5.7	.94	5	13

4.6.9 Inserting: The *i* Command

EXAMPLE 4.23

```
sed '/eastern/i\\
NEW ENGLAND REGION\\
-----------------------------------' datafile
northwest     NW    Charles Main       3.0 .98  3   34
western       WE    Sharon Gray        5.3 .97  5   23
southwest     SW    Lewis Dalsass      2.7 .8   2   18
southern      SO    Suan Chin          5.1 .95  4   15
southeast     SE    Patricia Hemenway  4.0 .7   4   17
NEW ENGLAND REGION

-----------------------------------
eastern       EA    TB Savage          4.4 .84  5   20
northeast     NE    AM Main Jr.        5.1 .94  3   13
north         NO    Margot Weber       4.5 .89  5   9
central       CT    Ann Stephens       5.7 .94  5   13
```

EXPLANATION

The *i* command is the insert command. If the pattern *eastern* is matched, the *i* command causes the text following the backslash to be inserted above the line containing *eastern*. A backslash is required after each line to be inserted, except the last one. (The extra backslash is for the C shell.)

4.6.10   Next: The *n* Command

EXAMPLE   4.24

```
sed '/eastern/{ n; s/AM/Archie/; }' datafile
northwest    NW    Charles Main       3.0  .98  3   34
western      WE    Sharon Gray        5.3  .97  5   23
southwest    SW    Lewis Dalsass      2.7  .8   2   18
southern     SO    Suan Chin          5.1  .95  4   15
southeast    SE    Patricia Hemenway  4.0  .7   4   17
eastern      EA    TB Savage          4.4  .84  5   20
northeast    NE    Archie Main Jr.    5.1  .94  3   13
north        NO    Margot Weber       4.5  .89  5   9
central      CT    Ann Stephens       5.7  .94  5   13
```

EXPLANATION

If the pattern *eastern* is matched on a line, the *n* command causes *sed* to get the next line of input (the line with *AM Main Jr.*), replace the pattern space with this line, substitute (*s*) *AM* with *Archie*, print the line, and continue.

4.6.11   Transform: The *y* Command

EXAMPLE   4.25

```
sed '1,3y/abcdefghijklmnopqrstuvwxyz/ABCDEFGHIJKL
MNOPQRSTUVWXYZ/' datafile
NORTHWEST    NW    CHARLES MAIN       3.0  .98  3   34
WESTERN      WE    SHARON GRAY        5.3  .97  5   23
SOUTHWEST    SW    LEWIS DALSASS      2.7  .8   2   18
southern     SO    Suan Chin          5.1  .95  4   15
southeast    SE    Patricia Hemenway  4.0  .7   4   17
eastern      EA    TB Savage          4.4  .84  5   20
northeast    NE    AM Main Jr.        5.1  .94  3   13
north        NO    Margot Weber       4.5  .89  5   9
central      CT    Ann Stephens       5.7  .94  5   13
```

EXPLANATION

For lines *1* through *3*, the *y* command translates all lowercase letters to uppercase letters. Regular expression metacharacters do not work with this command.

```
% cat datafile
```

northwest	NW	Charles Main	3.0	.98	3	34
western	WE	Sharon Gray	5.3	.97	5	23
southwest	SW	Lewis Dalsass	2.7	.8	2	18
southern	SO	Suan Chin	5.1	.95	4	15
southeast	SE	Patricia Hemenway	4.0	.7	4	17
eastern	EA	TB Savage	4.4	.84	5	20
northeast	NE	AM Main Jr.	5.1	.94	3	13
north	NO	Margot Weber	4.5	.89	5	9
central	CT	Ann Stephens	5.7	.94	5	13

4.6.12   Quit: The q Command

EXAMPLE 4.26

```
sed '5q' datafile
northwest    NW    Charles Main        3.0  .98  3  34
western      WE    Sharon Gray         5.3  .97  5  23
southwest    SW    Lewis Dalsass       2.7  .8   2  18
southern     SO    Suan Chin           5.1  .95  4  15
southeast    SE    Patricia Hemenway   4.0  .7   4  17
```

EXPLANATION

After the line 5 is printed, the *q* command causes the *sed* program to quit.

EXAMPLE 4.27

```
sed  '/Lewis/{ s/Lewis/Joseph/;q; }' datafile
northwest    NW    Charles Main      3.0  .98  3  34
western      WE    Sharon Gray       5.3  .97  5  23
southwest    SW    Joseph Dalsass    2.7  .8   2  18
```

EXPLANATION

When the pattern *Lewis* is matched on a line, first the substitution command (*s*) replaces *Lewis* with *Joseph*, and then the *q* command causes the *sed* program to quit.

4.6.13 Holding and Getting: The *h* and *g* Commands

```
sed -e '/northeast/h'  -e  '$G'  datafile
   northwest     NW    Charles Main        3.0  .98  3   34
   western       WE    Sharon Gray         5.3  .97  5   23
   southwest     SW    Lewis Dalsass       2.7  .8   2   18
   southern      SO    Suan Chin           5.1  .95  4   15
   southeast     SE    Patricia Hemenway   4.0  .7   4   17
   eastern       EA    TB Savage           4.4  .84  5   20
→  northeast     NE    AM Main Jr.         5.1  .94  3   13
   north         NO    Margot Weber        4.5  .89  5   9
   central       CT    Ann Stephens        5.7  .94  5   13
→  northeast     NE    AM Main Jr.         5.1  .94  3   13
```

As *sed* processes the file, each line is stored in a temporary buffer called the pattern space. Unless the line is deleted or suppressed from printing, the line will be printed to the screen after it is processed. The pattern space is then cleared and the next line of input is stored there for processing. In this example, after the line containing the pattern *northeast* is found, it is placed in the pattern space and the *h* command copies it and places it into another special buffer called the *holding buffer*. In the second *sed* instruction, when the last line is reached ($) the *G* command tells *sed* to get the line from the holding buffer and put it back in the pattern space buffer, appending it to the line that is currently stored there, in this case, the last line. Simply stated: Any line containing the pattern *northeast* will be copied and appended to the end of the file. (See Figure 4.1.)

```
% cat datafile
northwest        NW     Charles Main         3.0    .98    3    34
western          WE     Sharon Gray          5.3    .97    5    23
southwest        SW     Lewis Dalsass        2.7    .8     2    18
southern         SO     Suan Chin            5.1    .95    4    15
southeast        SE     Patricia Hemenway    4.0    .7     4    17
eastern          EA     TB Savage            4.4    .84    5    20
northeast        NE     AM Main Jr.          5.1    .94    3    13
north            NO     Margot Weber         4.5    .89    5     9
central          CT     Ann Stephens         5.7    .94    5    13
```

EXAMPLE 4.29

```
sed -e '/WE/{h; d; }' -e '/CT/{G; }' datafile
northwest        NW     Charles Main         3.0  .98    3    34
southwest        SW     Lewis Dalsass        2.7  .8     2    18
southern         SO     Suan Chin            5.1  .95    4    15
southeast        SE     Patricia Hemenway    4.0  .7     4    17
eastern          EA     TB Savage            4.4  .84    5    20
northeast        NE     AM Main Jr.          5.1  .94    3    13
north            NO     Margot Weber         4.5  .89    5     9
central          CT     Ann Stephens         5.7  .94    5    13
➤ western        WE     Sharon Gray          5.3  .97    5    23
```

EXPLANATION

If the pattern *WE* is found on a line, the *h* command causes the line to be copied from the pattern space into a holding buffer. When stored in the holding buffer, the line can be retrieved (*G* or *g* command) at a later time. In this example, when the pattern *WE* is found, the line in which it was found is stored in the pattern buffer first. The *h* command then puts a copy of the line in the holding buffer. The *d* command deletes the copy in the pattern buffer. The second command searches for *CT* in a line, and when it is found, *sed* gets (*G*) the line that was stored in the holding buffer and appends it to the line currently in the pattern space. Simply stated: The line containing *WE* is moved and appended after the line containing *CT*. (See "Holding and Exchanging: The h and x Commands" on page 87.)

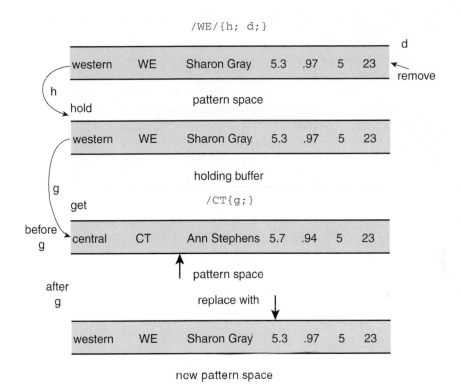

Figure 4.1 The pattern space and holding buffer. See Example 4.31.

EXAMPLE 4.30

```
sed -e '/northeast/h'  -e '$g'  datafile
  northwest    NW    Charles Main       3.0  .98  3   34
  western      WE    Sharon Gray        5.3  .97  5   23
  southwest    SW    Lewis Dalsass      2.7  .8   2   18
  southern     SO    Suan Chin          5.1  .95  4   15
  southeast    SE    Patricia Hemenway  4.0  .7   4   17
  eastern      EA    TB Savage          4.4  .84  5   20
➤ northeast    NE    AM Main Jr.        5.1  .94  3   13
  north        NO    Margot Weber       4.5  .89  5    9
➤ northeast    NE    AM Main Jr.        5.1  .94  3   13
```

EXPLANATION

As *sed* processes the file, each line is stored in a temporary buffer called the pattern space. Unless the line is deleted or suppressed from printing, the line will be printed to the screen after it is processed. The pattern space is then cleared and the next line of input is stored there for processing. In this example, after the line containing the pattern *northeast* is found, it is placed in the pattern space. The *h* command takes a copy of it and places it in another special buffer called the holding buffer. In the second *sed* instruction, when the last line is reached ($), the *g* command tells *sed* to get the line from the holding buffer and put it back in the pattern space buffer, replacing the line that is currently stored there, in this case, the last line. Simply stated: The line containing the pattern *northeast* is copied and moved to overwrite the last line in the file.

```
% cat datafile
```

northwest	NW	Charles Main	3.0	.98	3	34
western	WE	Sharon Gray	5.3	.97	5	23
southwest	SW	Lewis Dalsass	2.7	.8	2	18
southern	SO	Suan Chin	5.1	.95	4	15
southeast	SE	Patricia Hemenway	4.0	.7	4	17
eastern	EA	TB Savage	4.4	.84	5	20
northeast	NE	AM Main Jr.	5.1	.94	3	13
north	NO	Margot Weber	4.5	.89	5	9
central	CT	Ann Stephens	5.7	.94	5	13

EXAMPLE 4.31

```
sed -e '/WE/{h; d; }' -e '/CT/{g; }' datafile
```

northwest	NW	Charles Main	3.0	.98	3	34
southwest	SW	Lewis Dalsass	2.7	.8	2	18
southern	SO	Suan Chin	5.1	.95	4	15
southeast	SE	Patricia Hemenway	4.0	.7	4	17
eastern	EA	TB Savage	4.4	.84	5	20
northeast	NE	AM Main Jr.	5.1	.94	3	13
north	NO	Margot Weber	4.5	.89	5	9
western	WE	Sharon Gray	5.3	.97	5	23

EXPLANATION

If the pattern *WE* is found, the *h* command copies the line into the holding buffer; the *d* command deletes the line in the pattern space. When the pattern *CT* is found, the *g* command gets the copy in the holding buffer and overwrites the line currently in the pattern space. Simply stated: Any line containing the pattern *WE* will be moved to overwrite lines containing *CT*. (See Figure 4.1.)

4.6.14   Holding and Exchanging: The *h* and *x* Commands

EXAMPLE 4.32

```
sed -e '/Patricia/h'   -e '/Margot/x' datafile
northwest      NW     Charles Main        3.0  .98   3    34
western        WE     Sharon Gray         5.3  .97   5    23
southwest      SW     Lewis Dalsass       2.7  .8    2    18
southern       SO     Suan Chin           5.1  .95   4    15
southeast      SE     Patricia Hemenway   4.0  .7    4    17
eastern        EA     TB Savage           4.4  .84   5    20
northeast      NE     AM Main Jr.         5.1  .94   3    13
southeast      SE     Patricia Hemenway   4.0  .7    4    17
central        CT     Ann Stephens        5.7  .94   5    13
```

EXPLANATION

The *x* command exchanges (swaps) the contents of the holding buffer with the current pattern space. When the line containing the pattern *Patricia* is found, it will be stored in the holding buffer. When the line containing *Margot* is found, the pattern space will be exchanged for the line in the holding buffer. Simply stated: The line containing *Margot* will be replaced with the line containing *Patricia*.

4.7   *sed* Scripting

A *sed script* is a list of *sed* commands in a file. To let *sed* know your commands are in a file, when invoking *sed* at the command line, use the *–f* option followed by the name of the *sed* script. *Sed* is very particular about the way you type lines into the script. There cannot be any trailing whitespace or text at the end of the command. If commands are not placed on a line by themselves, they must be terminated with a semicolon. A line from the input file is copied into the pattern buffer, and all commands in the *sed* script are executed on that line. After the line has been processed, the next line from the input file is placed in the pattern buffer, and all commands in the script are executed on that line. *Sed* gets "garbled" if your syntax is incorrect.

The nice thing about *sed* scripts is that you don't have to worry about the shell's interaction as you do when at the command line. Quotes are not needed to protect *sed* commands from interpretation by the shell. In fact, you cannot use quotes in a *sed* script at all, unless they are part of a search pattern.

```
% cat datafile
northwest      NW    Charles Main         3.0   .98   3   34
western        WE    Sharon Gray          5.3   .97   5   23
southwest      SW    Lewis Dalsass        2.7   .8    2   18
southern       SO    Suan Chin            5.1   .95   4   15
southeast      SE    Patricia Hemenway    4.0   .7    4   17
eastern        EA    TB Savage            4.4   .84   5   20
northeast      NE    AM Main Jr.          5.1   .94   3   13
north          NO    Margot Weber         4.5   .89   5    9
central        CT    Ann Stephens         5.7   .94   5   13
```

4.7.1   sed Script Examples

EXAMPLE 4.33

```
% cat sedding1 (Look at the contents of the sed script.)
1   # My first sed script by Jack Sprat
2   /Lewis/a\
3      Lewis is the TOP Salesperson for April!!\
       Lewis is moving to the southern district next month.\
4      CONGRATULATIONS!
5   /Margot/c\
       *******************\
       MARGOT HAS RETIRED\
       *******************
6   1i\
    EMPLOYEE DATABASE\
    --------------------
7   $d

% sed -f sedding1 datafile    (Execute the sed script commands; the
                               input file is datafile.)
EMPLOYEE DATABASE
--------------------
northwest      NW    Charles Main        3.0  .98   3   34
western        WE    Sharon Gray         5.3  .97   5   23
southwest      SW    Lewis Dalsass       2.7  .8    2   18
Lewis is the TOP Salesperson for April!!
Lewis is moving to the southern district next month
CONGRATULATIONS!
southern       SO    Suan Chin           5.1  .95   4   15
southeast      SE    Patricia Hemenway   4.0  .7    4   17
eastern        EA    TB Savage           4.4  .84   5   20
northeast      NE    AM Main Jr.         5.1  .94   3   13
```

EXAMPLE 4.33 (CONTINUED)

```
********************
MARGOT HAS RETIRED
****************
```

EXPLANATION

1   This line is a comment. Comments must be on lines by themselves and start with a pound sign (#).

2   If a line contains the pattern *Lewis*, the next three lines are appended to that line.

3   Each line being appended, except the last one, is terminated with a backslash. The backslash must be followed immediately with a newline. If there is any trailing text, even one space after the newline, *sed* will complain.

4   The last line to be appended does not have the terminating backslash. This indicates to *sed* that this is the last line to be appended and that the next line is another command.

5   Any lines containing the pattern *Margot* will be replaced (*c* command) with the next three lines of text.

6   The next two lines will be inserted (*i* command) above line *1*.

7   The last line (*$*) will be deleted.

EXAMPLE 4.34

```
% cat sedding2 (Look at the contents of the sed script.)
# This script demonstrates the use of curly braces to nest addresses
# and commands. Comments are preceded by a pound sign (#) and must
# be on a line by themselves. Commands are terminated with a newline
# or semicolon.  If there is any text after a command, even one
# space, you receive an error message:
#      sed: Extra text at end of command:

1   /western/, /southeast/{
       /^ *$/d
       /Suan/{ h; d; }
    }
2    /Ann/g
3    s/TB \(Savage\)/Thomas \1/

% sed -f sedding2 datafile
northwest      NW      Charles Main        3.0  .98   3    34
western        WE      Sharon Gray         5.3  .97   5    23
southwest      SW      Lewis Dalsass       2.7  .8    2    18
southeast      SE      Patricia Hemenway   4.0  .7    4    17
eastern        EA      Thomas Savage       4.4  .84   5    20
```

EXAMPLE   4.34 (CONTINUED)

```
northeast     NE     AM Main Jr.      5.1 .94  3   13
north         NO     Margot Weber     4.5 .89  5    9
southern      SO     Suan Chin        5.1 .95  4   15
```

EXPLANATION

1   In the range of lines starting at *western* and ending at *southeast*, blank lines are deleted, and lines matching *Suan* are copied from the pattern buffer into the holding buffer, then deleted from the pattern buffer.

2   When the pattern *Ann* is matched, the g command copies the line in the holding buffer to the pattern buffer, overwriting what is in the pattern buffer.

3   All lines containing the pattern *TB Savage* are replaced with *Thomas* and the pattern that was tagged, *Savage*. In the search string, *Savage* is enclosed in escaped parentheses, tagging the enclosed string so that it can be used again. It is tag number 1, referenced by \1.

4.7.2   Review

Table 4.4 lists *sed* commands and what they do.

Table 4.4   *sed* Review

Command	What It Does
sed –n '/sentimental/p' filex	Prints to the screen all lines containing *sentimental*. The file *filex* does not change. Without the *–n* option, all lines with *sentimental* will be printed twice.
sed '1,3d' filex > newfilex	Deletes lines 1, 2, and 3 from *filex* and saves changes in *newfilex*.
sed '/[Dd]aniel/d' filex	Deletes lines containing *Daniel* or *daniel*.
sed –n '15,20p' filex	Prints only lines *15* through *20*.
sed '1,10s/Montana/MT/g' filex	Substitutes *Montana* with *MT* globally in lines *1* through *10*.
sed '/March/\!d' filex (csh) sed '/March/!d' filex (sh)	Deletes all lines not containing *March*. (The backslash is used only in the csh to escape the history character.)
sed '/report/s/5/8/' filex	Changes the first occurrence of *5* to *8* on all lines containing *report*.
sed 's/..../' filex	Deletes the first four characters of each line.
sed 's/...$//' filex	Deletes the last three characters of each line.
sed '/east/,/west/s/North/South/' filex	For any lines falling in the range from *east* to *west*, substitutes *North* with *South*.

Table 4.4 *sed* Review (continued)

Command	What It Does
sed –n '/Time off/w timefile' filex	Writes all lines containing *Time off* to the file *timefile*.
sed 's/\([Oo]ccur\)ence/\1rence/' file	Substitutes either *Occurence* or *occurence* with *Occurrence* or *occurrence*.
sed –n 'l' filex	Prints all lines showing nonprinting characters as \nn, where nn is the octal value of the character, and showing tabs as >.

UNIX TOOLS LAB EXERCISE

Lab 2: *sed* Exercise

```
Steve Blenheim:238-923-7366:95 Latham Lane, Easton, PA 83755:11/12/56:20300
Betty Boop:245-836-8357:635 Cutesy Lane, Hollywood, CA 91464:6/23/23:14500
Igor Chevsky:385-375-8395:3567 Populus Place, Caldwell, NJ 23875:6/18/68:23400
Norma Corder:397-857-2735:74 Pine Street, Dearborn, MI 23874:3/28/45:245700
Jennifer Cowan:548-834-2348:583 Laurel Ave., Kingsville, TX 83745:10/1/35:58900
Jon DeLoach:408-253-3122:123 Park St., San Jose, CA 04086:7/25/53:85100
Karen Evich:284-758-2857:23 Edgecliff Place, Lincoln, NB 92743:7/25/53:85100
Karen Evich:284-758-2867:23 Edgecliff Place, Lincoln, NB 92743:11/3/35:58200
Karen Evich:284-758-2867:23 Edgecliff Place, Lincoln, NB 92743:11/3/35:58200
Fred Fardbarkle:674-843-1385:20 Parak Lane, DeLuth, MN 23850:4/12/23:780900
Fred Fardbarkle:674-843-1385:20 Parak Lane, DeLuth, MN 23850:4/12/23:780900
Lori Gortz:327-832-5728:3465 Mirlo Street, Peabody, MA 34756:10/2/65:35200
Paco Gutierrez:835-365-1284:454 Easy Street, Decatur, IL 75732:2/28/53:123500
Ephram Hardy:293-259-5395:235 CarltonLane, Joliet, IL 73858:8/12/20:56700
James Ikeda:834-938-8376:23445 Aster Ave., Allentown, NJ 83745:12/1/38:45000
Barbara Kertz:385-573-8326:832 Ponce Drive, Gary, IN 83756:12/1/46:268500
Lesley Kirstin:408-456-1234:4 Harvard Square, Boston, MA 02133:4/22/62:52600
William Kopf:846-836-2837:6937 Ware Road, Milton, PA 93756:9/21/46:43500
Sir Lancelot:837-835-8257:474 Camelot Boulevard, Bath, WY 28356:5/13/69:24500
Jesse Neal:408-233-8971:45 Rose Terrace, San Francisco, CA 92303:2/3/36:25000
Zippy Pinhead:834-823-8319:2356 Bizarro Ave., Farmount, IL 84357:1/1/67:89500
Arthur Putie:923-835-8745:23 Wimp Lane, Kensington, DL 38758:8/31/69:126000
Popeye Sailor:156-454-3322:945 Bluto Street, Anywhere, USA 29358:3/19/35:22350
Jose Santiago:385-898-8357:38 Fife Way, Abilene, TX 39673:1/5/58:95600
Tommy Savage:408-724-0140:1222 Oxbow Court, Sunnyvale, CA 94087:5/19/66:34200
Yukio Takeshida:387-827-1095:13 Uno Lane, Ashville, NC 23556:7/1/29:57000
Vinh Tranh:438-910-7449:8235 Maple Street, Wilmington, VM 29085:9/23/63:68900
```

(Refer to the database called *datebook* on the CD.)

1. Change *Jon's* name to *Jonathan*.

2. Delete the first three lines.

3. Print lines *5* through *10*.

4. Delete lines containing *Lane*.

5. Print all lines where the birthdays are in *November* or *December*.

6. Append three stars to the end of lines starting with *Fred*.

7. Replace the line containing *Jose* with *JOSE HAS RETIRED*.

8. Change *Popeye*'s birthday to *11/14/46*.

9. Delete all blank lines.

10. Write a *sed* script that will:

   a. Insert above the first line the title *PERSONNEL FILE*.

   b. Remove the salaries ending in *500*.

   c. Print the contents of the file with the last names and first names reversed.

   d. Append at the end of the file *THE END*.

chapter
5

The *awk* Utility:
awk as a UNIX
Tool

5.1 What Is *awk*?

Awk is a programming language used for manipulating data and generating reports. The data may come from standard input, one or more files, or as output from a process. *Awk* can be used at the command line for simple operations, or it can be written into programs for larger applications. Because *awk* can manipulate data, it is an indispensable tool used in shell scripts and for managing small databases.

Awk scans a file (or input) line by line, from the first to the last line, searching for lines that match a specified pattern and performing selected actions (enclosed in curly braces) on those lines. If there is a pattern with no specific action, all lines that match the pattern are displayed; if there is an action with no pattern, all input lines specified by the action are executed upon.

5.1.1 What Does *awk* Stand for?

Awk stands for the first initials in the last names of each of the authors of the language, Alfred Aho, Brian Kernighan, and Peter Weinberger. They could have called it *wak* or *kaw*, but for whatever reason, *awk* won out.

5.1.2 Which *awk*?

There are a number of versions of *awk*: old *awk*, new *awk*, gnu *awk* (*gawk*), POSIX *awk*, and others. *Awk* was originally written in 1977, and in 1985, the original implementation was improved so that *awk* could handle larger programs. Additional features included user-defined functions, dynamic regular expressions, processing multiple input files, and more. On most systems, the command is *awk* if using the old version, *nawk* if using the new version, and *gawk* if using the gnu version.[1]

---

1. On SCO UNIX, the new version is spelled *awk*, and on Linux, the gnu version is spelled *awk*. This text pertains primarily to the new awk, *nawk*. The gnu implementation, *gawk*, is fully upward-compatible with *nawk*.

5.2 *awk*'s Format

An *awk* program consists of the *awk* command, the program instructions enclosed in quotes (or in a file), and the name of the input file. If an input file is not specified, input comes from standard input (*stdin*), the keyboard.

Awk instructions consist of patterns, actions, or a combination of patterns and actions. A pattern is a statement consisting of an expression of some type. If you do not see the keyword *if*, but you *think* the word *if* when evaluating the expression, it is a pattern. Actions consist of one or more statements separated by semicolons or newlines and enclosed in curly braces. Patterns cannot be enclosed in curly braces, and consist of regular expressions enclosed in forward slashes or expressions consisting of one or more of the many operators provided by *awk*.

Awk commands can be typed at the command line or in *awk* script files. The input lines can come from files, pipes, or standard input.

5.2.1 Input from Files

In the following examples, the percent sign (%) is the C shell prompt.

FORMAT

```
% nawk 'pattern' filename
% nawk '{action}' filename
% nawk 'pattern {action}' filename
```

Here is a sample file called *employees*:

EXAMPLE 5.1

```
% cat employees
Tom Jones      4424    5/12/66    543354
Mary Adams     5346    11/4/63    28765
Sally Chang    1654    7/22/54    650000
Billy Black    1683    9/23/44    336500

% nawk '/Mary/'  employees
Mary Adams     5346    11/4/63    28765
```

EXPLANATION

Nawk prints all lines that contain the pattern *Mary*.

EXAMPLE 5.2

```
% cat employees
Tom Jones      4424    5/12/66     543354
Mary Adams     5346    11/4/63     28765
Sally Chang    1654    7/22/54     650000
Billy Black    1683    9/23/44     336500

% nawk '{print $1}' employees
Tom
Mary
Sally
Billy
```

EXPLANATION

Nawk prints the first field of file *employees*, where the field starts at the left margin of the line and is delimited by whitespace.

EXAMPLE 5.3

```
% cat employees
Tom Jones      4424    5/12/66     543354
Mary Adams     5346    11/4/63     28765
Sally Chang    1654    7/22/54     650000
Billy Black    1683    9/23/44     336500

% nawk '/Sally/{print $1, $2}' employees
Sally Chang
```

EXPLANATION

Nawk prints the first and second fields of file *employees*, only if the line contains the pattern *Sally*. Remember, the field separator is whitespace.

5.2.2 Input from Commands

The output from a UNIX command or commands can be piped to *awk* for processing. Shell programs commonly use *awk* for manipulating commands.

FORMAT

```
% command | nawk 'pattern'
% command | nawk '{action}'
% command | nawk 'pattern {action}'
```

EXAMPLE 5.4

```
1  % df | nawk '$4 > 75000'
   /oracle    (/dev/dsk/c0t0d057 ):390780 blocks      105756 files
   /opt       (/dev/dsk/c0t0d058 ):1943994 blocks      49187 files

2  % rusers  | nawk '/root$/{print  $1}'
   owl
   crow
   bluebird
```

EXPLANATION

1   The *df* command reports the free disk space on file systems. The output of the *df* command is piped to *nawk* (new *awk*). If the fourth field is greater than 75,000 blocks, the line is printed.

2   The *rusers* command prints those logged on remote machines on the network. The output of the *rusers* command is piped to *nawk* as input. The first field is printed if the regular expression *root* is matched at the end of the line ($); that is, all machine names are printed where *root* is logged on.

5.3   Formatting Output

5.3.1   The *print* Function

The action part of the *awk* command is enclosed in curly braces. If no action is specified and a pattern is matched, *awk* takes the default action, which is to print the lines that are matched to the screen. The *print* function is used to print simple output that does not require fancy formatting. For more sophisticated formatting, the *printf* or *sprintf* functions are used. If you are familiar with C, then you already know how *printf* and *sprintf* work.

The *print* function can also be explicitly used in the action part of *awk* as *{print}*. The *print* function accepts arguments as variables, computed values, or string constants. Strings must be enclosed in double quotes. Commas are used to separate the arguments; if commas are not provided, the arguments are concatenated together. The comma evaluates to the value of the output field separator (*OFS*), which is by default a space.

The output of the *print* function can be redirected or piped to another program, and the output of another program can be piped to *awk* for printing. (See "Redirection" on page 16 and "Pipes" on page 19.)

```
% date
Wed Jul 28 22:23:16 PDT 2001

% date | nawk '{ print "Month: " $2 "\nYear: " , $6 }'
Month: Jul
Year: 2001
```

EXPLANATION

The output of the UNIX *date* command will be piped to *nawk*. The string *Month:* is printed, followed by the second field, the string containing the newline character, \n, and *Year:*, followed by the sixth field ($6).

Escape Sequences. Escape sequences are represented by a backslash and a letter or number. They can be used in strings to represent tabs, newlines, form feeds, and so forth (see Table 5.1).

Table 5.1 *print* Escape Sequences

Escape Sequence	Meaning
\b	Backspace.
\f	Form feed.
\n	Newline.
\r	Carriage return.
\t	Tab.
\047	Octal value 47, a single quote.
\c	*c* represents any other character, e.g., \".

```
Tom Jones      4424   5/12/66   543354
Mary Adams     5346   11/4/63   28765
Sally Chang    1654   7/22/54   650000
Billy Black    1683   9/23/44   336500

% nawk '/Sally/{print "\t\tHave a nice day, " $1, $2 "\!"}' employees
        Have a nice day, Sally Chang!
```

EXPLANATION

If the line contains the pattern *Sally*, the *print* function prints two tabs, the string *Have a nice day*, the first (where $1 is *Sally*) and second fields (where $2 is *Chang*), followed by a string containing two exclamation marks.

5.3.2 The *OFMT* Variable

When printing numbers, you may want to control the format of the number. Normally this would be done with the *printf* function, but the special *awk* variable, *OFMT*, can be set to control the printing of numbers when using the *print* function. It is set by default to "*%.6g*"—six significant digits to the right of the decimal are printed. (The following section describes how this value can be changed.)

EXAMPLE 5.7

```
% nawk  'BEGIN{OFMT="%.2f"; print 1.2456789, 12E-2}'
1.25  0.12
```

EXPLANATION

The *OFMT* variable is set so that floating point numbers (*f*) will be printed with two numbers following the decimal point. The percent sign (%) indicates a format is being specified.

5.3.3 The *printf* Function

When printing output, you may want to specify the amount of space between fields so that columns line up neatly. Since the *print* function with tabs does not always guarantee the desired output, the *printf* function can be used for formatting fancy output.

The *printf* function returns a formatted string to standard output, like the *printf* statement in C. The *printf* statement consists of a quoted control string that may be imbedded with format specifications and modifiers. The control string is followed by a comma and a list of comma-separated expressions that will be formatted according to the specifications stated in the control string. Unlike the *print* function, *printf* does not provide a newline. The escape sequence, \n, must be provided if a newline is desired.

For each percent sign and format specifier, there must be a corresponding argument. To print a literal percent sign, two percent signs must be used. See Table 5.2 for a list of *printf* conversion characters and Table 5.3 for *printf* modifiers. The format specifiers are preceded by a percent sign; see Table 5.4 for a list of format *printf* specifiers.

When an argument is printed, the place where the output is printed is called the *field*, and the *width* of the field is the number of characters contained in that field.

The pipe symbol (vertical bar) in the following examples, when part of the *printf* string, is part of the text and is used to indicate where the formatting begins and ends.

EXAMPLE 5.8

```
1    % echo "UNIX" | nawk ' {printf "|%-15s|\n", $1}'
     (Output)
     |UNIX           |
```

```
2    % echo "UNIX" | nawk '{ printf "|%15s|\n", $1}'
     (Output)
     |           UNIX|
```

EXPLANATION

1   The output of the *echo* command, *UNIX*, is piped to *nawk*. The *printf* function contains a control string. The percent sign alerts *printf* that it will be printing a *15-space*, left-justified string enclosed in vertical bars and terminated with a newline. The dash after the percent sign indicates left justification. The control string is followed by a comma and *$1*. The string *UNIX* will be formatted according to the format specification in the control string.

2   The string *UNIX* is printed in a right-justified, 15-space string, enclosed in vertical bars, and terminated with a newline.

EXAMPLE 5.9

```
% cat employees
Tom Jones      4424    5/12/66    543354
Mary Adams     5346    11/4/63    28765
Sally Chang    1654    7/22/54    650000
Billy Black    1683    9/23/44    336500

% nawk '{printf "The name is: %-15s ID  is %8d\n", $1, $3}' employees
The name is Tom            ID is4424
The name is Mary           ID is5346
The name is Sally          ID is1654
The name is Billy          ID is1683
```

EXPLANATION

The string to be printed is enclosed in double quotes. The first format specifier is *%-15s*. It has a corresponding argument, *$1*, positioned directly to the right of the comma after the closing quote in the control string. The percent sign indicates a format specification: The dash means left justify, the *15s* means 15-space string. At this spot, print a left-justified, 15-space string followed by the string *ID is* and a number.

The *%8d* format specifies that the decimal (integer) value of *$2* will be printed in its place within the string. The number will be right justified and take up eight spaces. Placing the quoted string and expressions within parentheses is optional.

Table 5.2 *printf* Conversion Characters

Conversion Character	Definition
c	Character.
s	String.
d	Decimal number.
ld	Long decimal number.
u	Unsigned decimal number.
lu	Long unsigned decimal number.
x	Hexadecimal number.
lx	Long hexidecimal number.
o	Octal number.
lo	Long octal number.
e	Floating point number in scientific notation (*e*-notation).
f	Floating point number.
g	Floating point number using either *e* or *f* conversion, whichever takes the least space.

Table 5.3 *printf* Modifiers

Character	Definition
−	Left-justification modifier.
#	Integers in octal format are displayed with a leading 0; integers in hexadecimal form are displayed with a leading 0*x*.
+	For conversions using *d*, *e*, *f*, and *g*, integers are displayed with a numeric sign + or −.
0	The displayed value is padded with zeros instead of whitespace.

Table 5.4 *printf* Format Specifiers

Format Specifier	What It Does
Given *x* = 'A', *y* = 15, *z* = 2.3, and $1 = Bob Smith:	
%c	Prints a single ASCII character. *printf("The character is %c\n",x) prints: The character is A.*
%d	Prints a decimal number. *printf("The boy is %d years old\n", y) prints: The boy is 15 years old.*
%e	Prints the *e* notation of a number. *printf("z is %e\n",z) prints: z is 2.3e+01.*
%f	Prints a floating point number. *printf("z is %f\n", 2.3 *2) prints: z is 4.600000.*
%o	Prints the octal value of a number. *printf("y is %o\n", y) prints: z is 17.*
%s	Prints a string of characters. *printf("The name of the culprit is %s\n", $1) prints: The name of the culprit is Bob Smith.*
%x	Prints the hex value of a number. *printf ("y is %x\n", y) prints: x is f.*

5.4 *awk* Commands from Within a File

If *awk* commands are placed in a file, the –*f* option is used with the name of the *awk* file, followed by the name of the input file to be processed. A record is read into *awk*'s buffer and each of the commands in the *awk* file are tested and executed for that record. After *awk* has finished with the first record, it is discarded and the next record is read into the buffer, and so on. If an action is not controlled by a pattern, the default behavior is to print the entire record. If a pattern does not have an action associated with it, the default is to print the record where the pattern matches an input line.

EXAMPLE 5.10

```
(The Database)
     $1          $2          $3          $4          $5
     Tom         Jones       4424        5/12/66     543354
     Mary        Adams       5346        11/4/63     28765
     Sally       Chang       1654        7/22/54     650000
     Billy       Black       1683        9/23/44     336500


     % cat awkfile
1    /^Mary/{print "Hello Mary!"}
2    {print $1, $2, $3}


     % nawk -f awkfile employees
     Tom Jones 4424
     Hello Mary!
     Mary Adams 5346
     Sally Chang 1654
     Billy Black 1683
```

EXPLANATION

1 If the record begins with the regular expression *Mary*, the string *Hello Mary*! is printed. The action is controlled by the pattern preceding it. Fields are separated by whitespace.

2 The first, second, and third field of *each* record are printed. The action occurs for each line because there is not a pattern controlling the action.

5.5 Records and Fields

5.5.1 Records

Awk does not see input data as an endless string of characters, but sees it as having a format or structure. By default, each line is called a *record* and is terminated with a newline.

The Record Separator. By default, the output and input record separator (line separator) is a carriage return, stored in the built-in *awk* variables ORS and RS, respectively. The ORS and RS values can be changed, but only in a limited fashion.

The $0 Variable. An entire record is referenced as $0 by *awk*. (When $0 is changed by substitution or assignment, the value of NF, the number of fields, may be changed.) The newline value is stored in *awk*'s built-in variable RS, a carriage return by default.

EXAMPLE 5.11

```
% cat employees
Tom Jones       4424       5/12/66       543354
Mary Adams      5346       11/4/63       28765
Sally Chang     1654       7/22/54       650000
Billy Black     1683       9/23/44       336500

% nawk '{print $0}' employees
Tom Jones       4424       5/12/66       543354
Mary Adams      5346       11/4/63       28765
Sally Chang     1654       7/22/54       650000
Billy Black     1683       9/23/44       336500
```

EXPLANATION

The *nawk* variable *$0* holds the current record. It is printed to the screen. By default, *nawk* would also print the record if the command were

```
% nawk '{print}' employees
```

The NR Variable.   The number of each record is stored in *awk's* built-in variable, *NR*. After a record has been processed, the value of *NR* is incremented by one.

EXAMPLE 5.12

```
% cat employees
Tom Jones       4424       5/12/66       543354
Mary Adams      5346       11/4/63       28765
Sally Chang     1654       7/22/54       650000
Billy Black     1683       9/23/44       336500

% nawk '{print NR, $0}'  employees
1 Tom Jones     4424       5/12/66       543354
2 Mary Adams    5346       11/4/63       28765
3 Sally Chang   1654       7/22/54       650000
4 Billy Black   1683       9/23/44       336500
```

EXPLANATION

Each record, *$0*, is printed as it is stored in the file and is preceded with the number of the record, *NR*.

5.5.2   Fields

Each record consists of words called *fields* which, by default, are separated by whitespace, that is, blank spaces or tabs. Each of these words is called a field, and *awk* keeps track of the number of fields in its built-in variable, *NF.* The value of *NF* can vary from line to line, and the limit is implementation-dependent, typically 100 fields per line. New fields can be created. The following example has four records (lines) and five fields (columns). Each record starts at the first field, represented as *$1*, then moves to the second field, *$2*, and so forth.

EXAMPLE 5.13

(Fields are represented by a dollar sign and the number of the field.)
(The Database)

$1	$2	$3	$4	$5
Tom	Jones	4424	5/12/66	543354
Mary	Adams	5346	11/4/63	28765
Sally	Chang	1654	7/22/54	650000
Billy	Black	1683	9/23/44	336500

```
% nawk '{print NR, $1, $2, $5}'  employees
1 Tom Jones 543354
2 Mary Adams 28765
3 Sally Chang 650000
4 Billy Black 336500
```

EXPLANATION

Nawk will print the number of the record (*NR*), and the first, second, and fifth fields (columns) of each line in the file.

EXAMPLE 5.14

```
% nawk  '{print $0, NF}'  employees
```

Tom Jones	44234	5/12/66	543354	5
Mary Adams	5346	11/4/63	28765	5
Sally Chang	1654	7/22/54	650000	5
Billy Black	1683	9/23/44	336500	5

EXPLANATION

Nawk will print each record (*$0*) in the file, followed by the number of fields.

5.5.3 Field Separators

The Input Field Separator. *Awk's* built-in variable, *FS*, holds the value of the input field separator. When the default value of *FS* is used, *awk* separates fields by spaces and/or tabs, stripping leading blanks and tabs. The *FS* can be changed by assigning a new value to it, either in a *BEGIN* statement or at the command line. For now, we will assign the new value at the command line. To change the value of *FS* at the command line, the *–F* option is used, followed by the character representing the new separator.

Changing the Field Separator at the Command Line.

EXAMPLE 5.15

```
% cat employees
Tom Jones:4424:5/12/66:543354
Mary Adams:5346:11/4/63:28765
Sally Chang:1654:7/22/54:650000
Billy Black:1683:9/23/44:336500

% nawk -F: '/Tom Jones/{print $1, $2}'  employees2
Tom Jones  4424
```

EXPLANATION

The *–F* option is used to reassign the value of the input field separator at the command line. When a colon is placed directly after the *–F* option, *nawk* will look for colons to separate the fields in the *employees* file.

Using More Than One Field Separator. You may specify more than one input separator. If more than one character is used for the field separator, *FS*, then the string is a regular expression and is enclosed in square brackets. In the following example, the field separator is a space, colon, or tab. (The old version of *awk* did not support this feature.)

EXAMPLE 5.16

```
% nawk -F'[ :\t]'  '{print $1, $2, $3}' employees
Tom Jones 4424
Mary Adams 5346
Sally Chang 1654
Billy Black 1683
```

EXPLANATION

The *–F* option is followed by a regular expression enclosed in brackets. If a space, colon, or tab is encountered, *nawk* will use that character as a field separator. The expression is surrounded by quotes so that the shell will not pounce on the metacharacters for its own. (Remember that the shell uses brackets for filename expansion.)

The Output Field Separator.   The default output field separator is a single space and is stored in *awk*'s internal variable, *OFS*. In all of the examples thus far, we have used the *print* statement to send output to the screen. The comma that is used to separate fields in *print* statements evaluates to whatever the *OFS* has been set. If the default is used, the comma inserted between $1 and $2 will evaluate to a single space and the *print* function will print the fields with a space between them. The *OFS* can be changed.

The fields are jammed together because the comma was not used to separate the fields. The *OFS* will not be evaluated unless the comma separates the fields.

EXAMPLE 5.17

```
% cat employees2
Tom Jones:4424:5/12/66:543354
Mary Adams:5346:11/4/63:28765
Sally Chang:1654:7/22/54:650000
Billy Black:1683:9/23/44:336500


(The Command Line)
% nawk -F: '/Tom Jones/{print $1, $2, $3, $4}' employees2
Tom Jones  4424 5/12/66  543354
```

EXPLANATION

The output field separator, a space, is stored in *nawk*'s *OFS* variable. The comma between the fields evaluates to whatever is stored in *OFS*. The fields are printed to standard output separated by a space.

EXAMPLE 5.18

```
% nawk -F: '/Tom Jones/{print $1 $2 $3 $4}' employees2
Tom Jones44245/12/66543354
```

EXPLANATION

```
% nawk -F: '/Tom Jones/{print $0}' employees2
Tom Jones:4424:5/12/66:543354
```

The $0 variable holds the current record exactly as it is found in the input file. The record will be printed as-is.

5.6   Patterns and Actions

5.6.1   Patterns

Awk patterns control what actions *awk* will take on a line of input. A pattern consists of a regular expression, an expression resulting in a true or false condition, or a combination of these. The default action is to print each line where the expression results in a true condition. When reading a pattern expression, there is an implied *if* statement. When an *if* is implied, there can be no curly braces surrounding it. When the *if* is explicit, it becomes an action statement and the syntax is different. (See "Conditional Statements" on page 165.)

EXAMPLE 5.19

```
% cat employees
Tom Jones      4424    5/12/66    543354
Mary Adams     5346    11/4/63    28765
Sally Chang    1654    7/22/54    650000
Billy Black    1683    9/23/44    336500


(The Command Line)
1    nawk '/Tom/' employees
     Tom Jones    4424   5/12/66   543354

2    nawk '$3 < 4000' employees
     Sally Chang 1654   7/22/54   650000
     Billy Black 1683   9/23/44   336500
```

EXPLANATION

1 If the pattern *Tom* is matched in the input file, the record is printed. The default action is to print the line if no explicit action is specified. This is equivalent to

   ```
   nawk '$0 ~ /Tom/{print $0}' employees
   ```

2 If the third field is less than *4000*, the record is printed.

5.6.2 Actions

Actions are statements enclosed within curly braces and separated by semicolons.[2] If a pattern precedes an action, the pattern dictates when the action will be performed. Actions can be simple statements or complex groups of statements. Statements are separated by semicolons, or by a newline if placed on their own line.

FORMAT

```
{ action }
```

---

2. On some versions of *awk*, actions must be separated by semicolons or newlines, and the statements within the curly braces also must be separated by semicolons or newlines. SVR4's *nawk* requires the use of semicolons or newlines to separate statements within an action, but does not require the use of semicolons to separate actions; for example, the two actions that follow do not need a semicolon:
```
nawk '/Tom/{print "hi Tom"};{x=5}'  file
```

EXAMPLE 5.20

```
{ print $1, $2 }
```

EXPLANATION

The action is to print fields *1* and *2*.

    Patterns can be associated with actions. Remember, actions are statements enclosed in curly braces. A pattern controls the action from the first open curly brace to the first closing curly brace. If an action follows a pattern, the first opening curly brace must be on the same line as the pattern. Patterns are *never* enclosed in curly braces.

FORMAT

```
pattern{ action statement; action statement; etc. }
      or
pattern{
      action statement
      action statement
}
```

EXAMPLE 5.21

```
% nawk '/Tom/{print "Hello there, "  $1}' employees
Hello there, Tom
```

EXPLANATION

If the record contains the pattern *Tom,* the string *Hello there, Tom* will print.

    A pattern with no action displays all lines matching the pattern. String-matching patterns contain regular expressions enclosed in forward slashes.

5.7   Regular Expressions

A *regular expression* to *awk* is a pattern that consists of characters enclosed in forward slashes. *Awk* supports the use of regular expression metacharacters (same as *egrep*) to modify the regular expression in some way. If a string in the input line is matched by the regular expression, the resulting condition is true, and any actions associated with the expression are executed. If no action is specified and an input line is matched by the regular expression, the record is printed. See Table 5.5.

EXAMPLE 5.22

```
% nawk  '/Mary/'  employees
Mary Adams      5346    11/4/63    28765
```

EXPLANATION

All lines in the *employees* file containing the regular expression pattern *Mary* are displayed.

EXAMPLE 5.23

```
% nawk  '/Mary/{print $1, $2}'  employees
Mary Adams
```

EXPLANATION

The first and second fields of all lines in the *employees* file containing the regular expression pattern *Mary* are displayed.

Table 5.5   *awk* Regular Expression Metacharacters

^	Matches at the beginning of string.
$	Matches at the end of string.
.	Matches for a single character.
*	Matches for zero or more of preceding character.
+	Matches for one or more of preceding character.
?	Matches for zero or one of preceding character.
[ABC]	Matches for any one character in the set of characters, i.e., A, B, or C.
[^ABC]	Matches character not in the set of characters, i.e., A, B, or C.
[A–Z]	Matches for any character in the range from A to Z.
A|B	Matches either A or B.
(AB)+	Matches one or more sets of AB.
*	Matches for a literal asterisk.
&	Used in the replacement string, to represent what was found in the search string.

EXAMPLE 5.24

```
% nawk  '/^Mary/'  employees
Mary Adams     5346    11/4/63   28765
```

EXPLANATION

All lines in the *employees* file that start with the regular expression *Mary* are displayed.

EXAMPLE 5.25

```
% nawk '/^[A-Z][a-z]+ /' employees
Tom Jones      4424    5/12/66    543354
Mary Adams     5346    11/4/63    28765
Sally Chang    1654    7/22/54    650000
Billy Black    1683    9/23/44    336500
```

EXPLANATION

All lines in the *employees* file where the line begins with an uppercase letter, followed by one or more lowercase letters, followed by a space are displayed.

5.7.1 The *match* Operator

The *match* operator, the tilde (~), is used to match an expression within a record or field.

EXAMPLE 5.26

```
% cat employees
Tom Jones      44234   5/12/66    543354
Mary Adams     5346    11/4/63    28765
Sally Chang    1654    7/22/54    650000
Billy Black    1683    9/23/44    336500

% nawk '$1 ~ /[Bb]ill/' employees
Billy Black    1683    9/23/44    336500
```

EXPLANATION

Any lines matching *Bill* or *bill* in the first field are displayed.

EXAMPLE 5.27

```
% nawk '$1 !~ /ly$/' employees
Tom Jones      4424    5/12/66    543354
Mary Adams     5346    11/4/63    28765
```

EXPLANATION

Any lines not matching *ly*, when *ly* is at the end of the first field are displayed.

5.8 *awk* Commands in a Script File

When you have multiple *awk* pattern/action statements, it is often much easier to put the statements in a script. The script is a file containing *awk* comments and statements. If statements and actions are on the same line, they are separated by semicolons. If statements are on separate lines, semicolons are not necessary. If an action follows a pattern, the opening curly brace must be on the same line as the pattern. Comments are preceded by a pound (#) sign.

EXAMPLE 5.28

```
% cat employees
Tom Jones:4424:5/12/66:54335
Mary Adams:5346:11/4/63:28765
Billy Black:1683:9/23/44:336500
Sally Chang:1654:7/22/54:65000
Jose Tomas:1683:9/23/44:33650

(The Awk Script)
% cat info
1    # My first awk script by Jack Sprat
     # Script name: info; Date: February 28, 2001
2    /Tom/{print  "Tom's birthday is "$3}
3    /Mary/{print NR, $0}
4    /^Sally/{print "Hi Sally. "  $1 " has a salary of  $" $4 "."}
     # End of info script

(The Command Line)
5    % nawk -F: -f info employees2
     Tom's birthday is 5/12/66
     2 Mary Adams:5346:11/4/63:28765
     Hi Sally. Sally Chang has a salary of $65000.
```

EXPLANATION

1   These are comment lines.

2   If the regular expression *Tom* is matched against an input line, the string *Tom's birthday is* and the value of the third field ($3) are printed.

3   If the regular expression *Mary* is matched against an input line, the action block prints *NR*, the number of the current record, and the record.

4   If the regular expression *Sally* is found at the beginning of the input line, the string *Hi Sally.* is printed, followed by the value of the first field ($1), the string *has a salary of $*, and the value of the fourth field ($4).

5   The *nawk* command is followed by the *–F:* option, specifying the colon to be the field separator. The *–f* option is followed by the name of the *awk* script. *Awk* will read instructions from the *info* file. The input file, *employees2,* is next.

5.9   Review

The examples in this section use a sample database, called *datafile*. In the database, the input field separator, *FS*, is whitespace, the default. The number of fields, *NF*, is 8. The number may vary from line to line, but in this file, the number of fields is fixed. The record separator, *RS*, is the newline, which separates each line of the file. *Awk* keeps track of the number of each record in the *NR* variable. The output field separator, *OFS*, is a space. If a comma is used to separate fields, when the line is printed, each field printed will be separated by a space.

5.9.1   Simple Pattern Matching

```
% cat datafile
northwest      NW    Joel Craig       3.0    .98    3    4
western        WE    Sharon Kelly     5.3    .97    5    23
southwest      SW    Chris Foster     2.7    .8     2    18
southern       SO    May Chin         5.1    .95    4    15
southeast      SE    Derek Johnson    4.0    .7     4    17
eastern        EA    Susan Beal       4.4    .84    5    20
northeast      NE    TJ Nichols       5.1    .94    3    13
north          NO    Val Shultz       4.5    .89    5    9
central        CT    Sheri Watson     5.7    .94    5    13
```

EXAMPLE 5.29

```
nawk '/west/'  datafile
northwest      NW    Joel Craig       3.0  .98  3    4
western        WE    Sharon Kelly     5.3  .97  5    23
southwest      SW    Chris Foster     2.7  .8   2    18
```

EXPLANATION

All lines containing the pattern *west* are printed.

EXAMPLE 5.30

```
nawk '/^north/' datafile
northwest    NW    Joel Craig      3.0  .98  3   4
northeast    NE    TJ Nichols      5.1  .94  3   13
north        NO    Val Shultz      4.5  .89  5   9
```

EXPLANATION
All lines beginning with the pattern *north* are printed.

EXAMPLE 5.31

```
nawk '/^(no|so)/' datafile
northwest    NW    Joel Craig      3.0  .98  3   4
southwest    SW    Chris Foster    2.7  .8   2   18
southern     SO    May Chin        5.1  .95  4   15
southeast    SE    Derek Johnson   4.0  .7   4   17
northeast    NE    TJ Nichols      5.1  .94  3   13
north        NO    Val Shultz      4.5  .89  5   9
```

EXPLANATION
All lines beginning with the pattern *no* or *so* are printed.

5.9.2 Simple Actions

EXAMPLE 5.32

```
nawk '{print $3, $2}' datafile
Joel NW
Sharon WE
Chris SW
May SO
Derek SE
Susan EA
TJ NE
Val NO
Sheri CT
```

EXPLANATION
The output field separator, *OFS*, is a space by default. The comma between $3 and $2 is translated to the value of the *OFS*. The third field is printed, followed by a space and the second field.

```
% cat datafile
northwest    NW    Joel Craig        3.0   .98   3   4
western      WE    Sharon Kelly      5.3   .97   5   23
southwest    SW    Chris Foster      2.7   .8    2   18
southern     SO    May Chin          5.1   .95   4   15
southeast    SE    Derek Johnson     4.0   .7    4   17
eastern      EA    Susan Beal        4.4   .84   5   20
northeast    NE    TJ Nichols        5.1   .94   3   13
north        NO    Val Shultz        4.5   .89   5   9
central      CT    Sheri Watson      5.7   .94   5   13
```

EXAMPLE 5.33

```
nawk '{print $3 $2}' datafile
JoelNW
SharonWE
ChrisSW
MaySO
DerekSE
SusanEA
TJNE
ValNO
SheriCT
```

EXPLANATION

The third field is followed by the second field. Since the comma does not separate fields $3 and $2, the output is displayed without spaces between the fields.

EXAMPLE 5.34

```
nawk 'print $1' datafile
nawk: syntax error at source line 1
 context is
         >>> print <<<   $1
nawk: bailing out at source line 1
```

EXPLANATION

This is the *nawk* (new *awk*) error message. *Nawk* error messages are much more verbose than those of the old *awk*. In this program, the curly braces are missing in the action statement.

EXAMPLE 5.35

```
awk 'print $1' datafile
awk: syntax error near line 1
awk: bailing out near line 1
```

EXPLANATION

This is the *awk* (old *awk*) error message. Old *awk* programs were difficult to debug since almost all errors produced this same message. The curly braces are missing in the action statement.

EXAMPLE 5.36

```
nawk '{print $0}' datafile
northwest    NW    Joel Craig       3.0   .98   3    4
western      WE    Sharon Kelly     5.3   .97   5    23
southwest    SW    Chris Foster     2.7   .8    2    18
southern     SO    May Chin         5.1   .95   4    15
southeast    SE    Derek Johnson    4.0   .7    4    17
eastern      EA    Susan Beal       4.4   .84   5    20
northeast    NE    TJ Nichols       5.1   .94   3    13
north        NO    Val Shultz       4.5   .89   5    9
central      CT    Sheri Watson     5.7   .94   5    13
```

EXPLANATION

Each record is printed. $0 holds the current record.

EXAMPLE 5.37

```
nawk '{print "Number of fields: "NF}' datafile
Number of fields: 8
Number of fields: 8
Number of fields: 8
Number of fields: 8
Number of fields: 8
Number of fields: 8
Number of fields: 8
Number of fields: 8
Number of fields: 8
```

EXPLANATION

There are 8 fields in each record. The built-in *awk* variable NF holds the number of fields and is reset for each record.

```
% cat datafile
```

northwest	NW	Joel Craig	3.0	.98	3	4
western	WE	Sharon Kelly	5.3	.97	5	23
southwest	SW	Chris Foster	2.7	.8	2	18
southern	SO	May Chin	5.1	.95	4	15
southeast	SE	Derek Johnson	4.0	.7	4	17
eastern	EA	Susan Beal	4.4	.84	5	20
northeast	NE	TJ Nichols	5.1	.94	3	13
north	NO	Val Shultz	4.5	.89	5	9
central	CT	Sheri Watson	5.7	.94	5	13

5.9.3 Regular Expressions in Pattern and Action Combinations

EXAMPLE 5.38

```
nawk '/northeast/{print $3, $2}' datafile
TJ NE
```

EXPLANATION

If the record contains (or matches) the pattern *northeast*, the third field, followed by the second field, is printed.

EXAMPLE 5.39

```
nawk '/E/' datafile
```

western	WE	Sharon Kelly	5.3	.97	5	23
southeast	SE	Derek Johnson	4.0	.7	4	17
eastern	EA	Susan Beal	4.4	.84	5	20
northeast	NE	TJ Nichols	5.1	.94	3	13

EXPLANATION

If the record contains an *E*, the entire record is printed.

EXAMPLE 5.40

```
nawk '/^[ns]/{print $1}' datafile
northwest
southwest
southern
southeast
northeast
north
```

EXPLANATION

If the record begins with an *n* or *s*, the first field is printed.

EXAMPLE 5.41

```
nawk '$5 ~ /\.[7-9]+/' datafile
southwest      SW      Chris Foster       2.7  .8   2    18
central        CT      Sheri Watson       5.7  .94  5    13
```

EXPLANATION

If the fifth field ($5) contains a literal period, followed by one or more numbers between 7 and 9, the record is printed.

EXAMPLE 5.42

```
nawk '$2 !~ /E/{print $1, $2}' datafile
northwest NW
southwest SW
southern SO
north NO
central CT
```

EXPLANATION

If the second field does not contain the pattern *E*, the first field followed by the second field ($1, $2) is printed.

```
% cat datafile
```

northwest	NW	Joel Craig	3.0	.98	3	4
western	WE	Sharon Kelly	5.3	.97	5	23
southwest	SW	Chris Foster	2.7	.8	2	18
southern	SO	May Chin	5.1	.95	4	15
southeast	SE	Derek Johnson	4.0	.7	4	17
eastern	EA	Susan Beal	4.4	.84	5	20
northeast	NE	TJ Nichols	5.1	.94	3	13
north	NO	Val Shultz	4.5	.89	5	9
central	CT	Sheri Watson	5.7	.94	5	13

EXAMPLE 5.43

```
nawk '$3 ~ /^Joel/{print $3 " is a nice guy."}' datafile
Joel is a nice guy.
```

EXPLANATION

If the third field ($3) begins with the pattern *Joel*, the third field followed by the string *is a nice guy.* is printed. Note that a space is included in the string if it is to be printed.

EXAMPLE 5.44

```
nawk '$8 ~ /[0-9][0-9]$/{print $8}' datafile
23
18
15
17
20
13
13
```

EXPLANATION

If the eighth field ($8) ends in two digits, it is printed.

EXAMPLE 5.45

```
nawk '$4 ~ /Chin$/{print "The price is $" $8 "."}' datafile
The price is $15.
```

EXPLANATION

If the fourth field ($4) ends with *Chin*, the string enclosed in double quotes (*"The price is $"*), the eighth field ($8), and the string containing a period are printed.

EXAMPLE 5.46

```
nawk '/TJ/{print $0}' datafile
northeast      NE     TJ Nichols          5.1 .94  3   13
```

EXPLANATION

If the record contains the pattern *TJ*, *$0* (the record) is printed.

5.9.4 Input Field Separators

% **cat datafile2**
Joel Craig:northwest:NW:3.0:.98:3:4
Sharon Kelly:western:WE:5.3:.97:5:23
Chris Foster:southwest:SW:2.7:.8:2:18
May Chin:southern:SO:5.1:.95:4:15
Derek Johnson:southeast:SE:4.0:.7:4:17
Susan Beal:eastern:EA:4.4:.84:5:20
TJ Nichols:northeast:NE:5.1:.94:3:13
Val Shultz:north:NO:4.5:.89:5:9
Sheri Watson:central:CT:5.7:.94:5:13

EXAMPLE 5.47

```
nawk '{print $1}' datafile2
Joel
Sharon
Chris
May
Derek
Susan
TJ
Val
Sheri
```

EXPLANATION

The default input field separator is whitespace. The first field (*$1*) is printed.

% cat datafile2
Joel Craig:northwest:NW:3.0:.98:3:4
Sharon Kelly:western:WE:5.3:.97:5:23
Chris Foster:southwest:SW:2.7:.8:2:18
May Chin:southern:SO:5.1:.95:4:15
Derek Johnson:southeast:SE:4.0:.7:4:17
Susan Beal:eastern:EA:4.4:.84:5:20
TJ Nichols:northeast:NE:5.1:.94:3:13
Val Shultz:north:NO:4.5:.89:5:9
Sheri Watson:central:CT:5.7:.94:5:13

EXAMPLE 5.48

```
nawk -F: '{print $1}' datafile2
```
Joel Craig
Sharon Kelly
Chris Foster
                    <more output here>
Val Shultz
Sheri Watson

EXPLANATION

The *–F* option specifies the colon as the input field separator. The first field (*$1*) is printed.

EXAMPLE 5.49

```
nawk '{print "Number of fields: "NF}' datafile2
```
Number of fields: 2
Number of fields: 2
Number of fields: 2
                    <more of the same output here>
Number of fields: 2
Number of fields: 2

EXPLANATION

Since the field separator is the default (whitespace) the number of fields for each record is 2. The only space is between the first and last name.

EXAMPLE 5.50

```
nawk -F: '{print "Number of fields: "NF}' datafile2
Number of fields: 7
Number of fields: 7
Number of fields: 7
          <more of the same output here>
Number of fields: 7
Number of fields: 7
```

EXPLANATION

Since the field separator is a colon, the number of fields in each record is 7.

EXAMPLE 5.51

```
nawk -F"[ :]" '{print $1, $2}' datafile2
Joel Craig northwest
Sharon Kelly western
Chris Foster southwest
May Chin southern
Derek Johnson southeast
Susan Beal eastern
TJ Nichols northeast
Val Shultz north
Sheri Watson central
```

EXPLANATION

Multiple field separators can be specified with *nawk* as a regular expression. Either a space or a colon will be designated as a field separator. The first and second fields (*$1*, *$2*) are printed.

```
% cat datafile
northwest      NW     Joel Craig         3.0    .98    3    4
western        WE     Sharon Kelly       5.3    .97    5    23
southwest      SW     Chris Foster       2.7    .8     2    18
southern       SO     May Chin           5.1    .95    4    15
southeast      SE     Derek Johnson      4.0    .7     4    17
eastern        EA     Susan Beal         4.4    .84    5    20
northeast      NE     TJ Nichols         5.1    .94    3    13
north          NO     Val Shultz         4.5    .89    5    9
central        CT     Sheri Watson       5.7    .94    5    13
```

5.9.5   *awk* Scripting

EXAMPLE 5.52

```
cat nawk.sc1
# This is a comment
# This is my first awk script
1   /^north/{print $1, $2, $3}
2   /^south/{print "The " $1 " district."}


nawk -f nawk.sc1 datafile
3   northwest NW Joel
    The southwest district.
    The southern district.
    The southeast district.
    northeast NE TJ
    north NO Val
```

EXPLANATION

1   If the record begins with the pattern *north*, the first, second, and third fields (*$1, $2, $3*) are printed.

2   If the record begins with the pattern *south*, the string *The*, followed by the value of the first field (*$1*), and the string *district.* are printed.

3   The *–f* option precedes the name of the *awk* script file, followed by the input file that is to be processed.

UNIX TOOLS LAB EXERCISE

Lab 3: *awk* Exercise

```
Mike Harrington:(510) 548-1278:250:100:175
Christian Dobbins:(408) 538-2358:155:90:201
Susan Dalsass:(206) 654-6279:250:60:50
Archie McNichol:(206) 548-1348:250:100:175
Jody Savage:(206) 548-1278:15:188:150
Guy Quigley:(916) 343-6410:250:100:175
Dan Savage:(406) 298-7744:450:300:275
Nancy McNeil:(206) 548-1278:250:80:75
John Goldenrod:(916) 348-4278:250:100:175
Chet Main:(510) 548-5258:50:95:135
Tom Savage:(408) 926-3456:250:168:200
Elizabeth Stachelin:(916) 440-1763:175:75:300
```

The database above contains the names, phone numbers, and money contributions to the party campaign for the past three months.

1. Print all the phone numbers.

2. Print *Dan's* phone number.

3. Print *Susan's* name and phone number.

4. Print all last names beginning with *D*.

5. Print all first names beginning with either a *C* or *E*.

6. Print all first names containing only four characters.

7. Print the first names of all those in the *916* area code.

8. Print *Mike's* campaign contributions. Each value should be printed with a leading dollar sign; e.g., $250 $100 $175.

9. Print last names followed by a comma and the first name.

10. Write an *awk* script called *facts* that:

    a. Prints full names and phone numbers for the *Savages*.

    b. Prints *Chet's* contributions.

    c. Prints all those who contributed $250 the first month.

chapter
6

The *awk* Utility: *awk* Programming Constructs

6.1   Comparison Expressions

Comparison expressions match lines where if the condition is true, the action is performed. These expressions use relational operators and are used to compare numbers or strings. Table 6.1 provides a list of the relational operators. The value of the expression is 1 if the expression evaluates true, and 0 if false.

6.1.1   Relational Operators

Table 6.1   Relational Operators

Operator	Meaning	Example
<	Less than.	$x < y$
<=	Less than or equal to.	$x <= y$
==	Equal to.	$x == y$
!=	Not equal to.	$x != y$
>=	Greater than or equal to.	$x >= y$
>	Greater than.	$x > y$
~	Matched by regular expression.	$x \sim /y/$
!~	Not matched by regular expression.	$x !\sim /y/$

EXAMPLE 6.1

```
(The Database)
% cat employee
Tom Jones      4423    5/12/66    543354
Mary Adams     5346    11/4/63    28765
Sally Chang    1654    7/22/54    650000
Billy Black    1683    9/23/44    336500

(The Command Line)
1   % nawk '$3 == 5346' employees
    Mary Adams   5346    11/4/63    28765

2   % nawk '$3 > 5000{print $1} ' employees
    Mary

3   % nawk '$2 ~ /Adam/ ' employees
    Mary Adams   5346    11/4/63    28765

4   % nawk '$2 !~ /Adam/ ' employees
    Tom Jones     4423    5/12/66    543354
    Sally Chang   1654    7/22/54    650000
    Billy Black   1683    9/23/44    336500
```

EXPLANATION

1   If the third field is equal to 5346, the condition is true and *awk* will perform the default action—print the line. When an *if* condition is implied, it is a conditional pattern test.

2   If the third field is greater than 5000, *awk* prints the first field.

3   If the second field matches the regular expression *Adam*, the record is printed.

4   If the second field does not match the regular expression *Adam,* the record is printed. If an expression is a numeric value and is being compared to a string value with an operator that requires a numeric comparison, the string value will be converted to a numeric value. If the operator requires a string value, the numeric value will be converted to a string value.

6.1.2   Conditional Expressions

A conditional expression uses two symbols, the question mark and the colon, to evaluate expressions. It is really just a short way to achieve the same result as doing an *if/else* statement. The general format is shown below.

FORMAT

```
conditional expression1 ? expression2 : expression3
```

This produces the same result as the *if/else* shown below. (A complete discussion of the *if/else* construct is given later.)

```
{
if (expression1)
        expression2
else
        expression3
}
```

```
nawk '{max=($1 > $2) ? $1 : $2; print max}' filename
```

If the first field is greater than the second field, the value of the expression after the question mark is assigned to *max*, otherwise the value of the expression after the colon is assigned to *max*.

This is comparable to

```
if ($1 > $2)
     max=$1
else
     max=$2
```

6.1.3   Computation

Computation can be performed within patterns. *Awk* performs all arithmetic in floating point. The arithmetic operators are provided in Table 6.2.

Table 6.2   Arithmetic Operators

Operator	Meaning	Example
+	Add	$x + y$
−	Subtract	$x - y$
*	Multiply	$x * y$
/	Divide	x / y
%	Modulus	$x \% y$
^	Exponentiation	$x ^ y$

EXAMPLE 6.3

```
nawk '$3 * $4 > 500' filename
```

EXPLANATION

Awk will multiply the third field (*$3*) by the fourth field (*$4*), and if the result is greater than *500*, it will display those lines. (*filename* is assumed to be a file containing the input.)

6.1.4 Compound Patterns

Compound patterns are expressions that combine patterns with logical operators (see Table 6.3). An expression is evaluated from left to right.

Table 6.3 Logical Operators

Operator	Meaning	Example
&&	Logical *and*	*a && b*
||	Logical *or*	*a || b*
!	*not*	*! a*

EXAMPLE 6.4

```
nawk '$2 > 5 && $2 <= 15' filename
```

EXPLANATION

Awk will display those lines that match both conditions; that is, where the second field (*$2*) is greater than *5 and* the second field (*$2*) is also less than or equal to *15*. With the && operator, *both* conditions must be true. (*filename* is assumed to be a file containing the input.)

EXAMPLE 6.5

```
nawk '$3 == 100 || $4 > 50' filename
```

EXPLANATION

Awk will display those lines that match one of the conditions; that is, where the third field is equal to *100 or* the fourth field is greater than *50*. With the \|\| operator, only one of the conditions must be true. (*filename* is assumed to be a file containing the input.)

EXAMPLE 6.6

```
nawk '!($2 < 100 && $3 < 20)' filename
```

EXPLANATION

If both conditions are true, *awk* will negate the expression and display those lines. So the lines displayed will have one or both conditions false. The unary *!* operator negates the result of the condition so that if the expression yields a true condition, the *not* will make it false, and vice versa. (*filename* is assumed to be a file containing the input.)

6.1.5 Range Patterns

Range patterns match from the first occurrence of one pattern to the first occurrence of the second pattern, then match for the next occurrence of the first pattern to the next occurrence of the second pattern, etc. If the first pattern is matched and the second pattern is not found, *awk* will display all lines to the end of the file.

EXAMPLE 6.7

```
nawk '/Tom/,/Suzanne/' filename
```

EXPLANATION

Awk will display all lines, inclusive, that range between the first occurrence of *Tom* and the first occurrence of *Suzanne*. If *Suzanne* is not found, *awk* will continue processing lines until the end of file. If, after the range between *Tom* and *Suzanne* is printed, *Tom* appears again, *awk* will start displaying lines until another *Suzanne* is found or the file ends.

6.1.6 A Data Validation Program

Using the *awk* commands discussed so far, the following password-checking program from the book, *The AWK Programming Language*,[1] illustrates how the data in a file can be validated.

---

1. Alfred V. Aho, Brian W. Kernighan, and Peter J. Weinberger, *The AWK Programming Language* (Boston: Addison-Wesley, 1988). © 1988 Bell Telephone Laboratories, Inc. Reprinted by permission of Pearson Education, Inc.

EXAMPLE 6.8

(The Password Database)

```
1   % cat /etc/passwd
    tooth:pwHfudo.eC9sM:476:40:Contract Admin.:/home/rickenbacker/tooth:/bin/csh
    lisam:9JY7OuS2f31HY:4467:40:Lisa M. Spencer:/home/fortune1/lisam:/bin/csh
    goode:v7Ww.nWJCeSIQ:32555:60:Goodwill Guest User:/usr/goodwill:/bin/csh
    bonzo:eTZbu6M2jM7VA:5101:911: SSTOOL Log account :/home/sun4/bonzo:/bin/csh
    info:mKZsrioPtW9hA:611:41:Terri Stern:/home/chewie/info:/bin/csh
    cnc:IN1IVqVj1bVv2:10209:41:Charles Carnell:/home/christine/cnc:/bin/csh
    bee:*:347:40:Contract Temp.:/home/chanel5/bee:/bin/csh
    friedman:oyuIiKoFTV0TE:3561:50:Jay Friedman:/home/ibanez/friedman:/bin/csh
    chambers:Rw7R1k77yUY4.:592:40:Carol Chambers:/usr/callisto2/chambers:/bin/csh
    gregc:nkLulOg:7777:30:Greg Champlin FE Chicago
    ramona:gbDQLdDBeRc46:16660:68:RamonaLeininge MWA CustomerService Rep:/
    home/forsh:
```

(The *Awk* Commands)

```
2   % cat /etc/passwd | nawk -F: ' \
3   NF != 7{\
4   printf("line %d, does not have 7 fields: %s\n",NR,$0)} \
5   $1 !~ /[A-Za-z0-9]/{printf("line %d, nonalphanumeric user id: %s\n",NR,$0)} \
6   $2 == "*" {printf("line %d, no password: %s\n",NR,$0)} '
```

(The Output)
line 7, no password: bee::347:40:Contract Temp.:/home/chanel5/bee:/bin/csh*
line 10, does not have 7 fields: gregc:nk2EYi7kLulOg:7777:30:Greg Champlin
FE Chicago
line 11, does not have 7 fields: ramona:gbDQLdDBeRc46:16660:68:Ramona
Leininger MWA Customer Service Rep:/home/forsh:

EXPLANATION

1   The contents of the */etc/passwd* file are displayed.

2   The *cat* program sends its output to *awk*. *Awk*'s field separator is a colon.

3   If the number of fields (*NF*) is not equal to 7, the following action block is executed.

4   The *printf* function prints the string *line <number>, does not have 7 fields:* followed by the number of the current record (*NR*) and the record itself (*$0*).

5   If the first field (*$1*) does not contain any alphanumeric characters, the *printf* function prints the string *nonalphanumeric user id:*, followed by the number of the record and the record.

6   If the second field (*$2*) equals an asterisk, the string *no passwd:* is printed, followed by the number of the record and the record itself.

6.2 Review

6.2.1 Equality Testing

```
% cat datafile
northwest      NW    Joel Craig       3.0   .98   3   4
western        WE    Sharon Kelly     5.3   .97   5   23
southwest      SW    Chris Foster     2.7   .8    2   18
southern       SO    May Chin         5.1   .95   4   15
southeast      SE    Derek Johnson    4.0   .7    4   17
eastern        EA    Susan Beal       4.4   .84   5   20
northeast      NE    TJ Nichols       5.1   .94   3   13
north          NO    Val Shultz       4.5   .89   5   9
central        CT    Sheri Watson     5.7   .94   5   13
```

EXAMPLE 6.9

```
nawk '$7 == 5' datafile
western        WE    Sharon Kelly     5.3  .97  5   23
eastern        EA    Susan Beal       4.4  .84  5   20
north          NO    Val Shultz       4.5  .89  5   9
central        CT    Sheri Watson     5.7  .94  5   13
```

EXPLANATION

If the seventh field ($7) is equal to the number 5, the record is printed.

EXAMPLE 6.10

```
nawk '$2 == "CT"{print $1, $2}' datafile
central        CT
```

EXPLANATION

If the second field is equal to the string *CT*, fields one and two ($1, $2) are printed. Strings must be quoted.

```
% cat datafile
northwest        NW     Joel Craig        3.0    .98    3    4
western          WE     Sharon Kelly      5.3    .97    5    23
southwest        SW     Chris Foster      2.7    .8     2    18
southern         SO     May Chin          5.1    .95    4    15
southeast        SE     Derek Johnson     4.0    .7     4    17
eastern          EA     Susan Beal        4.4    .84    5    20
northeast        NE     TJ Nichols        5.1    .94    3    13
north            NO     Val Shultz        4.5    .89    5    9
central          CT     Sheri Watson      5.7    .94    5    13
```

6.2.2   Relational Operators

EXAMPLE 6.11

```
nawk '$7 != 5' datafile
northwest      NW      Joel Craig        3.0  .98  3    4
southwest      SW      Chris Foster      2.7  .8   2    18
southern       SO      May Chin          5.1  .95  4    15
southeast      SE      Derek Johnson     4.0  .7   4    17
northeast      NE      TJ Nichols        5.1  .94  3    13
```

EXPLANATION

If the seventh field ($7) is not equal to the number 5, the record is printed.

EXAMPLE 6.12

```
nawk '$7 < 5 {print $4, $7}' datafile
Craig 3
Foster 2
Chin 4
Johnson 4
Nichols 3
```

EXPLANATION

If the seventh field ($7) is less than 5, fields 4 and 7 are printed.

EXAMPLE 6.13

```
nawk '$6 > .9 {print $1, $6}' datafile
northwest .98
western .97
southern .95
northeast .94
central .94
```

EXPLANATION

If the sixth field ($6) is greater than .9, fields 1 and 6 are printed.

EXAMPLE 6.14

```
nawk '$8 <= 17 { print $8}' datafile
4
15
17
13
9
13
```

EXPLANATION

If the eighth field ($8) is less than or equal to 17, it is printed.

EXAMPLE 6.15

```
nawk '$8 >= 17 {print $8}' datafile
23
18
17
20
```

EXPLANATION

If the eighth field is greater than or equal to 17, the eighth field is printed.

% **cat datafile**						
northwest	NW	Joel Craig	3.0	.98	3	4
western	WE	Sharon Kelly	5.3	.97	5	23
southwest	SW	Chris Foster	2.7	.8	2	18
southern	SO	May Chin	5.1	.95	4	15
southeast	SE	Derek Johnson	4.0	.7	4	17
eastern	EA	Susan Beal	4.4	.84	5	20
northeast	NE	TJ Nichols	5.1	.94	3	13
north	NO	Val Shultz	4.5	.89	5	9
central	CT	Sheri Watson	5.7	.94	5	13

6.2.3   Logical Operators

EXAMPLE 6.16

```
nawk '$8 > 10 && $8 < 17' datafile
southern      SO      May Chin        5.1  .95  4    15
northeast     NE      TJ Nichols      5.1  .94  3    13
central       CT      Sheri Watson    5.7  .94  5    13
```

EXPLANATION

If the eighth field ($8) is greater than 10 and less than 17, the record is printed. The record will be printed only if both expressions are true.

EXAMPLE 6.17

```
nawk '$2 == "NW" || $1 ~ /south/{print $1, $2}' datafile
northwest NW
southwest SW
southern SO
southeast SE
```

EXPLANATION

If the second field ($2) is equal to the string NW or the first field ($1) contains the pattern south, the first and second fields ($1, $2) are printed. The record will be printed if only one of the expressions is true.

6.2.4 Logical *not* Operator

EXAMPLE 6.18

```
nawk '!($8 == 13){print $8}' datafile
4
23
18
15
17
20
9
```

EXPLANATION

If the eighth field ($8) is equal to 13, the ! (not operator) *not*s the expression and prints the eighth field ($8). The ! is a unary negation operator.

6.2.5 Arithmetic Operators

EXAMPLE 6.19

```
nawk '/southern/{print $5 + 10}' datafile
15.1
```

EXPLANATION

If the record contains the regular expression *southern*, 10 is added to the value of the fifth field ($5) and printed. Note that the number prints in floating point.

EXAMPLE 6.20

```
nawk '/southern/{print $8 + 10}' datafile
25
```

EXPLANATION

If the record contains the regular expression *southern*, 10 is added to the value of the eighth field ($8) and printed. Note that the number prints in decimal.

```
% cat datafile
northwest    NW    Joel Craig       3.0    .98    3    4
western      WE    Sharon Kelly     5.3    .97    5    23
southwest    SW    Chris Foster     2.7    .8     2    18
southern     SO    May Chin         5.1    .95    4    15
southeast    SE    Derek Johnson    4.0    .7     4    17
eastern      EA    Susan Beal       4.4    .84    5    20
northeast    NE    TJ Nichols       5.1    .94    3    13
north        NO    Val Shultz       4.5    .89    5    9
central      CT    Sheri Watson     5.7    .94    5    13
```

EXAMPLE 6.21

```
nawk '/southern/{print $5 + 10.56}' datafile
15.66
```

EXPLANATION

If the record contains the regular expression *southern*, 10.56 is added to the value of the fifth field ($5) and printed.

EXAMPLE 6.22

```
nawk '/southern/{print $8 - 10}' datafile
5
```

EXPLANATION

If the record contains the regular expression *southern*, 10 is subtracted from the value of the eighth field ($8) and printed.

EXAMPLE 6.23

```
nawk '/southern/{print $8 / 2}' datafile
7.5
```

EXPLANATION

If the record contains the regular expression *southern*, the value of the eighth field ($8) is divided by 2 and printed.

EXAMPLE 6.24

```
nawk '/northeast/{print $8 / 3}' datafile
4.33333
```

EXPLANATION

If the record contains the regular expression *northeast*, the value of the eighth field ($8) is divided by 3 and printed. The precision is five places to the right of the decimal point.

EXAMPLE 6.25

```
nawk '/southern/{print $8 * 2}' datafile
30
```

EXPLANATION

If the record contains the regular expression *southern*, the eighth field ($8) is multiplied by 2 and printed.

EXAMPLE 6.26

```
nawk '/northeast/ {print $8 % 3}' datafile
1
```

EXPLANATION

If the record contains the regular expression *northeast*, the eighth field ($8) is divided by 3 and the remainder (modulus) is printed.

EXAMPLE 6.27

```
nawk '$3 ~ /^Susan/\
{print "Percentage: "$6 + .2 " Volume: " $8}' datafile
Percentage: 1.04 Volume: 20
```

EXPLANATION

If the third field ($3) begins with the regular expression *Susan*, the *print* function prints the result of the calculations and the strings in double quotes.

% **cat datafile**						
northwest	NW	Joel Craig	3.0	.98	3	4
western	WE	Sharon Kelly	5.3	.97	5	23
southwest	SW	Chris Foster	2.7	.8	2	18
southern	SO	May Chin	5.1	.95	4	15
southeast	SE	Derek Johnson	4.0	.7	4	17
eastern	EA	Susan Beal	4.4	.84	5	20
northeast	NE	TJ Nichols	5.1	.94	3	13
north	NO	Val Shultz	4.5	.89	5	9
central	CT	Sheri Watson	5.7	.94	5	13

6.2.6 Range Operator

EXAMPLE 6.28

```
nawk '/^western/,/^eastern/' datafile
western       WE    Sharon Kelly      5.3  .97  5    23
southwest     SW    Chris Foster      2.7  .8   2    18
southern      SO    May Chin          5.1  .95  4    15
southeast     SE    Derek Johnson     4.0  .7   4    17
eastern       EA    Susan Beal        4.4  .84  5    20
```

EXPLANATION

All records within the range beginning with the regular expression *western* are printed until a record beginning with the expression *eastern* is found. Records will start being printed again if the pattern *western* is found and will continue to print until *eastern* or end of file is reached.

6.2.7 Conditional Operator

EXAMPLE 6.29

```
nawk '{print ($7 > 4 ? "high "$7 : "low "$7)}' datafile
low 3
high 5
low 2
low 4
low 4
high 5
low 3
high 5
high 5
```

EXPLANATION

If the seventh field ($7) is greater than 4, the *print* function gets the value of the expression after the question mark (the string *high* and the seventh field), else the *print* function gets the value of the expression after the colon (the string *low* and the value of the seventh field).

6.2.8 Assignment Operators

EXAMPLE   6.30

```
nawk '$3 == "Chris"{ $3 = "Christian"; print}' datafile
southwest SW Christian Foster 2.7 .8 2 18
```

EXPLANATION

If the third field ($3) is equal to the string *Chris*, the action is to assign *Christian* to the third field ($3) and print the record. The double equal tests its operands for equality, whereas the single equal is used for assignment.

EXAMPLE   6.31

```
nawk '/Derek/{$8 += 12; print $8}' datafile
29
```

EXPLANATION

If the regular expression *Derek* is found, *12* is added and assigned to (+=) the eighth field ($8), and that value is printed. Another way to write this is: $8 = $8 + 12.

EXAMPLE   6.32

```
nawk '{$7 %= 3; print $7}' datafile
0
2
2
1
1
2
0
2
2
```

EXPLANATION

For each record, the seventh field ($7) is divided by 3, and the remainder of that division (modulus) is assigned to the seventh field and printed.

UNIX TOOLS LAB EXERCISE

Lab 4: *awk* Exercise

Mike Harrington:(510) 548-1278:250:100:175
Christian Dobbins:(408) 538-2358:155:90:201
Susan Dalsass:(206) 654-6279:250:60:50
Archie McNichol:(206) 548-1348:250:100:175
Jody Savage:(206) 548-1278:15:188:150
Guy Quigley:(916) 343-6410:250:100:175
Dan Savage:(406) 298-7744:450:300:275
Nancy McNeil:(206) 548-1278:250:80:75
John Goldenrod:(916) 348-4278:250:100:175
Chet Main:(510) 548-5258:50:95:135
Tom Savage:(408) 926-3456:250:168:200
Elizabeth Stachelin:(916) 440-1763:175:75:300

(Refer to the database called *lab4.data* on the CD.)

The database above contains the names, phone numbers, and money contributions to the party campaign for the past three months.

1 Print the first and last names of those who contributed over *$100* in the first month.

2. Print the names and phone numbers of those who contributed less than *$60* in the first month.

3. Print those who contributed between *$90* and *$150* in the third month.

4. Print those who contributed more than *$800* over the three-month period.

5. Print the names and phone numbers of those with an average monthly contribution greater than *$150*.

6. Print the first name of those not in the *916* area code.

7. Print each record preceded by the number of the record.

8. Print the name and total contribution of each person.

9. Add *$10* to *Elizabeth's* second contribution.

10. Change *Nancy McNeil's* name to *Louise McInnes*.

chapter
7

The *awk* Utility:
awk Programming

7.1   Variables

7.1.1   Numeric and String Constants

Numeric constants can be represented as integers, such as 243, floating point numbers, such as 3.14, or numbers using scientific notation, such as .723E–1 or 3.4e7. Strings, such as *Hello world*, are enclosed in double quotes.

Initialization and Type Coercion.   Just mentioning a variable in your *awk* program causes it to exist. A variable can be a string, a number, or both. When it is set, it becomes the type of the expression on the right-hand side of the equal sign.

   Uninitialized variables have the value zero or the value " ", depending on the context in which they are used.

```
name = "Nancy"   name is a string

x++              x is a number;
                 x is initialized to zero and incremented by 1

number = 35   number is a number
```

To coerce a string to be a number:

```
name + 0
```

To coerce a number to be a string:

```
number " "
```

All fields and array elements created by the *split* function are considered strings, unless they contain only a numeric value. If a field or array element is null, it has the string value of null. An empty line is also considered to be a null string.

7.1.2 User-Defined Variables

User-defined variables consist of letters, digits, and underscores, and cannot begin with a digit. Variables in *awk* are not declared. *Awk* infers data type by the context of the variable in the expression. If the variable is not initialized, *awk* initializes string variables to null and numeric variables to zero. If necessary, *awk* will convert a string variable to a numeric variable, and vice versa. Variables are assigned values with *awk*'s assignment operators. See Table 7.1.

Table 7.1 Assignment Operators

Operator	Meaning	Equivalence
=	$a = 5$	$a = 5$
+=	$a = a + 5$	$a += 5$
−=	$a = a - 5$	$a -= 5$
*=	$a = a * 5$	$a *= 5$
/=	$a = a / 5$	$a /= 5$
%=	$a = a \% 5$	$a \%= 5$
^=	$a = a ^ 5$	$a ^= 5$

The simplest assignment takes the result of an expression and assigns it to a variable.

FORMAT

```
variable = expression
```

EXAMPLE 7.1

```
% nawk '$1 ~  /Tom/ {wage = $2 * $3; print wage}'  filename
```

EXPLANATION

Awk will scan the first field for *Tom* and when there is a match, it will multiply the value of the second field by the value of the third field and assign the result to the user-defined variable *wage*. Since the multiplication operation is arithmetic, *awk* assigns *wage* an initial value of zero. (The % is the UNIX prompt and *filename* is an input file.)

Increment and Decrement Operators. To add one to an operand, the *increment operator* is used. The expression *x++* is equivalent to *x = x + 1*. Similarly, the *decrement operator* subtracts one from its operand. The expression *x– –* is equivalent to *x = x – 1*. This notation is useful in looping operations when you simply want to increment or decrement a counter. You can use the increment and decrement operators either preceding the operator, as in ++x, or after the operator, as in x++. If these expressions are used in assignment statements, their placement will make a difference in the result of the operation.

```
{x = 1;  y = x++ ; print x, y}
```

The ++ here is called a *post-increment operator*; *y* is assigned the value of one, and then *x* is increased by one, so that when all is said and done, **y will equal one, and x will equal two.**

```
{x = 1; y = ++x;  print x, y}
```

The ++ here is called a *pre-increment operator*; *x* is incremented first, and the value of two is assigned to *y*, so that when this statement is finished, **y will equal two, and x will equal two.**

User-Defined Variables at the Command Line. A variable can be assigned a value at the command line and passed into an *awk* script. For more on processing arguments, see "Processing Command Arguments (nawk)" on page 177, on *ARGV*, the array of command line arguments.

EXAMPLE 7.2

```
nawk –F: –f awkscript    month=4  year=2001 filename
```

EXPLANATION

The user-defined variables *month* and *year* are assigned the values 4 and 2001, respectively. In the *awk* script, these variables may be used as though they were created in the script. Note: If *filename* precedes the arguments, the variables will not be available in the *BEGIN* statements. (See "BEGIN Patterns" on page 145.)

The –v Option (nawk). The –v option provided by *nawk* allows command line arguments to be processed within a *BEGIN* statement. For each argument passed at the command line, there must be a –v option preceding it.

Field Variables. Field variables can be used like user-defined variables, except they reference fields. New fields can be created by assignment. A field value that is referenced and has no value will be assigned the null string. If a field value is changed, the $0 variable is recomputed using the current value of *OFS* as a field separator. The number of fields allowed is usually limited to 100.

EXAMPLE 7.3

```
% nawk ' { $5 = 1000 * $3 / $2;  print } '  filename
```

EXPLANATION

If $5 does not exist, *awk* will create it and assign the result of the expression *1000 * $3 / $2* to the fifth field (*$5*). If the fifth field exists, the result will be assigned to it, overwriting what is there.

EXAMPLE 7.4

```
% nawk ' $4 == "CA" { $4  = "California"; print}'  filename
```

EXPLANATION

If the fourth field (*$4*) is equal to the string *CA*, *awk* will reassign the fourth field to *California*. The double quotes are essential. Without them, the strings become user-defined variables with an initial value of null.

Built-In Variables.   Built-in variables have uppercase names. They can be used in expressions and can be reset. See Table 7.2 for a list of built-in variables.

Table 7.2 Built-In Variables

Variable Name	Variable Contents
ARGC	Number of command line argument.
ARGV	Array of command line arguments.
FILENAME	Name of current input file.
FNR	Record number in current file.
FS	The input field separator, by default a space.
NF	Number of fields in current record.
NR	Number of records so far.
OFMT	Output format for numbers.
OFS	Output field separator.
ORS	Output record separator.
RLENGTH	Length of string matched by *match* function.
RS	Input record separator.
RSTART	Offset of string matched by *match* function.
SUBSEP	Subscript separator.

EXAMPLE 7.5

```
(The Employees Database)
% cat employees2
Tom Jones:4423:5/12/66:543354
Mary Adams:5346:11/4/63:28765
Sally Chang:1654:7/22/54:650000
Mary Black:1683:9/23/44:336500


(The Command Line)
% nawk  -F:  '$1 == "Mary Adams"{print NR, $1, $2, $NF}' employees2

(The Output)
2  Mary Adams 5346   28765
```

EXPLANATION

The –F option sets the field separator to a colon. The *print* function prints the record number, the first field, the second field, and the last field ($NF).

7.1.3 *BEGIN* Patterns

The *BEGIN* pattern is followed by an action block that is executed *before awk* processes any lines from the input file. In fact, a *BEGIN* block can be tested without any input file, since *awk* does not start reading input until the *BEGIN* action block has completed. The *BEGIN* action is often used to change the value of the built-in variables, *OFS, RS, FS,* and so forth, to assign initial values to user-defined variables and to print headers or titles as part of the output.

EXAMPLE 7.6

```
% nawk 'BEGIN{FS=":"; OFS="\t"; ORS="\n\n"}{print $1,$2,$3}' file
```

EXPLANATION

Before the input file is processed, the field separator (*FS*) is set to a colon, the output field separator (*OFS*) to a tab, and the output record separator (*ORS*) to two newlines. If there are two or more statements in the action block, they should be separated with semicolons or placed on separate lines (use a backslash to escape the newline character if at the shell prompt).

EXAMPLE 7.7

```
% nawk 'BEGIN{print "MAKE YEAR"}'
make year
```

EXPLANATION

Awk will display *MAKE YEAR*. The *print* function is executed before *awk* opens the input file, and even though the input file has not been assigned, *awk* will still print *MAKE* and *YEAR*. When debugging *awk* scripts, you can test the *BEGIN* block actions before writing the rest of the program.

7.1.4 *END* Patterns

END patterns do not match any input lines, but execute any actions that are associated with the *END* pattern. *END* patterns are handled *after* all lines of input have been processed.

EXAMPLE 7.8

```
% nawk 'END{print "The number of records is " NR }' filename
The number of records is 4
```

EXPLANATION

The *END* block is executed after *awk* has finished processing the file. The value of *NR* is the number of the last record read.

EXAMPLE 7.9

```
% nawk '/Mary/{count++}END{print "Mary was found " count " times."}'\
  employees
Mary was found 2 times.
```

EXPLANATION

For every line that contains the pattern *sun*, the value of the *count* variable is incremented by one. After *awk* has processed the entire file, the *END* block prints the string *Sun was found*, the value of *count*, and the string *times*.

7.2 Redirection and Pipes

7.2.1 Output Redirection

When redirecting output from within *awk* to a UNIX file, the shell redirection operators are used. The filename must be enclosed in double quotes. When the > symbol is used, the file is opened and truncated. Once the file is opened, it remains open until explicitly closed or the *awk* program terminates. Output from subsequent *print* statements to that file will be appended to the file.

The >> symbol is used to open the file, but does not clear it out; instead it simply appends to it.

EXAMPLE 7.10

```
% nawk '$4 >= 70 {print $1, $2  > "passing_file" }' filename
```

EXPLANATION

If the value of the fourth field is greater than or equal to *70*, the first and second fields will be printed to the file *passing_ file*.

7.2.2 Input Redirection *(getline)*

The *getline* Function.   The *getline* function is used to read input from the standard input, a pipe, or a file other than the current file being processed. It gets the next line of input and sets the *NF, NR*, and the *FNR* built-in variables. The *getline* function returns one if a record is found and zero if EOF (end of file) is reached. If there is an error, such as failure to open a file, the *getline* function returns a value of *–1*.

EXAMPLE 7.11

```
% nawk 'BEGIN{ "date" | getline d; print d}' filename
Thu Jan 14 11:24:24 PST 2001
```

EXPLANATION

Will execute the UNIX *date* command, pipe the output to *getline*, assign it to the user-defined variable *d*, and then print *d*.

EXAMPLE 7.12

```
% nawk 'BEGIN{ "date " | getline d; split( d, mon) ; print mon[2]}'\
   filename
Jan
```

EXPLANATION

Will execute the *date* command and pipe the output to *getline*. The *getline* function will read from the pipe and store the input in a user-defined variable, *d*. The *split* function will create an array called *mon* out of variable *d* and then the second element of the array *mon* will be printed.

EXAMPLE 7.13

```
% nawk 'BEGIN{while("ls" | getline) print}'
a.out
db
dbook
getdir
file
sortedf
```

EXPLANATION

Will send the output of the *ls* command to *getline*; for each iteration of the loop, *getline* will read one more line of the output from *ls* and then print it to the screen. An input file is not necessary, since the *BEGIN* block is processed before *awk* attempts to open input.

EXAMPLE 7.14

```
(The Command Line)
1   % nawk 'BEGIN{ printf "What is your name?" ;\
      getline name < "/dev/tty"}\
2   $1 ~ name {print "Found " name " on line ", NR "."}\
3   END{print "See ya, " name "."}' filename

(The Output)
What is your name? Ellie       < Waits for input from user >
Found Ellie on line 5.
See ya, Ellie.
```

EXPLANATION

1   Will print to the screen *What is your name?* and wait for user response; the *getline* function will accept input from the terminal (*/dev/tty*) until a newline is entered, and then store the input in the user-defined variable *name*.

2   If the first field matches the value assigned to *name*, the *print* function is executed.

3   The *END* statement prints out *See ya,* and then the value *Ellie*, stored in variable *name,* is displayed, followed by a period.

EXAMPLE 7.15

```
(The Command Line)
% nawk 'BEGIN{while (getline < "/etc/passwd"  > 0 )lc++; print lc}'\
  file

(The Output)
16
```

EXPLANATION

Awk will read each line from the */etc/passwd* file, increment *lc* until EOF is reached, then print the value of *lc,* which is the number of lines in the *passwd* file.

Note: The value returned by *getline* is negative one if the file does not exist. If the end of file is reached, the return value is zero, and if a line was read, the return value is one. Therefore, the command

```
while ( getline < "/etc/junk")
```

would start an infinite loop if the file */etc/junk* did not exist, since the return value of negative one yields a true condition.

7.3 Pipes

If you open a pipe in an *awk* program, you must close it before opening another one. The command on the right-hand side of the pipe symbol is enclosed in double quotes. Only one pipe can be open at a time.

EXAMPLE 7.16

```
(The Database)
% cat names
john smith
alice cheba
george goldberg
susan goldberg
tony tram
barbara nguyen
elizabeth lone
dan savage
eliza goldberg
john goldenrod

(The Command Line)
% nawk '{print $1, $2 | "sort -r +1 -2 +0 -1 "}' names
```

EXAMPLE   7.16 (CONTINUED)

```
(The Output)
tony tram
john smith
dan savage
barbara nguyen
elizabeth lone
john goldenrod
susan goldberg
george goldberg
eliza goldberg
alice cheba
```

EXPLANATION

Awk will pipe the output of the *print* statement as input to the UNIX *sort* command, which does a reversed sort using the second field as the primary key and the first field as the secondary key. The UNIX command must be enclosed in double quotes. (See "sort" in Appendix A.)

7.4 Closing Files and Pipes

If you plan to use a file or pipe in an *awk* program again for reading or writing, you may want to close it first, since it remains open until the script ends. Once opened, the pipe remains open until *awk* exits. Therefore, statements in the *END* block will also be affected by the pipe. The first line in the *END* block closes the pipe.

EXAMPLE   7.17

```
(In Script)
1   { print $1, $2, $3 | " sort -r +1 -2 +0 -1"}
    END{
2   close("sort -r +1 -2 +0 -1")
     <rest of statements>  }
```

EXPLANATION

1   Awk pipes each line from the input file to the UNIX *sort* utility.

2   When the *END* block is reached, the pipe is closed. The string enclosed in double quotes must be identical to the pipe string where the pipe was initially opened.

The *system* Function.   The built-in *system* function takes a UNIX system command as its argument, executes the command, and returns the exit status to the *awk* program. It is similar to the C standard library function, also called *system()*. The UNIX command must be enclosed in double quotes.

```
system( "UNIX Command")
```

```
(In Script)
    {
1   system ( "cat" $1 )
2   system ( "clear" )
    }
```

1   The *system* function takes the UNIX *cat* command and the value of the first field in the input file as its arguments. The *cat* command takes the value of the first field, a filename, as its argument. The UNIX shell causes the *cat* command to be executed.

2   The *system* function takes the UNIX *clear* command as its argument. The shell executes the command, causing the screen to be cleared.

7.5 Review

7.5.1 Increment and Decrement Operators

```
% cat datafile
```

northwest	NW	Joel Craig	3.0	.98	3	4
western	WE	Sharon Kelly	5.3	.97	5	23
southwest	SW	Chris Foster	2.7	.8	2	18
southern	SO	May Chin	5.1	.95	4	15
southeast	SE	Derek Johnson	4.0	.7	4	17
eastern	EA	Susan Beal	4.4	.84	5	20
northeast	NE	TJ Nichols	5.1	.94	3	13
north	NO	Val Shultz	4.5	.89	5	9
central	CT	Sheri Watson	5.7	.94	5	13

```
% nawk '/^north/{count += 1; print count}' datafile
1
2
3
```

```
% cat datafile
northwest      NW     Joel Craig         3.0    .98    3    4
western        WE     Sharon Kelly       5.3    .97    5    23
southwest      SW     Chris Foster       2.7    .8     2    18
southern       SO     May Chin           5.1    .95    4    15
southeast      SE     Derek Johnson      4.0    .7     4    17
eastern        EA     Susan Beal         4.4    .84    5    20
northeast      NE     TJ Nichols         5.1    .94    3    13
north          NO     Val Shultz         4.5    .89    5    9
central        CT     Sheri Watson       5.7    .94    5    13
```

EXPLANATION

If the record begins with the regular expression *north*, a user-defined variable, *count*, is created; *count* is incremented by 1 and its value is printed.

EXAMPLE 7.20

```
% nawk '/^north/{count++; print count}' datafile
1
2
3
```

EXPLANATION

The auto-increment operator increments the user-defined variable *count* by 1. The value of *count* is printed.

EXAMPLE 7.21

```
% nawk '{x = $7--; print "x = "x ", $7 = "$7}' datafile
x = 3, $7 = 2
x = 5, $7 = 4
x = 2, $7 = 1
x = 4, $7 = 3
x = 4, $7 = 3
x = 5, $7 = 4
x = 3, $7 = 2
x = 5, $7 = 4
x = 5, $7 = 4
```

EXPLANATION

After the value of the seventh field ($7) is assigned to the user-defined variable *x*, the auto-decrement operator decrements the seventh field by one. The value of *x* and the seventh field are printed.

7.5.2 Built-In Variables

```
% nawk '/^north/{print "The record number is " NR}' datafile
The record number is 1
The record number is 7
The record number is 8
```

If the record begins with the regular expression *north*, the string *The record number is* and the value of *NR* (record number) are printed.

```
% nawk '{print NR, $0}' datafile
1 northwest    NW     Joel Craig        3.0   .98   3     4
2 western      WE     Sharon Kelly      5.3   .97   5     23
3 southwest    SW     Chris Foster      2.7   .8    2     18
4 southern     SO     May Chin          5.1   .95   4     15
5 southeast    SE     Derek Johnson     4.0   .7    4     17
6 eastern      EA     Susan Beal        4.4   .84   5     20
7 northeast    NE     TJ Nichols        5.1   .94   3     13
8 north        NO     Val Shultz        4.5   .89   5     9
9 central      CT     Sheri Watson      5.7   .94   5     13
```

The value of *NR*, the number of the current record, and the value of *$0*, the entire record, are printed.

```
% nawk 'NR==2,NR==5{print NR, $0}' datafile
2 western      WE     Sharon Kelly      5.3   97    5     23
3 southwest    SW     Chris Foster      2.7   8     2     18
4 southern     SO     May Chin          5.1   95    4     15
5 southeast    SE     Derek Johnson     4.0   7     4     17
```

If the value of *NR* is in the *range* between 2 and 5 (record numbers 2–5), the number of the record (*NR*) and the record (*$0*) are printed.

The awk Utility: awk Programming


```
% cat datafile
northwest    NW    Joel Craig       3.0    .98    3    4
western      WE    Sharon Kelly     5.3    .97    5    23
southwest    SW    Chris Foster     2.7    .8     2    18
southern     SO    May Chin         5.1    .95    4    15
southeast    SE    Derek Johnson    4.0    .7     4    17
eastern      EA    Susan Beal       4.4    .84    5    20
northeast    NE    TJ Nichols       5.1    .94    3    13
north        NO    Val Shultz       4.5    .89    5    9
central      CT    Sheri Watson     5.7    .94    5    13
```

EXAMPLE 7.25

```
% nawk '/^north/{print NR, $1, $2, $NF, RS}' datafile
1 northwest NW 4

7 northeast NE 13

8 north NO 9
```

EXPLANATION

If the record begins with the regular expression *north*, the number of the record (*NR*), followed by the first field, the second field, the value of the last record (*NF* preceded by a dollar sign) and the value of *RS* (a newline) are printed. Since the *print* function generates a newline by default, *RS* will generate another newline, resulting in double spacing between records.

% **cat datafile2**
Joel Craig:northwest:NW:3.0:.98:3:4
Sharon Kelly:western:WE:5.3:.97:5:23
Chris Foster:southwest:SW:2.7:.8:2:18
May Chin:southern:SO:5.1:.95:4:15
Derek Johnson:southeast:SE:4.0:.7:4:17
Susan Beal:eastern:EA:4.4:.84:5:20
TJ Nichols:northeast:NE:5.1:.94:3:13
Val Shultz:north:NO:4.5:.89:5:9
Sheri Watson:central:CT:5.7:.94:5:131.

EXAMPLE 7.26

```
% nawk -F: 'NR == 5{print NF}' datafile2
7
```

EXPLANATION

The field separator is set to a colon at the command line with the −F option. If the number of the record (NR) is 5, the number of fields (NF) is printed.

EXAMPLE 7.27

```
% nawk 'BEGIN{OFMT="%.2f";print 1.2456789,12E-2}' datafile2
1.25 0.12
```

EXPLANATION

The OFMT, output format variable for the print function, is set so that floating point numbers will be printed with a decimal-point precision of two digits. The numbers 1.23456789 and 12E−2 are printed in the new format.

```
% cat datafile
```

northwest	NW	Joel Craig	3.0	.98	3	4
western	WE	Sharon Kelly	5.3	.97	5	23
southwest	SW	Chris Foster	2.7	.8	2	18
southern	SO	May Chin	5.1	.95	4	15
southeast	SE	Derek Johnson	4.0	.7	4	17
eastern	EA	Susan Beal	4.4	.84	5	20
northeast	NE	TJ Nichols	5.1	.94	3	13
north	NO	Val Shultz	4.5	.89	5	9
central	CT	Sheri Watson	5.7	.94	5	13

EXAMPLE 7.28

```
% nawk '{$9 = $6 * $7; print $9}' datafile
2.94
4.85
1.6
3.8
2.8
4.2
2.82
4.45
4.7
```

EXPLANATION

The result of multiplying the sixth field ($6) and the seventh field ($7) is stored in a new field, $9, and printed. There were eight fields; now there are nine.

EXAMPLE 7.29

```
% nawk '{$10 = 100; print NF, $9, $0}' datafile
```

10	northwest	NW	Joel Craig	3.0	.98	3	4	100
10	western	WE	Sharon Kelly	5.3	.97	5	23	100
10	southwest	SW	Chris Foster	2.7	.8	2	18	100
10	southern	SO	May Chin	5.1	.95	4	15	100
10	southeast	SE	Derek Johnson	4.0	.7	4	17	100
10	eastern	EA	Susan Beal	4.4	.84	5	20	100
10	northeast	NE	TJ Nichols	5.1	.94	3	13	100
10	north	NO	Val Shultz	4.5	.89	5	9	100
10	central	CT	Sheri Watson	5.7	.94	5	13	100

EXPLANATION

The tenth field ($10) is assigned 100 for each record. This is a new field. The ninth field ($9) does not exist, so it will be considered a null field. The number of fields is printed (NF), followed by the value of $9, the null field, and the entire record ($0). The value of the tenth field is 100.

7.5.3 *BEGIN* Patterns

EXAMPLE 7.30

```
% nawk 'BEGIN{print "---------EMPLOYEES---------"}'
---------EMPLOYEES---------
```

EXPLANATION

The *BEGIN* pattern is followed by an action block. The action is to print out the string ---------*EMPLOYEES*--------- before opening the input file. Note that an input file has not been provided and *awk* does not complain.

EXAMPLE 7.31

```
% nawk 'BEGIN{print "\t\t---------EMPLOYEES-------\n"}\
  {print $0}' datafile
                ---------EMPLOYEES-------
```

northwest	NW	Joel Craig	3.0	.98	3	4
western	WE	Sharon Kelly	5.3	.97	5	23
southwest	SW	Chris Foster	2.7	.8	2	18
southern	SO	May Chin	5.1	.95	4	15
southeast	SE	Derek Johnson	4.0	.7	4	17
eastern	EA	Susan Beal	4.4	.84	5	20
northeast	NE	TJ Nichols	5.1	.94	3	13
north	NO	Val Shultz	4.5	.89	5	9
central	CT	Sheri Watson	5.7	.94	5	13

EXPLANATION

The *BEGIN* action block is executed first. The title ---------*EMPLOYEES*------- is printed. The second action block prints each record in the input file. When breaking lines, the backslash is used to suppress the carriage return. Lines can be broken at a semicolon or a curly brace.

% **cat datafile2**
Joel Craig:northwest:NW:3.0:.98:3:4
Sharon Kelly:western:WE:5.3:.97:5:23
Chris Foster:southwest:SW:2.7:.8:2:18
May Chin:southern:SO:5.1:.95:4:15
Derek Johnson:southeast:SE:4.0:.7:4:17
Susan Beal:eastern:EA:4.4:.84:5:20
TJ Nichols:northeast:NE:5.1:.94:3:13
Val Shultz:north:NO:4.5:.89:5:9
Sheri Watson:central:CT:5.7:.94:5:131.

EXAMPLE 7.32

```
% nawk 'BEGIN{ FS=":";OFS="\t"};/^Sharon/{print $1, $2, $8 }'\
   datafile2
Sharon Kelly      western      28
```

EXPLANATION

The *BEGIN* action block is used to initialize variables. The *FS* variable (field separator) is assigned a colon. The *OFS* variable (output field separator) is assigned a tab (\t). If a record begins with the regular expression *Sharon*, the first, second, and eighth fields ($1, $2, $8) are printed. Each field in the output is separated by a tab.

7.5.4 *END* Patterns

% **cat datafile**

northwest	NW	Joel Craig	3.0	.98	3	4
western	WE	Sharon Kelly	5.3	.97	5	23
southwest	SW	Chris Foster	2.7	.8	2	18
southern	SO	May Chin	5.1	.95	4	15
southeast	SE	Derek Johnson	4.0	.7	4	17
eastern	EA	Susan Beal	4.4	.84	5	20
northeast	NE	TJ Nichols	5.1	.94	3	13
north	NO	Val Shultz	4.5	.89	5	9
central	CT	Sheri Watson	5.7	.94	5	13

EXAMPLE 7.33

```
% nawk 'END{print "The total number of records is " NR}' datafile
The total number of records is 9
```

EXPLANATION

After *awk* has finished processing the input file, the statements in the *END* block are executed. The string *The total number of records is* is printed, followed by the value of *NR*, the number of the last record.

EXAMPLE 7.34

```
% nawk '/^north/{count++}END{print count}' datafile
3
```

EXPLANATION

If the record begins with the regular expression *north*, the user-defined variable *count* is incremented by one. When *awk* has finished processing the input file, the value stored in the variable *count* is printed.

7.5.5 *awk* Script with *BEGIN* and *END*

EXAMPLE 7.35

```
    # Second awk script-- awk.sc2
1   BEGIN{ FS=":"; OFS="\t"
       print "  NAME\t\tDISTRICT\tQUANTITY"
       print "_____\n"
    }

2      {print $1"\t  " $3"\t\t" $7}
       {total+=$7}
       /north/{count++}

3   END{
       print "-------------------------------------------"
       print "The total quantity is " total
       print "The number of northern salespersons is " count "."
    }
```

```
% cat datafile2
Joel Craig:northwest:NW:3.0:.98:3:4
Sharon Kelly:western:WE:5.3:.97:5:23
Chris Foster:southwest:SW:2.7:.8:2:18
May Chin:southern:SO:5.1:.95:4:15
Derek Johnson:southeast:SE:4.0:.7:4:17
Susan Beal:eastern:EA:4.4:.84:5:20
TJ Nichols:northeast:NE:5.1:.94:3:13
Val Shultz:north:NO:4.5:.89:5:9
Sheri Watson:central:CT:5.7:.94:5:131.
```

EXAMPLE 7.35 (CONTINUED)

```
(The Output)
4  % nawk -f awk.sc2 datafile2
   NAME          DISTRICT   QUANTITY

   Joel Craig       NW        4
   Sharon Kelly     WE        23
   Chris Foster     SW        18
   May Chin         SO        15
   Derek Johnson    SE        17
   Susan Beal       EA        20
   TJ Nichols       NE        13
   Val Shultz       NO        9
   Sheri Watson     CT        13
   --------------------------------------------
   The total quantity is 132
   The number of northern salespersons is 3.
```

EXPLANATION

1   The *BEGIN* block is executed first. The field separator (FS) and the output field separator (OFS) are set. Header output is printed.

2   The body of the *awk* script contains statements that are executed for each line of input coming from *datafile2*.

3   Statements in the *END* block are executed after the input file has been closed, i.e., before *awk* exits.

4   At the command line, the *nawk* program is executed. The *–f* option is followed by the script name, *awk.sc2*, and then by the input file, *datafile2*.

7.5.6 The *printf* Function

```
% nawk '{printf "$%6.2f\n",$6 * 100}' datafile
$ 98.00
$ 97.00
$ 80.00
$ 95.00
$ 70.00
$ 84.00
$ 94.00
$ 89.00
$ 94.00
```

EXPLANATION

The *printf* function formats a floating point number to be right-justified (the default) with a total of 6 digits, one for the decimal point, and two for the decimal numbers to the right of the period. The number will be rounded up and printed.

```
% nawk '{printf "|%-15s|\n",$4}' datafile
|Craig          |
|Kelly          |
|Foster         |
|Chin           |
|Johnson        |
|Beal           |
|Nichols        |
|Shultz         |
|Watson         |
```

EXPLANATION

A left-justified, 15-space string is printed. The fourth field ($4) is printed enclosed in vertical bars to illustrate the spacing.

% cat datafile						
northwest	NW	Joel Craig	3.0	.98	3	4
western	WE	Sharon Kelly	5.3	.97	5	23
southwest	SW	Chris Foster	2.7	.8	2	18
southern	SO	May Chin	5.1	.95	4	15
southeast	SE	Derek Johnson	4.0	.7	4	17
eastern	EA	Susan Beal	4.4	.84	5	20
northeast	NE	TJ Nichols	5.1	.94	3	13
north	NO	Val Shultz	4.5	.89	5	9
central	CT	Sheri Watson	5.7	.94	5	13

7.5.7 Redirection and Pipes

EXAMPLE 7.38

```
% nawk '/north/{print $1, $3, $4 > "districts"}' datafile
% cat districts
northwest Joel Craig
northeast TJ Nichols
north Val Shultz
```

EXPLANATION

If the record contains the regular expression *north*, the first, third, and fourth fields ($1, $3, $4) are printed to an output file called *districts*. Once the file is opened, it remains open until closed or the program terminates. The filename "*districts*" must be enclosed in double quotes.

EXAMPLE 7.39

```
% nawk '/south/{print $1, $2, $3 >> "districts"}' datafile
% cat districts
northwest Joel Craig
northeast TJ Nichols
north Val Shultz
southwest SW Chris
southern SO May
southeast SE Derek
```

EXPLANATION

If the record contains the pattern *south*, the first, second, and third fields ($1, $2, $3) are appended to the output file *districts*.

7.5.8 Opening and Closing a Pipe

EXAMPLE 7.40

```
# awk script using pipes -- awk.sc3
1   BEGIN{
2       printf " %-22s%s\n", "NAME", "DISTRICT"
        print "-------------------------------------"
3   }
4   /west/{count++}
5   {printf "%s %s\t\t%-15s\n", $3, $4, $1| "sort +1" }
6   END{
7       close "sort +1"
        printf "The number of sales persons in the western "
        printf "region is " count "."}
```

(The Output)
```
% nawk -f awk.sc3 datafile
```
```
1   NAME                          DISTRICT
2   -------------------------------------------------
3   Susan Beal                    eastern
    May Chin                      southern
    Joel Craig                    northwest
    Chris Foster                  southwest
    Derek Johnson                 southeast
    Sharon Kelly                  western
    TJ Nichols                    northeast
    Val Shultz                    north
    Sheri Watson                  central
    The number of sales persons in the western region is 3.
```

EXPLANATION

1   The special *BEGIN* pattern is followed by an action block. The statements in this block are executed first, before *awk* processes the input file.

2   The *printf* function displays the string *NAME* as a 22-character, left-justified string, followed by the string *DISTRICT*, which is right-justified.

3   The *BEGIN* block ends.

4   Now *awk* will process the input file, one line at a time. If the pattern *west* is found, the action block is executed, i.e., the user-defined variable *count* is incremented by one. The first time *awk* encounters the *count* variable, it will be created and given an initial value of zero.

5   The *print* function formats and sends its output to a pipe. After all of the output has been collected, it will be sent to the *sort* command

6   The *END* block is started.

7   The pipe (*sort +1*) must be closed with exactly the same command that opened it; in this example, "*sort +1*". Otherwise, the *END* statements will be sorted with the rest of the output.

UNIX TOOLS LAB EXERCISE

Lab 5: *nawk* Exercise

Mike Harrington:(510) 548-1278:250:100:175
Christian Dobbins:(408) 538-2358:155:90:201
Susan Dalsass:(206) 654-6279:250:60:50
Archie McNichol:(206) 548-1348:250:100:175
Jody Savage:(206) 548-1278:15:188:150
Guy Quigley:(916) 343-6410:250:100:175
Dan Savage:(406) 298-7744:450:300:275
Nancy McNeil:(206) 548-1278:250:80:75
John Goldenrod:(916) 348-4278:250:100:175
Chet Main:(510) 548-5258:50:95:135
Tom Savage:(408) 926-3456:250:168:200
Elizabeth Stachelin:(916) 440-1763:175:75:300

(Refer to the database called *lab5.data* on the CD.)

The database above contains the names, phone numbers, and money contributions to the party campaign for the past three months.

Write a *nawk* script to produce the following output:

```
% nawk -f nawk.sc db
              ***CAMPAIGN 1998 CONTRIBUTIONS***
------------------------------------------------------------------
NAME                 PHONE           Jan  |  Feb  |  Mar | Total Donated
------------------------------------------------------------------
Mike Harrington      (510) 548-1278  250.00  100.00  175.00   525.00
Christian Dobbins    (408) 538-2358  155.00   90.00  201.00   446.00
Susan Dalsass        (206) 654-6279  250.00   60.00   50.00   360.00
Archie McNichol      (206) 548-1348  250.00  100.00  175.00   525.00
Jody Savage          (206) 548-1278   15.00  188.00  150.00   353.00
Guy Quigley          (916) 343-6410  250.00  100.00  175.00   525.00
Dan Savage           (406) 298-7744  450.00  300.00  275.00  1025.00
Nancy McNeil         (206) 548-1278  250.00   80.00   75.00   405.00
John Goldenrod       (916) 348-4278  250.00  100.00  175.00   525.00
Chet Main            (510) 548-5258   50.00   95.00  135.00   280.00
Tom Savage           (408) 926-3456  250.00  168.00  200.00   618.00
Elizabeth Stachelin  (916) 440-1763  175.00   75.00  300.00   550.00
------------------------------------------------------------------
                            SUMMARY
------------------------------------------------------------------
The campaign received a total of $6137.00 for this quarter.
The average donation for the 12 contributors was $511.42.
The highest contribution was $300.00.
The lowest contribution was $15.00.
```

7.6   Conditional Statements

The conditional statements in *awk* were borrowed from the C language. They are used to control the flow of the program in making decisions.

7.6.1   *if* Statements

Statements beginning with the *if* construct are action statements. With *conditional patterns*, the *if* is implied; with a conditional *action* statement, the *if* is explicitly stated, and followed by an expression enclosed in parentheses. If the expression evaluates true (nonzero or non-null), the statement or block of statements following the expression is executed. If there is more than one statement following the conditional expression, the statements are separated either by semicolons or a newline, and the group of statements must be enclosed in curly braces so that the statements are executed as a block.

FORMAT

```
if (expression) {
    statement; statement; ...
    }
```

EXAMPLE   7.41

```
1   % nawk '{if ( $6 > 50 ) print $1 "Too high"}' filename

2   % nawk '{if ($6 > 20 && $6  <= 50){safe++; print "OK"}}' filename
```

EXPLANATION

1   In the *if* action block, the expression is tested. If the value of the sixth field is greater than *50*, the *print* statement is executed. Since the statement following the expression is a single statement, curly braces are not required. (*filename* represents the input file.)

2   In the *if* action block, the expression is tested. If the sixth field is greater than *20* *and* the sixth field is less than or equal to *50*, the statements following the expression are executed as a block and must be enclosed in curly braces.

7.6.2   *if/else* Statements

The *if/else* statement allows a two-way decision. If the expression after the *if* keyword is true, the block of statements associated with that expression are executed. If the first expression evaluates to false or zero, the block of statements after the *else* keyword is executed. If multiple statements are to be included with the *if* or *else*, they must be blocked with curly braces.

FORMAT

```
{if (expression) {
    statement; statement; ...
    }
else{
    statement; statement; ...
    }
}
```

EXAMPLE 7.42

```
1   % nawk '{if( $6 > 50) print   $1 " Too high" ;\
      else print "Range is OK"}' filename
2   % nawk '{if ( $6 > 50 ) { count++; print $3 } \
      else { x+5; print $2 } }' filename
```

EXPLANATION

1   If the first expression is true, that is, the sixth field ($6) is greater than 50, the
    print function prints the first field and *Too high*; otherwise, the statement after the
    else, *Range is OK*, is printed.

2   If the first expression is true, that is, the sixth field ($6) is greater than 50, the
    block of statements is executed; otherwise, the block of statements after the *else*
    is executed. Note that the blocks are enclosed in curly braces.

7.6.3 *if/else* and *else if* Statements

The *if/else* and *else if* statements allow a multiway decision. If the expression following
the keyword *if* is true, the block of statements associated with that expression is executed and control starts again after the last closing curly brace associated with the final
else. Otherwise, control goes to the *else if* and that expression is tested. When the first
else if condition is true, the statements following the expression are executed. If none of
the conditional expressions test true, control goes to the *else* statements. The *else* is
called the default action because if none of the other statements are true, the *else* block
is executed.

FORMAT

```
{if (expression) {
    statement; statement; ...
    }
else if (expression){
    statement; statement; ...
    }
else if (expression){
    statement; statement; ...
    }
else{
    statement
    }
}
```

EXAMPLE 7.43

```
(In the Script)
1   {if ( $3 > 89 && $3 < 101 ) Agrade++
2   else if ( $3 > 79 ) Bgrade++
3   else if ( $3 > 69 ) Cgrade++
4   else if ( $3 > 59 ) Dgrade++
5   else Fgrade++
    }
    END{print "The number of failures is" Fgrade }
```

EXPLANATION

1   The *if* statement is an action and must be enclosed in curly braces. The expression is evaluated from left to right. If the first expression is false, the whole expression is false; if the first expression is true, the expression after the logical *and* (*&&*) is evaluated. If it is true, the variable *Agrade* is incremented by one.

2   If the first expression following the *if* keyword evaluates to false (0), the *else if* expression is tested. If it evaluates to true, the statement following the expression is executed; that is, if the third field ($3) is greater than 79, *Bgrade* is incremented by one.

3   If the first two statements are false, the *else if* expression is tested, and if the third field ($3) is greater than 69, *Cgrade* is incremented.

4   If the first three statements are false, the *else if* expression is tested, and if the third field is greater than 59, *Dgrade* is incremented.

5   If none of the expressions tested above is true, the *else* block is executed. The curly brace ends the action block. *Fgrade* is incremented.

7.7 Loops

Loops are used to repeatedly execute the statements following the test expression if a condition is true. Loops are often used to iterate through the fields within a record and to loop through the elements of an array in the *END* block. *Awk* has three types of loops: the *while* loop, the *for* loop, and the special *for* loop, which will be discussed later when working with *awk* arrays.

7.7.1 *while* Loop

The first step in using a *while* loop is to set a variable to an initial value. The value is then tested in the *while* expression. If the expression evaluates to true (nonzero), the body of the loop is entered and the statements within that body are executed. If there is more than one statement within the body of the loop, those statements must be enclosed in curly braces. Before ending the loop block, the variable controlling the loop expression must be updated or the loop will continue forever. In the following example, the variable is reinitialized each time a new record is processed.

The *do/while* loop is similar to the *while* loop, except that the expression is not tested until the body of the loop is executed at least once.

EXAMPLE 7.44

```
% nawk '{ i  = 1; while ( i <= NF ) { print NF, $i ; i++ } }' filename
```

EXPLANATION

The variable *i* is initialized to one; while *i* is less than or equal to the number of fields (*NF*) in the record, the *print* statement will be executed, then *i* will be incremented by one. The expression will then be tested again, until the variable *i* is greater than the value of *NF*. The variable *i* is not reinitialized until *awk* starts processing the next record.

7.7.2 *for* Loop

The *for* loop and *while* loop are essentially the same, except the *for* loop requires three expressions within the parentheses: the initialization expression, the test expression, and the expression to update the variables within the test expression. In *awk*, the first statement within the parentheses of the *for* loop can perform only one initialization. (In C, you can have multiple initializations separated by commas.)

EXAMPLE 7.45

```
% nawk '{ for( i = 1; i <= NF; i++) print NF,$i }' filex
```

The variable *i* is initialized to one and tested to see whether it is less than or equal to the number of fields (*NF*) in the record. If so, the *print* function prints the value of *NF* and the value of $i (the $ preceding the *i* is the number of the *i*th field), then *i* is incremented by one. (Frequently the *for* loop is used with arrays in an *END* action to loop through the elements of an array.) See "Arrays" on page 171.

7.7.3 Loop Control

***break* and *continue* Statements.**   The *break* statement lets you break out of a loop if a certain condition is true. The *continue* statement causes the loop to skip any statements that follow if a certain condition is true, and returns control to the top of the loop, starting at the next iteration.

EXAMPLE 7.46

```
(In the Script)
1   {for ( x = 3; x <= NF; x++ )
         if ( $x < 0 ){ print "Bottomed out!"; break}
         # breaks out of for loop
    }

2   {for ( x = 3; x <= NF; x++ )
          if ( $x == 0 ) { print "Get next item"; continue}
          # starts next iteration of  the for loop
    }
```

1   If the value of the field $x is less than zero, the *break* statement causes control to go to the statement after the closing curly brace of the loop body; i.e., it breaks out of the loop.

2   If the value of the field $x is equal to zero, the *continue* statement causes control to start at the top of the loop and start execution, in the third expression at the *for* loop at *x++*.

7.8 Program Control Statements

7.8.1 *next* Statement

The *next* statement gets the next line of input from the input file, restarting execution at the top of the *awk* script.

EXAMPLE 7.47

```
(In Script)
{ if ($1 ~ /Peter/){next}
   else {print}
}
```

EXPLANATION

If the first field contains *Peter*, *awk* skips over this line and gets the next line from the input file. The script resumes execution at the beginning.

7.8.2 *exit* Statement

The *exit* statement is used to terminate the *awk* program. It stops processing records, but does not skip over an *END* statement. If the *exit* statement is given a value between 0 and 255 as an argument (exit 1), this value can be printed at the command line to indicate success or failure by typing:

EXAMPLE 7.48

```
(In Script)
   {exit (1) }

(The Command Line)
% echo $status       (csh)
1

$ echo $?     (sh/ksh)
1
```

EXPLANATION

An exit status of zero indicates success, and an exit value of nonzero indicates failure (a convention in UNIX). It is up to the programmer to provide the exit status in a program. The exit value returned in this example is 1.

7.9 Arrays

Arrays in *awk* are called *associative arrays* because the subscripts can be either numbers or strings. The subscript is often called the key and is associated with the value assigned to the corresponding array element. The keys and values are stored internally in a table where a hashing algorithm is applied to the value of the key in question. Due to the techniques used for hashing, the array elements are not stored in a sequential order, and when the contents of the array are displayed, they may not be in the order you expected.

An array, like a variable, is created by using it, and *awk* can infer whether it is used to store numbers or strings. Array elements are initialized with numeric value zero and string value null, depending on the context. You do not have to declare the size of an *awk* array. *Awk* arrays are used to collect information from records and may be used for accumulating totals, counting words, tracking the number of times a pattern occurred, and so forth.

7.9.1 Subscripts for Associative Arrays

Using Variables as Array Indexes.

EXAMPLE 7.49

```
(The Input File)
% cat employees
Tom Jones        4424    5/12/66    543354
Mary Adams       5346    11/4/63    28765
Cally Chang      1654    7/22/54    650000
Billy Black      1683    9/23/44    336500

(The Command Line)
1   % nawk '{name[x++]=$2};END{for(i=0; i<NR; i++)\
      print i, name[i]}' employees
    0 Jones
    1 Adams
    2 Chang
    3 Black

2   % nawk '{id[NR]=$3};END{for(x = 1; x <= NR; x++)\
      print id[x]}' employees
    4424
    5346
    1654
    1683
```

EXPLANATION

1   The subscript in array *name* is a user-defined variable, *x*. The ++ indicates a numeric context. *Awk* initializes *x* to zero and increments *x* by one *after* (post-increment operator) it is used. The value of the second field is assigned to each element of the *name* array. In the *END* block, the *for* loop is used to loop through the array, printing the value that was stored there, starting at subscript zero. Since the subscript is just a key, it does not have to start at zero. It can start at any value, either a number or a string.

2   The *awk* variable *NR* contains the number of the current record. By using *NR* as a subscript, the value of the third field is assigned to each element of the array for each record. At the end, the *for* loop will loop through the array, printing out the values that were stored there.

The Special *for* Loop.   The special *for* loop is used to read through an associative array in cases where the *for* loop is not practical; that is, when strings are used as subscripts or the subscripts are not consecutive numbers. The special *for* loop uses the subscript as a key into the value associated with it.

FORMAT

```
{for(item in arrayname){
    print arrayname[item]
    }
}
```

EXAMPLE 7.50

```
(The Input File)
% cat db
Tom Jones
Mary Adams
Sally Chang
Billy Black
Tom Savage
Tom Chung
Reggie Steel
Tommy Tucker

(The Command Line, for Loop)
1   % nawk '/^Tom/{name[NR]=$1};\
    END{for( i = 1; i <= NR; i++ )print name[i]}' db
    Tom



    Tom
```

EXAMPLE   7.50 (CONTINUED)

Tom

Tommy

```
(The Command Line, Special for Loop)
2    % nawk '/^Tom/{name[NR]=$1};\
       END{for(i in name){print name[i]}}' db
     Tom
     Tommy
     Tom
     Tom
```

EXPLANATION

1   If the regular expression *Tom* is matched against an input line, the *name* array is assigned a value. Since the subscript used is *NR*, the number of the current record, the subscripts in the array will not be in numeric order. Therefore, when printing the array with the traditional *for* loop, there will be null values printed where an array element has no value.

2   The special *for* loop iterates through the array, printing only values where there was a subscript associated with that value. The order of the printout is random because of the way the associative arrays are stored (hashed).

Using Strings as Array Subscripts.   A subscript may consist of a variable containing a string or literal string. If the string is a literal, it must be enclosed in double quotes.

EXAMPLE   7.51

```
(The Input File)
% cat datafile3
tom
mary
sean
tom
mary
mary
bob
mary
alex

(The Script)
    # awk.sc script
1   /tom/ { count["tom"]++ }
2   /mary/ { count["mary"]++ }
3   END{print "There are " count["tom"] " Toms in the file and
      " count["mary"]" Marys in the file."}
```

EXAMPLE 7.51 (CONTINUED)

```
(The Command Line)
    % nawk -f awk.sc datafile3
    There are 2 Toms in the file and 4 Marys in the file.
```

EXPLANATION

1   An array called *count* consists of two elements, *count["tom"]* and *count["mary"]*. The initial value of each of the array elements is zero. Every time *tom* is matched, the value of the array is incremented by one.

2   The same procedure applies to *count["mary"]*. Note: Only one *tom* is recorded for each line, even if there are multiple occurrences on the line.

3   The *END* pattern prints the value stored in each of the array elements.

Using Field Values as Array Subscripts.   Any expression can be used as a subscript in an array. Therefore, fields can be used. The program in Example 7.52 counts the frequency of all names appearing in the second field and introduces a new form of the *for* loop.

EXAMPLE 7.52

```
(The Input File)
% cat datafile4
4234    Tom     43
4567    Arch    45
2008    Eliza   65
4571    Tom     22
3298    Eliza   21
4622    Tom     53
2345    Mary    24

(The Command Line)
% nawk '{count[$2]++}END{for(name in count)print name,count[name] }'\
   datafile4
Tom 3
Arch 1
Eliza 2
Mary 1
```

EXPLANATION

The *awk* statement first will use the second field as an index in the *count* array. The index varies as the second field varies, thus the first index in the *count* array is *Tom* and the value stored in *count["Tom"]* is one.

Next, *count["Arch"]* is set to one, *count["Eliza"]* to one, and *count["Mary"]* to one. When *awk* finds the next occurrence of *Tom* in the second field, *count["Tom"]* is incremented, now containing the value 2. The same thing happens for each occurrence of *Arch, Eliza,* and *Mary*.

Figure 7.1 Using strings as subscripts in an array (Example 7.51).

```
for( index_value in array ) statement
```

The *for* loop found in the *END* block of the previous example works as follows: The variable *name* is set to the index value of the *count* array. After each iteration of the *for* loop, the *print* action is performed, first printing the *value of the index*, and then the *value stored* in that element. *(The order of the printout is not guaranteed.)*

EXAMPLE 7.53

```
(The Input File)
% cat datafile4
4334   Tom     43
4567   Arch    45
2008   Eliza   65
4571   Tom     22
3298   Eliza   21
4622   Tom     53
2345   Mary    24

(The Command Line)
% nawk  '{dup[$2]++; if (dup[$2] > 1){name[$2]++ }}\
  END{print "The duplicates were"\
  for (i in name){print i, name[i]}}' datafile4

(The Output)
Tom 2
Eliza 2
```

EXPLANATION

The subscript for the *dup* array is the value in the second field, that is, the name of a person. The value stored there is initially zero, and it is incremented by one each time a new record is processed. If the name is a duplicate, the value stored for that subscript will go up to two, and so forth. If the value in the *dup* array is greater than one, a new array called *name* also uses the second field as a subscript and keeps track of the number of names greater than one.

Arrays and the *split* Function. *Awk's* built-in *split* function allows you to split a string into words and store them in an array. You can define the field separator or use the value currently stored in *FS*.

FORMAT

```
split(string, array, field separator)
split (string, array)
```

EXAMPLE 7.54

```
(The Command Line)
% nawk BEGIN{ split( "3/15/2001", date, "/");\
  print "The month is " date[1] "and the year is "date[3]"} \
  filename

(The Output)
The month is 3 and the year is 2001.
```

EXPLANATION

The string *3/15/2001* is stored in the array *date*, using the forward slash as the field separator. Now *date[1]* contains *3*, *date[2]* contains *15*, and *date[3]* contains *2001*. The field separator is specified in the third argument; if not specified, the value of *FS* is used as the separator.

The delete Function.   The *delete* function removes an array element.

EXAMPLE 7.55

```
% nawk '{line[x++]=$2}END{for(x in line) delete(line[x])}'\
  filename
```

EXPLANATION

The value assigned to the array *line* is the value of the second field. After all the records have been processed, the special *for* loop will go through each element of the array, and the *delete* function will in turn remove each element.

Multidimensional Arrays (nawk).   Although *awk* does not officially support multi-dimensional arrays, a syntax is provided that gives the appearance of a multidimensional array. This is done by concatenating the indices into a string separated by the value of a special built-in variable, *SUBSEP*. The *SUBSEP* variable contains the value *"\034,"* an unprintable character that is so unusual that it is unlikely to be found as an index character. The expression *matrix[2,8]* is really the array *matrix[2 SUBSEP 8]*, which evaluates to *matrix["2\0348"]*. The index becomes a unique string for an associative array.

EXAMPLE 7.56

```
(The Input File)
1 2 3 4 5
2 3 4 5 6
6 7 8 9 10

(The Script)
1   {nf=NF
2   for(x = 1; x <= NF; x++ ){
3       matrix[NR, x] = $x
        }
    }
4   END { for (x=1; x <= NR; x++ ){
        for (y = 1; y <= nf; y++ )
            printf "%d ", matrix[x,y]
    printf"\n"
        }
    }

(The Output)
1 2 3 4 5
2 3 4 5 6
6 7 8 9 10
```

EXPLANATION

1   The variable *nf* is assigned the value of *NF*, the number of fields. (This program assumes a fixed number of five fields per record.)

2   The *for* loop is entered, storing the number of each field on the line in the variable *x*.

3   The *matrix* array is a two-dimensional array. The two indices, *NR* (number of the current record) and *x*, are assigned the value of each field.

4   In the *END* block, the two *for* loops are used to iterate through the *matrix* array, printing out the values stored there. This example does nothing more than demonstrate that multidimensional arrays can be simulated.

7.9.2 Processing Command Arguments (nawk)

ARGV.   Command line arguments are available to *nawk* (the new version of *awk*) with the built-in array called *ARGV*. These arguments include the command *nawk*, but not any of the options passed to *nawk*. The index of the *ARGV* array starts at zero. (This works only for *nawk*.)

ARGC.   *ARGC* is a built-in variable that contains the number of command line arguments.

EXAMPLE 7.57

```
(The Script)
# This script is called argvs
BEGIN{
    for ( i=0; i < ARGC; i++ ){
        printf("argv[%d] is %s\n", i, ARGV[i])
        }
    printf("The number of arguments, ARGC=%d\n", ARGC)
}


(The Output)
% nawk -f argvs datafile
argv[0] is nawk
argv[1] is datafile
The number of arguments, ARGC=2
```

EXPLANATION

In the *for* loop, *i* is set to zero, *i* is tested to see if it is less than the number of command line arguments (*ARGC*), and the *printf* function displays each argument encountered, in turn. When all of the arguments have been processed, the last *printf* statement outputs the number of arguments, *ARGC*. The example demonstrates that *awk* does not count command line options as arguments.

EXAMPLE 7.58

```
(The Command Line)
% nawk -f argvs datafile "Peter Pan" 12
argv[0] is nawk
argv[1] is datafile
argv[2] is Peter Pan
argv[3] is 12
The number of arguments, ARGC=4
```

EXPLANATION

As in the last example, each of the arguments is printed. The *nawk* command is considered the first argument, whereas the *–f* option and script name, *argvs*, are excluded.

EXAMPLE 7.59

```
(The Datafile)
% cat datafile5
Tom Jones:123:03/14/56
Peter Pan:456:06/22/58
Joe Blow:145:12/12/78
Santa Ana:234:02/03/66
Ariel Jones:987:11/12/66

(The Script)
% cat arging.sc
# This script is called arging.sc
1   BEGIN{FS=":"; name=ARGV[2]
2       print "ARGV[2] is "ARGV[2]
    }
    $1  ~ name { print $0 }

(The Command Line)
% nawk -f arging.sc datafile5 "Peter Pan"
ARGV[2] is Peter Pan
Peter Pan:456:06/22/58
nawk: can't open Peter Pan
input record number 5, file Peter Pan
source line number 2
```

EXPLANATION

1   In the *BEGIN* block, the variable *name* is assigned the value of *ARGV[2]*, *Peter Pan*.

2   *Peter Pan* is printed, but then *awk* tries to open *Peter Pan* as an input file after it has processed and closed the *datafile*. *Awk* treats arguments as input files.

EXAMPLE 7.60

```
(The Script)
% cat arging2.sc
BEGIN{FS=":"; name=ARGV[2]
    print "ARGV[2] is " ARGV[2]
    delete ARGV[2]
}
$1  ~ name { print $0 }

(The Command Line)
% nawk -f arging2.sc datafile "Peter Pan"
ARGV[2] is Peter Pan
Peter Pan:456:06/22/58
```

EXPLANATION

Awk treats the elements of the *ARGV* array as input files; after an argument is used, it is shifted to the left and the next one is processed, until the *ARGV* array is empty. If the argument is deleted immediately after it is used, it will not be processed as the next input file.

7.10 *awk* Built-In Functions

7.10.1 String Functions

The *sub* and *gsub* Functions.   The *sub* function matches the regular expression for the largest and leftmost substring in the record, and then replaces that substring with the substitution string. If a target string is specified, the regular expression is matched for the largest and leftmost substring in the target string, and the substring is replaced with the substitution string. If a target string is not specified, the entire record is used.

FORMAT

```
sub (regular expression, substitution string);
sub (regular expression, substitution string, target string)
```

EXAMPLE 7.61

```
1  % nawk '{sub(/Mac/, "MacIntosh"); print}' filename
2  % nawk '{sub(/Mac/, "MacIntosh", $1); print}' filename
```

EXPLANATION

1   The first time the regular expression *Mac* is matched in the record ($0), it will be replaced with the string *MacIntosh*. The replacement is made only on the first occurrence of a match on the line. (See *gsub* for multiple occurrences.)

2   The first time the regular expression *Mac* is matched in the first field of the record, it will be replaced with the string *MacIntosh*. The replacement is made only on the first occurrence of a match on the line for the target string. The *gsub* function substitutes a regular expression with a string globally, that is, for every occurrence where the regular expression is matched in each record ($0).

FORMAT

```
gsub(regular expression, substitution string)
gsub(regular expression, substitution string, target string)
```

EXAMPLE 7.62

```
1  % nawk '{ gsub(/CA/, "California"); print }' datafile
2  % nawk '{ gsub(/[Tt]om/, "Thomas", $1 ); print }' filename
```

EXPLANATION

1   Everywhere the regular expression *CA* is found in the record ($0), it will be replaced with the string *California*.

2   Everywhere the regular expression *Tom* or *tom* is found in the first field, it will be replaced with the string *Thomas*.

The *index* Function.   The *index* function returns the first position where a substring is found in a string. Offset starts at position 1.

FORMAT

```
index(string, substring)
```

EXAMPLE 7.63

```
% nawk '{ print index("hollow", "low") }' filename
4
```

EXPLANATION

The number returned is the *position* where the substring *low* is found in *hollow*, with the offset starting at one.

The *length* Function.   The *length* function returns the number of characters in a string. Without an argument, the *length* function returns the number of characters in a record.

FORMAT

```
length ( string )
length
```

EXAMPLE 7.64

```
% nawk '{ print length("hello") }' filename
5
```

EXPLANATION

The *length* function returns the number of characters in the string *hello*.

The *substr* Function.   The *substr* function returns the substring of a string starting at a position where the first position is one. If the length of the substring is given, that part of the string is returned. If the specified length exceeds the actual string, the string is returned.

FORMAT

```
substr(string, starting position)
substr(string, starting position, length of string)
```

EXAMPLE 7.65

```
% nawk ' { print substr("Santa Claus", 7, 6 )} ' filename
Claus
```

EXPLANATION

In the string *Santa Claus*, print the substring starting at position 7 with a length of 6 characters.

The *match* Function.   The *match* function returns the index where the regular expression is found in the string, or zero if not found. The *match* function sets the built-in variable *RSTART* to the starting position of the substring within the string, and *RLENGTH* to the number of characters to the end of the substring. These variables can be used with the *substr* function to extract the pattern. (Works only with *nawk*.)

FORMAT

```
match(string, regular expression)
```

EXAMPLE 7.66

```
% nawk 'END{start=match("Good ole USA", /[A-Z]+$/); print start}'\
  filename
10
```

EXPLANATION

The regular expression /[A–Z]+$/ says search for consecutive uppercase letters at the end of the string. The substring *USA* is found starting at the tenth character of the string *Good ole USA*. If the string cannot be matched, *0* is returned.

EXAMPLE 7.67

```
1   % nawk 'END{start=match("Good ole USA", /[A-Z]+$/);\
    print RSTART, RLENGTH}' filename
    10 3
2   % nawk 'BEGIN{ line="Good ole USA"}; \
    END{ match( line, /[A-Z]+$/);\
    print substr(line, RSTART,RLENGTH)}' filename
    USA
```

EXPLANATION

1   The *RSTART* variable is set by the *match* function to the starting position of the regular expression matched. The *RLENGTH* variable is set to the length of the substring.

2   The *substr* function is used to find a substring in the variable *line*, and uses the *RSTART* and *RLENGTH* values (set by the *match* function) as the beginning position and length of the substring.

The *split* Function.   The *split* function splits a string into an array using whatever field separator is designated as the third parameter. If the third parameter is not provided, *awk* will use the current value of *FS*.

FORMAT

```
split (string, array, field separator)
split (string, array)
```

EXAMPLE 7.68

```
% awk 'BEGIN{split("12/25/2001",date,"/");print date[2]}' filename
25
```

EXPLANATION

The *split* function splits the string *12/25/2001* into an array, called *date*, using the forward slash as the separator. The array subscript starts at *1*. The second element of the *date* array is printed.

The *sprintf* Function.   The *sprintf* function returns an expression in a specified format. It allows you to apply the format specifications of the *printf* function.

FORMAT

```
variable=sprintf("string with format specifiers ", expr1, expr2, \
... , expr2)
```

EXAMPLE 7.69

```
% awk '{line = sprintf ( "%-15s %6.2f ", $1 , $3 );\
 print line}'  filename
```

EXPLANATION

The first and third fields are formatted according to the *printf* specifications (a left-justified, *15*-space string and a right-justified, *6*-character floating point number). The result is assigned to the user-defined variable *line*. See "The printf Function" on page 161.

7.11 Built-In Arithmetic Functions

Table 7.3 lists the built-in arithmetic functions, where x and y are arbitrary expressions.

Table 7.3 Arithmetic Functions

Name	Value Returned
atan2(*x,y*)	Arctangent of *y/x* in the range.
cos(*x*)	Cosine of *x*, with *x* in radians.
exp(*x*)	Exponential function of *x, e*.
int(*x*)	Integer part of *x*; truncated toward 0 when *x* > 0.
log(*x*)	Natural (base *e*) logarithm of *x*.
rand( )	Random number *r*, where 0 < *r* < 1.
sin(*x*)	Sine of *x*, with *x* in radians.
sqrt(*x*)	Square root of *x*.
srand(*x*)	*x* is a new seed for *rand*( ).[a]

a. From Alfred V. Aho, Brian W. Kernighan, and Peter J. Weinberger, *The AWK Programming Language* (Boston: Addison-Wesley, 1988). © 1988 Bell Telephone Laboratories, Inc. Reprinted by permission of Pearson Education, Inc.

7.11.1 Integer Function

The *int* function truncates any digits to the right of the decimal point to create a whole number. There is no rounding off.

EXAMPLE 7.70

```
1   % awk 'END{print 31/3}' filename
    10.3333
2   % awk 'END{print int(31/3})' filename
    10
```

EXPLANATION

1   In the *END* block, the result of the division is to print a floating point number.

2   In the *END* block, the *int* function causes the result of the division to be truncated at the decimal point. A whole number is displayed.

7.11.2 Random Number Generator

The *rand* Function.   The *rand* function generates a pseudorandom floating point number greater than or equal to zero and less than one.

EXAMPLE 7.71

```
% nawk '{print rand()}' filename
0.513871
0.175726
0.308634

% nawk '{print rand()}' filename
0.513871
0.175726
0.308634
```

EXPLANATION

Each time the program runs, the same set of numbers is printed. The *srand* function can be used to seed the *rand* function with a new starting value. Otherwise, as in this example, the same sequence is repeated each time *rand* is called.

The *srand* Function.   The *srand* function without an argument uses the time of day to generate the seed for the *rand* function. *Srand(x)* uses *x* as the seed. Normally, *x* should vary during the run of the program.

EXAMPLE 7.72

```
% nawk 'BEGIN{srand()};{print rand()}' filename
0.508744
0.639485
0.657277

% nawk 'BEGIN{srand()};{print rand()}' filename
0.133518
0.324747
0.691794
```

EXPLANATION

The *srand* function sets a new seed for *rand*. The starting point is the time of day. Each time *rand* is called, a new sequence of numbers is printed.

EXAMPLE 7.73

```
% nawk 'BEGIN{srand()};{print 1 + int(rand() * 25)}' filename
6
24
14
```

EXPLANATION

The *srand* function sets a new seed for *rand*. The starting point is the time of day. The *rand* function selects a random number between 0 and 25 and casts it to an integer value.

7.12 User-Defined Functions *(nawk)*

A user-defined function can be placed anywhere in the script that a pattern action rule can.

FORMAT

```
function name ( parameter, parameter, parameter, ... ) {
    statements
    return expression
(The return statement and expression are optional)
}
```

Variables are passed by value and are local to the function where they are used. Only copies of the variables are used. Arrays are passed by address or by reference, so array elements can be directly changed within the function. Any variable used within the function that has *not* been passed in the parameter list is considered a global variable; that is, it is visible to the entire *awk* program, and if changed in the function, is changed throughout the program. The only way to provide local variables within a function is to include them in the parameter list. Such parameters are usually placed at the end of the list. If there is not a formal parameter provided in the function call, the parameter is initially set to null. The return statement returns control and possibly a value to the caller.

EXAMPLE 7.74

```
(The Command Line Display of grades File before Sort)
% cat  grades
44 55 66 22 77 99
100 22 77 99 33 66
55 66 100 99 88 45


(The Script)
% cat sorter.sc
    # Script is called sorter
    # It sorts numbers in ascending order
1   function sort ( scores, num_elements, temp, i, j ) {
        # temp, i, and j will be local and private,
        # with an initial value of null.
2       for( i = 2; i <= num_elements ; ++i ) {
3           for ( j = i; scores [j-1] > scores[j]; --j ){
                temp = scores[j]
                scores[j] = scores[j-1]
                scores[j-1] = temp
            }
4       }
5   }
6   {for ( i = 1; i <= NF; i++)
        grades[i]=$i
7   sort(grades, NF)     # Two arguments are passed
8   for( j = 1; j <= NF; ++j )
        printf( "%d ", grades[j] )
        printf("\n")
    }


(After the Sort)
% nawk -f sorter.sc grades
22 44 55 66 77 99
22 33 66 77 99 100
45 55 66 88 99 100
```

EXPLANATION

1   The function called *sort* is defined. The function can be defined anywhere in the script. All variables, except those passed as parameters, are global in scope. If changed in the function, they will be changed throughout the *awk* script. Arrays are passed by reference. Five formal arguments are enclosed within the parentheses. The array *scores* will be passed by reference, so that if any of the elements of the array are modified within the function, the original array will be modified. The variable *num_elements* is a local variable, a copy of the original. The variables *temp*, *i*, and *j* are local variables in the function.

2   The outer *for* loop will iterate through an array of numbers, as long as there are at least two numbers to compare.

3   The inner *for* loop will compare the current number with the previous number, *scores[j –1]*). If the previous array element is larger than the current one, *temp* will be assigned the value of the current array element, and the current array element will be assigned the value of the previous element.

4   The outer loop block ends.

5   This is the end of the function definition.

6   The first action block of the script starts here. The *for* loop iterates through each field of the current record, creating an array of numbers.

7   The *sort* function is called, passing the array of numbers from the current record and the number of fields in the current record.

8   When the *sort* function has completed, program control starts here. The *for* loop prints the elements in the sorted array.

7.13 Review

% **cat datafile**						
northwest	NW	Joel Craig	3.0	.98	3	4
western	WE	Sharon Kelly	5.3	.97	5	23
southwest	SW	Chris Foster	2.7	.8	2	18
southern	SO	May Chin	5.1	.95	4	15
southeast	SE	Derek Johnson	4.0	.7	4	17
eastern	EA	Susan Beal	4.4	.84	5	20
northeast	NE	TJ Nichols	5.1	.94	3	13
north	NO	Val Shultz	4.5	.89	5	9
central	CT	Sheri Watson	5.7	.94	5	13

EXAMPLE 7.75

```
% nawk '{if ( $8 > 15 ){ print $3 " has a high rating"}\
   else print $3 "---NOT A COMPETITOR---"}' datafile
```

Joel---NOT A COMPETITOR---
Sharon has a high rating
Chris has a high rating
May---NOT A COMPETITOR---
Derek has a high rating
Susan has a high rating
TJ---NOT A COMPETITOR---
Val---NOT A COMPETITOR---
Sheri---NOT A COMPETITOR---

EXPLANATION

The *if* statement is an action statement. If there is more than one statement following the expression, it must be enclosed in curly braces. (Curly braces are not required in this example, since there is only one statement following the expression.) The expression reads—*if* the eighth field is greater than 15, print the third field and the string *has a high rating*; *else* print the third field and *---NOT A COMPETITOR---*.

EXAMPLE 7.76

```
% nawk '{i=1; while(i<=NF && NR < 2){print $i; i++}}' datafile
```
northwest
NW
Joel
Craig
3.0
.98
3
4

EXPLANATION

The user-defined variable *i* is assigned 1. The *while* loop is entered and the expression tested. If the expression evaluates true, the *print* statement is executed; the value of the *i*th field is printed. The value of *i* is printed, next the value is incremented by 1, and the loop is reentered. The loop expression will become false when the value of *i* is greater than *NF* and the value of *NR* is two or more. The variable *i* will not be reinitialized until the next record is entered.

% **cat datafile**						
northwest	NW	Joel Craig	3.0	.98	3	4
western	WE	Sharon Kelly	5.3	.97	5	23
southwest	SW	Chris Foster	2.7	.8	2	18
southern	SO	May Chin	5.1	.95	4	15
southeast	SE	Derek Johnson	4.0	.7	4	17
eastern	EA	Susan Beal	4.4	.84	5	20
northeast	NE	TJ Nichols	5.1	.94	3	13
north	NO	Val Shultz	4.5	.89	5	9
central	CT	Sheri Watson	5.7	.94	5	13

EXAMPLE 7.77

```
% nawk '{ for( i=3 ; i <= NF && NR == 3 ; i++ ){ print $i }}' datafile
Chris
Foster
2.7
.8
2
18
```

EXPLANATION

This is similar to the *while* loop in functionality. The initialization, test, and loop control statements are all in one expression. The value of *i* (*i* = 3) is initialized once for the current record. The expression is then tested. If *i* is less than or equal to *NF*, and *NR* is equal to 3, the *print* block is executed. After the value of the ith field is printed, control is returned to the loop expression. The value of *i* is incremented and the test is repeated.

EXAMPLE 7.78

```
(The Command Line)
% cat nawk.sc4
# Awk script illustrating arrays
BEGIN{OFS="\t"}
{ list[NR] = $1 }      # The array is called list. The index in the
                       # number of the current record. The value of the
                       # first field is assigned to the array element.
END{ for( n = 1; n <= NR; n++){
        print list[n]} # for loop is used to loop
                       # through the array.
}
```

EXAMPLE 7.78 (CONTINUED)

```
(The Command Line)
% nawk -f nawk.sc4 datafile
northwest
western
southwest
southern
southeast
eastern
northeast
north
central
```

EXPLANATION

The array, *list*, uses NR as an index value. Each time a line of input is processed, the first field is assigned to the *list* array. In the *END* block, the *for* loop iterates through each element of the array.

EXAMPLE 7.79

```
(The Command Line)
% cat nawk.sc5
# Awk script with special for loop
/north/{name[count++]=$3}
END{ print "The number living in a northern district: " count
     print "Their names are: "
     for ( i in name )        # Special nawk for loop is used to
          print name[i]       # iterate through the array.
}

% nawk -f nawk.sc5 datafile
The number living in a northern district: 3
Their names are:
Joel
TJ
Val
```

EXPLANATION

Each time the regular expression *north* appears on the line, the *name* array is assigned the value of the third field. The index *count* is incremented each time a new record is processed, thus producing another element in the array. In the *END* block, the special *for* loop is used to iterate through the array.

% **cat datafile**						
northwest	NW	Joel Craig	3.0	.98	3	4
western	WE	Sharon Kelly	5.3	.97	5	23
southwest	SW	Chris Foster	2.7	.8	2	18
southern	SO	May Chin	5.1	.95	4	15
southeast	SE	Derek Johnson	4.0	.7	4	17
eastern	EA	Susan Beal	4.4	.84	5	20
northeast	NE	TJ Nichols	5.1	.94	3	13
north	NO	Val Shultz	4.5	.89	5	9
central	CT	Sheri Watson	5.7	.94	5	13

EXAMPLE 7.80

```
(The Command Line)
% cat nawk.sc6
# Awk and the special for loop
{region[$1]++}    # The index is the first field of each record

END{for(item in region){
      print region[item], item
    }
}

% nawk -f nawk.sc6 datafile
1 central
1 northwest
1 western
1 southeast
1 north
1 southern
1 northeast
1 southwest
1 eastern

% nawk -f nawk.sc6 datafile3
4 Mary
2 Tom
1 Alax
1 Bob
1 Sean
```

EXPLANATION

The *region* array uses the first field as an index. The value stored is the number of times each region was found. The *END* block uses the special *awk for* loop to iterate through the array called *region*.

UNIX TOOLS LAB EXERCISE

Lab 6: *nawk* Exercise

Mike Harrington:(510) 548-1278:250:100:175
Christian Dobbins:(408) 538-2358:155:90:201
Susan Dalsass:(206) 654-6279:250:60:50
Archie McNichol:(206) 548-1348:250:100:175
Jody Savage:(206) 548-1278:15:188:150
Guy Quigley:(916) 343-6410:250:100:175
Dan Savage:(406) 298-7744:450:300:275
Nancy McNeil:(206) 548-1278:250:80:75
John Goldenrod:(916) 348-4278:250:100:175
Chet Main:(510) 548-5258:50:95:135
Tom Savage:(408) 926-3456:250:168:200
Elizabeth Stachelin:(916) 440-1763:175:75:300

(Refer to the database called *lab6.data* on the CD.)

The database above contains the names, phone numbers, and money contributions to the party campaign for the past three months.

    1. Write a *nawk* script that will produce the following report:

```
            ***FIRST QUARTERLY REPORT***
            ***CAMPAIGN 1998 CONTRIBUTIONS***
-----------------------------------------------------------------
  NAME              PHONE       Jan  |  Feb  |  Mar  |  Total Donated
-----------------------------------------------------------------
Mike Harrington    (510) 548-1278  250.00  100.00  175.00    525.00
Christian Dobbins  (408) 538-2358  155.00   90.00  201.00    446.00
Susan Dalsass      (206) 654-6279  250.00   60.00   50.00    360.00
Archie McNichol    (206) 548-1348  250.00  100.00  175.00    525.00
Jody Savage        (206) 548-1278   15.00  188.00  150.00    353.00
Guy Quigley        (916) 343-6410  250.00  100.00  175.00    525.00
Dan Savage         (406) 298-7744  450.00  300.00  275.00   1025.00
Nancy McNeil       (206) 548-1278  250.00   80.00   75.00    405.00
John Goldenrod     (916) 348-4278  250.00  100.00  175.00    525.00
Chet Main          (510) 548-5258   50.00   95.00  135.00    280.00
Tom Savage         (408) 926-3456  250.00  168.00  200.00    618.00
Elizabeth Stachelin (916) 440-1763 175.00   75.00  300.00    550.00
-----------------------------------------------------------------
                            SUMMARY
-----------------------------------------------------------------
The campaign received a total of $6137.00 for this quarter.
The average donation for the 12 contributors was $511.42.
The highest total contribution was $1025.00 made by Dan Savage.
                    ***THANKS Dan***
The following people donated over $500 to the campaign.
They are eligible for the quarterly drawing!!
Listed are their names (sorted by last names) and phone numbers:
    John Goldenrod--(916) 348-4278
    Mike Harrington--(510) 548-1278
    Archie McNichol--(206) 548-1348
    Guy Quigley--(916) 343-6410
    Dan Savage  (406) 298-7744
    Tom Savage--(408) 926-3456
    Elizabeth Stachelin--(916) 440-1763
      Thanks to all of you for your continued support!!
```

7.14 Odds and Ends

Some data (e.g., that read in from tape or from a spreadsheet) may not have obvious field separators but may instead have fixed-width columns. To preprocess this type of data, the *substr* function is useful.

7.14.1 Fixed Fields

In the following example, the fields are of a fixed width, but are not separated by a field separator. The *substr* function is used to create fields.

EXAMPLE 7.81

```
% cat fixed
031291ax5633(408)987-0124
021589bg2435(415)866-1345
122490de1237(916)933-1234
010187ax3458(408)264-2546
092491bd9923(415)134-8900
112990bg4567(803)234-1456
070489qr3455(415)899-1426

% nawk '{printf substr($0,1,6)" ";printf substr($0,7,6)" ";\
  print substr($0,13,length)}' fixed
031291   ax5633   (408)987-0124
021589   bg2435   (415)866-1345
122490   de1237   (916)933-1234
010187   ax3458   (408)264-2546
092491   bd9923   (415)134-8900
112990   bg4567   (803)234-1456
070489   qr3455   (415)899-1426
```

EXPLANATION

The first field is obtained by getting the substring of the entire record, starting at the first character, offset by 6 places. Next, a space is printed. The second field is obtained by getting the substring of the record, starting at position 7, offset by 6 places, followed by a space. The last field is obtained by getting the substring of the entire record, starting at position *13* to the position represented by the length of the line. (The length function returns the length of the current line, *$0*, if it does not have an argument.)

Empty Fields.   If the data is stored in fixed-width fields, it is possible that some of the fields are empty. In the following example, the *substr* function is used to preserve the fields, regardless of whether they contain data.

EXAMPLE 7.82

```
1   % cat db
    xxx xxx
    xxx abc xxx
    xxx a    bbb
    xxx      xx


    % cat awkfix
    # Preserving empty fields. Field width is fixed.
    {
2   f[1]=substr($0,1,3)
3   f[2]=substr($0,5,3)
4   f[3]=substr($0,9,3)
5   line=sprintf("%-4s%-4s%-4s\n", f[1],f[2], f[3])
6   print line
    }
    % nawk -f awkfix db
    xxx xxx
    xxx abc xxx
    xxx a    bbb
    xxx      xx
```

EXPLANATION

1   The contents of the file *db* are printed. There are empty fields in the file.

2   The first element of the *f* array is assigned the substring of the record, starting at position *1* and offset by *3*.

3   The second element of the *f* array is assigned the substring of the record, starting at position *5* and offset by *3*.

4   The third element of the *f* array is assigned the substring of the record, starting at position *9* and offset by *3*.

5   The elements of the array are assigned to the user-defined variable *line* after being formatted by the *sprintf* function.

6   The value of *line* is printed and the empty fields are preserved.

Numbers with $, Commas, or Other Characters.   In the following example, the price field contains a dollar sign and comma. The script must eliminate these characters to add up the prices to get the total cost. This is done using the *gsub* function.

EXAMPLE 7.83

```
% cat vendor
access tech:gp237221:220:vax789:20/20:11/01/90:$1,043.00
alisa systems:bp262292:280:macintosh:new updates:06/30/91:$456.00
alisa systems:gp262345:260:vax8700:alisa talk:02/03/91:$1,598.50
apple computer:zx342567:240:macs:e-mail:06/25/90:$575.75
caci:gp262313:280:sparc station:network11.5:05/12/91:$1,250.75
datalogics:bp132455:260:microvax2:pagestation maint:07/01/90:$1,200.00
dec:zx354612:220:microvax2:vms sms:07/20/90:$1,350.00

% nawk -F: '{gsub(/\$/,"");gsub(/,/,""); cost +=$7};\

END{print "The total is $" cost}' vendor
$7474
```

EXPLANATION

The first *gsub* function globally substitutes the literal dollar sign (\\$) with the null string, and the second *gsub* function substitutes commas with a null string. The user-defined *cost* variable is then totalled by adding the seventh field to *cost* and assigning the result back to *cost*. In the *END* block, the string *The total cost is $* is printed, followed by the value of *cost*.[1]

7.14.2 Bundling and Unbundling Files

The Bundle Program.   In *The AWK Programming Language*, the program to bundle files together is very short and to the point. We are trying to combine several files into one file to save disk space, to send files through electronic mail, and so forth. The following *awk* command will print every line of each file, preceded with the filename.

EXAMPLE 7.84

```
% nawk '{ print FILENAME, $0 }' file1 file2 file3 > bundled
```

EXPLANATION

The name of the current input file, *FILENAME*, is printed, followed by the record (*$0*) for each line of input in *file1*. After *file1* has reached the end of file, *awk* will open the next file, *file2*, and do the same thing, and so on. The output is redirected to a file called *bundled*.

---

1. For details on how commas are added back into the program, see Alfred V. Aho, Brian W. Kernighan, and Peter J. Weinberger, *The AWK Programming Language* (Boston: Addison-Wesley, 1988), p. 72.

Unbundle. The following example displays how to unbundle files, or put them back into separate files.

EXAMPLE 7.85

```
%  nawk '$1 != previous { close(previous); previous=$1};\
   {print substr($0, index($0, " ") + 1) > $1}' bundled
```

EXPLANATION

The first field is the name of the file. If the name of the file is not equal to the value of the user-defined variable *previous* (initially null), the action block is executed. The file assigned to *previous* is closed, and *previous* is assigned the value of the first field. Then the *substr* of the record, the starting position returned from the index function (the position of the first space + 1), is redirected to the filename contained in the first field.

To bundle the files so that the filename appears on a line by itself, above the contents of the file use, the following command:

```
%  nawk '{if(FNR==1){print FILENAME;print $0}\
   else print $0}'  file1 file2 file3 > bundled
```

The following command will unbundle the files:

```
%  nawk 'NF==1{filename=$NF} ;\
   NF != 1{print $0 > filename}' bundled
```

7.14.3 Multiline Records

In the sample data files used so far, each record is on a line by itself. In the following sample datafile, called *checkbook*, the records are separated by blank lines and the fields are separated by newlines. To process this file, the record separator (*RS*) is assigned a value of null, and the field separator (*FS*) is assigned the newline.

EXAMPLE 7.86

```
(The Input File)
% cat checkbook
1/1/01
#125
-695.00
Mortgage

1/1/01
#126
-56.89
PG&E
```

EXAMPLE   7.86 (CONTINUED)

```
1/2/01
#127
-89.99
Safeway

1/3/01
+750.00
Pay Check

1/4/01
#128
-60.00
Visa
```

(The Script)
```
   % cat awkchecker
1  BEGIN{RS=""; FS="\n";ORS="\n\n"}
2  {print  NR, $1,$2,$3,$4}
```

(The Output)
```
% nawk -f awkchecker checkbook
1 1/1/01  #125  -695.00  Mortgage

2 1/1/01  #126  -56.89   PG&E

3 1/2/01  #127  -89.99   Safeway

4 1/3/01  +750.00  Pay Check

5 1/4/01  #128  -60.00   Visa
```

EXPLANATION

1   In the *BEGIN* block, the record separator (*RS*) is assigned null, the field separator (*FS*) is assigned a newline, and the output record separator (*ORS*) is assigned two newlines. Now each line is a field and each output record is separated by two newlines.

2   The number of the record is printed, followed by each of the fields.

7.14.4 Generating Form Letters

The following example is modified from a program in *The AWK Programming Language*.[2] The tricky part of this is keeping track of what is actually being processed. The input file is called *data.form*. It contains just the data. Each field in the input file is separated by

---

2. Alfred V. Aho, Brian W. Kernighan, and Peter J. Weinberger, *The AWK Programming Language* (Boston: Addison-Wesley, 1988). © 1988 Bell Telephone Laboratories, Inc. Reprinted by permission of Pearson Education, Inc.

colons. The other file is called *form.letter*. It is the actual form that will be used to create the letter. This file is loaded into *awk*'s memory with the *getline* function. Each line of the form letter is stored in an array. The program gets its data from *data.form*, and the letter is created by substituting real data for the special strings preceded by # and @ found in *form.letter*. A temporary variable, *temp*, holds the actual line that will be displayed after the data has been substituted. This program allows you to create personalized form letters for each person listed in *data.form*.

EXAMPLE 7.87

```
(The Awk Script)
% cat form.awk
# form.awk is an awk script that requires access to 2 files: The
# first file is called "form.letter." This file contains the
# format for a form letter. The awk script uses another file,
# "data.form," as its input file. This file contains the
# information that will be substituted into the form letters in
# the place of the numbers preceded by pound signs. Today's date
# is substituted in the place of "@date" in "form.letter."
1   BEGIN{ FS=":"; n=1
2   while(getline < "form.letter" >  0)
3       form[n++] = $0    # Store lines from form.letter in an array
4   "date" | getline d; split(d, today, " ")
            # Output of date is Fri Mar 2 14:35.50    PST 2001
5   thisday=today[2]". "today[3]", "today[6]
6   }
7   { for( i = 1; i < n; i++ ){
8       temp=form[i]
9       for ( j = 1; j <=NF; j++ ){
            gsub("@date", thisday, temp)
10          gsub("#" j, $j , temp )
        }
11  print temp
    }
    }
```

```
% cat form.letter
    The form letter, form.letter, looks like this:
*************************************************************
    Subject: Status Report for Project "#1"
    To: #2
    From: #3
    Date: @date
    This letter is to tell you, #2, that project "#1" is up to
    date.
    We expect that everything will be completed and ready for
    shipment as scheduled on #4.

    Sincerely,

    #3
*************************************************************
```

EXAMPLE 7.87 (CONTINUED)

The file, *data.form*, is awk's **input file** containing the data that will replace the #1-4 and the @date in *form.letter*.

% **cat data.form**
   Dynamo:John Stevens:Dana Smith, Mgr:4/12/2001
   Gallactius:Guy Sterling:Dana Smith, Mgr:5/18/2001

(The Command Line)

   % **nawk -f form.awk data.form**
   ****
   Subject: Status Report for Project "Dynamo"
   To: John Stevens
   From: Dana Smith, Mgr
   Date: Mar. 2, 2001
   This letter is to tell you, John Stevens, that project
   "Dynamo" is up to date.
   We expect that everything will be completed and ready for
   shipment as scheduled on 4/12/2001.

   Sincerely,

   Dana Smith, Mgr
   Subject: Status Report for Project "Gallactius"
   To: Guy Sterling
   From: Dana Smith, Mgr
   Date: Mar. 2, 2001
   This letter is to you, Guy Sterling, that project "Gallactius"
   is up to date.
   We expect that everything will be completed and ready for
   shipment as scheduled on 5/18/2001.

   Sincerely,

   Dana Smith, Mgr

EXPLANATION

1   In the *BEGIN* block, the field separator (*FS*) is assigned a colon; a user-defined variable *n* is assigned 1.

2   In the *while* loop, the *getline* function reads a line at a time from the file called *form.letter*. If *getline* fails to find the file, it returns a –1. When it reaches the end of file, it returns zero. Therefore, by testing for a return value of greater than one, we know that the function has read in a line from the input file.

3   Each line from *form.letter* is assigned to an array called *form*.

4   The output from the UNIX *date* command is piped to the *getline* function and assigned to the user-defined variable *d*. The *split* function then splits up the variable *d* with whitespace, creating an array called *today*.

EXPLANATION (CONTINUED)

5 The user-defined variable *thisday* is assigned the month, day, and year.

6 The *BEGIN* block ends.

7 The *for* loop will loop *n* times.

8 The user-defined variable *temp* is assigned a line from the *form* array.

9 The nested *for* loop is looping through a line from the input file, *data.form*, NF number of times. Each line stored in the *temp* variable is checked for the string *@date*. If *@date* is matched, the *gsub* function replaces it with today's date (the value stored in *this day*).

10 If a # and a number are found in the line stored in *temp*, the *gsub* function will replace the # and number with the value of the corresponding field in the input file, *data.form*. For example, if the first line stored is being tested, *#1* would be replaced with *Dynamo*, *#2* with *John Stevens*, *#3* with *Dana Smith*, *#4* with *4/12/2001*, and so forth.

11 The line stored in *temp* is printed after the substitutions.

7.14.5 Interaction with the Shell

Now that you have seen how *awk* works, you will find that *awk* is a very powerful utility when writing shell scripts. You can embed one-line *awk* commands or *awk* scripts within your shell scripts. The following is a sample of a Korn shell program embedded with *awk* commands.

EXAMPLE 7.88

```
!#/bin/ksh
# This korn shell script will collect data for awk to use in
# generating form letter(s). See above.
print "Hello $LOGNAME. "
print "This report is for the month and year:"
1   cal | nawk 'NR==1{print $0}'

    if [[ -f data.form  || -f formletter? ]]
    then
        rm data.form formletter?  2> /dev/null
    fi
    integer num=1
    while true
    do
        print "Form letter #$num:"
        read project?"What is the name of the project? "
        read sender?"Who is the status report from? "
        read recipient?"Who is the status report to? "
        read due_date?"What is the completion date scheduled? "
```

EXAMPLE 7.88 (CONTINUED)

```
        echo $project:$recipient:$sender:$due_date > data.form
        print -n "Do you wish to generate another form letter? "
        read answer
        if [[ "$answer" != [Yy]* ]]
        then
                break
        else
2               nawk -f form.awk  data.form  > formletter$num
        fi
        (( num+=1 ))
    done
    nawk -f form.awk data.form > formletter$num
```

EXPLANATION

1   The UNIX *cal* command is piped to *awk*. The first line that contains the current month and year is printed.

2   The *nawk* script *form.awk* generates form letters, which are redirected to a UNIX file.

7.15 Review

7.15.1 String Functions

```
% cat datafile
```

northwest	NW	Joel Craig	3.0	.98	3	4
western	WE	Sharon Kelly	5.3	.97	5	23
southwest	SW	Chris Foster	2.7	.8	2	18
southern	SO	May Chin	5.1	.95	4	15
southeast	SE	Derek Johnson	4.0	.7	4	17
eastern	EA	Susan Beal	4.4	.84	5	20
northeast	NE	TJ Nichols	5.1	.94	3	13
north	NO	Val Shultz	4.5	.89	5	9
central	CT	Sheri Watson	5.7	.94	5	13

EXAMPLE 7.89

```
% nawk 'NR==1{gsub(/northwest/,"southeast", $1) ;print}' datafile
southeast      NW      Joel Craig          3.0  .98   3   4
```

EXPLANATION

If this is the first record *(NR == 1)*, **globally substitute** the regular expression *northwest* with *southeast,* if *northwest* is found in the first field.

EXAMPLE 7.90

```
% nawk 'NR==1{print substr($3, 1, 3)}' datafile
Joe
```

EXPLANATION

If this is the first record, display the **substring** of the third field, starting at the first character, and extracting a length of 3 characters. The substring *Joe* is printed.

EXAMPLE 7.91

```
% nawk 'NR==1{print length($1)}' datafile
9
```

EXPLANATION

If this is the first record, the **length** (number of characters) in the first field is printed.

EXAMPLE 7.92

```
% nawk 'NR==1{print index($1,"west")}' datafile
6
```

EXPLANATION

If this is the first record, print the first position where the substring *west* is found in the first field. The string *west* starts at the sixth position (**index**) in the string *northwest.*

EXAMPLE 7.93

```
% nawk '{if(match($1,/^no/)){print substr($1,RSTART,RLENGTH)}}'\
  datafile
no
no
no
```

EXPLANATION

If the *match* function finds the regular expression /^no/ in the first field, the index position of the leftmost character is returned. The built-in variable *RSTART* is set to the index position and the *RLENGTH* variable is set to the length of the matched substring. The *substr* function returns the string in the first field starting at position *RSTART*, *RLENGTH* number of characters.

EXAMPLE 7.94

```
% nawk 'BEGIN{split("10/14/01",now,"/");print now[1],now[2],now[3]}'
10 14 01
```

EXPLANATION

The string *10/14/01* is **split** into an array called *now*. The delimiter is the forward slash. The elements of the array are printed, starting at the first element of the array.

% **cat datafile2**
Joel Craig:northwest:NW:3.0:.98:3:4
Sharon Kelly:western:WE:5.3:.97:5:23
Chris Foster:southwest:SW:2.7:.8:2:18
May Chin:southern:SO:5.1:.95:4:15
Derek Johnson:southeast:SE:4.0:.7:4:17
Susan Beal:eastern:EA:4.4:.84:5:20
TJ Nichols:northeast:NE:5.1:.94:3:13
Val Shultz:north:NO:4.5:.89:5:9
Sheri Watson:central:CT:5.7:.94:5:13

EXAMPLE 7.95

```
% nawk -F: '/north/{split($1, name, " ");\
print "First name: "name[1];\
print "Last name: " name[2];\
print "\n--------------------"}' datafile2


First name: Joel
Last name: Craig
--------------------
First name: TJ
Last name: Nichols
--------------------
First name: Val
last name: Shultz
--------------------
```

EXPLANATION

The input field separator is set to a colon (–F.). If the record contains the regular expression *north*, the first field is **split** into an array called *name*, where a space is the delimiter. The elements of the array are printed.

% **cat datafile**						
northwest	NW	Joel Craig	3.0	.98	3	4
western	WE	Sharon Kelly	5.3	.97	5	23
southwest	SW	Chris Foster	2.7	.8	2	18
southern	SO	May Chin	5.1	.95	4	15
southeast	SE	Derek Johnson	4.0	.7	4	17
eastern	EA	Susan Beal	4.4	.84	5	20
northeast	NE	TJ Nichols	5.1	.94	3	13
north	NO	Val Shultz	4.5	.89	5	9
central	CT	Sheri Watson	5.7	.94	5	13

EXAMPLE 7.96

```
% nawk '{line=sprintf("%10.2f%5s\n",$7,$2); print line}' datafile
3.00    NW
5.00    WE
2.00    SW
4.00    SO
4.00    SE
5.00    EA
3.00    NE
5.00    NO
5.00    CT
```

EXPLANATION

The *sprintf* function formats the seventh and the second fields ($7, $2) using the formatting conventions of the *printf* function. The formatted string is returned and assigned to the user-defined variable *line* and printed.

7.15.2 Command Line Arguments

EXAMPLE 7.97

```
% cat argvs.sc
# Testing command line arguments with ARGV and ARGC using a for loop.

BEGIN{
    for(i=0;i < ARGC;i++)
        printf("argv[%d] is %s\n", i, ARGV[i])
        printf("The number of arguments, ARGC=%d\n", ARGC)
}

% nawk -f argvs.sc datafile
argv[0] is nawk
argv[1] is datafile
The number of arguments, ARGC=2
```

EXPLANATION

The *BEGIN* block contains a *for* loop to process the **command line arguments**. *ARGC* is the number of arguments and *ARGV* is an array that contains the actual arguments. *Nawk* does not count options as arguments. The only valid arguments in this example are the *nawk* command and the input file, datafile.

EXAMPLE 7.98

```
% nawk 'BEGIN{name=ARGV[1]};\
  $0 ~ name {print $3 , $4}'  "Derek" datafile
nawk: can't open Derek
source line number 1


% nawk 'BEGIN{name=ARGV[1]; delete ARGV[1]};\
  $0 ~ name {print $3, $4}'  "Derek" datafile
Derek Johnson
```

EXPLANATION

1   The name *"Derek"* was set to the variable *name* in the *BEGIN* block. In the pattern-
    action block, *nawk* attempted to open *"Derek"* as an input file and failed.

2   After assigning *"Derek"* to the variable *name*, *ARGV[1]* is deleted. When starting
    the pattern-action block, *nawk* does not try to open *"Derek"* as the input file, but
    opens *datafile* instead.

% **cat datafile**						
northwest	NW	Joel Craig	3.0	.98	3	4
western	WE	Sharon Kelly	5.3	.97	5	23
southwest	SW	Chris Foster	2.7	.8	2	18
southern	SO	May Chin	5.1	.95	4	15
southeast	SE	Derek Johnson	4.0	.7	4	17
eastern	EA	Susan Beal	4.4	.84	5	20
northeast	NE	TJ Nichols	5.1	.94	3	13
north	NO	Val Shultz	4.5	.89	5	9
central	CT	Sheri Watson	5.7	.94	5	13

7.15.3 Reading Input *(getline)*

EXAMPLE 7.99

```
% nawk 'BEGIN{ "date" | getline d; print d}' datafile
Mon Jan 15 11:24:24 PST 2001
```

EXPLANATION

The UNIX *date* command is piped to the *getline* function. The results are stored in the
variable *d* and printed.

EXAMPLE 7.100

```
% nawk 'BEGIN{ "date " | getline d; split( d, mon) ;print mon[2]}'\
  datafile
Jan
```

EXPLANATION

The UNIX *date* command is piped to the *getline* function and the results are stored in *d*. The *split* function splits the string *d* into an array called *mon*. The second element of the array is printed.

EXAMPLE 7.101

```
% nawk 'BEGIN{ printf "Who are you looking for?" ; \
  getline name < "/dev/tty"};\
```

EXPLANATION

Input is read from the terminal, */dev/tty*, and stored in the array called *name*.

EXAMPLE 7.102

```
% nawk 'BEGIN{while(getline < "/etc/passwd"  > 0 ){lc++}; print lc}'\
  datafile
16
```

EXPLANATION

The *while* loop is used to loop through the */etc/passwd* file one line at a time. Each time the loop is entered, a line is read by *getline* and the value of the variable *lc* is incremented. When the loop exits, the value of *lc* is printed, i.e., the number of lines in the */etc/passwd* file. As long as the return value from *getline* is not *0*, i.e., a line has been read, the looping continues.

7.15.4 Control Functions

```
% nawk '{if ( $5 > 4.5) next; print $1}' datafile
northwest
southwest
southeast
eastern
north
```

If the fifth field is greater than 4.5, the next line is read from the input file (*datafile*) and processing starts at the beginning of the *awk* script (after the *BEGIN* block). Otherwise, the first field is printed.

```
% nawk '{if ($2 ~ /S/){print ; exit 0}}' datafile
southwest       SW      Chris   Foster  2.7     .8      2       18

% echo $status  ( csh ) or echo $? (sh or ksh)
0
```

If the second field contains an *S*, the record is printed and the *awk* program exits. The C shell status variable contains the exit value. If using the Bourne or Korn shells, the *$?* variable contains the exit status.

```
% cat datafile
northwest   NW   Joel Craig      3.0   .98   3   4
western     WE   Sharon Kelly    5.3   .97   5   23
southwest   SW   Chris Foster    2.7   .8    2   18
southern    SO   May Chin        5.1   .95   4   15
southeast   SE   Derek Johnson   4.0   .7    4   17
eastern     EA   Susan Beal      4.4   .84   5   20
northeast   NE   TJ Nichols      5.1   .94   3   13
north       NO   Val Shultz      4.5   .89   5   9
central     CT   Sheri Watson    5.7   .94   5   13
```

7.15.5 User-Defined Functions

EXAMPLE 7.105

```
(The Command Line)
% cat nawk.sc7
1   BEGIN{largest=0}
2   {maximum=max($5)}

3   function max ( num ) {
4       if ( num > largest){ largest=num }
        return largest
5   }
6   END{ print "The maximum is " maximum "."}

% nawk -f nawk.sc7 datafile
The maximum is 5.7.
```

EXPLANATION

1   In the *BEGIN* block, the user-defined variable *largest* is initialized to zero.

2   For each line in the file, the variable *maximum* is assigned the value returned from the function *max*. The function *max* is given $5 as its argument.

3   The user-defined function *max* is defined. The function statements are enclosed in curly braces. Each time a new record is read from the input file, *datafile*, the function *max* will be called.

4   It will compare the values in *num* and *largest* and return the larger of the two numbers.

5   The function definition block ends.

6   The *END* block prints the final value in *maximum*.

UNIX TOOLS LAB EXERCISE

Lab 7: *nawk* Exercise

Mike Harrington:(510) 548-1278:250:100:175
Christian Dobbins:(408) 538-2358:155:90:201
Susan Dalsass:(206) 654-6279:250:60:50
Archie McNichol:(206) 548-1348:250:100:175
Jody Savage:(206) 548-1278:15:188:150
Guy Quigley:(916) 343-6410:250:100:175
Dan Savage:(406) 298-7744:450:300:275
Nancy McNeil:(206) 548-1278:250:80:75
John Goldenrod:(916) 348-4278:250:100:175
Chet Main:(510) 548-5258:50:95:135
Tom Savage:(408) 926-3456:250:168:200
Elizabeth Stachelin:(916) 440-1763:175:75:300

(Refer to the database called *lab7.data* on the CD.)

The database above contains the names, phone numbers, and money contributions to the party campaign for the past three months.

1. Write a user-defined function to return the average of all the contributions for a given month. The month will be passed in at the command line.

8

The Interactive Bourne Shell

8.1   Startup

If the Bourne shell is your login shell, it follows a chain of processes before you see a shell prompt.

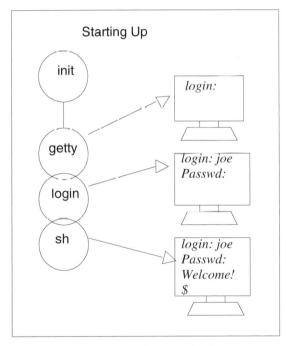

Figure 8.1   Starting the Bourne shell.

The first process to run is called *init*, PID 1. It gets instructions from a file called *inittab* (System V), or it spawns a *getty* process (BSD). These processes open up the terminal ports, providing a place where standard input comes from and a place where standard output and error go, and they put a login prompt on your screen. The */bin/login* program is then executed. The *login* program prompts for a password, encrypts and verifies the password, sets up an initial environment, and starts up the login shell, */bin/sh*, the last entry in the *passwd* file. The *sh* process looks for the system file, */etc/profile,* and executes its commands. It then looks in the user's home directory for an initialization file called *.profile*. After executing commands from *.profile*, the default dollar sign ($) prompt appears on your screen and the Bourne shell awaits commands.

8.1.1 The Environment

The environment of a process consists of variables, open files, the current working directory, functions, resource limits, signals, and so forth. It defines those features that are inherited from one shell to the next and the configuration for the working environment. The configuration for the user's shell is defined in the shell initialization files.

The Initialization Files.   After the Bourne shell program starts up, it first checks for the system file */etc/profile*. After executing the commands in that file, the initialization file, *.profile*, in the user's home directory, is executed. Skeleton files for initial setup can be found in */etc/skel* (SVR4).

The /etc/profile File.   The */etc/profile* file is a systemwide initialization file set up by the system administrator to perform tasks when the user logs on. It is executed when the Bourne shell starts up. It is available to all Bourne and Korn shell users on the system and normally performs such tasks as checking the mail spooler for new mail and displaying the message of the day from the */etc/motd* file. (The following examples will make more sense after you have completed this chapter.)

EXAMPLE 8.1

```
(Sample /etc/profile)
# The profile that all logins get before using their own .profile
1   trap " " 2 3
2   export LOGNAME PATH
3   if [ "$TERM" = " " ]
    then
        if /bin/i386
        then
            TERM=AT386    # Sets the terminal
        else
            TERM=sun
        fi
        export TERM
```

EXAMPLE 8.1 (CONTINUED)

```
        fi
        # Login and -su shells get /etc/profile services.
        # -rsh is given its environment in its own .profile.
4       case "$0" in
        -sh | -ksh | -jsh )
5           if [ ! -f .hushlogin ]
            then
                /usr/sbin/quota
                # Allow the user to break the Message-Of-The-
                # Day only.
6               trap "trap ' ' 2" 2
7               /bin/cat -s /etc/motd
                # Message of the day displayed
                trap " " 2
8               /bin/mail -E       # Checks for new mail
9               case $? in
                0)
                    echo "You have new mail. "
                ; ;
                2)
                    echo "You have mail. "
                ;;
                esac
            fi
        esac
10      umask 022
11      trap 2 3
```

EXPLANATION

1 The *trap* command controls signals coming into this program while it is running. If signals 2 (Control-C) or 3 (Control-\) are sent while the program is in execution, those signals will be ignored.

2 The variables *LOGNAME* and *PATH* are exported so that their values will be known in subshells started from this process.

3 The command */bin/i386* is executed. If the exit status of the command is zero, the terminal variable, *TERM*, is assigned the value *AT386*; if not, the *TERM* variable is assigned *sun*.

4 If the value of *$0*, the name of the program running the */etc/profile* file, is either a login or Bourne, Korn, or job shell, the following commands will be executed.

5 If the *.hushlogin* file does not exist, *quota* will be run to display the disk usage warnings if usage is over the quota.

6 The *trap* is reset so that the user can terminate the message of the day with Control-C.

7 After the message of the day has been displayed, the *trap* is reset to ignore Control-C.

8 The *mail* program checks for new incoming mail.

EXPLANATION (CONTINUED)

9   If the exit status ($?) of the *mail* program is *0* or *2*, the message "*You have new mail.*" or "*You have mail.*", respectively, is displayed.

10   The *umask* command is set to determine the initial permissions of files and directories when they are created.

11   The *trap* command sets signals 2 and 3 back to their defaults; i.e., to kill the program if either Control-C or Control-\ arrive.

The *.profile* File.   The *.profile* file is a user-defined initialization file executed once at login and found in your home directory. It gives you the ability to customize and modify the shell environment. Environment and terminal settings are normally put here, and if a window application or database application is to be initiated, it is started here. The settings in this file will be discussed in detail as the chapter progresses, but a brief synopsis of each line in the file is explained here.

EXAMPLE 8.2

```
(Sample .profile)

1    TERM=vt102
2    HOSTNAME=`uname -n`
3    EDITOR=/usr/ucb/vi
4    PATH=/bin:/usr/ucb:/usr/bin:/usr/local:/etc:/bin:/usr/bin:.
5    PS1="$HOSTNAME $ > "
6    export TERM HOSTNAME EDITOR PATH PS1
7    stty erase ^h
8    go () { cd $1; PS1=`pwd`; PS1=`basename $PS1`; }
9    trap '$HOME/.logout' EXIT
10   clear
```

EXPLANATION

1   The *TERM* variable is assigned the value of the terminal type, *vt102*.

2   Because the *uname –n* command is enclosed in backquotes, the shell will perform command substitution, i.e., the output of the command (the name of the host machine) will be assigned to the variable *HOSTNAME*.

3   The *EDITOR* variable is assigned */usr/ucb/vi*. Programs such as *mail* will now have this variable available when defining an editor.

4   The *PATH* variable is assigned the directory entries that the shell searches in order to find a UNIX program. If, for example, you type *ls*, the shell will search the *PATH* until it finds that program in one of the listed directories. If it never finds the program, the shell will tell you so.

5   The primary prompt is assigned the value of *HOSTNAME*, the machine name, and the $ and > symbols.

EXPLANATION (CONTINUED)

6 All of the variables listed are exported. They will be known by child processes started from this shell.

7 The *stty* command sets terminal options. The erase key is set to ^h, so that when you press the Backspace key, the letter typed preceding the cursor is erased.

8 A function called *go* is defined. The purpose of this function is to take one argument, a directory name, *cd* to that directory, and set the primary prompt to the present working directory. The *basename* command removes all but the last entry of the path. The prompt will show you the current directory.

9 The *trap* command is a signal handling command. When you exit the shell, that is, log out, the *.logout* file will be executed.

10 The *clear* command clears the screen.

The Prompts. When used interactively, the shell prompts you for input. When you see the prompt, you know that you can start typing commands. The Bourne shell provides two prompts: the primary prompt, a dollar sign ($), and the secondary prompt, a right angle bracket symbol (>). The prompts are displayed when the shell is running interactively. You can change these prompts. The variable *PS1* is the primary prompt set initially to a dollar sign ($). The primary prompt appears when you log on and the shell waits for you to type commands. The variable *PS2* is the secondary prompt, initially set to the right angle bracket character. It appears if you have partially typed a command and then pressed the carriage return. You can change the primary and secondary prompts.

The Primary Prompt. The dollar sign is the default primary prompt. You can change your prompt. Normally prompts are defined in *.profile*, the user initialization file.

EXAMPLE 8.3

```
1   $ PS1="`uname -n > `"
2   chargers >
```

EXPLANATION

1 The default primary prompt is a dollar sign ($). The *PS1* prompt is being reset to the name of the machine (*uname –n*) and a > symbol. (Don't confuse backquotes and single quotes.)

2 The new prompt is displayed.

The Secondary Prompt. The *PS2* prompt is the secondary prompt. Its value is displayed to standard error, which is the screen by default. This prompt appears when you have not completed a command and have pressed the carriage return.

EXAMPLE 8.4

```
1   $ echo "Hello
2   > there"
3   Hello
    there
4   $


5   $ PS2="----> "
6   $ echo 'Hi
7   ------>
    ------>
    ------> there'
    Hi


    there
    $
```

EXPLANATION

1   The double quotes must be matched after the string "*Hello*.

2   When a newline is entered, the secondary prompt appears. Until the closing dou-ble quotes are entered, the secondary prompt will be displayed.

3   The output of the *echo* command is displayed.

4   The primary prompt is displayed.

5   The secondary prompt is reset.

6   The single quote must be matched after the string '*Hi*.

7   When a newline is entered, the new secondary prompt appears. Until the closing single quote is entered, the secondary prompt will be displayed.

The Search Path.   The *path* variable is used by the Bourne shell to locate commands typed at the command line. The path is a colon-separated list of directories used by the shell when searching for commands. The search is from left to right. The dot at the end of the path represents the current working directory. If the command is not found in any of the directories listed in the path, the Bourne shell sends to standard error the message *filename: not found.* It is recommended that the path be set in the *.profile* file.

   If the dot is not included in the path and you are executing a command or script from the current working directory, the name of the script must be preceded with a *./,* such as *./program_name*, so that shell can find the program.

EXAMPLE 8.5

```
(Printing the PATH)
1  $ echo $PATH
/home/gsa12/bin:/usr/ucb:/usr/bin:/usr/local/bin:/usr/bin:/usr/local/bin:.

(Setting the PATH)
2  $ PATH=$HOME:/usr/ucb:/usr:/usr/bin:/usr/local/bin:.
3  $ export PATH
```

EXPLANATION

1 By echoing $PATH$, the value of the $PATH$ variable is displayed. The path consists of a list of colon-separated elements and is searched from left to right. The dot at the end of the path represents the user's current working directory.

2 To set the path, a list of colon-separated directories are assigned to the $PATH$ variable.

3 By exporting the path, child processes will have access to it.

The *hash* Command.   The *hash* command controls the internal hash table used by the shell to improve efficiency in searching for commands. Instead of searching the path each time a command is entered, the first time you type a command, the shell uses the search path to find the command, and then stores it in a table in the shell's memory. The next time you use the same command, the shell uses the hash table to find it. This makes it much faster to access a command than having to search the complete path. If you know that you will be using a command often, you can add the command to the hash table. You can also remove commands from the table. The output of the *hash* command displays both the number of times the shell has used the table to find a command (*hits*) and the relative cost (*cost*) of looking up the command, that is, how far down the search path it had to go before it found the command. The *hash* command with the *–r* option clears the hash table.

EXAMPLE 8.6

```
1  $ hash
   hits   cost    command
   3      8       /usr/bin/date
   1      8       /usr/bin/who
   1      8       /usr/bin/ls
2  $ hash vi
   3      8       /usr/bin/date
   1      8       /usr/bin/who
   1      8       /usr/bin/ls
   0      6       /usr/ucb/vi
3  $ hash -r
```

EXPLANATION

1　The *hash* command displays the commands currently stored in the internal hash table. The shell will not have to search the search path to find the commands listed when they are entered at the command line. This saves time. Otherwise, the shell has to go out to the disk to search the path. When you type a new command, the shell will search the path first, and then place it on the hash table. The next time you use that command, the shell finds it in memory.

2　The *hash* command can take arguments; the names of commands you want to guarantee get stored on the hash table ahead of time.

3　The *hash* command with the *−r* option clears the hash table.

The *dot* Command.　　The *dot* command is a built-in Bourne shell command. It takes a script name as an argument.The script will be executed in the environment of the current shell; that is, a child process will not be started. All variables set in the script will become part of the current shell's environment. Likewise, all variables set in the current shell will become part of the script's environment. The *dot* command is normally used to re-execute the *.profile* file if it has been modified. For example, if one of the settings, such as the *EDITOR* or *TERM* variable, has been changed since you logged on, you can use the *dot* command to re-execute the *.profile* without logging out and then logging back in.

EXAMPLE 8.7

```
$ . .profile
```

EXPLANATION

The *dot* command executes the initialization file, *.profile*, within this shell. Local and global variables are redefined within this shell. The *dot* command makes it unnecessary to log out and then log back in again.[1]

8.1.2　The Command Line

After logging on, the shell displays its primary prompt, a dollar sign, by default. The shell is your command interpreter. When the shell is running interactively, it reads commands from the terminal and breaks the command line into words. A command line consists of one or more words (tokens), separated by whitespace (blanks and/or tabs), and terminated with a newline, which is generated by pressing Enter. The first word is the command and subsequent words are the command's arguments. The command may be a UNIX executable program such as *ls* or *pwd*, a built-in command such as *cd* or *test*, or a shell script. The command may contain special characters, called *metacharacters*,

---

1. If the *.profile* were executed directly as a script, a subshell would be started. Then the variables would be set in the subshell, but not in the login shell (parent shell).

that the shell must interpret while parsing the command line. If a command line is long and you want to continue typing on the next line, the backslash character, followed by a newline, will allow you to continue typing on the next line. The secondary prompt will appear until the command line is terminated.

The Exit Status.   After a command or program terminates, it returns an exit status to the parent process. The exit status is a number between 0 and 255. By convention, when a program exits, if the status returned is zero, the command was successful in its execution. When the exit status is nonzero, the command failed in some way. The shell status variable, ?, is set to the value of the exit status of the last command that was executed. Success or failure of a program is determined by the programmer who wrote the program.

EXAMPLE 8.8

```
1   $ grep "john" /etc/passwd
    john:MgVyBsZJavdl6s:9496:40:John Doe:/home/falcon/john:/bin/sh
2   $ echo $?
    0
3   $ grep "nicky" /etc/passwd
4   $ echo $?
    1
5   $ grep "scott" /etc/passsswd
    grep: /etc/passsswd: No such file or directory
6   $ echo $?
    2
```

EXPLANATION

1   The *grep* program searches for the pattern *john* in the */etc/passwd* file and is successful. The line from */etc/passwd* is displayed.
2   The *?* variable is set to the exit value of the *grep* command. Zero indicates success.
3   The *grep* program cannot find user *nicky* in the */etc/passwd* file.
4   If the *grep* program cannot find the pattern, it returns an exit status of *1*.
5   The *grep* fails because the */etc/passsswd* file cannot be opened.
6   If *grep* cannot find the file, it returns an exit status of *2*.

Multiple Commands at the Command Line.   A command line can consist of multiple commands. Each command is separated by a semicolon, and the command line is terminated with a newline.

EXAMPLE 8.9

```
$ ls; pwd; date
```

EXPLANATION

The commands are executed from left to right, one after the other, until the newline is reached.

Grouping Commands.   Commands may also be grouped so that all of the output is either piped to another command or redirected to a file.

EXAMPLE 8.10

```
$ ( ls ; pwd; date ) > outputfile
```

EXPLANATION

The output of each of the commands is sent to the file called *outputfile*. The spaces inside the parentheses are necessary.

Conditional Execution of Commands.   With conditional execution, two command strings are separated by the special metacharacters, double ampersands (&&) and double vertical bars (||). The command on the right of either of these metacharacters will or will not be executed based on the exit condition of the command on the left.

EXAMPLE 8.11

```
$ cc prgm1.c -o prgm1 && prgm1
```

EXPLANATION

If the first command is successful (has a zero exit status), the command after the && is executed; i.e., if the *cc* program can successfully compile *prgm1.c*, the resulting executable program, *prgm1*, will be executed.

EXAMPLE 8.12

```
$ cc prog.c >& err || mail bob < err
```

EXPLANATION

If the first command fails (has a nonzero exit status), the command after the || is executed; i.e., if the *cc* program cannot compile *prog.c*, the errors are sent to a file called *err*, and user *bob* will be mailed the *err* file.

Commands in the Background.   Normally, when you execute a command, it runs in the foreground, and the prompt does not reappear until the command has completed execution. It is not always convenient to wait for the command to complete. By placing an ampersand (&) at the end of the command line, the shell will return the shell prompt immediately and execute the command in the background concurrently. You do not have to wait to start up another command. The output from a background job will be sent to the screen as it processes. Therefore, if you intend to run a command in the background, the output of that command might be redirected to a file or piped to another device, such as a printer, so that the output does not interfere with what you are doing.

The *$!* variable contains the PID number of the last job put in the background.

EXAMPLE 8.13

```
1   $ man sh | lp&
2   [1] 1557
3   $ kill -9 $!
```

EXPLANATION

1   The output of the *man* command (the manual pages for the *sh* command) is piped to the printer. The ampersand at the end of the command line puts the job in the background.

2   There are two numbers that appear on the screen: the number in square brackets indicates that this is the first job to be placed in the background; the second number is the PID, or the process identification number of this job.

3   The shell prompt appears immediately. While your program is running in the background, the shell is waiting for another command in the foreground.

4   The *!* variable evaluates to the PID of the job most recently put in the background. If you get it in time, you will kill this job before it goes to the print queue.

8.1.3 Metacharacters (Wildcards)

Metacharacters are special characters used to represent something other than themselves. Shell metacharacters are called *wildcards*. Table 8.1 lists metacharacters and what they do.

Table 8.1   Shell Metacharacters

Metacharacter	Meaning
\	Literally interprets the following character.
&	Processes in the background.
;	Separates commands.
$	Substitutes variables.
?	Matches for a single character.
[abc]	Matches for one character from a set of characters.
[!abc]	Matches for one character *not* from the set of characters.
*	Matches for zero or more characters.
(cmds)	Executes commands in a subshell.
{cmds}	Executes commands in current shell.

8.1.4 Filename Substitution

When evaluating the command line, the shell uses metacharacters to abbreviate filenames or pathnames that match a certain set of characters. The filename substitution metacharacters listed in Table 8.2 are expanded into an alphabetically listed set of filenames. The process of expanding the metacharacter into filenames is also called *filename substitution*, or *globbing*. If a metacharacter is used and there is no filename that matches it, the shell treats the metacharacter as a literal character.

Table 8.2 Shell Metacharacters and Filename Substitution

Metacharacter	Meaning
*	Matches zero or more characters.
?	Matches exactly one character.
[abc]	Matches one character in the set *a*, *b*, or *c*.
[a–z]	Matches one character in the range from *a* to *z*.
[! a–z]	Matches one character *not* in the range from *a* to *z*.
\	Escapes or disables the metacharacter.

The Asterisk.   The asterisk is a wildcard that matches for zero or more of any characters in a filename.

EXAMPLE 8.14

```
1   $ ls  *
    abc abc1 abc122 abc123 abc2 file1 file1.bak file2 file2.bak none
    nonsense nobody nothing nowhere one
2   $ ls  *.bak
    file1.bak file2.bak
3   $ echo a*
    ab abc1 abc122 abc123 abc2
```

EXPLANATION

1   The asterisk expands to all of the files in the present working directory. All of the files are passed as arguments to *is* and displayed.

2   All files starting with zero or more characters and ending with *.bak* are matched and listed.

3   All files starting with *a*, followed by zero or more characters, are matched and passed as arguments to the *echo* command.

The Question Mark.   The question mark represents a single character in a filename. When a filename contains one or more question marks, the shell performs filename substitution by replacing the question mark with the character it matches in the filename.

EXAMPLE 8.15

```
1   $ ls
    abc  abc122  abc2  file1.bak  file2.bak  nonsense  nothing  one
    abc1  abc123  file1  file2  none  noone  nowhere

2   $ ls a?c?
    abc1  abc2

3   $ ls ??
    ?? not found

4   $ echo  abc???
    abc122 abc123

5   $ echo ??
    ??
```

EXPLANATION

1   The files in the current directory are listed.
2   Filenames starting with *a*, followed by a single character, followed by *c* and a single character, are matched and listed.
3   Filenames containing exactly two characters are listed if found. Since there are no two-character files, the question marks are treated as a literal filename.
4   Filenames starting with *abc* and followed by exactly three characters are expanded and displayed by the *echo* command.
5   There are no files in the directory that contain exactly two characters. The shell treats the question mark as a literal question mark if it cannot find a match.

The Square Brackets.   The brackets are used to match filenames containing *one* character in a set or range of characters.

EXAMPLE 8.16

```
1   $ ls
    abc  abc122 abc2 file1.bak file2.bak nonsense nothing
    one  abc1 abc123 file1 file2 none noone nowhere

2   $ ls abc[123]
    abc1  abc2
```

EXAMPLE 8.16 (CONTINUED)

```
3   $ ls abc[1-3]
    abc1   abc2

4   $ ls [a-z][a-z][a-z]
    abc one

5   $ ls [!f-z] ???
    abc1   abc2

6   $ ls abc12[23]
    abc122 abc123
```

EXPLANATION

1   All of the files in the present working directory are listed.

2   All filenames containing four characters are matched and listed if the filename starts with *abc*, followed by *1*, *2*, or *3*. Only one character from the set in the brackets is matched.

3   All filenames containing four characters are matched and listed if the filename starts with *abc* and is followed by a number in the range from *1* to *3*.

4   All filenames containing three characters are matched and listed, if the filename contains exactly three lowercase alphabetic characters.

5   All filenames containing four characters are listed if the first character is *not* a lowercase letter between *f* and *z* ([*!f–z*], followed by three of any character (e.g., *???*).

6   Files are listed if the filenames contain *abc12* followed by 2 or 3.

Escaping Metacharacters.   To use a metacharacter as a literal character, the backslash may be used to prevent the metacharacter from being interpreted.

EXAMPLE 8.17

```
1   $ ls
    abc file1 youx
2   $ echo How are you?
    How are youx
3   $ echo How are you\?
    How are you?
4   $ echo  When does this line \
    > ever end\?
    When does this line ever end?
```

1   The files in the present working directory are listed. (Note the file *youx*.)

2   The shell will perform filename expansion on the *?*. Any files in the current directory starting with *y-o-u* and followed by exactly one character are matched and substituted in the string. The filename *youx* will be substituted in the string to read *How are youx* (probably not what you wanted to happen).

3   By preceding the question mark with a backslash, it is escaped, meaning that the shell will not try to interpret it as a wildcard.

4   The newline is escaped by preceding it with a backslash. The secondary prompt is displayed until the string is terminated with a newline. The question mark (*?*) is escaped to protect it from filename expansion.

8.1.5 Variables

There are two types of variables, local and environment variables. Some variables are created by the user and others are special shell variables.

Local Variables.   Local variables are given values that are known only to the shell in which they are created. Variable names must begin with an alphabetic or underscore character. The remaining characters can be alphabetic, decimal digits zero to nine, or an underscore character. Any other characters mark the termination of the variable name. When assigning a value, there can be no whitespace surrounding the equal sign. To set the variable to null, the equal sign is followed by a newline.[2]

A dollar sign is used in front of a variable to extract the value stored there.

Setting Local Variables.

```
1   $ round=world
    $ echo $round
    world

2   $ name="Peter Piper"
    $ echo $name
    Peter Piper

3   $ x=
    $ echo $x
```

---

2. A variable set to some value or to null will be displayed by using the *set* command, whereas an unset variable will not.

EXAMPLE 8.18 (CONTINUED)

```
4   $ file.bak="$HOME/junk"
    file.bak=/home/jody/ellie/junk: not found
```

EXPLANATION

1   The variable *round* is assigned the value *world*. When the shell encounters the dollar sign preceding a variable name, it performs variable substitution. The value of the variable is displayed.

2   The variable *name* is assigned the value *"Peter Piper"*. The quotes are needed to hide the whitespace so that the shell will not split the string into separate words when it parses the command line. The value of the variable is displayed.

3   The variable *x* is not assigned a value. It will be assigned null. The null value, an empty string, is displayed.

4   The period in the variable name is illegal. The only characters allowed in a variable name are numbers, letters, and the underscore. The shell tries to execute the string as a command.

The Scope of Local Variables.   A local variable is known only to the shell in which it was created. It is not passed on to subshells. The double dollar sign variable is a special variable containing the PID of the current shell.

EXAMPLE 8.19

```
1   $ echo $$
    1313
2   $ round=world
    $ echo $round
    world
3   $ sh              # Start a subshell

4   $ echo $$
    1326
5   $ echo $round

6   $ exit            # Exits this shell, returns to parent shell

7   $ echo $$
    1313
8   $ echo $round
    world
```

EXPLANATION

1 The value of the double dollar sign variable evaluates to the PID of the current shell. The PID of this shell is *1313*.

2 The local variable *round* is assigned the string value *world*, and the value of the variable is displayed.

3 A new Bourne shell is started. This is called a *subshell*, or *child shell*.

4 The PID of this shell is *1326*. The parent shell's PID is *1313*.

5 The variable *round* is not defined in this shell. A blank line is printed.

6 The *exit* command terminates this shell and returns to the parent shell. (Control-D will also exit this shell.)

7 The parent shell returns. Its PID is displayed.

8 The value of the variable *round* is displayed.

Setting Read-Only Variables.   A read-only variable cannot be redefined or unset.

EXAMPLE 8.20

```
1   $ name=Tom
2   $ readonly name
    $ echo $name
    Tom
3   $ unset name
    name: readonly
4   $ name=Joe
    name: readonly
```

EXPLANATION

1 The local variable *name* is assigned the value *Tom*.

2 The variable is made *readonly*.

3 A read-only variable cannot be unset.

4 A read-only variable cannot be redefined.

Environment Variables.   Environment variables are available to the shell in which they are created and any subshells or processes spawned from that shell. By convention, environment variables are capitalized. Environment variables are variables that have been exported.

The shell in which a variable is created is called the *parent shell*. If a new shell is started from the parent shell, it is called the *child shell*. Some of the environment variables, such as *HOME, LOGNAME, PATH,* and *SHELL*, are set before you log on by the */bin/login* program. Normally, environment variables are defined and stored in the *.profile* file in the user's home directory. See Table 8.3 for a list of environment variables.

Table 8.3 Bourne Shell Environment Variables

ENV Variable	Value
PATH	The search path for commands.
HOME	Home directory; used by *cd* when no directory is specified.
IFS	Internal field separators, normally space, tab, and newline.
LOGNAME	The user's login name.
MAIL	If this parameter is set to the name of a mail file and the *MAILPATH* parameter is not set, the shell informs the user of the arrival of mail in the specified file.
MAILCHECK	This parameter specifies how often (in seconds) the shell will check for the arrival of mail in the files specified by the *MAILPATH* or *MAIL* parameters. The default value is 600 seconds (10 minutes). If set to zero, the shell will check before issuing each primary prompt.
MAILPATH	A colon-separated list of filenames. If this parameter is set, the shell informs the user of the arrival of mail in any of the specified files. Each filename can be followed by a percent sign and a message that will be printed when the modification time changes. The default message is *You have mail*.
PWD	Present working directory.
PS1	Primary prompt string, which is a dollar sign by default.
PS2	Secondary prompt string, which is a right angle bracket by default.
SHELL	When the shell is invoked, it scans the environment for this name. The shell gives default values to *PATH*, *PS1*, *PS2*, *MAILCHECK*, and *IFS*. *HOME* and *MAIL* are set by *login*.

Setting Environment Variables.   To set environment variables, the *export* command is used either after assigning a value or when the variable is set. (Do not use the dollar sign on a variable when exporting it.)

EXAMPLE 8.21

```
1   $ TERM=wyse
    $ export TERM
2   $ NAME= "John Smith"
    $ export NAME
    $ echo $NAME
    John Smith
3   $ echo $$
    319                 # pid number for parent shell
4   $ sh
                        # Start a subshell
5   $ echo $$
    340                 # pid number for new shell
6   $ echo $NAME
    John Smith
7   $ NAME="April Jenner"
    $ export NAME
    $ echo $NAME
    April Jenner
8   $ exit              # Exit the subshell and go back to parent shell
9   $ echo $$
    319                 # pid number for parent shell
10  $ echo $NAME
    John Smith
```

EXPLANATION

1   The *TERM* variable is assigned *wyse*. The variable is exported. Now, processes started from this shell will inherit the variable.

2   The variable is defined and exported to make it available to subshells started from the shell.

3   The value of this shell's PID is printed.

4   A new Bourne shell is started. The new shell is called the *child*. The original shell is its *parent*.

5   The PID of the new Bourne shell is stored in the $$ variable and its value is echoed.

6   The variable, set in the parent shell, was exported to this new shell and is displayed.

7   The variable is reset to *April Jenner*. It is exported to all subshells, but will not affect the parent shell. Exported values are not propagated upward to the parent shell.

8   This Bourne child shell is exited.

9   The PID of the parent is displayed again.

10 The variable *NAME* contains its original value. Variables retain their values when exported from parent to child shell. The child cannot change the value of a variable for its parent.

Listing Set Variables.   There are two built-in commands that print the value of a variable: *set* and *env*. The *set* command prints all variables, local and global. The *env* command prints just the global variables.

EXAMPLE 8.22

```
1   $ env     (Partial list)
    LOGNAME=ellie
    TERMCAP=sun-cmd
    USER=ellie
    DISPLAY=:0.0
    SHELL=/bin/sh
    HOME=/home/jody/ellie
    TERM=sun-cmd
    LD_LIBRARY_PATH=/usr/local/OW3/lib
    PWD=/home/jody/ellie/perl


2   $ set
    DISPLAY=:0.0
    FMHOME=/usr/local/Frame-2.1X
    FONTPATH=/usr/local/OW3/lib/fonts
    HELPPATH=/usr/local/OW3/lib/locale:/usr/local/OW3/lib/help
    HOME=/home/jody/ellie
    HZ=100
    IFS=
    LANG=C
    LD_LIBRARY_PATH=/usr/local/OW3/lib
    LOGNAME=ellie
    MAILCHECK=600
    MANPATH=/usr/local/OW3/share/man:/usr/local/OW3/man:/
    usr/local/man:/usr/local/doctools/man:/usr/man
    OPTIND=1
    PATH=/home/jody/ellie:/usr/local/OW3/bin:/usr/ucb:/usr/local/
    doctools/bin:/usr/bin:/usr/local:/usr/etc:/etc:/usr/spool/
    news/bin:/home/jody/ellie/bin:/usr/lo
    PS1=$
    PS2=>
    PWD=/home/jody/ellie/kshprog/joke
    SHELL=/bin/sh
    TERM=sun-cmd
    TERMCAP=sun-cmd:te=\E[>4h:ti=\E[>4l:tc=sun:
    USER=ellie
    name=Tom
    place="San Francisco"
```

EXPLANATION

1   The *env* command lists all environment (exported) variables. These variables are, by convention, named with all uppercase letters. They are passed from the process in which they are created to any of its child processes.

2   The *set* command, without options, prints all *set* variables, local and exported (including variables set to null).

Unsetting Variables.   Both local and environment variables can be unset by using the *unset* command, unless the variables are set as read-only.

EXAMPLE 8.23

```
unset name; unset TERM
```

EXPLANATION

The *unset* command removes the variable from the shell's memory.

Printing the Values of Variables: The *echo* Command.   The *echo* command prints its arguments to standard output and is used primarily in Bourne and C shells. The Korn shell has a built-in *print* command. There are different versions of the *echo* command; for example, the Berkeley (BSD) *echo* is different from the System V *echo*. Unless you specify a full pathname, you will use the built-in version of the *echo* command. The built-in version will reflect the version of UNIX you are using. The System V *echo* allows the use of numerous escape sequences, whereas the BSD version does not. Table 8.4 lists the BSD *echo* option and escape sequences.

Table 8.4   BSD *echo* Option and System V Escape Sequences

Option	Meaning
BSD:	
−*n*	Suppress newline at the end of a line of output.
System V:	
\b	Backspace.
\c	Print the line without a newline.
\f	Form feed.
\n	Newline.
\r	Return.
\t	Tab.
\v	Vertical tab.
\\	Backslash.

EXAMPLE 8.24

```
1   $ echo The username is $LOGNAME.
    The username is ellie.

2   $ echo "\t\tHello there\c"   # System V
    Hello there$

3   $ echo -n "Hello there"      # BSD
    Hello there$
```

EXPLANATION

1   The *echo* command prints its arguments to the screen. Variable substitution is performed by the shell before the *echo* command is executed.

2   The System V version of the *echo* command supports escape sequences similar to those of the C programming language. The $ is the shell prompt.

3   The *–n* option to the *echo* command indicates the BSD version of the *echo* command is being used. The line is printed without the newline. The escape sequences are not supported by this version of *echo*.

Variable Expansion Modifiers.   Variables can be tested and modified by using special modifiers. The modifier provides a shortcut conditional test to check if a variable has been set, and then assigns a value to the variable based on the outcome of the test. See Table 8.5 for a list of variable modifiers.

Table 8.5   Variable Modifiers

Modifier	Value
${variable:–word}	If *variable* is set and is non-null, substitute its value; otherwise, substitute *word*.
${variable:=word}	If *variable* is set or is non-null, substitute its value; otherwise, set it to *word*. The value of *variable* is substituted permanently. Positional parameters may not be assigned in this way.
${variable:+word}	If *parameter* is set and is non-null, substitute *word*; otherwise, substitute nothing.
${variable:?word}	If *variable* is set and is non-null, substitute its value; otherwise, print *word* and exit from the shell. If *word* is omitted, the message *parameter null or not set* is printed.

Using the colon with any of the modifiers (–, =, +, ?) checks whether the variable is not set or is *null;* without the colon, a variable set to null is considered to be set.

EXAMPLE 8.25

```
(Assigning Temporary Default Values)
1   $ fruit=peach
2   $ echo ${fruit:-plum}
    peach

3   $ echo ${newfruit:-apple}
    apple
4   $ echo $newfruit

5   $ echo $EDITOR       # More realistic example
6   $ echo ${EDITOR:-/bin/vi}
    /bin/vi
7   $ echo $EDITOR

8   $ name=
    $ echo ${name-Joe}
9   $ echo ${name:-Joe}
    Joe
```

EXPLANATION

1   The variable *fruit* is assigned the value *peach*.

2   The special modifier will check to see if the variable *fruit* has been set. If it has, the value is printed; if not, *plum* is substituted for *fruit* and its value is printed.

3   The variable *newfruit* has not been set. The value *apple* will be temporarily substituted for *newfruit*.

4   The setting was only temporary. The variable *newfruit* is not set.

5   The environment variable *EDITOR* has not been set.

6   The : modifier substitutes *EDITOR* with */bin/vi*.

7   The *EDITOR* was never set. Nothing prints.

8   The variable *name* is set to null. By not prefixing the modifier with a colon, the variable is considered to be set, even if to null, and the new value *Joe* is not assigned to *name*.

9   The colon causes the modifier to check that a variable is either *not* set or is set to null. In either case, the value *Joe* will be substituted for *name*.

EXAMPLE 8.26

```
(Assigning Permanent Default Values)
1   $ name=
2   $ echo   ${name:=Patty}
    Patty
3   $ echo $name
    Patty
4   $ echo ${EDITOR:=/bin/vi}
    /bin/vi
5   $ echo $EDITOR
    /bin/vi
```

EXPLANATION

1 The variable *name* is assigned the value *null*.

2 The special modifier *:=* will check to see if the variable name has been set. If it has been set, it will not be changed; if it is either null or not set, it will be assigned the value to the right of the equal sign. *Patty* is assigned to *name* since the variable is set to null. The setting is permanent.

3 The variable *name* still contains the value *Patty*.

4 The value of the variable *EDITOR* is set to */bin/vi*.

5 The value of the variable *EDITOR* is displayed.

EXAMPLE 8.27

```
(Assigning Temporary Alternate Value)
1   $ foo=grapes
2   $ echo ${foo:+pears}
    pears
3   $ echo $foo
    grapes
    $
```

EXPLANATION

1 The variable *foo* has been assigned the value *grapes*.

2 The special modifier *:+* will check to see if the variable has been set. If it has been set, *pears* will temporarily be substituted for *foo*; if not, null is returned.

3 The variable *foo* now has its original value.

EXAMPLE 8.28

```
(Creating Error Messages Based On Default Values)
1   $ echo ${namex:?"namex is undefined"}
    namex: namex is undefined
2   $ echo ${y?}
    y: parameter null or not set
```

EXPLANATION

1   The *:?* modifier will check to see if the variable has been set. If not, the string to the right of the *?* is printed to standard error, after the name of the variable. If in a script, the script exits.

2   If a message is not provided after the *?*, the shell sends a default message to standard error.

Positional Parameters.   Normally, the special built-in variables, often called *positional parameters*, are used in shell scripts when passing arguments from the command line, or used in functions to hold the value of arguments passed to the function. See Table 8.6. The variables are called positional parameters because they are denoted by their position on the command line. The Bourne shell allows up to nine positional parameters. The name of the shell script is stored in the *$0* variable. The positional parameters can be set and reset with the *set* command.

Table 8.6   Positional Parameters

Positional Parameter	Meaning
$0	References the name of the current shell script.
$1–$9	Denotes positional parameters *1* through *9*.
$#	Evaluates to the number of positional parameters.
*$**	Evaluates to all the positional parameters.
$@	Means the same as *$**, except when double quoted.
"$"*	Evaluates to *"$1 $2 $3"*.
"$@"	Evaluates to *"$1" "$2" "$3"*.

EXAMPLE 8.29

```
1   $ set tim bill ann fred
    $ echo $*        # Prints all the positional parameters
                     # tim bill ann fred.


2   $ echo $1        # Prints the first positional parameter.
    tim
3   $ echo $2 $3     # Prints the second and third
    bill ann         # positional parameters.
4   $ echo $#        # Prints the total number of
    4                # positional parameters.


5   $ set a b c d e f g h i j k l m
    $ echo  $10      # Prints the first positional parameter
    a0               # followed by a zero.
6   $ echo  $*
    a b c d e f g h i j k l m


7   $ set file1 file2 file3
    $ echo  \$$#
    $3
8   $ eval echo  \$$#
    file3
```

EXPLANATION

1 The *set* command assigns values to positional parameters. The $* special variable contains all of the parameters set.

2 The value of the first positional parameter, *tim*, is displayed.

3 The value of the second and third parameters, *bill* and *ann,* are displayed.

4 The $# special variable contains the number of positional parameters currently set.

5 The *set* command resets all of the positional parameters. The original set is destroyed. Positional parameters cannot be numbered beyond nine. The value of the first positional parameter is printed, followed by the number zero.

6 The $* allows you to print all of the parameters, even past nine.

7 The positional parameters are reset to *file1*, *file2*, and *file3*. The dollar sign is escaped; $# is the number of arguments. The *echo* command displays $3.

8 The *eval* command parses the command line a second time before executing the command. The first time parsed, the shell substitutes \$$# with $3, and the second time, the shell substitutes the value of $3 with *file3*.

Other Special Variables. The shell has special variables consisting of a single character. The dollar sign preceding the character allows you to access the value stored in the variable. See Table 8.7.

Table 8.7 Special Variables

Variable	Meaning
$	The PID of the shell
–	The *sh* options currently set
?	The exit value of last executed command
!	The PID of the last job put in the background

EXAMPLE 8.30

```
1   $ echo The pid of this shell is $$
    The pid of this shell is 4725

2   $ echo The options for this shell are $-
    The options for this shell are s

3   $ grep dodo /etc/passwd
    $ echo $?
    1

4   $ sleep 25&
    4736
    $ echo $!
    4736
```

EXPLANATION

1   The $ variable holds the value of the PID for this process.
2   The – variable lists all options for this interactive Bourne shell.
3   The *grep* command searches for the string *dodo* in the */etc/passwd* file. The *?* variable holds the exit status of the last command executed. Since the value returned from *grep* is *1*, *grep* is assumed to have failed in its search. An exit status of zero indicates a successful exit.
4   The *!* variable holds the PID number of the last command placed in the background. The *&* appended to the *sleep* command sends the command to the background.

8.1.6 Quoting

Quoting is used to protect special metacharacters from interpretation. There are three methods of quoting: the backslash, single quotes, and double quotes. The characters listed in Table 8.8 are special to the shell and must be quoted.

Table 8.8 Special Metacharacters Requiring Quotes

Metacharacter	Meaning
;	Command separator
&	Background processing
( )	Command grouping; creates a subshell
{ }	Command grouping; does not create a subshell
|	Pipe
<	Input redirection
>	Output redirection
newline	Command termination
space/tab	Word delimiter
$	Variable substitution character
* [ ] ?	Shell metacharacters for filename expansion

Single and double quotes must be matched. Single quotes protect special metacharacters, such as $, *, ?, |, >, and <, from interpretation. Double quotes also protect special metacharacters from being interpreted, but allow variable and command substitution characters (the dollar sign and backquotes) to be processed. Single quotes will protect double quotes and double quotes will protect single quotes.

The Bourne shell does not let you know if you have mismatched quotes. If running interactively, a secondary prompt appears when quotes are not matched. If in a shell script, the file is scanned and if the quote is not matched, the shell will attempt to match it with the next available quote; if the shell cannot match it with the next available quote, the program aborts and the message *'end of file' unexpected* appears on the terminal. Quoting can be a real hassle for even the best of shell programmers! See Appendix C for shell quoting rules.

The Backslash.   The backslash is used to quote (or escape) a single character from interpretation. The backslash is not interpreted if placed in single quotes. The backslash will protect the dollar sign ($), backquotes (` `), and the backslash from interpretation if enclosed in double quotes.

EXAMPLE 8.31

```
1   $ echo Where are you going\?
    Where are you going?

2   $ echo Start on this line and \
    >  go to the next line.
    Start on this line and go to the next line.

3   $ echo \\
    \

4   $ echo '\\'
    \\

5   $ echo '\$5.00'
    \$5.00

6   $ echo "\$5.00"
    $5.00
```

EXPLANATION

1   The backslash prevents the shell from performing filename substitution on the question mark.
2   The backslash escapes the newline, allowing the next line to become part of this line.
3   Since the backslash itself is a special character, it prevents the backslash following it from interpretation
4   The backslash is not interpreted when enclosed in single quotes.
5   All characters in single quotes are treated literally. The backslash does not serve any purpose here.
6   When enclosed in double quotes, the backslash prevents the dollar sign from being interpreted for variable substitution.

Single Quotes.   Single quotes must be matched. They protect all metacharacters from interpretation. To print a single quote, it must be enclosed in double quotes or escaped with a backslash.

EXAMPLE 8.32

```
1   $ echo 'hi there
    > how are you?
    > When will this end?
    > When the quote is matched
    > oh'
```

EXAMPLE 8.32 (CONTINUED)

```
hi there
how are you?
When will this end?
When the quote is matched
oh
```

2 `$ echo 'Don\'t  you need $5.00?'`
   Don't you need $5.00?

3 `$ echo 'Mother yelled, "Time to eat!"'`
   Mother yelled, "Time to eat!"

EXPLANATION

1 The single quote is not matched on the line. The Bourne shell produces a secondary prompt. It is waiting for the quote to be matched.

2 The single quotes protect all metacharacters from interpretation. The apostrophe in *Don't* is escaped with a backslash. Otherwise, it would match the first quote, and the single quote at the end of the string would not have a mate. In this example, the $ and the ? are protected from the shell and will be treated as literals.

3 The single quotes protect the double quotes in this string.

Double Quotes.   Double quotes must be matched, will allow variable and command substitution, and protect any other special metacharacters from being interpreted by the shell.

EXAMPLE 8.33

1 `$ name=Jody`
2 `$ echo "Hi $name, I'm glad to meet you!"`
   Hi Jody, I'm glad to meet you!

3 `$ echo "Hey $name, the time is `date`"`
   Hey Jody, the time is Wed Dec 14 14:04:11 PST 1998

EXPLANATION

1 The variable *name* is assigned the string *Jody*.

2 The double quotes surrounding the string will protect all special metacharacters from interpretation, with the exception of $ in *$name*. Variable substitution is performed within double quotes.

3 Variable substitution and command substitution are both performed when enclosed within double quotes. The variable *name* is expanded, and the command in backquotes, *date*, is executed.

8.1.7 Command Substitution

Command substitution is used when assigning the output of a command to a variable or when substituting the output of a command within a string. All three shells use back-quotes to perform command substitution.[3]

EXAMPLE 8.34

```
1   $ name=`nawk -F:  '{print $1}' database`
    $ echo $name
    Ebenezer Scrooge

2   $ set `date`
3   $ echo $*
    Fri Oct 19 09:35:21 PDT 2001

4   $ echo $2 $6
    Oct 2001
```

EXPLANATION

1   The *nawk* command is enclosed in backquotes. It is executed and its output is assigned to the variable *name*, as a string, and displayed.

2   The *set* command assigns the output of the *date* command to positional parameters. Whitespace separates the list of words into its respective parameters.

3   The $* variable holds all of the positional parameters. The output of the *date* command was stored in the $* variable. Each parameter is separated by whitespace.

4   The second and sixth parameters are printed.

8.1.8 An Introduction to Functions

Although the Bourne shell does not have an *alias* mechanism for abbreviating commands, it does support functions (introduced to the shell in SVR2). Functions are used to execute a group of commands with a name. They are like scripts, only more efficient. Once defined, they become part of the shell's memory so that when the function is called, the shell does not have to read it in from the disk as it does with a file. Often functions are used to improve the modularity of a script (discussed in the programming section of this chapter). Once defined, they can be used again and again. Functions are often defined in the user's initialization file, *.profile*. They must be defined before they are invoked, and cannot be exported.

Defining Functions.   The function name is followed by a set of empty parentheses. The definition of the function consists of a set of commands separated by semicolons

---

3. The Korn shell allows backquotes for command substitution for upward-compatibility, but provides an alternate method as well.

and enclosed in curly braces. The last command is terminated with a semicolon. Spaces around the curly braces are required.

FORMAT

```
function_name () { commands ; commands; }
```

EXAMPLE 8.35

```
1   $ greet () { echo "Hello $LOGNAME, today is `date`; }
2   $ greet
    Hello ellie, today is Thu Oct 4 19:56:31 PDT  2001
```

EXPLANATION

1 The function is called *greet*.

2 When the *greet* function is invoked, the command(s) enclosed within the curly braces are executed.

EXAMPLE 8.36

```
1   $ fun () { pwd; ls; date; }
2   $ fun
    /home/jody/ellie/prac
    abc      abc123    file1.bak    none       nothing   tmp
    abc1     abc2      file2        nonsense   nowhere   touch
    abc122   file1     file2.bak    noone      one
    Sat Feb 24 11:15:48 PST 2001

3   $ welcome () { echo "Hi $1 and $2"; }
4   $ welcome tom joe
    Hi tom and joe

5   $ set jane nina lizzy
6   $ echo $*
    jane nina lizzy

7   $ welcome tom joe
    hi tom and joe

8   $ echo  $1 $2
    jane nina
```

EXPLANATION

1 The function *fun* is named and defined. The name is followed by a list of commands enclosed in curly braces. Each command is separated by a semicolon. A space is required after the first curly brace or you will get a syntax error. A function must be defined before it can be used.

EXPLANATION (CONTINUED)

2 The function behaves just like a script when invoked. Each of the commands in the function definition are executed in turn.

3 There are two positional parameters used in the function *welcome*. When arguments are given to the function, the positional parameters are assigned those values.

4 The arguments to the function, *tom* and *joe*, are assigned to *$1* and *$2*, respectively. The positional parameters in a function are private to the function and will not interfere with any used outside the function.

5 The positional parameters are set at the command line. These variables have nothing to do with the ones set in the function.

6 *$** displays the values of the currently set positional parameters.

7 The function *welcome* is called. The values assigned to the positional parameters are *tom* and *joe*.

8 The positional variables assigned at the command line are unaffected by those set in the function.

Listing and Unsetting Functions.   To list functions and their definitions, use the *set* command. The function and its definition will appear in the output, along with the exported and local variables. Functions and their definitions are unset with the *unset* command.

8.1.9 Standard I/O and Redirection

When the shell starts up, it inherits three files: *stdin*, *stdout*, and *stderr*. Standard input normally comes from the keyboard. Standard output and standard error normally go to the screen. There are times when you want to read input from a file or send output or error to a file. This can be accomplished by using I/O redirection. See Table 8.9 for a list of redirection operators.

Table 8.9   Redirection Operators

Redirection Operator	What It Does
<	Redirect input.
>	Redirect output.
>>	Append output.
2>	Redirect error.
1>&2	Redirect output to where error is going.
2>&1	Redirect error to where output is going.

EXAMPLE 8.37

```
1   $ tr '[A-Z]'  '[a-z]' < myfile
                                    # Redirect  input

2   $ ls > lsfile            # Redirect output
    $ cat lsfile
    dir1
    dir2
    file1
    file2
    file3

3   $ date >> lsfile         # Redirect and append otuput
    $ cat lsfile
    dir1
    dir2
    file1
    file2
    file3
    Mon Sept 17 12:57:22 PDT 2001


4   $ cc prog.c 2> errfile    Redirect error

5   $ find . -name \*.c -print > foundit 2> /dev/null
    # Redirect output to foundit, and error to /dev/null.

6   $ find . -name \*.c -print > foundit 2>&1
    # Redirect output and send standard error to where output is going

7   $ echo "File needs an argument" 1>&2
    # Send standard output to error
```

EXPLANATION

1   Instead of getting input from the keyboard, standard input is redirected from the file *myfile* to the UNIX *tr* command. All uppercase letters are converted to lower-case letters.

2   Instead of sending output to the screen, the *ls* command redirects its output to the file *lsfile*.

3   The output of the *date* command is redirected and appended to *lsfile*.

4   The file *prog.c* is compiled. If the compile fails, the standard error is redirected to the file *errfile*. Now you can take your error file to the local guru for an explanation (of sorts)!

EXPLANATION (CONTINUED)

5   The *find* command starts searching in the current working directory for filenames ending in *.c*, and prints the filenames to a file named *foundit*. Errors from the *find* command are sent to */dev/null*.

6   The *find* command starts searching in the current working directory for filenames ending in *.c*, and prints the filenames to a file named *foundit*. The errors are also sent to *foundit*.

7   The *echo* command sends its message to standard error. Its standard output is merged with standard error.

The *exec* Command and Redirection.   The *exec* command can be used to replace the current program with a new one without starting a new process. Standard output or input can be changed with the *exec* command without creating a subshell (see Table 8.10). If a file is opened with *exec*, subsequent *read* commands will move the file pointer down the file a line at a time until the end of the file. The file must be closed to start reading from the beginning again. However, if using UNIX utilities such as *cat* and *sort*, the operating system closes the file after each command has completed. For examples on how to use *exec* commands in scripts, see "Looping Commands" on page 280.

Table 8.10   The *exec* Command

exec *Command*	*What It Does*
exec ls	*ls* will execute in place of the shell. When *ls* is finished, the shell in which it was started does not return.
exec < filea	Open *filea* for reading standard input.
exec > filex	Open *filex* for writing standard output.
exec 3< datfile	Open *datfile* as file descriptor 3 for reading input.
sort <&3	*Datfile* is sorted.
exec 4>newfile	Open *newfile* as file descriptor (fd) 4 for writing.
ls >&4	Output of *ls* is redirected to *newfile*.
exec 5<&4	Make fd 5 a copy of fd 4.
exec 3<&–	Close fd 3.

EXAMPLE   **8.38**

```
1   $ exec date
    Sun Oct 14 10:07:34  PDT 2001
     <Login prompt appears if you are in your login shell >
```

EXAMPLE   8.38 (CONTINUED)

```
2   $ exec > temp
    $ ls
    $ pwd
    $ echo Hello
3   $ exec > /dev/tty
4   $ echo Hello
    Hello
```

EXPLANATION

1   The *exec* command executes the *date* command in the current shell (it does not fork a child shell). Since the *date* command is executed in place of the current shell, when the *date* command exits, the shell terminates. If a Bourne shell had been started from the C shell, the Bourne shell would exit and the C shell prompt would appear. If you are in your login shell when you try this, you will be logged out. If you are working interactively in a shell window, the window exits.

2   The *exec* command opens standard output for the current shell to the *temp* file. Output from *ls*, *pwd*, and *echo* will no longer go to the screen, but to *temp*.

3   The *exec* command reopens standard output to the terminal. Now, output will go to the screen as shown in line 4.

4   Standard output has been directed back to the terminal (*/dev/tty*).

EXAMPLE   8.39

```
1   $ cat doit
    pwd
    echo hello
    date
2   $ exec < doit
    /home/jody/ellie/shell
    hello
    Sun Oct 14 10:07:34  PDT 2001
3   %
```

EXPLANATION

1   The contents of a file called *doit* are displayed.

2   The *exec* command opens standard input to the file called *doit*. Input is read from the file instead of from the keyboard. The commands from the file *doit* are executed in place of the current shell. When the last command exits, so does the shell. See Figure 8.2.

3   The Bourne shell exited when the *exec* command completed. The C shell prompt appeared. It was the parent shell. If you had been in your login shell when the *exec* finished, you would be logged out; if in a window, the window would have disappeared.

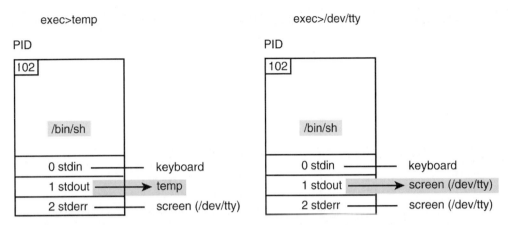

Figure 8.2 The *exec* command.

EXAMPLE 8.40

```
1   $ exec 3> filex
2   $ who >& 3
3   $ date >& 3
4   $ exec 3>&-
5   $ exec 3< filex
6   $ cat <&3
    ellie    console  Oct  7       09:53
    ellie    ttyp0    Oct  7       09:54
    ellie    ttyp1    Oct  7       09:54
    ellie    ttyp2    Oct 11       15:42
    Sun Oct 14 13:31:31  PDT 2001
7   $ exec 3<&-
8   $ date >& 3
    Sun Oct 14 13:41:14  PDT 2001
```

EXPLANATION

1   File descriptor 3 (fd 3) is assigned to *filex* and opened for redirection of output. See Figure 8.3.

2   The output of the *who* command is sent to fd 3, *filex*.

3   The output of the *date* command is sent to fd 3; *filex* is already opened, so the output is appended to *filex*.

4   Fd 3 is closed.

5   The *exec* command opens fd 3 for reading input. Input will be redirected from *filex*.

6   The *cat* program reads from fd 3, assigned to *filex*.

7   The *exec* command closes fd 3. (Actually, the operating system will close the file once end of file is reached.)

8   When attempting to send the output of the *date* command to fd 3, the output goes to the screen, since the file descriptor was closed.

Figure 8.3 *exec* and file descriptors.

8.1.10 Pipes

A *pipe* takes the output from the command on the left-hand side of the pipe symbol and sends it to the input of the command on the right-hand side of the pipe symbol. A pipe-line can consist of more than one pipe.

   The purpose of the next three commands is to count the number of people logged on (*who*), save the output of the command in a file (*tmp*), use the *wc –l* to count the number of lines in the *tmp* file (*wc –l*), and then remove the *tmp* file (i.e., find the number of people logged on). See Figures 8.4 and 8.5.

EXAMPLE 8.41

```
1   $ who > tmp
2   $ wc -l tmp
    4 tmp
3   $ rm tmp


# Using a pipe saves disk space and time.

4   $ who | wc -1
    4


5   $ du . | sort -n | sed -n '$p'
    72388   /home/jody/ellie
```

EXPLANATION

1   The output of the *who* command is redirected to the *tmp* file.

2   The *wc –l* command displays the number of lines in *tmp*.

3   The *tmp* file is removed.

4   With the pipe facility, you can perform all three of the preceding steps in one step. The output of the *who* command is sent to an anonymous kernel buffer; the *wc –l* command reads from the buffer and sends its output to the screen.

5   The output of the *du* command, the number of disk blocks used per directory, is piped to the *sort* command and sorted numerically. It is then piped to the *sed* command, which prints the last line of the output it receives.

Figure 8.4 The pipe.

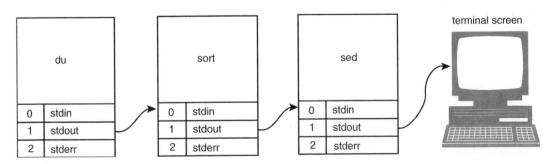

Figure 8.5 Multiple pipes (filter).

8.1.11 The *here document* and Redirecting Input

The *here document* accepts inline text for a program expecting input, such as *mail, sort,* or *cat,* until a user-defined terminator is reached. It is often used in shell scripts for creating menus. The command receiving the input is appended with a << symbol, followed by a user-defined word or symbol, and a newline. The next lines of text will be the lines of input to be sent to the command. The input is terminated when the user-defined word or symbol is then placed on a line by itself in the leftmost column (it cannot have spaces surrounding it). The word is used in place of Control-D to stop the program from reading input.

   If the terminator is preceded by the <<– operator, leading tabs, and only tabs, may precede the final terminator. The user-defined terminating word or symbol must match exactly from "here" to "here." The following examples illustrate the use of the *here document* at the command line to demonstrate the syntax. It is much more practical to use them in scripts.

EXAMPLE 8.42

```
1   $ cat << FINISH              ←┐      # FINISH is a user-defined
2   > Hello there $LOGNAME        |         terminator
3   > The time is `date`          |
    > I can't wait to see you!!!  |
4   > FINISH                     ←┘      # terminator matches first

5   Hello there ellie                    # FINISH on line 1.
    The time is Thu Feb 8 19:42:16 PST 2001
    I can't wait to see you!!!
6   $
```

EXPLANATION

1   The UNIX *cat* program will accept input until the word *FINISH* appears on a line by itself.

2   A secondary prompt appears. The following text is input for the *cat* command. Variable substitution is performed within the *here document.*

3   Command substitution, *`date`*, is performed within the *here document.*

4   The user-defined terminator *FINISH* marks the end of input for the *cat* program. It cannot have any spaces before or after it and is on a line by itself.

5   The output from the *cat* program is displayed.

6   The shell prompt reappears.

EXAMPLE 8.43

```
1   $ cat <<- DONE
    >   Hello there
    >   What's up?
    >   Bye now The time is `date`.
2   >   DONE
    Hello there
    What's up?
    Bye now The time is Thu Feb 8 19:48:23 PST 2001.
    $
```

EXPLANATION

1   The *cat* program accepts input until *DONE* appears on a line by itself. The <<– operator allows the input and final terminator to be preceded by one or more tabs.

2   The final matching terminator, *DONE*, is preceded by a tab. The output of the *cat* program is displayed on the screen.

8.2 Programming with the Bourne Shell

8.2.1 The Steps in Creating a Shell Script

A shell script is normally written in an editor and consists of commands interspersed with comments. Comments are preceded by a pound sign and consist of text used to document what is going on.

The First Line. The first line at the top left corner of the script will indicate the program that will be executing the lines in the script. This line is commonly written as

```
#!/bin/sh
```

The *#!* is called a magic number and is used by the kernel to identify the program that should be interpreting the lines in the script. This line must be the top line of your script.

Comments. *Comments* are lines preceded by a pound sign (#) and can be on a line by themselves or on a line following a script command. They are used to document your script. It is sometimes difficult to understand what the script is supposed to do if it is not commented. Although comments are important, they are often too sparse or not used at all. Try to get used to commenting what you are doing not only for someone else, but also for yourself. Two days from now you may not recall exactly what you were trying to do.

Executable Statements and Bourne Shell Constructs.   A Bourne shell program consists of a combination of UNIX commands, Bourne shell commands, programming constructs, and comments.

Making the Script Executable.   When you create a file, it is not given the execute permission. You need this permission to run your script. Use the *chmod* command to turn on the execute permission.

EXAMPLE 8.44

```
1   $ chmod +x myscript
2   $ ls -lF  myscript
    -rwxr-xr-x   1  ellie   0 Jul  13:00 myscript*
```

EXPLANATION

1   The *chmod* command is used to turn on the execute permission for the user, group, and others.

2   The output of the *ls* command indicates that all users have execute permission on the *myscript* file. The asterisk at the end of the filename also indicates that this is an executable program.

A Scripting Session.   In the following example, the user will create a script in the editor. After saving the file, the execute permissions are turned on, and the script is executed. If there are errors in the program, the shell will respond immediately.

EXAMPLE 8.45

```
(The Script)
% cat greetings
1   #!/bin/sh
2   # This is the first Bourne shell program of the day.
    # Scriptname: greetings
    # Written by:  Barbara Born
3   echo "Hello $LOGNAME, it's nice talking to you."
4   echo "Your present working directory is `pwd`."
    echo "You are working on a machine called `uname -n`."
    echo "Here is a list of your files."
5   ls      # List files in the present working directory
6   echo  "Bye for now $LOGNAME. The time is `date +%T`!"

(The Command Line)
    $ chmod +x greetings
    $ greetings
3   Hello barbara, it's nice talking to you.
4   Your present working directory is /home/lion/barbara/prog
    You are working on a machine called lion.
    Here is a list of your files.
```

EXAMPLE 8.45 (CONTINUED)

```
5   Afile       cplus   letter    prac
    Answerbook  cprog   library   prac1
    bourne      joke    notes     perl5
6   Bye for now barbara. The time is 18:05:07!
```

EXPLANATION

1   The first line of the script, *#!/bin/sh*, lets the kernel know what interpreter will execute the lines in this program, in this case the sh (Bourne shell) interpreter.

2   The comments are nonexecutable lines preceded by a pound sign. They can be on a line by themselves or appended to a line after a command.

3   After variable substitution is performed by the shell, the *echo* command displays the line on the screen.

4   After command substitution is performed by the shell, the *echo* command displays the line on the screen.

5   The *ls* command is executed. The comment will be ignored by the shell.

6   The *echo* command displays the string enclosed within double quotes. Variables and command substitution (backquotes) are expanded when placed within double quotes. In this case, the quotes were really not necessary.

8.2.2 Reading User Input

The *read* command is a built-in command used to read input from the terminal or from a file (see Table 8.11). The *read* command takes a line of input until a newline is reached. The newline at the end of a line will be translated into a null byte when read. You can also use the *read* command to cause a program to stop until the user enters a carriage return. To see how the *read* command is most effectively used for reading lines of input from a file, see "Looping Commands" on page 280.

Table 8.11   The *read* Command

Format	Meaning
read answer	Reads a line from standard input and assigns it to the variable *answer*.
read first last	Reads a line from standard input to the first whitespace or newline, putting the first word typed into the variable *first* and the rest of the line into the variable *last*.

EXAMPLE 8.46

```
(The Script)
$ cat nosy
    #!/bin/sh
    # Scriptname: nosy
    echo "Are you happy? \c"
1   read answer
    echo "$answer is the right response."
    echo "What is your full name? \c"
2   read first middle last
    echo "Hello  $first"
--------------------------------------------------------------
(The Output)
    $ nosy
    Are you happy? Yes
1   Yes is the right response.
2   What is your full name? Jon Jake Jones
    Hello Jon
```

EXPLANATION

1   The *read* command accepts a line of user input and assigns the input to the variable *answer*.

2   The *read* command accepts input from the user and assigns the first word of input to the variable *first*, the second word of input to the variable *middle*, and all the rest of the words up to the end of the line to the variable *last*.

EXAMPLE 8.47

```
(The Script)
$ cat printer_check
    #!/bin/sh
    # Scriptname: printer_check
    # Script to clear a hung up printer for SVR4
1   if [ $LOGNAME != root ]
    then
        echo "Must have root privileges to run this program"
        exit 1
    fi
2   cat << EOF
    Warning: All jobs in the printer queue will be removed.
    Please turn off the printer now. Press return when you
    are ready to continue. Otherwise press Control C.
    EOF
3   read ANYTHING       # Wait until the user turns off the printer
    echo
4   /etc/init.d/lp stop         # Stop the printer
5   rm -f /var/spool/lp/SCHEDLOCK /var/spool/lp/temp*
    echo
```

EXAMPLE 8.47 (CONTINUED)

```
      echo "Please turn the printer on now."
  6   echo "Press return to continue"
  7   read ANYTHING            # Stall until the user turns the printer
                               # back on
      echo                     # A blank line is printed
  8   /etc/init.d/lp start     # Start the printer
```

EXPLANATION

1 Checks to see if user is *root*. If not, sends an error and exits.

2 Creates a *here document*. Warning message is displayed on the screen.

3 The *read* command waits for user input. When the user presses Enter, the variable *ANYTHING* accepts whatever is typed. The variable is not used for anything. The *read* in this case is used to wait until the user turns off the printer, comes back, and presses Enter.

4 The *lp* program stops the printer daemon.

5 The *SCHEDLOCK* file must be removed before the scheduler can start again, as well as temporary files in */var/spool/lp*.

6 The user is asked to press Return when ready.

7 Whatever the user types is read into the variable *ANYTHING*, and when *Enter* is pressed, the program will resume execution.

8 The *lp* program starts the print daemons.

8.2.3 Arithmetic

Arithmetic is not built into the Bourne shell. If you need to perform simple integer arithmetic calculations, the UNIX *expr* command is most commonly used in Bourne shell scripts. For floating point arithmetic, the *awk* or *bc* programs can be used. Because arithmetic was not built in, the performance of the shell is degraded when iterating through loops a number of times. Each time a counter is incremented or decremented in a looping mechanism, it is necessary to fork another process to handle the arithmetic.

Integer Arithmetic and the *expr* Command.   The *expr* command is an expression-handling program. When used to evaluate arithmetic expressions, it can perform simple integer operations (see Table 8.12). Each of its arguments must be separated by a space. The +, −, *, /, and % operators are supported, and the normal programming rules of associativity and precedence apply.

Table 8.12   The *expr* Command Arithmetic Operators

Operator	Function
* / %	Multiplication, division, modulus.
+ −	Addition, substraction.

EXAMPLE 8.48

```
1   $ expr 1 + 4
    5

2   $ expr 1+4
    1+4

3   $ expr 5 + 9 / 3
    8

4   $ expr 5 * 4
    expr: syntax error

5   $ expr 5 \* 4 - 2
    18

6   $ expr 11 % 3
    2

7   $ num=1
    $ num=`expr $num + 1`
    $ echo $num
    2
```

EXPLANATION

1   The *expr* command evaluates the expression. The two numbers are added.
2   Since there are no spaces between the operator, the expression is evaluated as a string.
3   Addition and division are combined. The division is performed first and then the addition.
4   The asterisk (*) is evaluated by the shell as one of its wildcards, causing the *expr* command to fail.
5   The asterisk (*) is escaped with a backslash to prevent shell interpretation. The *expr* command performs arithmetic.
6   The modulus operator (%) returns the remainder after division is performed.
7   The variable *num* is assigned *1*. The *expr* command adds one to the value of the variable and assigns the result to *num*. The value of *num* is echoed to the screen.

Floating Point Arithmetic.   The *bc*, *awk*, and *nawk* utilities are useful if you need to perform more complex calculations.

EXAMPLE 8.49

```
(The Command Line)
1   $ n=`echo "scale=3; 13 / 2" | bc`
    $ echo $n
    6.500

2   product=`nawk -v x=2.45 -v y=3.123 'BEGIN{printf "%.2f\n",x*y}'`
    $ echo $product
    7.65
```

EXPLANATION

1   The output of the *echo* command is piped to the *bc* program. The scale is set to 3, which is the number of significant digits to the right of the decimal point that will be printed. The calculation is to divide *13* by *2*. The entire pipeline is enclosed in backquotes. Command substitution will be performed and the output assigned to the variable *n*.

2   The *nawk* program gets its values from the argument list passed in at the command line, *x=2.45 y=3.123*. (The *–v* switch works with *nawk*, not *awk*.) After the numbers are multiplied, the *printf* function formats and prints the result with a precision of two places to the right of the decimal point. The output is assigned to the variable *product*.

8.2.4   Positional Parameters and Command Line Arguments

Information can be passed into a script via the command line. Each word (separated by whitespace) following the script name is called an argument.

Command line arguments can be referenced in scripts with positional parameters; for example, $1 for the first argument, $2 for the second argument, $3 for the third argument, and so on. The $# variable is used to test for the number of parameters, and $* is used to display all of them. Positional parameters can be set or reset with the *set* command. When the *set* command is used, any positional parameters previously set are cleared out. See Table 8.13.

Table 8.13   Positional Parameters

Positional Parameter	What It References
$0	References the name of the script.
$#	Holds the value of the number of positional parameters.
$*	Lists all of the positional parameters.
$@	Means the same as $*, except when enclosed in double quotes.
"$*"	Expands to a single argument (e.g., "$1 $2 $3").
"$@"	Expands to separate arguments (e.g., "$1" "$2" "$3").
$1 ... $9	References up to nine positional parameters.

EXAMPLE 8.50

```
(The Script)
    #!/bin/sh
    # Scriptname: greetings
    echo "This script is called $0."
1   echo "$0   $1 and $2"
    echo "The number of positional parameters is $#"
    -------------------------------------------------------------
(The Command Line)
    $ chmod +x greetings
2   $ greetings
    This script is called  greetings.
    greetings  and
    The number of positional paramters is

3   $ greetings Tommy
    This script is called greetings.
    greetings Tommy and
    The number of positional parameters is 1

4   $ greetings Tommy  Kimberly
    This script is called greetings.
    greetings Tommy and Kimberly
    The number of positional parameters is 2
```

EXPLANATION

1   In the script *greetings*, positional parameter *$0* references the script name, *$1* the first command line agreement, and *$2* the second command line agreement.

2   The *greetings* script is executed without any arguments passed. The output illustrates that the script is called *greetings* (*$0* in the script) and that *$1* and *$2* were never assigned anything; therefore, their values are null and nothing is printed.

3   This time, one argument is passed, *Tommy*. *Tommy* is assigned to positional parameter *1*.

4   Two arguments are entered, *Tommy* and *Kimberly*. *Tommy* is assigned to *$1* and *Kimberly* is assigned to *$2*.

The *set* Command and Positional Parameters.   The *set* command with arguments resets the positional parameters.[4] Once reset, the old parameter list is lost. To unset all of the positional parameters, use *set – –*. *$0* is always the name of the script.

---

4. Remember, without arguments, the *set* command displays all the variables that have been set for this shell, local and exported. With options, the *set* command turns on and off shell control options such as *–x* and *–v*.

EXAMPLE   8.51

```
(The Script)
    $ cat args
    #!/bin/sh
    # Scriptname: args
    # Script to test command line arguments
1   echo The name of this script is $0.
2   echo The arguments are $*.
3   echo The first argument is $1.
4   echo The second argument is $2.
5   echo The number of arguments is $#.
6   oldargs=$*                 # Save parameters passed in from the
                               # command line
7   set Jake Nicky Scott    # Reset the positional parameters
8   echo All the positional parameters are $*.
9   echo The number of postional parameters is $#.
10  echo "Good-bye for now, $1 "
11  set `date`         #  Reset the positional parameters
12  echo The date is $2 $3, $6.
13  echo "The value of \$oldargs is $oldargs."
14  set $oldargs
15  echo $1 $2 $3

(The Output)
    $ args a b c d
1   The name of this script is args.
2   The arguments are a b c d.
3   The first argument is a.
4   The second argument is b.
5   The number of arguments is 4.
8   All the positional parameters are Jake Nicky Scott.
9   The number of positional parameters is 3.
10  Good-bye for now, Jake
12  The date is Mar 25, 2001.
13  The value of $oldargs is a b c d.
```

EXPLANATION

1   The name of the script is stored in the *$0* variable.

2   *$** represents all of the positional parameters.

3   *$1* represents the first positional parameter (command line argument).

4   *$2* represents the second positional parameter.

5   *$#* is the total number of positional parameters (command line arguments).

6   All positional parameters are saved in a variable called *oldargs*.

7   The *set* command allows you to reset the positional parameters, clearing out the old list. Now, *$1* is *Jake*, *$2* is *Nicky*, and *$3* is *Scott*.

8   *$** represents all of the parameters, *Jake*, *Nicky*, and *Scott*.

9   *$#* represents the number of parameters, 3.

EXPLANATION (CONTINUED)

10 *$1* is *Jake*.

11 After command substitution is performed, i.e., *date* is executed, the positional parameters are reset to the output of the *date* command.

12 The new values of *$2*, *$3*, and *$6* are displayed.

13 The values saved in *oldargs* are printed.

14 The *set* command creates positional parameters from the value stored in *oldargs*.

15 The first three positional parameters are displayed.

EXAMPLE 8.52

```
(The Script)
    $ cat checker
    #!/bin/sh
    # Scriptname: checker
    # Script to demonstrate the use of special variable
    # modifiers and arguments
1   name=${1:?"requires an argument" }
    echo Hello $name

(The Command Line)
2   $ checker
    ./checker: 1: requires an argument
3   $ checker Sue
    Hello Sue
```

EXPLANATION

1 The special variable modifier *:?* will check whether *$1* has a value. If not, the script exits and the message is printed.

2 The program is executed without an argument. *$1* is not assigned a value; an error is displayed.

3 The *checker* program is given a command line argument, *Sue*. In the script, *$1* is assigned *Sue*. The program continues.

How $* and $@ Differ.   The $* and $@ differ only when enclosed in double quotes. When $* is enclosed within double quotes, the parameter list becomes a single string. When $@ is enclosed within double quotes, each of the parameters is quoted; that is, each word is treated as a separate string.

EXAMPLE 8.53

```
1   $ set 'apple pie' pears peaches
2   $ for i in $*
    > do
    > echo $i
    > done
    apple
    pie
    pears
    peaches


3   $ set 'apple pie' pears peaches
4   $ for i in "$*"
    > do
    > echo $i
    > done
    apple pie pears peaches


5   $ set 'apple pie' pears peaches
6   $ for i in $@
    > do
    > echo $i
    > done
    apple
    pie
    pears
    peaches


7   $ set 'apple pie' pears peaches
8   $ for i in "$@"          # At last!!
    > do
    > echo $i
    > done
    apple pie
    pears
    peaches
```

EXPLANATION

1   The positional parameters are set.

2   When $* is expanded, the quotes surrounding *apple pie* are stripped; *apple* and *pie* become two separate words. The *for* loop assigns each of the words, in turn, to the variable *i*, and then prints the value of *i*. Each time through the loop, the word on the left is shifted off, and the next word is assigned to the variable *i*.

3   The positional parameters are set.

4   By enclosing $* in double quotes, the entire parameter list becomes one string, "*apple pie pears peaches*". The entire list is assigned to *i* as a single word. The loop makes one iteration.

5 The positional parameters are set.

6 Unquoted, $@ and $* behave the same way (see line 2 of this explanation).

7 The positional parameters are set.

8 By surrounding $@ with double quotes, each of the positional parameters is treated as a quoted string. The list would be "*apple pie*," "*pears*," "*peaches*." The desired result is finally achieved.

8.2.5 Conditional Constructs and Flow Control

Conditional commands allow you to perform some task(s) based on whether a condition succeeds or fails. The *if* command is the simplest form of decision-making; the *if/else* commands allow a two-way decision; and the *if/elif/else* commands allow a multiway decision.

The Bourne shell expects a command to follow an *if*. The command can be a system command or a built-in command. The exit status of the command is used to evaluate the condition.

To evaluate an expression, the built-in *test* command is used. This command is also linked to the bracket symbol. Either the *test* command is used, or the expression can be enclosed in set of single brackets. Shell metacharacters (wildcards) are not expanded by the *test* command. The result of a command is tested, with zero status indicating success and nonzero status indicating failure. See Table 8.14.

Testing Exit Status. The following examples illustrate how the exit status is tested.

EXAMPLE 8.54

```
(At the Command Line)
1   $ name=Tom
2   $ grep "$name"  /etc/passwd
    Tom:8ZKX2F:5102:40:Tom Savage:/home/tom:/bin/ksh
3   $ echo $?
    0            Success!

4   $ test $name != Tom
5   $ echo $?
    1            Failure

6   $ [ $name = Tom ]         # Brackets replace the test command
7   $ echo $?
    0            Success

8   $ [ $name =  [Tt]?m ]     # Wildcards are not evaluated
9   $ echo  $?                # by the test command
    1
```

EXPLANATION

1   The variable *name* is assigned the string *Tom*.

2   The *grep* command will search for string *Tom* in the *passwd* file.

3   The *?* variable contains the exit status of the last command executed, in this case, the exit status of *grep*. If *grep* is successful in finding the string *Tom*, it will return an exit status of zero. The *grep* command was successful.

4   The *test* command is used to evaluate strings, numbers, and perform file testing. Like all commands, it returns an exit status. If the exit status is zero, the expression is true; if the exit status is one, the expression evaluates to false. There *must* be spaces surrounding the equal sign. The value of *name* is tested to see if it is not equal to *Tom*.

5   The test fails and returns an exit status of one.

6   The brackets are an alternate notation for the *test* command. There must be spaces after the first bracket. The expression is tested to see if *$name* evaluates to the string *Tom*.

7   The exit status of the test is zero. The test was successful because *$name* is equal to *Tom*.

8   The *test* command does not allow wildcard expansion. Since the question mark is treated as a literal character, the test fails. *Tom* and *[Tt]?m* are not equal.

9   The exit status is one indicating that the text in line 8 failed.

The *test* Command.   The *test* command is used to evaluate conditional expressions, returning true or false. It will return a zero exit status for true and a nonzero exit status for false. The *test* command or brackets can be used.

Table 8.14   String, Integer, and File Testing

Test Operator	Test For
String Test:	
string1 = string2	*String1* is equal to *String2* (*space surrounding = required*).
string1 != string2	*String1* is not equal to *String2* (*space surrounding != required*).
string	*String* is not null.
−z string	Length of *string* is zero.
−n string	Length of *string* is nonzero.
Example:	*test −n $word* or *[−n $word]*.
	test tom = sue or *[tom = sue]*.

Table 8.14   String, Integer, and File Testing (continued)

Test Operator	Test For
Integer Test:	
int1 –eq int2	*Int1* is equal to *int2*.
int1 –ne int2	*Int1* is not equal to *int2*.
int1 –gt int2	*Int1* is greater than *int2*.
int1 –ge int2	*Int1* is greater than or equal to *int2*.
int1 –lt int2	*Int1* is less than *int2*.
int1 –le int2	*Int1* is less than or equal to *int2*.
File Test:	
–b filename	Block special file.
–c filename	Character special file.
–d filename	Directory existence.
–f filename	Regular file existence and not a directory.
–g filename	Set-group-ID is set.
–k filename	Sticky bit is set.
–p filename	File is a named pipe.
–r filename	File is readable.
–s filename	File is nonzero size.
–u filename	Set-user-ID bit is set.
–w filename	File is writeable.
–x filename	File is executable.

The *if* Command.   The simplest form of conditional is the *if* command. The command or UNIX utility following the *if* construct is executed and its exit status is returned. The exit status is usually determined by the programmer who wrote the utility. If the exit status is zero, the command succeeded and the statement(s) after the *then* keyword are executed. In the C shell, the expression following the *if* command is a Boolean-type expression as in C. But in the Bourne and Korn shells, the statement following the *if* is a command or group of commands. If the exit status of the command being evaluated is zero, the block of statements after the *then* is executed until *fi* is reached. The *fi* terminates the *if* block. If the exit status is nonzero, meaning that the command failed in some way, the statement(s) after the *then* keyword are ignored and control goes to the line directly after the *fi* statement. It is important that you know the exit status of the commands being tested. For example, the exit status of *grep* is reliable in letting you know whether *grep* found the pattern it was searching for in a file. If *grep* is successful in its search, it returns a zero exit status; if not, it returns one. The *sed* and *awk* programs also search for patterns, but they will report a successful exit status regardless of whether they find the pattern. The criteria for success with *sed* and *awk* is correct syntax, not functionality.[5]

FORMAT

```
if command
then
     command
     command
fi
----------------------------------

if test expression
then
     command
fi

          or

if [ expression ]
then
     command
fi
     ----------------------------
```

EXAMPLE 8.55

```
1    if ypmatch "$name" passwd > /dev/null 2>&1
2    then
          echo Found $name!
3    fi
```

---

5. Unlike the C shell, the Bourne shell does not support an *if* statement without a *then*, even for a simple statement.

EXPLANATION

1   The *ypmatch* command is an NIS (Sun's Network Information Services) command that searches for its argument, *name*, in the NIS *passwd* database on the server machine. Standard output and standard error are redirected to */dev/null*, the UNIX bit bucket. If *ypmatch* is not supported on your system, try

```
if grep "$name" /etc/passwd > /dev/null 2>&1
```

2   If the exit status of the *ypmatch* command is zero, the program goes to the *then* statement and executes commands until *fi* is reached.

3   The *fi* terminates the list of commands following the *then* statement.

EXAMPLE 8.56

```
1    echo   "Are you okay (y/n) ?"
     read answer
2    if [ "$answer" = Y -o "$answer" = y  ]
     then
         echo   "Glad to hear it."
3    fi
```

EXPLANATION

1   The user is asked the question and told to respond. The *read* command waits for a response.

2   The *test* command, represented by square brackets, is used to test expressions. It returns an exit status of zero if the expression is true and nonzero if the expression is false. If the variable *answer* evaluates to *Y* or *y*, the commands after the *then* statement are executed. (The *test* command does not allow the use of wildcards when testing expressions, and spaces must surround the square brackets. (and the = operators.) See Table 8.14.

      $answer is double quoted to hold it together as a single string. The *test* command fails if more than one word appears before the = operator. For example, if the user entered *yes, you betcha*, the *answer* variable would evaluate to three words, causing the *test* to fail, *unless $answer* is enclosed in double quotes.

3   The *fi* terminates the list of commands following the *then* statement.

The *exit* Command and the *?* Variable.   The *exit* command is used to terminate the script and return to the command line. You may want the script to exit if some condition occurs. The argument given to the *exit* command is a number ranging from 0 to 255. If the program exits with zero as an argument, the program exited with success. A nonzero argument indicates some kind of failure. The argument given to the *exit* command is stored in the shell's *?* variable.

EXAMPLE 8.57

```
(The Script)
$ cat bigfiles
    # Name: bigfiles
    # Purpose: Use the find command to find any files in the root
    # partition that have not been modified within the past n (any
    # number within 30 days) days and are larger than 20 blocks
    # (512-byte blocks)

1   if  [ $# -ne 2 ]
    then
        echo  "Usage: $0 mdays size " 1>&2
        exit 1
2   fi
3   if  [ $1 -lt 0 -o $1 -gt 30 ]
    then

        echo "mdays is out of range"
        exit 2
4   fi
5   if [ $2 -le 20 ]
    then
        echo "size is out of range"
        exit 3
6   fi
7   find / -xdev -mtime $1 -size +$2 -print

(The Command Line)
$ bigfiles
Usage: bigfiles mdays size

$ echo $?
1

$ bigfiles 400 80
mdays is out of range

$ echo $?
2

$ bigfiles 25 2
size is out of range

$ echo $?
3

$ bigfiles 2 25
(Output of find prints here)
```

EXPLANATION

1 The statement reads: *If the number of arguments is not equal to 2, print the error message and send it to standard error, then exit the script with an exit status of 1.*

2 The *fi* marks the end of the block of statements after *then*.

3 The statement reads: *If the value of the first positional parameter passed in from the command line is less than 0 or greater than 30, then print the message and exit with a status of 2.* See Table 8.14 for numeric operators.

4 The *fi* ends the *if* block.

5 The statement reads: *If the value of the second positional parameter passed in at the command line is less than or equal to 20 (512-byte blocks), then print the message and exit with a status of 3.*

6 The *fi* ends the *if* block.

7 The *find* command starts its search in the root directory. The *–x dev* option prevents *find* from searching other partitions. The *–mtime* option takes a number argument, which is the number of days since the file was modified, and the *–size* option takes a number argument, which is the size of the file in 512-byte blocks.

Checking for Null Values.   When checking for null values in a variable, use double quotes to hold the null value or the *test* command will fail.

EXAMPLE 8.58

```
(The Script)

1  if [ "$name" = "" ]
       # Alternative to  [ ! "$name" ]  or  [ -z "$name" ]
   then
       echo The name variable is null
   fi

(From System showmount program, which displays all remotely mounted
systems)

   remotes=`/usr/sbin/showmount`
2  if [ "X${remotes}" != "X" ]
   then
       /usr/sbin/wall ${remotes}
                 ...
3  fi
```

EXPLANATION

1   If the *name* variable evaluates to null, the test is true. The double quotes are used to represent null.

2   The *showmount* command lists all clients remotely mounted from a host machine. The command will list either one or more clients, or nothing. The variable *remotes* will either have a value assigned or will be null. The letter *X* precedes the variable *remotes* when being tested. If *remotes* evaluates to null, no clients are remotely logged on and *X* will be equal to *X*, causing the program to start execution again on line 3. If the variable has a value, for example, the hostname *pluto*, the expression would read *if Xpluto != X*, and the *wall* command would be executed. (All users on remote machines will be sent a message.) The purpose of using *X* in the expression is to guarantee that even if the value of *remotes* is null, there will always be a placeholder on either side of the *!=* operator in the expression.

3   The *fi* terminates the *if*.

The *if/else* Command.   The *if/else* commands allow a two-way decision-making process. If the command after the *if* fails, the commands after the *else* are executed.

FORMAT

```
if command
then
     command(s)
else
     command(s)
fi
```

EXAMPLE 8.59

```
(The Script)
    #!/bin/sh
1   if ypmatch "$name" passwd > /dev/null 2>&1 6
2   then
        echo Found $name!
3   else
4       echo  "Can't find $name."
        exit 1
5   fi
```

---

6. If using NIS+, the command would read: *If nismatch "$name" passwd.org_dir.*

EXPLANATION

1   The *ypmatch* command searches for its argument, *name*, in the NIS *passwd* database. Since the user does not need to see the output, standard output and standard error are redirected to */dev/null*, the UNIX bit bucket.

2   If the exit status of the *ypmatch* command is zero, program control goes to the *then* statement and executes commands until *else* is reached.

3   The commands under the *else* statement are executed if the *ypmatch* command fails to find *$name* in the *passwd* database; that is, the exit status of *ypmatch* must be nonzero for the commands in the *else* block to be executed.

4   If the value in *$name* is not found in the *passwd* database, this *echo* statement is executed and the program exits with a value of one, indicating failure.

5   The *fi* terminates the *if*.

EXAMPLE 8.60

```
(The Script)
$ cat idcheck
#!/bin/sh
# Scriptname: idcheck
# purpose:check user ID to see if user is root.
# Only root has a uid of 0.
# Format for id output:uid=9496(ellie) gid=40 groups=40
# root's uid=0
```

```
1   id=`id | nawk -F'[=()' '{print $2}'`        # Get user ID
    echo your user id is: $id
2   if [ $id -eq 0 ]
    then
3       echo "you are superuser."
4   else
        echo "you are not superuser."
5   fi
```

```
    (The Command Line)
6   $ idcheck
    your user id is: 9496
    you are not superuser.
7   $ su
    Password:
8   # idcheck
    your user id is: 0
    you are superuser
```

EXPLANATION

1   The *id* command is piped to the *nawk* command. *Nawk* uses an equal sign and open parenthesis as field separators, extracts the user ID from the output, and assigns the output to the variable *id*.

2   If the value of *id* is equal to zero, then line 3 is executed

4   If ID is not equal to zero, the *else* statements are executed.

5   The *fi* marks the end of the *if* command.

6   The *idcheck* script is executed by the current user, whose UID is *9496*.

7   The *su* command switches the user to *root*.

8   The # prompt indicates that the superuser (root) is the new user. The UID for root is *0*.

The *if/elif/else* Command.   The *if/elif/else* commands allow a multiway decision-making process. If the command following the *if* fails, the command following the *elif* is tested. If that command succeeds, the commands under its *then* statement are executed. If the command after the *elif* fails, the next *elif* command is checked. If none of the commands succeeds, the *else* commands are executed. The *else* block is called the default.

FORMAT

```
if   command
then
     command(s)
elif command
then
     commands(s)
elif command
then
     command(s)
else
     command(s)
fi
```

EXAMPLE 8.61

```
(The Script)
$ cat tellme
    #!/bin/sh
    # Scriptname: tellme
1   echo -n "How old are you? "
    read age
2   if [ $age -lt  0 -o $age -gt 120 ]
    then
        echo  "Welcome to our planet! "
        exit 1
    fi
```

EXAMPLE 8.61 (CONTINUED)

```
3   if [ $age -ge 0 -a  $age -lt 13 ]
    then
        echo "A child is a garden of verses"
    elif [ $age -ge 12 -a $age -lt  20 ]
    then
        echo "Rebel without a cause"
    elif [ $age  -gt 20 -a  $age -lt  30 ]
    then
        echo "You got the world by the tail!!"
    elif [ $age -ge  30 -a  $age -lt 40 ]
    then
        echo "Thirty something..."
4   else
        echo "Sorry I asked"
5   fi
```

```
(The Output)
$ tellme
How old are you? 200
Welcome to our planet!

$ tellme
How old are you? 13
Rebel without a cause

$ tellme
How old are you? 55
Sorry I asked
```

EXPLANATION

1   The user is asked for input. The input is assigned to the variable *age*.

2   A numeric test is performed within the square brackets. If *age* is less than *0* or greater than *120*, the *echo* command is executed and the program terminates with an exit status of one. The interactive shell prompt will appear.

3   A numeric test is performed within the square brackets. If *age* is greater than *0* and less than *13*, the *test* command returns exit status zero, true, and the statement after the *then* is executed. Otherwise, program control goes to the *elif*. If that test is false, the next *elif* is tested.

4   The *else* construct is the default. If none of the above statements are true, the *else* commands will be executed.

5   The *fi* terminates the initial *if* statement.

File Testing.   Often when writing scripts, your script will require that there are certain files available and that those files have specific permissions, are of a certain type, or have other attributes. (See Table 8.14.) You will find file testing a necessary part of writing dependable scripts.

When *if* statements are nested, the *fi* statement always goes with the nearest *if* statement. Indenting the nested *ifs* makes it easier to see which *if* statement goes with which *fi* statement.

EXAMPLE 8.62

```
(The Script)
    #!/bin/sh
    file=./testing


1 ┌─if [ -d $file ]
  │  then
  │       echo "$file is a directory"
2 │  elif [ -f $file ]
  │  then
3 │    ┌─if [   -r $file -a -w $file -a -x $file ]
  │    │  then    # nested if command
  │    │      echo "You have read, write, and execute \
  │    │      permission on $file."
4 │    └─ fi
5 │  else
  │       echo "$file is neither a file nor a directory."
6 └─fi
```

EXPLANATION

1   If the file *testing* is a directory, print *testing is a directory*.

2   If the file *testing* is not a directory, *else if* the file is a plain file, then...

3   If the file *testing* is readable, writeable, and executable, then...

4   The *fi* terminates the innermost *if* command.

5   The *else* commands are executed *if* lines 1 and 2 are not true.

6   This *fi* goes with the first *if*.

The *null* Command.   The *null* command, represented by a colon, is a built-in, do-nothing command that returns an exit status of zero. It is used as a placeholder after an *if* command when you have nothing to say, but need a command or the program will produce an error message because it requires something after the *then* statement. Often the null command is used as an argument to the *loop* command to make the loop a forever loop.

EXAMPLE 8.63

```
(The Script)
1   name=Tom
2   if grep "$name" databasefile > /dev/null 2>&1
    then
3       :
4   else
        echo  "$1 not found in databasefile"
        exit 1
    fi
```

EXPLANATION

1   The variable *name* is assigned the string *Tom*.

2   The *if* command tests the exit status of the *grep* command. If *Tom* is found in the database file, the *null* command, a colon, is executed and does nothing.

3   The colon is the *null* command. It does nothing other than returning a *0* exit status.

4   What we really want to do is print an error message and exit if *Tom* is *not* found. The commands after the *else* will be executed if the *grep* command fails.

EXAMPLE 8.64

```
(The Command Line)
1   $ DATAFILE=
2   $ : ${DATAFILE:=$HOME/db/datafile}
    $ echo $DATAFILE
    /home/jody/ellie/db/datafile
3   $ : ${DATAFILE:=$HOME/junk}
    $ echo $DATAFILE
    /home/jody/ellie/db/datafile
```

EXPLANATION

1   The variable *DATAFILE* is assigned null.

2   The colon command is a "do-nothing" command. The modifier (:=) returns a value that can be assigned to a variable or used in a test. In this example, the expression is passed as an argument to the do-nothing command. The shell will perform variable substitution; that is, assign the pathname to *DATAFILE* if *DATAFILE* does not already have a value. The variable *DATAFILE* is permanently set.

3   Since the variable has already been set, it will not be reset with the default value provided on the right of the modifier.

EXAMPLE 8.65

```
(The Script)
$ cat wholenum
    #!/bin/sh
1   # Name:wholenum
    # Purpose:The expr command tests that the user enters an integer
    echo "Enter a number."
    read number
2   if expr "$number" + 0 > /dev/null 2>&1
    then
3       :
    else
4       echo "You did not enter an integer value."
        exit 1
5   fi
```

EXPLANATION

1.   The user is asked to enter an integer. The number is assigned to the variable *number*.

2.   The *expr* command evaluates the expression. If addition can be performed, the number is a whole number and *expr* returns a successful exit status. All output is redirected to the bit bucket */dev/null*.

3.   If *expr* is successful, it returns a zero exit status, and the colon command does nothing.

4.   If the *expr* command fails, it returns a nonzero exit status, the *echo* command displays the message, and the program exits.

5.   The *fi* ends the *if* block.

8.2.6 The *case* Command

The *case* command is a multiway branching command used as an alternative to *if/elif* commands. The value of the *case* variable is matched against *value1, value2*, and so forth, until a match is found. When a value matches the *case* variable, the commands following the value are executed until the double semicolons are reached. Then execution starts after the word *esac* (*case* spelled backwards).

    If the *case* variable is not matched, the program executes the commands after the *)*, the default value, until ;; or *esac* is reached. The *)* value functions the same as the *else* statement in *if/else* conditionals. The *case* values allow the use of shell *wildcards* and the vertical bar (pipe symbol) for *or*ing two values.

FORMAT

```
case variable in
value1)
    command(s)
    ;;
value2)
    command(s)
    ;;
*)
command(s)
    ;;
esac
```

EXAMPLE 8.66

```
(The Script)
$ cat colors
    #!/bin/sh
    # Scriptname: colors
1   echo -n "Which color do you like?"
    read color
2   case "$color" in
3   [Bb]l??)
4       echo I feel $color
        echo The sky is $color
5       ;;
6   [Gg]ree*)
        echo  $color is for trees
        echo  $color is for seasick;;
7   red | orange)              # The vertical bar means "or"
        echo  $color is very warm!;;
8   *)
        echo  No such color as $color;;
9   esac
10  echo  "Out of case"
```

EXPLANATION

1   The user is asked for input. The input is assigned to the variable *color*.

2   The *case* command evaluates the expression *$color*.

3   If the color begins with a *B* or *b*, followed by the letter *l* and any two characters, the *case* expression matches the first value. The value is terminated with a single closed parenthesis. The wildcards are shell metacharacters used for filename expansion.

4   The statements are executed if the value in line number 3 matches the *case* expression.

5   The double semicolons are required after the last command in this block of commands. Control branches to line 10 when the semicolons are reached. The script is easier to debug if the semicolons are on their own line.

EXPLANATION (CONTINUED)

6   If the *case* expression matches a *G* or *g*, followed by the letters *ree* and ending in zero or more of any other characters, the *echo* commands are executed. The double semicolons terminate the block of statements and control branches to line 10.

7   The vertical bar is used as an *or* conditional operator. If the *case* expression matches either *red* or *orange*, the *echo* command is executed.

8   This is the default value. If none of the above values match the *case* expression, the commands after the *)* are executed.

9   The *esac* statement terminates the *case* command.

10 After one of the *case* values are matched, execution continues here.

Creating Menus with the *here document* and *case* Command.   The *here document* and *case* command are often used together. The *here document* is used to create a menu of choices that will be displayed to the screen. The user will be asked to select one of the menu items, and the *case* command will test against the set of choices to execute the appropriate command.

EXAMPLE 8.67

```
(The .profile File)
    echo "Select a terminal type: "
1   cat << ENDIT
        1) vt 120
        2) wyse50
        3) sun
2   ENDIT
3   read choice
4   case "$choice" in
5   1)  TERM=vt120
        export TERM
        ;;
    2)  TERM=wyse50
        export TERM
        ;;
6   3)  TERM=sun
        export TERM
        ;;
7   esac
8   echo "TERM is $TERM."

(The Output)
$ . .profile
Select a terminal type:
1) vt120
2) wyse50
3) sun
3                   <-- User input
TERM is sun.
```

EXPLANATION

1   If this segment of script is put in the *.profile*, when you log on, you will be given a chance to select the proper terminal type. The *here document* is used to display a menu of choices.

2   The user-defined *ENDIT* terminator marks the end of the *here document*.

3   The *read* command stores the user input in the variable *TERM*.

4   The *case* command evaluates the variable *TERM* and compares that value with one of the values preceding the closing parenthesis: *1, 2,* or ***.

5   The first value tested is 1. If there is a match, the terminal is set to a *vt120*. The *TERM* variable is exported so that subshells will inherit it.

6   A default value is not required. The *TERM* variable is normally assigned in */etc/profile* at login time. If the choice is 3, the terminal is set to a *sun*.

7   The *esac* terminates the *case* command.

8   After the *case* command has finished, this line is executed.

8.2.7 Looping Commands

Looping commands are used to execute a command or group of commands a set number of times or until a certain condition is met. The Bourne shell has three types of loops: the *for* loop, the *while* loop, and the *until* loop.

The *for* Command.   The *for* looping command is used to execute commands a finite number of times on a list of items. For example, you might use this loop to execute the same commands on a list of files or usernames. The *for* command is followed by a user-defined variable, the keyword *in*, and a list of words. The first time in the loop, the first word from the wordlist is assigned to the variable, and then shifted off the list. Once the word is assigned to the variable, the body of the loop is entered, and commands between the *do* and *done* keywords are executed. The next time around the loop, the second word is assigned to the variable, and so on. The body of the loop starts at the *do* keyword and ends at the *done* keyword. When all of the words in the list have been shifted off, the loop ends and program control continues after the *done* keyword.

FORMAT

```
for variable in word_list
do
    command(s)
done
```

EXAMPLE   8.68

```
(The Script)
$ cat forloop
    #!/bin/sh
    # Scriptname: forloop
1   for pal in Tom Dick Harry Joe
2   do
3       echo "Hi $pal"
4   done
5   echo "Out of loop"

(The Output)
$ forloop
Hi Tom
Hi Dick
Hi Harry
Hi Joe
Out of loop
```

EXPLANATION

1. This *for* loop will iterate through the list of names, *Tom*, *Dick*, *Harry*, and *Joe*, shifting each one off (to the left and assigning its value to the user-defined variable, *pal*) after it is used. As soon as all of the words are shifted and the wordlist is empty, the loop ends and execution starts after the *done* keyword. The first time in the loop, the variable *pal* will be assigned the word *Tom*. The second time through the loop, *pal* will be assigned *Dick*, the next time *pal* will be assigned *Harry*, and the last time *pal* will be assigned *Joe*.

2. The *do* keyword is required after the wordlist. If it is used on the same line, the list must be terminated with a semicolon. Example:

    ```
    for pal in Tom Dick Harry Joe; do
    ```

3. This is the body of the loop. After *Tom* is assigned to the variable *pal*, the commands in the body of the loop (i.e., all commands between the *do* and *done* keywords) are executed.

4. The *done* keyword ends the loop. Once the last word in the list (*Joe*) has been assigned and shifted off, the loop exits.

5. Control resumes here when the loop exits.

EXAMPLE   8.69

```
(The Command Line)
1   $ cat mylist
    tom
    patty
    ann
    jake
```

EXAMPLE 8.69 (CONTINUED)

```
(The Script)
$ cat mailer
    #!/bin/sh
    # Scriptname: mailer
2   for person in `cat mylist`
    do
3       mail $person < letter
        echo  $person was sent a letter.
4   done
5   echo "The letter has been sent."
```

EXPLANATION

1 The contents of a file, called *mylist*, are displayed.

2 Command substitution is performed and the contents of *mylist* becomes the wordlist. The first time in the loop, *tom* is assigned to the variable *person*, then it is shifted off to be replaced with *patty*, and so forth.

3 In the body of the loop, each user is mailed a copy of a file called *letter*.

4 The *done* keyword marks the end of this loop iteration.

5 When all of the users in the list have been sent mail and the loop has exited, this line is executed.

EXAMPLE 8.70

```
(The Script)
    #!/bin/sh
    # Scriptname: backup
    # Purpose:
    # Create backup files and store them in a backup directory
1   dir=/home/jody/ellie/backupscripts
2   for file in memo[1-5]
    do
        if [ -f $file ]
        then
            cp $file $dir/$file.bak
            echo "$file is backed up in $dir"
        fi
    done

(The Output)
memo1 is backed up in /home/jody/ellie/backupscripts
memo2 is backed up in /home/jody/ellie/backupscripts
memo3 is backed up in /home/jody/ellie/backupscripts
memo4 is backed up in /home/jody/ellie/backupscripts
memo5 is backed up in /home/jody/ellie/backupscripts
```

EXPLANATION

1   The variable *dir* is assigned.

2   The wordlist will consist of all files in the current working directory with names starting with *memo* and ending with a number between *1* and *5*. Each filename will be assigned, one at time, to the variable *file* for each iteration of the loop.

3   When the body of the loop is entered, the file will be tested to make sure it exists and is a real file. If so, it will be copied into the directory */home/jody/ellie/backup-scripts* with the *.bak* extension appended to its name.

The $* and $@ Variables in Wordlists.   When expanded, the $* and $@ are the same unless enclosed in double quotes. $* evaluates to one string, whereas $@ evaluates to a list of separate words.

EXAMPLE 8.71

```
(The Script)
$ cat greet
    #!/bin/sh
    # Scriptname: greet
1   for name in $*          # Same as for name in $@
2   do
        echo Hi $name
3   done

(The Command Line)
$ greet Dee Bert Lizzy Tommy
Hi Dee
Hi Bert
Hi Lizzy
Hi Tommy
```

EXPLANATION

1   $* and $@ expand to a list of all the positional parameters, in this case, the arguments passed in from the command line: *Dee*, *Bert*, *Lizzy*, and *Tommy*. Each name in the list will be assigned, in turn, to the variable *name* in the *for* loop.

2   The commands in the body of the loop are executed until the list is empty.

3   The *done* keyword marks the end of the loop body.

EXAMPLE 8.72

```
(The Script)
$ cat permx
    #!/bin/sh
    # Scriptname:permx
1   for file            # Empty wordlist
    do
2       if [ -f $file -a ! -x $file ]
        then
```

EXAMPLE 8.72 (CONTINUED)

```
3                    chmod +x $file
                     echo $file now has execute permission
        fi
   done


(The Command Line)
4    $ permx *
     addon now has execute permission
     checkon now has execute permission
     doit now has execute permission
```

EXPLANATION

1   If the *for* loop is not provided with a wordlist, it iterates through the positional parameters. This is the same as *for file* in *$**.

2   The filenames are coming in from the command line. The shell expands the asterisk (*) to all filenames in the current working directory. If the file is a plain file and does not have execute permission, line 3 is executed.

3   Execute permission is added for each file being processed.

4   At the command line, the asterisk will be evaluated by the shell as a wildcard and all files in the current directory will be replaced for the *. The files will be passed as arguments to the *permx* script.

The *while* Command.   The *while* evaluates the command immediately following it and, if its exit status is zero, the commands in the body of the loop (commands between *do* and *done*) are executed. When the *done* keyword is reached, control is returned to the top of the loop and the *while* command checks the exit status of the command again. Until the exit status of the command being evaluated by the *while* becomes nonzero, the loop continues. When the exit status reaches nonzero, program execution starts after the *done* keyword.

FORMAT

```
while command
do
    command(s)
done
```

EXAMPLE 8.73

```
(The Script)
$ cat num
    #!/bin/sh
    # Scriptname: num
1   num=0          # Initialize num
2   while  [ $num -lt 10 ]              # Test num with test command
    do
        echo  -n $num
3       num=`expr  $num + 1`           # Increment num
    done
    echo "\nAfter loop exits, continue running here"

(The Output)
0123456789
After loop exits, continue running here
```

EXPLANATION

1   This is the initialization step. The variable *num* is assigned *0*.

2   The *while* command is followed by the *test* (square brackets) command. If the value of *num* is less than *10*, the body of the loop is entered.

3   In the body of the loop, the value of *num* is incremented by one. If the value of *num* never changes, the loop would iterate infinitely or until the process is killed.

EXAMPLE 8.74

```
(The Script)
    #!/bin/sh
    # Scriptname: quiz
1   echo "Who was the chief defense lawyer in the OJ case?"
    read answer
2   while [ "$answer" != "Johnny" ]
3   do
        echo  "Wrong try again!"
4       read answer
5   done
6   echo You got it!

(The Output)
$ quiz
Who was the chief defense lawyer in the OJ case? Marcia
Wrong try again!
Who was the chief defense lawyer in the OJ case?  I give up
Wrong try again!
Who was the chief defense lawyer in the OJ case?  Johnny
You got it!
```

EXPLANATION

1   The *echo* command prompts the user, *Who was the chief defense lawyer in the OJ case?* The *read* command waits for input from the user. The input will be stored in the variable *answer*.

2   The *while* loop is entered and the *test* command, the bracket, tests the expression. If the variable *answer* does not equal the string *Johnny*, the body of the loop is entered and commands between the *do* and *done* are executed.

3   The *do* keyword is the start of the loop body.

4   The user is asked to re-enter input.

5   The *done* keyword marks the end of the loop body. Control is returned to the top of the *while* loop, and the expression is tested again. As long as $answer does not evaluate to *Johnny*, the loop will continue to iterate. When the user enters *Johnny*, the loop ends. Program control goes to line 6.

6   When the body of the loop ends, control starts here.

EXAMPLE 8.75

```
(The Script)
$ cat sayit
    #!/bin/sh
    # Scriptname: sayit
    echo Type q to quit.
    go=start
1   while [ -n "$go" ]    # Make sure to double quote the variable
    do
2       echo -n I love you.
3       read word
4       if [ "$word" = q -o "$word" = Q ]
        then
                echo "I'll always love you!"
                go=
        fi
    done
```

```
(The Output)
$ sayit
Type q to quit.
I love you.        When user presses the Enter key, the program continues
I love you.
I love you.
I love you.
I love you.q
I'll always love you!
$
```

1   The command after the *while* is executed and its exit status tested. The *–n* option to the *test* command tests for a nonnull string. Since *go* initially has a value, the test is successful, producing a zero exit status. If the variable *go* is not enclosed in double quotes and the variable is null, the *test* command would complain:

```
go: test: argument expected
```

2   The loop is entered. The string *I love you.* is echoed to the screen.

3   The *read* command waits for user input.

4   The expresson is tested. If the user enters a *q* or *Q*, the string *I'll always love you!* is displayed, and the variable *go* is set to null. When the *while* loop is re-entered, the test is unsuccessful since the variable is null. The loop terminates. Control goes to the line after the *done* statement. In this example, the script will terminate since there are no more lines to execute.

The *until* Command.   The *until* command is used like the *while* command, but executes the loop statements only if the command after *until* fails, i.e., if the command returns an exit status of nonzero. When the *done* keyword is reached, control is returned to the top of the loop and the *until* command checks the exit status of the command again. Until the exit status of the command being evaluated by *until* becomes zero, the loop continues. When the exit status reaches zero, the loop exits, and program execution starts after the *done* keyword.

```
until command
do
     command(s)
done
```

EXAMPLE 8.76

```
    #!/bin/sh
1   until who | grep linda
2   do
        sleep 5
3   done
    talk linda@dragonwings
```

EXPLANATION

1   The *until* loop tests the exit status of the last command in the pipeline, *grep*. The *who* command lists who is logged on this machine and pipes its output to *grep*. The *grep* command will return a zero exit status (success) only when it finds user *linda*.

2   If user *linda* has not logged on, the body of the loop is entered and the program sleeps for five seconds.

3   When *linda* logs on, the exit status of the *grep* command will be zero and control will go to the statements following the *done* keyword.

EXAMPLE 8.77

```
(The Script)
$ cat hour
    #!/bin/sh
    # Scriptname: hour
1   hour=1
2   until [ $hour  -gt 24 ]
    do
3       case "$hour" in
        [0-9] |1[0-1])echo  "Good morning!"
            ;;
        12) echo  "Lunch time."


            ;;
        1[3-7])echo  "Siesta time."
            ;;
        *)  echo  "Good night."
            ;;
        esac
4       hour=`expr $hour + 1`
5   done

(The Output)
$ hour
Good morning!
Good morning!
    ...
Lunch time.
Siesta time.
    ...
Good night.
    ...
```

EXPLANATION

1   The variable *hour* is initialized to *1*.

2   The *test* command tests if the hour is greater than *24*. If the hour is not greater than *24*, the body of the loop is entered. The *until* loop is entered if the command following it returns a nonzero exit status. Until the condition is true, the loop continues to iterate.

3   The *case* command evaluates the *hour* variable and tests each of the *case* statements for a match.

4   The *hour* variable is incremented before control returns to the top of the loop.

5   The *done* command marks the end of the loop body.

Looping Commands.   If some condition occurs, you may want to break out of a loop, return to the top of the loop, or provide a way to stop an infinite loop. The Bourne shell provides loop control commands to handle these kinds of situations.

The *shift* Command.   The *shift* command shifts the parameter list to the left a specified number of times. The *shift* command without an argument shifts the parameter list once to the left. Once the list is shifted, the parameter is removed permanently. Often, the *shift* command is used in a *while* loop when iterating through a list of positional parameters.

FORMAT

```
shift [n]
```

EXAMPLE 8.78

```
(Without a Loop)
(The Script)
1   set joe mary tom sam
2   shift
3   echo $*
4   set `date`
5   echo  $*
6   shift 5
7   echo  $*
8   shift 2

(The Output)
3   mary tom sam
5   Fri Sep 9 10:00:12 PDT 2001
7   2001
8   cannot shift
```

EXPLANATION

1   The *set* command sets the positional parameters. *$1* is assigned *joe*, *$2* is assigned *mary*, *$3* is assigned *tom*, and *$4* is assigned *sam*. *$** represents all of the parameters.

2   The *shift* command shifts the positional parameters to the left; *joe* is shifted off.

3   The parameter list is printed after the shift.

4   The *set* command resets the positional parameters to the output of the UNIX *date* command.

5   The new parameter list is printed.

6   This time the list is shifted 5 times to the left.

7   The new parameter list is printed.

8   By attempting to shift more times than there are parameters, the shell sends a message to standard error.

EXAMPLE   8.79

```
(With a Loop)
(The Script)
$ cat doit
    #!/bin/sh
    # Name: doit
    # Purpose: shift through command line arguments
    # Usage: doit [args]
1   while [  $# -gt  0 ]
    do
2       echo  $*
3       shift
4   done

(The Command Line)
$ doit a b c d e
a b c d e
b c d e
c d e
d e
e
```

EXPLANATION

1   The *while* command tests the numeric expression. If the number of positional parameters (*$#*) is greater than *0*, the body of the loop is entered. The positional parameters are coming from the command line as arguments. There are five.

2   All positional parameters are printed.

3   The parameter list is shifted once to the left.

EXPLANATION (CONTINUED)

4   The body of the loop ends here; control returns to the top of the loop. Each time the loop is entered, the *shift* command causes the parameter list to be decreased by one. After the first shift, $# (number of positional parameters) is four. When $# has been decreased to zero, the loop ends.

EXAMPLE 8.80

```
(The Script)
$ cat dater
    #!/bin/sh
    # Scriptname: dater
    # Purpose: set positional parameters with the set command
    # and shift through the parameters.
1   set `date`
2   while [ $# -gt 0 ]
    do
3       echo $1
4       shift
    done


(The Output)
$ dater
Sat
Oct
13
12:12:13
PDT
2001
```

EXPLANATION

1   The *set* command takes the output of the *date* command and assigns the output to positional parameters $1 through $6.

2   The *while* command tests whether the number of positional parameters ($#) is greater than 0. If true, the body of the loop is entered.

3   The *echo* command displays the value of $1, the first positional parameter.

4   The *shift* command shifts the parameter list once to the left. Each time through the loop, the list is shifted until the list is empty. At that time, $# will be zero and the loop terminates.

The *break* Command.   The built-in *break* command is used to force immediate exit from a loop, but not from a program. (To leave a program, the *exit* command is used.) After the *break* command is executed, control starts after the *done* keyword. The *break* command causes an exit from the innermost loop, so if you have nested loops, the *break* command takes a number as an argument, allowing you to break out of a specific outer loop. If you are nested in three loops, the outermost loop is loop number 3, the next nested loop is loop number 2, and the innermost nested loop is loop number 1. The *break* is useful for exiting from an infinite loop.

FORMAT

```
break [n]
```

EXAMPLE 8.81

```
1   while true; do
2       echo Are you ready to move on\?
        read answer
3       if [  "$answer"  =  Y -o "$answer" = y  ]
        then
4           break
5       else
            ....commands...
        fi
6   done
7   print "Here we are"
```

EXPLANATION

1   The *true* command is a UNIX command that always exits with zero status. It is often used to start an infinite loop. It is okay to put the *do* statement on the same line as the *while* command, as long as a semicolon separates them. The body of the loop is entered.

2   The user is asked for input. The user's input is assigned to the variable *answer.*

3   If *$answer* evaluates to Y or y, control goes to line 4.

4   The *break* command is executed, the loop is exited, and control goes to line 7. The line *Here we are* is printed. Until the user answers with a Y or y, the program will continue to ask for input. This could go on forever!

5   If the test fails in line 3, the *else* commands are executed. When the body of the loop ends at the *done* keyword, control starts again at the top of the *while* at line 1.

6   This is the end of the loop body.

7   Control starts here after the *break* command is executed.

The *continue* Command.   The *continue* command returns control to the top of the loop if some condition becomes true. All commands below the *continue* will be ignored. If nested within a number of loops, the *continue* command returns control to the innermost loop. If a number is given as its argument, control can then be started at the top of any loop. If you are nested in three loops, the outermost loop is loop number 3, the next nested loop is loop number 2, and the innermost nested loop is loop number 1.[7]

_____

7. If the *continue* command is given a number higher than the number of loops, the loop exits.

FORMAT

```
continue [n]
```

EXAMPLE 8.82

```
(The mailing List)
$ cat mail_list
ernie
john
richard
melanie
greg
robin


(The Script)
    #!/bin/sh
    # Scriptname: mailem
    # Purpose: To send a list
1   for name in `cat  mail_list`
    do
2       if [    "$name" = "richard" ] ; then
3           continue
        else
4           mail $name < memo
        fi
5   done
```

EXPLANATION

1 After command substitution, *cat mail_list*, the *for* loop will iterate through the list of names from the file called *mail_list*.

2 If the name matches *richard*, the *continue* command is executed and control goes back to top of the loop where the loop expression is evalutated. Since *richard* has already been shifted off the list, the next user, *melanie*, will be assigned to the variable *name*. The string *richard* does not need to be quoted here because it is only one word. But, it is good practice to quote the string after the test's = operator because if the string consisted of more than one word, for example, *richard jones*, the *test* command would produce an error message:

```
test: unknown operator richard
```

3 The *continue* command returns control to the top of the loop, skipping any commands in the rest of the loop body.

4 All users in the list, except *richard*, will be mailed a copy of the file *memo*.

5 This is the end of the loop body.

Nested Loops and Loop Control.   When using nested loops, the *break* and *continue* commands can be given a numeric, integer argument so that control can go from the inner loop to an outer loop.

EXAMPLE 8.83

```
(The Script)
$ cat months
    #!/bin/sh
    # Scriptname: months
1   for month in Jan Feb Mar Apr May Jun Jul Aug Sep Oct Nov Dec
    do
2       for week in  1 2 3 4
        do
            echo -n "Processing the month of $month. Okay? "
            read ans
3           if [ "$ans" = n  -o -z "$ans" ]
            then
4               continue 2
            else
                echo -n "Process week $week of $month? "
                read ans
                if [ "$ans" = n -o -z "$ans" ]
                then
5                   continue
                else
                    echo "Now processing week $week of $month."
                    sleep 1
                        # Commands go here
                    echo "Done processing..."
                fi
            fi
6       done
7   done
```

```
(The Output)
$ months
Processing the month of Jan. Okay?
Processing the month of Feb. Okay? y
Process week 1 of Feb? y
Now processing week 1 of Feb.
Done processing...
Processing the month of Feb. Okay? y
Process week 2 of Feb? y
Now processing week 2 of Feb.
Done processing...
Processing the month of Feb. Okay? n
Processing the month of Mar. Okay? n

Processing the month of Apr. Okay? n
Processing the month of May. Okay? n
```

EXPLANATION

1 The outer *for* loop is started. The first time in the loop, *Jan* is assigned to *month*.

2 The inner *for* loop starts. The first time in this loop, *1* is assigned to *week*. The inner loop iterates completely before going back to the outer loop.

3 If the user enters either an *n* or presses Enter, line 4 is executed.

4 The *continue* command with an argument of 2 starts control at the top of the second outermost loop. The *continue* without an argument returns control to the top of the innermost loop.

5 Control is returned to the innermost *for* loop.

6 This *done* terminates the innermost loop.

7 This *done* terminates the outermost loop.

I/O Redirection and Subshells.   Input can be piped or redirected to a loop from a file. Output can also be piped or redirected to a file from a loop. The shell starts a sub shell to handle I/O redirection and pipes. Any variables defined within the loop will not be known to the rest of the script when the loop terminates.

Redirecting the Output of the Loop to a File.

EXAMPLE 8.84

```
(The Command Line)
1   $ cat memo
    abc
    def
    ghi


(The Script)
$ cat numbers
    #!/bin/sh
    # Program name: numberit
    # Put line numbers on all lines of memo
2   if [ $# -lt  1 ]
    then
3       echo  "Usage: $0 filename " >&2
        exit 1
    fi
4   count=1                          # Initialize count
5   cat $1 | while read line
    # Input is coming from file on command line
    do
6       [ $count -eq 1 ] && echo "Processing file $1..." > /dev/tty
7       echo $count $line
8       count=`expr $count + 1`
9   done > tmp$$                      # Output is going to a temporary file
```

EXAMPLE   8.84 (CONTINUED)

```
10  mv tmp$$ $1

(The Command Line)
11  $ numberit memo
    Processing file memo...


12  $ cat memo
    1 abc
    2 def
    3 ghi
```

EXPLANATION

1   The contents of file *memo* are displayed.

2   If the user did not provide a command line argument when running this script, the number of arguments ($#) will be less than one and the error message appears.

3   The usage message is sent to *stderr* (>&2) if the number of arguments is less than *1*.

4   The *count* variable is assigned the value *1*.

5   The UNIX *cat* command displays the contents of the filename stored in *$1*, and the output is piped to the *while* loop. The *read* command is assigned the first line of the file the first time in the loop, the second line of the file the next time through the loop, and so forth. The *read* command returns a zero exit status if it is successful in reading input and one if it fails.

6   If the value of *count* is *1*, the *echo* command is executed and its output is sent to */dev/tty*, the screen.

7   The *echo* command prints the value of *count*, followed by the line in the file.

8   The *count* is incremented by one.

9   The output of this entire loop, each line of the file in *$1*, is redirected to the file *tmp$$*, with the exception of the first line of the file, which is redirected to the terminal, */dev/tty*.[8]

10 The *tmp* file is renamed to the filename assigned to *$1*.

11 The program is executed. The file to be processed is called *memo*.

12 The file *memo* is displayed after the script has finished, demonstrating that line numbers have been prepended to each line.

---

8. $$ expands to the PID number of the current shell. By appending this number to the filename, the filename is made unique.

EXAMPLE 8.85

```
(The File)
$ cat testing
apples
pears
peaches

(The Script)
    #!/bin/sh
    # This program demonstrates the scope of variables when
    # assigned within loops where the looping command uses
    # redirection. A subshell is started when the loop uses
    # redirection, making all variables created within the loop
    # local to the shell where the loop is being executed.
1   while read line
    do
2       echo $line      # This line will be redirected to outfile
3       name=JOE
4   done < testing > outfile   # Redirection of input and output
5   echo Hi there $name

(The Output)
5   Hi there
```

EXPLANATION

1   If the exit status of the *read* command is successful, the body of the *while* loop is entered. The *read* command is getting input from the file *testing*, named after the *done* on line 4. Each time through the loop, the *read* command reads another line from the file *testing*.

2   The value of *line* will be redirected to *outfile* in line 4.

3   The variable *name* is assigned *JOE*. Since redirection is utilized in this loop, the variable is local to the loop.

4   The *done* keyword consists of the redirection of input from the file *testing*, and the redirection of output to the file *outfile*. All output from this loop will go to *outfile*.

5   When out of the loop, *name* is undefined. It was local to the *while* loop and known only within the body of that loop. Since the variable *name* has no value, only the string *Hi there* is displayed.

Piping the Output of a Loop to a UNIX Command.   Output can be either piped to another command(s) or redirected to a file.

EXAMPLE 8.86

```
(The Script)
    #!/bin/sh
1   for i in 7 9 2 3 4  5
2   do
        echo  $i
3   done | sort -n
```

```
(The Output)
2
3
4
5
7
9
```

EXPLANATION

1   The *for* loop iterates through a list of unsorted numbers.

2   In the body of the loop, the numbers are printed. This output will be piped into
     the UNIX *sort* command, a numerical sort.

3   The pipe is created after the *done* keyword. The loop is run in a subshell.

Running Loops in the Background.   Loops can be executed to run in the background. The program can continue without waiting for the loop to finish processing.

EXAMPLE 8.87

```
(The Script)
    #!/bin/sh
1   for person in bob jim joe sam
    do
2       mail $person < memo
3   done &
```

EXPLANATION

1   The *for* loop shifts through each of the names in the wordlist: *bob, jim, joe,* and
     sam. Each of the names is assigned to the variable *person*, in turn.

2   In the body of the loop, each person is sent the contents of the *memo* file.

3   The ampersand at the end of the *done* keyword causes the loop to be executed in
     the background. The program will continue to run while the loop is executing.

The *exec* Command and Loops.   The *exec* command can be used to open or close
standard input or output without creating a subshell. Therefore, when starting a loop,

any variables created within the body of the loop will remain when the loop completes. When using redirection in loops, any variables created within the loop are lost.

The *exec* command is often used to open files for reading and writing, either by name or by file descriptor number. Recall that file descriptors 0, 1, and 2 are reserved for standard input, output, and error. If a file is opened, it will receive the next available file descriptor. For example, if file descriptor 3 is the next free descriptor, the new file will be assigned file descriptor 3.

EXAMPLE 8.88

```
(The File)
1  $ cat tmp
   apples
   pears
   bananas
   pleaches
   plums

(The Script)
$ cat speller
   #!/bin/sh
   # Scriptname: speller
   # Purpose: Check and fix spelling errors in a file
2  exec < tmp                 # Opens the tmp file
3  while read line            # Read from the tmp file
   do
4      echo $line
5      echo -n "Is this word correct? [Y/N] "
6      read answer < /dev/tty    # Read from the terminal
7      case "$answer" in
8      [Yy]*)
9          continue;;
       *)
           echo "What is the correct spelling? "
10         read word < /dev/tty
11         sed "s/$line/$word/g" tmp > error
12         mv error tmp
13         echo $line has been changed to $word.
       esac
14 done
```

EXPLANATION

1   The contents of the *tmp* file are displayed.
2   The *exec* command changes standard input (file descriptor 0) so that instead of input coming from the keyboard, it is coming from the *tmp* file.
3   The *while* loop starts. The *read* command gets a line of input from the *tmp* file.
4   The value stored in the *line* variable is printed.
5   The user is asked if the word is correct.

EXPLANATION (CONTINUED)

6   The *read* gets the user's response from the terminal, */dev/tty*. If the input is not re-
     directed directly from the terminal, it will continue to be read from the file *tmp*,
     still opened for reading.

7   The *case* command evalutates the user's answer.

8   If the variable answer evaluates to a string starting with a *Y* or *y*, the *continue* state-
     ment on the next line will be executed.

9   The *continue* statement causes the program to go to the beginning of the *while*
     loop on line 3.

10   The user is again asked for input (the correct spelling of the word). The input is
     redirected from the terminal, */dev/tty*.

11   The *sed* command will replace the value of *line* with the value of *word* wherever it
     occurs in the *tmp* file, and send the output to the *error* file.

12   The error file will be renamed *tmp*, thus overwriting the old contents of *tmp* with
     the contents of the *error* file.

13   This line is displayed to indicate that the change has been made.

14   The *done* keyword marks the end of the loop body.

IFS and Loops.   The shell's internal field separator (*IFS*) evaluates to spaces, tabs,
and the newline character. It is used as a word (token) separator for commands that
parse lists of words, such as *read, set,* and *for*. It can be reset by the user if a different
separator will be used in a list. Before changing its value, it is a good idea to save the
original value of the *IFS* in another variable. Then it is easy to return to its default value,
if needed.

EXAMPLE 8.89

```
(The Script )
$ cat runit
    #/bin/sh
    # Script is called runit.
    # IFS is the internal field separator and defaults to
    # spaces, tabs, and newlines.
    # In this script it is changed to a colon.
1   names=Tom:Dick:Harry:John
2   OLDIFS="$IFS"    # Save the original value of IFS
3   IFS=":"
4   for persons in $names
    do
5       echo  Hi $persons
    done
6   IFS="$OLDIFS"               # Reset the IFS to old value
7   set Jill Jane Jolene        # Set positional parameters
8   for girl in $*
    do
```

EXAMPLE 8.89 (CONTINUED)

```
9       echo Howdy $girl
    done
```

```
(The Output)
$ runit
5   Hi Tom
    Hi Dick
    Hi Harry
    Hi John
9   Howdy Jill
    Howdy Jane
    Howdy Jolene
```

EXPLANATION

1   The *names* variable is set to the string *Tom:Dick:Harry:John*. Each of the words is separated by a colon.

2   The value of *IFS*, whitespace, is assigned to another variable, *OLDIFS*. Since the value of the *IFS* is whitespace, it must be quoted to preserve it.

3   The *IFS* is assigned a colon. Now the colon is used to separate words.

4   After variable substitution, the *for* loop will iterate through each of the names, using the colon as the internal field separator between the words.

5   Each of the names in the wordlist are displayed.

6   The *IFS* is reassigned its original value stored in *OLDIFS*.

7   The positional parameters are set. *$1* is assigned *Jill*, *$2* is assigned *Jane*, and *$3* is assigned *Jolene*.

8   *$** evaluates to all the positional parameters, *Jill, Jane*, and *Jolene*. The *for* loop assigns each of the names to the *girl* variable, in turn, through each iteration of the loop.

9   Each of the names in the parameter list is displayed.

8.2.8 Functions

Functions were introduced to the Bourne shell in AT&T's UNIX System VR2. A function is a name for a command or group of commands. Functions are used to modularize your program and make it more efficient. You may even store functions in another file and load them into your script when you are ready to use them.

Here is a review of some of the important rules about using functions.

1. The Bourne shell determines whether you are using a built-in command, a function, or an executable program found out on the disk. It looks for built-in commands first, then functions, and last, executables.

2. A function must be defined before it is used.

3. The function runs in the current environment; it shares variables with the script that invoked it, and lets you pass arguments by assigning them as positional parameters. If you use the exit command in a function, you exit the entire script. If, however, either the input or output of the function is redirected or the function is enclosed within backquotes (command substitution), a subshell is created and the function and its variables and present working directory are known only within the subshell. When the function exits, any variables set there will be lost, and if you have changed directories, you will revert to the directory you were in before invoking the function. If you exit the function, you return to where the script left off when the function was invoked.

4. The *return* statement returns the exit status of the last command executed within the function or the value of the argument given, and cannot exceed a value of 255.

5. Functions exist only in the shell where they are defined; they cannot be exported to subshells. The *dot* command can be used to execute functions stored in files.

6. To list functions and definitions, use the *set* command.

7. Traps, like variables, are global within functions. They are shared by both the script and the functions invoked in the script. If a trap is defined in a function, it is also shared by the script. This could have unwanted side effects.

8. If functions are stored in another file, they can be loaded into the current script with the *dot* command.

FORMAT

```
function_name () { commands ; commands; }
```

EXAMPLE 8.90

```
dir () { echo "Directories: " ; ls -l | nawk '/^d/ {print $NF}' ; }
```

EXPLANATION

The name of the function is *dir*. The empty parentheses are necessary syntax for naming the function but have no other purpose. The commands within the curly braces will be executed when *dir* is typed. The purpose of the function is to list only the subdirectories below the present working directory. The spaces surrounding the curly braces are required.

To Unset a Function.   To remove a function from memory, the *unset* command is used.

FORMAT

```
unset function_name
```

Function Arguments and the Return Value. Since the function is executed within the current shell, the variables will be known to both the function and the shell. Any changes made to your environment in the function will also be made to the shell. Arguments can be passed to functions by using positional parameters. The positional parameters are private to the function; that is, arguments to the function will not affect any positional parameters used outside the function.

The *return* command can be used to exit the function and return control to the program at the place where the function was invoked. (Remember, if you use *exit* anywhere in your script, including within a function, the script terminates.) The return value of a function is really just the value of the exit status of the last command in the script, unless you give a specific argument to the *return* command. If a value is assigned to the *return* command, that value is stored in the *?* variable and can hold an integer value between zero and 255. Because the *return* command is limited to returning only an integer between zero and 255, you can use command substitution to capture the output of a function. Place the entire function in backquotes and assign the output to a variable just as you would if getting the output of a UNIX command.

EXAMPLE 8.91

```
(Using the return Command)
(The Script)
$ cat do_increment
    #!/bin/sh
    # Scriptname: do_increment
1   increment ()  {
2      sum=`expr $1 + 1`
3      return $sum  # Return the value of sum to the script.
    }
4   echo  -n "The sum is "
5   increment 5     # Call function increment; pass 5 as a
                     # parameter. 5 becomes $1 for the increment
                     # function.
6   echo $?          # The return value is stored in $?
7   echo  $sum      # The variable "sum" is known to the function,
                     # and is also known to the main script.


(The Output)
     $ do_increment
4,6   The sum is 6
7     6
```

EXPLANATION

1   The function called *increment* is defined.

2   When the function is called, the value of the first argument, $1, will be incremented by one and the result assigned to *sum*.

3   The *return* built-in command, when given an argument, returns to the main script after the line where the function was invoked. It stores its argument in the *?* variable.

4   The string is echoed to the screen.

EXPLANATION (CONTINUED)

5. The *increment* function is called with an argument of *5*.

6. When the function returns, its exit status is stored in the *?* variable. The exit status is the exit value of the last command executed in the function unless an explicit argument is used in the *return* statement. The argument for *return* must be an integer between 0 and 255.

7. Although the *sum* was defined in the function *increment*, it is global in scope, and therefore also known within the script that invoked the function. Its value is printed.

EXAMPLE 8.92

```
(Using Command Substitution)
(The Script)
$ cat do_square
    #!/bin/sh
    # Scriptname: do_square
1   function square {
    sq=`expr $1 \* $1`
    echo  "Number to be squared is $1."
2   echo  "The result is $sq "
    }
3   echo "Give me a number to square. "
    read number
4   value_returned=`square $number` # Command substitution
5   echo   $value_returned

(The Output)
$ do_square
3   Give me a number to square.
    10
5   Number to be squared is 10. The result is 100
```

EXPLANATION

1. The function called *square* is defined. Its function, when called, is to multiply its argument, *$1*, by itself.

2. The result of squaring the number is printed.

3. The user is asked for input. This is the line where the program starts executing.

4. The function *square* is called with a number (input from the user) as its argument. Command substitution is performed because the function is enclosed in backquotes. The output of the function, both of its *echo* statements, is assigned to the variable *value_returned*.

5. The command substitution removes the newline between the strings *Number to be squared is 10.* and *The result is 100.*

8.2.9 Functions and the *dot* Command

Storing Functions.   Functions are often defined in the *.profile* file, so that when you log in, they will be defined. Functions cannot be exported, but they can be stored in a file. Then when you need the function, the *dot* command is used with the name of the file to activate the definitions of the functions within it.

EXAMPLE 8.93

```
1  $ cat myfunctions
2  go() {
       cd $HOME/bin/prog
       PS1=''`pwd` > '
       ls
   }
3  greetings() { echo "Hi $1! Welcome to my world." ; }

4  $ . myfunctions
5  $ greetings george
   Hi george! Welcome to my world.
```

EXPLANATION

1   The file *myfunctions* is displayed. It contains two function definitions.

2   The first function defined is called *go*. It sets the primary prompt to the present working directory.

3   The second function defined is called *greetings*. It will greet the name of the user passed in as an argument.

4   The *dot* command loads the contents of the file *myfunctions* into the shell's memory. Now both functions are defined for this shell.

5   The *greetings* function is invoked and executed.

EXAMPLE 8.94

```
(The .dbfunctions file  shown below contains functions to be used by
the main program)
1  $ cat .dbfunctions
2  addon () {    # Function is named and defined in file .dbfunctions
3     while true
      do
          echo "Adding information "
          echo "Type the full name of employee "
          read name
          echo "Type address for employee "
          read address
          echo "Type start date for employee (4/10/88 ) :"
          read startdate
          echo $name:$address:$startdate
          echo -n "Is this correct? "
```

EXAMPLE 8.94 (CONTINUED)

```
            read ans
            case "$ans"  in
            [Yy]*)
                        echo "Adding info..."
                        echo $name:$address:$startdate>>datafile
                  sort -u datafile -o datafile
                  echo -n "Do you want to go back to the main menu? "
                  read ans
                  if [ $ans = Y -o $ans = y ]
                  then
4                       return          # Return to calling program
                  else

5                       continue        # Go to the top of the loop
                  fi
                  ;;
            *)
                  echo "Do you want to try again? "
                  read answer
            case "$answer" in
            [Yy]*) continue;;
            *) exit;;
            esac
                  ;;
      esac
   done
6 }   # End of function definition
-------------------------------------------------------------
(The Command Line)
7 $ more mainprog
   #!/bin/sh
   # Scriptname: mainprog
   # This is the main script that will call the function, addon

   datafile=$HOME/bourne/datafile
8 . .dbfunctions          # The dot command reads the dbfunctions file
                          # into memory
   if [ ! -f $datafile ]
   then
      echo "`basename $datafile` does not exist" 1>&2
      exit 1
   fi
9 echo "Select one: "
   cat <<EOF
      [1] Add info
      [2] Delete info
      [3] Exit
```

EXAMPLE 8.94 (CONTINUED)

```
        EOF
        read choice
        case $choice in
10        1)  addon            # Calling the addon function
              ;;
          2)  delete           # Calling the delete function
              ;;

          3)  update
              ;;
          4)
              echo Bye
              exit 0
              ;;
          *)  echo Bad choice
              exit 2
              ;;
        esac
        echo Returned from function call
        echo The name is $name
        # Variable set in the function are known in this shell.
```

EXPLANATION

1 The *.dbfunctions* file is displayed.

2 The *addon* function is defined. Its function is to add new information to the file *datafile*.

3 A *while* loop is entered. It will loop forever unless a loop control statement such as *break* or *continue* is included in the body of the loop.

4 The *return* command sends control back to the calling program where the function was called.

5 Control is returned to the top of the *while* loop.

6 The closing curly brace ends the function definition.

7 This is the main script. The function *addon* will be used in this script.

8 The *dot* command loads the file *.dbfunctions* into the program's memory. Now the function *addon* is defined for this script and available for use. It is as though you had just defined the function right here in the script.

9 A menu is displayed with the *here document*. The user is asked to select a menu item.

10 The *addon* function is invoked.

8.2.10 Trapping Signals

While your program is running, if you press Control-C or Control-\, your program terminates as soon as the signal arrives. There are times when you would rather not have the program terminate immediately after the signal arrives. You could arrange to ignore the signal and keep running or perform some sort of cleanup operation before actually exiting the script. The *trap* command allows you to control the way a program behaves when it receives a signal.

A *signal* is defined as an asynchronous message that consists of a number that can be sent from one process to another, or by the operating system to a process if certain keys are pressed or if something exceptional happens.[9] The *trap* command tells the shell to terminate the command currently in execution upon the receipt of a signal. If the *trap* command is followed by commands within quotes, the command string will be executed upon receipt of a specified signal. The shell reads the command string twice, once when the trap is set, and again when the signal arrives. If the command string is surrounded by double quotes, all variable and command substitution will be performed when the trap is set the first time. If single quotes enclose the command string, variable and command substitution do not take place until the signal is detected and the trap is executed.

Use the command *kill –l* to get a list of all signals. Table 8.15 provides a list of signal numbers and their corresponding names.

FORMAT

```
trap 'command; command' signal-number
```

EXAMPLE 8.95

```
trap 'rm tmp*; exit 1'  1 2 15
```

EXPLANATION

When any of the signals *1* (hangup), *2* (interrupt), or *15* (software termination) arrive, remove all the *tmp* files and exit.

If an interrupt signal comes in while the script is running, the *trap* command lets you handle the signal in several ways. You can let the signal behave normally (default), ignore the signal, or create a handler function to be called when the signal arrives.

---

9. Bolsky, Morris I., and Korn, David G., *The New KornShell Command and Programming Language* (Englewood Cliffs, NJ: Prentice Hall PTR, 1995), p. 327.

Table 8.15 Signal Numbers and Signals

1) *HUP*	12) *SYS*	23) *POLL*
2) *INT*	13) *PIPE*	24) *XCPU*
3) *QUIT*	14) *ALRM*	25) *XFSZ*
4) *ILL*	15) *TERM*	26) *VTALRM*
5) *TRAP*	16) *URG*	27) *PROF*
6) *IOT*	17) *STOP*	28) *WINCH*
7) *EMT*	18) *TSTP*	29) *LOST*
8) *FPE*	19) *CONT*	30) *USR1*
9) *KILL*	20) *CHLD*	31) *USR2*
10) *BUS*	21) *TTIN*	
11) *SEGV*	22) *TTOU*	

Resetting Signals.   To reset a signal to its default behavior, the *trap* command is followed by the signal name or number.

EXAMPLE 8.96

```
trap 2
```

EXPLANATION

Resets the default action for signal 2, *SIGINT*, which is used to kill a process, i.e., Control-C.

EXAMPLE 8.97

```
trap 'trap 2' 2
```

EXPLANATION

Sets the default action for signal 2 (*SIGINT*) to execute the command string within quotes when the signal arrives. The user must press Control-C twice to terminate the program. The first *trap* catches the signal, the second *trap* resets the trap back to its default action, which is to kill the process.

Ignoring Signals.   If the *trap* command is followed by a pair of empty quotes, the signals listed will be ignored by the process.

EXAMPLE 8.98

```
trap " "  1  2
```

EXPLANATION

Signals *1* and *2* will be ignored by the shell.

Listing Traps.   To list all traps and the commands assigned to them, type *trap*.

EXAMPLE 8.99

```
(The Script)
$ cat trapping
   #/bin/sh
   # Scriptname: trapping
   # Script to illustrate the trap command and signals
1  trap 'echo "Control-C will not terminate $0."' 2
2  trap 'echo "Control-\ will not terminate $0."' 3

3  echo "Enter any string after the prompt."
   echo "When you are ready to exit, type \"stop\"."
4  while true
   do
        echo  -n "Go ahead...> "
        read reply
5       if [ "$reply" = stop ]
        then
6            break
        fi
7  done

(The Output)
$ trapping
Enter any string after the prompt.
When you are ready to exit, type "stop".
Go ahead...> this is it^C
Control-C will not terminate trapping.
Go ahead...> this is never it ^\
Control-\ will not terminate trapping.
Go ahead...> stop
$
```

EXPLANATION

1 The first *trap* catches the *INT* signal, Control-C. If ^C is pressed while the program is running, the command enclosed in quotes will be executed. Instead of aborting, the program will print *Control-C will not terminate trapping*, and continue to prompt the user for input.

2 The second *trap* command will be executed when the user presses Conrtrol-\, the *QUIT* signal. The string *Control-\ will not terminate trapping* will be displayed, and the program will continue to run. This signal, by default, kills the process and produces a core file.

3 The user is prompted for input.

4 The *while* loop is entered and a prompt, *Go ahead...>*, is displayed.

5 The user input is assigned to the *reply* variable and, if its value matches *stop*, the loop exits and the program terminates. This is the way we will get out of this program unless it is killed with the *kill* command.

6 The *break* command causes the body of the loop to be exited with control starting after line 7. In this case, the program is at its end.

7 This is the end of the *while* loop.

Traps in Functions.   If you use a trap to handle a signal in a function, it will affect the entire script, once the function is called. The trap is global to the script. In the following example, the trap is set to ignore the interrupt key, ^C. This script had to be killed with the *kill* command to stop the looping. It demonstrates potential undesirable side effects when using traps in functions.

EXAMPLE 8.100

```
(The Script)
    #!/bin/sh
1   trapper () {
        echo "In trapper"
2       trap 'echo "Caught in a trap!"' 2
        # Once set, this trap affects the entire script. Anytime
        # ^C is entered, the script will ignore it.
    }
3   while :
    do
        echo "In the main script"
4       trapper
5       echo "Still in main"
        sleep 5
    done
```

EXAMPLE 8.100 (CONTINUED)

```
(The Output)
$ trapper
In the main script
In trapper
Still in main
^CCaught in a trap!
In the main script
In trapper
Still in main
^CCaught in a trap!
In the main script
```

EXPLANATION

1   The *trapper* function is defined. All variables and traps set in the function are global to the script.

2   The *trap* command will ignore signal 2, the interrupt key (^C). If ^C is pressed, the message *Caught in a trap* is printed, and the script continues forever.

3   The main script starts a forever loop.

4   The function *trapper* is called.

5   When the function returns, execution starts here.

Debugging.   By using the *–n* option to the *sh* command, you can check the sytnax of your scripts without really executing any of the commands. If there is a syntax error in the script, the shell will report the error. If there are no errors, nothing is displayed.

The most commonly used method for debugging scripts is to use the *set* command with the *–x* option, or to use the *–x* option as an argument to the *sh* command, followed by the script name. See Table 8.16 for a list of debugging options. These options allow an execution trace of your script. Each command from your script is displayed after substitution has been performed, and then the command is executed. When a line from your script is displayed, it is preceded with a plus (+) sign.

With the verbose option turned on, or by invoking the Bourne shell with the *–v* option (*sh –v* scriptname), each line of the script will be displayed just as it was typed in the script, and then executed.

Table 8.16   Debugging Options

Command	Option	What It Does
sh –x scriptname	Echo option	Displays each line of script after variable substitutions and before execution.
sh –v scriptname	Verbose option	Displays each line of script before execution, just as you typed it.
sh –n scriptname	Noexec option	Interprets but does not execute commands.

Table 8.16 Debugging Options (continued)

Command	Option	What It Does
set −x	Turns on echo	Traces execution in a script.
set +x	Turns off echo	Turns off tracing.

EXAMPLE 8.101

```
(The Script)
$ cat todebug
    #!/bin/sh
1   # Scriptname: todebug
    name="Joe Blow"
    if  [ "$name" = "Joe Blow" ]
    then
        echo "Hi $name"
    fi

    num=1
    while [ $num -lt 5 ]
    do
        num=`expr $num + 1`
    done
    echo The grand total is $num

(The Output)
2   $ sh -x todebug
    + name=Joe Blow
    + [ Joe Blow = Joe Blow ]
    + echo Hi Joe Blow

    Hi Joe Blow
    num=1
    + [ 1 -lt 5 ]
    + expr 1 + 1
    num=2
    + [ 2 -lt 5 ]
    + expr 2 + 1
    num=3
    + [ 3 -lt 5 ]
    + expr 3 + 1
     num=4
    + [ 4 -lt 5 ]
    + expr 4 + 1
     num=5
    + [ 5 -lt 5 ]
    + echo The grand total is 5
    The grand total is 5
```

EXPLANATION

1   The script is called *todebug*. You can watch the script run with the –x switch turned on. Each iteration of the loop is displayed and the values of variables are printed as they are set and when they change.

2   The *sh* command starts the Bourne shell with the –x option. Echoing is turned on. Each line of the script will be displayed to the screen prepended with a plus sign (+). Variable substitution is performed before the line is displayed. The result of the execution of the command appears after the line has been displayed.

8.2.11 Processing Command Line Options with *getopts*

If you are writing scripts that require a number of command line options, positional parameters are not always the most efficient. For example, the UNIX *ls* command takes a number of command line options and arguments. (An option requires a leading dash; an argument does not.) Options can be passed to the program in several ways: *ls –laFi, ls –i –a –l –F, ls –ia –F,* and so forth. If you have a script that requires arguments, positional parameters might be used to process the arguments individually, such as *ls –l –i –F* . Each dash option would be stored in *$1, $2,* and *$3,* respectively. But, what if the user listed all of the options as one dash option, as in *ls –liF?* Now the *–liF* would all be assigned to *$1* in the script. The *getopts* function makes it possible to process command line options and arguments in the same way they are processed by the *ls* program.[10] The *getopts* function will allow the *runit* program to process its arguments using any variety of combinations.

EXAMPLE 8.102

```
(The Command Line )
1   $ runit -x -n  200 filex

2   $ runit -xn200 filex

3   $ runit -xy

4   $ runit -yx -n 30

5   $ runit -n250 -xy filey

( any other combination of these arguments )
```

---

10. See the UNIX manual pages (Section 3) for the C library function *getopt*.

EXPLANATION

1 The program *runit* takes four arguments: *x* is an option, *n* is an option requiring a number argument after it, and *filex* is an argument that stands alone.

2 The program *runit* combines the options *x* and *n* and the number argument *200*; *filex* is also an argument.

3 The program *runit* is invoked with the *x* and *y* options combined.

4 The program *runit* is invoked with the *y* and *x* options combined; the *n* option is passed separately, as is the number argument, *30*.

5 The program *runit* is invoked with the *n* option combined with the number argument, the *x* and *y* options are combined, and the *filey* is separate.

Before getting into all the details of the *runit* program, we examine the line from the program where *getopts* is used to see how it processes the arguments.

EXAMPLE 8.103

```
(A Line from the Script Called "runit")
while getopts :xyn: name
```

EXPLANATION

- *x*, *y*, and *n* are the options.
- Options typed at the command line begin with a dash.
- Any options that do not contain a dash tell *getopts* that the option list is at an end.
- Each time *getopts* is called, it places the next option it finds, without the dash, in the variable *name*. (You can use any variable name here.) If an illegal argument is given, *name* is assigned a question mark.
- *OPTIND* is a special variable that is initialized to one and is incremented each time *getopts* completes processing a command line argument to the number of the next argument *getopts* will process.
- The *OPTARG* variable contains the value of a legal argument.

***getopts* Scripts.**   The following examples illustrate how *getopts* processes arguments.

EXAMPLE 8.104

```
(The Script)
$ cat opts1
    #!/bin/sh
    # Program opts1
    # Using getopts -- First try --
1   while getopts xy options
    do
2       case $options in
3       x) echo "you entered -x as an option";;
        y) echo "you entered -y as an option";;
        esac
    done

(The Command Line)
4   $ opts1 -x
    you entered -x as an option
5   $ opts1 -xy
    you entered -x as an option
    you entered -y as an option
6   $ opts1 -y
    you entered -y as an option
7   $ opts1 -b
    opts1:   illegal option --  b
8   $ opts1 b
```

EXPLANATION

1   The *getopts* command is used as a condition for the *while* command. The valid op-
    tions for this program are listed after the *getopts* command; they are *x* and *y*. Each
    option is tested in the body of the loop, one after the other. Each option will be
    assigned to the variable *options*, without the leading dash. When there are no
    longer any arguments to process, *getopts* will exit with a nonzero status, causing
    the *while* loop to terminate.

2   The *case* command is used to test each of the possible options found in the *options*
    variable, either *x* or *y*.

3   If *x* was an option, the string *You entered x as an option* is displayed.

4   At the command line, the *opts1* script is given a *x* option, a legal option to be pro-
    cessed by *getopts*.

5   At the command line, the *opts1* script is given a *xy* option; *x* and *y* are legal options
    to be processed by *getopts*.

6   At the command line, the *opts1* script is given a *y* option, a legal option to be pro-
    cessed by *getopts*.

7   The *opts1* script is given a *b* option, an illegal option. *Getopts* sends an error mes-
    sage to *stderr*.

8   An option without a dash prepended to it is not an option and causes *getopts* to
    stop processing arguments.

EXAMPLE 8.105

```
(The Script)
$ cat opts2
   #!/bin/sh
   # Program opts2
   # Using getopts -- Second try --
1  while getopts xy options 2> /dev/null
   do
2      case $options in
       x) echo "you entered -x as an option";;
       y) echo "you entered -y as an option";;
3      \?) echo "Only -x and -y are valid options"  1>&2;;
       esac
   done

(The Command Line)
   $ opts2 -x
   you entered -x as an option

   $ opts2 -y
   you entered -y as an option

   $ opts2 xy

   $ opts2 -xy
   you entered -x as an option
   you entered -y as an option

4  $ opts2 -g
   Only -x and -y are valid options

5  $ opts2 -c
   Only -x and -y are valid options
```

EXPLANATION

1   If there is an error message from *getopts*, it is redirected to */dev/null*.

2   If the option is a bad option, a question mark will be assigned to the *options* variable. The *case* command can be used to test for the question mark, allowing you to print your own error message to standard error.

3   If the *options* variable is assigned the question mark, the *case* statement is executed. The question mark is protected with the backslash so that the shell does not see it as a wildcard and try to perform filename substitution.

4   *g* is not a legal option. A question mark is assigned to the variable *options*, and the error message is displayed.

5   *c* is not a legal option. A question mark is assigned to the variable *options*, and the error message is displayed.

EXAMPLE 8.106

```
(The Script)
$ cat opts3
   #!/bin/sh
   # Program opts3
   # Using getopts -- Third try --
1  while getopts dq: options
   do
       case $options in
2          d) echo "-d is a valid switch ";;
3          q) echo "The argument for -q is $OPTARG";;
           \?) echo "Usage:opts3 -dq filename ... " 1>&2;;
       esac
   done

(The Command Line)
4  $ opts3 -d
   -d is a valid switch

5  $ opts3 -q  foo
   The argument for -q is foo

6  $ opts3 -q
   Usage:opts3 -dq filename ...

7  $ opts3 -e
   Usage:opts3 -dq filename ...

8  $ opts3 e
```

EXPLANATION

1   The *while* command tests the exit status of *getopts*; if *getopts* can successfully process an argument, it returns zero exit status, and the body of the *while* loop is entered. The colon appended to the argument list means that the *q* option requires an argument. The argument will be stored in the special variable, *OPTARG*.

2   One of the legal options is *d*. If *d* is entered as an option, the *d* (without the dash) is stored in the *options* variable.

3   One of the legal options is *q*. The *q* option requires an argument. There must be a space between the *q* option and its argument. If *q* is entered as an option followed by an argument, the *q*, without the dash, is stored in the *options* variable and the argument is stored in the *OPTARG* variable. If an argument does not follow the *q* option, the question mark is stored in the variable *options*.

4   The *d* option is a legal option to *opts3*.

5   The *q* option with an argument is also a legal option to *opts3*.

6   The *q* option without an argument is an error.

7   The *e* option is invalid. A question mark is stored in the *options* variable if the option is illegal.

EXPLANATION (CONTINUED)

8   The option is prepended with neither a dash nor a plus sign. The *getopts* command will not process it as an option and returns a nonzero exit status. The *while* loop is terminated.

EXAMPLE 8.107

```
$ cat opts4
    #!/bin/sh
    # Program opts4
    # Using getopts -- Fourth try --
1   while getopts xyz: arguments 2>/dev/null
    do
        case $arguments in
2       x) echo "you entered -x as an option.";;
        y) echo "you entered y as an option.";;
3       z) echo "you entered -z as an option."
            echo "\$OPTARG is $OPTARG.";;
4       \?) echo "Usage opts4 [-xy] [-z  argument]"
            exit 1;;
        esac
    done
5   echo "The initial value of \$OPTIND is 1.
        The final value of \$OPTIND is $OPTIND.
        Since this reflects the number of the next command line
        argument,the number of arguments passed was
        'expr $OPTIND - 1'. "
```

```
(The Command Line)
$ opts4 -xyz foo
you entered -x as an option.
you entered y as an option
you entered -z as an option.
$OPTARG is foo.
The initial value of $OPTIND is 1.
The final value of $OPTIND is 3.
Since this reflects the number of the next command
line argument, the number of arguments passed was 2.
$ opts4 -x -y -z  boo
you entered -x as an option.
you entered -y as an option.
you entered -z as an option.
$OPTARG is boo.
The initial value of $OPTIND is 1.
The final value of $OPTIND is 5.
Since this reflects the number of the next command
line argument,the number of arguments passed was 4.
$ opts4 -d
Usage: opts4  [-xy] [-z argument]
```

EXPLANATION

1   The *while* command tests the exit status of *getopts*; if *getopts* can successfully process an argument, it returns zero exit status, and the body of the *while* loop is entered. The colon appended to the *z* option tells *getopts* that an argument must follow the –*z* option. If the option takes an argument, the argument is stored in the *getopts* built-in variable *OPTARG*.

2   If *x* is given as an option, it is stored in the variable *arguments*.

3   If *z* is given as an option with an argument, the argument is stored in the built-in variable *OPTARG*.

4   If an invalid option is entered, the question mark is stored in the variable *arguments*, and an error message is displayed.

5   The special *getopts* variable, *OPTIND*, holds the number of the next option to be processed. Its value is always one more than the actual number of command line arguments.

8.2.12   The *eval* Command and Parsing the Command Line

The *eval* command evaluates a command line, performs all shell substitutions, and then executes the command line. It is used when normal parsing of the command line is not enough.

EXAMPLE   8.108

```
1   $ set a b c d
2   $ echo The last argument is \$$#
3   The last argument is $4

4   $ eval echo The last argument is \$$#
    The last argument is d

5   $ set -x
    $ eval echo The last argument is \$$#
    + eval echo the last argument is $4
    + echo the last argument is d
    The last argument is d
```

EXPLANATION

1   Four positional parameters are set.

2   The desired result is to print the value of the last positional parameter. The \$ will print a literal dollar sign. The $# evaluates to 4, the number of positional parameters. After the shell evaluates the $#, it does not parse the line again to get the value of $4.

EXPLANATION (CONTINUED)

3   *$4* is printed instead of the last argument.

4   After the shell performs variable substitution, the *eval* command performs the variable substitution and then executes the *echo* command.

5   Turn on the echoing to watch the order of parsing.

EXAMPLE 8.109

```
(From SVR4 Shutdown Program)
1   eval '/usr/bin/id | /usr/bin/sed 's/[^a-z0-9=].*//''
2   if [ "${uid:=0}" -ne 0 ]
    then
3       echo $0: Only root can run $0
        exit 2
    fi
```

EXPLANATION

1   This is a tricky one. The *id* program's output is sent to *sed* to extract the *uid* part of the string. The output for *id* is:

     uid=9496(ellie) gid=40 groups=40
     uid=0(root) gid=1(daemon) groups=1(daemon)

     The *sed* regular expression reads: *Find any character that is not a letter, number, or an equal sign and remove that character and all characters following it.* The result is to substitute everything from the first opening parenthesis to the end of the line with nothing. What is left is either *uid=9496* or *uid=0*.

     After *eval* evaluates the command line, it then executes the resulting command:

     uid=9496
     or
     uid=0

     For example, if the user's ID is *root*, the command executed would be *uid=0*. This creates a local variable in the shell called *uid* and assigns zero to it.

2   The value of the *uid* variable is tested for zero, using command modifiers.

3   If the *uid* is not zero, the *echo* command displays the script name (*$0*) and the message.

8.2.13 Shell Invocation Options

When the shell is started using the *sh* command, it can take options to modify its behavior. See Table 8.17.

Table 8.17   Shell Invocation Options

Option	Meaning
−i	Shell is in the interactive mode. *QUIT* and *INTERRUPT* are ignored.
−s	Commands are read from standard input and output is sent to standard error.
−c string	Commands are read from string.

8.2.14 The *set* Command and Options

The *set* command can be used to turn shell options on and off, as well as for handling command line arguments. To turn an option on, the dash (−) is prepended to the option; to turn an option off, the plus sign (+) is prepended to the option. See Table 8.18 for a list of *set* options.

EXAMPLE 8.110

```
1   $ set -f

2   $ echo *
    *

3   $ echo ??
    ??

4   $ set +f
```

EXPLANATION

1   The *f* option is turned on, disabling filename expansion.
2   The asterisk is not expanded.
3   The question marks are not expanded.
4   The *f* is turned off; filename expansion is enabled.

Table 8.18   The *set* Command Options

Option	Meaning
–a	Marks variables that have been modified or exported.
–e	Exits the program if a command returns a nonzero status.
–f	Disables globbing (filename expansion).
–h	Locates and remembers function commands as functions when they are defined, not just when they are executed.
–k	All keyword arguments are placed in the environment for a command, not just those that precede the command name.
–n	Reads commands but does not execute them; used for debugging.
–t	Exits after reading and executing one command.
–u	Treats *unset* variables as an error when performing substitution.
–v	Prints shell input lines as they are read; used for debugging.
–x	Prints commands and their arguments as they are being executed. Used for debugging.
– –	Does not change any of the flags.

8.2.15 Shell Built-In Commands

The shell has a number of commands that are built into its source code. Since the commands are built-in, the shell doesn't have to locate them on disk, making execution much faster. The built-in commands are listed in Table 8.19.

Table 8.19   Built-In Commands

Command	What It Does
:	Do-nothing command; returns exit status zero.
. file	The *dot* command reads and executes command from file.
break [n]	See *looping*.
continue [n]	See *looping*.
cd	Change directory.
echo [args]	Echo arguments.
eval command	Shell scans the command line twice before execution.

Table 8.19   Built-In Commands (continued)

Command	What It Does
exec command	Runs command in place of this shell.
exit [n]	Exit the shell with status *n*.
export [var]	Make *var* known to subshells.
hash	Controls the internal hash table for quicker searches for commands.
kill [–signal process]	Sends the signal to the PID number or job number of the process. See */usr/include/sys/signal.h* for a list of signals.
getopts	Used in shell scripts to parse command line and check for legal options.
login [username] *newgrp [arg]*	Sign onto the system. Logs a user into a new group by changing the real group and effective group ID.
pwd	Print present working directory.
read [var]	Read line from standard input into variable *var*.
readonly [var]	Make variable *var* read-only. Cannot be reset.
return [n]	Return from a function where *n* is the exit value given to the return.
set	See Table 8.18.
shift [n]	Shift positional parameters to the left *n* times.
stop pid	Halt execution of the process number PID.
suspend	Stops execution of the current shell (but not if a login shell).
times	Print accumulated user and system *times* for processes run from this shell.
trap [arg] [n]	When shell receives signal *n* (0, 1, 2, or 15), execute *arg*.
type [command]	Prints the type of command; e.g., *pwd* has a built-in shell, in *ksh*, an alias for the command *whence –v*.
umask [octal digits]	User file creation mode mask for owner, group, and others.
unset [name]	*Unset* value of variable or function.
wait [pid#n]	Wait for background process with PID number *n* and report termination status.
ulimit [options size]	Set maximum limits on processes.
umask [mask]	Without argument, print out file creation mask for permissions.

BOURNE SHELL LAB EXERCISES

Lab 8: Getting Started

1. What process puts the login prompt on your screen?
2. What process assigns values to *HOME*, *LOGNAME*, and *PATH*?
3. How do you know what shell you are using?
4. Where is your login shell assigned? (What file?)
5. Explain the difference between the */etc/profile* and *.profile* file. Which one is executed first?
6. Edit your *.profile* file as follows:
    a. Welcome the user.
    b. Add your home directory to the path if it is not there.
    c. Set the erase function to the Backspace key using *stty.*
    d. Type: *.profile*
       What is the function of the dot command?

Lab 9: Shell Metacharacters

1. Make a directory called *wildcards. Cd* to that directory and type at the prompt:

```
touch ab abc a1 a2 a3 a11 a12 ba ba.1 ba.2 filex filey AbC ABC
ABc2 abc
```

2. Write and test the command that will do the following:
    a. List all files starting with *a.*
    b. List all files ending in at least one digit.
    c. List all files starting with an *a* or *A.*
    d. List all files ending in a period, followed by a digit.
    e. List all files containing just two of the letter *a.*
    f   List three character files where all letters are uppercase.
    g. List files ending in *10, 11,* or *12.*
    h. List files ending in x or y.
    i. List all files ending in a digit, an uppercase letter, or a lowercase letter.
    j. List all files *not* starting with a *b* or *B.*
    k. Remove two-character files starting with *a* or *A.*

Lab 10: Redirection

1. What are the names of the three file streams associated with your terminal?
2. What is a file descriptor?
3. What command would you use to do the following:
    a. Redirect the output of the *ls* command to a file called *lsfile?*
    b. Redirect and append the output of the *date* command to *lsfile?*
    c. Redirect the output of the *who* command to *lsfile?* What happened?
4. Perform the following:
    a. Type *cp* all by itself. What happens?

b. Save the error message from the above example to a file.

c. Use the *find* command to find all files, starting from the parent directory, of type *directory*. Save the standard output in a file called *found* and any errors in a file called *found.errs*.

d. Take the output of three commands and redirect the output to a file called *gottem_all*.

e. Use a pipe(s) with the *ps* and *wc* commands to find out how many processes you are currently running.

Lab 11: First Script

1. Write a script called *greetme* that will do the following:

   a. Contain a comment section with your name, the name of this script, and the purpose of this script.

   b. Greet the user.

   c. Print the date and the time.

   d. Print a calendar for this month.

   e. Print the name of your machine.

   f. Print the name and release of this operating system, (*cat /etc/motd*).

   g. Print a list of all files in your parent directory.

   h. Print all the processes *root* is running.

   i. Print the value of the *TERM*, *PATH*, and *HOME* variables.

   j. Print your disk usage (*du*).

   k. Use the *id* command to print your group ID.

   l. Print *Please couldn't you loan me $50.00?*

   m. Tell the user *Good bye* and the current hour (see *man* pages for the *date* command).

2. Make sure your script is executable.

   ```
   chmod +x greetme
   ```

3. What was the first line of your script? Why do you need this line?

Lab 12: Command Line Arguments

1. Write a script called *rename* that will take two arguments: the first argument is the name of the original file and the second argument is the new name for the file.

   If the user does not provide two arguments, a usage message will appear on the screen and the script will exit. Here is an example of how the script works:

   ```
   $ rename
   Usage: rename oldfilename newfilename
   $

   $ rename file1 file2
   file1 has been renamed file2
   Here is a listing of the directory:
   a file2
   b file.bak
   ```

2. The following *find* command (SunOS) will list all files in the *root* partition that are larger than 100K and that have been modified in the last week. (Check your *man* pages for the correct *find* syntax on your system.)

    ```
    find / -xdev -mtime -7 -size +200 -print
    ```

    Write a script called *bigfiles* that will take two arguments: One will be the *mtime* and one the *size* value. An appropriate error message will be sent to *stderr* if the user does not provide two arguments.

3. If you have time, write a script called *vib* that creates backup files for *vi*. The backup files will have the extension *.bak* appended to the original name.

Lab 13: Getting User Input

1. Write a script called *nosy* that will do the following:
    a. Ask the user's full name—first, last, and middle name.
    b. Greet the user by his or her first name.
    c. Ask the user's year of birth and calculate his or her age (use *expr*).
    d. Ask the user's login name and print his or her user ID (*from /etc/passwd*).
    e. Tell the user his or her home directory.
    f. Show the user the processes he or she is running.
    g. Tell the user the day of the week, and the current time in nonmilitary time. The output should resemble

        The day of the week is Tuesday and the current time is 04:07:38 PM.

2. Create a text file called *datafile* (unless this file has already been provided for you). Each entry consists of fields separated by colons. The fields are as follows:
    a. First and last name
    b. Phone number
    c. Address
    d. Birth date
    e. Salary

3. Create a script called *lookup* that will do the following:
    a. Contain a comment section with the script name, your name, the date, and the reason for writing this script. The reason for writing this script is to display the datafile in sorted order.
    b. Sort the *datafile* by last names.
    c. Show the user the contents of the *datafile*.
    d. Tell the user the number of entries in the file.

4. Try the *–x* and *–v* options for debugging your script. How did you use these commands? How do they differ?

Lab 14: Conditional Statements

1. Write a script called *checking* that will do the following:
    a. Take a command line argument: a user's login name.

    b. Test to see if a command line argument was provided.

    c. Check to see if the user is in the */etc/passwd* file. If so, it will print

        Found <user> in the /etc/passwd file.

      Otherwise, it will print

        No such user on our system.

2. In the *lookup* script, ask the user if he or she would like to add an entry to the *datafile*. If the answer is *yes* or *y*:

    a. Prompt the user for a new name, phone, address, birth date, and salary. Each item will be stored in a separate variable. You will provide the colons between the fields and append the information to the *datafile*.

    b. Sort the file by last names. Tell the user you added the entry, and show him or her the line preceded by the line number.

Lab 15: Conditionals and File Testing

1. Rewrite *checking*. After checking whether the named user is in the */etc/passwd* file, the program will check to see if the user is logged on. If so, the program will print all the processes that are running; otherwise, it will tell the user

    <user> is not logged on.

2. The *lookup* script depends on the *datafile* in order to run. In the *lookup* script, check to see if the *datafile* exists and if it is readable and writeable. Add a menu to the *lookup* script to resemble the following:

    [1] Add entry.
    [2] Delete entry.
    [3] View entry.
    [4] Exit.

    a. You already have the *Add entry* part of the script written. The *Add entry* routine should now include code that will check to see if the name is already in the *datafile* and if it is, tell the user so. If the name is not there, add the new entry.

    b. Now write the code for the *Delete entry*, *View entry*, and *Exit* functions.

    c. The *Delete* part of the script should first check to see if the entry exists before trying to remove it. If it does not exist, notify the user; otherwise, remove the entry and tell the user you removed it. On exit, make sure that you use a digit to represent the appropriate exit status.

    d. How do you check the exit status from the command line?

Lab 16: The Case Statement

1. The *ps* command is different on UCB and AT&T UNIX. On AT&T UNIX, the command to list all processes is

```
ps -ef
```

On UCB UNIX, the command is

```
ps -aux
```

Write a program called *systype* that will check for a number of different system types. The cases to test for will be

AIX
IRIX
HP–UX
SCO
OSF1
ULTRIX
SunOS (Solaris / SunOS)
OS

Solaris, HP–UX, SCO, and IRIX are AT&T-type systems. The rest are BSDish.

The version of UNIX you are using will be printed to *stdout*. The system name can be found with the *uname –s* command or from the */etc/motd* file.

Lab 17: Loops

Select one of the following:

1. Write a program called *mchecker* to check for new mail and write a message to the screen if new mail has arrived.

    a. The program will get the size of the mail spool file for the user. (The spool files are found in */usr/mail/$LOGNAME* on AT&T systems and */usr/spool/mail/$USER* on UCB systems. Use the *find* command if you cannot locate the file.) The script will execute in a continuous loop, once every 30 seconds. Each time the loop executes, it will compare the size of the mail spool file with its size from the previous loop. If the new size is greater than the old size, a message will be printed on your screen, saying *Username, You have new mail.*

    The size of a file can be found by looking at the output from *ls –l*, *wc –c* or from the *find* command.

2. Write a program called *dusage* that will mail a list of users, one at a time, a listing of the number of blocks they are currently using. The list of users will be in a file called *potential_hogs*. One of the users listed in the *potential_hogs* file will be *admin*.

    a. Use file testing to check that *potential_hogs* file exists and is readable.

    b. A loop will be used to iterate through the list of users. Only those users who are using over 500 blocks will be sent mail. The user *admin* will be skipped over (i.e., he or she does not get a mail message). The mail message will be stored in a *here document* in your *dusage* script.

    c. Keep a list of the names of each person who received mail. Do this by creating a log file. After everyone on the list has been sent mail, print the number of people who received mail and a list of their names.

Lab 18: Functions

1. Rewrite the *systype* program from Lab 9 as a function that returns the name of the system. Use this function to determine what options you will use with the *ps* command in the *checking* program.

2. The *ps* command to list all processes on AT&T UNIX is

   ```
   ps -ef
   ```

3. On BSD UNIX, the command is

   ```
   ps -aux
   ```

4. Write a function called *cleanup* that will remove all temporary files and exit the script. If the interrupt or hangup signal is sent while the program is running, the *trap* command will call the *cleanup* function.

5. Use a *here document* to add a new menu item to the *lookup* script to resemble the following:

   [1] Add entry
   [2] Delete entry
   [3] Change entry
   [4] View entry
   [5] Exit

   Write a function to handle each of the items in the menu. After the user has selected a valid entry and the function has completed, ask if the user would like to see the menu again. If an invalid entry is entered, the program should print

   Invalid entry, try again.

   and the menu will be redisplayed.

6. Create a submenu under *View entry* in the *lookup* script. The user will be asked if he or she would like to view specific information for a selected individual:

   a) Phone
   b) Address
   c) Birthday
   d) Salary

7. Use the *trap* command in a script to perform a cleanup operation if the interrupt signal is sent while the program is running.

chapter
9

The C Shell

9.1 The Interactive C Shell

Before the C shell displays a prompt, it is preceded by a number of processes. See Figure 9.1.

9.1.1 Startup

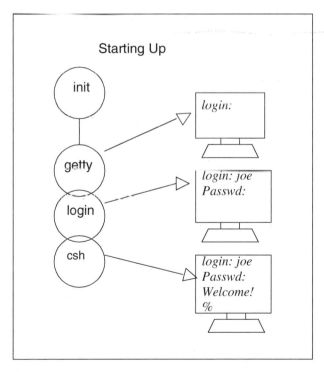

Figure 9.1 System startup and the C shell.

After the system boots, the first process to run is called *init*; it is assigned process identification number (PID) 1. It gets instructions from a file called *inittab* (System V) or spawns a *getty* process (BSD). These processes are responsible for opening up the terminal ports, for providing a place where input comes from (*stdin*), where standard output (*stdout*) and error (*stderr*) go, and for putting a login prompt on your screen. The */bin/login* program is then executed. The login program prompts for a password, encrypts and verifies your password, sets up an initial working environment, and then initiates the shell, */bin/csh*. The C shell looks in the user's home directory for a file called *.cshrc*, an initialization file allowing you to customize the C shell environment you will be working in. After executing commands in the *.cshrc* file, commands in the *.login* file are executed. The *.cshrc* file will be executed every time a new C shell is started. The *.login* file is executed only once when the user logs on, and also contains commands and variables to initialize the user's environment. After executing commands from those files, the percent sign prompt appears on your screen and the C shell awaits commands.

9.1.2 The Environment

Initialization Files.   After the *csh* program starts, it is programmed to execute two files in the user's home directory: the *.cshrc* file and the *.login* file. These files allow users to initialize their own environments.

The *.cshrc* File.   The *.cshrc* file contains C shell variable settings and is executed every time a *csh* subshell is started. Aliases and history are normally set here.

EXAMPLE 9.1

```
(The .cshrc File)
1   if ( $?prompt ) then
2       set prompt = "\! stardust > "
3       set history = 32
4       set savehist = 5
5       set noclobber
6       set filec fignore = ( .o )
7       set cdpath = ( /home/jody/ellie/bin /usr/local/bin /usr/bin )
8       set ignoreeof
9       alias m more
        alias status 'date;du -s'
        alias cd 'cd \!*;set prompt = "\! <$cwd> "'
    endif
```

EXPLANATION

1   If the prompt has been set (*$?prompt*), the shell is running interactively; i.e., it is not running in a script.

2   The primary prompt is set to the number of the current history event, the name *stardust*, and a > character. This will change the % prompt, the default.

EXPLANATION (CONTINUED)

3 The *history* variable is set to *32*. This controls the number of history events that will appear on the screen. The last 32 commands you entered will be displayed when you type *history* (see "Command Line History" on page 340).

4 Normally, when you log out, the history list is cleared. The *savehist* variable allows you to save a specified number of commands from the end of the history list. In this example, the last 5 commands will be saved in a file in your home directory, the *.history* file, so that when you log in again, the shell can check to see if that file exists and put the history lines saved at the top of the new history list.

5 The *noclobber* variable is set to protect the user from inadvertently removing files when using redirection. For example, *sort myfile > myfile* will destroy *myfile*. With *noclobber* set, the message *file exists* will appear on the screen.

6 The *filec* variable is used for filename completion so that you only need to type the first number of significant characters in a filename, press the ESC key, and the shell will complete the rest of the filename. By pressing ^D (Control-D) when typing in the filename, the C shell will display a list of files that match that string. The *fignore* variable allows you to exclude files that you do not want affected by filename completion. In this case, all the *.o* filenames (object files) will not be affected by *filec*, even though *filec* is set (see "Filename Completion: The filec Variable" on page 355).

7 The *cdpath* variable is assigned a list of path elements. When changing directories, if you specify just the directory name, and that directory is not a subdirectory directly below the current working directory, the shell will search the *cdpath* directory entries to see if it can find the directory in any of those locations and then will change the directory.

8 The *ignoreeof* variable prevents you from logging out with ^D. UNIX utilities that accept input from the keyboard, such as the *mail* program, are terminated by pressing ^D. Often, on a slow system, the user will be tempted to press ^D more than once. The first time, the *mail* program would be terminated, the second time, the user is logged out. By setting *ignoreeof*, you are required to type *logout* to log out.

9 The *aliases* are set to give a shorthand notation for a single command or group of commands. Now when you type the alias, the command(s) assigned to it will be executed. The alias for the *more* command is *m*. Every time you type *m*, the *more* command is executed. The *status* alias prints the date and a summary of the user's disk usage. The *cd* alias creates a new prompt every time the user changes directory. The new prompt will contain the number of the current history event (\!*) and the current working directory, *$cwd* surrounded by < >. (see "Aliases" on page 345).

The *.login* File. The *.login* file is executed one time when you first log in. It normally contains environment variables and terminal settings. It is the file where window applications are usually started. Since environment variables are inherited by processes spawned from this shell and only need to be set once, and terminal settings do not have to be reset for every process, those settings belong in the *.login* file.

EXAMPLE 9.2

```
(The .login File)
1   stty -istrip
2   stty erase ^H
3   #
    # If possible start the windows system.
    # Give a user a chance to bail out
    #
4   if ( `tty` == "/dev/console" ) then
5       if ( $TERM == "sun" || $TERM == "AT386" ) then
6           if ( ${?OPENWINHOME} == 0 ) then
7               setenv OPENWINHOME /usr/openwin
8           endif
        echo ""
9       echo -n "Starting OpenWindows in 5 seconds\
            (type Control-C to interrupt)"
10      sleep 5
        echo ""
11      $OPENWINHOME/bin/openwin
12      clear
13      logout
        endif
    endif
```

EXPLANATION

1   The *stty* command sets options for the terminal. Input characters will not be stripped to seven bits if *-istrip* is an option.

2   The *stty* command sets the Backspace key (Control-H) to erase characters.

3   Any line beginning with a # is a comment. It is not an executable statement.

4   If the current terminal window (*tty*) is the console (*/dev/console*), the next line is executed; otherwise, program control goes to the last *endif*.

5   If the value of the *TERM* variable is equal to *sun* or *AT386*, then the next line is executed.

6   If the *OPENWINHOME* environment variable has not been set (*$?* is *0* if not set, and *1* if set), the next line is executed.

7   The *OPENWINHOME* environment variable is set to */usr/openwin*.

8   This *endif* ends the *if* on line 5.

9   The line is displayed on the screen, letting the user know that *OpenWindows* is starting unless Control-C is typed within the next 5 seconds.

10 The program sleeps (stops execution) for 5 seconds.

11 The *openwin* program is started. A set of terminal windows (shell and command tool windows and a console window) will appear on the screen.

12 After closing windows, the screen will be cleared.

13 The user will be logged out.

The Search Path.   The *path* variable is used by the shell to locate commands typed at the command line. The search is from left to right. The dot represents the current working directory. If the command is not found in any of the directories listed in the path, or in the present working directory, the shell sends the message *Command not found* to standard error. It is recommended that the path be set in the *.login* file.[1] The search path is set differently in the C shell than it is in the Bourne and Korn shells. Each of the elements is separated by whitespace.

```
set path = (/usr/bin /usr/ucb /bin /usr .)
echo $path
/usr/bin /usr/ucb /bin /usr .
```

The environment variable *PATH* will display as:

```
echo $PATH
/usr/bin:/usr/ucb:/bin:.
```

The C shell internally updates the environment variable for *PATH* to maintain compatibility with other programs (such as the Bourne or Korn shells) that may be started from this shell and will need to use the *path* variable.

The *rehash* Command.   The shell builds an internal hash table consisting of the contents of the directories listed in the search path. (If the dot is in the search path, the files in the dot directory, the current working directory, are not put in the hash table.) For efficiency, the shell uses the hash table to find commands that are typed at the command line, rather than searching the path each time. If a new command is added to one of the directories already listed in the search path, the internal hash table must be recomputed. This is done by typing

```
% rehash
```

(The % is the C shell prompt.) The hash table is also automatically recomputed when you change your path at the prompt or start another shell.

The *hashstat* Command.   The *hashstat* command displays performance statistics to show the effectiveness of its search for commands from the hash table. The statistics are in terms of "hits" and "misses." If the shell finds most of its commands you use at the end of your path, it has to work harder than if they were at the front of the path, resulting in a higher number of misses than hits. In such cases, you can put the most heavily hit directory toward the front of the path to improve performance.

```
% hashstat
2 hits, 13 misses, 13%
```

---

1. Do not confuse the search path variable with the *cdpath* variable set in the *.cshrc* file.

The *source* Command.   The *source* command is a shell built-in command, that is, part of the shell's internal code. It is used to execute a command or set of commands from a file. Normally, when a command is executed, the shell forks a child process to execute the command, so that any changes made will not affect the original shell, called the parent shell. The *source* command causes the program to be executed in the current shell, so that any variables set within the file will become part of the environment of the current shell. The *source* command is normally used to reexecute the *.cshrc* or *.login* if either has been modified. For example, if the *path* is changed after logging in, type

```
% source .login or .cshrc
```

The Shell Prompts.   The C shell has two prompts: the *primary* prompt, a percent sign (%), and the *secondary* prompt, a question mark (?). The primary prompt is the one displayed on the terminal after you have logged in; it waits for you to type commands. The primary prompt can be reset. If you are writing scripts at the prompt that require C shell programming constructs, for example, decision-making or looping, the secondary prompt will appear so that you can continue onto the next line. It will continue to appear after each newline, until the construct has been properly terminated. The secondary prompt cannot be reset.   *IT IS ALWAYS ?*

The Primary Prompt.   When running interactively, the prompt waits for you to type a command and press the Enter key. If you do not want to use the default prompt, reset it in the *.cshrc* file and it will be set for this and all other C subshells. If you only want it set for this login session, set it at the shell prompt.

EXAMPLE 9.3
```
1   % set prompt = "$LOGNAME > "
2   ellie >
```
EXPLANATION
1   The primary prompt is assigned the user's login name, followed by a > symbol and a space.
2   The new prompt is displayed.

The Secondary Prompt.   The secondary prompt appears when you are writing on-line scripts at the prompt. Whenever shell programming constructs are entered, followed by a newline, the secondary prompt appears and continues to appear until the construct is properly terminated. Writing scripts correctly at the prompt takes practice. Once the command is entered and you press Enter, you cannot back up, and the C shell history mechanism does not save commands typed at the secondary prompt.

EXAMPLE 9.4

```
1   % foreach pal (joe tom ann)
2   ? mail $pal < memo
3   ? end
4   %
```

EXPLANATION

1   This is an example of on-line scripting. Because the C shell is expecting further input after the *foreach* loop is entered, the secondary prompt appears. The *foreach* loop processes each word in the parenthesized list.

2   The first time in the loop, *joe* is assigned to the variable *pal*. The user *joe* is sent the contents of *memo* in the mail. Then next time through the loop, *tom* is assigned to the variable *pal*, and so on.

3   The *end* statement marks the end of the loop. When all of the items in the parenthesized list have been processed, the loop ends and the primary prompt is displayed.

4   The primary prompt is displayed.

9.1.3 The Command Line

After logging in, the C shell displays its primary prompt, by default a percent sign. The shell is your command interpreter. When the shell is running interactively, it reads commands from the terminal and breaks the command line into words. A command line consists of one or more words (or tokens) separated by whitespace (blanks and/or tabs) and terminated with a newline, generated by pressing the Enter key. The first word is the command, and subsequent words are the command's options and/or arguments. The command may be a UNIX executable program such as *ls* or *pwd*, an alias, a built-in command such as *cd* or *jobs*, or a shell script. The command may contain special characters, called *metacharacters*, that the shell must interpret while parsing the command line. If the last character in the command line is a backslash, followed by a newline, the line can be continued to the next line.[2]

The Exit Status.   After a command or program terminates, it returns an *exit status* to the parent process. The exit status is a number between 0 and 255. By convention, when a program exits, if the status returned is zero, the command was successful in its execution. When the exit status is nonzero, the command failed in some way. The C shell status variable is set to the value of the exit status of the last command that was executed. Success or failure of a program is determined by the programmer who wrote the program.

---

2. The length of the command line can be 256 characters or more; it can be even higher on different versions of UNIX.

EXAMPLE 9.5

```
1 % grep "ellie" /etc/passwd
  ellie:GgMyBsSJavd16s:9496:40:Ellie Quigley:/home/jody/ellie
2 % echo $status
  0
3 % grep "nicky" /etc/passwd
4 % echo $status
  1
5 % grep "scott" /etc/passsswd
  grep: /etc/passsswd: No such file or directory
6 % echo $status
  2
```

EXPLANATION

1 The *grep* program searches for the pattern *ellie* in the */etc/passwd* file and is successful. The line from */etc/passwd* is displayed.

2 The status variable is set to the exit value of the *grep* command; *0* indicates success.

3 The *grep* program cannot find user *nicky* in the */etc/passwd* file.

4 The *grep* program cannot find the pattern, so it returns an exit status of *1*.

5 The *grep* fails because the file */etc/passsswd* cannot be opened.

6 *Grep* cannot find the file, so it returns an exit status of *2*.

Command Grouping. A command line can consist of multiple commands. Each command is separated by a semicolon and the command line is terminated with a newline.

EXAMPLE 9.6

```
% ls; pwd; cal 2001
```

EXPLANATION

The commands are executed from left to right until the newline is reached.

Commands may also be grouped so that all of the output is either piped to another command or redirected to a file. The shell executes commands in a subshell.

EXAMPLE 9.7

```
1 % ( ls ; pwd; cal 2001 ) > outputfile
2 % pwd; ( cd / ; pwd ) ; pwd
  /home/jody/ellie
  /
  /home/jody/ellie
```

EXPLANATION

1   The output of each of the commands is sent to the file called *outputfile*. Without the parentheses, the output of the first two commands would go to the screen, and only the output of the *cal* command would be redirected to the output file.

2   The *pwd* command displays the present working directory. The parentheses cause the commands enclosed within them to be processed by a subshell. The *cd* command is built into the shell. While in the subshell, the directory is changed to *root* and the present working directory is displayed. When out of the subshell, the present working directory of the original shell is displayed.

Conditional Execution of Commands.   With conditional execution, two command strings are separated by two special metacharacters, double ampersand and double vertical (*&&* and *||*). The command on the right of either of these metacharacters will or will not be executed based on the exit condition of the command on the left.

EXAMPLE 9.8

```
% grep '^tom:' /etc/passwd && mail tom < letter
```

EXPLANATION

If the first command is successful (has a zero exit status), the second command after the *&&* is executed. If the *grep* command successfully finds *tom* in the *passwd* file, the command on the right will be executed: The *mail* program will send *tom* the contents of the *letter* file.

EXAMPLE 9.9

```
% grep '^tom:' /etc/passwd || echo "tom is not a user here."
```

EXPLANATION

If the first command fails (has a nonzero exit status), the second command after the *||* is executed. If the *grep* command does not find *tom* in the *passwd* file, the command on the right will be executed: The *echo* program will print *tom is not a user here.* to the screen.

Commands in the Background.   Normally, when you execute a command, it runs in the foreground, and the prompt does not reappear until the command has completed execution. It is not always convenient to wait for the command to complete. By placing an ampersand at the end of the command line, the shell will return the shell prompt immediately so that you do not have to wait for the last command to complete before starting another one. The command running in the background is called a *background job* and its output will be sent to the screen as it processes. It can be confusing if two commands are sending output to the screen concurrently. To avoid confusion, you can send the output of the job running in the background to a file or pipe it to another device such

as a printer. It is often handy to start a new shell window in the background, so you will
have access to both the window from which you started and the new shell window.

EXAMPLE 9.10

```
1   % man xview | lp&
2   [1] 1557
3   %
```

EXPLANATION

1   The output from the man pages for the *xview* program is piped to the printer. The
    ampersand at the end of the command line puts the job in the background.

2   There are two numbers that appear on the screen: The number in square brackets
    indicates that this is the first job to be placed in the background, and the second
    number is the PID of this job.

3   The shell prompt appears immediately. While your program is running in the
    background, the shell is prompting you for another command in the foreground.

9.1.4 Command Line History

The history mechanism is built into the C shell. It keeps a numbered list of the commands (called *history events*) that you have typed at the command line. You can recall a
command from the history list and reexecute it without retyping the command. The history substitution character, the exclamation point, is often called the *bang* character. The
history built-in command displays the history list.

EXAMPLE 9.11

```
(The Command Line)
% history
1 cd
2 ls
3 more /etc/fstab
4 /etc/mount
5 sort index
6 vi index
```

EXPLANATION

The history list displays the last commands that were typed at the command line. Each
event in the list is preceded with a number.

Setting History.   The C shell *history* variable is set to the number of events you want
to save from the history list and display on the screen. Normally, this is set in the *.cshrc*
file, the user's initialization file.

EXAMPLE   9.12

```
set history=50
```

EXPLANATION

The last *50* commands typed at the terminal are saved and may be displayed on the screen by typing the *history* command.

Saving History.   To save history events across logins, set the *savehist* variable. This variable is normally set in the *.cshrc* file, the user's initialization file.

EXAMPLE   9.13

```
set savehist=25
```

EXPLANATION

The last *25* commands from the history list are saved and will be at the top of the history list the next time you log in.

Displaying History.   The *history* command displays the events in the history list. The history command also has options that control the number of events and the format of the events that will be displayed. The numbering of events does not necessarily start at one. If you have 100 commands on the history list, and you have set the history variable to 25, you will only see the last 25 commands saved.

EXAMPLE   9.14

```
% history
1 ls
2 vi file1
3 df
4 ps -eaf
5 history
6 more /etc/passwd
7 cd
8 echo $USER
9 set
```

EXPLANATION

The history list is displayed. Each command is numbered.

EXAMPLE 9.15

```
% history -h       # Print without line numbers
ls
vi file1
df
ps -eaf
history
more /etc/passwd
cd
echo $USER
set
history -n
```

EXPLANATION
The history list is displayed without line numbers.

EXAMPLE 9.16

```
% history -r       # Print the history list in reverse
11 history -r
10 history -h
 9 set
 8 echo $USER
 7 cd
 6 more /etc/passwd
 5 history
 4 ps -eaf
 3 df
 2 vi file1
 1 ls
```

EXPLANATION
The history list is displayed in reverse order.

EXAMPLE 9.17

```
% history 5        # Prints the last 5 events on the history list
 7   echo $USER
 8   cd
 9   set
10   history -n
11   history 5
```

EXPLANATION
The last five commands on the history list are displayed.

Reexecuting Commands. To reexecute a command from the history list, the exclamation point (bang) is used. If you type two exclamation points (!!), the last command is reexecuted. If you type the exclamation point followed by a number, the number is associated with the command from the history list and the command is executed. If you type an exclamation point and a letter, the last command that started with that letter is executed. The caret (^) is also used as a shortcut method for editing the previous command.

EXAMPLE 9.18

```
1   % date
    Mon Feb  8 12:27:35 PST 2001

2   % !!
    date
    Mon Feb  8 12:28:25 PST 2001

3   % !3
    date
    Mon Feb  8 12:29:26 PST 2001

4   % !d
    date
    Mon Feb  8 12:30:09 PST 2001

5   % dare
    dare: Command not found.

6   % ^r^t
    date
    Mon Feb  8 12:33:25 PST 2001
```

EXPLANATION

1   The UNIX *date* command is executed at the command line. The history list is updated. This is the last command on the list.

2   The *!!* (bang bang) gets the last command from the history list; the command is reexecuted.

3   The third command on the history list is reexecuted.

4   The last command on the history list that started with the letter *d* is reexecuted.

5   The command is mistyped.

6   The carets are used to substitute letters from the last command on the history list. The first occurrence of an *r* is replaced with a *t*.

EXAMPLE 9.19

```
1   % cat  file1 file2 file3

        <Contents of files displayed here>

    % vi !:1
    vi file1

2   % cat file1 file2 file3

        <Contents of file, file2, and file3 are displayed here>

    % ls !:2
    ls file2
    file2

3   % cat file1 file2 file3
    % ls  !:3
    ls file3
    file3

4   % echo a b c
    a b c
    % echo !$
    echo c
    c

5   % echo a b c
    a b c
    % echo !^
    echo a
    a

6   % echo a b c
    a b c
    % echo !*
    echo a b c
    a b c

7   % !!:p
    echo a b c
```

EXPLANATION

1   The *cat* command displays the contents of *file1* to the screen. The history list is updated. The command line is broken into words, starting with word number zero. If the word number is preceded by a colon, that word can be extracted from the history list. The *!:1* notation means, *get the first argument from the last command on the history list and replace it in the command string.* The first argument from the last command is *file1.* (Word *0* is the command itself.)

2   The *!:2* is replaced with the second argument of the last command, *file2,* and given as an argument to *ls. file2* is printed. (*file2* is the third word.)

3   *ls !:3* reads, *go to the last command on the history list and get the fourth word (words start at zero) and pass it to the* ls *command as an argument* (*file3* is the fourth word).

4   The bang (*!*) with the dollar sign (*$*) refers to the last argument of the last command on the history list. The last argument is *c.*

5   The caret (*^*) represents the first argument after the command. The bang (*!*) with the *^* refers to the first argument of the last command on the history list. The first argument of the last command is *a.*

6   The asterisk (*) represents all arguments after the command. The bang (*!*) with the * refers to all of the arguments of the last command on the history list.

7   The last command from the history list is printed but not executed. The history list is updated. You could now perform caret substitutions on that line.

9.1.5 Aliases

An *alias* is a C shell user-defined abbreviation for a command. Aliases are useful when a command has a number of options and arguments or the syntax is difficult to remember. Aliases set at the command line are not inherited by subshells. Aliases are normally set in the *.cshrc* file. Since the *.cshrc* is executed when a new shell is started, any aliases set there will get reset for the new shell. Aliases may also be passed into shell scripts, but will cause potential portability problems unless they are directly set within the script.

Listing Aliases.   The *alias* built-in command lists all set aliases. The alias is printed first, followed by the real command or commands it represents.

EXAMPLE 9.20

```
% alias
co        compress
cp        cp -i
ls1       enscript -B -r -Porange -f Courier8 !* &
mailq     /usr/lib/sendmail -bp
mroe      more
mv        mv -i
rn        /usr/spool/news/bin/rn3
uc        uncompress
```

EXAMPLE 9.20 (CONTINUED)

```
uu      uudecode
vg      vgrind -t -s11 !:1 | lpr -t
weekly (cd /home/jody/ellie/activity; ./weekly_report; echo Done)
```

EXPLANATION

The *alias* command lists the alias (nickname) for the command in the first column and the real command the alias represents in the second column.

Creating Aliases. The *alias* command is used to create an alias. The first argument is the name of the alias, the nickname for the command. The rest of the line consists of the command or commands that will be executed when the alias is executed. Multiple commands are separated by a semicolon, and commands containing spaces and meta-characters are surrounded by single quotes.

EXAMPLE 9.21

```
1   % alias m more
2   % alias mroe more
3   % alias lF 'ls -alF'
4   % alias cd  'cd \!*; set prompt = "$cwd   >"'
    % cd ..
    /home/jody >  cd /            # New prompt displayed
    / >
```

EXPLANATION

1   The nickname for the *more* command is set to *m*.

2   The alias for the *more* command is set to *mroe*. This is handy if you can't spell.

3   The alias definition is enclosed in quotes because of the whitespace. The alias *lF* is a nickname for the command *ls –alF*.

4   When *cd* is executed, the alias for *cd* will cause *cd* to go to the directory named as an argument and will then reset the prompt to the current working directory followed by the string >. The *!** is used by the alias in the same way it is used by the history mechanism. The backslash prevents the history mechanism from evaluating the *!** first before the alias has a chance to use it. The *\!** represents the arguments from the most recent command on the history list.

Deleting Aliases. The *unalias* command is used to delete an alias. To temporarily turn off an alias, the alias name is preceded by a backslash.

EXAMPLE 9.22

```
1   % unalias mroe
2   % \cd ..
```

EXPLANATION

1   The *unalias* command deletes the alias *mroe* from the list of defined aliases.

2   The alias *cd* is temporarily turned off for this execution of the command only.

Alias Loop.   An alias loop occurs when an alias definition references another alias that references back to the original alias.

EXAMPLE 9.23

```
1   % alias m more
2   % alias mroe m
3   % alias m mroe          # Causes a loop
4   % m datafile
    Alias loop.
```

EXPLANATION

1   The alias is *m*. The alias definition is *more*. Every time *m* is used, the *more* command is executed.

2   The alias is *mroe*. The alias definition is *m*. If *mroe* is typed, the alias *m* is invoked and the *more* command is executed.

3   This is the culprit. If alias *m* is used, it invokes alias *mroe*, and alias *mroe* references back to *m*, causing an alias loop. Nothing bad happens. You just get an error message.

4   Alias *m* is used. It is circular. M calls *mroe* and *mroe* calls *m*, then *m* calls *mroe*, etc., etc. Rather than looping forever, the C shell catches the problem and displays an error message.

9.1.6 Job Control

Job control is a powerful feature of the C shell that allows you to run programs, called *jobs*, in the background or foreground. Normally, a command typed at the command line runs in the foreground, and will continue until it has finished. If you have windows, job control may not be necessary, since you can simply open another window to start a new task. On the other hand, with a single terminal, job control is a very useful feature. For a list of job commands, see Table 9.1.

Table 9.1 Job Control Commands

Command	Meaning
jobs	Lists all the jobs running.
^Z (Control-Z)	Stops (suspends) the job; the prompt appears on the screen.
bg	Starts running the stopped job in the background.
fg	Brings a background job to the foreground.
kill	Sends the kill signal to a specified job.

The Ampersand and Background Jobs.   If you expect a command to take a long time to complete, you can append the command with an ampersand and the job will execute in the background. The C shell prompt returns immediately and now you can type another command. Now the two commands are running concurrently, one in the background and one in the foreground. They both send their standard output to the screen. If you place a job in the background, it is a good idea to redirect its output either to a file or pipe it to a device such as a printer.

EXAMPLE 9.24

```
1   % find . -name core -exec rm {} \; &
2   [1]  543
3   %
```

EXPLANATION

1   The *find* command runs in the background. (Without the *–print* option, the *find* command does not send any output to the screen).[3]

2   The number in square brackets indicates this is the first job to be run in the background and the PID for this process is 543.

3   The prompt returns immediately. The shell waits for user input.

The Suspend Key Sequence and Background Jobs.   To suspend a program, the suspend key sequence, ^Z, is issued. The job is now suspended (stopped), the shell prompt is displayed, and the program will not resume until the *fg* or *bg* commands are issued. (When using the *vi* editor, the ZZ command writes and saves a file. Do not confuse this with ^Z, which would suspend the *vi* session.) If you try to log out when a job is suspended, the message *There are stopped jobs* appears on the screen.

---

3. The *find* syntax requires a semicolon at the end of an *exec* statement. The semicolon is preceded by a backslash to prevent the shell from interpreting it.

The *jobs* Command.   The C shell built-in command, *jobs*, displays the programs that are currently active and either running or suspended in the background. *Running* means the job is executing in the background. When a job is *stopped*, it is suspended; it is not in execution. In both cases, the terminal is free to accept other commands.

EXAMPLE 9.25

```
(The Command Line)
1   % jobs
2   [1] + Stopped vi filex
    [2] - Running sleep 25

3   % jobs -l
    [1] + 355  Stopped vi filex
    [2] - 356  Running sleep 25

4   [2] Done sleep 25
```

EXPLANATION

1   The *jobs* command lists the currently active jobs.

2   The notation *[1]* is the number of the first job; the plus sign indicates that the job is not the most recent job to be placed in the background; the dash indicates that this is the most recent job put in the background; *Stopped* means that this job was suspended with ^Z and is not currently active.

3   The *–l* option (long listing) displays the number of the job as well as the PID of the job. The notation *[2]* is the number of the second job, in this case, the last job placed in the background. The dash indicates that this is the most recent job. The *sleep* command is running in the background.

4   After *sleep* has been running for 25 seconds, the job will complete and a message saying that it has finished appears on the screen.

The Foreground and Background Commands.   The *fg* command brings a background job into the foreground. The *bg* command starts a suspended job running in the background. A percent sign and the number of a job can be used as arguments to *fg* and *bg* if you want to select a particular job for job control.

EXAMPLE 9.26

```
1   % jobs
2   [1] + Stopped vi filex
    [2] - Running cc prog.c -o prog
3   % fg %1
    vi filex
    (vi session starts)
4   % kill %2
    [2] Terminated cc prog.c -o prog
```

EXAMPLE 9.26 (CONTINUED)

```
5   % sleep 15
    (Press ^z)
    Stopped
6   % bg
    [1] sleep 15 &
    [1] Done    sleep 15
```

EXPLANATION

1   The *jobs* command lists currently running processes, called jobs.

2   The first job stopped is the *vi* session, the second job is the *cc* command.

3   The job numbered *[1]* is brought to the foreground. The number is preceded with a percent sign.

4   The *kill* command is built-in. It sends the *TERM* (terminate) signal, by default, to a process. The argument is either the number or the PID of the process.

5   The *sleep* command is stopped by pressing ^Z. The *sleep* command is not using the CPU and is suspended in the background.

6   The *bg* command causes the last background job to start executing in the background. The *sleep* program will start the countdown in seconds before execution resumes.[4]

9.1.7   Metacharacters

Metacharacters are special characters that are used to represent something other than themselves. As a rule of thumb, characters that are neither letters nor numbers may be metacharacters. The shell has its own set of metacharacters, often called *shell wildcards*. Shell metacharacters can be used to group commands together, to abbreviate filenames and pathnames, to redirect and pipe input/output, to place commands in the background, and so forth. Table 9.2 presents a partial list of shell metacharacters.

Table 9.2   Shell Metacharacters

Metacharacter	Purpose	Example	Meaning
$	Variable substitution	*set name=Tom echo* *$name* *Tom*	Sets the variable *name* to *Tom*; displays the value stored there.
!	History substitution	*!3*	Reexecutes the third event from the history list.

---

4. Programs such as *grep*, *sed*, and *awk* have a set of metacharacters, called regular expression metacharacters, for pattern matching. These should not be confused with shell metacharacters.

Table 9.2   Shell Metacharacters (continued)

Metacharacter	Purpose	Example	Meaning
*	Filename substitution	rm *	Removes all files.
?	Filename substitution	ls ??	Lists all two-character files.
[ ]	Filename substitution	cat f[123]	Displays contents of f1, f2, f3.
;	Command separator	ls;date;pwd	Each command is executed in turn.
&	Background processing	lp mbox&	Printing is done in the background. Prompt returns immediately.
>	Redirection of output	ls > file	Redirects standard output to file. *>> APPEND*
<	Redirection of input	ls < file	Redirects standard input from file.
>&	Redirection of output and error	ls >& file	Redirects both output and errors to file. *>>& APPEND BOTH stdout stderr*
>!	If noclobber is set, override it	ls >! file	If file exists, truncate and overwrite it, even if noclobber is set.
>>!	If noclobber is set, override it	ls >>! file	If file does not exist, create it; even if noclobber is set. *>>&!*
( )	Groups commands to be executed in a subshell	(ls ; pwd) >tmp	Executes commands and sends output to tmp file.
{ }	Groups commands to be executed in this shell	{ cd /; echo $cwd }	Changes to root directory and displays current working directory.

Filename Substitution.   When evaluating the command line, the shell uses meta-characters to abbreviate filenames or pathnames that match a certain set of characters. The filename substitution metacharacters listed in Table 9.3 are expanded into an alpha-betically listed set of filenames. The process of expanding a metacharacter into filenames is also called *globbing*. Unlike the other shells, when the C shell cannot substitute a file-name for the metacharacter it is supposed to represent, the shell reports *No match*.

Table 9.3 Shell Metacharacters and Filename Substitution

Metacharacter	Meaning
*	Matches zero or more characters.
?	Matches exactly one character.
[abc]	Matches one character in the set: *a*, *b*, or *c*.
[a–z]	Matches one character in the range *a* to *z*.
{a, ile,ax}	Matches for a character or set of characters.
~	Substitutes the user's home directory for tilde.
\	Escapes or disables the metacharacter.

9.1.8 Expanding the Metacharacters

The shell performs filename substitution by evaluating its metacharacters and replacing them with the appropriate letters or digits in a filename.

The Asterisk.   The asterisk matches zero or more characters in a filename.

EXAMPLE 9.27

```
1   % ls
    a.c b.c abc ab3 file1 file2 file3 file4 file5

2   % echo *
    a.c b.c abc ab3 file1 file2 file3 file4 file5

3   % ls  *.c
    a.c b.c

4   % rm  z*p
    No match.
```

EXPLANATION

1   All the files in the current directory are listed.
2   The *echo* program prints all its arguments to the screen. The asterisk (also called a *splat*) is a wildcard that means, *match for zero or more of any characters found in a filename*. All the files in the directory are matched and echoed to the screen.
3   Filenames ending in *.c* are listed.
4   Since none of the files in the directory start with *z*, the shell reports *No match*.

The Question Mark.   The question mark matches exactly one character in a filename.

EXAMPLE 9.28

```
1   % ls
    a.c b.c abc ab3 file1 file2 file3 file4 file5

2   % ls ???
    abc ab3

3   % echo How are you?
    No match.

4   % echo How are you\?
    How are you?
```

EXPLANATION

1   All the files in the current directory are listed.

2   The question mark matches for a single-character filename. Any filenames consisting of three characters are listed.

3   The shell looks for a filename spelled *y-o-u* followed by one character. There is not a file in the directory that matches these characters. The shell prints *No match*.

4   The backslash preceding the question mark is used to turn off the special meaning of the question mark. Now the shell treats the question mark as a literal character.

The Square Brackets.   The square brackets match a filename for one character from a set or range of characters.

EXAMPLE 9.29

```
1   % ls
    a.c b.c abc ab3 file1 file2 file3 file4 file5 file10
    file11  file12

2   % ls file[123]
    file1 file2 file3

3   % ls [A-Za-z][a-z][1-5]
    ab3

4   % ls file1[0-2]
    file10 file11 file12
```

EXPLANATION

1   All the files in the current directory are listed.

2   Filenames starting with *file* and follwed with a *1*, *2*, or *3* are matched and listed.

EXPLANATION (CONTINUED)

3   Filenames starting with a letter (either uppercase or lowercase) followed by a low-
      ercase letter, and followed by a number between *1* and *5* are matched and listed.

4   Filenames starting with *file1* and followed by a *0, 1,* or *2* are listed.

The Curly Braces.   The curly braces (*{}*)match for a character or string of characters
in a filename.

EXAMPLE 9.30

```
1   % ls
    a.c b.c abc ab3 ab4 ab5 file1 file2 file3 file4 file5 foo
    faa fumble

2   % ls f{oo,aa,umble}
    foo faa fumble

3   % ls a{.c,c,b[3-5]}
    a.c ab3 ab4 ab5
```

EXPLANATION

1   All the files in the current directory are listed.

2   Files starting with *f* and followed by the strings *oo, aa,* or *umble* are listed. Spaces
      inside the curly braces will cause the error message *Missing }.*

3   Files starting with *a* followed by *.c, c,* or *b3, b4,* or *b5* are listed. (The square brack-
      ets can be used inside the curly braces.)

Escaping Metacharacters.   The backslash is used to escape the special meaning of
a single character. The escaped character will represent itself.

EXAMPLE 9.31

```
1   % gotta light?
    No match.
2   % gotta light\?
    gotta: Command not found.
```

EXPLANATION

1   This is a little UNIX joke. The question mark is a file substitution metacharacter
      and evaluates to a single character. The shell looks for a file in the present working
      directory that contains the characters *l-i-g-h-t,* followed by a single character. If
      the shell cannot find the file, it reports *No match.* This shows you something about
      the order in which the shell parses the command line. The metacharacters are
      evaluated before the shell tries to locate the *gotta* command.

EXPLANATION (CONTINUED)

2   The backslash protects the metacharacter from interpretation, often called escaping the metacharacter. Now the shell does not complain about a *No match,* but searches the path for the *gotta* command, which is not found.

Tilde Expansion.   The tilde character by itself expands to the full pathname of the user's home directory. When the tilde is prepended to a username, it expands to the full pathname of that user's home directory. When prepended to a path, it expands to the home directory and the rest of the pathname.

EXAMPLE 9.32

```
1   % echo ~
    /home/jody/ellie

2   % cd ~/desktop/perlstuff
    % pwd
    /home/jody/ellie/desktop/perlstuff

3   % cd ~joe
    % pwd
    /home/bambi/joe
```

EXPLANATION

1   The *tilde* expands to the user's home directory.
2   The tilde followed by a pathname expands to the user's home directory, followed by */desktop/perlstuff.*
3   The tilde followed by a username expands to the home directory of the user. In this example, the directory is changed to that user's home directory.

Filename Completion: The *filec* Variable.   When running interactively, the C shell provides a shortcut method for typing a filename or username. The built-in *filec* variable, when set, is used for what is called filename completion. If you type the first few significant characters of a file in the current working directory and press the ESC key, the shell fills in the rest of the filename, provided that there are not a number of other files beginning with the same characters. If you type Control-D after the partial spelling of the file, the shell will print out a list of files that match those characters. The terminal beeps if there are multiple matches. If the list begins with a tilde, the shell attempts to expand that list to a username.

EXAMPLE 9.33

```
1   % set filec
2   % ls
    rum rumple rumplestilsken run2
```

EXAMPLE 9.33 (CONTINUED)

```
3   % ls ru[ESC]5      # terminal beeps
4   % ls rum^D
    rum rumple rumplestilsken
5   % ls rump[ESC]
    rumple
6   % echo ~ell[ESC]
    /home/jody/ellie
```

EXPLANATION

1   The special C shell variable *filec* is set. Filename completion can be used.

2   The files in the present working directory are listed.

3   Filename completion is attempted. The letters *r* and *u* are not unique; that is, the shell does not know which one to pick, so it causes the terminal to beep.

4   After the letters *r-u-m* are typed, ^D is pressed. A list of all filenames beginning with *rum* are displayed.

5   The first filename starting with *rump* is completed and displayed.

6   If a tilde precedes a partially spelled username, the shell will attempt to complete the spelling of the user's name and display the user's home directory.

Turning Off Metacharacters with *noglob*.   If the *noglob* variable is set, filename substitution is turned off, meaning that all metacharacters represent themselves; they are not used as wildcards. This can be useful when searching for patterns in programs like *grep, sed,* or *awk,* which may contain metacharacters that the shell may try to expand.

EXAMPLE 9.34

```
1   % set noglob
2   % echo * ?? [] ~
    * ?? [] ~
```

EXPLANATION

1   The variable *noglob* is set. It turns off the special meaning of the wildcards.

2   The metacharacters are displayed as themselves without any interpretation.

9.1.9 Redirection and Pipes

Normally, standard output (*stdout*) from a command goes to the screen, standard input (*stdin*) comes from the keyboard, and error messages (*stderr*) go to the screen. The shell allows you to use the special redirection metacharacters to redirect the input/output to

---

5. [ESC] stands for Escape key.

or from a file. The redirection operators (<, >, >>, >&) are followed by a filename. This file is opened by the shell before the command on the left-hand side is executed.

Pipes, represented by a vertical bar (|) symbol, allow the output of one command to be sent to the input of another command. The command on the left-hand side of the pipe is called the *writer* because it writes to the pipe. The command on the right-hand side of the pipe is the *reader* because it reads from the pipe. See Table 9.4 for a list of redirection and pipe metacharacters.

Table 9.4   Redirection Metacharacters

Metacharacter	*Meaning*
command < *file*	Redirects input from *file* to *command*.
command > *file*	Redirects output from *command* to *file*.
command >& *file*	Redirects output and errors to *file*.
command >> *file*	Redirects output of *command* and appends it to *file*.
command >>& *file*	Redirects and appends output and errors of *command* to *file*.
command << WORD	Redirects input from first WORD to terminating WORD to *command*.
<input>	User input goes here. It will be treated as a doubly quoted string of text.
WORD	WORD marks the termination of input to command.
command | *command*	Pipes output of first *command* to input of second *command*
command |& *command*	Pipes output and errors of first *command* to input of second *command*.
command >! *file*	If the *noclobber* variable is set, override its effects for this command and either open or overwrite *file*.
command >>! *file*	Override *noclobber* variable; if *file* does not exist, it is created and output from *command* is appended to it.
command >>&! *file*	Override *noclobber* variable; if *file* does not exist, it is created and both output and errors are appended to it.

Redirecting Input.   Instead of the input coming from the terminal keyboard, it can be redirected from a file. The shell will open the file on the right-hand side of the < symbol and the program on the left will read from the file. If the file does not exist, the error *No such file or directory* will be reported by the C shell.

FORMAT

```
command < file
```

EXAMPLE 9.35

```
mail bob < memo
```

EXPLANATION

The file *memo* is opened by the shell, and the input is redirected to the *mail* program. Simply, the user *bob* is sent a file called *memo* by the *mail* program.

The *here document*.   The *here document* is another way to redirect input to a command. It is used in shell scripts for creating menus and processing input from other programs. Normally, programs that accept input from the keyboard are terminated with Control-D (^d). The *here document* provides an alternate way of sending input to a program and terminating the input without typing ^D. The << symbol is followed by a user-defined word, often called a *terminator*. Input will be directed to the command on the left-hand side of the << symbol until the user-defined terminator is reached. The final terminator is on a line by itself, and cannot be surrounded by any spaces. Variable and command substitution are performed within the *here document*. (Normally, *here documents* are used in shell scripts to create menus and provide input to commands such as *mail, bc, ex, ftp*, etc.)

FORMAT

```
command << MARK
        ... input ...
MARK
```

EXAMPLE 9.36

```
(Without the here document)
(The Command Line)
1   % cat
2   Hello There.
    How are you?
    I'm tired of this.
3   ^D

(The Output)
4   Hello There.
    How are you?
    I'm tired of this.
```

EXPLANATION

1   The *cat* program, without arguments, waits for keyboard input.

EXPLANATION (CONTINUED)

2   The user types input at the keyboard.

3   The user types ^D to terminate input to the *cat* program.

4   The *cat* program sends its output to the screen.

EXAMPLE 9.37

```
(With the here document)
(The Command Line)
1   % cat << DONE
2   Hello There.
    How are you?
    I'm tired of this.
3   DONE

(The Output)
4   Hello There.
    How are you?
    I'm tired of this.
```

EXPLANATION

1   The *cat* program will receive input from the first *DONE* to the terminating *DONE*.
    The words are user-defined terminators.

2   These lines are input. When the word *DONE* is reached, no more input is accepted.

3   The final terminator marks the end of input. There cannot be any spaces on either
    side of this word.

4   The text between the first word *DONE* and the final word *DONE* is the output of
    the *cat* command (from "here" to "here") and is sent to the screen. The final
    DONE must be against the left margin with no space or other text to the right of it.

EXAMPLE 9.38

```
(The Command Line)
1   % set name = steve
2   % mail $name << EOF
3   Hello there, $name
4   The hour is now `date +%H`
5   EOF
```

EXPLANATION

1   The shell variable *name* is assigned the username *steve*. (Normally, this example
    would be included in a shell script.)

2   The variable *name* is expanded within the *here document*.

EXPLANATION (CONTINUED)

3   The *mail* program will receive input until the terminator EOF is reached.

4   Command substitution is performed within the *here document*; that is, the command within the backquotes is executed and the output of the command is replaced within the string.

5   The terminator EOF is reached, and input to the *mail* program is stopped.

Redirecting Output.   By default, the standard output of a command or commands normally goes to the terminal screen. To redirect standard output from the screen to a file, the > symbol is used. The command is on the left-hand side of the > symbol, and a filename is on the right-hand side. The shell will open the file on the right-hand side of the > symbol. If the file does not exist, the shell will create it; if it does exist, the shell will open the file and truncate it. Often files are inadvertently removed when using redirection. (A special C shell variable, called *noclobber*, can be set to prevent redirection from clobbering an existing file. See Table 9.5.)

FORMAT

```
command > file
```

EXAMPLE 9.39

```
cat file1 file2 > file3
```

EXPLANATION

The contents of *file1* and *file2* are concatenated and the output is sent to *file3*. Remember that the shell opens *file3* before it attempts to execute the *cat* command. If *file3* already exists and contains data, the data will be lost. If *file3* does not exist, it will be created.

Appending Output to an Existing File.   To append output to an existing file, the >> symbol is used. If the file on the right-hand side of the >> symbol does not exist, it is created; if it does exist, the file is opened and output is appended to the end of the file.

FORMAT

```
command >> file
```

EXAMPLE 9.40

```
date >> outfile
```

EXPLANATION

The standard output of the *date* command is redirected and appended to *outfile*.

Redirecting Output and Error.   The *>&* symbol is used to redirect both standard output and standard error to a file. Normally, a command is either successful and sends its output to *stdout*, or fails and sends its error messages to *stderr*. Some recursive programs, such as *find* and *du*, send both standard output and errors to the screen as they move through the directory tree. By using the *>&* symbol, both standard output and standard error can be saved in a file and examined. The C shell does not provide a symbol for redirection of only standard error, but it is possible to get just the standard error by executing the command in a subshell. See Figure 9.2.

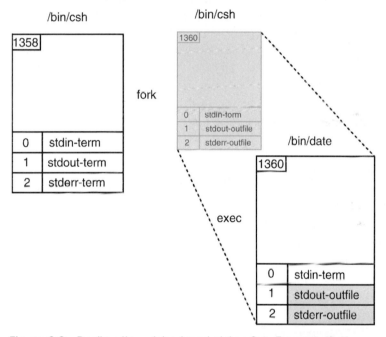

Figure 9.2   Redirecting *stdout* and *stderr*. See Example 9.41.

EXAMPLE   9.41

```
1   % date
    Tue Aug 3 10:31:56  PDT  2001
2   % date >& outfile
3   % cat outfile
    Tue Aug 3 10:31:56  PDT  2001
```

EXPLANATION

1   The output of the *date* command is sent to standard output, the screen.

2   The output and errors are sent to *outfile*.

3   Since there were no errors, the standard output is sent to *outfile* and the contents of the file are displayed.

EXAMPLE 9.42

```
1   % cp file1 file2
2   % cp file1
    Usage: cp [-ip] f1 f2; or: cp [-ipr] f1 ... fn d2

3   % cp file1 >& errorfile
4   % cat errorfile
    Usage: cp [-ip] f1 f2; or: cp [-ipr] f1 ... fn d2
```

EXPLANATION

1   To copy a file, the *cp* command requires both a source file and a destination file. The *cp* command makes a copy of *file1* and puts the copy in *file2*. Since the *cp* command is given the correct syntax, nothing is displayed to the screen. The copy was successful.

2   This time the destination file is missing and the *cp* command fails, sending an error to *stderr*, the terminal.

3   The *>&* symbol is used to send both *stdout* and *stderr* to *errorfile*. Since the only output from the command is the error message, that is what is saved in *errorfile*.

4   The contents of errorfile are displayed, showing that it contains the error message produced by the *cp* command.

Separating Output and Errors.   Standard output and standard error can be separated by enclosing the command in parentheses. When a command is enclosed in parentheses, the C shell starts up a subshell, handles redirection from within the subshell, and then executes the command. By using the technique shown in Example 9.43, the standard output can be separated from the errors.

EXAMPLE 9.43

```
(The Command Line)
1   % find . -name '*.c' -print >& outputfile
2   % (find . -name '*.c' -print > goodstuff) >& badstuff
```

EXPLANATION

1   The *find* command will start at the current directory, searching for all files ending in *.c,* and will print the output to *outputfile*. If an error occurs, that will also go into *outputfile*.

2   The *find* command is enclosed within parentheses. The shell will create a subshell to handle the command. Before creating the subshell, the words outside the parentheses will be processed; that is, the *badstuff* file will be opened for both standard output and error. When the subshell is started, it inherits the standard input, output, and errors from its parent. The subshell then has standard input coming from the keyboard, and both standard output and standard error going to the *badstuff* file. Now the subshell will handle the > operator. The *stdout* will be assigned the file *goodstuff*. The output is going to *goodstuff*, and the errors are going to *badstuff*. See Figure 9.3.

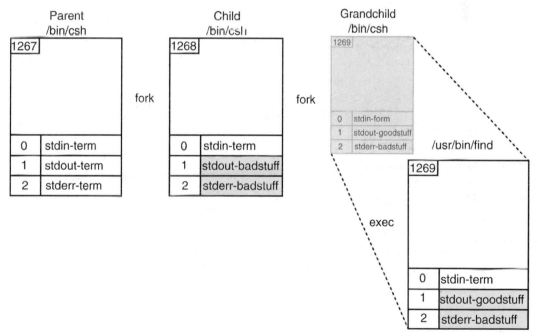

Figure 9.3   Separating *stdout* and *stderr*.

The *noclobber* Variable.   The special C shell built-in variable *noclobber*, when set, protects you from clobbering files with redirection. See Table 9.5.

Table 9.5 The *noclobber* Variable

noclobber *Is Not Set*	*File Exists*	*File Does Not Exist*
command > file	*file* is overwritten.	*file* is created.
command >> file	*file* is appended to.	*file* is created.
noclobber *Is Set*		
command > file	Error message.	*file* is created.
command >> file	*file* is appended to.	Error message.
***Overwriting* noclobber**		
command >! file	If the *noclobber* variable is set, override its effects for this *command* and either open or truncate *file*, redirecting output of *command* to *file*.	
command >>! file	Override *noclobber* variable; if *file* does not exist, it is created and output from *command* is appended to it. (See Example 9.44.)	

EXAMPLE 9.44

```
1   % cat filex
    abc
    123

2   % date > filex
3   % cat filex
    Wed Aug 5 11:51:04  PDT 2001

4   % set noclobber
5   % date > filex
    filex: File exists.

6   % ls >! filex    # Override noclobber for this command only
    % cat filex
    abc
    ab1
    dir
    filex
    plan.c
```

EXAMPLE   9.44 (CONTINUED)

```
7   % ls > filex
    filex:  File exists.

8   % unset noclobber      # Turn off noclobber permanently
```

EXPLANATION

1   The contents of *filex* are displayed on the screen.

2   The output of the *date* command is redirected to *filex*. The file is truncated and its original contents overwritten.

3   The contents of *filex* are displayed.

4   The *noclobber* variable is set.

5   Since *filex* already exists and *noclobber* is set, the shell reports that the file exists and will not allow it to be overwritten.

6   The output of *ls* is redirected to *filex* because the >! operator overrides the effects of *noclobber*.

7   The effects of the >! symbol were temporary. It does not turn off *noclobber*. It simply overrides *noclobber* for the command where it is implemented.

8   The *noclobber* variable is unset.

9.1.10 Variables

C shell variables hold only strings or a set of strings. Some variables are built into the shell and can be set by turning them on or off, such as the *noclobber* or *filec* variable. Others are assigned a string value, such as the *path* variable. You can create your own variables and assign them to strings or the output of commands. Variable names are case-sensitive and may contain up to 20 characters consisting of numbers, letters, and the underscore.

There are two types of variables: local and environment. The scope of a variable is its visibility. A local variable is visible to the shell where it is defined. The scope of environment variables is often called *global*. Their scope is for this shell and all processes spawned (started) from this shell.

The dollar sign ($) is a special metacharacter that, when preceding a variable name, tells the shell to extract the value of that variable. The *echo* command, when given the variable as an argument, will display the value of the variable after the shell has processed the command line and performed variable substitution.

The special notation $?, when prepended to the variable name, lets you know whether the variable has been set. If a one is returned, it means true, the variable has been set. If a zero is returned, it means false, the variable has not been set.

EXAMPLE 9.45

```
1  % set filec
2  % set history = 50
3  % set name = George
4  % set machine = `uname -n`
5  % echo  $?machine
   1
6  % echo  $?blah
   0
```

EXPLANATION

1   Sets the built-in variable *filec* for filename completion.

2   Sets the built-in variable *history* to *50* to control the number of events displayed.

3   Sets the user-defined variable *name* to *George*.

4   Sets the user-defined variable *machine* to the output of the UNIX command. The command is in backquotes, telling the shell to perform command substitution.

5   The *$?* is prepended to the variable name to test whether or not the variable has been set. Since the test yields a one (true), the variable has been set.

6   The *$?* yields zero (false). The variable has not been set.

Curly Braces.   Curly braces insulate a variable from any characters that may follow it.

EXAMPLE 9.46

```
1  % set var = net
   % echo $var
   net

2  % echo $varwork
   varwork: Undefined variable.

3  % echo ${var}work
   network
```

EXPLANATION

1   The curly braces surrounding the variable name insulate the variable from characters that follow it.

2   A variable called *varwork* has not been defined. The shell prints an error message.

3   The curly braces shield the variable from characters appended to it. *$var* is expanded and the string *work* is appended.

Local Variables.   Local variables are known only in the shell where they were created. If a local variable is set in the *.cshrc* file, the variable will be reset every time a new C shell is started. By convention, local variables are named with lowercase letters.

Setting Local Variables. If the string being assigned contains more than one word, it must be quoted; otherwise, only the first word will be assigned to the variable. It does not matter if there are spaces around the equal sign, but if there is a space on one side of the equal sign, there must be one on the other side.

EXAMPLE 9.47

```
1   % set round = world
2   % set name = "Santa Claus"

3   % echo $round
    world

4   % echo $name
    Santa Claus

5   % csh              # Start a subshell
6   % echo $name
    name: Undefined variable.
```

EXPLANATION

1   The local variable *round* is assigned the value *world*.

2   The local variable *name* is assigned the value *Santa Claus*. The double quotes keep the shell from evaluating the whitespace between *Santa* and *Claus*.

3   The dollar sign prepended to the variable allows the shell to perform variable substitution, that is, to extract the value stored in the variable.

4   Variable substitution is performed.

5   A new C shell (called a subshell) process is started.

6   In the subshell, the variable *name* has not been defined. It was defined in the parent shell as a local variable.

The *set* Command. The *set* command prints all local variables set for this shell.

EXAMPLE 9.48

```
(The Command Line)
% set
argv       ()
cwd        /home/jody/ellie
fignore    .o
filec
history    500
home       /home/jody/ellie
hostname   jody
ignoreeof
noclobber
```

EXAMPLE 9.48 (CONTINUED)

```
notify
path        (/home/jody/ellie /bin /usr/local /usr/usr/bin/usr/etc .)
prompt      jody%
shell       /bin/csh
status      0
term        sun-cmd
user        ellie
```

EXPLANATION

All of the local variables set for this shell are printed. Most of these variables are set in the *.cshrc* file. The *argv, cwd, shell, term, user,* and *status* variables are preset, built-in variables.

Built-In Local Variables. The shell has a number of predefined variables with their own definitions. Some of the variables are either on or off. For example, if you set *noclobber*, the variable is on and effective, and when you unset *noclobber*, it is turned off. Some variables require a definition when set. Built-in variables are usually set in the *.cshrc* file if they are to be effective for different C shells. Some of the built-in variables already discussed include *noclobber, cdpath, history, filec,* and *noglob*. For a complete list, see Table 9.16 on page 423.

Environment Variables. Environment variables are often called *global* variables. They are defined in the shell where they were created and inherited by all shells spawned from that shell. Although environment variables are inherited by subshells, those defined in subshells are not passed back to parent shells. Inheritance is from parent to child, not the other way around (like real life). By convention, environment variables are named with capital letters.

EXAMPLE 9.49

```
(The Command Line)
1   % setenv TERM wyse
2   % setenv PERSON "Joe Jr."
3   % echo $TERM
    wyse
4   % echo $PERSON
    Joe Jr.
5   % echo $$        # $$ evaluates to the PID of the current shell
    206
6   % csh            # Start a subshell
7   % echo $$
    211
8   % echo $PERSON
    Joe Jr.
```

EXAMPLE 9.49 (CONTINUED)

```
9   % setenv PERSON "Nelly Nerd"
10  % echo $PERSON
    % Nelly Nerd
11  % exit              # Exit the subshell
12  % echo $$
    206
13  % echo $PERSON      # Back in parent shell
    Joe Jr.
```

EXPLANATION

1   The shell environment variable *TERM* is set to a *wyse* terminal.

2   The user-defined variable *PERSON* is set to *Joe Jr.* The quotes are used to protect the space.

3   The dollar sign ($) prepended to the variable name allows the shell to evaluate the contents of the variable, called variable substitution.

4   The value of the environment variable *PERSON* is printed.

5   The $$ variable contains the PID of the current shell. The PID is *206*.

6   The *csh* command starts a new C shell, called a subshell.

7   The PID of the current shell is printed. Since this is a new C shell, it has a different PID number. The PID is *211*.

8   The environment variable *PERSON* was inherited by the new shell.

9   The *PERSON* variable is reset to *Nelly Nerd.* This variable will be inherited by any shells spawned from this shell.

10 The new value of the *PERSON* variable is printed.

11 This C shell is exited.

12 The original C shell is running; to attest to that, the PID *206* is printed. It is the same as it was before the subshell was started.

13 The *PERSON* variable contains its original value.

Printing Environment Variables. The *printenv* (UCB) and *env* (SVR4) commands print all the environment variables set for this shell and its subshells. The *setenv* command prints variables and their values on both the UCB and SVR4 versions of the C shell.

EXAMPLE 9.50

```
% env
FONTPATH=/usr/local/OW3/lib/fonts
HELPPATH=/usr/local/OW3/lib/locale:/usr/local/OW3/lib/help
HOME=/home/jody/ellie
LD_LIBRARY_PATH=/usr/local/OW3/lib
LOGNAME=ellie
MANPATH=/ur/local/man:/usr/local/man:/usr/local/doctools/man:/usr/man
```

EXAMPLE 9.50 (CONTINUED)

```
NOSUNVIEW=0
OPENWINHOME=/usr/local/OW3
PATH=/bin:/usr/local:/usr:/usr/bin:/usr/etc:/home/5bin:/usr/
    doctools:/usr:.
PWD=/home/jody/ellie
SHELL=/bin/csh
TERM=sun-cmd
USER=ellie
WINDOW_PARENT=/dev/win0
WINDOW_TTYPARMS=
WMGR_ENV_PLACEHOLDER=/dev/win3
```

EXPLANATION

The environment variables are set for this session and all processes that are started from this shell. Many applications require the setting of environment variables. For example, the *man* command has a *MANPATH* variable set to the location that *man* pages can be found, and the *openwin* program has an environment variable set to the place where its fonts are stored. When any of these programs are executed, the information in these variables is passed to them.

Arrays.   In the C shell, an array is simply a list of words, separated by spaces or tabs, and enclosed in parentheses. The elements of the array are numbered by subscripts starting at one. If there is not an array element for a subscript, the message *Subscript out of range* is displayed. Command substitution will also create an array. If the $# notation precedes an array name, the number of elements in the array is displayed.

EXAMPLE 9.51

```
1   % set fruit = ( apples pears peaches plums )
2   % echo $fruit
    apples pears peaches plums

3   % echo $fruit[1]          # Subscripts start at 1
    apples

4   % echo $fruit[2-4]        # Prints the 2nd, 3rd, and 4th elements
    pears peaches plums

5   $ echo $fruit[6]
    Subscript out of range.

6   % echo $fruit[*]          # Prints all elements of the array
    apples pears peaches plums
```

EXAMPLE 9.51 (CONTINUED)

```
7   % echo $#fruit            # Prints the number of elements
    4

8   % echo $fruit[$#fruit]    # Prints the last element
    plums

9   % set fruit[2] = bananas     # Reassigns the second element
    % echo $fruit
    apples bananas peaches plums

10  % set path = ( ~ /usr/bin /usr /usr/local/bin . )
    % echo $path
    /home/jody/ellie /usr/bin /usr /usr/local/bin .

11  % echo $path[1]
    /home/jody/ellie
```

EXPLANATION

1   The wordlist is enclosed within parentheses. Each word is separated by whitespace. The array is called *fruit*.

2   The words in the *fruit* array are printed.

3   The first element of the *fruit* array is printed. The subscripts start at one.

4   The second, third, and fourth elements of the wordlist are printed. The dash allows you to specify a range.

5   The array does not have six elements. The subscript is out of range.

6   All elements of the *fruit* array are printed.

7   The $# preceding the array is used to obtain the number of elements in the array. There are four elements in the *fruit* array.

8   Since the subscript *$#fruit* evaluates to the total number of elements in the array, if that value is used as an index value of the array, i.e., *[$#fruit]*, the last element of the *fruit* array is printed.

9   The second element of the array is assigned a new value. The array is printed with its replaced value, *bananas*.

10 The *path* variable is a special C shell array of directories used to search for commands. By creating an array, the individual elements of the path can be accessed or changed.

11 The first element of *path* is printed.

The *shift* Command and Arrays. If the built-in *shift* command takes an array name as its argument, it shifts off (to the left) the first element of the array. The length of the array is decreased by one. (Without an argument, the *shift* command shifts off the first element of the built-in *argv* array. See "Command Line Arguments" on page 394.)

EXAMPLE 9.52

```
1   % set names = ( Mark Tom Liz Dan Jody )

2   % echo $names
    Mark Tom Liz Dan Jody

3   % echo $names[1]
    Mark

4   % shift   names

5   % echo $names
    Tom Liz Dan Jody

6   % echo $names[1]
    Tom

7   % set days = ( Monday Tuesday )

8   % shift days

9   % echo $days
    Tuesday

10  % shift days

11  % echo $days

12  % shift days
    shift: no more words.
```

EXPLANATION

1   The array is called *names*. It is assigned the list of words in parentheses. Each word is separated by whitespace.

2   The array is printed.

3   The first element of the array is printed.

4   The array is shifted to the left by one element. The word *Mark* is shifted off.

5   The array was decreased by one element after the *shift*.

6   The first element of the array, after the *shift*, is *Tom*.

7   An array called *days* is created. It has two elements, *Monday* and *Tuesday*.

8   The array *days* is shifted one to the left.

9   The array is printed. *Tuesday* is the only element left.

10 The array *days* is shifted again. The array is empty.

11 The *days* array is empty.

12 This time, attempting to shift causes the shell to send an error message indicating that it cannot shift elements from an empty array.

Creating an Array from a String. You may want to create a wordlist out of a quoted string. This is accomplished by placing the string variable within a set of parentheses.

EXAMPLE 9.53

```
1   % set name = "Thomas Ben Savage"
    % echo $name[1]
    Thomas Ben Savage

2   % echo $name[2]
    Subscript out of range.

3   % set name = ( $name )

4   % echo $name[1] $name[2] $name[3]
    Thomas Ben Savage
```

EXPLANATION

1   The variable *name* is assigned the string *Thomas Ben Savage*.
2   When treated as an array, there is only one element, the entire string.
3   The variable is enclosed in parentheses, creating an array of words, called *name*.
4   The three elements of the new array are displayed.

9.1.11 Special Variables

Built into the C shell are several variables consisting of one character. The $ preceding the character allows variable interpretation. See Table 9.6.

Table 9.6 Variables and Their Meanings

Variable	Example	Meaning
$?var	echo $?name	Returns *1* if variable has been set, *0* if not.
$#var	echo $#fruit	Prints the number of elements in an array.
$$	echo $$	Prints the PID of the current shell.
$<	set name = $<	Accepts a line of input from user up to newline.

EXAMPLE 9.54

```
1   % set num
    % echo $?num
    1
```

EXAMPLE   9.54 (CONTINUED)

```
2   % echo $path
    /home/jody/ellie    /usr/bin/    usr/local/bin
    % echo $#path
    3

3   % echo $$
    245

    % csh              # Start a subshell
    % echo $$
    248

4   % set name = $<
    Christy Campbell
    % echo $name
    Christy Campbell
```

EXPLANATION

1   The variable *num* is set to null. The $? preceding the variable evaluates to one if the variable has been set (either to null or some value), and to zero if the variable has not been set.

2   The *path* variable is printed. It is an array of three elements. The $# preceding the variable extracts and prints the number of elements in the array.

3   The $$ is the PID of the current process, in this case, the C shell.

4   The $< variable accepts a line of input from the user up to, but not including, the newline, and stores the line in the *name* variable. The value of the *name* variable is displayed.

Pathname Variable Modifiers.   If a pathname is assigned to a variable, it is possible to manipulate the pathname variable by appending special C shell extensions to it. The pathname is divided into four parts: *head*, *tail*, *root*, and *extension*. See Table 9.7 for examples of pathname modifiers and what they do.

Table 9.7   Pathname Modifiers

```
set pn = /home/ellie/prog/check.c
```

Modifier	Meaning	Example	Result
:r	root	echo $pn:r	/home/ellie/prog/check
:h	head	echo $pn:h	/home/ellie/prog
:t	tail	echo $pn:t	check.c
:e	extension	echo $pn:e	c
:g	global	echo $p:gt	(See Example 9.55)

EXAMPLE 9.55

```
1  % set pathvar = /home/danny/program.c

2  % echo $pathvar:r
   /home/danny/program

3  % echo $pathvar:h
   /home/danny

4  % echo $pathvar:t
   program.c

5  % echo $pathvar:e
   c

6  % set pathvar = ( /home/* )
   echo $pathvar
   /home/jody /home/local /home/lost+found /home/perl /home/tmp

7  % echo $pathvar:gt
   jody   local   lost+found   perl tmp
```

EXPLANATION

1   The variable *pathvar* is set to */home/danny/program.c*.
2   When *:r* is appended to the variable, the extension is removed when displayed.
3   When *:h* is appended to the variable, the head of the path is displayed; that is, the last element of the path is removed.
4   When *:t* is appended to the variable, the tail end of the path (the last element) is displayed.
5   When *:e* is appended to the variable, the extension is displayed.
6   The variable is set to */home/**. The asterisk expands to all the pathnames in the current directory starting in */home/*.
7   When *:gt* is appended to the variable, the tail end of each (global) of the path elements is displayed.

9.1.12 Command Substitution

A string or variable can be assigned the output of a UNIX command by placing the command in backquotes. This is called *command substitution*. (On the keyboard, the backquote is normally below the tilde character.) If the output of a command is assigned to a variable, it is stored as a wordlist (see "Arrays" on page 370), not a string, so that each of the words in the list can be accessed separately. To access a word from the list, a subscript is appended to the variable name. Subscripts start at one.

EXAMPLE 9.56

```
1   % echo The name of my machine is `uname -n`.
    The name of my machine is stardust.

2   % echo The present working directory is `pwd`.
    The present working directory is /home/stardust/john.

3   % set d = `date`
    % echo $d
    Sat Jun 20 14:24:21 PDT 2001

4   % echo $d[2] $d[6]
    Jun 2001

5   % set d = "`date`"
    % echo $d[1]
    Sat Jun 20 14:24:21 PDT 2001
```

EXPLANATION

1   The UNIX command *uname –n* is enclosed in backquotes. When the shell encounters the backquotes, it will execute the enclosed command, *uname –n*, and substitute the output of the command, *stardust*, into the string. When the *echo* command prints its arguments to standard output, the name of the machine will be one of its arguments.

2   The UNIX command *pwd* is executed by the shell and the output is substituted in place within the string.

3   The local variable *d* is assigned the output of the *date* command. The output is stored as a list of words (an array).

4   Elements 2 and 6 of the *d* array are printed. The subscripts start at one.

5   Since the output is enclosed in double quotes, it is a single string rather than a wordlist.

Wordlists and Command Substitution.   When a command is enclosed in backquotes and assigned to a variable, the resulting value is an array (wordlist). Each element of the array can be accessed by appending a subscript to the array name. The subscripts start at one. If a subscript that is greater than the number of words in the array is used, the C shell prints *Subscript out of range*. If the output of a command consists of more than one line, the newlines are stripped from each line and replaced with a single space.

EXAMPLE 9.57

```
1   % set d = `date`
    % echo $d
    Fri Aug 29 14:04:49 PDT 2001
```

EXAMPLE 9.57 (CONTINUED)

```
3   % echo $d[1-3]
    Fri Aug 29

4   % echo $d[6]
    2001

4   % echo $d[7]
    Subscript out of range.

5   % echo The calendar for the month of November is `cal 11 2001`"
    The calendar for month of November is November 2001 S M Tu W
    Th F S 1 2 3 4 5 6 7 8 9 10 11 12 13 14 15 16 17 18 19 20 21
    22 23 24 25 26 27 28 29 30
```

EXPLANATION

1   The variable *d* is assigned the output of the UNIX *date* command. The output is stored as an array. The value of the variable is displayed.

2   The first three elements of the array are displayed.

3   The sixth element of the array is displayed.

4   There are not seven elements in the array. The shell reports that the subscript is out of range.

5   The output spans more than one line. Each newline is replaced with a space. This may not be the output you expected.

EXAMPLE 9.58

```
1   % set machine = `rusers | awk '/tom/{print $1}'`

2   % echo $machine
    dumbo bambi dolphin

3   % echo $#machine
    3

4   % echo $machine[$#machine]
    dolphin

5   % echo $machine
    dumbo bambi dolphin

6   % shift $machine
    % echo $machine
    bambi dolphin
```

EXAMPLE   9.58 (CONTINUED)

```
7   % echo $machine[1]
    bambi

8   % echo $#machine
    2
```

EXPLANATION

1   The output of the *rusers* command is piped to *awk*. If the regular expression *tom* is found, *awk* prints the first field. The first field, in this case, is the name of the machine(s) where user *tom* is logged on.

2   User *tom* is logged on three machines. The names of the machines are displayed.

3   The number of elements in the array is accessed by preceding the array name with $#. There are three elements in the array.

4   The last element of the array is displayed. The number of elements in the array (*$#machine*) is used as a subscript.

5   The array is displayed.

6   The *shift* command shifts the array to the left. The first element of the array is dropped and the subscripts are renumbered, starting at one.

7   The first element of the array after the *shift* is displayed.

8   After the *shift*, the length of the array has decreased by one.

9.1.13 Quoting

The C shell has a whole set of metacharacters that have some special meaning. In fact, almost any character on your keyboard that is not a letter or a number has some special meaning for the shell. Here is a partial list:

```
* ? [ ] $ ~ ! ^ & { } ( ) > < | ; : %
```

The backslash and quotes are used to escape the interpretation of metacharacters by the shell. Whereas the backslash is used to escape a single character, the quotes can be used to protect a string of characters. There are some general rules for using quotes:

1.   Quotes are paired and must be matched on a line. The backslash character can be used to escape a newline so that a quote can be matched on the next line.

2.   Single quotes will protect double quotes, and double quotes will protect single quotes.

3.   Single quotes protect all metacharacters from interpretation, with the exception of the history character (*!*).

4.   Double quotes protect all metacharacters from interpretation, with the exception of the history character (*!*), the variable substitution character ($), and the backquotes (used for command substitution).

The Backslash. The backslash is used to escape the interpretation of a single character and, in the C shell, is the only character that can be used to escape the history character, the exclamation point (also called the bang). Often the backslash is used to escape the newline character. Backslash interpretation does not take place within quotes.

EXAMPLE 9.59

```
1   % echo Who are you?
    echo: No match.

2   % echo Who are you\?
    Who are you?

3   % echo This is a very,very long line and this is where I\
    break the line.
    This is a very, very long line and this is where I
        I break the line.

4   % echo "\\abc"
    \\abc
    % echo '\\abc'
    \\abc
    % echo \\abc
    \abc
```

EXPLANATION

1   The question mark is used for filename expansion. It matches for a single character. The shell is looking for a file in the current directory that is spelled *y-o-u*, followed by a single character. Since there is not a file by that name in the directory, the shell complains that it could not find a match with *No match*.

2   The shell will not try to interpret the question mark, since it is escaped with the backslash.

3   The string is continued to the next line by escaping the newline with a backslash.

4   If the backslash is enclosed in either single or double quotes, it is printed. When not enclosed in quotes, the backslash escapes itself.

Single Quotes. Single quotes must be matched on the same line and will escape all metacharacters with the exception of the history (bang) character (*!*). The history character is not protected because the C shell evaluates history before it does quotes, but not before backslashes.

EXAMPLE 9.60

```
1  % echo 'I need $5.00'
   I need $5.00

2  % echo 'I need $500.00 now\!\!'
   I need $500.00 now!!

3  % echo 'This is going to be a long line so
   Unmatched '.

4  % echo 'This is going to be a long line so \
   I used the backslash to suppress the newline'
   This is going to be a long line so
   I used the backslash to suppress the newline
```

EXPLANATION

1 The string is enclosed in single quotes. All characters, except the history (bang) character (!), are protected from shell interpretation.

2 The !! must be protected from shell interpretation by using the backslash character.

3 The quotes must be matched on the same line, or the shell reports *Unmatched*.

4 If the line is to be continued, the backslash character is used to escape the newline character. The quote is matched at the end of the next line. Even though the shell ignored the newline, the *echo* command did not.

Double Quotes. Double quotes must be matched, will allow variable and command substitution, and hide everything else except the history (bang) character (!). The backslash will not escape the dollar sign when enclosed in double quotes.

EXAMPLE 9.61

```
1  % set name = Bob
   % echo "Hi $name"
   Hi Bob

2  % echo "I don't have time."
   I don't have time.

3  % echo "WOW!"        # Watch the history metacharacter!
   ": Event not found.

4  % echo "Whoopie\!"
   Whoopie!

5  % echo "I need \$5.00"
   I need \.00
```

EXPLANATION

1. The local variable *name* is assigned the value *Bob*. The double quotes allow the dollar sign to be used for variable substitution.
2. The single quote is protected within double quotes.
3. Double or single quotes will not protect the exclamation point from shell interpretation. The built-in *history* command is looking for the last command that began with a double quote and that event was not found.
4. The backslash is used to protect the exclamation point.
5. The backslash does not escape the dollar sign when used within double quotes.

The Quoting Game.   As long as the quoting rules are adhered to, double quotes and single quotes can be used in a variety of combinations in a single command.

EXAMPLE 9.62

```
1   % set name = Tom

2   % echo "I can't give $name" ' $5.00\!'
    I can't give Tom $5.00!

3   % echo She cried, \"Oh help me\!' "', $name.
    She cried, "Oh help me!", Tom.
```

EXPLANATION

1. The local variable *name* is assigned *Tom*.
2. The single quote in the word *can't* is protected when enclosed within double quotes. The shell would try to perform variable substitution if the dollar sign in *$5.00* were within double quotes. Therefore, the string *$5.00* is enclosed in single quotes so that the dollar sign will be a literal. The exclamation point is protected with a backslash since neither double nor single quotes can protect it from shell interpretation.
3. The first conversational quotes are protected by the backslash. The exclamation point is also protected with a backslash. The last conversational quotes are enclosed in a set of single quotes. Single quotes will protect double quotes.

Steps to Successful Quoting.   In a more complex command, it is often difficult to match quotes properly unless you follow the steps listed here. (See Appendix C.)

1. Know the UNIX command and its syntax. Before variable substitution, hard code the values into the command line to see if you get the expected results.

```
% nawk -F: '/^Zippy Pinhead/{print "Phone is " $2}' datafile 408-123 4567
```

2. If the UNIX command worked correctly, then plug in the variables. At this
point, do not remove or change any quotes. Simply put the variables in place of
the words they represent. In this example, replace *Zippy Pinhead* with *$name*.

```
% set name = "Zippy Pinhead"
% nawk -F: '/^$name/{print "Phone is " $2}' datafile
```

3. Play the quoting game as follows: Starting at the left-hand side with the first
single quote, insert a matching single quote just before the dollar sign in *$name*.
Now you have a set of matched quotes.

```
nawk -F: '/^'$name/{print "Phone is " $2}' datafile
```

Now, right after the last letter, *e* in *$name*, place another single quote. (Believe
me, this works.) This quote matches the quote after the closing curly brace.

```
% nawk -F: '/^'$name'/{print "Phone is  " $2}' datafile
```

Count the number of single quotes, starting at the left-hand side. You have four,
a nice even number. Everything within each set of single quotes is ignored by the
shell. The quotes are matched as follows:

```
% nawk -F: '$1 ~ /'$name'/{print $2}' filename
```

4. Last step: Double quote the variables. Surround each variable very snugly
within a set of double quotes. The double quotes protect the whitespace in the
expanded variable; for example, the space in *Zippy Pinhead* is protected.

```
% nawk -F: '$1 ~ /'"$name"'/{print $2}' filename
```

Quoting Variables.   The *:x* and *:q* modifiers are used when it is necessary to quote
variables.

Quoting with the *:q* Modifier.   The *:q* modifier is used to replace double quotes.

EXAMPLE   9.63

```
1    % set name = "Daniel Savage"          ⎫— TWO FORMS OF DOUBLE
2    % grep $name:q database                ⎭        QUOTE
       same as
3    % grep "$name" database

4    % set food = "apple pie"

5    % set dessert = ( $food "ice cream")   ⎫— A LIST, LIKE PERL,
                                             ⎭  HERE → AN ARRAY.
6    % echo $#dessert       ⎫— NUMBER ELEMENTS IN ARRAY
     3
7    % echo $dessert[1]     ⎫— FIRST ITEM
     apple

8    % echo $dessert[2]
     pie

9    % echo $dessert[3]              — THIS QUOTES $food, MAKING
     ice cream                           IT ONE ITEM.

10   % set dessert = ($food:q "ice cream")

11   % echo $#dessert
     2
12   % echo $dessert[1]
     apple pie
13   % echo $dessert[2]
     ice cream
```

EXPLANATION

1   The variable is assigned the string *Daniel Savage*.

2   When *:q* is appended to the variable, the variable is quoted. This is the same as enclosing the variable in double quotes.

3   The double quotes surrounding the variable *$name* allow variable substitution to take place, but protect any whitespace characters. Without the double quotes, the *grep* program will search for *Daniel* in a file called *Savage* and a file called *database*.

4   The variable *food* is assigned the string *apple pie*.

5   The variable *dessert* is assigned an array (wordlist) consisting of *apple pie* and *ice cream*.

6   The number of elements in the *dessert* array is three. When the *food* variable was expanded, the quotes were removed. There are three elements, *apple, pie*, and *ice cream*.

7   The first element of the array is printed. The variable expands to separated words if not quoted.

8   The second element of the array is printed.

EXPLANATION (CONTINUED)

9   Since *"ice cream"* is quoted, it is treated as one word.

10 The *dessert* array is assigned *apple pie* and *ice cream*. The *:q* can be used to quote the variable in the same way double quotes quote the variable; i.e., *$food:q* is the same as *"$food"*.

11 The array consists of two strings, *apple pie* and *ice cream*.

12 The first element of the array, *apple pie*, is printed.

13 The second element of the array, *ice cream*, is printed.

Quoting with the *:x* Modifier.   If you are creating an array and any of the words in the list contain metacharacters, *:x* prevents the shell from interpreting the metacharacters when performing variable substitution

EXAMPLE 9.64

```
1   % set  things = "*.c  a??  file[1-5]"
    % echo $#things
    1

2   % set newthings = ( $things )
    set: No match.

3   % set newthings = ( $things:x )
4   % echo $#newthings
    3

5   % echo "$newthings[1] $newthings[2] $newthings[3] "
    *.c  a??   file[1-5]

6   %  grep $newthings[2]:q filex
    The question marks in a?? would be used for filename expansion
    it is not quoted
```

EXPLANATION

1   The variable *things* is assigned a string. Each string contains a wildcard. The number of elements in the variable is one, one string.

2   When attempting to create an array out of the string *things*, the C shell tries to expand the wildcard characters to perform filename substitution within *things* and produces a *No match*.

3   The *:x* extension prevents the shell from expanding the wildcards in the *things* variable.

4   The array *newthings* consists of three elements.

5   To print the elements of the array, they must be quoted or, again, the shell will try to expand the wildcards.

6   The *:q* quotes the variable just as though the variable were surrounded by double quotes. The *grep* program will print any lines containing the pattern *a??* in file *filex*.

9.2 Programming with the C Shell

9.2.1 Steps in Creating a Shell Script

A shell script is normally written in an editor and consists of commands interspersed with comments. Comments are preceded by a pound sign and consist of text used to document what is going on.

The First Line. At the top left corner, the line preceded by #! (often called *shbang*) indicates the program that will be executing the lines in the script. This line is commonly

```
#!/bin/csh
```

The #!, also called a *magic number*, is used by the kernel to identify the program that should be interpreting the lines in the script. When a program is loaded into memory, the kernel will examine the first line. If the first line is binary data, the program will be executed as a compiled program; if the first line contains the #!, the kernel will look at the path following the #! and start that program as the interpreter. If the path is */bin/csh*, the C shell will interpret the lines in the program. This line must be the top line of your script or the line will be treated as a comment line.

When the script starts, the *.cshrc* file is read first and executed, so that anything set within that file will become part of your script. You can prevent the *.cshrc* from being read into your script by using the –*f* (fast) option to the C shell program. This option is written as

```
#!/bin/csh -f
```

Comments. Comments are lines preceded by a pound sign (#). They are used to document your script. It is sometimes difficult to understand what the script is supposed to do if it is not commented. Although comments are important, they are often too sparse or not even used at all. Try to get used to commenting what you are doing not only for someone else, but also for yourself. Two days from now you may not remember exactly what you were trying to do.

Making the Script Executable. When you create a file, it is not given execute permission. You need this permission to run your script. Use the *chmod* command to turn on execute permission.

```
EXAMPLE  9.65
```

```
1   % chmod +x myscript
2   % ls -lF  myscript
    -rwxr--xr--x    1  ellie  0 Jul  13:00 myscript*
```

EXPLANATION

1   The *chmod* command is used to turn on execute permission for the user, the group, and others.

2   The output of the *ls* command indicates that all users have execute permission on the *myscript* file. The asterisk at the end of the filename (resulting from the –F option) also indicates that this is an executable program.

An Example Scripting Session.   In the following example, the user will create the script in the editor. After saving the file, the execute permissions are turned on with the *chmod* command, and the script is executed. If there are errors in the program, the C shell will respond immediately.

EXAMPLE 9.66

```
(The Script - info)
   #!/bin/csh -f
   # This script is called info
1  echo Hello ${LOGNAME}!
2  echo The hour is `date +%H`
3  echo "This machine is `uname -n`"
4  echo The calendar for this month is
5  cal
6  echo The processes you are running are:
7  ps -ef | grep  "^ *$LOGNAME"
8  echo "Thanks for coming. See you soon\!\!"

   (The Command Line)
   % chmod +x info
   % info
1  Hello ellie!
2  The hour is 09
3  This machine is jody
4  The calendar for this month is
5       July 2001
   S    M   Tu   W   Th    F    S
                        1    2    3
    4    5    6    7    8    9   10
   11   12   13   14   15   16   17
   18   19   20   21   22   23   24
   25   26   27   28   29   30   31
7  The processes you are running are:
   < output of ps prints here >
8  Thanks for coming. See you soon!!
```

EXPLANATION

1   The user is greeted. The variable *LOGNAME* holds the user's name. On BSD systems, *USER* is used. The curly braces shield the variable from the exclamation point. The exclamation point does not need to be escaped because it will not be interpreted as a history character unless there is a character appended to it.

2   The *date* command is enclosed in backquotes. The shell will perform command substitution and the date's output, the current hour, will be substituted into the *echo* string.

3   The *uname –n* command displays the machine name.

4   The *cal* command is not enclosed in backquotes because when the shell performs command substitution, the newlines are all stripped from the output. This produces a strange-looking calendar. By putting the *cal* command on a line by itself, the formatting is preserved.

5   The calendar for this month is printed.

6, 7   The user's processes are printed. Use *ps –aux* for BSD.

8   The string is printed. Note that the two exclamation points are prepended with backslashes. This is necessary to prevent history substitution.

9.2.2 Reading User Input

The $< Variable.   To make a script interactive, a special C shell variable is used to read standard input into a variable. The $< symbol reads a line from standard input up to but not including the newline, and assigns the line to a variable.[6]

EXAMPLE 9.67

```
(The Script - greeting)
    #/bin/csh  -f
    # The greeting script
1   echo -n "What is your name? "
2   set name = $<
3   echo Greetings to you, $name.

(The Command Line)
    % chmod +x greeting
    % greeting
1   What is your name?  Dan Savage
3   Greetings to you, Dan Savage.
```

---

6. Another way to read one line of input is `setvariable = 'head -1'`.

EXPLANATION

1   The string is echoed to the screen. The *–n* option causes the *echo* command to suppress the newline at the end of the string. On some versions of *echo*, use a \c at the end of the string to suppress the newline; e.g., *echo hello\c*.

2   Whatever is typed at the terminal, up to a newline is stored as a string in the *name* variable.

3   The string is printed after variable substitution is performed.

Creating a Wordlist from the Input String.   Since the input from the $< variable is stored as a string, you may want to break the string into a wordlist.

EXAMPLE 9.68

```
1   % echo What is your full name\?

2   % set name = $<
    Lola Justin Lue

3   % echo Hi $name[1]
    Hi Lola Justin Lue

4   % echo $name[2]
    Subscript out of range.

5   % set name = ( $name )

6   % echo Hi $name[1]
    Hi Lola

7   % echo $name[2] $name[3]
    Justin Lue
```

EXPLANATION

1   The user is asked for input.

2   The special variable $< accepts input from the user in a string format.

3   Since the value *Lola Justin Lue* is stored as a single string, the subscript *[1]* displays the whole string. Subscripts start at one.

4   The string consists of one word. There are not two words, so by using a subscript of *[2]*, the shell complains that the *Subscript is out of range.*

5   To create a wordlist, the string is enclosed in parentheses. An array is created. The string is broken up into a list of words and assigned to the variable *name.*

6   The first element of the array is printed.

7   The second and third elements of the array are printed.

9.2.3 Arithmetic

There is not really a need to do math problems in a shell script, but sometimes arithmetic is necessary, e.g., to increment or decrement a loop counter. The C shell supports integer arithmetic only. The @ symbol is used to assign the results of calculations to numeric variables.

Arithmetic Operators.   The following operators in Table 9.8 are used to perform integer arithmetic operations. They are the same operators as found in the C programming language. See Table 9.13 on page 397 for operator precedence. Also borrowed from the C language are shortcut assignment operators, shown in Table 9.9.

Table 9.8   Operators

Function	Operator
Addition	+
Subtraction	−
Division	/
Multiplication	*
Modulus	%
Left shift	<<
Right shift	>>

Table 9.9   Shortcut Operations

Operator	Example	Equivalent to
+=	@ num += 2	@ num = $num + 2
−=	@ num −= 4	@ num = $num − 4
*=	@ num *= 3	@ num = $num * 3
/=	@ num /= 2	@ num = $num / 2
++	@ num++	@ num = $num + 1
− −	@ num− −	@ num = $num − 1

EXAMPLE 9.69

```
1   % @ sum = 4 + 6
    echo $sum
    10

2   % @ sum++
    echo $sum
    11

3   % @ sum += 3
    echo $sum
    14

4   % @ sum--
    echo $sum
    13

5   % @ n = 3+4
    @: Badly formed number
```

EXPLANATION

1   The variable *sum* is assigned the result of adding *4* and *6*. (The space after the @ is required.)
2   The variable *sum* is incremented by *1*.
3   The variable *sum* is incremented by *3*.
4   The variable *sum* is decremented by *1*.
5   Spaces are required after the @ symbol and surrounding the operator.

Floating Point Arithmetic.   Since floating point arithmetic is not supported by this shell, if you should need more complex mathematical operations, you can use UNIX utilities.

The *bc* and *nawk* utilities are useful if you need to perform complex calculations.

EXAMPLE 9.70

```
(The Command Line)
1   set n=`echo "scale=3; 13 / 2" | bc`
    echo $n
    6.500

2   set product=`nawk -v x=2.45 -v y=3.124 'BEGIN{\
    printf "%.2f\n", x * y }'`

    % echo $product
    7.65
```

EXPLANATION

1   The output of the *echo* command is piped to the *bc* program. The scale is set to *3*; that is, the number of significant digits to the right of the decimal point that will be printed. The calculation is to divide *13* by *2*. The entire pipeline is enclosed in backquotes. Command substitution will be performed and the output assigned to the variable *n*.

2   The *nawk* program gets its values from the argument list passed in at the command line. Each argument passed to *nawk* is preceded by the *–v* switch; for example, *–v x=2.45* and *–v y=3.124*. After the numbers are multiplied, the *printf* function formats and prints the result with a precision of *2* places to the right of the decimal point. The output is assigned to the variable *product*.

9.2.4 Debugging Scripts

C shell scripts often fail because of some simple syntax error or logic error. Options to the *csh* command are provided to help you debug your programs. See Table 9.10.

Table 9.10   Echo (*–x*) and Verbose (*–v*)

As options to csh	
csh –x scriptname	Display each line of script after variable substitution and before execution.
csh –v scriptname	Display each line of script before execution, just as you typed it.
csh –n scriptname	Interpret but do not execute commands.
As arguments to the set command	
set echo	Display each line of script after variable substitution and before execution.
set verbose	Display each line of script before execution, just as you typed it.
As the first line in a script	
#!/bin/csh –xv	Turns on both echo and verbose. These options can be invoked separately or combined with other *csh* invocation arguments.

EXAMPLE 9.71

```
(The -v and -x Options)
1   % cat practice
    #!/bin/csh
    echo Hello $LOGNAME
    echo The date is `date`
    echo Your home shell is $SHELL
    echo Good-bye $LOGNAME


2   % csh -v practice
    echo Hello $LOGNAME
    Hello ellie
    echo The date is `date`
    The date is Sun May 23 12:24:07 PDT  2001
    echo Your login shell is $SHELL
    Your login shell is /bin/csh
    echo Good-bye $LOGNAME
    Good-bye ellie


3   % csh -x practice
    echo Hello ellie
    Hello ellie
    echo The date is `date`
    date
    The date is Sun May 23 12:24:15 PDT  2001
    echo Your login shell is /bin/csh
    Your login shell is /bin/csh
    echo Good-bye ellie
    Good-bye ellie
```

EXPLANATION

1   The contents of the C shell script are displayed. Variable and command substitu-
    tion lines are included so that you can see how *echo* and *verbose* differ.

2   The –*v* option to the *csh* command causes the *verbose* feature to be enabled. Each
    line of the script is displayed as it was typed in the script, and then the line is
    executed.

3   The –*x* option to the *csh* command enables echoing. Each line of the script is dis-
    played after variable and command substitution are performed, and then the line
    is executed. Since this feature allows you to examine what is being replaced as a
    result of command and variable substitution, it is used more often than the *verbose*
    option.

EXAMPLE 9.72

```
(Echo and Verbose)
1   % cat practice
    #!/bin/csh
    echo Hello $LOGNAME
    echo The date is 'date'
    set echo
    echo Your home shell is $SHELL
    unset echo
    echo Good-bye $LOGNAME

    % chmod +x practice

2   % practice
    Hello ellie
    The date is Sun May 26 12:25:16 PDT  2001
--> echo Your login shell is /bin/csh
--> Your login shell is /bin/csh
--> unset echo
    Good-bye ellie
```

EXPLANATION

1   The *echo* option is set and unset within the script. This enables you to debug certain sections of your script where you have run into a bottleneck, rather than echoing each line of the entire script.

2   The – –> marks where the echoing was turned on. Each line is printed after variable and command substitution and then executed.

EXAMPLE 9.73

```
1   % cat practice
    #!/bin/csh
    echo Hello $LOGNAME
    echo The date is 'date'
    set verbose
    echo Your home shell is $SHELL
    unset verbose
    echo Good-bye $LOGNAME

2   % practice
    Hello ellie
    The date is Sun May 23 12:30:09 PDT  2001
--> echo Your login shell is $SHELL
--> Your login shell is /bin/csh
- -> unset verbose
    Good-bye ellie
```

EXPLANATION

1   The *verbose* option is set and unset within the script.
2   The – –> marks where *verbose* was turned on. The lines are printed just as they were typed in the script and then executed.

9.2.5   Command Line Arguments

Shell scripts can take command line arguments. Arguments are used to modify the behavior of the program in some way. The C shell assigns command line arguments to positional parameters and enforces no specific limit on the number of arguments that can be assigned (the Bourne shell sets a limit of nine positional parameters). Positional parameters are number variables. The scriptname is assigned to $0, and any words following the scriptname are assigned to $1, $2, $3 . . . ${10}, ${11}, and so on. $1 is the first command line argument. In addition to using positional parameters, the C shell provides the *argv* built-in array.

Positional Parameters and *argv*.   If using the *argv* array notation, a valid subscript must be provided to correspond to the argument being passed in from the command line or the error message *Subscript out of range* is sent by the C shell. The *argv* array does not include the scriptname. The first argument is $*argv[1]*, and the number of arguments is represented by $#*argv*. (There is no other way to represent the number of arguments.) See Table 9.11 for a list of command line arguments.

Table 9.11   Command Line Arguments

Argument	Meaning
$0	The name of the script.
$1, $2, . . . ${10}...	The first and second positional parameters are referenced by the number preceded by a dollar sign. The curly braces shield the number 10 so that it does not print the first positional parameter followed by a zero.
$*	All the positional parameters.
$argv[0]	Not valid; nothing is printed. C shell array subscripts start at 1.
$argv[1] $argv[2]...	The first argument, second argument, etc.
$argv[*]	All arguments.
$argv	All arguments.
$#argv	The number of arguments.
$argv[$#argv]	The last argument.

EXAMPLE 9.74

```
(The Script)
#!/bin/csh -f
# The greetings script
# This script greets a user whose name is typed in at the
# command line.

1    echo $0 to you $1 $2 $3
2    echo Welcome to this day `date | awk '{print $1, $2, $3}'`
3    echo Hope you have a nice day, $argv[1]\!
4    echo Good-bye $argv[1] $argv[2] $argv[3]

(The Command Line)
    % chmod +x greetings

    % greetings Guy Quigley
1   greetings to you Guy Quigley
2   Welcome to this day Fri Aug 28
3   Hope you have a nice day, Guy!
4   Subscript out of range
```

EXPLANATION

1   The name of the script and the first three positional parameters are to be displayed. Since there are only two positional parameters coming in from the command line, *Guy* and *Quigley*, *$1* becomes *Guy*, *$2* becomes *Quigley*, and *$3* is not defined.

2   The *awk* command is quoted with single quotes so that the shell does not confuse *awk*'s field numbers *$1*, *$2*, and *$3* with positional parameters. (Do not confuse *awk*'s field designators *$1*, *$2*, and *$3* with the shell's positional parameters.)

3   The *argv* array is assigned values coming in from the command line. *Guy* is assigned to *argv[1]* and its value is displayed. You can use the *argv* array to represent the command line arguments within your script, or you can use positional parameters. The difference is that positional parameters do not produce an error if you reference one that has no value, whereas an unassigned *argv* value causes the script to exit with the *Subscript out of range* error message.

4   The shell prints the error *Subscript out of range* because there is no value for *argv[3]*.

9.2.6 Flow Control and Conditional Constructs

When making decisions, the *if, if/else, if/else if,* and *switch* commands are used. These commands control the flow of the program by allowing decision-making based on whether an expression is true or false.

Testing Expressions.   An expression consists of a set of operands separated by operators. Operators and precedence are listed in Tables 9.12 and 9.13. To test an expression, the expression is surrounded by parentheses. The C shell evaluates the expression, resulting in either a zero or nonzero numeric value. If the result is *nonzero*, the expression is *true*; if the result is *zero*, the expression is *false*.

Table 9.12   Comparison and Logical Operators

Operator	Meaning	Example
==	Is equal to	$x == $y
!=	Is not equal to	$x != $y
>	Is greater than	$x > $y
>=	Is greater than or equal to	$x >= $y
<	Is less than	$x < $y
<=	Is less than or equal to	$x <= $y
=~	String matches	$ans =~ [Yy]*
!~	String does not match	$ans !~ [Yy]*
!	Logical *not*	! $x
||	Logical *or*	$x || $y
&&	Logical *and*	$x && $y

When evaluating an expression with the logical *and* (&&), the shell evaluates from left to right. If the first expression (before the &&) is false, the shell assigns false as the result of the entire expression, never checking the remaining expressions. If the first expression is false, the whole expression is false when using the logical *and* (&&) operator. Both expressions surrounding a logical && operator must be true for the entire expression to evaluate to true.

When evaluating an expression with the logical *or* (||), if the first expression to the left of the || is true, the shell assigns *true* to the entire expression and never checks further. In a logical || expression, only one of the expressions must be true.

The logical *not* is a unary operator; that is, it evaluates one expression. If the expression to the right of the *not* operator is true, the expression becomes false. If it is false, the expression becomes true.

Precedence and Associativity.   Like C, the C shell uses precedence and associativity rules when testing expressions. If you have an expression with a mix of different operators, such as the following:

```
@  x = 5 + 3 * 2
echo $x
11
```

the shell reads the operators in a certain order. *Precedence* refers to the order of importance of the operator. *Associativity* refers to whether the shell reads the expression from left to right or right to left when the precedence is equal.[7] Other than in arithmetic expressions (which you will not readily need in shell scripts anyway), the order of associativity is from left to right if the precedence is equal. You can change the order by using parentheses. (See Table 9.13.)

```
@ x = ( 5 + 3 ) * 2
echo $x
16
```

Expressions can be numeric, relational, or logical. Numeric expressions use the following arithmetic operators:

```
+ - * /   ++ -- %
```

Relational expressions use the operators that yield either a true (nonzero) or false (zero) result:

```
>   <   >=   <-   ==   !=
```

Logical expressions use these operators:

```
!   &&  ||
```

Table 9.13 Operator Precedence

Precedence	Operator	Meaning
High	( )	Change precedence; group
	˜	Complement
	!	Logical not, negation
	* / %	Multiply, divide, modulo
	+ -	Add, subtract
	<< >>	Bitwise left and right shift
	> >= < <=	Relational operators: greater than, less than
	== !=	Equality: equal to, not equal to

7. Associativity in arithmetic expressions is right to left in cases of equal precedence.

Table 9.13   Operator Precedence (continued)

Precedence	Operator	Meaning
	=~ !~	Pattern matching: matches, does not match
	&	Bitwise *and*
	^	Bitwise exclusive *or*
	|	Bitwise inclusive *or*
	&&	Logical *and*
Low	||	Logical *or*

The *if* Statement.   The simplest form of conditional is the *if* statement. After the *if* is tested, and if the expression evaluates to true, the commands after the *then* keyword are executed until the *endif* is reached. The *endif* keyword terminates the block. The *if* statement may be nested as long as every single *if* statement is terminated with a matching *endif*. The *endif* goes with the nearest enclosing *if*.

FORMAT

```
if ( expression ) then
    command
    command
endif
```

EXAMPLE 9.75

```
(In the Script: Checking for Arguments)
1   if ( $#argv != 1 ) then
2       echo "$0 requires an argument"
3       exit 1
4   endif
```

EXPLANATION

1   This line reads: *If the number of arguments ($#argv) passed in from the command line is not equal to one, then...*

2   If the first line is true, this line and line 3 are executed.

3   The program exits with a value of one, meaning it failed.

4   Every *if* block is closed with an *endif* statement.

Testing and Unset or Null Variables.   The $? special variable is used to test if a variable has been set. It will return true if the variable is set to null.

EXAMPLE 9.76

```
(From .cshrc File)
if ( $?prompt ) then
    set history = 32
endif
```

EXPLANATION

The *.cshrc* file is executed every time you start a new *csh* program. *$?* is used to check to see if a variable has been set. In this example, the shell checks to see if the prompt has been set. If the prompt is set, you are running an interactive shell, not a script. The prompt is only set for interactive use. Since the history mechanism is only useful when running interactively, the shell will not set history if you are running a script.

EXAMPLE 9.77

```
(The Script)
    echo -n "What is your name? "
1   set name = $<
2   if ( "$name" != "" ) then
        grep "$name" datafile
    endif
```

EXPLANATION

1   The user is asked for input. If the user just presses Enter, the variable *name* is set, but it is set to null.

2   The variable is double quoted so that if the user enters more than one word in *name*, the expression will still be evaluated. If the quotes were removed and the user entered first and last name, the shell would exit the script with the error message *if: Expression syntax*. The empty double quotes represent a null string

The *if/else* Statements.   The *if/else* construct is a two-way branching control structure. If the expression after the *if* command is true, the block following it is executed; otherwise, the block after the *else* is executed. The *endif* matches the innermost *if* statement and terminates the statement.

FORMAT

```
if ( expression ) then
    command
else
    command
endif
```

EXAMPLE 9.78

```
1   if ( $answer =~ [Yy]* ) then
2       mail bob < message
3   else
4       mail john < datafile
5   endif
```

EXPLANATION

1 This line reads: *If the value of $answer matches a Y or a y, followed by zero or more characters, then go to line 2; otherwise, go to line 3.* (The * is a shell metacharacter.)

2 The user *bob* is mailed the contents of the file *message*.

3 The commands under the *else* are executed if line 1 is not true.

4 The user *john* is mailed the contents of the file *datafile*.

5 The *endif* block ends the *if* block.

Debugging Expressions.   The –*x* option (called *echoing*) to the C shell allows you to trace what is going on in your script as it executes. If you are unsure what is going on, this is a good way to debug your script.

EXAMPLE 9.79

```
    (The Script: Using Logical Expressions and Checking Values)
    #!/bin/csh -f
    # Scriptname: logical
    set x = 1
    set y = 2
    set z = 3
1   if ( ( "$x" && "$y" ) || ! "$z" ) then
        # Note: grouping and parentheses
2       echo TRUE
    else
        echo FALSE
    endif

    (The Output)
3   % csh -x logical
    set x = 1
    set y = 2
    set z = 3
    if  ( ( 1 && 2 ) || ! 3 )  then
    echo TRUE
    TRUE
    else
    %
```

EXPLANATION

1 The logical expression is being evaluated. The first expression is enclosed in parentheses (not necessary since *&&* is of higher precedence than ||). The parentheses do not require spaces when nested, but the negation operator (*!*) must have a space after it.

2 If the expression evaluates true, this line is executed.

3 The *csh* program is executed with the *–x* switch. This turns on echoing. Every line in your script is echoed back to you after variable substitution has been performed.

The *if* Statement and a Single Command. If an expression is followed by a single command, the *then* and *endif* keywords are not necessary.

FORMAT

```
if ( expression ) single command
```

EXAMPLE 9.80

```
if ($#argv == 0) exit 1
```

EXPLANATION

The expression is tested. If the number of command line arguments, *$#argv*, is equal to zero, the program is exited with a status of one.

The *if/else if* Statements. The *if/else if* construct offers a multiway decision-making mechanism. A number of expressions can be tested, and when one of the expressions evaluated is true, the block of statements that follow is executed. If none of the expressions are true, the *else* block is executed.

FORMAT

```
if ( expression ) then
    command
    command
else if ( expression ) then
    command
    command
else
    command
endif
```

EXAMPLE 9.81

```
(The Script: grade)
   #!/bin/csh -f
   # This script is called grade
   echo -n "What was your grade? "
   set grade = $<
1  if ( $grade >= 90 && $grade <= 100 ) then
       echo "You got an A\!"
2  else if ( $grade > 79 ) then
       echo "You got a B"
3  else if ( $grade > 69 ) then
       echo "You're average"
   else
4       echo "Better study"
5  endif
```

EXPLANATION

1   If *grade* is greater than or equal to *90 and grade* is less than or equal to *100*, then *You got an A!* is printed. *Both* expressions surrounding the *&&* must be true or program control will go to the *else if* on line 2.

2   If line 1 is false, test the expression (line 2), and if it is true, *You got a B* is printed.

3   If line 1 and 2 are both false, try this one. If this expression is true, then *echo You're average* is printed.

4   If all of the above expressions test false, the statements in the *else* block are executed.

5   The *endif* ends the entire *if* construct.

Exit Status and the Status Variable.   Every UNIX command returns an exit status. If the command was successful, it returns an exit status of zero. If the command failed, it returns a nonzero exit status. You can test to see whether the command succeeded or failed by looking at the value of the C shell status variable. The status variable contains the exit status of the last command executed.

EXAMPLE 9.82

```
1  % grep ellie /etc/passwd
   ellie:pHAZk66gA:9496:41:Ellie:/home/jody/ellie:/bin/csh
2  % echo $status
   0                      # Zero shows that grep was a success

3  % grep joe /etc/passwd
4  % echo $status
   1                      # Nonzero shows that grep failed
```

EXPLANATION

1   The *grep* program found *ellie* in the */etc/passwd* file.

EXPLANATION (CONTINUED)

2   The *grep* program, if it finds the pattern *ellie*, returns a zero status when it exits.

3   The *grep* program did not find *joe* in the */etc/passwd* file.

4   The *grep* program returns a nonzero status if the pattern is not found.

Exiting from a Shell Script.   In your shell script, the *exit* command will take you back to the shell prompt. The *exit* command takes an integer value to indicate the type of exit. A nonzero argument indicates failure; zero indicates success. The number must be between 0 and 255.

EXAMPLE 9.83

```
(The checkon Shell Script)
    #!/bin/csh -f
1   if ( $#argv != 1 ) then
2          echo "$0 requires an argument"
3          exit 2
4   endif


(At the command line)
5   % checkon
    checkon requires an argument
6   % echo $status
    2
```

EXPLANATION

1   If the number of arguments passed in from the command line ($#argv) is not equal to one, then go to line 2.

2   The *echo* prints the scriptname ($0) and the string *requires an argument*.

3   The program exits back to the prompt with a value of 2. This value will be stored in the *status* variable of the parent shell.

4   The end of the conditional *if*.

5   At the command line, the program *checkon* is executed without an argument.

6   The program exits with a value of 2, which is stored in the *status* variable.

Using the Status Variable in a Script.   The *status* variable can be used in a script to test the status of a command. The *status* variable is assigned the value of the last command that was executed.

EXAMPLE 9.84

```
(The Script)
    #!/bin/csh -f
```

EXAMPLE 9.84 (CONTINUED)

```
1    ypmatch  $1  passwd >& /dev/null
2    if ( $status == 0 ) then
3         echo Found $1 in the NIS database
     endif
```

EXPLANATION

1   The *ypmatch* program checks the NIS database to see if the name of the user, passed in as the first argument, is in the database.

2   If the *status* returned from the last command is zero, the *then* block is executed.

3   This line is executed if the *if* test expression evaluated to be true.

Evaluating Commands within Conditionals.   The C shell evaluates *expressions* in conditionals. To evaluate *commands* in conditionals, curly braces must enclose the command. If the command is successful, that is, returns an exit status of zero, the curly braces tell the shell to evaluate the expression as true (*1*).[8] If the command fails, the exit status is nonzero, and the expression is evaluated as false (*0*).

It is important, when using a command in a conditional, to know the exit status of that command. For example, the *grep* program returns an exit status of zero when it finds the pattern it is searching for, one when it cannot find the pattern, and two when it cannot find the file. When *awk* or *sed* are searching for patterns, those programs return zero whether or not they are successful in the pattern search. The criterion for success with *awk* and *sed* is based on whether or not the syntax is right; that is, if you typed the command correctly, the exit status of *awk* and *sed* is zero.

If the exclamation mark is placed before the expression, it *nots* the entire expression so that if true, it is now false, and vice versa. Make sure a space follows the exclamation mark, or the C shell will invoke the history mechanism.

FORMAT

```
if  { ( command ) }  then
    command
    command
endif
```

{ } COMMAND EVALUATION

EXAMPLE 9.85

```
     #!/bin/csh -f
1    if  { ( who | grep $1 >& /dev/null ) } then
2         echo $1 is logged on and running:
3         ps -ef | grep "^ *$1"        # ps -aux for BSD
4    endif
```

---

8. The command's exit status is inverted by the shell so that the expression yields a true or false result.

EXPLANATION

1 The *who* command is piped to the *grep* command. All of the output is sent to /dev/null, the UNIX "bit bucket." The output of the *who* command is sent to *grep*; *grep* searches for the name of the user stored in the *$1* variable (first command line argument). If *grep* is successful and finds the user, an exit status of zero is returned. The shell will then invert the exit status of the *grep* command to yield one, or true. If the shell evaluates the expression to be true, it executes the commands between the *then* and *endif*.

2 If the C shell evaluates the expression in line 1 to be true, lines 2 and 3 are executed.

3 All the processes running and owned by *$1* are displayed.

4 The *endif* ends the *if* statements.

FORMAT

```
if ! { (command) } then
```

EXAMPLE 9.86

```
1   if   !   {  (  ypmatch $user passwd >& /dev/null  )  }  then
2       echo $user is not a user here.
        exit 1
3   endif
```

EXPLANATION

1 The *ypmatch* command is used to search the NIS *passwd* file, if you are using a network. If the command succeeds in finding the user (*$user*) in the *passwd* file, the expression evaluates to be true. The exclamation point (*!*) preceding the expression *nots* or complements the expression; that is, makes it false if it is true, and vice versa.

2 If the expression is not true, the user is not found and this line is executed.

3 The *endif* ends this *if* block.

The *goto*. A *goto* allows you to jump to some label in the program and start execution at that point. Although *gotos* are frowned upon by many programmers, they are sometimes useful for breaking out of nested loops.

EXAMPLE 9.87

```
(The Script)
    #!/bin/csh -f
1   startover:
2   echo "What was your grade? "
```

EXAMPLE 9.87 (CONTINUED)

```
    set grade = $<
3   if ( "$grade" < 0 || "$grade" > 100 ) then
4       echo "Illegal grade"
5       goto startover
    endif
    if ( $grade >= 89 ) then
        echo "A for the genius\!"
    else if ( $grade >= 79 ) then
        .. < Program continues >
```

EXPLANATION

1   The label is a user-defined word with a colon appended. The label is called *start-over*. During execution of the program, the label is ignored by the shell, unless the shell is explicitly directed to go to the label.

2   The user is asked for input.

3   If the expression is true, (the user entered a grade less than *0* or greater than *100*), the string *Illegal grade* is printed, and the *goto* starts execution at the named label, *startover*. The program continues to execute from that point.

4   The *if* expression tested false, so this line is printed.

5   The *goto* sends control to line 1 and execution starts after the label, *startover*.

File Testing.   The C shell has a built-in set of options for testing attributes of files, such as, *Is it a directory, a plain file (not a directory), or a readable file,* and so forth. For other types of file tests, the UNIX *test* command is used. The built-in options for file inquiry are listed in Table 9.14.

Table 9.14   File Testing

Test Flag	(What It Tests) True If
–r	Current user can read the file.
–w	Current user can write to the file.
–x	Current user can execute the file.
–e	File exists.
–o	Current user owns the file.
–z	File is zero length.
–d	File is a directory.
–f	File is a plain file.

EXAMPLE 9.88

```
    #!/bin/csh -f
1   if ( -e file ) then
        echo file exists
    endif

2   if ( -d file ) then
        echo file is a directory
    endif

3   if ( ! -z file ) then
        echo file is not of zero length
    endif
4   if ( -r file && -w file ) then
        echo file is readable and writeable
    endif
```

EXPLANATION

1 The statement reads, *if the file exists, then ...*
2 The statement reads, *if the file is a directory, then ...*
3 The statement reads, *if the file is not of zero length, then* ...
4 The statement reads, *if the file is readable and writeable, then ... .* The file testing flags cannot be stacked, as in *–rwx* file. A single option precedes the filename (e.g., *–r file && –w file && –x file*).

The *test* Command and File Testing. The UNIX *test* command includes options that were built-in to the C shell, as well as a number of options that were not. See Table 9.15 for a list of test options. You may need these additional options when testing less common attributes of files such as block and special character files, or *setuid* files. The *test* command evaluates an expression and returns an exit status of either zero for success or one for failure. When using the *test* command in an *if* conditional statement, curly braces must surround the command so that the shell can evaluate the exit status properly.[9]

To use the *test* command in a conditional statement, use curly braces as you would for any other command for the C shell to evaluate the exit status properly.

---

9. A common error is to name your script *test*. If your search path contains the UNIX *test* command first, it will execute it. The *test* command either displays an error or nothing at all if the syntax is correct.

Table 9.15 File Testing with the *test* Command

Option	Meaning—Tests True If
–b	File is a block special file.
–c	File is a character special file.
–d	File exists and is a directory file.
–f	File exists and is a plain file.
–g	File has the set-group-ID bit set.
–k	File has the sticky bit set.
–p	File is a named pipe.
–r	Current user can read the file.
–s	File exists and is not empty.
–t n	n is file descriptor for terminal.
–u	File has the set-user-ID bit set.
–w	Current user can write to the file.
–x	Current user can execute the file.

EXAMPLE 9.89

```
1  if { test  -b file } echo file is a block device file

2  if { test -u file }  echo file has the set-user-id bit set
```

EXPLANATION

1   The statement reads, *if the file is a block special file (found in /dev), then ...*
2   The statement reads, *if the file is a setuid program (set user ID), then ...*

Nesting Conditionals.   Conditional statements can be nested. Every *if* must have a corresponding *endif* (*else if* does not have an *endif*). It is a good idea to indent nested statements and line up the *if*s and *endif*s so that you can read and test the program more effectively.

EXAMPLE 9.90

```
(The Script)
    #!/bin/csh -f
    # Scriptname: filecheck

    # Usage: filecheck filename

    set file=$1
1   if ( ! -e $file ) then
        echo "$file does not exist"
        exit 1
    endif
2   if ( -d $file ) then
        echo "$file is a directory"
3   else if (-f $file) then
4       if ( -r $file && -x $file ) then      # Nested if construct
            echo "You have read and execute permission on $file"
5       endif
    else
        print "$file is neither a plain file nor a directory."
6   endif
```

```
(The Command Line)
$ filecheck testing
You have read and execute permission of file testing.
```

EXPLANATION

1   If *file* (after variable substitution) is a file that does not exist (note the *not* operator, *!*), the commands under the *then* keyword are executed. An exit value of one means that the program failed.

2   If the *file* is a directory, print *testing is a directory.*

3   If the *file* is not a directory, *else if* the file is a plain file, *then* ... the next statement is executed, another *if*.

4   This *if* is nested in the previous *if*. If *file* is readable, writeable, and executable, *then* ... . This *if* has its own *endif* and is lined up to indicate where it belongs.

5   The *endif* terminates the innermost *if* construct.

6   The *endif* terminates the outermost *if* construct.

The *switch* Command.   The *switch* command is an alternative to using the *if–then–else if* construct. Sometimes the *switch* command makes a program clearer to read when handling multiple options. The value in the *switch* expression is matched against the expressions, called *labels*, following the *case* keyword. The *case* labels will accept constant expressions and wildcards. The label is terminated with a colon. The *default* label is optional, but its action is taken if none of the other cases match the *switch* expression. The *breaksw* is used to transfer execution to the *endsw*. If a *breaksw* is omitted and a label is matched, any statements below the matched label are executed until either a *breaksw* or *endsw* is reached.

FORMAT

```
switch (variable)
case constant:
    commands
    breaksw
case constant:
    commands
    breaksw
endsw
```

EXAMPLE 9.91

```
(The Script - colors)
    #!/bin/csh -f
    # This script is called colors
1   echo -n "Which color do you like? "
2   set color = $<
3   switch ("$color")
4   case bl*:
        echo I feel $color
        echo The sky is $color
5       breaksw
6   case red:              # Is is red or is it yellow?
7   case yellow:
8       echo The sun is sometimes $color.
9       breaksw
10  default:
11      echo $color not one of the categories.
12      breaksw
13  endsw
```

```
(The Command Line)
% colors
```

```
(The Output)
1   Which color do you like? red
8   The sun is sometimes red.
1   Which color do you like? Doesn't matter
11  Doesn't matter is not one of the categories.
```

EXPLANATION

1   The user is asked for input.

2   The input is assigned to the *color* variable.

3   The *switch* statement evaluates the variable. The variable is enclosed in double quotes in case the user entered more than one word. The *switch* statement evaluates a single word or string of words if the string of words is held together with double quotes.

EXPLANATION (CONTINUED)

4   The *case* label is *bl**, meaning that the *switch* expression will be matched against any set of characters starting with *b*, followed by an *l*. If the user entered *blue*, *black*, *blah*, *blast*, etc., the commands under this *case* label would be executed.

5   The *breaksw* transfers program control to the *endsw* statement.

6   If the *switch* statement matches this label, *red*, the program starts executing statements until the *breaksw* on line 9 is reached. Line 8 will be executed. *The sun is sometimes red* is displayed.

7   If line 4 is not matched, cases *red* and *yellow* are tested.

8   If either label, *red* or *yellow*, is matched, this line is executed.

9   The *breaksw* transfers program control to the *endsw* statement.

10 The default label is reached if none of the case labels matches the *switch* expression. This is like the *if/else if/else* construct.

11 This line is printed if the user enters something not matched in any of the above cases.

12 This *breaksw* is optional since the switch will end here. It is recommended to leave the *breaksw* here so that if more cases are added later, it will not be overlooked.

13 The *endsw* terminates the *switch* statement.

Nesting Switches. Switches can be nested; i.e., a *switch* statement and its cases can be contained within another *switch* statement as one of its cases. There must be an *endsw* to terminate each *switch* statement. A *default* case is not required.

EXAMPLE 9.92

```
(The Script: systype)
  #!/bin/csh -f
  # This script is called systype
  # Program to determine the type of system you are on.
  echo "Your system type is. "
1  set release = (`uname -r`)
2  switch (`uname -s`)
3  case SunOS:
4      switch ("$release")
5      case 4.*:
              echo "SunOS $release"
              breaksw
6      case [56].*:
              echo "Solaris $release"
              breaksw
7      endsw
       breaksw
   case HP*:
       echo HP-UX
       breaksw
```

412 Chapter 9 • The C Shell

```
        case Linux:
            echo Linux
            breaksw
8   endsw

(The Command Line)
% systype
Your system type:
SunOS 4.1.2
```

EXPLANATION

1   The variable *release* is assigned the output of *uname -r*, the release number for the version of the operating system.

2   The *switch* command evaluates the output of *uname -s*, the name of the operating system.

3   If the system type is *SunOS*, the *case* command on line 3 is executed.

4   The value of the variable *release* is evaluated in each of the cases for a match.

5   The *case* for all release versions 4 are tested.

6   The *case* for all release versions 5 and 6 are tested.

7   The inner *switch* statement is terminated.

8   The outer *switch* statement is terminated.

9.2.7 Loops

Looping constructs allow you to execute the same statements a number of times. The C shell supports two types of loops: the *foreach* loop and the **while** loop. The *foreach* loop is used when you need to execute commands on a list of items, one item at a time, such as a list of files or a list of usernames. The *while* loop is used when you want to keep executing a command until a certain condition is met.

The *foreach* Loop.   The *foreach* command is followed by a variable and a wordlist enclosed in parentheses. The first time the loop is entered, the first word in the list is assigned to the variable. The list is shifted to the left by one and the body of the loop is entered. Each command in the loop body is executed until the *end* statement is reached. Control returns to the top of the loop. The next word on the list is assigned to the variable, the commands after the *foreach* line are executed, the end is reached, control returns to the top of the *foreach* loop, the next word in the wordlist is processed, and so on. When the wordlist is empty, the loop ends.

FORMAT

```
foreach variable (wordlist)
      commands
end
```

EXAMPLE 9.93

```
1    foreach person (bob sam sue fred)
2        mail $person < letter
3    end
```

EXPLANATION

1   The *foreach* command is followed by a variable, *person*, and a wordlist enclosed in parentheses. The variable *person* will be assigned the value *bob* the first time the *foreach* loop is entered. Once *bob* has been assigned to *person*, *bob* is shifted off (to the left) and *sam* is at the beginning of the list. When the *end* statement is reached, control starts at the top of the loop, and *sam* is assigned to the variable *person*. This procedure continues until *fred* is shifted off, at which time the list is empty and the loop is over.

2   The user *bob* will be mailed the contents of the file *letter* the first time through the loop.

3   When the *end* statement is reached, loop control is returned to the *foreach*, and the next element in the list is assigned to the variable *person*.

EXAMPLE 9.94

```
(The Command Line)
% cat maillist
tom
dick
harry
dan

(The Script - mailtomaillist)
    #!/bin/csh -f
    # This script is called mailtomaillist
1    foreach person (`cat maillist`)
2        mail $person <<EOF
        Hi $person,
        How are you?  I've missed you. Come on over
        to my place.
        Your pal,
                $LOGNAME@`uname -n`
    EOF
3    end
```

EXPLANATION

1   Command substitution is performed within the parentheses. The contents of the file *maillist* become the wordlist. Each name in the wordlist (*tom, dick, harry, dan*) is assigned, in turn, to the variable *person*. After the looping statements are executed and the *end* is reached, control returns to the *foreach*, a name is shifted off from the list, and assigned to the variable *person*. The next name in the list replaces the one that was just shifted off. The list therefore decreases in size by one. This process continues until all the names have been shifted off and the list is empty.

2   The *here document* is used. Input is sent to the *mail* program from the first *EOF* to the terminating *EOF*. (It is important that the last *EOF* is against the left-hand margin and has no surrounding whitespace.) Each person in the list will be sent the *mail* message.

3   The *end* statement for the *foreach* loop marks the end of the block of lines that is executed within this loop. Control returns to the top of the loop.

EXAMPLE 9.95

```
1   foreach file (*.c)
2       cc $file -o $file:r
    end
```

REMOVE .C EXTENSION

EXPLANATION

1   The wordlist for the *foreach* command is a list of files in the current directory ending in *.c* (i.e., all the C source files).

2   Each file in the list will be compiled. If, for example, the first file to be processed is *program.c*, the shell will expand the *cc* command line to

```
cc program.c -o program
```

The *:r* causes the *.c* extension to be removed.

EXAMPLE 9.96

```
(The Command Line)
1   % runit f1 f2 f3 dir2 dir3

(The Script)
    #!/bin/csh -f
    # This script is called runit.
    # It loops through a list of files passed as
    # arguments.

2   foreach arg ($*)
```

EXAMPLE 9.96 (CONTINUED)

```
3      if ( -e $arg ) then
       ...              Program code continues here

       else
       ...              Program code continues here
       endif
4    end
5    echo "Program continues here"
```

EXPLANATION

1   The scriptname is *runit*; the command line arguments are *f1, f2, f3, dir2*, and *dir3*.

2   The $* variable evaluates to a list of all the arguments (positional parameters) passed in at the command line. The *foreach* command processes, in turn, each of the words in the wordlist, *f1, f2, f3, dir2*, and *dir3*. Each time through the loop, the first word in the list is assigned to the variable *arg*. After a word is assigned, it is shifted off (to the left) and the next word is assigned to *arg*, until the list is empty.

3   The commands in this block are executed for each item in the list until the *end* statement is reached.

4   The *end* statement terminates the loop after the wordlist is empty.

5   After the loop ends, the program continues to run.

The *while* Loop. The *while* loop evaluates an expression, and as long as the expression is true (nonzero), the commands below the *while* command will be executed until the *end* statement is reached. Control will then return to the *while* expression, the expression will be evaluated, and if still true, the commands will be executed again, and so on. When the *while* expression is false, the loop ends and control starts after the *end* statement.

EXAMPLE 9.97

```
(The Script)
    #!/bin/csh -f
1   set num = 0
2   while ($num < 10)
3       echo $num
4       @ num++          # See arithmetic.
5   end
6   echo "Program continues here"
```

EXPLANATION

1   The variable *num* is set to an initial value of zero.

2   The *while* loop is entered and the expression is tested. If the value of *num* is less than *10*, the expression is true, and lines 3 and 4 are executed.

3   The value of *num* is displayed each time through the loop.

EXPLANATION (CONTINUED)

4 The value of the variable *num* is incremented. If this statement were omitted, the loop would continue forever.

5 The *end* statement terminates the block of executable statements. When this line is reached, control is returned to the top of the *while* loop and the expression is evaluated again. This continues until the *while* expression is false (i.e., when *$num* is *10*).

6 Program execution continues here after the loop terminates.

EXAMPLE 9.98

```
(The Script)
    #!/bin/csh -f
1   echo -n  "Who wrote \"War and Peace\"?"
2   set answer = $<
3   while ("$answer" != "Tolstoy")
        echo "Wrong, try again\!"
4       set answer = $<
5   end
6   echo Yeah!
```

EXPLANATION

1 The user is asked for input.

2 The variable *answer* is assigned whatever the user inputs.

3 The *while* command evaluates the expression. If the value of *$answer* is not equal to the string *Tolstoy* exactly, the message *Wrong, try again!* is printed and the program waits for user input.

4 The variable *answer* is assigned the new input. This line is important. If the value of the variable *answer* never changes, the loop expression will never become false, thus causing the loop to spin infinitely.

5 The *end* statement terminates the block of code inside the *while* loop.

6 If the user enters *Tolstoy*, the loop expression tests false, and control goes to this line. *Yeah!* is printed.

The *repeat* Command.   The *repeat* command takes two arguments, a number and a command. The *command* is executed *that* number of times.

EXAMPLE 9.99

```
% repeat 3 echo hello
hello
hello
hello
```

EXPLANATION

The *echo* command is executed three times.

9.2.8 Looping Commands

The *shift* Command.   The *shift* command, without an array name as its argument, shifts the *argv* array by one word from the left, thereby decreasing the size of the *argv* array by one. Once shifted off, the array element is lost.

EXAMPLE 9.100

```
(The Script)
    #!/bin/csh -f
    # Script is called loop.args
1   while ($#argv)
2       echo $argv
3       shift
4   end

(The Command Line)
5   % loop.args a b c d e
    a b c d e
    b c d e
    c d e
    d e
    e
```

EXPLANATION

1   $#*argv* evaluates to the number of command line arguments. If there are five command line arguments, *a, b, c, d,* and *e,* the value of $#*argv* is 5 the first time in the loop. The expression is tested and yields 5, true.

2   The command line arguments are printed.

3   The *argv* array is shifted one to the left. There are only four arguments left, starting with *b.*

4   The end of the loop is reached, and control goes back to the top of the loop. The expression is reevaluated. This time, $#*argv* is 4. The arguments are printed, and the array is shifted again. This goes on until all of the arguments are shifted off. At that time, when the expression is evaluated, it will be 0, which is false, and the loop exits.

5   The arguments *a, b, c, d,* and *e* are passed to the script via the *argv* array.

The *break* Command.   The *break* command is used to break out of a loop so that control starts after the *end* statement. It breaks out of the innermost loop. Execution continues after the *end* statement of the loop.

EXAMPLE 9.101

```
    #!/bin/csh -f
    # This script is called baseball
1   echo -n "What baseball hero died in August 1995? "
2   set answer = $<
3   while ("$answer" !~ [Mm]*)
4         echo "Wrong\! Try again."
          set answer = $<
5         if ( "$answer" =~ [Mm]* ) break
6   end
7   echo "You are a scholar."
```

EXPLANATION

1   The user is asked for input.

2   The input from the user is assigned to the variable *answer* (answer: Mickey Mantle).

3   The *while* expression reads: *While the value of answer does not begin with a big M or little m, followed by zero or more of any character, enter the loop.*

4   The user gets to try again. The variable is reset.

5   If the variable *answer* matches *M* or *m*, *break* out of the loop. Go to the *end* statement and start executing statements at line 7.

6   The *end* statement terminates this block of statements after the loop.

7   After the loop exits, control starts here and this line is executed.

EXAMPLE 9.102

```
    #!/bin/csh -f
    # This script is called database
1   while (1)
        echo "Select a menu item"
2       cat << EOF
    1) Append
    2) Delete
    3) Update
    4) Exit
    EOF
3       set choice = $<
4       switch ($choice)
        case 1:
              echo "Appending"
5             break                # Break out of loop; not a breaksw
        case 2:
              echo "Deleting"
              break
        case 3:
              echo "Updating"
              break
```

EXAMPLE   9.102 (CONTINUED)

```
        case 4:
                exit 0
        default:
6               echo "Invalid choice. Try again.
        endsw
7   end
8   echo "Program continues here"
```

EXPLANATION

1   This is called an *infinite* loop. The expression always evaluates to one, which is true.

2   This is a *here document*. A menu is printed to the screen.

3   The user selects a menu item.

4   The *switch* command evaluates the variable.

5   If the user selects a valid choice, between 1 and 4, the command after the appropriate matching *case* label is executed. The *break* statement causes the program to break out of the loop and start execution on line 8. Don't confuse this with the *breaksw* statement, which merely exits the switch at *endsw*.

6   If the *default case* is matched, that is, none of the cases are matched, program control goes to the end of the loop and then starts again at the top of the *while*. Since the expression after the *while* always evaluates true, the body of the loop is entered and the menu is displayed again.

7   End of the *while* loop statements.

8   After the loop is exited, this line is executed.

Nested Loops and the *repeat* Command.   Rather than a *goto*, the *repeat* command can be used to break out of nested loops. The *repeat* command will not do this with the *continue* command.

EXAMPLE   9.103

```
(Simple Script)
    #!/bin/csh -f
1 ─ while (1)
  │     echo "Hello, in 1st loop"
2 │   ─ while (1)
  │ │         echo "In 2nd loop"
  │ │       ─ while (1)
  │ │       │     echo "In 3rd loop"
  │ │       │     repeat 3 break
  │ │       └ end
  │ └ end
  └ end
5   echo "Out of all loops"
```

EXAMPLE   9.103 (CONTINUED)

```
(The Output)
Hello, in 1st loop
In 2nd loop
In 3rd loop
Out of all loops
```

EXPLANATION

1   Start the first *while* loop.

2   Enter the second nested *while* loop.

3   Enter the third nested *while* loop.

4   The *repeat* command will cause *break* to be executed three times; it will break first out of this innermost loop, then the second loop, and last, the first loop. Control continues at line 5.

5   Program control starts here after loop terminates.

The *continue* Command.   The *continue* statement starts execution at the top of the innermost loop.

EXAMPLE   9.104

```
1   set done = 0
2   while ( ! $done )
        echo "Are you finished yet?"
        set answer = $<
3       if ("$answer" =~ [Nn]*) continue
4       set done = 1
5   end
```

EXPLANATION

1   The variable *done* is assigned zero.

2   The expression is tested. It reads: *while (! 0)*. Not 0 is evaluated as true (logical *not*).

3   If the user entered *No, no,* or *nope* (anything starting with *N* or *n*), the expression is true and the *continue* statement returns control to the top of the loop where the expression is reevaluated.

4   If *answer* does not start with *N* or *n*, the variable *done* is reset to one. When the end of the loop is reached, control starts at the top of the loop and the expression is tested. It reads: *while (! 1)*. Not 1 is false. The loop exits.

5   This marks the end of the *while* loop.

EXAMPLE 9.105

```
(The Script)
    #!/bin/csh -f
1   if ( ! -e memo ) then
        echo  "memo file non existent"
        exit 1
    endif
2   foreach person (anish bob don karl jaye)
3       if ("$person" =~ [Kk]arl) continue
4       mail -s "Party time"  $person < memo
    end
```

EXPLANATION

1   A file check is done. If the file *memo* does not exist, the user is sent an error message and the program exits with a status of 1.

2   The loop will assign each person in the list to the variable *person*, in turn, and then shift off the name in the list to process the next one.

3   If the person's name is *Karl* or *karl*, the *continue* statement starts execution at the top of the *foreach* loop (*Karl* is not sent the memo because his name was shifted off after being assigned to *person*). The next name in the list is assigned to *person*.

4   Everyone on the mailing list is sent the memo, except *karl*.

9.2.9 Interrupt Handling

If a script is interrupted with the Interrupt key, it terminates and control is returned to the C shell, that is, you get your prompt back. The *onintr* command is used to process interrupts within a script. It allows you to ignore the interrupt (^C) or transfer control to another part of the program before exiting. Normally, the *interrupt* command is used with a label to "clean up" before exiting. The *onintr* command without arguments restores the default action.

EXAMPLE 9.106

```
(The Script)
1   onintr  finish
2      < Script continues here >
3   finish:
4   onintr -          # Disable further interrupts
5   echo Cleaning temp files
6   rm $$tmp* ; exit 1
```

EXPLANATION

1   The *onintr* command is followed by a label name. The label *finish* is a user-defined label; control will be transferred to the *finish* label if an interrupt occurs. Usually this line is at the beginning of the script. It is not in effect until it is executed in the script.

EXPLANATION (CONTINUED)

2   The rest of the script lines are executed unless ^C (Interrupt key) is pressed while the program is in execution, at which time, control is transferred to the label.

3   This is the label; when the interrupt comes in, the program will continue to run, executing the statements below the label.

4   To shield this part of the script from interrupts, the *onintr* – is used. If Control-C is entered now, it will be ignored.

5   This line is echoed to the screen.

6   All *tmp* files are removed. The *tmp* files are prefixed with the shell's PID ($$) number and suffixed with any number of characters. The program exits with a status of 1.

9.2.10 *setuid* Scripts

Whoever runs a *setuid* program temporarily (as long as he or she is running the *setuid* program) becomes the owner of that program and has the same permissions as the owner. The *passwd* program is a good example of a *setuid* program. When you change your password, you temporarily become *root*, but only during the execution of the *passwd* program. That is why you are able to change your password in the */etc/passwd* (or */etc/shadow*) file, which normally is off-limits to regular users.

Shell programs can be written as *setuid* programs. You might want to do this if you have a script that is accessing a file containing information that should not be accessible to regular users, such as salary or personal information. If the script is a *setuid* script, the person running the script can have access to the data, but it is still restricted from others. A *setuid* program requires the following steps:

1. In the script, the first line is

```
#!/bin/csh -feb
```

The -feb options:

```
-f   fast start up; don't execute .cshrc
-e   abort immediately if interrupted
-b   this is a setuid script
```

2. Next, change the permissions on the script so that it can run as a *setuid* program:

```
% chmod 4755 script_name
          or
% chmod +srx script_name
% ls -l
-rwsr-xr-x   2 ellie        512 Oct 10 17:18 script_name
```

9.2.11 Storing Scripts

After creating successful scripts, it is customary to collect them in a common script directory and change your path so that the scripts can be executed from any location.

EXAMPLE 9.107

```
1   % mkdir ~/bin
2   % mv myscript ~/bin
3   % vi .login

    In .login reset the path to add ~/bin.
4       set path = ( /usr/ucb /usr /usr/etc ~/bin . )

5   (At command line)
    % source .login
```

EXPLANATION

1 Make a directory under your home directory called *bin*, or any other name you choose.

2 Move any error-free scripts into the *bin* directory. Putting buggy scripts here will just cause problems.

3 Go into your *.login* file and reset the path.

4 The new path contains the directory *~/bin*, which is where the shell will look for executable programs. Since it is near the end of the path, a system program that may have the same name as one of your scripts will be executed first.

5 By sourcing the *.login*, the *path* changes are affected; it is not necessary to log out and back in again.

9.2.12 Built-In Commands

Rather than residing on disk like UNIX commands, built-in commands are part of the C shell's internal code and are executed from within the shell. If a built-in command occurs as any component of a pipeline except the last, it is executed in a subshell. See Table 9.16 for a list of built-in commands.

Table 9.16 Built-In Commands and Their Meanings

Built-In Command	Meaning
:	Interpret null command, but perform no action.
alias	A nickname for a command.
bg [%job]	Run the current or specified jobs in the background.
break	Break out of the innermost *foreach* or *while* loop.
breaksw	Break from a switch, resuming after the *endsw*.

Table 9.16 Built-In Commands and Their Meanings (continued)

Built-In Command	*Meaning*
case label:	A label in a switch statement.
cd [dir] *chdir [dir]*	Change the shell's working directory to *dir*. If no argument is given, change to the home directory of the user.
continue	Continue execution of the nearest enclosing *while* or *foreach*.
default:	Label the *default* case in a switch statement. The *default* should come after all case labels.
dirs [–l]	Print the directory stack, most recent to the left; the first directory shown is the current directory. With the –*l* argument, produce an unabbreviated printout; use of the ~ notation is suppressed.
echo [–n] list	Write the words in *list* to the shell's standard output, separated by space characters. The output is terminated with a newline unless the –*n* option is used.
eval command	Run *command* as standard input to the shell and execute the resulting commands. This is usually used to execute commands generated as the result of command or variable substitution, since parsing occurs before these substitutions (e.g., *eval 'tset -s options'*).
exec command	Execute *command* in place of the current shell, which terminates.
exit [(expr)]	Exit the shell, either with the value of the status variable or with the value specified by *expr*.
fg [% job]	Bring the current or specified *job* into the foreground.
foreach var (wordlist)	See "The foreach Loop" on page 412.
glob wordlist	Perform filename expansion on wordlist. Like *echo*, but no *escapes* (\\) are recognized. Words are delimited by null characters in the output.
goto label	See "The goto" on page 405.
hashstat	Print a statistics line indicating how effective the internal hash table has been at locating commands (and avoiding *execs*). An *exec* is attempted for each component of the path where the hash function indicates a possible hit, and in each component that does not begin with a backslash.
history [–hr] [n]	Display the *history* list; if *n* is given, display only the *n* most recent events.
–r	Reverse the order of the printout to be most recent first rather than oldest first.
–h	Display the history list without leading numbers. This is used to produce files suitable for sourcing using the –*h* option to source.
if (expr)	See "Flow Control and Conditional Constructs" on page 395.

Table 9.16   Built-In Commands and Their Meanings (continued)

Built-In Command	Meaning
else if (expr2) then	See "Flow Control and Conditional Constructs" on page 395.
jobs [–l]	List the active *jobs* under job control.
–l	List IDs in addition to the normal information.
kill [–sig] [pid] *[%job]* ... *kill –l*	Send the *TERM* (terminate) signal, by default or by the signal specified, to the specified ID, the job indicated, or the current job. Signals are given either by number or name. There is no default. Typing *kill* does not send a signal to the current job. If the signal being sent is *TERM* (terminate) or *HUP* (hangup), then the job or process is sent a *CONT* (continue) signal as well.
–l	List the signal names that can be sent.
limit [–h] [resource *[max–use]]*	*Limit* the consumption by the current process or any process it spawns, each not to exceed *max use* on the specified *resource*. If *max–use* is omitted, print the current *limit*; if *resource* is omitted, display all *limits*.
–h	Use hard limits instead of the current limits. Hard limits impose a ceiling on the values of the current limits. Only the superuser may raise the hard limits. Resource is one of: *cputime*, maximum CPU seconds per process; *filesize*, largest single file allowed; *datasize*, maximum data size (including stack) for the process; *stacksize*, maximum stack size for the process; *coredump*, maximum size of a core dump; and *descriptors*, maximum value for a file descriptor.
login [username|–p]	Terminate a *login* shell and invoke *login(1)*. The *.logout* file is not processed. If *username* is omitted, *login* prompts for the name of a user.
–p	Preserve the current environment (variables).
logout	Terminate a *login* shell.
nice [+n|–n] *[command]*	Increment the process priority value for the shell or *command* by n. The higher the priority value, the lower the priority of a process and the slower it runs. If *command* is omitted, *nice* increments the value for the current shell. If no increment is specified, *nice* sets the *nice* value to 4. The range of *nice* values is from –20 through 19. Values of n outside this range set the value to the lower or higher boundary, respectively.
+n	Increment the process priority value by n.
–n	Decrement by n. This argument can be used only by the superuser.
nohup [command]	Run *command* with *HUPs* (hangups) ignored. With no arguments, ignore *HUPs* throughout the remainder of a script.
notify [%job]	*Notify* the user asynchronously when the status of the current or of a specified *job* changes.

Table 9.16   Built-In Commands and Their Meanings (continued)

Built-In Command	Meaning
*onintr [–	label]*	Control the action of the shell on interrupts. With no arguments, *onintr* restores the default action of the shell on interrupts. (The shell terminates shell scripts and returns to the terminal command input level.) With the minus sign argument, the shell ignores all interrupts. With a *label* argument, the shell executes a *goto label* when an interrupt is received or a child process terminates because it was interrupted.
popd [+n]	Pop the directory stack and *cd* to the new top directory. The elements of the directory stack are numbered from zero, starting at the top.
+n	Discard the *n*th entry in the stack.
*pushd [+n	dir]*	Push a directory onto the directory stack. With no arguments, exchange the top two elements.
+n	Rotate the *n*th entry to the top of the stack and *cd* to it.
dir	Push the current working directory onto the stack and change to *dir*.
rehash	Recompute the internal hash table of the contents of directories listed in the *path* variable to account for new commands added.
repeat count command	Repeat command *count* times.
set [var [= value]]	See "Variables" on page 365.
setenv [VAR [word]]	See "Variables" on page 365. The most commonly used environment variables, *USER, TERM,* and *PATH*, are automatically imported to and exported from the *csh* variables, *user*, *term*, and *path*; there is no need to use *setenv* for these. In addition, the shell sets the *PWD* environment variable from the *csh* variable *cwd* whenever the latter changes.
shift [variable]	The components of *argv*, or *variable*, if supplied, are shifted to the left, discarding the first component. It is an error for *variable* not to be set, or to have a null value.
source [–h] name	Read commands from *name*. *Source* commands may be nested, but if they are nested too deeply, the shell may run out of file descriptors. An error in a sourced file at any level terminates all nested *source* commands. Used commonly to reexecute the *.login* or *.cshrc* files to ensure variable settings
–h	are handled within the current shell, i.e., shell does not create a child shell (fork). Place commands from the filename on the history list without executing them.
stop [%job] ...	*Stop* the current or specified background *job*.

Table 9.16 Built-In Commands and Their Meanings (continued)

Built-In Command	Meaning
suspend	Stop the shell in its tracks, much as if it had been sent a stop signal with ^Z. This is most often used to stop shells started by *su*.
switch (string)	See "The switch Command" on page 409.
time [command]	With no argument, print a summary of *time* used by this C shell and its children. With an optional *command*, execute *command* and print a summary of the *time* it uses.
umask [value]	Display the file creation mask. With *value*, set the file creation mask. *Value*, given in octal, is *xored* with the permissions of 666 for files and 777 for directories to arrive at the permissions for new files. Permissions cannot be added via *umask*.
unalias pattern	Discard aliases that match (filename substitution) *pattern*. All aliases are removed by *unalias* *
unhash	Disable the internal hash table.
unlimit [–h] [resource]	Remove a limitation on *resource*. If no *resource* is specified, all resource limitations are removed. See the description of the *limit* command for the list of *resource* names.
–h	Remove corresponding hard limits. Only the superuser may do this.
unset pattern	Remove variables whose names match (filename substitution) *pattern*. All variables are removed by '*unset* *'; this has noticeably distasteful side effects.
unsetenv variable	Remove *variable* from the environment. Pattern matching, as with *unset*, is not performed.
wait	*Wait* for background jobs to finish (or for an interrupt) before prompting.
while (expr)	See "The while Loop" on page 415.
%[job] [&]	Bring the current or indicated *job* to the foreground. With the ampersand, continue running *job* in the background.
@ [var =expr] *@ [var[n] =expr]*	With no arguments, display the values for all shell variables. With arguments, the variable *var*, or the *n*th word in the value of *var*, is set to the value that *expr* evaluates to.

C SHELL LAB EXERCISES

Lab 19: Getting Started

1. What does the *init* process do?
2. What is the function of the *login* process?
3. How do you know what shell you are using?
4. How can you change your login shell?
5. Explain the difference between the *.cshrc* and *.login* files. Which one is executed first?
6. Edit your *.cshrc* file as follows:
    a. Create three of your own aliases.
    b. Reset your prompt.

Set the following variables and put a comment after each variable explaining what it does:

```
noclobber      # Protects clobbering files from redirection overwriting
history
ignoreeof
savehist
filec
```

7. Type the following:
    ```
    source .cshrc
    ```
    What does the *source* command do?
8. Edit your *.login* file as follows:
    a. Welcome the user.
    b. Add your home directory to the path if it is not there.
    c. Source the *.login* file.
9. Type *history*. What is the output?
    a. How do you reexecute the last command?
    b. Now type: *echo a b c*

Use the *history* command to reexecute the *echo* command with only its last argument, *c*.

Lab 20: Shell Metacharacters

1. Type at the prompt:
    ```
    touch ab abc a1 a2 a3 a11 a12 ba ba.1 ba.2 filex filey AbC ABC
    ABc2 abc
    ```
2. Write and test the command that will do the following:
    a. List all files starting with *a*.
    b. List all files ending in at least one digit.
    c. List all files starting with an *a* or *A*.
    d. List all files ending in a period, followed by a digit.

    e. List all files containing just two of the letter *a*.

    f. List three character files where all letters are uppercase.

    g. List files ending in *11* or *12*.

    h. List files ending in *x* or *y*.

    i. List all files ending in a digit, an uppercase letter, or a lowercase letter.

    j. List all files containing a *b*.

    k. Remove two character files starting with *a*.

Lab 21: Redirection

1. What are the names of the three file streams associated with your terminal?

2. What is a file descriptor?

3. What command would you use to do the following:

    a. Redirect the output of the *ls* command to a file called *lsfile*?

    b. Redirect and append the output of the *date* command to *lsfile*?

    c. Redirect the output of the *who* command to *lsfile*? What happened?

4. What happens when you type *cp* all by itself?

    a. How do you save the error message from the above example to a file?

5. Use the *find* command to find all files, starting from the parent directory, and of type *directory*. Save the standard output in a file called *found* and any errors in a file called *found.errs*.

6. What is *noclobber*? How do you override it?

7. Take the output of three commands and redirect the output to a file called *gotemail*.

8. Use a pipe(s) with the *ps* and *wc* commands to find out how many processes you are currently running.

Lab 22: First Script

1. Write a script called *greetme* that will do the following:

    a. Greet the user.

    b. Print the date and time.

    c. Print a calendar for this month.

    d. Print the name of your machine.

    e. Print a list of all files in your parent directory.

    f. Print all the processes you are running.

    g. Print the value of the *TERM*, *PATH*, and *HOME* variables.

    h. Print *Please couldn't you loan me $50.00?*

    i. Tell the user *Good bye* and the current hour. (See *man* pages for the *date* command.)

2. Make sure your script is executable.

```
chmod +x greetme
```

3. What was the first line of your script?

Lab 23: Getting User Input

1. Write a script called *nosy* that will do the following:
    a. Ask the user's full name—first, last, and middle name.
    b. Greet the user by his or her first name.
    c. Ask the user's year of birth and calculate the user's age.
    d. Ask the user's login name and print user's ID (*from /etc/passwd*).
    e. Tell the user his or her home directory.
    f. Show the user the processes he or she is running.
    g. Tell the user the day of the week, and the current time in nonmilitary time.

   The output should resemble the following:

   The day of the week is Tuesday and the current time is 04:07:38 PM.

2. Create a text file called *datafile* (unless this file has already been provided for you.) Each entry consists of fields separated by colons. The fields are:
    a. First and last name
    b. Phone number
    c. Address
    d. Birth date
    e. Salary

3. Create a script called *lookup* that will do the following:
    a. Contain a comment section with the scriptname, your name, the date, and the reason for writing this script. The reason for writing this script is to display the *datafile* in sorted order.
    b. Sort the *datafile* by last names.
    c. Show the user the contents of the *datafile*.
    d. Tell the user the number of entries in the file.

4. Try the *echo* and *verbose* commands for debugging your script. How did you use these commands?

Lab 24: Command Line Arguments

1. Write a script called *rename* that will do the following:
    a. Take two filenames as command line arguments, the first file is the old file and the second file is the new one.
    b. Rename the old filename with the new filename.
    c. List the files in the directory to show the change.

2. Write a script called *checking* that will do the following:
    a. Take a command line argument, a user's login name.
    b. Test to see if a command line argument was provided.
    c. Check to see if the user is in the */etc/passwd* file. If so, print the following:
       Found <user> in the /etc/passwd file.
       Otherwise, print the following:
       No such user on our system.

Lab 25: Conditionals and File Testing

1. In the *lookup* script, ask the user if he or she would like to add an entry to the *datafile*. If *yes* or *y*:

   a. Prompt the user for a new name, phone, address, birth date, and salary. Each item will be stored in a separate variable. You will provide the colons between the fields and append the information to the *datafile*.

   b. Sort the file by last names. Tell the user you added the entry, and show the line preceded by the line number.

2. Rewrite *checking*.

   a. After checking whether the named user is in the */etc/passwd* file, the program will check to see if he or she is logged on. If so, the program will print all the processes that are running; otherwise it will tell the user the following:

      <user> is not logged on."

3. The *lookup* script depends on the *datafile* in order to run. In the *lookup* script, check to see if the *datafile* exists and if it is readable and writeable

4. Add a menu to the *lookup* script to resemble the following:

   ```
   [1] Add entry
   [2] Delete entry
   [3] View entry
   [4] Exit
   ```

5. You already have the *Add entry* part of the script written. The *Add entry* routine should now include code that will check to see if the name is already in the *datafile* and if it is, tell the user so. If the name is not there, add the new entry.

6. Now write the code for the *Delete entry*, *View entry*, and *Exit* functions.

7. The *Delete* part of the script should first check to see if the entry exists before trying to remove it. If the entry does not exist, notify the user; otherwise, remove the entry and tell the user you removed it. On exit, make sure that you use a digit to represent the appropriate exit status.

8. How do you check the exit status from the command line?

Lab 26: The *switch* Statement

1. Rewrite the following script using a *switch* statement.

   ```
   #!/bin/csh -f
   # Grades program
   echo -n "What was your grade on the test? "
   set score = $<
   if ( $grade >= 90 && $grade <= 100 ) then
       echo You got an A\!
   else if ( $grade >= 80 && $grade < 89 ) then
       echo You got a B.
   else if ( $grade >= 79 && $grade < 79 ) then
       echo "You're average."
   else if ( $grade >= 69 && $grade < 69 ) then
       echo Better study harder
   else
       echo Better luck next time.
   endif
   ```

2. Rewrite the *lookup* script using switch statements for each of the menu items.

Lab 27: Loops

1. Write a program called *picnic* that will mail a list of users, one at a time, an invitation to a picnic. The list of users will be in a file called *friends*. One of the users listed in the *friends* file will be Popeye.

   a. The invitation will be in another file, called *invite*.

   b. Use file testing to check that both files exist and are readable.

   c. A loop will be used to iterate through the list of users. When Popeye is reached, he will be skipped over (i.e., he does not get an invitation), and the next user on the list sent an invitation, and so forth.

   d. Keep a list with the names of each person who received an invitation. Do this by building an array. After everyone on the list has been sent mail, print the number of people who received mail and a list of their names.

   Bonus: If you have time, you may want to customize your *invite* file so that each user receives a letter containing his or her name. For example, the message might start:

   Dear John,
   I hope you can make it to our picnic....

   To do this your *invite* file may be written:

   Dear XXX,
   I hope you can make it to our picnic....

   With *sed* or *awk,* you could then substitute *XXX* with the user name. (It might be tricky putting the capital letter in the user name, since user names are always lowercase.)

2. Add a new menu item to the *lookup* script to resemble the following:

   [1] Add entry
   [2] Delete entry
   [3] Change entry
   [4] View entry
   [5] Exit

   After the user has selected a valid entry, when the function has completed, ask the user if he or she would like to see the menu again. If an invalid entry is entered, the program should print the following:

   Invalid entry, try again.

   The menu will be redisplayed.

3. Create a submenu under *View entry* in the *lookup* script. The user will be asked if he would like to view specific information for a selected individual:

   a) Phone
   b) Address
   c) Birth date
   d) Salary

4. Add the *onintr* command to your script using a label. When the program starts execution at the label, any temporary files will be removed, the user will be told *Good–bye*, and the program will exit.

10

The Korn Shell

10.1 Interactive Korn Shell

Before the Korn shell displays a prompt, it is preceded by a number of processes. See Figure 10.1.

10.1.1   Startup

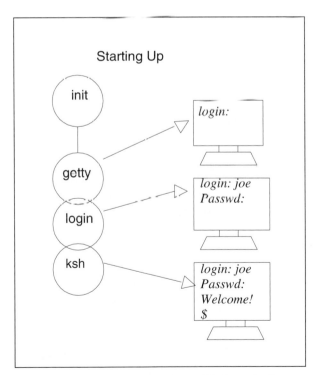

Figure 10.1   System startup and the Korn shell.

The first process to run is called *init*, PID 1. It gets instructions from a file called *inittab* (System V) or spawns a *getty* (BSD) process. These processes open up the terminal ports, provide a place where input comes from, *stdin*, and the place where standard output (*stdout*) and standard error (*stderr*) go, and put a login prompt on your screen. The */bin/login* program is then executed. The *login* program prompts you for a password, encrypts and verifies the password, sets up an initial environment, and starts up the login shell, */bin/ksh*, the last entry in the *passwd* file. The *ksh* program looks for the system file, */etc/profile,* and executes its commands. It then looks in the user's home directory for an initialization file called *.profile*, and an environment file, conventionally called *.kshrc*. After executing commands from those files, the dollar sign prompt appears on your screen and the Korn shell awaits commands.

10.1.2   The Environment

The Initialization Files.   After executing the commands in */etc/profile*, the initialization files in the user's home directory are executed. The *.profile* is executed, followed by the *ENV* file, commonly called the *.kshrc* file.

The /etc/profile File.   The */etc/profile* is a systemwide readable file set up by the system administrator to perform tasks when the user logs on and the Korn shell starts up. It is available to all Bourne and Korn shell users on the system, and normally performs such tasks as checking the mail spooler for new mail and displaying the message of the day from the */etc/motd* file. The following text is an example of the */etc/profile*. See Chapter 8, "The Interactive Bourne Shell," for a complete explanation of each line of */etc/profile*.

EXAMPLE

```
# The profile that all logins get before using their own .profile
trap " " 2 3
export LOGNAME PATH  # Initially set by /bin/login
if [ "$TERM" = " " ]
then
    if /bin/i386
    then     # Set the terminal type
        TERM=AT386
    else
        TERM=sun
    fi
    export TERM
fi
# Login and -su shells get /etc/profile services.
# -rsh is given its environment in the .profile.
case "$0" in
-sh | -ksh | -jsh )
    if [ ! -f .hushlogin ]
    then
        /usr/sbin/quota
```

EXAMPLE (CONTINUED)

```
                # Allow the user to break the Message-Of-The-Day only.
                    trap "trap ' ' 2" 2
                    /bin/cat -s /etc/motd
                    # Display the message of the day
                    trap " " 2
                    /bin/mail -E
                    case $? in
                    0)         # Check for new mail
                        echo "You have new mail. "
                                ;;
                    2)  echo "You have mail. "
                                ;;
                    esac
            fi
    esac
    umask 022
    trap 2 3
```

The .profile File.   The *.profile* file is a user-defined initialization file, that is executed once at login (by the Bourne and Korn shells) and is found in your home directory. It gives you the ability to customize and modify your working environment. Environment variables and terminal settings are normally set here, and if a window application or *dbm* is to be initiated, it is started here. If the *.profile* file contains a special variable called *ENV*, the filename that is assigned to that variable will be executed next. The *ENV* file is often named *.kshrc*; it contains aliases and *set −o* commands. The *ENV* file is executed every time a *ksh* subshell is spawned. The lines from the following files may not be meaningful to you now, but all of the concepts, such as exporting variables, history, the search path, and so on, will be discussed in detail throughout the text of this book.

EXAMPLE 10.1

```
 1   set -o allexport
 2   TERM=vt102
 3   HOSTNAME=$(uname -n)
 4   HISTSIZE=50
 5   EDITOR=/usr/ucb/vi
 6   ENV=$HOME/.kshrc
 7   PATH=$HOME/bin:/usr/ucb:/usr/bin:\
     /usr/local:/etc:/bin:/usr/bin:/usr/local\
     /bin:/usr/hosts:/usr/5bin:/usr/etc:/usr/bin:.
 8   PS1="$HOSTNAME ! $ "
 9   set +o allexport
10   alias openwin=/usr/openwin/bin/openwin
11   trap '$HOME/.logout' EXIT
12   clear
```

EXPLANATION

1   By setting the *allexport* option, all variables created will automatically be exported (made available to subshells).

2   The terminal is set to *vt102*.

3   The variable *HOSTNAME* is assigned the name of this machine, $(uname –n).

4   The *HISTSIZE* variable is assigned *50*; 50 lines from the history file will be displayed on the terminal when the user types *history*.

5   The *EDITOR* variable is assigned the pathname for the *vi* editor. Programs such as *mail* allow you to select an editor in which to work.

6   The *ENV* variable is assigned the path to the home directory (*$HOME*) and the name of the file that contains further Korn shell customization settings. After the *.profile* is executed, the *ENV* file is executed. The name of the *ENV* file is your choice; it is commonly called *.kshrc*.

7   The search path is defined. It is a colon-separated list of directories used by the shell in its search for commands typed at the prompt or in a script file. The shell searches each element of the path from left to right for the command. The dot at the end represents the current working directory. If the command cannot be found in any of the listed directories, the shell will look in the current directory.

8   The primary prompt, by default a dollar sign ($), is set to the name of the host machine, the number of the current command in the history file, and a dollar sign ($).

9   The *allexport* option is turned off.

10 An alias is a nickname for a command. The alias for *openwin* is assigned the full pathname of the *openwin* command, which starts Sun's window application.

11 The *trap* command will execute the *.logout* file when you exit this shell, that is, when you log out. The *.logout* file is a user-defined file containing commands that are executed at the time of logging out. For example, you may want to record the time you log out, clean up a temporary file, or simply say *So long*.

12 The *clear* command clears the screen.

The *ENV* File.   The *ENV* variable is assigned the name of a file that will be executed every time an interactive *ksh* or *ksh* program (script) is started. The *ENV* variable is set in the *.profile* and is assigned the name of the file that will contain special *ksh* variables and aliases. The name is conventionally *.kshrc*, but you can call it anything you want. (The *ENV* file is not processed when the privileged option is on. See Table 10.1.)

EXAMPLE 10.2

```
1   set -o trackall
2   set -o vi
3   alias l='ls -laF'
    alias ls='ls -aF'
```

EXAMPLE 10.2 (CONTINUED)

```
    alias hi='fc -l'
    alias c=clear
4   function pushd { pwd > $HOME/.lastdir.$$ ; }
    function popd { cd $(< $HOME/.lastdir.$$) ;
           rm $HOME/.lastdir.$$; pwd; }
    function psg { ps -ef | egrep $1 | egrep -v egrep; }
    function vg { vgrind -s11 -t $* | lpr -t ; }
```

EXPLANATION

1   The *set* option for tracked aliases is turned on. (For a complete description, see
    "Aliases" on page 453.)

2   The *set* option for the *vi* editor is turned on for in-line editing of the history file.
    (See "Command Line History" on page 444.)

3   The aliases (nicknames) for the commands are defined.

4   The functions are named and defined. (See "Functions" on page 489.)

The *set -o* Options.   The *set* command can take options if the *–o* switch is used.
Options allow you to customize the shell environment. They are either on or off, and are
normally set in the *ENV* file.

FORMAT

```
    set -o option Turns on the option.
    set +o option  Turns off the option
    set -[a-z] Abbreviation for an option; the minus turns it on
    set +[a-z] Abbreviation for an option; the plus turns it off
```

EXAMPLE 10.3

```
    set -o allexport
    set +o allexport
    set -a
    set +a
```

EXPLANATION

1   Sets the *allexport* option. This option causes all variables to be automatically ex-
    ported to subshells.

2   Unsets the *allexport* option. All variables will now be local to the current shell.

3   Sets the *allexport* option. Same as 1. Not every option has an abbreviation (see
    Table 10.1).

4   Unsets the *allexport* option. Same as 2.

Table 10.1 Options

Name of Option	Abbreviation	What It Does
allexport	−*a*	Causes variables set to be automatically exported.
bgnice		Background jobs are run with a lower priority.
emacs		For command line editing, uses the *emacs* built-in editor.
errexit	−*e*	If a command returns a nonzero exit status (fails), executes the *ERR* trap, if set, and exits. Not set when reading initialization files.
gmacs		For command editing, uses the *gmacs* built-in editor.
ignoreeof		Prevents logout with ^D; must type *exit* to exit the shell.
markdirs		Puts a trailing backslash (/) on directory names when filename expansion is used.
monitor	−*m*	Allows job control.
noclobber		Protects files from being overwritten when redirection is used.
noexec	−*n*	Reads commands, but does not execute them. Used to check the syntax of scripts. Not on when running interactively.
noglob	−*f*	Disables pathname expansion; i.e., turns off wildcards.
nolog		Does not store function definitions in the history file.
notify		Notifies user when background job finishes (only in versions newer than 1988).
nounset		Displays an error when expanding a variable that has not been set.
privileged	−*p*	When set, the shell does not read the *.profile* or ENV file; used with *setuid* scripts.
trackall		Enables alias tracking.
verbose	−*v*	Turns on the *verbose* mode for debugging.
vi		For command line editing, uses the *vi* built-in editor.
xtrace	−*x*	Turns on the echo mode for debugging.

10.1.3 The Prompts

The Korn shell provides four prompts. The primary and secondary prompts are used when the Korn shell is running interactively. You can change these prompts. The variable *PS1* is the primary prompt, set initially to a dollar sign ($). It appears when you log on and waits for you to type commands. The variable *PS2* is the secondary prompt, initially set to the > character. It appears if you have partially typed a command and then pressed Enter. You can change the primary and secondary prompts.

The Primary Prompt. $ is the default primary prompt. You can change your prompt. Normally, prompts are defined in *.profile*.

EXAMPLE 10.4

```
1   $ PS1="$(uname -n) ! $ "
2   jody 1141 $
```

EXPLANATION

1   The default primary prompt is a $. The *PS1* prompt is being reset to the name of the machine $(*uname –n*), the number of the current history number, and the $. The exclamation point evaluates to the current history number. (To print an exclamation point, type two exclamation points (*!!*) in the *PS1* definition.)

2   The new prompt is displayed.

The Secondary Prompt. The *PS2* prompt is the secondary prompt. Its value is displayed to standard error (the screen). This prompt appears when you have not completed a command and have pressed the carriage return.

EXAMPLE 10.5

```
1   $ print "Hello
2   > there"
3   Hello
    there
4   $

5   $ PS2="----> "
6   $ print "Hi
7   ------>
    ------>
    ------> there"
    Hi


    there
    $
```

EXPLANATION

1 The double quotes must be matched after the string *"Hello.*

2 When a newline is entered, the secondary prompt appears. Until the closing double quotes are entered, the secondary prompt will be displayed.

3 The output of the *print* command is displayed.

4 The primary prompt is displayed.

5 The secondary prompt is reset.

6 The double quotes must be matched after the string *"Hi.*

7 When a newline is entered, the new secondary prompt appears. Until the closing double quotes are entered, the secondary prompt will be displayed.

10.1.4   The Search Path

To execute a command typed at the command line or within a shell script, the Korn shell searches the directories listed in the *PATH* variable. The *PATH* is a colon-separated list of directories, searched by the shell from left to right. The dot in the *PATH* represents the current working directory. If the command is not found in any of the directories listed in the path, the shell sends the message *ksh: filename: not found* to standard error. It is recommended that the path be set in the *.profile* file. To speed up the searching process, the Korn shell has implemented tracked aliases. See "Tracked Aliases" on page 455.

EXAMPLE 10.6

```
$ echo $PATH
/home/gsa12/bin:/usr/ucb:/usr/bin:/usr/local/bin:.
```

EXPLANATION

The Korn shell will search for commands starting in */home/gsa12/bin*. If the command is not found there, */usr/ucb* is searched, then */usr/bin*, */usr/local/bin*, and finally the user's home directory represented by the period.

The Dot Command.   The dot command (.) is a built-in Korn shell command. It takes a scriptname as an argument. The script will be executed in the environment of the current shell. A child process will not be started. The dot command is normally used to reexecute the *.profile* file or the *ENV* file, if either of those files has been modified. For example, if one of the settings in either file has been changed after you have logged on, you can use the dot command to reexecute the initialization files without logging out and then logging back in.

EXAMPLE 10.7

```
$ . .profile
$ . .kshrc
$ . $ENV
```

EXPLANATION

Normally a child process is started when commands are executed. The dot command executes each of the initialization files, *.profile,* the *ENV* file (*.kshrc*), in the current shell. Local and global variables in these files are defined within this shell. Otherwise, the user would have to log out and log back in to cause these files to be executed for the login shell. The dot command makes that unnecessary.

10.1.5   The Command Line

After logging in, the Korn shell displays its primary prompt, a dollar sign by default. The shell is your command interpreter. When the shell is running interactively, it reads commands from the terminal and breaks the command line into words. A command line consists of one or more words (or tokens), separated by whitespace (blanks and/or tabs), and terminated with a newline, generated by pressing Enter. The first word is the command, and subsequent words are the command's arguments. The command may be a UNIX executable program such as *ls* or *pwd*, a built-in command such as *cd* or *jobs*, or a shell script. The command may contain special characters, called metacharacters, which the shell must interpret while parsing the command line. If a command line is too long, the backslash character, followed by a newline, will allow you to continue typing on the next line. The secondary prompt will appear until the command line is terminated.

The Order of Processing Commands.   The first word on the command line is the command to be executed. The command may be a keyword, a special built-in command or utility, a function, a script, or an executable program. The command is executed according to its type in the following order:[1]

1. Keyword (such as *if, while, until*).
2. Aliases (see *typeset –f*).
3. Built-in commands.
4. Functions.
5. Scripts and executables.

The special built-in commands and functions are defined within the shell, and therefore are executed from within the current shell, making them much faster in execution.

---

1. A built-in command will override a function; therefore, an alias must be defined to the name of the function. (See "Aliases" on page 453.) In the 1994 version of the Korn shell, the order of processing functions and built-ins was reversed, thus alleviating this problem.

Scripts and executable programs such as *ls* and *pwd* are stored on disk, and the shell must locate them within the directory hierarchy by searching the *PATH* environment variable; the shell then forks a new shell that executes the script. To find out the type of command you are using, use the built-in command, *whence –v* , or its alias, *type*. (See Example 10.8.)

EXAMPLE 10.8

```
$ type print
print is a shell builtin
$ type test
test is a shell builtin
$ type ls
ls is a tracked alias for /usr/bin/ls
$ type type
type is an exported alias for whence -v
$ type bc
bc is /usr/bin/bc
$ type if
if is a keyword
```

The Exit Status.   After a command or program terminates, it returns an exit status to the parent process. The exit status is a number between 0 and 255. By convention, when a program exits, if the status returned is zero, the command was successful in its execution. When the exit status is nonzero, the command failed in some way. The Korn shell status variable *?* is set to the value of the exit status of the last command that was executed. Success or failure of a program is determined by the programmer who wrote the program. In shell scripts, you can explicitly control the exit status by using the *exit* command.

EXAMPLE 10.9

```
1   $ grep "ellie" /etc/passwd
    ellie:GgMyBsSJavdl6s:9496:40:Ellie Quigley:/home/jody/ellie
2   $ echo $?
    0

3   $ grep "nicky" /etc/passwd
4   $ echo $?
    1

5   $ grep "scott" /etc/passsswd
    grep: /etc/passsswd: No such file or directory
6   $ echo $?
    2
```

EXPLANATION

1 The *grep* program searches for the pattern *ellie* in the */etc/passwd* file and is successful. The line from */etc/passwd* is displayed.

2 The *?* variable is set to the exit value of the *grep* command. Zero indicates success.

3 The *grep* program cannot find user *nicky* in the */etc/passwd* file.

4 If the *grep* program cannot find the pattern, it returns an exit status of one.

5 The *grep* fails because the file */etc/passsswd* cannot be opened.

6 If *grep* cannot find the file, it returns an exit status of two.

Multiple Commands and Command Grouping.   A command line can consist of multiple commands. Each command is separated by a semicolon, and the command line is terminated with a newline.

EXAMPLE 10.10

```
$ ls; pwd; date
```

EXPLANATION

The commands are executed from left to right until the newline is reached. Commands may also be grouped so that all of the output is either piped to another command or redirected to a file.

EXAMPLE 10.11

```
$ ( ls ; pwd; date ) > outputfile
```

EXPLANATION

The output of each of the commands is sent to the file called *outputfile*.

Conditional Execution of Commands.   With conditional execution, two command strings are separated by two special metacharacters, && and ||. The command on the right of either of these metacharacters will or will not be executed based on the exit condition of the command on the left.

EXAMPLE 10.12

```
$ cc prgm1.c -o prgm1 && prgm1
```

EXPLANATION

If the first command is *successful* (has a zero exit status), the command after the && is executed.

EXAMPLE 10.13

```
$ cc prog.c >& err || mail bob < err
```

EXPLANATION

If the first command *fails* (has a nonzero exit status), the command after the || is executed.

Commands in the Background.   Normally, when you execute a command, it runs in the foreground, and the prompt does not reappear until the command has completed execution. It is not always convenient to wait for the command to complete. By placing an ampersand (&) at the end of the command line, the shell will return the shell prompt immediately and execute the command in the background concurrently. You do not have to wait to start up another command. The output from a background job will be sent to the screen as it processes. Therefore, if you intend to run a command in the background, the output of that command should be redirected to a file or piped to another device such as a printer so that the output does not interfere with what you are doing.

EXAMPLE 10.14

```
1    $ man ksh | lp&
2    [1] 1557
3    $
```

EXPLANATION

1   The output of the manual pages for the Korn shell is piped to the printer. The ampersand at the end of the command line puts the job in the background.

2   Two numbers appear on the screen: the number in square brackets indicates that this is the first job to be placed in the background; the second number is the PID, the process identification number, of this job.

3   The Korn shell prompt appears immediately. While your program is running in the background, the shell is waiting for another command in the foreground.

10.1.6   Command Line History

The history mechanism keeps a numbered record of the commands that you have typed at the command line in a history file. You can recall a command from the history file and reexecute it without retyping the command. The *history* built-in command displays the history list. The default name for the history file is *.sh_history,* and it is located in your home directory.

The *HISTSIZE* variable, accessed when *ksh* first accesses the history file, specifies how many commands can be accessed from the history file. The default size is 128. The *HIST-FILE* variable specifies the name of the command history file (*~/.sh_history* is the default) where commands are stored. The history file grows from one login session to the next; it becomes very large unless you clean it out. The history command is a preset alias for the *fc –l* command.

The *history* Command/Redisplay Commands. The built-in *history* command lists previously typed commands preceded by a number. The command can take arguments to control the display.

EXAMPLE 10.15

```
1   $ history          # Same as fc -l
    1 ls
    2 vi file1
    3 df
    4 ps -eaf
    5 history
    6 more /etc/passwd
    7 cd
    8 echo $USER
    9 set
    10 history

2   $ history -n        # Print without line numbers
    ls
    vi file1
    df
    ps -eaf
    history
    more /etc/passwd
    cd
    echo $USER
    set
    history
    history -n

3   $ history 8         # List from 8th command to present
    8    echo $USER
    9    set
    10   history
    11   history -n
    12   history 8

4   $ history -3        # List this command and the 3 preceding it
    10   history
    11   history -n
    12   history 8
    13   history -3
```

EXAMPLE 10.15 (CONTINUED)

```
5   $ history -1 -5          # List last 5 commands, preceding this one
    13  history -3           # in reversed order.
    12  history 8
    11  history -n
    10  history
    9   set

6   $ history -5 -1          # Print last 5 commands, preceding this one
    10  history              # in order.
    11  history -n
    12  history 8
    13  history -3
    14  history -1 -5

7   $ history                # (Different history list)
    78  date
    79  ls
    80  who
    81  echo hi
    82  history

8   $ history ls echo        # Display from most recent ls command to
    79  ls                   # most recent echo command.
    80  who
    81  echo hi

9   $ history -r ls echo     # -r reverses the list
    81  echo hi
    80  who
    79  ls
```

Reexecuting Commands with the *r* Command.   The *r* command redoes the last command typed at the command line. If the *r* command is followed by a space and a number, the command at that number is reexecuted. If the *r* command is followed by a space and a letter, the last command that began with that letter is executed. Without any arguments, the *r* command reexecutes the most previous command on the history list.

EXAMPLE 10.16

```
1   $ r date
    date
    Mon Feb 15 12:27:35 PST 2001

2   $ r 3    redo command number 3
    df
    Filesystem    kbytes    used      avail     capacity    Mounted on
    /dev/sd0a     7735      6282      680       90%         /
    /dev/sd0g     144613    131183    0         101%        /usr
    /dev/sd2c     388998    211395    138704    60%         /home.

3   $ r vi           # Redo the last command that began with pattern vi.
4   $ r vi file1=file2    # Redo last command that began with vi
                          # and substitute the first occurrence of
                          # file1 with file2.
```

EXPLANATION

1   The last command, *date*, is reexecuted.
2   The third command in the history file is executed.
3   The last command, starting with the string *vi*, is executed.
4   The string *file1* is replaced with the string *file2*. The last command, *vi file1*, is replaced with *vi file2*.

Command Line Editing.   The Korn shell provides two built-in editors, *emacs* and *vi*, that allow you to interactively edit your history list. To enable the *vi* editor, add the *set* command listed below and put this line in your *.profile* file. The *emacs* built-in editor works on lines in the history file one line at a time, whereas the *vi* built-in editor works on commands consisting of more than one line. To set *vi*, type

```
set -o vi
```

   or

```
VISUAL=vi
```

   or

```
EDITOR=/usr/bin/vi
```

If using *emacs*, type

```
set -o emacs
```

   or

```
VISUAL=emacs
```

   or

```
EDITOR=/usr/bin/emacs
```

Note that *set –o vi* overrides *VISUAL*, and *VISUAL* overrides *EDITOR*.

The *vi* Built-In Editor.   To edit the history list, press the Esc key and use the standard keys that you would use in *vi* for moving up and down, left and right, deleting, inserting, and changing text. See Table 10.2. After making the edit, press the Enter key. The command will be executed and added to the bottom of the history list. To scroll upward in the history file, press the Esc key and then the K key.

Table 10.2   *vi* Commands

Command	Function
Moving Through the History File	
Esc k *or* +	Move up the history list.
Esc j *or* –	Move down the history list.
G	Move to first line in history file.
5G	Move to fifth command in history file for *string*.
/string	Search upward through history file.
?	String search downward through history file.
Moving Around on a Line	
h	Move left on a line.
l	Move right on a line.
b	Move backward a word.
e or w	Move forward a word.
^ or 0	Move to beginning of first character on the line.
$	Move to end of line.
Editing with vi	
a A	Append text.
i I	Insert text.

Table 10.2 *vi* Commands (continued)

Command	Function
Editing with vi	
dd dw x	Delete text into a buffer (line, word, or character).
cc C	Change text.
u U	Undo.
yy Y	Yank (copy a line into buffer).
p P	Put yanked or deleted line down below or above the line.
r R	Replace a letter or any amount of text on a line.

The *emacs* Built-In Editor. To start moving backward through the history file, press ^P. To move forward, press ^N . Use *emacs* editing commands to change or correct text, then press Enter and the command will be reexecuted. See Table 10.3.

Table 10.3 *emacs* Commands

Command	Function
Moving Through the History File	
Ctrl-P	Move up history file.
Ctrl-N	Move down history file.
Ctrl-B	Move backward one character.
Ctrl-R	Search backwards for string.
Esc B	Move back one word.
Ctrl-F	Move forward one character.
Esc F	Move forward one word.
Ctrl-A	Move to the beginning of the line.
Ctrl-E	Move to the end of the line.
Esc <	Move to the first line of the history file.
Esc >	Move to the last line of the history file.

Table 10.3 *emacs* Commands (continued)

Command	Function
Editing with emacs	
Ctrl-U	Delete the line.
Ctrl-Y	Put the line back.
Ctrl-K	Delete from cursor to the end line.
Ctrl-D	Delete a letter.
Esc D	Delete one word forward.
Esc H	Delete one word backward.
Esc space	Set a mark at cursor position.
Ctrl-X Ctrl-X	Exchange cursor and mark.
Ctrl-P Ctrl-Y	Push region from cursor to mark into a buffer (Ctrl-P) and put it down (Ctrl-Y).

FCEDIT[2] and Editing Commands.   The *fc* command is a built-in command that can be used with the *FCEDIT* variable (typically set in the *.profile* file) to invoke the editor of your choice for editing the history file. This can be any editor on your system. The *FCEDIT* variable is set to the full pathname of your favorite editor. If *FCEDIT* is not set, the default editor, */bin/ed,* is invoked when you type the *fc* command.

The *FCEDIT* variable should be set to the chosen editor. You can specify a number of items from the history list that you want to edit. After you edit the commands, the Korn shell will execute the whole file. Any commands that are preceded by a pound sign (#) will be treated as comments and will not be executed. See Table 10.4 for more on commenting and filename expansion.

---

2. On versions of the Korn shell newer than 1988, the *FCEDIT* variable has been renamed *HISTEDIT*, and the *fc* command has been renamed *hist*.

EXAMPLE 10.17

```
1   $ FCEDIT=/usr/bin/vi
2   $ pwd
3   $ fc
```
<Starts up the full-screen vi editor with the pwd command on line 1>

```
4   $ history
    1 date
    2 ls -l
    3 echo "hello"
    4 pwd

5   $ fc -3 -1          # Start vi, edit, write/quit, and execute
                        # last 3 commands.
```

EXPLANATION

1   The *FCEDIT* variable can be assigned the pathname for any of the UNIX text editors you have on your system, such as *vi, emacs, textedit*, etc. If not set, the *ed* editor is the default.

2   The *pwd* command is typed at the command line. It will be placed in the *history* file.

3   The *fc* command caused the editor (set in *FCEDIT*) to be invoked with the last command typed in the editor window. If the user writes and quits the editor, any commands typed there will be executed.

4   The *history* command lists recently typed commands.

5   The *fc* command is used to start up the editor with the last three commands from the *history* file in the editor's buffer.

10.1.7   Commenting and Filename Expansion

Filename expansion is a mechanism that allows the user to type part of a filename and press the escape key to see the rest of the filename(s). In the examples, [Esc] represents the escape key.

Table 10.4   Using the Esc Key and Filename Expansion

Combination	Result
command [Esc]#	# precedes command with a #; puts it on the history list commented; command will not be executed.
command [Esc]_	Underscore inserts the last word of the last command at the cursor position.
command [Esc] 2_	Inserts the second word of the last command at the cursor position.
word[Esc] *	*replaces the current word with all files matched.
word[Esc] \	\ replaces the current word with the first filename that starts with the same characters; filename expansion.
word[Esc]=	Displays all filenames beginning with the same character as the current word and displays them in a numbered list.

EXAMPLE 10.18

```
        (Press the Esc Key for [Esc].

1   $ ls a[Esc]=
    1) abc
    2) abc1
    3) abc122
    4) abc123
    5) abc2

2   $ ls a[Esc]*
    ls abc abc1 abc122 abc123 abc2
    abc    abc1   abc122 abc123 abc2

3   $ print apples pears peaches
    apples pears peaches

4   $ print [Esc]_
    print peaches
    peaches

5   $ print apples pears peaches plums
    apples pears peaches
```

EXAMPLE 10.18 (CONTINUED)

```
6   $ print [Esc]2_
    print pears
    pears
```

EXPLANATION

1   By typing an *a*, followed by the Esc key and an equal sign (=), all files starting with *a* are numbered and listed. (The numbers do not really serve any special purpose.)

2   By typing an *a*, then the Esc key and an asterisk (*), the filenames starting with *a* are displayed.

3   The *print* command displays its arguments: *apples, pears*, and *peaches*.

4   The Esc key, followed by an underscore (_), is replaced with the last argument.

5   The *print* command displays its arguments: *apples, pears*, and *peaches*.

6   The Esc key, followed by the number 2 and an underscore, is replaced by the second argument. The command (*print*) is the first argument, starting at word zero.

10.1.8 Aliases

An alias is a Korn shell or user-defined abbreviation for a command. The alias name contains alphanumeric characters. Default aliases are provided by the shell and can be redefined or unset. Unlike the C shell aliases, the Korn shell does not support passing arguments. (If you need to use arguments, see "Functions" on page 556.)

Aliases can be exported to subshells by storing them in the *ENV* file. (The commands in the *ENV* file are executed every time a new shell is spawned.) In the 1988 version of the Korn shell, the *–x* option allows aliases to be exported to subshells as long as the new shell is not a separate invocation of *ksh*. Tracked aliases are provided by the Korn shell to speed up the time it takes the shell to search the path. Aliases can alias themselves; that is, they are recursive.

Listing Aliases.   The alias built-in command lists all set aliases.

EXAMPLE 10.19

```
 1   $ alias
 2   autoload=typeset -fu
 3   false=let 0
 4   functions=typeset -f
 5   hash=alias -t
 6   history=fc -l
 7   integer=typset -i
 8   r=fc -e -
 9   stop=kill -STOP
10   suspend=kill -STOP $$
11   true=:
12   type=whence -v
```

EXPLANATION

1   The *alias* command, without arguments, lists all aliases. This is a list of preset aliases, including those you have set.

2   The *autoload* alias is used for invoking functions dynamically.

3   The *false* alias is used in expressions testing for a false condition.

4   The *functions* alias lists all functions and their definitions.

5   The *hash* alias lists all tracked aliases.

6   The *history* alias lists all commands in the history file, *.sh_history*, preceded by a number.

7   The *integer* alias allows you to create integer-type variables.

8   The *r* alias lets you redo a previous command from the history list.

9   The *stop* alias causes a process to be suspended if a job number or PID is provided to the *kill* command. The job can be resumed in the foreground by typing *fg*.

10 The *suspend* alias suspends the current job by sending the *STOP* signal and the PID ($$) of this process to the *kill* command.

11 The *true* alias is set to the do-nothing command, often used to start an infinite loop.

12 The *type* alias indicates the type of command you are executing: an alias, a binary executable, and so forth.

Creating an Alias.   The user can create aliases in the Korn shell. An alias is a nickname for an existing command or commands. The real command(s) is substituted for the alias when the shell evaluates the command line.

EXAMPLE 10.20

```
1   $ alias cl='clear'
2   $ alias l='ls -laF'
3   $ alias ls='ls -aF'
4   $ \ls ..
```

EXPLANATION

1   The alias *cl* is an alias for *clear*.

2   The alias is *l*. The letter *l* is a nickname for the command *ls –laF*.

3   The alias *ls* is assigned the command *ls –aF*.

4   The backslash turns off the meaning of the alias for the execution of this line. The real *ls* command, not the alias, is executed.

Removing an Alias. The *unalias* command deletes an alias.

EXAMPLE 10.21

```
unalias cl
```

EXPLANATION

The alias *cl* is removed from the list of set aliases.

Tracked Aliases. To reduce the amount of time needed to do a search of the path, the Korn shell creates an alias when a command is first encountered and sets the alias equal to the full pathname of the command. This is called a *tracked alias.* [3]

The Korn shell has some preset tracked aliases that are defined when it is installed. To use tracked aliases, the *set –o trackall* command is issued; it is normally set in the *ENV* file. To see all tracked aliases, type *alias –t*.

EXAMPLE 10.22

```
$ alias -t
chmod=/bin/chmod
ls=/bin/ls
vi=/usr/ucb/vi
who=/bin/who
```

EXPLANATION

The *–t* option to the built-in *alias* command displays those commands that have been aliased via the tracking mechanism. When the user types any of these commands, the shell will not search the path, but use the alias definition to invoke the command.

10.1.9   Job Control

Job control is used to control the execution of background and foreground jobs.

To use Korn shell job control, the monitor option (*set –o monitor*) must be set on systems that do not support job control. See Table 10.5 for job control commands.

---

3. Tracked aliases will be undefined if the *PATH* variable is reset.

EXAMPLE 10.23

```
1   $ vi
    [1]  + Stopped              # vi

2   $ sleep 25&
    [2] 4538


3   $ jobs
    [2]  +  Running             # sleep 25&
    [1]  -  Stopped             # vi

4   $ jobs -l
    [2]  + 4538   Running       # sleep 25&
    [1]  - 4537   Stopped       # vi


5   $ fg %1
```

EXPLANATION

1   After the *vi* editor is invoked, you can press ^Z (Control-Z) to suspend the *vi* session. The editor will be suspended in the background, and after the message *Stopped* appears, the shell prompt will appear immediately.

2   The ampersand at the end of the command causes the *sleep* command, with an argument of 25, to execute in the background. The notation [2] means that this is the second job to be run in the background and the PID of this job is *4538*.

3   The *jobs* command displays the jobs currently in the background.

4   The *jobs* command with the *–l* option displays the processes (jobs) running in the background and the PID numbers of those jobs.

5   The *fg* command followed by a percent sign and the job number will bring that numbererd job into the foreground. Without a number, *fg* brings the most recently backgrounded job back into the foreground.

Table 10.5   Job Control Commands

Command	Meaning
jobs	Lists all unfinished processes in a numerically ordered list where the number of the job is enclosed in brackets.
jobs –l	Same as *jobs*, but includes the PID number of the job.
^Z	Stops the current job.
fg %n	Runs background job in foreground.
bg %n	Runs job in background.
wait %n	Waits for job number *n* to finish.
kill %n	Kills job number *n*.

10.1.10 Metacharacters

Metacharacters are special characters used to represent something other than themselves. Table 10.6 lists some common Korn shell metacharacters and their functions.

Table 10.6 Shell Metacharacters

Command	Function
\	Literal interpretation of the following character.
&	Background processing.
;	Command separator.
$	Variable substitution.
?	Match for a single character.
[abc]	Match for one from a set of characters.
[!abc]	Match for one *not* from the set of characters.
*	Match for zero or more characters.
(cmds)	Execute commands in a subshell.
{cmds}	Execute commands in current shell.

EXAMPLE 10.24

```
1  $ ls -d *     all files are displayed
   abc    abc122   abc2   file1.bak file2.bak nonsense   nothing one
   abc1 abc123   file1    file2    none     noone

2  $ print hello \      # The carriage return is escaped
   > there
   hello there

3  $ rusers&             # Process the rusers command in the background
   [1]    4334
   $

4  $ who; date; uptime     # Commands are executed one at a time
   ellie   console Feb 10 10:46
   ellie   ttyp0    Feb 15 12:41
   ellie   ttyp1    Feb 10 10:47
   ellie   ttyp2    Feb 5  10:53
   Mon Feb 15 17:16:43 PST 2001
   5:16pm up 5 days, 6:32, 1 user, load average: 0.28, 0.23, 0.01

5  $ print $HOME        # The value of the HOME variable is printed
   /home/jody/ellie
```

EXAMPLE 10.24 (CONTINUED)

```
6   $ print $LOGNAME   # The value of the LOGNAME variable is printed
    ellie

7   $ ( pwd; cd / ; pwd )
    /home/jody/ellie
    /
    $ pwd
    /home/jody/ellie

8   $ { pwd; cd /; pwd; }
    /home/jody/ellie
    /
    $ pwd
    /

9   $ ( date; pwd; ls ) > outfile
    $ cat outfile
    Mon Feb 15 15:56:34 PDT 2001
    /home/jody/ellie
    foo1
    foo2
    foo3
```

EXPLANATION

1   The asterisk matches all the files in the current directory. (The *–d* option to the *ls* command prevents the contents of subdirectories from being displayed.)

2   The backslash escapes the newline so that the command line can be continued on the next line.

3   The ampersand (*&*) causes the *rusers* program to be executed in the background; the shell prompt returns immediately. Both processes will run concurrently.

4   Each command is separated by a semicolon. Each command will be executed one at a time.

5   If a dollar sign precedes the variable, the shell will perform variable substitution. The value of the *env* variable, *HOME*, is displayed. The *HOME* variable contains the full pathname of the user's home directory.

6   Again, the dollar sign precedes the variable name. The value of the *LOGNAME* variable is the user's login name.

7   The parentheses indicate that the enclosed commands will be executed in a subshell. The *cd* command is built into the shell, so that each shell that is invoked has its own copy of *cd*. The *pwd* command prints the present working directory, */home/jody/ellie*. After *cd*ing to the *root* directory, the *pwd* command displays that the new directory is *root*. After the subshell exits, the output of the *pwd* command in the parent shell indicates that the directory is still set to */home/jody/ellie* as it was before entering the subshell.

8   The curly braces indicate that the enclosed commands will be executed in the current shell. The *pwd* command prints the present working directory, */home/jody/ellie*. After *cd*ing to the *root* directory, the *pwd* command displays that the new directory is *root*. After the commands within the curly braces exit, the output of the *pwd* command indicates that the directory is still set to the root directory.

9   The parentheses are used to group the commands so that the output of all three commands is sent to *outfile*.

10.1.11   Filename Substitution (Wildcards)

When evaluating the command line, the shell uses metacharacters to abbreviate filenames or pathnames that match a certain set of characters, often called *wildcards*. The filename substitution metacharacters listed in Table 10.7 are expanded into an alphabetically listed set of filenames. The process of expanding a metacharacter into filenames is also called filename substitution, or *globbing*. If a metacharacter is used and there is no filename that matches it, the Korn shell treats the metacharacter as a literal character.

Table 10.7   Shell Metacharacters and Filename Substitution

Metacharacter	Meaning
*	Matches zero or more characters.
?	Matches exactly one character.
[abc]	Matches one character in the set, *a*, *b*, or *c*.
[a–z]	Matches one character in the range: any character in the set between *a* and *z*.
~	Substitutes the user's home directory for ~.
\	Escapes or disables the metacharacter.

The Asterisk.   The asterisk is a wildcard that matches for zero or more of any character in a filename.

EXAMPLE 10.25

```
1   $ ls *
    abc abc1 abc122 abc123 abc2 file1 file1.bak file2 file2.bak none
    nonsense noone nothing nowhere one

2   $ ls *.bak
    file1.bak file2.bak

3   $ print a*c
    abc
```

EXPLANATION

1   The asterisk expands to all of the files in the present working directory. All of the files are passed to *ls* and displayed.

2   All files starting with zero or more characters and ending with *.bak* are matched and listed.

3   All files starting with *a*, followed by zero or more characters, and ending in *c* are matched and passed as arguments to the *print* command.

The Question Mark.   The question mark represents a single character in a filename. When a filename contains one or more question marks, the shell performs filename substitution by replacing the question mark with the character it matches in the filename.

EXAMPLE 10.26

```
1   $ ls
    abc abc1 abc122 abc123 abc2 file1 file1.bak file2 file2.bak
    none nonsense noone nothing nowhere one

2   $ ls a?c?
    abc1 abc2

3   $ ls ??
    ?? not found

4   $ print abc???
    abc122 abc123

5   $ print ??
    ??
```

EXPLANATION

1 The files in the current directory are listed.

2 Filenames containing four characters are matched and listed if the filename starts with an *a*, followed by a single character, followed by a *c* and a single character.

3 Filenames containing exactly two characters are listed. There are none, so the two question marks are treated as literal characters. Since there is no file in the directory called *??*, the shell sends the message *?? not found*.

4 Filenames containing six characters are matched and printed, starting with *abc* and followed by exactly three of any character.

5 The *ksh print* function gets the two question marks as an argument. The shell tries to match for any filenames with exactly two characters. There are no files in the directory that contain exactly two characters. The shell treats the question mark as a literal question mark if it cannot find a match. The two literal question marks are passed as arguments to the *print* command.

The Square Brackets.   Brackets are used to match filenames containing *one* character from a set or range of characters.

EXAMPLE 10.27

```
1  $ ls
   abc abc1 abc122 abc123 abc2 file1 file1.bak file2 file2.bak
   none nonsense noone nothing nowhere one
2  $ ls abc[123]
   abc1 abc2

3  $ ls abc[1-3]
   abc1 abc2

4  $ ls [a-z][a-z][a-z]
   abc one

5  $ ls [!f-z]???
   abc1 abc2

6  $ ls abc12[2-3]
   abc122 abc123
```

EXPLANATION

1 All of the files in the present working directory are listed.

2 All four-character names are matched and listed if the filename starts with *abc*, followed by *1*, *2*, or *3*. Only one character from the set in the brackets is matched for a filename.

3 All four-character filenames are matched and listed if the filename starts with *abc*, and is followed by a number in the range from *1* to *3*.

EXPLANATION (CONTINUED)

4 All three-character filenames are matched and listed, if the filename contains exactly three lowercase alphabetic characters.

5 All four-character files are listed if the first character is *not* a letter between *f* and *z*, followed by three of any character (*???*).

6 Files are listed if the filenames contain *abc12*, followed by 2 or 3.

Escaping the Metacharacters.   To use a metacharacter as a literal character, use the backslash to prevent the metacharacter from being interpreted.

EXAMPLE 10.28

```
1  $ ls
   abc file1 youx

2  $ print How are you?
   How are youx

3  $ print How are you\?
   How are you?

4  $ print When does this line \
   > ever end\?
   When does this line ever end?
```

EXPLANATION

1 The files in the present working directory are listed. Note the file *youx*.

2 The shell will perform filename expansion on the question mark. Any files in the current directory starting with *y-o-u* and followed by exactly one character are matched and substituted in the string. The filename *youx* will be substituted in the string to read, *How are youx* (probably not what you wanted to happen).

3 By preceding the question mark (*?*) with a backslash, it is escaped, meaning that the shell will not try to interpret it as a wildcard.

4 The newline is escaped by preceding it with a backslash. The secondary prompt is displayed until the string is terminated with a newline. The question mark (*?*) is escaped to protect it from filename expansion.

Tilde and Hyphen Expansion.   The tilde character was adopted by the Korn shell (from the C shell) for pathname expansion. The tilde by itself evaluates to the full pathname of the user's home directory. When the tilde is appended with a username, it expands to the full pathname of that user.

The hyphen character refers to the previous working directory; *OLDPWD* also refers to the previous working directory.

EXAMPLE 10.29

```
1   $ echo ~
    /home/jody/ellie

2   $ echo ~joe
    /home/joe

3   $ echo ~+
    /home/jody/ellie/perl

4   $ echo ~-
    /home/jody/ellie/prac

5   $ echo $OLDPWD
    /home/jody/ellie/prac

6   $ cd -
    /home/jody/ellie/prac
```

EXPLANATION

1 The tilde evaluates to the full pathname of the user's home directory.
2 The tilde preceding the username evaluates to the full pathname of *joe's* home directory.
3 The ~+ notation evaluates to the full pathname of the working directory.
4 The ~- notation evaluates to the previous working directory.
5 The *OLDPWD* variable contains the previous working directory.
6 The hyphen refers to the previous working directory; *cd* to go to the previous working directory and display the directory.

New *ksh* Metacharacters.   The new Korn shell metacharacters are used for file-name expansion in a way that is similar to the regular expression metacharacters of *egrep* and *awk*. The metacharacter preceding the characters enclosed in parentheses controls what the pattern matches. See Table 10.8.

EXAMPLE 10.30

```
1   $ ls
    abc abc1 abc122 abc123 abc2 file1 file1.bak file2 file2.bak none
    nonsense noone nothing nowhere one

2   $ ls abc?(1|2)
    abc   abc1 abc2

3   $ ls abc*([1-5])
    abc    abc1   abc122 abc123 abc2
```

EXAMPLE 10.30 (CONTINUED)

```
4  $ ls abc+([1-5])
   abc1   abc122 abc123 abc2

5  $ ls no@(thing|ne)
   none    nothing

6  $ ls no!(one|nsense)
   none    nothing nowhere
```

EXPLANATION

1 All the files in the present working directory are listed.

2 Matches filenames starting with *abc* and followed by *zero characters or one* of either of the patterns in parentheses. Matches *abc* , *abc1*, or *abc2*.

3 Matches filenames starting with *abc* and followed by *zero or more* numbers between *1* and *5*. Matches *abc, abc1, abc122, abc123*, and *abc2*.

4 Matches filenames starting with *abc* and followed by *one or more* numbers between *1* and *5*. Matches *abc1, abc122, abc123*, and *abc2*.

5 Matches filenames starting with *no* and followed by exactly *thing* or *ne*. Matches *nothing* or *none*.

6 Matches filenames starting with *no* and followed by anything except *one* or *nsense*. Matches *none, nothing,* and *nowhere*.

Table 10.8 Regular Expression Wildcards

Regular Expression	Meaning
abc?(2|9)1	? matches zero or one occurrences of any pattern in the parentheses. The vertical bar represents an *or* condition; e.g., either *2* or *9*. Matches *abc21, abc91,* or *abc1*.
abc*([0–9])	* matches zero or more occurrences of any pattern in the parentheses. Matches *abc* followed by zero or more digits; e.g., *abc, abc1234, abc3, abc2,* etc.
abc+([0–9])	+ matches one or more occurrences of any pattern in the parentheses. Matches *abc* followed by one or more digits; e.g., *abc3, abc123,* etc.
no@(one|ne)	@ matches exactly one occurrence of any pattern in the parentheses. Matches *noone* or *none*.
no!(thing|where)	! matches all strings *except* those matched by any of the pattern in the parentheses. Matches *no, nobody,* or *noone,* but not *nothing* or *nowhere*.

The *noglob* Variable.   If the *noglob* variable is set, filename substitution is turned off, meaning that all metacharacters represent themselves; they are not used as wild-cards. This can be useful when searching for patterns containing metacharacters in programs like *grep, sed*, or *awk*. If *noglob* is not set, all metacharacters must be escaped with a backslash if they are not to be interpreted.

EXAMPLE 10.31

```
1   % set -o noglob        # or set -f

2   % print * ?? [] ~ $LOGNAME
    * ?? [] /home/jody/ellie ellie

3   % set +o noglob   # or set +f
```

EXPLANATION

1   The *noglob* variable is set. It turns off the special meaning of the wildcards for file-name expansion. You can use the *–f* option to set the command to achieve the same results.

2   The filename expansion metacharacters are displayed as themselves without any interpretation. Note that the tilde and the dollar sign are still expanded.

3   The *noglob* option is reset. Filename metacharacters will be expanded.

10.1.12 Variables

Local Variables.   Local variables are given values that are known only to the shell in which they are created. Variable names must begin with an alphabetic or underscore character. The remaining characters can be alphabetic, decimal digits zero to nine, or an underscore character. Any other characters mark the termination of the variable name.

Setting and Referencing Local Variables.   When assigning a value to a variable, there can be no whitespace surrounding the equal sign. To set the variable to null, the equal sign is followed by nothing. If more than one word is assigned to a variable, it must be quoted to protect the whitespace; otherwise, the shell prints an error message and the variable is undefined.

If a dollar sign is prepended to the variable name, the value assigned to that variable can be referenced. If other characters are attached to a variable name, curly braces are used to shield the name of the variable from the extra characters.

EXAMPLE 10.32

```
1   $ state=Cal
    $ echo $state
    Cal
```

EXAMPLE 10.32 (CONTINUED)

```
2   $ name="Peter Piper"
    $ echo $name
    Peter Piper


3   $ x=
    $ echo $x
# Blank line appears when a variable is either unset or set to null

    $
4   $ state=Cal
    $ print ${state}ifornia
    California
```

EXPLANATION

1   The variable *state* is assigned the value *Cal* . When the shell encounters the dollar sign preceding a variable name, it performs variable substitution. The value of the variable is displayed.

2   The variable *name* is assigned the value *"Peter Piper"*. The quotes are needed to hide the whitespace so that the shell will not split the string into separate words when it parses the command line. The value of the variable is displayed.

3   The variable *x* is not assigned a value. It will be assigned a null string. The null value, an empty string, is displayed. The same output would be displayed if the variable had not been set at all.

4   The variable *state* is assigned the value *Cal*. The variable is enclosed in curly braces to shield it from the characters that are appended. The value of the variable *Cal* is displayed with *ifornia* appended.

The Scope of Local Variables.   A local variable is known only to the shell in which it was created. It is not passed on to subshells. The $$ variable is a special variable containing the PID (process identification number) of the current shell.

EXAMPLE 10.33

```
1   $ echo $$
    1313


2   $ round=world
    $ echo $round
    world


3   $ ksh      # Start a subshell

4   $ echo $$
    1326


5   $ echo $round
```

EXAMPLE 10.33 (CONTINUED)

```
6   $ exit        # Exits this shell, returns to parent shell

7   $ echo $$
    1313

8   $ echo $round
    world
```

EXPLANATION

1   The value of the $$ variable evaluates to the PID of the current shell. The PID of this shell is *1313*.

2   The local variable *round* is assigned the string value *world* and the value of the variable is displayed.

3   A new Korn shell is invoked. This is called a *subshell*, or *child shell*.

4   The PID of this shell is *1326*. The parent shell's PID is *1313*.

5   The variable *round* is not defined in this shell.

6   The *exit* command terminates this shell and returns to the parent shell. If the *ignoreeof* option is not set, Control-D will also exit this shell.

7   The parent shell returns. Its PID is displayed.

8   The value of the variable is displayed.

Setting Read-Only Variables.   A read-only variable cannot be redefined or unset. It can be set with the *readonly* or *typeset –r* built-in commands. You may want to set variables to *readonly* for security reasons when running in privileged mode.

EXAMPLE 10.34

```
1   $ readonly name=Tom
    $ print $name
    Tom

2   $ unset name
    ksh: name: is read only

3   $ name=Joe
    ksh name: is read only

4   $ typeset -r PATH
    $ PATH=${PATH}:/usr/local/bin
    ksh: PATH: is read only
```

1   The *readonly* local variable *name* is assigned the value *Tom*.

2   A *readonly* variable cannot be unset.

3   A *readonly* variable cannot be redefined.

4   The *PATH* variable is set to be *readonly*. Any effort to unset or change the variable will produce an error message.

Environment Variables.   Environment variables are available to the shell in which they are created and any subshells or processes spawned from that shell. By convention, environment variables are capitalized.

The shell in which a variable is created is called the *parent shell*. If a new shell is started from the parent shell, it is called the *child shell*. Some of the environment variables, such as *HOME*, *LOGNAME*, *PATH*, and *SHELL*, are set before you log in by the */bin/login* program. Normally, environment variables are set in the *.profile* file in the user's home directory.

Setting Environment Variables.   To set environment variables, the *export* command is used either after assigning a value or when the variable is set. All variables in a script can be exported by turning on the *allexport* option to the *set* command.

EXAMPLE   10.35

```
 1   $ TERM=wyse ; export TERM
 2   $ export NAME ="John Smith"
     $ print $NAME
     John Smith
 3   $ print $$
     319
 4   $ ksh
 5   $ print $$
     340
 6   $ print $NAME
     John Smith
 7   $ NAME="April Jenner"
     $ print $NAME
     April Jenner
 8   $ exit
 9   $ print $$
     319
10   $ print $NAME
     John Smith
```

EXPLANATION

1 The *TERM* variable is assigned *wyse*. The variable is exported. Now processes started from this shell will inherit the variable.

2 The variable is exported and defined in the same step. (New with the Korn shell.)

3 The value of this shell's PID is printed.

4 A new Korn shell is started. The new shell is called the *child*. The original shell is its *parent*.

5 The PID of the new Korn shell, stored in the $$ (*340*) variable, is printed.

6 The variable was exported to the new shell and is displayed.

7 The variable is reset to *April Jenner* and displayed.

8 This Korn child shell is exited. The parent shell will return.

9 The PID of the parent, *319*, is displayed again.

10 The variable *NAME* contains its original value. Variables retain their values when exported from parent to child. The child cannot change the value of a variable for its parent.

Special Environment Variables.   The Korn shell assigns default values to the environment variables, *PATH, PS1, PS2, PS3, PS4, MAILCHECK, FCEDIT, TMOUT*, and *IFS*. The *SHELL, LOGNAME, USER*, and *HOME* are set by the */bin/login* program. You can change the values of the defaults and set the others listed in Table 10.9.

Table 10.9 Korn Shell Environment Variables

Variable Name	Meaning
_ (underscore)	The last argument of the previous command.
CDPATH	The search path for the *cd* command. A colon-separated list of directories used to find a directory if the / , ./, or ../ is not at the beginning of the pathname.
COLUMNS	If set, defines the width of the edit window for shell edit modes and the select command.
EDITOR	Pathname for a built-in editor: *emacs, gmacs*, or *vi*.
ENV	A variable set to the name of a file, containing functions and aliases, that the Korn shell will invoke when the *ksh* program is invoked. On versions newer than 1988, this file is only executed when *ksh* is invoked interactively, not for noninteractive shells. The variable is not expanded if the privileged option is turned on.
ERRNO	System error number. Its value is the error number of the most recently failed system call.
FCEDIT	Default editor name for the *fc* command. On versions newer than 1988, this variable is called *HISTEDIT*, and the *fc* command is *hist*.

Table 10.9 Korn Shell Environment Variables (continued)

Variable Name	Meaning
FPATH	A colon-separated list of directories that defines the search path for directories containing auto-loaded functions.
HISTEDIT	For versions of the Korn shell newer than 1988, the new name for FCEDIT.
HISTFILE	Specifies file in which to store command history.
HISTSIZE	Maximum number of commands from the history that can be accessed; default is 128.
HOME	Home directory; used by cd when no directory is specified.
IFS	Internal field separators, normally SPACE, TAB, and NEWLINE, used for field splitting of words resulting from command substitution, lists in loop constructs, and reading input.
LINENO	Current line number in script.
LINES	Used in select loops for vertically displaying menu items; default is 24.
MAIL	If this parameter is set to the name of a mail file and the MAILPATH parameter is not set, the shell informs the user of the arrival of mail in the specified file.
MAILCHECK	This parameter specifies how often (in seconds) the shell will check for the arrival of mail in the files specified by the MAILPATH or MAIL parameters. The default value is 600 seconds (10 minutes). If set to zero, the shell will check before issuing each primary prompt.
MAILPATH	A colon-separated list of filenames. If this parameter is set, the shell informs the user of the arrival of mail in any of the specified files. Each filename can be followed by a % and a message that will be printed when the modification time changes. The default message is *You have mail*.
OLDPWD	Last working directory.
PATH	The search path for commands; a colon-separated list of directories the shell uses to search for the command you want to execute.
PWD	Present working directory; set by cd.
PPID	Process ID of the parent process.
PS1	Primary prompt string, by default $.
PS2	Secondary prompt string, by default >.
PS3	Selection prompt string used with the select command, by default #?.
PS4	Debug prompt string used when tracing is turned on, by default +.

Table 10.9 Korn Shell Environment Variables (continued)

Variable Name	Meaning
RANDOM	Random number generated each time the variable is referenced.
REPLY	Set when read is not supplied arguments.
SHELL	When the shell is invoked, it scans the environment for this name. The shell gives default values to *PATH*, *PS1*, *PS2*, *MAILCHECK*, and *IFS*. *HOME* and *MAIL* are set by *login*.
TMOUT	Specifies number of seconds to wait for input before exiting.
VISUAL	Specifies editor for in-line command editing: *emacs*, *gmacs*, or *vi*.

Listing Set Variables. There are three built-in commands that print the value of variables: *set, env,* and *typeset*. The *set* command prints all variables, local and global. The *env* command prints only global variables. The *typeset* command prints all variables, integers, functions, and exported variables. The *set –o* command prints all options set for the Korn shell.

EXAMPLE 10.36

```
1   $ env        # Partial list
    LOGNAME=ellie
    TERMCAP=sun-cmd:te=\E[>4h:ti=\E[>4l:tc=sun:
    USER=ellie
    DISPLAY=:0.0
    SHELL=/bin/ksh
    HOME=/home/jody/ellie
    TERM=sun-cmd
    LD_LIBRARY_PATH=/usr/local/OW3/lib
    PWD=/home/jody/ellie/perl

2   $ typeset
    export MANPATH
    export PATH
    integer ERRNO
    export FONTPATH
    integer OPTIND
    function LINENO
    export OPENWINHOME
    export LOGNAME
    function SECONDS
    integer PPID
    PS3
    PS2
    export TERMCAP
    OPTARG
```

EXAMPLE 10.36 (CONTINUED)

```
       export USER
       export DISPLAY
       function RANDOM
       export SHELL
       integer TMOUT
       integer MAILCHECK

3   $ set
    DISPLAY=:0.0
    ERRNO=10
    FCEDIT=/bin/ed
    FMHOME=/usr/local/Frame-2.1X
    FONTPATH=/usr/local/OW3/lib/fonts
    HELPPATH=/usr/local/OW3/lib/locale:/usr/local/OW3/lib/help
    HOME=/home/jody/ellie
    IFS=
    LD_LIBRARY_PATH=/usr/local/OW3/lib
    LINENO=1
    LOGNAME=ellie
    MAILCHECK=600
    MANPATH=/usr/local/OW3/share/man:/usr/local/OW3/man:/
    usr/local/man:/usr/local/doctools/man:/usr/man
    OPTIND=1
    PATH=/home/jody/ellie:/usr/local/OW3/bin:/usr/ucb:/
    usr/local/doctools/bin:/usr/bin:/usr/local:/usr/etc:/etc:/
    usr/spool/news/bin:/home/jody/ellie/bin:/usr/lo
    PID=1332
    PS1=$
    PS2=>
    PS3=#?
    PS4=+
    PWD=/home/jody/ellie/kshprog/joke
    RANDOM=4251
    SECONDS=36
    SHELL=/bin/ksh
    TERM=sun-cmd
    TERMCAP=sun-cmd:te=\E[>4h:ti=\E[>4l:tc=sun:
        TMOUT=0
    USER=ellie
    _=pwd
    name=Joe
    place=San Francisco
    x=

4   set -o
    allexport        off
```

EXAMPLE 10.36 (CONTINUED)

```
bgnice          on
emacs           off
errexit         off
gmacs           off
ignoreeof       off
interactive     on
keyword         off
markdirs        off
monitor         on
noexec          off
noclobber       off
noglob          off
nolog           off
nounset         off
privileged      off
restricted      off
trackall        off
verbose         off
viraw           off
xtrace          off
```

EXPLANATION

1   The *env* command lists all environment (exported) variables. These variables are, by convention, named with uppercase letters. They are passed from the process in which they are created to any of the child processes.

2   The *typeset* command displays all variables and their attributes, functions, and integers. The *typeset* command with the + option displays only the names of the variables.

3   The *set* command, without options, prints all set variables, local and exported, including variables set to null.

4   The *set* command with the *–o* option lists all built-in variables that are set to *on* or *off*. To turn options off, use the plus sign (+), and to turn options on, use the minus sign (–); for example, *set –o allexport* turns on the *allexport* option.

Unsetting Variables.   Both local and environment variables can be unset by using the *unset* command (unless the variables are set to *readonly*).

EXAMPLE 10.37

```
unset name; unset TERM
```

EXPLANATION

The variables *name* and *Term* are no longer defined for this shell

Printing the Values of Variables.   The *echo* command (used in Bourne and C shells) is still effective in this shell, but the *print* command has more options and is more efficient. Both the *echo* command and *print* command are built-in to the shell. The *print* command has a number of options to control its output. They are listed in Table 10.10.

Table 10.10   Print Options

Option	Meaning
−r	Prevents escape sequences.
−R	Prevents *ksh* from treating a −2 or −x as a *print* argument; turns off the dash if preceding an argument (except −n); \t, \c, \c are not recognized as special and appear unchanged when printed without the \.
−un	Redirects output to file descriptor *n*.
−n	No newline in output; like echo −n.
−p	Sends output to a coprocess or pipe (&|) rather than to standard output.
−s	Output is appended to the history file as a command rather than to standard output.
−	Any arguments that follow are not print options. The dash allows arguments that contain a hyphen, e.g., −2.
−f	For versions newer than 1988, used to emulate *printf*.

EXAMPLE 10.38

```
1   $ print Hello my friend and neighbor!
    Hello my friend and neighbor!

2   $ print "Hello          friends"
    Hello          friends

3   $ print -r "\n"
    \n

4   $ print -s "date +%H"
    $ history -2
    132 print -s "date +%H"
    133 date +%H
    134 history -2
    $ r 133
    09
```

EXAMPLE 10.38 (CONTINUED)

```
5    $ print -n $HOME
     /home/jody/ellie

6    $ var=world
     $ print ${var}wide
     worldwide

7    $ print -x is an option
     ksh: print: bad option(s)

8    $ print - -x is an option
     -x is an option
```

EXPLANATION

1   The shell parses the command line, breaks the command line into words (tokens) separated by space, and passes the words as arguments to the *print* command. The shell removes all the extra whitespace between words.

2   The quotes create a single string. The shell evaluates the string as a single word and the whitespace is preserved.

3   This is the raw option. Any escape sequences, such as \r, are not interpreted.

4   The *–s* option appends the *print* command's arguments to the history file as a command. The string "*date +%H*" is the argument to the *print* command. The *date* string is appended to the history list as a command and then executed with the *r* command (history's *redo* command).

5   The *–n* option suppresses the newline. The Korn shell prompt is on the same line as the output from the *print* command.

6   The local variable is assigned the value *world*. The braces insulate the variable from characters appended to it.

7   When the first argument to the *print* function begins with a dash, the *print* command interprets the argument as one of its options, unless an additional preceding dash is provided.

8   The dash as an option allows you to use a dash as the first character in the string to be printed.

Escape Sequences.   Escape sequences consist of a character preceded by a backslash and have a special meaning when enclosed within quotes. (See Table 10.11.)

The *print* command, without the *–r* and *–R* options, formats output when any of the following escape sequences are placed within a string. The string must be enclosed in double or single quotes.

EXAMPLE 10.39

```
1  $ print '\t\t\tHello\n'
            Hello

   $

2  $ print "\aTea \tTime!\n\n"
   Ding ( bell rings ) Tea        Time!
```

EXPLANATION

1 The backslash characters must be quoted with either single or double quotes. The \t escape sequence represents a tab, and \n represents a newline. The output is three tabs, followed by the string *Hello*, and a newline.

2 The \a escape sequence causes a bell to ring (\07) and the \t creates a tab. The two \n sequences will print two newline characters.

Table 10.11 Escape Sequences

Backslash Character	Meaning
\a	Bell character.
\b	Backspace.
\c	Suppress newline and ignore any arguments that follow \c.
\f	Formfeed.
\n	Newline.
\r	Return.
\t	Tab.
\v	Vertical tab.
\\	Backslash.
\0x	Eight-bit character with a 1-, 2-, or 3-digit ASCII value, as in print \0124.
\E	Only on versions newer than 1988; used for an escape sequence.

Variable Expressions and Expansion Modifiers. Variable expressions can be tested and modified by using special modifiers. The modifier provides a shortcut conditional test to check whether a variable has been set, and then, depending on the modifier, may assign a default value to the variable. These expressions can be used with conditional constructs such as *if* and *elif*. See Table 10.12.

The colon does not have to be used with the modifier. Using the colon with the modifier checks whether the variable is not set or is *null*; without the colon, a variable set to null is considered a set variable.

Table 10.12 Variable Expressions and Modifiers

Expression	Function
${variable:–word}	If *variable* is set and is nonnull, substitute its value; otherwise, substitute *word*.
${variable:=word}	If *variable* is not set or is null, set it to *word*; the value of *variable* is substituted permanently. Positional parameters may not be assigned in this way.
${variable:+word}	If *variable* is set and is nonnull, substitute *word*; otherwise substitute nothing.
${variable:?word}	If *variable* is set and is nonnull, substitute its value; otherwise, print *word* and exit from the shell. If *word* is omitted, the message *parameter null or not set* is printed.

EXAMPLE 10.40

```
(Using Temporary Default Values)
1   $ fruit=peach

2   $ print ${fruit:-plum}
    peach

3   $ print ${newfruit:-apple}
    apple

4   $ print $newfruit

5   $ print ${TERM:-vt120}
    sun-cmd
```

EXPLANATION

1   The variable *fruit* is assigned the value *peach*.
2   The special modifier will check to see if the variable *fruit* has been set. If it has, the value *peach* is printed; if not, *plum* is printed.
3   The variable *newfruit* has not been set. The value *apple* will be printed.
4   The variable *newfruit* was not set, so nothing prints. In step 3, the expression was simply replaced with the word *apple* and printed.
5   If the *TERM* variable has not been set, a default value *vt120* will be displayed. In this example, the terminal has already been set to *sun–cmd*, a Sun workstation.

EXAMPLE 10.41

```
(Assigning Permanent Default Values)
1   $ name=

2   $ print ${name:=Patty}
    Patty

3   $ print $name
    Patty

4   $ print ${TERM:=vt120}
    vt120

    $ print $TERM
    vt120
```

EXPLANATION

1   The variable *name* is assigned the value *null*.

2   The special modifier *:=* will check to see if the variable name has been set to some value other than null. If it has been set, it will not be changed; if it is either null or not set, it will be assigned the value to the right of the equal sign. *Patty* is assigned to *name* since the variable is set to null. The setting is permanent.

3   The variable *name* still contains the value *Patty*.

4   If the variable *TERM* is not set, it will be assigned the default value *vt120* permanently.

EXAMPLE 10.42

```
(Assigning Temporary Alternate Value)
1   $ foo=grapes
2   $ print ${foo:+pears}
    pears
    $ print $foo
    grapes
```

EXPLANATION

1   The variable *foo* has been assigned the value *grapes*.

2   The special modifier *:+* will check to see if the variable has been set. If it has been set, it will temporarily be reset to *grapes*. If it has not been set, null is returned.

EXAMPLE 10.43

```
(Creating Error Messages Based on Default Values)
1   $ print ${namex:?"namex is undefined"}
    ksh: namex: namex is undefined

2   $ print ${y?}
    ksh: y: parameter null or not set
```

EXPLANATION

1   The *:?* modifier will check to see if the variable has been set. If not, the string to the right of the *?* is printed to standard error, after the name of the variable. If in a script, the script exits.

2   If a message is not provided after the *?*, the Korn shell sends a default message to standard error. Without the colon, the *?* modifier would consider a variable set to null a set variable, and the message would not be printed.

EXAMPLE 10.44

```
(Line from a System Script)
if [ "${uid:=0}" -ne 0 ]
```

EXPLANATION

If the UID (user ID) has a value, it will not be changed; if it does not have a value, it will be assigned the value zero (superuser). The value of the variable will be tested for nonzero. This line was taken from the */etc/shutdown* program (SVR4/Solaris 2.5). It is here to give you an example of how variable modifiers are used.

Variable Expansion of Substrings.   Pattern matching arguments are used to strip off certain portions of a string from either the front or end of the string. The most common use for these operators is stripping off pathname elements from the head or tail of the path. See Table 10.13.

Table 10.13   Variable Expansion Substrings

Expression	Function
${variable%pattern}	Matches the *smallest trailing portion* of the value of *variable* to *pattern* and removes it.
${variable%%pattern}	Matches the *largest trailing portion* of the value of *variable* to *pattern* and removes it.
${variable#pattern}	Matches the *smallest leading portion* of the value of *variable* to *pattern* and removes it.
${variable##pattern}	Matches the *largest leading portion* of the value of *variable* to *pattern* and removes it.

EXAMPLE   10.45

```
1   $ pathname="/usr/bin/local/bin"
2   $ print ${pathname%/bin*}
    /usr/bin/local
```

EXPLANATION

1   The local variable *pathname* is assigned */usr/bin/local/bin*.

2   The % removes the *smallest trailing portion* of *pathname* containing the pattern */bin*, followed by zero or more characters; that is, it strips off */bin*.

EXAMPLE   10.46

```
1   $ pathname="usr/bin/local/bin"
2   $ print ${pathname%%/bin*}
    /usr
```

EXPLANATION

1   The local variable *pathname* is assigned */usr/bin/local/bin*.

2   The %% removes the *largest trailing portion* of *pathname* containing the pattern */bin*, followed by zero or more characters; that is, it strips off */bin/local/bin*

EXAMPLE   10.47

```
1   $ pathname=/home/lilliput/jake/.cshrc
2   $ print ${pathname#/home}
    /lilliput/jake/.cshrc
```

EXPLANATION

1   The local variable *pathname* is assigned */home/liliput/jake/.cshrc*.

2   The # removes the *smallest leading portion* of *pathname* containing the pattern */home*; that is, */home* is stripped from the beginning of the path variable.

EXAMPLE   10.48

```
1   $ pathname=/home/liliput/jake/.cshrc
2   $ print ${pathname##*/}
    .cshrc
```

EXPLANATION

1   The local variable *pathname* is assigned */home/liliput/jake/.cshrc*.

2   The ## removes the *largest leading portion* of *pathname* containing zero or more characters up to and including the last slash; that is, it strips off */home/lilliput/jake* from the path variable.

Variable Attributes: The *typeset* Command. The attributes of a variable, such as its case, width, and left or right justification, can be controlled by the *typeset* command. When the *typeset* command changes the attributes of a variable, the change is permanent. The *typeset* function has a number of other functions. See Table 10.14.

EXAMPLE 10.49

```
1  $ typeset -u name="john doe"
   $ print "$name"
   JOHN DOE            # Changes all characters to uppercase.


2  $ typeset -l name
   $ print $name
   john doe            # Changes all characters to lowercase.


3  $ typeset -L4 name
   $ print $name
   john                # Left-justified fixed-width 4-character field.


4  $ typeset -R2 name
   $ print $name       # Right-justified fixed-width 2-character field.
   hn


5  $ name="John Doe"
   $ typeset -Z15 name         # Null-padded sting, 15-space field.
        width
   $ print "$name"
    John Doe


6  $ typeset -LZ15 name        # Left-justified, 15-space field width.
   $ print "$name$name"
   John Doe        John Doe


7  $ integer n=25
   $ typeset -Z15 n            # Left-justified, zero-padded integer.
   $ print "$n"
   000000000000025


8  $ typeset -lL1 answer=Yes   # Left justify one lowercase letter.
   $ print $answer
   y
```

EXPLANATION

1 The *–u* option to the *typeset* command converts all characters in a variable to uppercase.

2 The *–l* option to the *typeset* command converts all characters in a variable to lowercase.

3 The *–L* option to the *typeset* command converts the variable *name* to a left-justified, four-character string, *john*.

EXPLANATION (CONTINUED)

4   The *–R* option to the *typeset* command converts the variable *name* to a right-justified, two-character string, *hn*.

5   The variable *name* is set to *John Doe*. The *–Z* option to the *typeset* command will convert the string to a null-padded, 15-space string. The variable is quoted to preserve whitespace.

6   The variable *name* is converted to a left-justified, 15-space, null-padded string.

7   The variable *n* is an integer (see *typeset –i*, Table 10.14) assigned the value 25. The *typeset* command will convert the integer *n* to a zero-filled, 15-space, left-justified number.

8   The variable *answer* is assigned the value *Yes* and converted to a lowercase, left-justified, one-character string. (This can be very useful when handling user input in a script.)

Table 10.14   Other Uses of the *typeset* Command

Command	What It Does
typeset	Displays all variables.
typeset –i num	Will only accept integer values for *num*.
typeset –x	Displays exported variables.
typeset a b c	If defined in a function, creates *a*, *b*, and *c* to be local variables.
typeset –r x=foo	Sets *x* to *foo* and then makes it read-only.

Positional Parameters.   Normally, the special built-in variables, often called *positional parameters*, are used in shell scripts when passing arguments from the command line, or used in functions to hold the value of arguments passed to the function. The variables are called positional parameters because they are referenced by numbers 1, 2, 3, and so on, representing their respective positions in the parameter list. See Table 10.15.

The name of the shell script is stored in the *$0* variable. The positional parameters can be set and reset with the *set* command.

Table 10.15   Positional Parameters

Expression	Function
$0	References the name of the current shell script.
$1–$9	Positional parameters *1–9*.
${10}	Positional parameter *10*.
$#	Evaluates to the number of positional parameters.
$*	Evaluates to all the positional parameters.
$@	Same as *$**, except when double quoted.
"$*"	Evaluates to *"$1 $2 $3"*, etc.
"$@"	Evaluates to *"$1" "$2" "$3"*, etc.

EXAMPLE 10.50

```
1   $ set tim bill ann fred
    $ print $*          # Prints all the positional parameters.
    tim bill ann fred

2   $ print $1          # Prints the first position.
    tim

3   $ print $2 $3       # Prints the second and third position.
    bill ann

4   $ print $#          # Prints the total number of positional
    4                   # parameters.

5   $ set a b c d e f g h i j k l m
    $ print $10         # Prints the first positional parameter
    a0                  # followed by a 0.

    $ print ${10} ${11} # Prints the 10th and 11th positions.
    j k

6   $ print $#
    13

7   $ print $*
    a b c d e f g h i j k l m
```

EXAMPLE 10.50 (CONTINUED)

```
8    $ set file1 file2 file3
     $ print \$$#
     $3

9    $ eval print \$$#
     file3
```

EXPLANATION

1   The *set* command assigns values to positional parameters. The $* special variable contains all of the parameters set.

2   The value of the first positional parameter, *tim*, is displayed.

3   The value of the second and third parameters, *bill* and *ann*, are displayed.

4   The $# special variable contains the number of positional parameters currently set.

5   The *set* command resets all of the positional parameters. The original parameter list is cleared. To print any positional parameters beyond 9, the curly braces are used to keep the two digits together. Otherwise, the value of the first positional parameter is printed, followed by the number appended to it.

6   The number of positional parameters is now *13*.

7   The values of all the positional parameters are printed.

8   The dollar sign is escaped; $# is the number of arguments. The *print* command displays $3, a literal dollar sign followed by the number of positional parameters.

9   The *eval* command parses the command line a second time before executing the command. The first time parsed by the shell, the print would display $3; the second time, after *eval*, the *print* displays the value of $3, *file3*.

10.1.13 Other Special Variables

The Korn shell has some special built-in variables, as shown in Table 10.16.

Table 10.16   Special Variables

Variable	Meaning
$$	PID of the shell.
$–	*ksh* options currently set.
$?	Exit value of last executed command.
$!	PID of last job put in background.

EXAMPLE 10.51

```
1   $ print The pid of this shell is $$
    The pid of this shell is 4725

2   $ print The options for this korn shell are $-
    The options for this korn shell are ismh

3   $ grep dodo /etc/passwd
    $ print $?
    1

4   $ sleep 25&
    [1]     400
    $ print $!
    400
```

EXPLANATION

1 The $$ variable holds the value of the PID for this process.

2 The $– variable lists all options for this interactive Korn shell.

3 The *grep* command searches for the string *dodo* in the */etc/passwd* file. The ? variable holds the exit status of the last command executed. Since the value returned from *grep* is one, *grep* is assumed to have failed in its search. An exit status of zero indicates a successful exit.

4 The & appended to the *sleep* command causes the command to be executed in the background. The $! variable holds the PID number of the last command placed in the background.

10.1.14 Quotes

Quotes are used to protect special metacharacters from interpretation. They can cause major debugging hassles in all shell scripts. Single quotes must be matched. They protect special metacharacters from being interpreted by the shell. Double quotes also must be matched. They protect most characters from interpretation by the shell, but allow variable and command substitution characters to be processed. Single quotes will protect double quotes, and double quotes will protect single quotes. The Korn shell, unlike the Bourne shell, will inform you if you have mismatched quotes by sending an error message to standard error with the line where it detects that the quotes were mismatched.

The Backslash. The backslash is used to protect (or escape) a single character from interpretation.

EXAMPLE 10.52

```
1   $ print Where are you going\?
    Where are you going?
2   $ print Start on this line and \
    > go to the next line.
    Start on this line and go to the next line.
```

EXPLANATION

1   The special metacharacter ? is escaped with the backslash. It will not be interpret-ed for filename expansion by the shell.

2   The newline is escaped. The next line will become part of the first line. The > is the Korn shell's secondary prompt.

Single Quotes.   Single quotes must be matched. They protect all metacharacters from interpretation. To print a single quote, it must be enclosed in double quotes or escaped with a backslash.

EXAMPLE 10.53

```
1   $ print 'hi there
    > how are you?
    > When will this end?
    > When the quote is matched
    > oh'
    hi there
    how are you?
    When will this end?
    When the quote is matched
    oh

2   $ print 'Do you need $5.00?'
    Do you need $5.00?

3   $ print 'Mother yelled, "Time to eat!"'
    Mother yelled, "Time to eat!"
```

EXPLANATION

1   The single quote is not matched on the line. The Korn shell produces a secondary prompt. It is waiting for the quote to be matched.

2   The single quotes protect all metacharacters from interpretation. In this example, the $ and the ? are protected from the shell and will be treated as literals.

3   The single quotes protect the double quotes in this string. The double quotes here are conversational quotes.

Double Quotes.   Double quotes must be matched, will allow variable and command substitution, and protect any other special metacharacters from being interpreted by the shell.[4]

```
1   $ name=Jody
2   $ print "Hi $name, I'm glad to meet you!"
    Hi Jody, I'm glad to meet you!

3   $ print "Hey $name, the time is `date`"
    Hey Jody, the time is Fri Dec 18 14:04:11 PST 2001
```

EXPLANATION

1   The variable *name* is assigned the string *Jody*.

2   The double quotes surrounding the string will protect all special metacharacters from interpretation, with the exception of $ in *$name*. Variable substitution is performed within double quotes.

3   Variable substitution and command substitution are both performed when enclosed within double quotes. The variable *name* is expanded and the command in backquotes, *date*, is executed.

10.1.15 Command Substitution

Command substitution is used when assigning the output of a command to a variable, or when substituting the output of a command into a string. The Bourne and C shells use backquotes to perform command substitution. The Korn shell does allow the backquote format (calling it "obsolescent"), but placing the command in parentheses is the preferred method because it has simpler quoting rules and makes nesting commands easier.

FORMAT

```
`Unix command`        # Old method with backquotes

$(Unix command)       # New method
```

---

4. Using backquotes for command substitution is an old form still used in the Bourne and C shells. Although still legal syntax, the Korn shell introduces a new method shown in this section.

EXAMPLE 10.55

```
(Old Way)
1   $ print "The hour is `date +%H`"
    The hour is 09


2   $ name=`nawk -F: ''{print $1}' database`
    $ print $name
    Ebenezer Scrooge


3   $ ls `ls /etc`
    shutdown


4   $ set `date`


5   $ print $*
    Sat Oct 13 09:35:21 PDT 2001


6   $ print $2 $6
    Oct 2001
```

EXPLANATION

1   The output of the *date* command is substituted into the string.

2   The output of the *nawk* command is assigned to the variable *name*, and displayed.

3   The output of the *ls* command, enclosed in backquotes, is a list of files from the */etc* directory. The filenames will be arguments to the first *ls* command. All files with the same name in */etc* as are in the current directory are listed.

4   The *set* command assigns the output of the *date* command to positional parameters. Whitespace separates the list of words into its respective parameters.

5   The $* variable holds all of the parameters. The output of the *date* command was stored in the $* variable. Each parameter is separated by whitespace.

6   The second and sixth parameters are printed.

The *ksh alternate* for using backquotes in command substitution is presented in Example 10.56.

EXAMPLE 10.56

```
(The New ksh Way)
1   $ d=$(date)
    print $d
    Sat Oct 20 09:35:21 PDT 2001


2   $ line = $(< filex)


3   $ print The time is $(date +%H)
    The time is 09
```

EXAMPLE 10.56 (CONTINUED)

```
4    $ machine=$(uname -n)
     $ print $machine
     jody

5    $ dirname="$(basename $(pwd)) "        # Nesting commands
     $ print $dirname
     bin
```

EXPLANATION

1 The *date* command is enclosed within parentheses. The output of the command is returned to the expression, assigned to the variable *d,* and displayed.

2 The input from the file is assigned to the variable *line.* The < *filex* notation has the same effect as `cat filex`. Command substitution is performed within the parentheses when the parentheses are preceded with a dollar sign.

3 The UNIX *date* command and its hour argument, *+%H,* are enclosed within parentheses. Command substitution is performed, and the results are placed within the *print* string.

4 Command substitution has been performed. The output of the UNIX *uname* command is assigned to the variable *machine.*

5 To set the variable *dirname* to the name (only) of the present working directory, command substitution is nested. The *pwd* command is executed first, passing the full pathname of the present working directory as an argument to the UNIX command *basename.* The *basename* command strips off all but the last element of a pathname. Nesting commands within backquotes is not allowed.

10.1.16 Functions

This section introduces functions so that you can use them interactively or store them in your initialization files. Later, when discussing scripts, functions will be covered in more depth. Functions can be used when an alias is not enough, that is, for passing arguments. Functions are often defined in the user's initialization file, *.profile.* They are like miniscripts, but unlike scripts, functions run in the current environment; that is, the shell does not fork a child process to execute a function. All variables are shared with the shell that invoked the function. Often functions are used to improve the modularity of a script. Once defined, they can be used repeatedly and even stored in another directory.

Functions must be defined before they are invoked; there are two formats used to define them. One format came from the Bourne shell and the other is new with the Korn shell. Functions can be exported from one invocation of the shell to the next. The *typeset* function and *unset* command can be used to list and unset functions. See Table 10.17.

Table 10.17 The *typeset* Command and Functions

Command	Function
typeset –f	Lists functions and their definitions; *functions* is an alias for *typeset –f*.
typeset +f	Lists only function names.
unset –f name	Unset a function.

Defining Functions. There are two acceptable formats for defining functions: the Bourne shell format (still allowed for upward compatibility) and the new Korn shell format. A function must be defined before it can be used.

FORMAT

```
(Bourne Shell)
functionname() { commands ; commands; }5

(Korn Shell)
function functionname { commands; commands; }
```

EXAMPLE 10.57

```
1   $ function fun { pwd; ls; date; }

2   $ fun
    /home/jody/ellie/prac
    abc        abc123    file1.bak   none        nothing   tmp
    abc1       abc2      file2       nonsense    nowhere   touch
    abc122     file1     file2.bak   noone       one
    Tue Feb 9 11:15:48 PST 2001

3   $ function greet { print "Hi $1 and $2"; }

4   $ greet tom joe              # Here $1 is tom and $2 is joe
    Hi tom and joe

5   $ set jane nina lizzy
6   $ print $*
    jane nina lizzy

7   $ greet tom joe
    Hi tom and joe

8   $ print $1 $2
    jane nina
```

5. The POSIX standard defines functions with the Bourne shell syntax, but variables and traps cannot be local in scope, as with the new Korn shell definition.

EXPLANATION

1   The function *fun* is named and defined. The name is followed by a list of commands enclosed in curly braces. Each command is separated by a semicolon. There must be a space after the first curly brace or you will get a syntax error such as *ksh: syntax error: `}' unexpected*. A function must be defined before it can be used.

2   The function behaves like a script or an alias when invoked. Each of the commands in the function definition is executed in turn.

3   There are two positional parameters used in the function *greet*. When arguments are given to the function, the positional parameters are assigned those values.

4   The arguments to the function *tom* and *joe* are assigned to $1 and $2, respectively. The positional parameters in a function are private to the function and will not interfere with any used outside the function.

5   The positional parameters are set at the command line. These variables have nothing to do with the ones set in the function.

6   $* displays the values of the currently set positional parameters.

7   The function *greet* is called. The values assigned to the positional parameters $1 and $2 are *tom* and *joe*, respectively.

8   The positional variables assigned at the command line are unaffected by those set in the function.

Functions and Aliases.   When processing the command line, the shell looks for aliases before special built-in commands and for special built-ins before functions. If a function has the same name as a built-in, the built-in will take priority over the function. An alias for a special built-in can be defined, and then the function name can be given the name of the alias to override the order of processing.

EXAMPLE 10.58

```
(The ENV File)
1   alias cd=_cd
2   function _cd {
3   \cd $1
4   print $(basename $PWD)
5   }

(The Command Line)
$ cd /
/
$ cd $HOME/bin
bin
$ cd ..
ellie
```

EXPLANATION

1 The alias for *cd* is assigned *_cd*.

2 The function *_cd* is defined. The opening curly brace marks the start of the function definition.

3 If an alias is preceded by a backslash, alias substitution is not performed. The backslash precedes *cd* to execute the built-in *cd* command, not the alias. Without the backslash, the function would be recursive and the shell would display an error message: *cd_: recursion too dee*p. *$1* is the argument (name of a directory) passed to *cd*.

4 The name of the directory (not the full pathname) is printed.

5 The closing curly brace marks the end of the function definition.

Listing Functions.   To list functions and their definitions, use the *typeset* command.

EXAMPLE   10.59

```
(The Command Line)
1   $ typeset -f
    function fun
    {
    pwd; ls; date; }
    function greet
    {
    print "hi $1 and $2"; }

2   $ typeset +f
    fun
    greet
```

EXPLANATION

1 The *typeset* command, with the *–f* option, lists the function and its definition.

2 The *typeset* command, with the *+f* option, lists only the names of defined functions.

Unsetting Functions.   When a function is unset, it will be removed from the shell's memory.

EXAMPLE   10.60

```
(The Command Line)
1   $ typeset -f
    function fun
    {
        pwd; ls; date; }
    function greet
    {
    print "hi $1 and $2"; }
```

EXAMPLE 10.60 (CONTINUED)

2 $ **unset -f fun**

3 $ **typeset -f**
   function greet
   {
   print "hi $1 and $2"; }

EXPLANATION

1 The *typeset –f* command displays the function and its definition. Two functions, *fun* and *greet*, are displayed.

2 The built-in command *unset*, with the *–f* option, undefines the *fun* function, removing it from the shell's memory.

3 The *fun* function is no longer shown as one of the functions defined when the *typeset –f* command is executed.

10.1.17 Standard I/O and Redirection

The shell opens three files (called *streams*) whenever a program is started: *stdin, stdout,* and *stderr.* Standard input normally comes from the keyboard and is associated with file descriptor 0. Standard output normally goes to the screen, file descriptor 1. Standard error normally goes to the screen, file descriptor 2. Standard input, output, and error can be redirected to or from a file. See Table 10.18 for a list of redirection operators.

Table 10.18 Redirection

Operator	Function
<	Redirect input.
>	Redirect output.
>>	Append output.
2>	Redirect error.
1>&2	Redirect output to where error is going.
2>&1	Redirect error to where output is going.

EXAMPLE 10.61

```
(The Command Line)
1   $ tr '[A-Z]' '[a-z]' < myfile   # Redirect input

2   $ ls > lsfile           # Redirect output
    $ cat lsfile
    dir1
    dir2
    file1
    file2
    file3

3   $ date >> lsfile        # Redirect and append output
    $ cat lsfile
    dir1
    dir2
    file1
    file2
    file3
    Mon Sept 17 12:57:22 PDT 2001

4   $ cc prog.c 2> errfile            # Redirect error

5   $ find . -name \*.c -print > founditfile 2> /dev/null

6   $ find . -name \*.c -print > foundit 2>&1

7   $ print "File needs an argument" 1>&2

8   $ function usage { print "Usage: $0 [-y] [-g] filename" 1>&2 ;
          exit 1; }
```

EXPLANATION

1   The standard input is redirected from the file *myfile* to the UNIX *tr* command. All uppercase letters are converted to lowercase letters.

2   The *ls* command redirects its output to the file *lsfile*.

3   The output of the *date* command is redirected and appended to *lsfile*.

4   The file *prog.c* is compiled. If the compile fails, standard error is redirected to *errfile*.

5   The *find* command starts searching in the current working directory for filenames ending in *.c* and prints the files to a filenamed *founditfile*. Errors from the *find* command are sent to */dev/null*.

6   The *find* command starts searching in the current working directory for filenames ending in *.c* and prints the files to a filenamed *foundit*. The standard error (file descriptor 2) is being sent to the same place that the standard output (file descriptor 1) is being sent, to the file called *foundit*.

EXPLANATION (CONTINUED)

7   The *print* command sends its message to standard error. Standard output is merged with standard error; that is, standard output is being redirected to the place where standard error goes, the terminal. This makes it possible to separate error messages from "good" output.

8   The function *usage* is defined. This function, when called, will print a usage message, send the output to standard error, and exit. This type of function is often used in scripts.

The *exec* Command and Redirection.   The *exec* command can be used to replace the current program with the one being *execed*. Another use for the *exec* command is to change standard output or input without creating a subshell. If a file is opened with *exec*, subsequent *read* commands will move the file pointer down the file a line at a time until end of file. The file must be closed to start reading from the beginning again. However, if using UNIX utilities such as *cat* and *sort*, the operating system closes the file after each command has completed. See Table 10.19 for *exec* functionality.

Table 10.19   *exec* Commands

Command	Function
exec ls	*ls* will execute in place of the shell. When *ls* is finished, the shell in which it was started does not return.
exec < filea	Open *filea* for reading standard input.
exec > filex	Open *filex* for writing standard output.
exec 2> errors	Open *errors* for writing standard error.
exec 2> /dev/console	Sends all error messages to the *console*.
exec 3< datfile	Open *datfile* as file descriptor 3 for reading input.
sort <&3	*datfile* is sorted.
exec 4>newfile	Open *newfile* as file descriptor 4 for writing.
ls >&4	Output of *ls* is redirected to *newfile*.
exec 5<&4	Make *fd* 5 a copy of *fd* 4. Both descriptors refer to *newfile*.
exec 3<&–	Close file descriptor 3, *datfile*.

10.1.18 Redirection and the Child Shell

When the output of a command is redirected from the screen to a file, the Korn shell creates a child (fork) shell to rearrange the file descriptors, as shown in Figure 10.2.

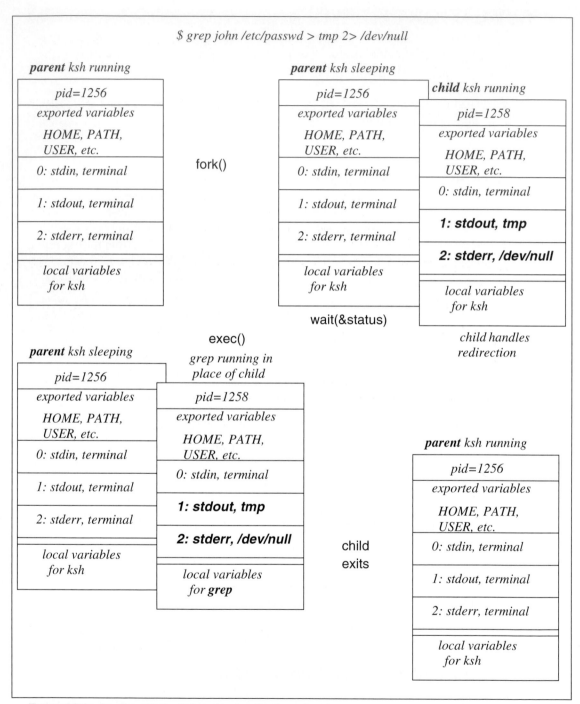

Figure 10.2   Redirection of standard output and errors.

10.1.19 Pipes

A pipe takes the output from the command on the left-hand side of the pipe symbol and sends it to the input of a command on the right-hand side of the pipe symbol. A pipeline can consist of more than one pipe.

EXAMPLE 10.62

```
1   $ who > tmp

2   $ wc -l tmp
    4 tmp

3   $ rm tmp

4   $ who | wc -l        # Using the pipe
```

EXPLANATION

The purpose of lines 1 through 3 is to count the number of people logged on (*who*), save the output of the command in a file (*tmp*), use the *wc –l* to count the number of lines in the tmp file (*wc –l*), and then remove the tmp file; that is, find the number of people logged on. The pipe performs the same task in one command.

1   The output of the *who* command is redirected to the *tmp* file.
2   The *wc –l* command displays the number of lines in *tmp*.
3   The *tmp* file is removed.
4   With the pipe facility, you can perform all three of the above steps, 1,2, and 3, in one step. The output of the *who* command is sent to an anonymous kernel buffer (instead of to a temporary file that requires disk space); the *wc –l* command reads from the buffer and sends its output to the screen.

EXAMPLE 10.63

```
1   $ ls | more
    < lists (ls) all files one page at a time (more) >

2   $ du ~ | sort -n | sed -n '$p'
    72388   /home/jody/ellie

3   $ cat | lp  or  cat | lpr
```

EXPLANATION

1 The *ls* output is piped to the *more* command, which accepts input. Output is displayed one page at a time.

2 The output of the *du* command (disk usage) is sorted numerically and piped to the *sed* command (stream editor), which displays only the last line ($p).

3 The *cat* command reads from standard input; its output is piped to the line printer (*lp* in SVR4 and *lpr* in BSD).

10.1.20 The *here document* and Redirecting Input

A *here document* captures in-line input for programs such as *mail, sort*, and *cat*. Input is placed between two words or symbols. The first word is preceded by a UNIX command and the << symbol. The next line(s) consist of the input to be received by the command. The last line consists of a second word that exactly matches the first word. This word is called the final terminator and marks the end of input. It is used in the same way Control-D is used to terminate input. There can be no spaces surrounding the final terminator. If the first word is preceded by the <<–, leading tabs (and only tabs) may precede the final terminator. Normally, *here documents* are used in shell scripts, rather than interactively. A good use for a *here document* is to create a menu in a script.

FORMAT

```
UNIX command << TERMINATOR
    lines of input
    input
TERMINATOR
```

EXAMPLE 10.64

```
(The Command Line)
1   $ cat << FINISH# FINISH is a user-defined terminator
2   > Hello there $LOGNAME
3   > The time is $(date)
    > I can't wait to see you!!!
4   > FINISH
5   Hello there ellie
    The time is Sun Feb 7 19:42:16 PST 2001
    I can't wait to see you!!
6   $
```

EXPLANATION

1   The UNIX *cat* program will accept input until the word *FINISH* appears on a line by itself.

2   Variable substitution is performed within the *here document*. The > is the Korn shell's secondary prompt.

3   Command substitution is performed within the *here document*.

4   The user-defined terminator, *FINISH*, marks the end of input for the *cat* program. It cannot have any spaces before or after it and is on a line by itself.

5   The output from the *cat* program is displayed.

6   The shell prompt reappears.

EXAMPLE 10.65

```
(From the .profile File)
1   print "Select a terminal type"
2   cat << EOF
      [1] sun
      [2] ansi
      [3] wyse50
3   EOF
4   read TERM
    ...
```

EXPLANATION

1   The user is asked to select a terminal type.

2   The menu will appear on the screen. This is a *here document*, meaing from *here* until the matching *EOF* on line 3 is reached, input will be given to the *cat* command. You could use a series of echo commands to get the same results, but visually, the *here document* is nicer.

3   *EOF* is a user-defined terminator, marking the end of the *here document*. It must be at the left margin with no spaces surrounding it.

4   The user input will be read in from the keyboard and assigned to *TERM*.

EXAMPLE 10.66

```
(The Command Line)
1   $ cat <<- DONE
    >Hello there
    >What's up?
    >Bye now The time is $(date).

2   >       DONE
```

EXAMPLE 10.66 (CONTINUED)

```
3    Hello there
     What's up?
     Bye now The time is Sun Feb 7 19:48:23 PST 2001.
```

EXPLANATION

1   The *cat* program accepts input until *DONE* appears on a line by itself. The <<– operator allows the final terminator to be preceded by one or more tabs. (The > is the shell's secondary prompt.)

2   The final matching *DONE* terminator is preceded by a tab. From the first *DONE* on line 1 to the last *DONE* on this line, the text in between is sent as input to the *cat* command.

3   The output of the *cat* program is displayed on the screen.

10.1.21 Timing Commands

The *time* Command.   The *time* command is a *ksh* built-in command. The *time* command prints the following to standard error: elapsed time, the user time, and the system time used to execute a command.

EXAMPLE 10.67

```
1    $ time sleep 3
     real   0m3.15s     took 3.15 seconds to run
     user   0m0.01s     sleep used its own code for .01 seconds
     sys    0m0.08s     and kernel code for .08 seconds

2    $ time ps –ef | wc –1     # time is measured for all commands in
     38                        # the pipeline
     real   0m1.03s
     user   0m0.01s
     sys    0m0.10s
```

EXPLANATION

1   The *time* command will display the total amount of time elapsed to run the command, the time the user part of the program took to run, and the time the kernel spent running the program. The *sleep* command took *3.15* seconds to run.

2   The time is measured for the *ps* command and *wc* command.

10.1.22 The *TMOUT* Variable

The *TMOUT* variable is an integer type. It can be set to force users to type commands within a certain period of time. *TMOUT*, by default, is set to zero, allowing the user an infinite amount of time to type commands after the *PS1* prompt. If *TMOUT* is set to a value greater than zero, the shell will terminate after the time has expired. Sixty additional seconds will be allotted as the grace period before actually exiting the shell.

EXAMPLE 10.68

```
$ TMOUT=600
time out in 60 seconds due to inactivity
ksh: timed out waiting for input
```

EXPLANATION

The *TMOUT* variable is set to *600* seconds. If the user does nothing for 600 seconds, a message will appear on the screen and then an additional 60 seconds grace period will be allotted before the shell exits. If you do this at the prompt, your current shell exits.

10.2 Programming with the Korn Shell

Writing shell scripts requires a few steps, as outlined in the following section.

10.2.1 The Steps in Creating a Shell Script

A shell script is normally written in an editor and consists of commands interspersed with comments. Comments are preceded by a pound sign.

The First Line. At the top-left corner, to indicate the program that will be executing the lines in the script, #!/bin/ksh is commonly used. The #! is called a magic number and is used by the kernel to identify the program that should be interpreting the lines in the script. This line must be the top line of your script. The Korn shell also provides a number of invocation options that control how the shell behaves. These options are listed at the end of this chapter.

Comments. Comments are lines preceded by a pound sign. They are used to document your script. It is sometimes difficult to understand what the script is supposed to do if it is not commented. Although comments are important, they are often too sparse or not even used at all. Try to get used to commenting what you are doing, not only for someone else, but also for yourself.

Executable Statements and Korn Shell Constructs. A Korn shell program consists of a combination of UNIX commands, Korn shell commands, programming constructs, and comments.

Naming and Storing Scripts. When naming scripts, it is a good idea to give the script a meaningful name and one that does not conflict with other UNIX commands or aliases. For example, you may want to call the script *test* because it is merely performing some simple test procedure, but *test* is a built-in command and you may find you are executing the wrong *test*. Additionally, if you name the file *foo, goo, boobar,* and so forth, in a few days or even hours you may not have any idea what is in that script!

After you have tested your script and found it "bug-free," make a directory where you can store the scripts, then set the path so that your scripts can be executed from anywhere in the directory hierarchy.

EXAMPLE 10.69

```
1   $ mkdir ~/bin
2   $ mv myscript ~/bin

(In .profile)
3   export PATH=${PATH}:~/bin

4   $ . .profile
```

EXPLANATION

1   A common place to store scripts is in a directory under your home directory called *bin*.

2   The script, called *myscript*, is moved into the new *bin* directory.

3   The new directory is added to the *PATH* variable in the *.profile* initialization file.

4   The *dot* command causes the *.profile* file to be executed in the current environment so that you do not have to log out and then back in to enable the new setting.

Making a Script Executable.   When you create a file, it is not automatically given execute permission (regardless of how *umask* is set). You need this permission to run your script. Use the *chmod* command to turn on execute permission.

EXAMPLE 10.70

```
1   $ chmod +x myscript
2   $ ls -lF myscript
    -rwxr--xr--x  1 ellie       0 Jul 12 13:00 joker*
```

EXPLANATION

1   The *chmod* command is used to turn on execute permission for the user, group, and others.

2   The output of the *ls* command indicates that all users have execute permission on the *joker* file. The asterisk at the end of the filename also indicates that this is an executable program.

Using a Script as an Argument to *ksh*.   If you don't make a script executable, you can execute it by passing it as an argument to the *ksh* command:

EXAMPLE 10.71

```
(The Command Line)
$ ksh myscript
```

EXPLANATION

If the *ksh* program is given a scriptname as its argument, it will execute the script and the *#!* line is not necessary or even used.

A Scripting Session.   In Example 10.72, the user will create a script in the editor. After saving the file, the execute permissions are turned on, and the script is executed. If there are errors in the program, the Korn shell will respond immediately.

EXAMPLE 10.72

```
(The Script)
1   #!/bin/ksh
2   # This is the first Korn shell program of the day.
    # Scriptname: greetings
    # Written by: Karen Korny
3   print "Hello $LOGNAME, it's nice talking to you."
4   print "Your present working directory is $(pwd)."
    print "You are working on a machine called $(uname -n)."
    print "Here is a list of your files."
5   ls      # List files in the present working directory
    print "Bye for now $LOGNAME. The time is $(date +%T)!"

(The Command Line)
    $ chmod +x greetings
    $ greetings
3   Hello karen, it's nice talking to you.
4   Your present working directory is /home/lion/karen/junk
    Your are working on a machine called lion.
    Here is a list of your files.
5   Afile         cplus   letter     prac
    Answerbook    cprog   library    prac1
    bourne        joke    notes      perl5
    Bye for now karen. The time is 18:05:07!
```

EXPLANATION

1   The first line of the script, *#!/bin/ksh*, lets the kernel know what interpreter will execute the lines in this program.

2　The comments are nonexecutable lines preceded by a #. They can be on a line by themselves or inserted in a line after a command.

3　The *print* command displays the line on the screen, after variable substitution is performed by the shell.

4　The *print* command displays the line on the screen, after command substitution is performed by the shell.

5　The *ls* command is executed. The comment, any text on the line after the pound sign (#), will be ignored by the shell.

10.2.2　Reading User Input

The *read* command is used to take input from the terminal or from a file until the newline is reached. The Korn shell provides some additional options for the *read* command. See Table 10.20 for different *read* formats. See Table 10.21 for *read* options.

Table 10.20　The *read* Format

Format	Meaning
read answer	*Reads* a line from standard input and assigns it to the variable *answer*.
read first last	*Reads* a line from standard input to the first whitespace or newline, putting the first word typed into the variable *first* and the rest of the line into the variable *last*.
read response?"Do you feel okay?"	*Displays* the string *Do you feel okay?* to standard error and waits for user to type a reply, then puts the reply in the variable *response*. This form of *read* requires and accepts only one variable. Whatever the user types, until the newline, will be stored in *response*.
read –u3 line	*Reads* a line from file descriptor 3 into variable *line*.
read	*Reads* input into a built-in variable, *REPLY*.

Table 10.21 The *read* Options

Options	Meaning
–r	Treats newline character, the \n, as a literal.
–s	Copies a line into the history file.
–un	Reads from file descriptor n; the default is *fd 0*, or standard input.
–p	Reads a line of input from a coprocess.

On Versions of ksh Newer than 1988:

–A	Stores the fields as an array, index starting at zero.
–t sec	Puts a limit of seconds on the user's response time.
–d char	Used as an alternate delimiter for terminating input; newline is the default.

EXAMPLE 10.73

```
(The Script)
    #!/bin/ksh
    # Scriptname: nosy
    print -n "Are you happy? "
1   read answer
    print "$answer is the right response."
    print -n "What is your full name? "

2   read first middle last
    print "Hello $first"
    print -n "Where do you work? "
3   read

4   print I guess $REPLY keeps you busy!

5   read place?"Where do you live? "
    # New ksh read and print combined
    print Welcome to $place, $first $last


(The Output)
    $ nosy
    Are you happy? Yes
1   Yes is the right response.
2   What is your full name? Jon Jake Jones
    Hello Jon
3   Where do you work? Tandem
```

EXAMPLE 10.73 (CONTINUED)

```
4    I guess Tandem keeps you busy!
5    Where do you live? Timbuktu
     Welcome to Timbuktu, Jon Jones
```

EXPLANATION

1   The *read* command accepts a line of user input and assigns the input to the variable *answer*.

2   The *read* command accepts input from the user and assigns the first word of input to the variable *first*, assigns the second word of input to the variable *middle*, and all the rest of the words to the end of the line to the variable *last*.

3   The *read* command, without an argument, accepts a line of input from the user and assigns the input to the built-in variable *REPLY*.

4   After the shell has performed variable substitution, the *print* function prints the string, showing the value of the built-in *REPLY* variable.

5   If the variable following the *read* command is appended with a question mark (*?*), the string after the question mark is displayed as a prompt. The user input is stored in the variable *place*.

Read and File Descriptors.   When the system boots up, three files called streams (*stdin*, *stdout*, and *stderr*) are opened and assigned to an array of file descriptors. The first three file descriptors, 0, 1, and 2, are for standard input, standard output, and standard error, respectively. The next file descriptor available is file descriptor 3. The *–u* option allows the *read* command to read directly from the file descriptor.

EXAMPLE 10.74

```
(The Command Line)
1    $ cat filex
     Captain Kidd
     Scarlett O'Hara


2    $ exec 3< filex
     # filex is assigned to file descriptor 3 for reading


3    $ read -u3 name1
     # read from filex and store input in variable, name1


4    $ print $name1
     Captain Kidd


5    $ read -u3 name2
     $ print $name2
     Scarlett O'Hara
```

EXAMPLE 10.74 (CONTINUED)

```
6   $ exec 3<&-                    # Close file descriptor 3

7   $ read -u3 line
    ksh: read: bad file unit number
```

EXPLANATION

1   The contents of *filex* are displayed.

2   The *exec* command is used to open file descriptor 3 for reading from *filex*.

3   The *read* command reads one line directly from unit 3 (file descriptor 3, *filex*) and assigns that line to the variable *name1*.

4   The line stored in *name1* is printed.

5   The file *filex* is still open, and this *read* command reads the next line from the file and stores that line in the variable *name2*.

6   File descriptor 3 (unit 3) is closed. *filex* is no longer open.

7   Since file descriptor 3 (*filex*) has been closed, the *read* command fails when attempting to read input from that descriptor into variable *line*.

Reading through Files.   Example 10.75 uses the *read* command with a *while* loop. The loop will iterate through the file one line at a time. When end of file is reached, the loop terminates. The files are opened with descriptors (units) for reading.

EXAMPLE 10.75

```
(The Files)
1   $ cat names
    Merry Melody
    Nancy Drew
    Rex Allen
    $ cat addresses
    150 Piano Place
    5 Mystery Lane
    130 Cowboy Terrace
-----------------------------------------------------------------
(The Script)
    #!/bin/ksh
    # Scriptname: readit
2   while read -u3 line1 && read -u4 line2
    do
3       print "$line1:$line2"
4   done 3<$1 4<$2
-----------------------------------------------------------------
```

EXAMPLE 10.75 (CONTINUED)

```
(The Command Line)
5  $ readit names addresses
   Merry Melody:150 Piano Place
   Nancy Drew:5 Mystery Lane
   Rex Allen:130 Cowboy Terrace
```

EXPLANATION

1   The contents of two files, *names* and *addresses,* are displayed.

2   The *while* loop is started. The *read* command reads a line of input from file descriptor *3* (unit 3) and, if successful, reads another line from file descriptor *4*. The file descriptors (units) are assigned filenames on line 4. The filenames are being passed as arguments, or positional parameters 1 and 2.

3   The value of the first variable, a colon, and the value of the second variable are displayed.

4   The input assigned to file descriptor *3* is the first command line argument, *names.* The input assigned to file descriptor *4* is the second command line argument, *addresses.*

5   The script is executed with command line arguments (the names of two files).

10.2.3   Arithmetic

The Korn shell supports both integer and floating point arithmetic, but floating point arithmetic is available only on versions of the Korn shell newer than 1988. The *typeset* command is used for assigning types. See Table 10.22 for the *typeset* command.

Table 10.22   *typeset* and Arithmetic

typeset Command	Alias	Meaning
typeset –i variable	*integer* variable	Variable is only allowed integer assignment.
typeset –i#		# is the base number for the integer.
On Versions of ksh Newer than 1988:		
typeset –F variable		Floating point number assignment.
typeset –E variable	*float* variable	Floating point number assignment.

The Integer Type.   Variables can be declared as integers with the *typeset –i* command or its alias, *integer*. If you attempt to assign any string value, *ksh* returns an error. If you assign a floating point number, the decimal point and the fractional value will be truncated. The *integer* alias can be used instead of *typeset –i*. Numbers can also be represented in different bases such as *binary, octal,* and *hex.*

EXAMPLE 10.76

```
1   $ typeset -i num or integer num       # integer is an alias for
                                          # typeset -i

2   $ num=hello
    /bin/ksh: hello: bad number

3   $ num=5 + 5
    /bin/ksh: +: not found

4   $ num=5+5
    $ echo $num
    10

5   $ num=4*6
    $ echo $num
    24

6   $ num="4 * 6"
    $ echo $num
    24

7   $ num=6.789
    $ echo $num
    6
```

EXPLANATION

1   The *typeset* command with the *–i* option creates an integer variable *num*.

2   Trying to assign the string *hello* to the integer variable *num* causes an error.

3   The whitespace must be quoted or removed unless the (( )) operators are used (see "Arithmetic Operators and the let Command" on page 511).

4   The whitespace is removed and arithmetic is performed.

5   Multiplication is performed and the result assigned to *num*.

6   The whitespace is quoted so that the multiplication can be performed and to keep the shell from expanding the wildcard (*).

7   Since the variable is set to integer, the fractional part of the number is truncated.

Using Different Bases.   Numbers can be represented in decimal (base 10), octal (base 8), and so forth, by using the *typeset* command and with the *–i* option and the base number.[6]

```
1   $ num=15
2   $ typeset -i2 num      # binary
    $ print $num
    2#1111

3   $ typeset -i8 num      # octal
    $ print $num
    8#17

4   $ typeset -i16 num     # hex
    $ print $num
    16#f

5   $ read number
    2#1101
    $ print $number
    2#1101

6   $ typeset -i number
    $ print $number
    2#1101

7   $ typeset -i10 number    # decimal
    $ print $number
    13

8   $ typeset -i8 number     # octal
    $ print $number
    8#15
```

EXPLANATION

1   The variable *num* is assigned the value *15*.

2   The *typeset* command converts the number to a binary format. The display is the base of the number (2), followed by a pound sign (#), and the value of the number in binary.

3   The *typeset* command converts the number to an octal format and displays the value of the number in base *8*.

4   The *typeset* command converts the number to hexadecimal format and displays the value of the number in base *16*.

---

6. Bases greater than 36 are available on versions of the Korn shell that are newer than 1988.

EXPLANATION (CONTINUED)

5   The *read* command accepts input from the user. The input is entered in binary format, stored in the variable *number*, and displayed in binary format.

6   The *typeset* command converts *number* to an integer. It still displays in binary format.

7   The *typeset* command converts *number* to a decimal integer and displays it.

8   The *typeset* command converts *number* to octal and displays its value in base 8.

Listing Integers.   The *typeset* command with only the –*i* argument will list all preset integers and their values, as shown in the following display.

```
$ typeset -i
ERRNO=2
LINENO=1
MAILCHECK=600
OPTIND-1
PPID-4081
RANDOM=25022
SECONDS=47366
TMOUT=0
n=5
number=#15
```

Arithmetic Operators and the *let* Command.   The *let* command is a Korn shell built-in command that is used to perform integer arithmetic. This replaces the Bourne shell integer testing. The alternative and preferred way to use the *let* command is with the (( )) operator.

Table 10.23   *let* Operators

Operator	Meaning
–	Unary minus.
!	Logical *not*.
~	Bitwise *not*.
* / %	Multiply, divide, remainder.
+ –	Add, subtract.
<< >>	Bitwise left shift, right shift.
<= >= < > == !=	Comparison operators.
& ^ |	Bitwise *and*; exclusive *or*.
&& || !	Logical *and*; logical *or*; unary *not*.
=	Assignment.
*= /= %= += –= <<= >>= &= ^= |=	Shortcut assignment.

Note: The ++ and −− operators are supported on versions of *ksh* that are newer than 1988.

EXAMPLE 10.78

```
1   $ i=5

2   $ let i=i+1
    $ print $i
    6

3   $ let "i = i + 2"
    $ print $i
    8

4   $ let "i+=1"
    $ print $i
    9
```

EXPLANATION

1   The variable *i* is assigned the value *5*.
2   The *let* command will add *1* to the value of *i*. The $ (dollar sign) is not required for variable substitution when performing arithmetic.
3   The quotes are needed if the arguments contain whitespace.
4   The shortcut operator, +=, is used to add *1* to the value of *i*.

EXAMPLE 10.79

```
    (The Command Line)
1   $ (( i = 9 ))

2   $ (( i = i * 6 ))
    $ print $i
    54

3   $ (( i > 0 && i <= 10 ))

4   $ print $?
    1
    $ j=100

5   $ (( i < j || i == 5 ))

6   $ print $?
    0

7   $ if (( i < j && i == 54 ))
    > then
    > print True
    >fi
    True
    $
```

EXPLANATION

1   The variable *i* is assigned the value *9*. The (( )) operators are an alternate form of the *let* command. Since the expression is enclosed in double parentheses, spaces are allowed between the operators.

2   The variable *i* is assigned the product of *i*6*.

3   The numeric expressions are tested. If both expressions are true, zero exit status is returned.

4   The special *?* variable holds the exit status of the last command (the *let* command) executed. Since the value is one, the command failed (evaluated as false).

5   The numeric expressions are tested. If one of the expressions is true, zero exit status is returned.

6   The special *?* variable holds the exit status of the last command (the *let* command) executed. Since the value is zero, the command succeeded (evaluated as true).

7   The *if* conditional command precedes the *let* command. The secondary prompt appears while waiting for the command to be completed. If the exit status is zero, the commands after the *then* statement are executed; otherwise, the primary prompt returns.

10.2.4   Positional Parameters and Command Line Arguments

Command line arguments can be referenced in scripts with positional parameters; for example, $1 is set to the first argument, $2 to the second argument, and $3 to the third argument. Positional parameters can be reset with the *set* command. See Table 10.24.

Table 10.24   Positional Parameters

Variable	Function
$0	References the name of the script.
$#	Holds the value of the number of positional parameters.
$*	Contains a list of all the positional parameters.
$@	Means the same as $*, except when enclosed in double quotes.
"$*"	Expands to a single argument, e.g., *"$1 $2 $3"*.
"$@"	Expands to separate arguments, e.g., *"$1" "$2" "$3"*.

The *set* Command and Positional Parameters.   The *set* command sets the positional parameters. If the positional parameters have already been set, the *set* command will reset them, removing any values in the old list. To unset all of the positional parameters, use *set – –*.

EXAMPLE   10.80

```
        (The Script)
        $ cat args
        #!/bin/ksh
        # Script to test command line arguments
1       print The name of this script is $0.
2       print The arguments are $*.
3       print The first argument is $1.
4       print The second argument is $2.
5       print The number of arguments is $#.
6       oldparameters=$*
7       set Jake Nicky Scott
8       print All the positional parameters are $*.
9       print The number of positional parameters is $#.
10      print $oldparameters
11      set --
12      print Good-bye for now, $1.
13      set $oldparameters
14      print $*


        (The Output)
        $ args a b c d
1       The name of this script is args.
2       The arguments are a b c d.
3       The first argument is a.
4       The second argument is b.
5       The number of arguments is 4.
8       All the positional parameters are Jake Nicky Scott.
9       The number of positional parameters is 3.
10      a b c d
12      Good-bye for now ,.
14      a b c d
        $
```

EXPLANATION

1   The name of the script is stored in the *$0* variable.

2   *$** (and *$@*) both represent all of the positional parameters.

3   *$1* represents the first positional parameter (command line argument).

4   *$2* represents the second positional parameter.

5   *$#* is the total number of positional parameters (command line arguments).

EXPLANATION (CONTINUED)

6　The variable *oldparameters* is assigned all of the positional parameters ($*). Later on, if you want to get back your original parameters, you can do so by typing *set $oldparameters*.

7　Reset positional parameters with the *set* command. The *set* command completely clears all previously set parameters. *Jake* is assigned to $1, *Nicky* is assigned to $2, and *Scott* is assigned to $3.

8　The new positional parameters are printed.

9　The number of positional parameters is printed.

10　The original parameters were stored in the variable *oldparameters*. They are printed.

11　All parameters are unassigned.

12　$1 has no value. The parameters list was cleared with the *set* – – command.

13　A new parameter list is assigned by substituting the values in *oldparameters* to the parameter list with the *set* command.

14　All the positional parameters are printed.

EXAMPLE 10.81

```
(How $* and $@ Differ)
1   $ set 'apple pie' pears peaches
2   $ for i in $*
    > do
    > echo $i
    > done
    apple
    pie
    pears
    peaches


3   $ set 'apple pie' pears peaches
4   $ for i in "$*"
    > do
    > echo $i
    > done
    apple pie pears peaches


5   $ set 'apple pie' pears peaches
6   $ for i in $@
    > do
    > echo $i
    > done
```

EXAMPLE 10.81 (CONTINUED)

```
    apple
    pie
    pears
    peaches

7   $ set 'apple pie' pears peaches
8   $ for i in "$@"              # At last!!
    > do
    > echo $i
    > done
    apple pie
    pears
    peaches
```

EXPLANATION

1   The positional parameters are set. When the $* is expanded, the quotes are stripped and *apple pie* becomes two separate words. The *for* loop assigns each of the words, in turn, to the variable *i* and then prints the value of *i*. Each time through the loop, the word on the left is shifted off, and the next word is assigned to *i*.

2   If $* is surrounded by double quotes, all of the words in the list become one single string, and the whole string is assigned to the variable *i*.

3   The positional parameters are set.

4   By enclosing $* in double quotes, the entire parameter list becomes one string.

5   The positional parameters are set.

6   Unquoted, the $@ behaves the same way as the $*.

7   The positional parameters are set.

8   By surrounding $@ with double quotes, each of the positional parameters is treated as a quoted string. The list would consist of *"apple pie," "pears,"* and *"peaches."* Each of the quoted words is assigned to *i*, in turn, as the loop goes through each iteration.

10.2.5   Testing Exit Status and the $? Variable

The ? variable contains a number value (between 0 and 255) representing the exit status of the last command that exited. If the exit status is zero, the command exited with success; if nonzero, the command failed in some way. You can test the exit status of commands and use the *test* command to test the exit status of expressions.

The following examples illustrate how the exit status is tested. The single brackets are used in the Bourne shell, and although perfectly acceptable in the Korn shell, Dr. Korn provides you with the new double-bracket notation for testing expressions.

EXAMPLE 10.82

```
(The Command Line)
1   $ name=Tom
2   $ grep "$name" datafile
    Tom Savage:408-124-2345
3   $ print $?
    0                          # Success!

4   $ test $name = Tom

5   $ print $?
    0                          # Success

6   $ test $name != Tom
    $ print $?
    1                          # Failure

7   $ [ $name = Tom ]          # Brackets instead of the test command
8   $ print $?
    0

9   $ [[ $name = [Tt]?m ]]     # New ksh test command
10  $ print $?
    0
```

EXPLANATION

1   The string *Tom* is assigned to the variable *name*.

2   The *grep* command will search for string *Tom* in the *datafile*, and if successful in its search, will display the line found.

3   The *?* variable, accessed by *$?*, contains the exit status of the last command executed, in this case, the exit status of *grep*. If *grep* is successful in finding the string *Tom*, it will return an exit status of zero. The *grep* command was successful.

4   The *test* command is used to evaluate strings and numbers, and to perform file testing. It returns an exit status of zero if the expression is true, and an exit status of one if the expression fails. There must be spaces surrounding the equal sign.

5   The value of *name* is tested to see if it is equal to *Tom*. The *test* command returns an exit status of *0*, meaning that *$name* does evaluate to *Tom*.

6   The value of *name* is tested to see if it is equal to *Tom*. The *test* command returns an exit status of *1*, meaning that *name* is not equal to *Tom*.

7   The brackets are an alternate notation for the *test* command. There must be spaces after the first bracket. The expression is tested to see if *$name* evaluates to the string *Tom*.

8   The exit status of the test is zero. The test was successful because *$name* is equal to *Tom*.

9 The new Korn shell *test* command, *[[*, is used. The new *test* allows shell metacharacter expansion. If the variable matches *Tom, tom, Tim, tim*, and so on, the test will return a successful status, zero.

10 The variable *name* did match a string beginning with *T* or *t* and ending in *m*, resulting in a successful exit status (*$?*) of *0*.

10.2.6   Conditional Constructs and Flow Control

Conditional commands allow you to perform some task(s) based on whether or not a condition succeeds or fails. The *if* command is the simplest form of decision making. The *if/else* commands allow a two-way decision construct, and the *if/elif/else* commands allow a multiway decision construct.

The Korn shell expects a command to follow an *if*. The command can be a system command or a built-in command. The exit status of the command is used to evaluate the condition. To evaluate an expression, the built-in *test* command is used. This command is also linked to the *[* and the *[[* symbols. The Bourne shell encloses an expression in a set of single brackets: *[* and *]*. The Korn shell has a more sophisticated method for testing expressions. The expression is enclosed in double brackets: *[[* and *]]*. In the single brackets, the expansion of wildcards is not allowed; with the double brackets (Korn shell only), wildcard expansion is supported and a new set of operators have been added. The result of a command is tested, with zero status indicating success, and nonzero status indicating failure.

The Old *test* Command.   The *test* command is used to evaluate conditional expressions, returning true or false. It returns zero exit status for true, and nonzero exit status for false. Either the *test* command or the brackets can be used. The Korn shell introduced a new way of testing expressions with double brackets. For backward-compatibility with the Bourne shell, the older form of *test* can be used with either the *test* command or the single brackets. However, the preferred method for Korn shell programmers is the new *test* with double brackets. A complete list to test operators (both old and new style) are listed in Table 10.25.

Table 10.25   Testing and Logical Operators

test	Tests For
String Testing:	
string1 = string2	*string1* is equal to *string2*.
string1 != string2	*string1* is not equal to *string2*.
string	*string* is not null.
−z string	length of *string* is zero.
−n string	length of *string* is nonzero.

Table 10.25 Testing and Logical Operators (continued)

test	Tests For
	Examples: *test −n $word* or [*−n $word*] *test tom = sue* or [*tom = sue*]

Integer Testing (Old-Style test Used with Bourne Shell):

int1 −eq int2	*int1* is equal to *int2*.
int1 −ne int2	*int1* is not equal to *int2*.
int1 −gt int2	*int1* is greater than *int2*.
int1 −ge int2	*int1* is greater than or equal to *int2*.
int1 −lt int2	*int1* is less than *int2*.
int1 −le int2	*int1* is less than or equal to *int2*.

Logical Operators (Old-Style test).

!	*Not* operator.
−a	*And* operator.
−o	*Or* operator.

File Testing (Old-Style test):

−b filename	Block special file.
−c filename	Character special file.
−d filename	Directory existence.
−f filename	File existence and not a directory.
−g filename	Set-group-ID is set.
−h filename	Symbolic link.
−k filename	Sticky bit is set.
−p filename	File is a named pipe.
−r filename	File is readable.
−s filename	File is nonzero size.
−u filename	Set-user-ID bit is set.
−w filename	File is writeable.
−x filename	File is executable.

The New *test* Command. With the *[[...]]* compound *test* command, additional operators are available. Wildcards can be used in string-matching tests, and many of the errors from the old *test* have been eliminated. New *string test* operators are listed in Table 10.26.

Table 10.26   String Testing (New-Style Test)

String Testing Operator	Tests For
string = pattern	string matches pattern.[a]
string != pattern	string does not match pattern.
string1 < string2	ASCII value of string1 is less than string2.
string1 > string2	ASCII value of string1 is greater than string2.
−z string	string is zero in length, null parameter.
−n string	string is nonzero in length, nonnull parameter.

a.   On versions newer than 1988, the == operator is permitted.

EXAMPLE 10.83

```
(The Script)
   read answer
1  if [[ $answer = [Yy]* ]]       # Test for Yes or yes or Y or y, etc.
   then...


   Example:
   (The Script)
   guess=Noone
2  if [[ $guess != [Nn]o@(one|body) ]]      # Test for Noone, noone
   then. . .                                # or Nobody, nobody...


   Example:
   (The Command Line)
3  [[ apples < oranges ]]
   print $?
   0
4  [[ apples > oranges ]]
   print $?
   1
5  $ name="Joe Shmoe"
   $ [ $name = "Abe Lincoln" ]            # old style
   ksh: Shmoe: unknown test operator

6  $ [[ $name = "Abe Lincoln" ]]          # new style
   $ echo $?
   1
```

EXPLANATION

1   The *answer* read in from the user is tested to see if it matches anything starting with Y or y.

EXPLANATION (CONTINUED)

2   The variable *guess* is tested. If it is not equal to a string starting with *N* or *n*, followed by an *o*, and exactly *one* or *body*, for example, *noone* or *nobody*, the *then* command would be executed.

3   The string *apples* is tested to see if it comes before *oranges* in the ASCII collating sequence. It does.

4   The string *apples* is tested to see if it comes after *oranges* in the ASCII collating sequences. It does not.

5   In the old-style *test*, the variable *name* is split into separate words. Since the = operator expects a single string as its left operand, the *test* command fails. To fix the problem, the variable should be enclosed in double quotes.

6   In the new-style *test*, the variable is not split up into separate words; therefore, double quotes are not required around *$name*.

File Testing with Binary Operators.   The binary operators for testing files require two operands (i.e., a file on either side of the operator). See Table 10.27 for a list of binary file testing operators.

Table 10.27   Binary File Testing and Logical Operators

Operators	Tests For
Binary File Testing	
file1 –nt file2	True if *file1* is newer than *file2*.
file1 –ot file2	True if *file1* is older than *file2*.
file1 –ef file2	True if *file1* is another name for *file2*.

Logical Operators.   The Korn shell, like C, provides logical testing of the truth or falsity of expressions. They are listed in Table 10.28.

Table 10.28   Logical Operators

Operators	Tests For
&&	The *and* operator evaluates the expression on the left-hand side of *&&*; if true, the expression on the right side of *&&* is tested and must also be true. If one expression is false, the expression is false. The *&&* operator replaces *–a*; e.g., ((($x && $y) > 5)).
||	The *or* operator evaluates the expression on the left-hand side of the || operator; if true, the expression is true; if false, the expression on the right-hand side of the || is evaluated; if true, the expression is true. Only if both expressions are false will the expression evaluate to false. The || operator replaces *–o*; e.g., ((($x || $y).

File Testing.   The Korn shell provides a number of built-in test commands for checking the attributes of files, such as existence, type, permissions, etc. The file testing options (also called *flags*) are listed in Table 10.29.

Table 10.29   File Testing (New *test* Flags)

test *Flag*	*Tests For*
Korn Shell Only:	
–a *file*	*file* exists.
–e *file*	*file* exists (versions newer than 1988).
–L *file*	*file* exists and is a symbolic link.
–O *file*	You are the owner of *file*.
–G *file*	Your group ID is the same as *file*'s.
–S *file*	*file* exists and is a socket.
Bourne and Korn Shells:	
–r *file*	*file* exists and is readable.
–w *fle*	*file* exists and is writeable.
–x *file*	*file* exists and is executable.
–f *file*	*file* exists and is not a directory.
–d *file*	*file* exists and is a directory.
–b *file*	*file* exists and is a block special file.
–c *file*	*file* exists and is a character special file.
–p *file*	*file* exists and is a named pipe.
–u *file*	*file* exists and is setuid.
–g *file*	*file* exists and is setgid.
–k *file*	*file* exists and sticky bit is set.
–s *file*	*file* has a nonzero size.

EXAMPLE 10.84

```
    (The Script)
1   file=/etc/passwd
2   if [[ -f $file && (-r $file || -w $file) ]]
    then
3     print $file is a plain file and is either readable or writeable
    fi
```

EXPLANATION

1   The variable *file* is assigned */etc/passwd*.

2   The file test operators test if the file is a plain file and is either readable or write-able. The parentheses are used for grouping. In the old *test*, the parentheses had to be escaped with a backslash.

3   If both of the tests are true, the file is a plain file, and it is either readable or writeable, this line is executed.

The *if* Command.   The simplest form of conditional is the *if* command. The command following the *if* keyword is executed and its exit status is returned. If the exit status is zero, the command succeeded and the statement(s) after the *then* keyword are executed.

In the C shell and C language, the expression following the *if* command is a Boolean-type expression. But in the Bourne and Korn shells, the statement following the *if* is a command or group of commands. The exit status of the last command of the *if* line is used to determine whether or not to continue and execute commands under the *then* statement. If the exit status of the last command on the *if* line is zero, the commands under the *then* statement are executed. The *fi* terminates the command list to be executed after the *then*. If the exit status is nonzero, meaning that the command failed in some way, the statement(s) after the *then* statement are ignored and control goes to the line directly after the *fi* statement.

Conditional commands can be nested. Every *if* must have a corresponding *fi*. The *fi* is paired with the closest *if*. Using indentation to format your *if* blocks helps when debugging your programs.

FORMAT

```
if command
then      # Testing command exit status
    command
    command
fi
-------------------------------------

if test expression
then      # Using the test command to test expressions
```

FORMAT (CONTINUED)

```
        command
fi

            or

if [ expression ]
then                    # Using the old-style test command--
    command             # brackets replace the word test
fi
-----------------------------------
if [[ expression ]]
then                    # New-style brackets for testing expressions
    command
fi
------------------------------------------------
if command
then
...
    if command
    then
    ...
        if command          # Nested conditionals
        then
        ...
        fi
    fi
fi
```

EXAMPLE 10.85

```
1   if ypmatch $name passwd > /dev/null 2>&1
2   then
        echo Found $name!
3   fi
```

EXPLANATION

1   The *ypmatch* command is an NIS command that searches for its argument, *name*, in the NIS *passwd* database on the server machine. Standard output and standard error are redirected to */dev/null*, the UNIX bit bucket.

2   If the exit status of the *ypmatch* command is zero, the program goes to the *then* statement and executes commands until *fi* is reached.

3   The *fi* terminates the list of commands following the *then* statement.

Using the Old-Style Bourne *test*. If you have been programming in the Bourne shell, the Korn shell is backward-compatible, allowing your Bourne shell scripts to be executed properly by the Korn shell. Many Bourne shell programmers, when converting to Korn shell, still use the old-style *test* command when evaluating expressions. If you are reading or maintaining scripts, you may find the old syntax alive and well. Therefore, a brief discussion of the old syntax may help you, even if you are writing your own scripts with the new Korn shell *test* command.

EXAMPLE 10.86

```
      #!/bin/ksh
      # Scriptname: are_you_ok
1     print "Are you ok (y/n) ?"
      read answer
2     if [ "$answer" = Y -o "$answer" = y ]      # Old-style test
      then
           print "Glad to hear it."
3     fi
```

EXPLANATION

1 The user is asked the question, *Are you ok (y/n) ?*. The *read* command causes the program to wait for user input.

2 The *test* command, represented by a [, is used to test expressions and returns an exit status of zero if the expression is true and nonzero if the expression is false. If the variable *answer* evaluates to Y or y, the commands after the *then* statement are executed. (The *test* command does not allow the use of wildcards when testing expressions.)

3 The *fi* terminates the list of commands following the *then* statement.

Using the New-Style Korn *test*. The new Korn shell-style testing allows expressions to contain shell metacharacters and Korn shell operators such as && and ||.

EXAMPLE 10.87

```
      #!/bin/ksh
      # Scriptname: are_you_ok2
1     print "Are you ok (y/n) ?"
      read answer
2     if [[ "$answer" = [Yy]* ]]               # New-style test
      then
           print "Glad to hear it."
3     fi
```

EXPLANATION

1   The user is asked the question, *Are you ok (y/n) ?*. The *read* command causes the program to wait for user input.

2   The *[[ ]]* is a special Korn shell construct used to test expressions. If the *answer* evaluates to *Y* or *y* followed by any number of characters, the commands after the *then* statement are executed.

3   The *fi* statement terminates the *if*.

Using the Old-Style Bourne *test* with Numbers.   To test numeric expressions, the old-style Bourne shell *test* command and its operators are still acceptable in the Korn shell, but the new-style *let* command is preferred.

EXAMPLE 10.88

```
1   if [ $# -lt 1 ]
    then
          print "$0: Insufficient arguments " 1>&2
          exit 1
2   fi
```

EXPLANATION

1   The statement reads: *If the number of arguments is less than 1, print the error message and send it to standard error. Then exit the script.* The old style of testing integers is used with the *test* command.

2   The *fi* marks the end of the block of statements after *then*.

The *let* Command and Testing Numbers.   Although it is still acceptable to use single square brackets and old-style Bourne shell numeric operators for testing numeric expressions, the preferred Korn shell method is to use the double parentheses and the new C-language–style numeric operators when testing *numeric* expressions. Note that the double brackets are only used for testing *string* expressions and for file tests (see Table 10.29).

EXAMPLE 10.89

```
1   if (( $# < 1 ))
    then
          print "$0: Insufficient arguments " 1>&2
          exit 1
2   fi
```

EXPLANATION

1   The statement reads: *If the number of arguments is less than 1, print the error mes-sage and send it to standard error. Then exit the script.* This is the preferred way to perform numeric tests in the Korn shell.

2   The *fi* marks the end of the block of statements after *then*.

The *if/else* Command.   The if/*else* command allows a two-way decision-making process. If the command after the *if* fails, the commands after the *else* are executed.

FORMAT

```
if command
then
    command(s)
else
    command(s)
fi
```

EXAMPLE 10.90

```
1    if ypmatch "$name" passwd > /dev/null 2>&1
2    then
            print Found $name!
3    else
4            print "Can't find $name."
            exit 1
5    fi
```

EXPLANATION

1   The *ypmatch* command searches for its argument, *$name,* in the NIS *passwd* data-base. Standard output and standard error are redirected to */dev/null,* the UNIX bit bucket.

2   If the exit status of the *ypmatch* command is zero, program control goes to the *then* statement and executes commands until *else* is reached.

3   The commands under the *else* statement are executed if the *ypmatch* command fails to find *name* in the *passwd* database; that is, the exit status of *ypmatch* must be nonzero for the commands in the *else* block to be executed.

4   The *print* function sends output to the screen and the program exits.

5   This marks the end of the *if* construct.

The *if/elif/else* Command.   The if/*elif/else* command allows a multiway decision-making process. If the command following the *if* fails, the command following the *elif* is tested. If that command succeeds, the commands under its *then* statement are executed. If the command after the *elif* fails, the next *elif* command is checked. If none of the com-mands succeed, the *else* commands are executed. The *else* block is called the default.

FORMAT

```
if command
then
    command(s)
elif command
then
    commands(s)
elif command
then
    command(s)
else
    command(s)
fi
```

FORMAT

```
if [[ string expression ]]      or       if (( numeric expression ))
then
    command(s)
elif [[ string expression ]]    or       elif (( numeric expression ))
then
    commands(s)
elif [[ string expression ]]    or       elif(( numeric expression ))
then
    command(s)
else
    command(s)
fi
```

EXAMPLE 10.91

```
(The Script)
    #!/bin/ksh
    # Scriptname: tellme
1   read age?"How old are you? "
2   if (( age < 0 || age > 120 ))
    then
        print "Welcome to our planet! "
        exit 1
    fi
3   if (( age >= 0 && age < 13 ))
    then
        print "A child is a garden of verses"
```

EXAMPLE 10.91 (CONTINUED)

```
        elif (( age > 12 && age < 20 ))
        then
            print "Rebel without a cause"
        elif (( age >= 20 && age < 30 ))
        then
            print "You got the world by the tail!!"
        elif (( age >= 30 && age < 40 ))
        then
            print "Thirty something..."
    4   else
            print "Sorry I asked"
    5   fi

(The Output)
$ tellme
How old are you? 200
Welcome to our planet!

$ tellme
How old are you? 13
Rebel without a cause

$ tellme
How old are you? 55
Sorry I asked
```

EXPLANATION

1   The user is asked for input. The input is assigned to the variable *age*.

2   A numeric test is performed within the double parentheses. If *age* is less than zero or greater than *120*, the *print* command is executed and the program terminates with an exit status of one. The interactive shell prompt will appear. Note that the dollar sign ($) is not required to perform variable substitution when using the (( )) operators.

3   A numeric test is performed within the double parentheses. If *age* is greater than zero and less than *13*, the *let* command returns exit status zero, true.

4   The *else* construct is the default. If none of the above statements are true, the *else* commands will be executed.

5   The *fi* terminates the initial *if* statement.

The *exit* Command.   The *exit* command is used to terminate the script and get back to the command line. You may want the script to exit if some condition does not test true. The argument to the *exit* command is an integer, ranging from zero to 255. When the program exits, the exit number is stored in the shell's ? variable.

EXAMPLE 10.92

```
(The Script)
    #!/bin/ksh
    # Scriptname: filecheck
    # Purpose: Check to see if a file exists,what type it is,
    # and its permissions.

1   file=$1      # Variable is set to first command line argument
2   if [[ ! -a $file ]]
    then
        print "$file does not exist"
        exit 1
    fi
3   if [[ -d $file ]]
    then
        print "$file is a directory"
4   elif [[ -f $file ]]
    then
5       if [[ -r $file && -w $file && -x $file ]]
        then
            print "You have read, write, and execute permission on
            file $file"
        else
6           print "You don't have the correct permissions"
            exit 2
        fi
    else
7       print "$file is neither a file nor a directory. "
        exit 3
8   fi


(The Command Line)
9   $ filecheck testing
    testing does not exist
10  $ echo $?
    1
```

EXPLANATION

1 The first command line argument passed to this program (*$1*) is assigned to the variable *file*.

2 The *test* command follows the *if*. If *$file* (after variable substitution) is a file that does not exist (note the *not* operator, *!*), the commands under the *then* keyword are executed. An exit value of one means that the program failed in some way (in this case, the test failed).

3 If the file is a directory, *print* that it is a directory.

4 If the file is not a directory, *else if* the file is a plain file, *then*...

5 If the file is readable, writeable, and executable, *then*...

EXPLANATION (CONTINUED)

6   The *fi* terminates the innermost *if* command. The program exits with an argument of two if the file does not have *read, write*, and *execute* permission.

7   The *else* commands are executed if lines 2 and 3 fail. The program exits with a value of three.

8   This *fi* goes with the *if* on line 3 in the example.

9   The file called *testing* does not exist.

10 The *$?* variable holds the exit status, *one*.

The *null* Command.   The *null* command is a colon. It is a built-in, do-nothing command that returns an exit status of zero. It is used as a placeholder after an *if* command when you have nothing to say, but need a command or the program will produce an error message because it requires something after the *then* statement. Often the *null* command is used as an argument to the *loop* command to make the loop a forever loop or for testing variable expression modifiers such as *{EDITOR:–/bin/vi}*.

EXAMPLE 10.93

```
(The Script)
1    name=Tom
2    if grep "$name" databasefile > /dev/null 2>&1
     then
3        :
4    else
         print "$1 not found in databasefile"
         exit 1
     fi
```

EXPLANATION

1   The string *Tom* is assigned to the variable *name*.

2   The *if* command tests the exit status of the *grep* command. If *Tom* is found in *databasefile*, the null command is executed and does nothing.

3   The colon is the *null* command. It always exits with a zero exit status.

4   What we really want to do is print an error message and exit if *Tom* is not found. The commands after the *else* will be executed if the *grep* command fails.

EXAMPLE 10.94

```
(The Script)
1    : ${EDITOR:=/bin/vi}
2    echo $EDITOR
```

EXPLANATION

1. The colon command takes an argument that is evaluated by the shell. The expression ${EDITOR:=/bin/vi} is used as an argument to the colon command. If the variable *EDITOR* has been previously set, its value will not be changed; if it has not been set, the value */bin/vi* will be assigned to it. The Korn shell would have responded with an error such as *ksh: /bin/vi: not found* if the colon command had not preceded the expression.

2. The value of the *EDITOR* variable is displayed.

10.2.7 The *case* Command

The *case* command is a multiway branching command used as an alternative to the *if/elif* commands. The value of the *case* variable is matched against *value1*, *value2*, and so forth until a match is found. When a value matches the *case* variable, the commands following the value are executed until the double semicolons are reached. Then, instruction starts after the word *esac* (*case* spelled backwards).

If a *case* variable is not matched, the program executes commands after the *)* , the default value, until the double semicolons or *esac* is reached. The *)* value serves the same purpose as the *else* statement in *if/else* conditionals. The case values can use shell wildcards and the vertical bar (pipe symbol) for *or*ing two values.

FORMAT

```
case variable in
value1)
    command(s);;
value2)
    command(s);;
*)
    command(s);;
esac
```

EXAMPLE 10.95

```
(The Script)
    #!/bin/ksh
    # Scriptname: xtermcolor
    # Sets the xterm foreground color (the color of the prompt and
    # input typed for interactive windows.
1   read color?"Choose a foreground color for your terminal?"
2   case "$color" in
3   *[Bb]l??)
4       xterm -fg blue -fn terminal &
5           ;;
6   *[Gg]reen)
        xterm -fg darkgreen -fn terminal &
            ;;
```

EXAMPLE 10.95 (CONTINUED)

```
7   red | orange)                        # The vertical bar means "or"
       xterm -fg "$color" -fn terminal &
       ;;
8   *)  xterm -fn terminal &             # default
       ;;
9   esac
10  print "Out of case..."
```

EXPLANATION

1   The user is asked for input. The input is assigned to the variable *color*.

2   The *case* command evaluates the expression *$color*.

3   If *color* begins with a *B* or *b*, followed by the letter *l* and any two characters, the *case* expression matches the first value. The value is terminated with a single closed parenthesis. The wildcards are shell metacharacters.

4   The statement is executed if the value in line 3 matches the *case* expression. The *xterm* command sets the foreground color to blue.

5   The double semicolons are required after the last command in this block of commands. Control branches to line 10, after the semicolons are reached.

6   If the *case* expression matches a *G* or *g*, followed by the letters *r-e-e-n*, the *xterm* window foreground color is set to dark green. The double semicolons terminate the block of statements and control branches to line 10.

7   The vertical bar is used as an *or* conditional operator. If the *case* expression matches either *red* or *orange*, the *xterm* command is executed.

8   This is the default value. If none of the above values match the *case* expression, the command(s) after the ***) value are executed. The default color for the terminal foreground is black.

9   The *esac* statement (*case* spelled backwards) terminates the *case* command.

10 After one of the values is matched, execution continues here.

The *case* Command and the *here document*.   Often the *here document* is used to create a menu. After the user has selected a choice from the menu, the *case* command is used to match against one of the choices. The Korn shell also provides a *select* loop for creating menus.

EXAMPLE 10.96

```
(The .profile File)
    print "Select a terminal type "
1   cat << EOF
        1) vt120
        2) wyse50
        3) ansi
        4) sun
```

```
2   EOF
3   read TERM
4   case "$TERM" in
    1)  export TERM=vt120
        ;;
    2)  export TERM=wyse50
        ;;
    3)  export TERM=ansi
        ;;
    *)  export TERM=sun
        ;;
5   esac
    print "TERM is $TERM"
```

EXPLANATION

1   A *here document* is used to display a menu of choices.
2   EOF is the user-defined terminator. Input for the *here document* stops here.
3   The *read* command waits for user input and assigns it to the *TERM* variable.
4   The *case* command evaluates the variable *TERM* and matches it against one of the numbers in the list. If a match is found, the terminal is set.
5   The *case* command terminates with *esac*.

10.2.8   Looping Commands

The looping commands are used to execute a command or group of commands a set number of times, or until a certain condition is met. The Korn shell has four types of loops: the *for* loop, *while* loop, *until* loop, and *select* loop.

The *for* Command.   The *for* looping command is used to execute commands for each member of a set of arguments. You might use this loop to execute the same commands on a list of files or usernames. The *for* command is followed by a user-defined variable, the keyword *in*, and a list of words. The first time in the loop, the first word from the wordlist is assigned to the variable, and then shifted off. The next time around the loop, the second word is assigned to the variable, and so on. The body of the loop starts at the *do* keyword and ends at the *done* keyword. When all of the words in the list have been shifted off, the loop ends and program control continues after the *done* keyword.

FORMAT

```
for variable in wordlist
do
    command(s)
done
```

EXAMPLE 10.97

```
(The Script)
1   for pal in Tom Dick Harry Joe
2   do
3       print "Hi $pal"
4   done
5   print "Out of loop"

(The Output)
    Hi Tom
    Hi Dick
    Hi Harry
    Hi Joe
    Out of loop
```

EXPLANATION

1   This *for* loop will iterate through the list of names, *Tom, Dick, Harry, and Joe,* shifting each one off (to the left) after it is assigned to the variable *pal*. As soon as all of the words are shifted and the wordlist is empty, the loop ends and execution starts after the *done* keyword. The word following the *for* command, *pal*, is a variable that will be assigned the value after the *in* keyword, one at a time, for each iteration of the loop. The first time in the loop, the variable *pal* will be assigned the word *Tom*. The second time through the loop, *pal* will be assigned *Dick*, the next time *pal* will be assigned *Harry*, and the last time, *pal* will be assigned *Joe*.

2   The *do* keyword is required after the wordlist. If it is used on the same line, the list must be terminated with a semicolon. For example:
    for pal in Tom Dick Harry Joe; do

3   This is the body of the loop. After *Tom* is assigned to the variable *pal*, the commands in the body of the loop, that is, all commands between the *do* and the *done* keywords, are executed.

4   The *done* keyword ends the loop. If there are no words left to be processed in the wordlist on line 1, the loop exits, and execution starts at line 5.

5   This line is executed when the loop terminates.

EXAMPLE 10.98

```
(The Command Line)
1   $ cat mylist
    tom
    patty
    ann
    jake
---------------------------------------------------------------
```

EXAMPLE 10.98 (CONTINUED)

```
(The Script)
2   for person in $(< mylist)     #same as for person in `cat mylist`
    do
3       mail $person < letter
        print $person was sent a letter.
4   done
5   print "The letter has been sent."
```

EXPLANATION

1   The contents of a file, called *mylist*, are displayed.

2   Command substitution is performed and the contents of *mylist* become the wordlist. The first time in the loop, *tom* is assigned to the variable *person*, and then shifted off, to be replaced with *patty*, and so on.

3   In the body of the loop, each user is mailed a copy of a file called *letter*.

4   The *done* keyword marks the end of this loop iteration.

5   When all of the users in the list have been sent mail, the loop will exit, and this line will be executed.

EXAMPLE 10.99

```
1   for file in *.c
2   do
        if [[ -f $file ]] ; then
            cc $file -o ${file%.c}
        fi
    done
```

EXPLANATION

1   The wordlist will consist of all files in the current working directory ending with the extension *.c* (C source files). Each filename will be assigned to variable *file*, in turn, for each iteration of the loop.

2   When the body of the loop is entered, the file will be tested to make sure it exists and is a real file. If so, it will be compiled. *${file%.c}* expands to the filename without its extension.

The $* and $@ Variables in Wordlists.   When expanded, the $* and $@ are the same unless enclosed in double quotes. "$*" evaluates to one string, whereas "$@" evaluates to a list of separate words.

EXAMPLE 10.100

```
(The Script)
    #!/bin/ksh
1   for name in $*      # or for name in $@
2   do
        echo Hi $name
3   done
-----------------------------------------------------------------
(The Command Line)
$ greet Dee Bert Lizzy Tommy
Hi Dee
Hi Bert
Hi Lizzy
Hi Tommy
```

EXPLANATION

1   $* and $@ expand to a list of all the positional parameters, in this case, the arguments passed in from the command line: *Dee*, *Bert*, *Lizzy*, and *Tommy*. Each name in the list will be assigned, in turn, to the *name* variable in the *for* loop.

2   The commands in the body of the loop are executed until the list is empty.

3   The *done* keyword marks the end of the loop body.

The *while* Command.   The *while* evaluates the command immediately following it, and if its exit status is zero, the commands in the body of the loop (commands between *do* and *done*) are executed. When the *done* keyword is reached, control is returned to the top of the loop and the *while* command checks the exit status of the command again. Until the exit status of the command being evaluated by the *while* becomes nonzero, the loop continues. When the exit status reaches nonzero, program execution starts after the *done* keyword. If the exit status never becomes nonzero, the loop goes around and around infinitely. (Of course, pressing Control-C or Control-\ will stop the looping.)

FORMAT

```
while command
do
    command(s)
done
```

EXAMPLE 10.101

```
(The Script)
1   num=0                       # Initialize num
2   while (( num < 10 ))        # Test num with the let
    do
        print -n $num
```

EXAMPLE 10.101 (CONTINUED)

```
3      (( num=num + 1 ))          # Increment num
     done
     print "\nAfter loop exits, continue running here"

(The Output)
0123456789
After loop exits, continue running here
```

EXPLANATION

1   This is the initialization step. The variable *num* is assigned zero.

2   The *while* command is followed by the *let* command. If the value of *num* is less than 10, the body of the loop is entered.

3   In the body of the loop, the value of *num* is incremented by one. If the value of *num* was never changed, the loop would iterate infinitely or until the process was killed.

EXAMPLE 10.102

```
(The Script)
     #!/bin/ksh
     # Scriptname: quiz
1    read answer?"Who was the U.S. President in 1992? "
2    while [[ $answer != "Bush" ]]
3    do
         print "Wrong try again!"
4        read answer
5    done
6    print Good guess!

(The Output)
$ quiz
Who was the U.S. President in 1992? George
Wrong try again!
Who was the U.S. President in 1992? I give up
Wrong try again!
Who was the U.S. President in 1992? Bush
Good guess!
```

EXPLANATION

1   The *read* command prints the string after the question mark (?), *Who was the U.S. President in 1992?*, and waits for input from the user. The input will be stored in the variable *answer*.

2   The *while* loop is entered and the test command, *[[*, evaluates the expression. If the variable *answer* does not equal the string *Bush*, the body of the loop is entered and commands between the *do* and *done* are executed.

EXPLANATION (CONTINUED)

3   The *do* keyword is the start of the loop body.

4   The user is asked to reenter input.

5   The *done* keyword marks the end of the loop body. Control is returned to the top of the *while* loop, and the expression is tested again. As long as *$answer* does not evaluate to *Bush*, the loop will continue to iterate. When the user's input is *Bush*, the loop ends. Program control goes to line 6.

EXAMPLE 10.103

```
(The Script)
1   go=1
    print Type q to quit.
2   while let go or (( go ))
    do
        print I love you.
        read word
3       if [[ $word = [qQ]* ]]
        then
            print "I'll always love you"
4           go=0
        fi
5   done

(The Output)
$ sayit
Type q to quit.
I love you.
I love you.
I love you.
I love you.
I love you.
q
I'll always love you
$
```

EXPLANATION

1   The variable *go* is assigned *1*.

2   The loop is entered. The *let* command tests the expression. The expression evaluates to one. The program goes into the body of the *while* loop and executes commands from the *do* keyword to the *done* keyword.

3   If the user enters a *q* or *Q* as input to the variable *word*, the commands between *then* and *fi* are executed. Anything else will cause *I love you.* to be displayed.

4   The variable *go* is assigned zero. When program control starts at the top of the *while* loop, the expression will be tested. Since the expression evaluates to false, the loop exits and the script starts execution after the *done* keyword on line 5.

5   The *done* marks the end of the body of the loop.

The *until* Command.   The *until* command is used like the *while* command, but evaluates the exit status in the opposite way. The *until* evaluates the command immediately following it, and if its exit status is not zero, the commands in the body of the loop (commands between *do* and *done*) are executed. When the *done* keyword is reached, control is returned to the top of the loop and the *until* command checks the exit status of the command again. Until the exit status of the command being evaluated by *until* becomes zero, the loop continues. When the exit status reaches zero, program execution starts after the *done* keyword.

FORMAT

```
until command
do
    command(s)
done
```

EXAMPLE 10.104

```
#!/bin/ksh
1  until who | grep linda
2  do
       sleep 5
3  done
   talk linda@dragonwings
```

EXPLANATION

1   The *until* loop tests the exit status of the last command in the pipeline, *grep*. The *who* command lists who is logged on this machine and pipes its output to *grep*. The *grep* command will return zero exit status (success) only when it finds user *linda*.

2   If user *linda* has not logged in, the body of the loop is entered and the program sleeps for 5 seconds.

3   When *linda* logs on, the exit status of the *grep* command will be zero and control will go to the statements following the *done* keyword.

EXAMPLE 10.105

```
    #!/bin/ksh
1   hour=0
2   until (( hour > 23 ))
    do
3       case "$hour" in
        [0-9]|1[0-1]) print "Good morning!"
                ;;
        12) print "Lunch time"
                ;;
        1[3-7]) print "Siesta time"
                ;;
        *) print "Good night"
                ;;
        esac
4       (( hour+=1 ))
5   done
```

EXPLANATION

1   The *hour* variable is assigned zero. The variable must be initialized before being used in the *until* loop.

2   The *until* command is followed by the *let* command. If the *hour* is not greater than 23, that is, the exit status is nonzero, the loop body is entered.

3   The *case* command matches the value of the *hour* variable against one of the *hour* values, or matches the default, executing the command that applies.

4   The *hour* is incremented by one; otherwise, the *hour* will never become greater than 23 and the loop will never exit. Control is returned to the *until* command and the *hour* is evaluated again.

5   The *done* keyword marks the end of the loop. When the *hour* is greater than 23, control will go to the line under the *done*, if there is one; otherwise, the program is exited.

The *select* Command and Menus. The *here document* is an easy method for creating menus, but the Korn shell introduces a new loop, called the *select* loop, which is used primarily for creating menus. A menu of numerically listed items is displayed to standard error. The PS3 prompt is used to prompt the user for input; by default, PS3 is #?. After the PS3 prompt is displayed, the shell waits for user input. The input should be one of the numbers in the menu list. The input is stored in the special Korn shell *REPLY* variable. The number in the *REPLY* variable is associated with the string to the right of the parentheses in the list of selections.[7]

The *case* command is used with the *select* command to allow the user to make a selection from the menu and, based on that selection, execute commands. The *LINES* and *COLUMNS* variables can be used to determine the layout of the menu items displayed

---

7. If you want the menu to reappear when the loop starts again, set the *REPLY* variable to null just before the *done* keyword.

on the terminal. The output is displayed to standard error, each item preceded by a number and closing parenthesis, and the PS3 prompt is displayed at the bottom of the menu. Since the *select* command is a looping command, it is important to remember to use either the *break* command to get out of the loop, or the *exit* command to exit the script.

FORMAT

```
select var in wordlist
do
     command(s)
done
```

EXAMPLE 10.106

```
(The Script)
    #!/bin/ksh
    # Program name: goodboys
1   PS3="Please choose one of the three boys : "
2   select choice in tom dan guy
3   do
4       case $choice in
        tom)
            print Tom is a cool dude!
5           break;;              # break out of the select loop
6        dan | guy )
            print Dan and Guy are both sweethearts.
            break;;
          *)
7           print " $REPLY is not one of your choices" 1>&2
            print "Try again."
            ;;
8        esac
9   done
```

```
(The Command Line)
$ goodboys
1) tom
2) dan
3) guy
Please choose one of the three boys : 2
Dan and Guy are both sweethearts.

$ goodboys
1) tom
2) dan
3) guy
Please choose one of the three boys : 4
4 is not one of your choices
Try again.
Please choose one of the three boys : 1
Tom is a cool dude!
$
```

EXPLANATION

1 The *PS3* variable is assigned the prompt that will appear below the list of menu selections. After the prompt is displayed, the program waits for user input. The input is stored in the built-in variable called *REPLY*.

2 The *select* command is followed by the variable *choice*. This syntax is similar to that of the *for* loop. The variable *choice* is assigned, in turn, each of the items in the list that follows it, in this case, *tom*, *dan*, and *guy*. It is this wordlist that will be displayed in the menu, preceded by a number and a right parenthesis.

3 The *do* keyword indicates the start of the body of the loop.

4 The first command in the body of the *select* loop is the *case* command. The *case* command is normally used with the *select* loop. The value in the *REPLY* variable is associated with one of the choices: 1 is associated with *tom*, 2 is associated with *dan*, and 3 is associated with *guy*.

5 If *tom* is the choice, after printing the string *Tom is a cool dude!*, the *break* command causes the *select* loop to be exited. Program control starts after the *done* keyword.

6 If either menu item, 2 (*dan*) or 3 (*tom*), is selected, the *REPLY* variable contains the user's selection. If the selection is not 1, 2, or 3, an error message is sent to standard error. The user is asked to try again and control starts at the beginning of the *select* loop.

7 The end of the *case* command.

8 The end of the *select* loop.

EXAMPLE 10.107

```
(The Script)
    #!/bin/ksh
    # Program name: ttype
    # Purpose: set the terminal type
    # Author: Andy Admin
1   COLUMNS=60
2   LINES=1
3   PS3="Please enter the terminal type: "
4   select choice in wyse50 vt200 vt100 sun
    do
5       case $REPLY in
        1)
6           export TERM=$choice
            print "TERM=$choice"
            break;;                    # break out of the select loop
        2 | 3 )
            export TERM=$choice
```

EXAMPLE 10.107 (CONTINUED)

```
               print "TERM=$choice"
               break;;
          4)
               export TERM=$choice
               print "TERM=$choice"
               break;;
          *)
7              print "$REPLY is not a valid choice. Try again" 1>&2
                  ;;
          esac
8    done


(The Command Line)
$ ttype
1) wyse50    2) vt200   3) vt100     4) sun
Please enter the terminal type : 4
TERM=sun


$ ttype
1) wyse50    2) vt200   3) vt100     4) sun
Please enter the terminal type : 3
TERM=vt100


$ ttype
1) wyse50    2) vt200   3) vt100     4) sun
Please enter the terminal type : 7
7 is not a valid choice. Try again.
Please enter the terminal type: 2
TERM=vt200
```

EXPLANATION

1   The *COLUMNS* variable is set to the width of the terminal display in columns for menus created with the *select* loop. The default is 80.

2   The *LINES* variable controls the vertical display of the *select* menu on the terminal. The default is 24 lines. By changing the *LINES* value to *1*, the menu items will be printed on one line, instead of vertically as in the last example.

3   The *PS3* prompt is set and will appear under the menu choices.

4   The *select* loop will print a menu with four selections: *wyse50*, *vt200*, *vt100*, and *sun*. The variable *choice* will be assigned one of these values based on the user's response held in the *REPLY* variable. If *REPLY* is 1, *wyse50* is assigned to *choice*; if *REPLY* is 2, *vt200* is assigned to *choice*; if *REPLY* is 3, *vt100* is assigned to *choice*; and if *REPLY* is 4, *sun* is assigned to *choice*.

5   The *REPLY* variable evaluates to the user's input selection.

6   The terminal type is assigned, exported, and printed.

EXPLANATION (CONTINUED)

7   If the user does not enter a number between 1 and 4, he or she will be prompted again. Note that the menu does not appear, just the *PS3* prompt. To make the menu reappear, set the *REPLY* variable to null. Type above line 8: *REPLY =*

8   The end of the *select* loop.

Looping Commands.   If some condition occurs, you may want to break out of a loop, return to the top of the loop, or provide a way to stop an infinite loop. The Korn shell provides loop control commands to control loops.

The *shift* Command.   The *shift* command shifts the parameter list to the left a specified number of times. The *shift* command without an argument shifts the parameter list once to the left. Once the list is shifted, the parameter is removed permanently. Often the *shift* command is used in *while* loops when iterating through a list of positional parameters.

FORMAT

```
shift [n]
```

EXAMPLE 10.108

```
(Without a Loop)
(The Script)
   #!/bin/ksh
   # Scriptname: doit0
1  set joe mary tom sam
2  shift
3  print $*
4  set $(date)
5  print $*
6  shift 5
7  print $*
8  shift 2

(The Output)
   $ doit0
3  mary tom sam
5  Sun Sep 9 10:00:12 PDT 2001
7  2001
8  ksh: shift: bad number
```

EXPLANATION

1   The *set* command sets the positional parameters. *$1* is assigned *joe*, *$2* is assigned *mary*, *$3* is assigned *tom*, and *$4* is assigned *sam*.

2   The *shift* command shifts the positional parameters to the left; *joe* is shifted off.

3   The parameter list is printed after the *shift*. *$** represents all of the parameters.

EXPLANATION (CONTINUED)

4   The *set* command resets the positional parameters to the output of the UNIX *date* command.

5   The new parameter list is printed.

6   This time the list is shifted five times to the left.

7   The new parameter list is printed.

8   By attempting to shift more times than there are parameters, the shell sends a message to standard error.

EXAMPLE   10.109

```
(With a Loop)
(The Script)
    #!/bin/ksh
    # Usage: doit [args]
1   while (( $# > 0 ))
    do
2       print $*
3       shift
4   done
(The Command Line)
$ doit a b c d e
a b c d e
b c d e
c d e
d e
e
```

EXPLANATION

1   The *while* command tests the numeric expression. If the number of positional parameters ($#) is greater than zero, the body of the loop is entered. The positional parameters are coming from the command line as arguments. There are five.

2   All the positional parameters are printed.

3   The parameter list is shifted once to the left.

4   The body of the loop ends here; control returns to the top of the loop. The parameter list has decreased by one. After the first shift, $# is four. When $# has been decreased to zero, the loop ends.

The *break* Command.   The built-in *break* command is used to force immediate exit from a loop, but not from a program. (To leave a program, the *exit* command is used.) After the *break* command is executed, control starts after the *done* keyword. The *break* command causes an exit from the innermost loop, so if you have nested loops, the *break* command takes a number as an argument, allowing you to exit out of any number of outer loops. The *break* is useful for exiting from an infinite loop.

FORMAT

```
break [n]
```

EXAMPLE 10.110

```
1   while true; do
2       read answer? Are you ready to move on\?
3       if [[ $answer = [Yy]* ]]; then
            break
4       else
            ....commands...
        fi
5   done
6   print "Here we are"
```

EXPLANATION

1　The *true* command is a UNIX command, and an alias for the colon command in the Korn shell. It always exits with zero status and is often used to start an infinite loop. (The null command (:) can be used to do the same thing.) The body of the loop is entered.

2　The user is asked for input. The user's input is assigned to the variable *answer*.

3　If *answer* evaluates to *Y, y, Yes, Yup,* or *Ya* (anything beginning with Y or y), the *break* command is executed and control goes to line 6. The line *Here we are* is printed. Until the user answers something that starts with a Y or y, the program will continue to ask for input. This could go on forever!

4　If the test fails in line 3, the *else* commands are executed. When the body of the loop ends at the *done* keyword, control starts again at the top of the *while* at line 1.

5　The end of the loop body.

6　Control starts here after the *break* command is executed.

The *continue* Command.　The *continue* command starts back at the top of the loop if some condition becomes true. All commands below the *continue* will be ignored. The *continue* command returns control to the top of the innermost loop; if nested within a number of loops, the *continue* command may take a number as its argument. Control can be started at the top of any number of outer loops.

FORMAT

```
continue [n]
```

EXAMPLE 10.111

```
(The Mailing List)
$ cat mail_list
ernie
john
richard
melanie
greg
robin

(The Script)
    # Scriptname: mailtomaillist
    #!/bin/ksh
1   for name in $(< mail_list)
    do
2     if [[ "$name" = "richard" ]] then
3         continue
      else
4         mail $name < memo
      fi
5   done
```

EXPLANATION

1 The *for* loop will iterate through a list of names stored in a file called *mail_list*.
   Each time a name from the list is assigned to the variable *name*, it is shifted off the
   list and replaced by the next name on the list.

2 The *name* matches *richard*; the *continue* command is executed. Since *richard* has
   already been shifted off, the next user, *melanie*, is assigned to the variable *name*.

3 The *continue* command returns control to the top of the loop, skipping any commands in the rest of the loop body.

4 All users in the list, except *richard*, will be mailed a copy of the file *memo*.

5 The end of loop body.

Nested Loops.   If using nested loops, the *break* and *continue* commands let you control which loop to terminate.

EXAMPLE 10.112

```
(The Script)
   #!/bin/ksh
1  while true ; do ◄─────────────┐
         < Commands here>          │
2      for user in tom dick harry joe
       do
           if [[ $user = [Dd]* ]]
           then
3              continue 2 ─────────┘
                   < Commands here >
4              while true
               do
                   < Commands here>
5                  break 3 ───┐
6              done           │
7          fi                 │
       done                   │
8  done ──────────────────────┘
9  print Out of loop ◄────────
```

EXPLANATION

1 The *true* command always returns an exit status of zero. The loop is designed to go forever unless you use loop control commands.

2 The *for* loop is entered.

3 The *for* loop will loop through each of the names in the list. If the user variable begins with a *D* or *d*, the *continue* command causes control to go to the top of the *while* loop. Without an argument, the *continue* command would start control at the top of the *for* loop. The argument 2 tells the shell to go to the top of the second enclosing loop and restart execution there.

4 The *while* loop is nested. The *true* command always exits with zero status. The loop will go forever.

5 The *break* command terminates the outermost *while* loop. Execution starts at line 9.

6 The *done* keyword marks the end of the innermost *while* loop.

7 This *done* keyword marks the end of the *for* loop.

8 This *done* keyword marks the end of outermost *while* loop.

9 Out of the loop.

I/O Redirection and Loops. The Korn shell allows you to use redirection and pipes in loops. Unlike the Bourne shell, the loop runs in this shell, not a subshell. Variables set within the loop will still be set when the loop exits.

Redirect the Output of a Loop to a File.   Instead of sending the output of a loop to the screen, it can be redirected to a file or a pipe. See Example 10.113.

EXAMPLE   10.113

```
    (The Command Line)
1   $ cat memo
    abc
    def
    ghi
-------------------------------------------------------------------
(The Script)
    #!/bin/ksh
    # Program name: numberit
    # Put line numbers on all lines of memo
2   if (( $# < 1 ))
    then
        print "Usage: $0 filename " >&2
        exit 1
    fi
3   integer count=1                 # Initialize count
4   cat $1 | while read line        # Input is coming from memo
    do
5       (( count == 1 )) && print "Processing file $1..." > /dev/tty
6       print $count $line
7       (( count+=1 ))
8   done > tmp$$                     # Output is going to a temporary file
9   mv tmp$$ $1

(The Command Line)
10  $ numberit memo
    Processing file memo...

11  $ cat memo
    1 abc
    2 def
    3 ghi
```

EXPLANATION

1   The contents of file *memo* are displayed.

2   If the number of arguments is less than one, a usage message is sent to standard error, the screen.

3   The *count* variable is declared an integer and is assigned the value *1*.

4   The UNIX *cat* command displays the contents of the filename stored in *$1*, and the output is piped to the *while* loop. The *read* command is assigned the first line of the file the first time in the loop, the second line of the file the next time through the loop, and so forth.

EXPLANATION (CONTINUED)

5　The output of this *print* statement is sent to */dev/tty*, the screen. If not explicitly redirected to */dev/tty*, the output will be redirected to *tmp$$* on line 8.

6　The *print* function prints the value of *count*, followed by the line in the file.

7　The *count* variable is incremented by *1*.

8　The output of this entire loop, with the exception of line 3, is redirected to the file *tmp$$* (where *$$* evaluates to the PID of this process). The *tmp* file is given a unique name by appending the PID of this process to its name.

9　The *tmp* file is renamed to the name of the file that was assigned to *$1*.

10　The program is executed. The file to be processed is called *memo*.

11　The file is displayed with line numbers.

Pipe the Output of a Loop to a UNIX Command.　The output of a loop can be redirected from the screen to a pipe. See Example 10.114.

EXAMPLE 10.114

```
(The Script)
1   for i in 7 9 2 3 4 5
2   do
        print $i
3   done | sort -n

(The Output)
2
3
4
5
7
9
```

EXPLANATION

1　The *for* loop iterates through a list of unsorted numbers.

2　In the body of the loop, the numbers are printed. This output will be piped into the UNIX *sort* command.

3　The pipe is created after the *done* keyword.

Running Loops in the Background.　If the loop is going to take a while to process, it can be run as a background job so that the rest of the program can continue.

EXAMPLE 10.115

```
1   for person in bob jim joe sam
    do
2       mail $person < memo
3   done &
```

EXPLANATION

1 The *for* loop shifts through each of the names in the wordlist: *bob, jim, joe*, and *sam*. Each of the names is assigned to the variable *person*, in turn.

2 In the body of the loop, each person is sent the contents of the file *memo*.

3 The ampersand at the end of the *done* keyword causes the loop to be executed in the background. The program will continue to run while the loop is executing.

The *exec* Command and Loops.   The *exec* command can be used to close standard input or output without creating a subshell.

EXAMPLE 10.116

```
(The File)
1   cat tmp
    apples
    pears
    bananas
    peaches
    plums
    -----------------------------------------------------------
(The Script)
    #!/bin/ksh
    # Scriptname: speller
    # Purpose: Check and fix spelling errors in a file
    #

2   exec < tmp          # Opens the tmp file
3   while read line     # Read from the tmp file
    do
4       print $line
5       print -n "Is this word correct? [Y/N] "
6       read answer < /dev/tty    # Read from the terminal
    case $answer in
    [Yy]*)
        continue
            ;;
    *)
        print "New word? "
```

EXAMPLE 10.116 (CONTINUED)

```
7            read word < /dev/tty
             sed "s/$line/$word/" tmp > error
             mv error tmp

8            print $word has been changed.
                   ;;
         esac
    done
```

EXPLANATION

1 The contents of the *tmp* file are displayed.
2 The *exec* command changes standard input (file descriptor 0), so that instead of input coming from the keyboard, it is coming from the *tmp* file.
3 The *while* loop starts. The *read* command gets a line of input from the *tmp* file.
4 The value stored in the *line* variable is printed to the screen.
5 The user is asked if the word is correct.
6 The *read* command gets the user's response from the terminal, */dev/tty*. If the input is not redirected directly from the terminal, it will continue to be read from the file *tmp*, still opened for input.
7 The user is again asked for input, and the input is redirected from the terminal, */dev/tty*.
8 The new word is displayed.

The *IFS* and Loops.   The *IFS*, the shell's internal field separator, evaluates to spaces, tabs, and the newline character. It is used as a word (token) separator for commands that parse lists of words such as *read, set, for,* and *select*. It can be reset by the user if a different separator will be used in a list. It is a good idea to save the original value of the *IFS* in another variable before changing it. Then it is easy to return to its default value.

EXAMPLE 10.117

```
(The Script)
    #!/bin/ksh
    # Script is called runit.
    # IFS is the internal field separator and defaults to
    # spaces, tabs, and newlines.
    # In this script it is changed to a colon.
1   names=Tom:Dick:Harry:John
2   OLDIFS="$IFS"                # Save the original value of IFS
3   IFS=":"
4   for persons in $names
    do
```

EXAMPLE 10.117 (CONTINUED)

```
5       print Hi $persons
     done
6    IFS="$OLDIFS"                # Reset the IFS to old value

7    set Jill Jane Jolene         # Set positional parameters
8    for girl in $*
     do
         print Howdy $girl
     done

(The Output)
$ runit

Hi Tom
Hi Dick
Hi Harry
Hi John
Howdy Jill
Howdy Jane
Howdy Jolene
```

EXPLANATION

1   The *names* variable is set to the string *Tom:Dick:Harry:John*. Each of the words is separated by a colon.

2   The value of *IFS* is assigned to another variable, *OLDIFS*. Since the value of the *IFS* is whitespace, it must be quoted to preserve the whitespace.

3   The *IFS* is assigned a colon. Now the colon is used to separate words.

4   After variable substitution, the *for* loop will iterate through each of the names using the colon as the internal field separator between the words.

5   Each of the names in the wordlist is displayed.

6   *IFS* is reassigned its original values, stored in *OLDIFS*.

7   The positional parameters are set. *$1* is assigned *Jill*, *$2* is assigned *Jane*, and *$3* is assigned *Jolene*.

8   *$** evaluates to all the positional parameters, *Jill, Jane,* and *Jolene*. The *for* loop assigns each of the names to the *girl* variable, in turn, through each iteration of the loop.

10.2.9   Arrays

Korn shell arrays are one-dimensional arrays that may contain up to 1,024 (size varies) elements consisting of words or integers. The index starts at zero. Each element of an array can be set or unset individually. Values do not have to be set in any particular order. For example, you can assign a value to the tenth element before you assign a value to the first element. An array can be set using the *set* command with the –*A* option.

Associative arrays are supported under versions of the Korn shell that are more recent than 1988.

EXAMPLE 10.118

```
(The Command Line)
1   $ array[0]=tom
    $ array[1]=dan
    $ array[2]=bill

2   $ print ${array[0]}      # Curly braces are required.
    tom

3   $ print ${array[1]}
    dan

4   $ print ${array[2]}
    bill

5   $ print ${array[*]}      # Display all elements.
    tom dan bill

6   $ print ${#array[*]}     # Display the number of elements.
    3
```

EXPLANATION

1   The first three elements of the array are assigned values. The index starts at zero.
2   The value of the first array element, *tom*, is printed. Make sure you remember to surround the variable with curly braces. $array[0] would print *tom[0]*.
3   The value of the second element of the array, *dan*, is printed.
4   The value of the third element of the array, *bill*, is printed.
5   All elements in the array are printed.
6   The number of elements in the array are printed. An array can be declared with *typeset* if you know the size and type.

EXAMPLE 10.119

```
(At The Command Line)
1   $ typeset -i ints[4]       # Declare an array of four integers.
2   $ ints[0]=50
    $ ints[1]=75
    $ ints[2]=100
3   $ ints[3]=happy
    ksh: happy: bad number
```

  1   The *typeset* command creates an array of *4* integers.

  2   Integer values are assigned to the array.

  3   A string value is assigned to the fourth element of the array, and the Korn shell sends a message to standard error.

Creating Arrays with the *set* Command.   You can assign the values of an array using the *set* command. The first word after the *–A* option is the name of the array; the rest of the words are the elements of the array.

EXAMPLE 10.120

```
(The Command Line)
1   $ set -A fruit apples pears peaches

2   $ print ${fruit[0]}
    apples

3   $ print ${fruit[*]}
    apples pears peaches

4   $ fruit[1]=plums

5   $ print ${fruit[*]}
    apples plums peaches
```

EXPLANATION

  1   The *set* command with the *–A* option creates an array. The name of the array, *fruit*, follows the *–A* option. Each of the elements of the *fruit* array follow its name.

  2   Subscripts start at zero. Curly braces are required around the variable for it to be evaluated properly. The first element of the array is printed.

  3   When the asterisk is used as a subscript, all elements of the array are displayed.

  4   The second element of the array is reassigned the value *plums*.

  5   All elements of the array are displayed.

10.2.10 Functions

Korn shell functions are similar to those used in the Bourne shell, and are used to modularize your program. A function is a collection of one or more commands that can be executed simply by entering the function's name, similar to a built-in command. Here is a review of some of the important rules about using functions.

   1. The Korn shell executes built-in commands first, then functions, and then executables. Functions are read into memory once when they are defined, not every time they are referenced.

2. A function must be defined before it is used; therefore, it is best to place function definitions at the beginning of the script.

3. The function runs in the current environment; it shares variables with the script that invoked it, and lets you pass arguments by setting them as positional parameters. The present working directory is that of the calling script. If you change the directory in the function, it will be changed in the calling script.

4. In the Korn shell, you can declare local variables in the function using the *typeset* command. *Ksh* functions can be exported to subshells.

5. The *return* statement returns the exit status of the last command executed within the function or the value of the argument given, and cannot exceed a value of 255.

6. To list functions and definitions, use the preset alias, *functions.*

7. Traps are local to functions and will be reset to their previous value when the function exits (not so with the Bourne shell).

8. Functions can be recursive, that is, call themselves. Recursion should be handled carefully. The Korn shell will warn you otherwise with the message, *recursion too deep.*

9. Functions can be autoloaded; they are defined only if referenced. If never referenced, they are not loaded into memory.

10. Versions of the Korn shell that are more recent than 1988 also support discipline functions, passing variables by reference, and compound variables. A built-in command is no longer found before a function of the same name. In older versions it was necessary to use a combination of aliases and functions to write a function that would override a built-in command.[8]

Defining Functions. A function must be defined before it can be invoked. Korn shell functions are defined with the keyword *function* preceding the function name. The curly braces must have a space on the inside of each brace. (Please see Bourne shell functions for the older-style function definition, still compatible in Korn shell scripts.)

FORMAT

```
function function_name { commands; commands; }
```

EXAMPLE 10.121

```
function usage { print "Usage $0 [-y] [-g] " ; exit 1; }
```

EXPLANATION

The function name is *usage.* It is used to print a diagnostic message and exit the script if the script does not receive the proper arguments, either *-y* or *-g.*

---

8. Korn, David G., and Bolsky, Morris I., *The Korn Shell Command and Programming Language* (Englewood Cliffs, NJ: Prentice-Hall, Inc., 1988), p. 77.

Listing and Unsetting Functions.   To list local function definitions, type: *typeset –f*. To list exported function definitions, type: *typeset –fx*. To unset a function, type: *unset –f function_name*. See the *typeset* command, Table 10.30 on page 561.

Local Variables and the Return Value.   The *typeset* command can be used to create local variables. These variables will be known only in the function where they are created. Once out of the function, the local variables are undefined.

The return value of a function is really just the value of the exit status of the last command in the script unless a specific *return* command is used. If a value is assigned to the *return* command, that value is stored in the *?* variable. It can hold an integer value between 0 and 255. Because the *return* command is limited to returning only integer values, you can use command substitution to return the output of a function and assign the output to a variable, just as you would if getting the output of a UNIX command.

EXAMPLE 10.122

```
(The Script)
   #!/bin/ksh
   # Scriptname: do_increment
   # Using the return Command)
1  function increment {
2     typeset sum       # sum is a local variable.
      (( sum = $1 + 1 ))
3     return $sum       # Return the value of sum to the script.
   }

   print -n "The sum is "
4  increment 5          # Call the function increment and pass 5 as a
                        # parameter. 5 becomes $1 for the increment
                        # function.
5  print $?             # The return value is stored in the ? variable
6  print $sum           # The variable "sum" was local to the
                        # function, and is undefined in the main
                        # script. Nothing is printed.

(The Output)
   $ do_increment
5  The sum is 6
   6
```

EXPLANATION

1   The function called *increment* is defined.

2   The *typeset* command defines the variable *sum* to be local to this function.

3   The *return* built-in command, when given an argument, returns to the main script after the line where the function was invoked and stores its argument in the *?* variable. In the script, the *increment* function is called with an argument.

4   The *increment* function is called with an argument of 5.

EXPLANATION (CONTINUED)

5   The exit status of the function is stored in *?* unless an explicit argument is given
    to the *return* command. The *return* command argument specifies a return status
    for the function, its value is stored in the *?* variable, and it must be an integer be-
    tween 0 and 255.

6   Since *sum* was defined as a local variable in the function *increment*, it is not defined
    in the script that invoked the function. Nothing is printed.

EXAMPLE 10.123

```
(Using Command Substitution)
(The Script)
    # Scriptname: do_square
    #!/bin/ksh
1   function square {
    (( sq = $1 * $1 ))
        print "Number to be squared is $1."
2       print "The result is $sq "
    }

3   read number?"Give me a number to square. "
4   value_returned=$(square $number)
5   print $value_returned


(The Output)
    $ do_square
5   Number to be squared is 10. The result is 100
```

EXPLANATION

1   The function called *square* is defined. It will multiply its argument times itself.

2   The result of squaring the number is printed.

3   The user is asked for input.

4   The function *square* is called with a number (input from the user) as its argument.
    Command substitution is performed because the function is enclosed in paren-
    theses preceded by a *$*. The output of the function (both of its *print* statements)
    is assigned to the variable *value_returned*.

5   The command substitution removes the newline between the strings *Number to be
    squared is* and *The result is 100*.

Exported Functions.   Function definitions are not inherited by subshells unless you
define them in the *ENV* file with the *typeset* command, e.g., *typeset –fx function_names*.

You can export functions with *typeset –fx* from the current Korn shell to a script, or from one script to another, but not from one invocation of *ksh* to the next (e.g., a separate invocation means that if you type *ksh* at the prompt, a brand new shell is started up). Exported function definitions will not be inherited by the new shell.

EXAMPLE 10.124

```
(The First Script)
   $ cat calling_script
   #!/bin/ksh


1  function sayit { print "How are ya $1?" ; }
2  typeset -fx sayit    # Export sayit to other scripts
3  sayit Tommy
4  print "Going to other script"
5  other_script         # Call other_script
   print "Back in calling script"
**************************************************************
(The Second Script)
   $ cat other_script
            NOTE: This script cannot be invoked with #!/bin/ksh
6  print "In other script "
7  sayit Dan
8  print "Returning to calling script"


(The Output)
   $ calling_script
3  How are ya Tommy?
4  Going to other script
6  In other script
7  How are ya Dan?
8  Returning to calling script
   Back in calling script
```

EXPLANATION

1   The function *sayit* is defined. It will accept one argument to be stored in *$1*.

2   The *typeset* command with the *–fx* option allows the function to be exported to any script called from this script.

3   The function *sayit* is invoked with *Tommy* as an argument. *Tommy* will be stored in *$1* in the function.

4   After the *sayit* function terminates, the program resumes here.

5   The script, called *other_script*, is executed.

EXPLANATION (CONTINUED)

6   We are now in the other script. This script is called from the first script, *sayit*. It cannot start with the line #!/*bin/ksh* because this line causes a ksh subshell to be started, and exporting functions does not work if a separate Korn shell is invoked.

7   The function *sayit* is invoked. *Dan* is passed as an argument, which will be stored in *$1* in the function.

8   After this line is printed, *other_script* terminates and control goes back to the calling script at the line where it left off after the function was invoked.

10.2.11 The *typeset* Command and Function Options

The *typeset* command is used to display function attributes.

Table 10.30 *typeset* and Function Options

Option	What It Does
typeset –f	Displays all functions and their values. Must have a history file, as all function definitions are stored there.
typeset +f	Displays just function names.
typeset –fx	Displays all function definitions that will be exported across shell scripts, but not as a separate invocation of *ksh*.
typeset –fu func	*func* is the name of a function that has not yet been defined.

Autoloaded Functions.   An autoloaded function is not loaded into your program until you reference it. The autoloaded function can be defined in a file somewhere else and the definition will not appear in your script, allowing you to keep the script small and compact. To use autoload, you need to set the *FPATH* variable in your *ENV* file. The *FPATH* variable contains a search path for directories containing function files. The files in this directory have the same names as the functions defined within them.

The *autoload* alias for *typeset –fu* specifies that the function names that have not yet been defined are to be autoloaded functions. After the *autoload* command is executed with the function as its argument, you must invoke the function to execute the commands contained in it. The primary advantage of autoloading functions is better performance, since the Korn shell does not have to read the function definition if it has never been referenced.[9]

---

9. Bolsky, Morris, and Korn, David, *The New Kornshell*. (Upper Saddle River, NJ: Prentice Hall, 1995), p. 78.

EXAMPLE 10.125

```
(The Command Line)
1   $ mkdir functionlibrary
2   $ cd functionlibrary
3   $ vi foobar

(In Editor)
4   function foobar { pwd; ls; whoami; }    # function has the same
                                            # name as the file.

(In .profile File)
5   export FPATH=$HOME/functionlibrary      # This path is searched for
                                            # functions.

(In Your Script)
6   autoload foobar
7   foobar
```

EXPLANATION

1   Make a directory in which to store functions.

2   Go to the directory.

3   *foobar* is a file in *functionlibrary*. The file *foobar* contains the definition of function *foobar*. The filename and function name must match.

4   The function *foobar* is defined in the file called *foobar*.

5   In the user's *.profile* initialization file, the *FPATH* variable is assigned the path where the functions are stored. This is the path the Korn shell will search when autoloading a function. *FPATH* is exported.

6   In your script, the function *foobar* is brought into the program's memory.

7   The function *foobar* is invoked.

A number of functions can be stored in one file; for example, calculation functions may be contained in a file called *math*. Since the function must have the same name as the file in which it is stored, you may create hard links to the function file. Each function name will be a link to the file in which the function is defined. For example, if a function in the *math* file is called *square*, use the UNIX *ln* command to give the *math* file another name, *square*. Now the *math* file and *square* file can be referenced, and in either case you are referencing the file by the corresponding function name. Now the *square* function can be autoloaded by its own name.

EXAMPLE 10.126

```
(The Command Line)
1   $ ln math square add divide
2   $ ls -i
    12256 add
    12256 math
    12256 square
    12256 divide
3   $ autoload square; square
```

EXPLANATION

1   The UNIX *ln* (link) command lets you give a file alternate names. The *math* file and *square* are the same file. The link count is incremented by one for each link created.

2   A listing shows that all files have the same inode number, meaning they are all one file but can be accessed with different names.

3   Now, when the *square* file is autoloaded, the function *square* has the same name and will be invoked. None of the other functions defined in the file can be referenced until they, in turn, have been specifically autoloaded by name.

10.2.12 Trapping Signals

While your program is running, if you press Control-C or Control-\, the program terminates as soon as the signal arrives. There are times when you would rather not have the program terminate immediately after the signal arrives. You could arrange to ignore the signal and keep running, or perform some sort of cleanup operation before actually exiting the script. The *trap* command allows you to control the way a program behaves when it receives a signal.

A signal is defined as an asynchronous message that consists of a number that can be sent from one process to another, or by the operating system to a process if certain keys are pressed or if something exceptional happens.[10] The *trap* command tells the shell to terminate the command currently in execution upon the receipt of a signal. If the *trap* command is followed by commands within single quotes, those commands will be executed upon receipt of a specified signal. Use the command *kill –l* to get a list of all signals and the numbers corresponding to them.

FORMAT

```
trap 'command; command' signal
```

---

10. Bolsky, Morris I., and Korn, David G., *The New KornShell Command and Programming Language* (Englewood Cliffs, NJ: Prentice Hall PTR, 1995), p. 327.

EXAMPLE 10.127

```
trap 'rm tmp*$$; exit 1' 1 2 15
```

EXPLANATION

When any of the signals *1* (hangup), *2* (interrupt), or *15* (software termination) arrives, remove all the *tmp* files and then *exit*.

If an interrupt comes in while the script is running, the *trap* command lets you handle the interrupt signal in several ways. You can let the signal behave normally (default), ignore the signal, or create a handler function to be called when the signal arrives. See Table 10.31 for a list of signal numbers and their corresponding names.

Table 10.31 Signals[a] *(Type: kill –1)*

1) *HUP*	12) *SYS*	23) *POLL*
2) *INT*	13) *PIPE*	24) *XCPU*
3) *QUIT*	14) *ALRM*	25) *XFSZ*
4) *ILL*	15) *TERM*	26) *VTALRM*
5) *TRAP*	16) *URG*	27) *PROF*
6) *IOT*	17) *STOP*	28) *WINCH*
7) *EMT*	18) *TSTP*	29) *LOST*
8) *FPE*	19) *CONT*	30) *USR1*
9) *KILL*	20) *CHLD*	31) *USR2*
10) *BUS*	21) *TTIN*	
11) *SEGV*	22) *TTOU*	

a. The output of this command may differ slightly with the operating system.

Pseudo or Fake Signals.   The three fake signals are not real signals, but are generated by the shell to help debug a program. They are treated like real signals by the *trap* command and defined in the same way. See Table 10.32 for a list of pseudo signals.

Table 10.32 Korn Shell Fake Trap Signals

Signal	What It Does
DEBUG	Executes *trap* commands after every script command.
ERR	Executes *trap* commands if any command in the script returns a nonzero exit status.
0 or EXIT	Executes *trap* commands if the shell exits.

Signal names such as *HUP* and *INT* are normally prefixed with *SIG*, for example, *SIGHUP, SIGINT,* and so forth. The Korn shell allows you to use symbolic names for the signals, which are the signal names without the *SIG* prefix, or you can use the numeric value for the signal. See Example 10.128.

Resetting Signals.   To reset a signal to its default behavior, the *trap* command is followed by the signal name or number. *Traps* set in functions are local to functions; that is, they are not known outside the function where they were set.

EXAMPLE 10.128

```
trap 2  or  trap INT
```

EXPLANATION

Resets the default action for signal 2, *SIGINT.* The default action is to kill the process when the interrupt key (Control-C) is pressed.

Ignoring Signals.   If the *trap* command is followed by a pair of empty quotes, the signals listed will be ignored by the process.

EXAMPLE 10.129

```
trap " " 1 2   or   trap "" HUP INT
```

EXPLANATION

Signals *1* (*SIGHUP*) and 2 (*SIGINT*) will be ignored by the shell process.

Listing Traps.   To list all traps and the commands assigned to them, type *trap.*

EXAMPLE 10.130

```
(The Script)
    #!/bin/ksh
    # Scriptname: trapping
    # Script to illustrate the trap command and signals
    # Can use the signal numbers or ksh abbreviations seen
    # below. Cannot use SIGINT, SIGQUIT, etc.
1   trap 'print "Control-C will not terminate $PROGRAM."' INT
2   trap 'print "Control-\ will not terminate $PROGRAM."' QUIT
3   trap 'print "Control-Z will not terminate $PROGRAM."' TSTP
4   print "Enter any string after the prompt.\
    When you are ready to exit, type \"stop\"."
5   while true
    do
6       print -n "Go ahead...> "
7       read
8       if [[ $REPLY = [Ss]top ]]
        then
9           break
        fi
10  done
```

```
(The Output)
    $ trapping
4   Enter any string after the prompt.
    When you are ready to exit, type "stop".
6   Go ahead...> this is it^C
1   Control-C will not terminate trapping.
6   Go ahead...> this is it again^Z
3   Control-Z will not terminate trapping.
6   Go ahead...> this is never it^\
2   Control-\ will not terminate trapping.
6   Go ahead...> stop
    $
```

EXPLANATION

1   The first *trap* catches the *INT* signal, Control-C. If Control-C is pressed while the program is running, the command enclosed in quotes will be executed. Instead of aborting, the program will print *Control-C will not terminate trapping* and continue to prompt the user for input.

2   The second *trap* command will be executed when the user presses Control-\, the *QUIT* signal. The string *Control-\ will not terminate trapping* will be displayed and the program will continue to run. This signal, *SIGQUIT* by default, kills the process and produces a core file.

3   The third *trap* command will be executed when the user presses Control-Z, the *TSTP* signal. The string *Control-Z will not terminate trapping* will be displayed, and the program will continue to run. This signal normally causes the program to be suspended in the background if job control is implemented.

4   The user is prompted for input.

5   The *while* loop is entered.

6   The string *Go ahead...>* is printed and the program waits for input (see *read* next line).

7   The *read* command assigns user input to the built-in *REPLY* variable.

8   If the value of *REPLY* matches *Stop* or *stop*, the *break* command causes the loop to exit and the program will terminate. Entering *Stop* or *stop* is the only way we will get out of this program unless it is killed with the *kill* command.

9   The *break* command causes the body of the loop to be exited.

10 The *done* keyword marks the end of the loop.

EXAMPLE 10.131

```
(The Script)
    $ cat trap.err
    #!/bin/ksh
    # This trap checks for any command that exits with a non-zero
    # status and then prints the message.
1   trap 'print "You gave me a non-integer. Try again. "' ERR
2   typeset -i number      # Assignment to number must be integer
3   while true
    do
4       print -n "Enter an integer. "
5       read -r number 2> /dev/null
6       if (( $? == 0 ))      # Was an integer read in?
        then                  # Was the exit status zero?
7           break
        fi
    done
8   trap - ERR            # Unset pseudo trap for ERR
    n=$number
9   if grep ZOMBIE /etc/passwd > /dev/null 2>&1
    then
        :
    else
10      print "\$n is $n. So long"
    fi

(The Output)
    $ trap.err
4   Enter an integer. hello
1   You gave me a non-integer. Try again.
```

EXAMPLE 10.131 (CONTINUED)

```
4    Enter an integer. good-bye
1    You gave me a non-integer. Try again.
4    Enter an integer. \\\
1    You gave me a non-integer. Try again.
4    Enter an integer. 5
10   $n is 5. So long.


     $ trap.err
4    Enter an integer. 4.5
10   $n is 4. So long.
```

EXPLANATION

1 The *ERR* (fake or pseudo) signal will print the message in double quotes any time a command in the program returns a nonzero exit status, that is, fails.

2 The *typeset* command with the *–i* option creates an integer variable, *number*, which can only be assigned integers.

3 The exit status of the *true* command is always zero; the body of the *while* loop is entered.

4 The user is asked to type in an integer.

5 The *read* command reads user input and assigns it to the *number* variable. The number must be an integer; if not, an error message will be sent to */dev/null*. The *–r* option to the *read* command allows you to enter a negative number (starting with the minus sign).

6 If the exit status from the *read* command is zero, a number was entered, and the *if* statements will be executed.

7 The *break* command is executed and the loop exits.

8 The *trap* for the fake Korn shell signal *ERR* is unset.

9 When *grep* fails, it returns a nonzero exit status; if we had not unset the *ERR* trap, the script would have printed *You gave me a non-integer. Try again. So long* if the *grep* failed to find *ZOMBIE* in the */etc/passwd* file.

10 This line is printed if the *grep* failed. Note that if a floating point number such as 4.5 is entered, the number is truncated to an integer.

Traps and Functions.   If *trap* is used in a function, the *trap* and its commands are local to the function.

EXAMPLE 10.132

```
(The Script)
    #!/bin/ksh
1   function trapper {
        print "In trapper"
2       trap 'print "Caught in a trap!"' INT
        print "Got here."
        sleep 25
    }
3   while :
    do
        print "In the main script"
4       trapper    # Call the function
5       print "Still in main"
        sleep 5
        print "Bye"
    done
-   -------------------------------------   ----------
(The Output)
$ functrap
In the main script
In trapper
Got here.
^CCaught in a trap!
$
```

EXPLANATION

1 The function *trapper* is defined. It contains the *trap* command.

2 The *trap* command will be executed if Control-C is entered. The *print* command within the *trap* is executed and the program continues execution. Control-C is entered while the *sleep* command is running. Normally, the program will continue to run just after the command where it was interrupted (with the exception of the *sleep* command, which causes the program to abort). The *trap* has no effect on lines starting after 4.

3 In the main part of the script, a *while* loop is started. The colon is a do-nothing command that always returns a zero exit status. The loop will go forever.

4 Once in the loop, the function *trapper* is called.

5 The *trap* command within the *trapper* function will have no effect in this part of the program because the trap is local to the function. If the function exits normally (i.e., ^C is not pressed), execution will continue here. The default behavior for ^C will cause the script to abort if the signal is sent here or to any of the lines that follow.

10.2.13 Coprocesses

A coprocess is a special two-way pipeline that allows shell scripts to write to the standard input of another command and to read from its standard output. This provides a way to create a new interface for an existing program. The append operator, |&, is placed at the end of the command to initiate the command as a coprocess. Normal redirection and background processing should not be used on coprocesses. The *print* and *read* commands require a *–p* switch to read from and write to a coprocess. The output must be sent to standard output and have a newline at the end of each message of output. The standard output must be flushed after each message is sent to standard output. You can run multiple coprocesses by using the *exec* command with the *>&p* or *<&p* operator. To open file descriptor 4 as a coprocess, you would enter *exec 4>&p*.

EXAMPLE 10.133

```
(The Script)
    #!/bin/ksh
    # Scriptname: mycalculator
    # A simple calculator -- uses the bc command to perform the
    # calculations
    # Since the shell performs operations on integers only,
    # this program allows
    # you to use floating point numbers by writing to and reading
    # from the bcprogram.

1   cat << EOF
    **************************************************
2         WELCOME TO THE CALCULATOR PROGRAM
    **************************************************
3   EOF

4   bc |&                       # Open coprocess

5   while true
    do
6       print "Select the letter for one of the operators below "
7       cat <<- EOF
            a) +
            s) -
            m) *
            d) /
            e) ^
    EOF
8       read op
9       case $op in
            a) op="+";;
            s) op="-";;
            m) op="*";;
            d) op="/";;
```

EXAMPLE   10.133 (CONTINUED)

```
              e) op="^";;
              *) print "Bad operator"
                     continue;;
        esac
10    print -p scale=3                    # write to the coprocess
11    print "Please enter two numbers: "  # write to standard out
12    read num1 num2                      # read from standard in
13    print -p "$num1" "$op" "$num2"      # write to the coprocess
14    read -p result                      # read from the coprocess
15    print $result
16    print -n "Continue (y/n)? "
17    read answer
18    case $answer in
      [Nn]* )
19        break;;
      esac
20  done
21  print Good-bye
```

(The Output)
```
$ mycalculator
      ******************************************************
1         WELCOME TO THE CALCULATOR PROGRAM
      ******************************************************
6     Select one of the operators below
7         a) +
          s) -
          m) *
          d) /
          e) ^
      e
11    Please enter two numbers:
      2.3 4
      27.984
16    Continue (y/n)? y
6     Select one of the operators below
7         a) +
          s) -
          m) *
          d) /
          e) ^
      d
11    Please enter two numbers:
      2.1 4.6
      0.456
16    Continue (y/n)? y
6     Select one of the operators below
7         a) +
          s) -
```

EXAMPLE 10.133 (CONTINUED)

```
        m)  *
        d)  /
        e)  ^
    m
11  Please enter two numbers:
    4 5
    20
16  Continue (y/n)? n
    Good-bye
```

EXPLANATION

1   The *here document* is used to display a menu.

2   This text is printed as a header to the menu below.

3   EOF is a user-defined terminator, marking the end of the *here document*.

4   The *bc* command (desk calculator) is opened as a coprocess. It is executed in the background.

5   A *while* loop is started. Since the *true* command always returns a successful exit status of 0, the loop will continue indefinitely until a break or exit is reached.

6   The user is prompted to select an item from a menu to be displayed.

7   Another *here document* displays a list of math operations the user can choose for the *bc* program.

8   The *read* command assigns user input to the variable *op*.

9   The *case* command matches for one of the *op* values and assigns an operator to *op*.

10 The *print* command, with the –p option, pipes output, *scale=3*, to the coprocess, the *bc* command. The *bc* command accepts the *print* output as input and sets the *scale* to 3. (The *scale* defines the number of significant digits to the right of the decimal point in a number that will be displayed by *bc*.)

11 The user is prompted to enter two numbers.

12 The *read* command assigns user input to the variables *num1* and *num2*.

13 The *print –p* command sends the arithmetic expression to the *bc* coprocess.

14 The shell reads from the *bc* coprocess (*read –p*) and assigns the input to the variable *result*.

15 The result of the calculation (*$result*) is printed.

16 The user is asked about continuing.

17 The user enters input. It is assigned to the variable *answer*.

18 The *case* command evaluates the variable *answer*.

19 If the user had entered *No* or *no* or *nope*, etc., the *break* command would be executed, and the *while* loop would be terminated with control sent to line 21.

20 The *done* keyword marks the end of the *while* loop.

21 This line is printed when the loop terminates.

10.2.14 Debugging

By turning on the *noexec* option or using the *–n* argument to the *ksh* command, you can check the syntax of your scripts without really executing any of the commands. If there is a syntax error in the script, the shell will report the error. If there are no errors, nothing is displayed.

The most commonly used method for debugging scripts is to turn on the *xtrace* option or to use the *ksh* command with the *–x* option. These options allow an execution trace of your script. Each command from your script is displayed after variable substitution has been performed, and then the command is executed. When a line from your script is displayed, it is preceded with the value of the PS4 prompt, a plus (+) sign. The PS4 prompt can be changed.

With the *verbose* option turned on, or by invoking the Korn shell with the *–v* option (*ksh –v scriptname*), each line of the script will be displayed, just as it was typed in the script, and then executed. See Table 10.33 for debug commands.

Table 10.33 Debug Commands and Options

Command	Function	How It Works
ksh –x scriptname	Invokes *ksh* with *echo* option.	Displays each line of the script after variable substitution and before execution.
ksh –v scriptname	Invokes *ksh* with *verbose* option.	Displays each line of the script before execution, just as you typed it.
ksh –n scriptname	Invokes *ksh* with *noexec* option.	Interprets but does not execute commands.
set –x or *set –o xtrace*	Turns on *echo* option.	Traces execution in a script.
set +x	Turns off *echo*.	Turns off tracing.
typeset –ft	Turns on tracing.	Traces execution in a function.
export PS4='$LINENO '	The PS4 prompt by default is a +.	You can reset the prompt. In this example, a line number will be printed for each line.
trap 'print $LINENO ' DEBUG	Prints value of *$LINENO* for each line in the script.	For each script command, the trap action is performed. See format for *trap*.
trap 'print Bad input' ERR		If a nonzero exit status is returned, the *trap* is executed.
trap 'print Exiting from $0' EXIT		Prints message when script or function exits.

EXAMPLE 10.134

```
(The Script)
    #!/bin/ksh
    # Scriptname: todebug
1   name="Joe Blow"
2   if [[ $name = [Jj]* ]] then
        print Hi $name
    fi


    num=1
3   while (( num < 5 ))
    do
4       (( num=num+1 ))
    done
5   print The grand total is $num


(The Output)
1   $ ksh -x todebug
2   + name=Joe Blow
    + [[ Joe Blow = [Jj]* ]]
    + print Hi Joe Blow
    Hi Joe Blow
    + num=1           The + is the PS4 prompt
    + let num < 5
    + let num=num+1
    + let num < 5
    + let num=num+1
    + let num < 5
    + let num=num+1
    + let num < 5
    + let num=num+1
    + let num < 5
    + print The grand total is 5
    The grand total is 5
```

EXPLANATION

1   The Korn shell is invoked with the –x option. Echoing is turned on. Each line of the script will be displayed on the screen, followed by the result of executing that line. Variable substitution is performed. Alternatively, the –x option can be used in the script instead of at the command line; e.g., #!/bin/ksh –x

2   The lines are preceded by the plus (+) sign, the PS4 prompt.

3   The *while* loop is entered. It will loop 4 times.

4   The value of *num* is incremented by by 1.

5   After the *while* loop exits, this line is printed.

EXAMPLE   10.135

```
(The Script)
    #!/bin/ksh
    # Scriptname: todebug2
1   trap 'print "num=$num on line $LINENO"' DEBUG
    num=1
    while (( num < 5 ))
    do
        (( num=num+1 ))
    done
    print The grand total is $num

(The Output)
    $ todebug2
2   num=1 on line 3
    num=1 on line 4
    num=2 on line 6
    num=2 on line 4
    num=3 on line 6
    num=3 on line 4
    num=4 on line 6
    num=4 on line 4
    num=5 on line 6
    num=5 on line 4
    The grand total is 5
    num=5 on line 8
    num=5 on line 8
```

EXPLANATION

1   *LINENO* is a special Korn shell variable that holds the number of the current script line. The *DEBUG* signal, used with the *trap* command, causes the string enclosed in single quotes to be executed every time a command in the script is executed.

2   As the *while* loop executes, the value of the variable *num* and the line of the script are displayed.

10.2.15 Processing Command Line Options with *getopts*

If you are writing scripts that require a number of command line options, positional parameters are not always most efficient. For example, the UNIX *ls* command takes a number of command line options and arguments. (An option requires a leading dash; an argument does not.) Options can be passed to the program in several ways: *ls –laFi, ls –i –a –l –F, ls –ia –F,* and so forth. If you have a script that requires arguments, positional parameters might be used to process the arguments individually, such as *ls –l –i –F.* Each dash option would be stored in *$1, $2,* and *$3,* respectively. But, what if the user listed all of the options as one dash option, as in *ls –liF*? Now the *–liF* would all be assigned to *$1* in the script. The *getopts* function makes it possible to process command line options and arguments in the same way they are processed by the *ls* program.[11] The *getopts* function will allow the *runit* program to process its arguments using a variety of combinations.

EXAMPLE 10.136

```
(The Command Line)

1   $ runit -x -n 200 filex

2   $ runit -xn200 filex

3   $ runit -xy

4   $ runit -yx -n 30

5   $ runit -n250 -xy filey

(any other combination of these arguments )
```

EXPLANATION

1   The program *runit* takes four arguments; *x* is an option, *n* is an option requiring a number argument after it, and *filex* is an argument that stands alone.

2   The program *runit* combines the options *x* and *n* and the number argument *200*; *filex* is also an argument.

3   The program *runit* combines the *x* and *y* options.

4   The program *runit* combines the *y* and *x* options; the *n* option is passed separately as is the number argument, *30*.

5   The program *runit* combines the *n* option with the number argument; the *x* and *y* options are combined and the *filey* is separate.

Before getting into all the details of the *runit* program, we examine the line from the program where *getopts* is used to see how it processes the arguments. The following is a line from the script called *runit*:

```
while getopts :xyn: name
```

1. *x*, *y*, and *n* are the options.
2. Options typed at the command line begin with either – or +.
3. Any options that do not contain a + or – tell *getopts* that the option list is at an end.
4. The colon after an option says that the option requires an argument; that is, the –*n* option requires an argument.

---

11. See Section 3 of the UNIX manual for the C library function *getopt*.

5. The colon before an option list says that if you type an illegal option, *getopts* will allow the programmer to handle it. For example, in the command *runit –p*, where *–p* is not one of the legal options, *getopts* will tell you so programmatically. The shell does not print an error message.

6. Each time *getopts* is called, it places the next option it finds, without the dash, in the variable *name*. (You can use any variable name here.) If there is a plus sign prepended to the option, then it goes into *name* with the plus sign. If an illegal argument is given, *name* is assigned a question mark; if a required argument is missing, *name* is assigned a colon.

7. *OPTIND* is a special variable that is initialized to one and is incremented each time *getopts* completes processing a command line argument to the number of the next argument *getopts* will process.

8. The *OPTARG* variable contains the value of a legal argument, or if an illegal option is given, the value of the illegal option is stored in *OPTARG*.

Sample *getopts* Scripts.   The following sample scripts illustrate how *getopts* processes arguments.

EXAMPLE   10.137

```
(The Script)
    #!/bin/ksh
    # Program opts1
    # Using getopts -- First try --
1   while getopts xy options
    do
2   case $options in
3      x) print "you entered -x as an option";;
       y) print "you entered -y as an option";;
    esac
    done
--------------------------------------------------------------------
(The Command Line)
4   $ opts1 -x
    you entered -x as an option

5   $ opts1 -xy
    you entered -x as an option
    you entered -y as an option

6   $ opts1 -y
    you entered -y as an option

7   $ opts1 -b
    opts1[3]: getopts: b bad option(s)

8   $ opts1 b
```

EXPLANATION

1   The *getopts* command is used as a condition for the *while* command. The valid options for this program are listed after the *getopts* command; they are *x* and *y*. Each option is tested in the body of the loop, one after the other. Each option will be assigned to the variable *options*, without the leading dash. When there are no longer any arguments to process, *getopts* will exit with a nonzero status, causing the *while* loop to terminate.

2   The *case* command is used to test each of the possible options found in the *options* variable, either *x* or *y*.

3   If *x* was an option, the string *you entered x as an option* is displayed.

4   At the command line, the *opts1* script is given an *x* option, a legal option to be processed by *getopts*.

5   At the command line, the *opts1* script is given an *xy* option, legal options to be processed by *getopts*.

6   At the command line, the *opts1* script is given a *y* option, a legal option to be processed by *getopts*.

7   The *opts1* script is given a *b* option, an illegal option. *Getopts* sends an error message.

8   An option without a – or + prepended to it is not an option and causes *getopts* to stop processing arguments.

EXAMPLE 10.138

```
(The Script)
    #!/bin/ksh
    # Program opts2
    # Using getopts -- Second try --
1   while getopts :xy options
    do
2       case $options in
        x) print "you entered -x as an option";;
        y) print "you entered -y as an option";;
3       \?) print $OPTARG is not a valid option 1>&2;;
        esac
    done
--------------------------------------------------------------------
(The Command Line)

    $ opts2 -x
    you entered -x as an option

    $ opts2 -y
    you entered -y as an option
```

EXAMPLE 10.138 (CONTINUED)

```
    $ opts2 xy
    $ opts2 -xy
    you entered -x as an option
    you entered -y as an option

4   $ opts2 -g
    g is not a valid option

5   $ opts2 -c
    c is not a valid option
```

EXPLANATION

1   The colon preceding the option list prevents the Korn shell from printing an error message for a bad option. However, if the option is a bad option, a question mark will be assigned to the *options* variable.

2   The *case* command can be used to test for the question mark, allowing you to print your own error message to standard error.

3   If the *options* variable is assigned the question mark, this *case* statement is executed. The question mark is protected with the backslash so that the Korn shell does not see it as a wildcard and try to perform filename substitution.

4   *g* is not a legal option. The question mark is assigned to the *options* variable, and *OPTARG* is assigned the illegal option *g*.

5   *c* is not a legal option. The question mark is assigned to the *options* variable, and *OPTARG* is assigned the illegal option *c*.

EXAMPLE 10.139

```
(The Script)
    #!/bin/ksh
    # Program opts3
    # Using getopts -- Third try --
1   while getopts :d options
    do
        case $options in
2       d) print -R "-d is the ON switch";;
3       +d) print -R "+d is the OFF switch";;
        \?) print $OPTARG is not a valid option;;
        esac
    done
  # Need the -R option with print or the shell tries to use -d as a
  # print option
-----------------------------------------------------------------
```

EXAMPLE 10.139 (CONTINUED)

```
(The Command Line)
4  $ opts3 -d
   -d is the ON switch

5  $ opts3 +d
   +d is the OFF switch

6  $ opts3 -e
   e is not a valid option

7  $ opts3 e
```

EXPLANATION

1 The *while* command tests the exit status of *getopts*; if *getopts* can successfully process an argument, it returns zero exit status, and the body of the *while* loop is entered. The colon prepended to the *d* option tells *getopts* not to print an error message if the user enters an invalid option.

2 One of the legal options is *–d*. If *–d* is entered as an option, the *d* (without the dash) is stored in the *options* variable. (The *–R* option to the *print* command allows the first character in the *print* string to be a dash.)

3 One of the legal options is *+d*. If *+d* is entered as an option, the *d* (with the plus sign) is stored in the *options* variable.

4 The *–d* option is a legal option to *opts3*.

5 The *+d* option is also a legal option to *opts3*.

6 The *–e* option is invalid. A question mark is stored in *options* if the option is illegal. The illegal argument is stored in *OPTARG*.

7 The option is prepended with neither a dash nor a plus sign. The *getopts* command will not process it as an option and returns a nonzero exit status. The *while* loop is terminated.

EXAMPLE 10.140

```
(The Script)
   #!/bin/ksh
   # Program opts4
   # Using getopts -- Fourth try --
1  alias USAGE='print "usage: opts4 [-x] filename " >&2'
2  while getopts :x: arguments
   do
   case $arguments in
3      x) print "$OPTARG is the name of the argument ";;
```

EXAMPLE 10.140 (CONTINUED)

```
4          :) print "Please enter an argument after the -x option" >&2
           USAGE ;;
5          \?) print "$OPTARG is not a valid option." >&2
           USAGE;;
       esac
6      print "$OPTIND" # The number of the next argument to be processed
       done
-----------------------------------------------------------------
(The Command Line)
7      $ opts4 -x
       Please enter an argument after the -x option
       usage: opts4 [-x] filename
       2
8      $ opts4 -x filex
       filex is the name of the argument
       3
9      $ opts4 -d
       d is not a valid option.
       usage: opts4 [-x] filename
       1
```

EXPLANATION

1   The alias *USAGE* is assigned the diagnostic error message that will be printed if *getopts* fails.

2   The *while* command tests the exit status of *getopts*; if *getopts* can successfully process an argument, it returns zero exit status, and the body of the *while* loop is entered. The colon prepended to the *x* option tells *getopts* not to print an error message if the user enters an invalid option. The colon appended to the *x* option tells *getopts* that an argument should follow the *x* option. If the option takes an argument, the argument is stored in the *getopts* built-in variable, *OPTARG*.

3   If the *x* option was given an argument, the argument is stored in the *OPTARG* variable and will be printed.

4   If an argument was not provided after the *x* option, a colon is stored in the variable *arguments*. The appropriate error message is displayed.

5   If an invalid option is entered, the question mark is stored in the variable *arguments* and an error message is displayed.

6   The special *getopts* variable, *OPTIND*, holds the number of the next option to be processed. Its value is always one more than the actual number of command line arguments.

7   The *x* option requires an argument. An error message is printed.

8   The name of the argument is *filex*. The variable *OPTARG* holds the name of the argument *filex*.

9   The option *d* is invalid. The usage message is displayed.

10.2.16 Security

Privileged Scripts.   A script is privileged if the Korn shell is invoked with the −*p* option. When the privileged option is used and the real UID and/or the real GID are not the same as the effective UID or effective GID, the *.profile* will not be executed and a system file called */etc/suid_profile* will be executed instead of the *ENV* file.

Restricted Shells.   When the Korn shell is invoked with the −*r* option, the shell is restricted. When the shell is restricted, the *cd* command cannot be used and the *SHELL*, *ENV*, and *PATH* variables cannot be modified or unset; commands cannot be executed if the first character is a backslash; and the redirection operators (>, <, |, >>) are illegal. This option cannot be unset or set with the *set* command. The command *rksh* will invoke a restricted shell.

10.2.17 Built-In Commands

The Korn shell has a number of built-in commands, as shown in Table 10.34.

Table 10.34   Built-In Commands and Their Functions

Command	*Function*
:	Do-nothing command; returns exit status zero.
. *file*	The dot command reads and executes a command from *file*.
break	See *looping*.
continue	See *looping*.
cd	Changes directory.
echo [args]	Displays arguments.
eval command	Shell scans the command line twice before execution.
exec command	Runs *command* in place of this shell.
exit [n]	Exit the shell with status *n*.
export [var]	Makes *var* known to subshells.
fc −e [editor] [lnr] first last	Used to edit commands in the history list. If no editor is specified, the value of *FCEDIT* is used; if *FCEDIT* is not set, */bin/ed* is used. Usually history is aliased to *fc −l*.

Table 10.34 Built-In Commands and Their Functions (continued)

Command	Function
	Examples:
	fc –l Lists the last 16 commands on the history list.
	fc –e emacs grep Reads the last *grep* command into the *emacs* editor.
	fc 25 30 Reads commands 25 through 30 into the editor specified in *FCEDIT*, by default the *ed* editor.
	fc –e – Reexecutes the last command.
	fc –e – Tom=Joe 28 Replaces *Tom* with *Joe* in history command 28.
	fg Brings the last background job to the foreground.
	fg %n Brings job number *n* to the foreground. Type *jobs* to find the correct job number.
jobs [–l]	Lists the active *jobs* by number and with the *–l* option by PID number.
	Examples:
	$ jobs
	[3] + Running sleep 50&
	[1] – Stopped vi
	[2] Running sleep%
kill [–signal process]	Sends the signal to the PID number or job number of process. See */usr/include/sys/signal.h* for a list of signals.
	Signals:
	SIGHUP1 /* hangup (disconnect) */
	SIGINT 2 /* interrupt */
	SIGQUIT 3 /* quit */
	SIGILL 4 /* illegal instruction (not reset when caught) */
	SIGTRAP 5 /* trace trap (not reset when caught) */
	SIGIOT 6 /* IOT instruction */
	SIGABRT 6 /* used by abort, replace *SIGIOT* in the future */
	SIGEMT 7 /* EMT instruction */
	SIGFPE 8 /* floating point exception */
	SIGKILL 9 /* kill (cannot be caught or ignored) */
	SIGBUS 10 /* bus error */
	SIGSEGV 11 /* segmentation violation */
	SIGSYS 12 /* bad argument to system call */
	SIGPIPE 13 /* write on a pipe with no one to read it */
	SIGALRM 14 /* alarm clock */
	SIGTERM 15 /* software termination signal from kill */
	SIGURG 16 /* urgent condition on I/O channel */
	SIGSTOP 17 /* sendable stop signal not from tty */
	SIGTSTP 18 /* stop signal from tty */
	SIGCONT 19 /* continue a stopped process */

Table 10.34   Built-In Commands and Their Functions (continued)

Command	Function
	(To use the *kill* command and a signal name, strip off the *SIG* prefix and precede the signal name with a dash.) Examples: *kill –INT %3* *kill –HUP 1256* *kill –9 %3* *kill %1*
getopts	Used in shell scripts to parse command line and check for legal options.
hash	Lists all tracked aliases.
login [username]	
newgrp [arg]	Changes your real group ID to the group ID.
print –[nrRsup]	Replacement for *echo*. See *print*.
pwd	Print present working directory.
read [var]	Read line from standard input into variable *var*.
readonly [var]	Make variable *var readonly*. Cannot be reset.
return [n]	Exit value given to a function.

set [–aefhknoptuvx– [–o option] [–A arrayname] [arg]]

Examples:

set	Lists all variables and their values.
set +	Lists all variables without their values.
set –o	Lists all option settings.
set a b c	Resets positional parameters $1, $2, $3.
set –s	Sorts $1, $2, and $3 alphabetically.
set –o vi	Sets the *vi* option.
set –xv	Turns on the *xtrace* and *verbose* options for debugging.
set – –	Unsets all positional parameters.
set – – "$x"	Sets $1 to the value of *x*, even if *x* is *–x*.
set == $x	Does pathname expansion on each item in *x* and then sets the positional parameters to each item.
set –A name tom dick harry	*name[0]* is set to *tom*. *name[1]* is set to *dick*. *name[2]* is set to *harry*.

Table 10.34   Built-In Commands and Their Functions (continued)

Command	Function
	Examples *(continued)*:
	set +A name joe *name[0]* is reset to *joe*, the rest of the array is left alone.
	name[1] is *dick*.
	name[2] is *harry*.
	(To set options, use the *−o* flag; to unset options, use the *+o* flag.)
	Example:
	set −o ignoreeof
	Options:
	allexport After setting this, exports any variable defined or changed.
	bgnice Runs background jobs with a lesser priority; used instead of *nice*.
	emacs Sets the *emacs* built-in editor.
	errexit The shell exits when a command returns a nonzero exit status.
	gmacs Sets the built-in *gmacs* editor.
	ignoreeof Ignores the *EOF* (Control-D) key from terminating the shell. Must use *exit* to exit.
	keyword Adds *keyword* arguments occurring anywhere on the command line to the environment of the shell.
	markdirs Puts a trailing backslash on all directory names resulting from filename expansion.
	monitor Sets job control.
	noclobber Prevents overwriting files using the redirection operator, >. Use >| to force overwrite.
	noexec Same as *ksh −n*; reads commands but does not execute them. Used to check for syntax errors in shell scripts.
	noglob Disables pathname expansion with *ksh* wildcard metacharacters.
	nolog Function definitions will not be stored in the history file.
	nounset Displays an error if a variable has not been set.
	privileged Turns on privileged mode for setuid programs.
	trackall *Ksh* causes each command to become a tracked alias; automatically turned on for interactive shells.
	verbose Echos each line of input to standard error; useful in debugging.
	vi Sets the *vi* built-in editor.
	viraw Specifies *vi* character at a time input.
	xtrace Expands each command and displays it in the PS4 prompt, with variables expanded.

Table 10.34   Built-In Commands and Their Functions (continued)

Command	Function
shift [n]	*Shifts* positional parameters to the left *n* times.
times	Prints accumulated user and system *times* for processes run from this shell.
trap [arg] [n]	When shell receives signal *n* (0, 1, 2, or 15), *arg* is executed.
type [command]	Prints the type of command; e.g., *pwd* is a built-in shell. In *ksh*, an alias for *whence –v.*
typeset [options] [var]	Sets attributes and values for shell variables and functions.
ulimit [options size]	Sets maximum limits on processes.

<u>Examples:</u>

ulimit –a	Display all limits:
	Time (seconds) unlimited.
	File (blocks) unlimited.
	Data (kbytes) 524280.
	Stack (kbytes) 8192.
	Memory (kbytes) unlimited.
	Coredump (blocks) unlimited.

<u>Other Options:</u>

–c size	Limits core dumps to size blocks.
–d size	Limits the data size (of executables) to size blocks.
–f size	Limits the size of files to size blocks (default).
–m size	Limits the size of physical memory to size *K* bytes.
–s size	Limits the size of the stack area to size *K* bytes.
–t secs	Limits process execution time to *secs* seconds.

Command	Function
umask [mask]	Without argument, prints out file creation mask for permissions.
umask [octal digits]	User file creation mode mask for owner, group, and others.
unset [name]	*Unsets* value of variable or function.
wait [pid#n]	*Waits* for background process with PID number *n* and report termination status.
whence [command]	Prints information about the command, like *ucb whereis.*

<u>Examples:</u>

whence –v happy	*happy* is a function
whence –v addon	*addon* is an undefined function
whence –v ls	*ls* is a tracked alias for */bin/ls*
whence ls	*/bin/ls*

10.2.18 Korn Shell Invocation Arguments

When the Korn shell is involved, it can take options to control its behavior. See Table 10.35.

Table 10.35 Arguments to *ksh*

Command	*Function*
−*a*	Automatically exports all variables.
−*c cmd*	Executes a command string.
−*e*	Exits when a command returns a nonzero status.
−*f*	Turns off globbing, the expansion of filename metacharacters.
−*h*	Causes commands to be treated as tracked aliases.
−*i*	Sets the interactive mode.
−*k*	Sets the keyword option. All the key arguments to commands will be made part of the environment.
−*m*	Causes commands executed in the background to be run in a separate process group, and will continue to run even if Control-C or logout is attempted. Sends a message that the job has terminated when done.
−*n*	Can be used for debugging. Commands are scanned, but not executed. Can be used with −*x* and −*v* options.
−*o*	Allows options to be set by the names listed in the table above with the *set* command.
−*p*	Turns on privileged mode. Used for running *setuid* programs.
−*r*	Sets the restricted mode.
−*s*	Reads command from *stdin*, the default.
−*t*	Causes the shell to exit after executing the first command found in shell input and the −*c* option is specified.
−*u*	Any reference to an unset variable is considered an error.
−*v*	Each line of a script or standard input is printed before any parsing, variable substitution, or other processing is performed. Output is written to standard error. Used for debugging.
−*x*	Each line of a script or standard input is printed before it is executed. Filename expansion, variable substitution, and command substitution are shown in the output. All output is prepended with the value of the PS4 prompt, a plus sign followed by a space. Lines are written to standard error.

KORN SHELL LAB EXERCISES

Lab 28: Getting Started

1. What shell are you using? How do you know?

2. Do you have a *.profile* and/or a *.kshrc* file in your home directory? What is the difference between the *.profile* and *.kshrc*? What is the *ENV* file and how can you invoke it if you make changes in it?

3. What is the default primary prompt? What is the default secondary prompt? Change your primary prompt at the command line so that it contains your login name.

4. What is the purpose of setting each of the following variables?

    a. *set –o ignoreeof*

    b. *set –o noclobber*

    c. *set –o trackall*

    d. *set –o monitor*

    e. *set –o vi*

    Why are these variables set in the *ENV* file? What is the purpose of the *PATH*? What are the elements of your *PATH* variable?

5. What is the difference between a local and an environment variable? How do you list all your variables? How do you list only environment variables? To list all your current option settings, type the following:

    ```
    set -o
    ```

    Which set options are turned on?

6. Create a local variable called *myname* that contains your full name. Now *export* the variable. Type the following at the prompt:

    ```
    ksh
    ```

    Was the variable *name* exported? Type *exit* to get back to the parent shell. Make the variable *name* readonly. What is a *readonly* variable?

7. What are positional parameters normally used for? Type the following:

    ```
    set apples pears peaches plums
    ```

    Using the positional parameters, print *plums*. Print *apples peaches*. Print *apples pears peaches plums*. Print the number of parameters. Reset the positional parameters to a list of veggies. Print the whole list of veggies. What happened to the *fruit* list?

    Type the following:

    ```
    set --
    print $*
    ```

    What happened?

8. Print the PID of the current shell. Type the following at the prompt:

    ```
    grep $LOGNAME /etc/passwd
    echo $?
    ```

    What does the *$?* tell you. What does the exit status tell you about the execution of a command?

9. Change both the primary and secondary prompt in your *.profile*. How do you reexecute the *.profile* file without logging out and logging back in?

Lab 29: History

1. What is your *HISTSIZE* variable set to? What is your *HISTFILE* variable set to? Check your *.kshrc* file to see if *set –o vi* is there. If it has not been set, set it in the *.kshrc* file and reexecute the file by typing the following:

```
.  .kshrc
```

2. Type the following commands at the command line:

```
ls
date
who
cal 2 1993
date +%T
```

Type *history* or *fc –l*. What do these commands do? Print your history list in reverse. Print your history list without numbers. Print the current command and the five preceding it. Print everything from the tenth command to the present. Print everything between the most recent *ls* command to the most recent *cal* command.

3. Using the *r* command, reexecute the last command. Reexecute the last command that started with the letter *d*. Change the *cal* command *year* output to *1897*. Change the *date* command *+%T* argument to find the current hour.

4. If your history is set, press the Esc key at the command line and use the K key to move up through the history list. Change the *ls* command to *ls –alF* and reexecute it.

5. Check to see if the *FCEDIT* variable has been set by typing the *env* command. If it has not been set, type the following at the command line:

```
export FCEDIT=vi
```

Now type the following at the command line:

```
fc -1 -4
```

What happened?

6. How do you *comment* a line from your history list, so that it will be placed on the list without being executed?

7. At the command line, type the following:

```
touch a1 a2 a3 apples bears balloons a4 a45
```

Now using the history Esc sequences shown in Tables 10.2 and 10.3, print all the files beginning with an *a*.

   a. Print the first file beginning with *a*.

   b. Print a list of all files beginning with *a*.

   c. Print the first file beginning with *b*.

   d. Print a command and comment it.

8. At the command line, type the following:

```
print a b c d e
```

9. Using the history *Esc underscore* command, change the command to the following:

```
print e
```

Using the history *Esc underscore* command, change the first command to output:

```
print c
```

Lab 30: Aliases and Functions

1. What command lists all the aliases currently set?
2. What command lists all the *tracked* aliases?
3. Create aliases for the following commands:

```
date +%T
history -n
ls -alF
rm -i
cp -i
print
```

4. How do you export an alias?
5. Create a function that contains the following commands:

```
ls -F
print -n "The time is"
date +%T
print -n "Your present working directory is"
pwd
```

6. Execute the function.
7. Now create your own functions, using positional parameters to pass arguments.
8. What command lists the functions and their definitions?
9. Try some of the *print* options.

Lab 31: Shell Metacharacters

1. Create a directory called *meta*. *Cd* to that directory. Use *touch* to create the following files:

```
abc abc1 abc2 abc2191 Abc1 ab2 ab3 ab345 abc29 abc9 abc91
abc21xyz abc2121 noone nobody nothing nowhere
```

2. Do the following:
   a. List all files that start with a lower case *a*.
   b. List all files starting with upper case *A* followed by two characters.
   c. List all files that end in a number.
   d. List all files that match one number after *abc*.
   e. List all files that match *nothing* or *noone*.
   f. List all files that match one or more numbers after *abc*.
   g. List all files that do not contain the pattern *abc*.
   h. List all files that contain *ab* followed by a 3 or 4.
   i. List all files starting with *a* or *A*, followed by *b*, and ending in one number.
   j. What is the error message if there is not a match?

Lab 32: Tilde Expansion, Quotes, and Command Substitution

1. Use the *tilde* to do the following:
    a. Print your home directory.
    b. Print your neighbor's home directory.
    c. Print your previous working directory.
    d. Print your current working directory.
2. What variable holds the value of your present working directory? What variable holds the value of your previous working directory?
3. Use the – to go to your previous working directory.
4. Use the *print* command to send the following output to the screen. (The word enclosed in < > is a variable name that will be expanded, and words enclosed in [ ] are output of commands that have been executed; i.e., use command substitution.)

```
Hi <LOGNAME> how's your day going?
"No, <LOGNAME> you can't use the car tonight!", she cried.
The time is [ Sun Feb 21 13:19:27 PST 2001 ]
The name of this machine is [ eagle ] and
the time is [ 31:19:27 ]
```

5. Create a *file* that contains a list of user names. Now create a variable called *nlist* which contains the list of user names, extracted by using command substitution.
    a. Print out the value of the variable. How does command substitution affect the formatting of a list?
    b. Test this by setting a variable to the output of the *ps –eaf* command.
    c. What happened to the formatting?

Lab 33: Redirection

1. Go into the editor and create the following two-line text file called *ex6*:

```
Last time I went to the beach I found a sea shell.
While in Kansas I found a corn shell.
```

2. Now append this line to your *ex6* file: The *National Enquirer* says someone gave birth to a shell, called the born shell.
3. Mail the *ex6* file to yourself.
4. Using a pipe, count the number of lines (*wc –l*) in your *ex6* file.
5. To list all set options, type the following:

```
set -o
```

Do you have the *noclobber* variable set? If not, type the following:

```
set -o noclobber
```

What happened?

6. Type the following at the command line:

```
cat << FINIS
How are you $LOGNAME
The time is `date`Bye!!
FINIS
```

What printed?

7. Now try this using tabs:

```
cat <<- END
         hello there
         how are you
  END
```

What printed?

8. Type the following at the command line:

```
kat file 2> error || print kat failed
```

What happened? Why?

9. Now type the following at the command line:

```
cat zombie 2> errorfile || print cat failed
```

What happened? Why? How does the && operator work? Try your own command to test it.

10. Use the *find* command to print all files that begin with an *a* from the root directory down. Put the standard output in a file called *foundit* and send the errors to */dev/null*.

Lab 34: Job Control

1. At the command line type the following:

```
mail <user>Press control-z
```

Now type:

```
jobs
```

What is the number in the square brackets?

2. Now type:

```
sleep 300
jobs
bg
```

What does *bg* do? What do the + and – signs indicate?

3. Kill the *mail* job using job control.

4. Go into the editor. Type ^Z to stop the job.
Now bring the stopped *vi* job back into the *foreground*. What command did you type?

5. Type the following command:

```
jobs -l
```

What is the output?

6. What is the *TMOUT* variable used for?

7. How much time was spent by the kernel when executing the following command:

```
(sleep 5 ; ps -eaf )
```

Lab 35: Writing the *info* Shell Script

1. Write a program called *info*. Make sure you make the program executable with the *chmod* command before you try to execute it.
2. The program should contain *comments*.
3. The program should do the following when executed:
    a. Output the number of users logged on.
    b. Output the time and date.
    c. Output the present working directory.
    d. List all directory files in the parent directory.
    e. Print out the name of the shell being used.
    f. Print a line from the password file containing your login name.
    g. Print your user ID.
    h. Print the name of this machine.
    i. Print your disk usage.
    j. Print a calendar for this month.
    k. Tell the user *good bye* and print the hour in nonmilitary time.

Lab 36: Variable Expansion of Substrings

1. Write a script that will do the following:
    a. Set a variable called *mypath* to your home directory.
    b. Print the value of *mypath*.
    c. Print just the last element of the path in *mypath*.
    d. Print the first element of the path in *mypath*.
    e. Print all but the last element of the variable *mypath*.

Lab 37: The *lookup* Script

1. Create a file called *datafile* if it has not been provided for you on the CD. It will consist of colon-separated fields:
    a. First and last name
    b. Phone number
    c. Address (street, city, state, and zip)
    d. Birth date (04/12/66)
    e. Salary
2. Put 10 entries in your file. Write a script called *lookup* that will do the following:
    a. Welcome the user.
    b. Print the names and phone numbers for all the users in the *datafile*.
    c. Print the number of lines in the *datafile*.
    d. Tell the user *good bye*.

Lab 38: Using *typeset*

1. Write a script that will do the following:
   a. Ask the user to type in his or her first and last name.
   b. Store the answers in two variables.
   c. Use the new *ksh read* command.
2. Use the *typeset* command to convert the first and last name variables to all lowercase letters.
3. Test to see if the person's name is t*om jones*. If it is, print *Welcome, Tom Jones*; if it is not, print, *Are you happy today, FIRSTNAME LASTNAME?*. (The user's first and last names are converted to uppercase letters.)
4. Have the user type in an answer to the question and use the new *ksh test* command to see whether the answer is *yes* or *no*. If *yes*, have your script say something nice to him or her, and if *no*, tell the user to go home and give the current time of day.
5. Rewrite the *lookup* script.
   a. The script will ask the user if he or she would like to add an entry to the *datafile*.
   b. If the user answers *yes* or *y*, ask for the following input:
   Name
   Phone number
   Address
   Birth date
   Salary
   A variable for each item will be assigned the user input.

EXAMPLE

```
print -n "What is the name of the person you are adding to the file?"
read name The information will be appended to the datafile.
```

Lab 39: The *if/else* Construct and the *let* Command

1. Write a script called *grades* that will ask the user for his or her numeric grade on a test.
   a. The script will test that the grade is within the possible grade range, 0 to 100.
   b. The script will tell the user if he or she got an A, B, C, D, or F.
2. Write a script called *calc* that will perform the functions of a simple calculator. The script will provide a simple menu:

   [a] Add
   [s] Subtract
   [m] Multiply
   [d] Divide
   [r] Remainder

3. The user will choose one of the letters from the menu.
4. The user will then be asked to enter two integers between 0 and 100.
5. If the numbers are out of the range, an error message will be printed and the script will exit.
6. The program will perform the arithmetic on the two integers.
7. The answer will be printed in base 10, 8, and 16.

Lab 40: The *case* Statement

1. Write a script *timegreet* that will do the following:

   a. Provide a comment section at the top of the script, with your name, the date, and the purpose of this program.

   b. Convert the following program using *case* statements:

```
# The timegreet script by Ellie Quigley
you=$LOGNAME
hour=`date | awk '{print substr($4, 1, 2)}'`
print "The time is: $(date)"
if (( hour > 0 && $hour < 12 ))
then
    print "Good morning, $you!"
elif (( hour == 12 ))
then
    print "Lunch time!"
elif (( hour > 12 && $hour < 16 ))
then
    print "Good afternoon, $you!"
else
    print "Good night, $you!"
fi
```

2. Rewrite the *lookup* script, replacing the *if/elif* construct with the *case* command. Add one more menu item:

   1) Add Entry
   2) Delete Entry
   3) Update Entry
   4) View Entry
   5) Exit

Lab 41: The *select* Loop

1. Write a script that will do the following:

   a. Provide a comment section at the top of the script, with your name, the date, and the purpose of this program.

   b. Use the *select* loop to provide a menu of foods. The output will resemble the following:

   $ foods
   1) steak and potatoes
   2) fish and chips
   3) soup and salad
   Please make a selection. 1
   Stick to your ribs
   Watch your cholesterol
   Enjoy your meal.

```
$ foods
1) steak and potatoes
2) fish and chips
3) soup and salad
Please make a selection. 2
British are coming
```
Enjoy your meal.

```
$ foods
1) steak and potatoes
2) fish and chips
3) soup and salad
Please make a selection. 3
Health foods...
Dieting is so boring.
```
Enjoy your meal.

```
$ foods
1) steak and potatoes
2) fish and chips
3) soup and salad
Please make a selection. 5
Not on the menu today!
```

2. Rewrite the *lookup* script using the *select* command to create a main menu and a sub menu. The menu will resemble the following:

```
1) Add Entry
2) Delete Entry
3) Update Entry
4) View Entry
      a) Name
      b) Phone
      c) Address
      d) Birthday
      e) Salary
5) Exit
```

Lab 42: Autoloading Functions

Steps for autoloading a function:

1. Make a directory called *myfunctions*.
2. Change directory to *myfunctions* and use the editor to create a file called *goodbye*.
3. Insert in the *goodbye* file a function called *goodbye*, spelled exactly the same as the filename.
4. The *goodbye* function contains:

```
function goodbye {
print The current time is $(date)
print "The name of this script is $0"
print See you later $1
print Your machine is `uname -n`
}
```

5. Write and quit the editor. You now have a file containing a function with the same name.
6. Go to your home directory. Modify the *.kshrc* file in the editor by typing the following line:

   ```
   FPATH=$HOME/myfunctions
   ```

7. Exit the editor, and to execute the *.kshrc* in the current environment, use the *dot* command.
8. In the *timegreet* script you have already written, include the following lines:

   ```
   autoload goodbye
   goodbye $LOGNAME
   ```

9. Run the *timegreet* script. The *goodbye* function output will appear.
10. Create functions for each of the menu items in the *lookup* script. Store the functions in a file called *lookup_functions* in a directory called *myfunctions*.
11. Autoload the functions in your *lookup* script and make the function calls for the corresponding cases.
12. Use the *trap* command so that if the user enters a menu selection other than an integer value, the *trap* command will print an error to the screen, and cause the script to ask the user to reenter the correct data type.

chapter
11

The Interactive *bash* Shell

11.1 Introduction

With an interactive shell, the standard input, output, and error are tied to a terminal. When using the Bourne Again (*bash*) shell interactively, you type UNIX commands at the *bash* prompt and wait for a response. *Bash* provides you with a large assortment of built-in commands and command line shortcuts, such as history, aliases, file and command completion, command line editing, and many more. Some of the features were present in the standard UNIX Bourne shell but the GNU project has expanded the shell to include a number of new features as well adding POSIX compliancy. With the release of *bash* 2.x, so many features of the UNIX Korn shell and C shell have been included that the *bash* shell is a fully functional shell at both the interactive and programming level, while upwardly compatible with the standard Bourne shell. For UNIX users, *bash* offers an alternative to the standard shells, *sh*, *csh*, and *ksh*.[1]

This chapter focuses on how you interact with *bash* at the command line and how to customize your working environment. You will learn how to take advantage of all shortcuts and built-in features in order to create an efficient and fun working environment. The next chapter takes you a step further. Then you will be ready to write *bash* shell scripts to further tailor the working environment for yourself by automating everyday tasks and developing sophisticated scripts, and if you are an administrator, doing the same not only for yourself but also for whole groups of users.

11.1.1 Versions of *bash*

The Bourne Again shell is a Capricorn, born on January 10, 1988, fathered by Brian Fox and later adopted by Chet Ramey, who now officially maintains *bash*, enhances it, and fixes bugs. The first version of *bash* was 0.99. The current version (as of this writing) is version 2.04. Major enhancements were completed in version 2.0, but there are a num-

---

1. Although bash is traditionally the default shell for Linux platforms, it now comes bundled with Solaris 8.

ber of operating systems that are still using version 1.14.7. All versions are freely available under the GNU public license. To see what version you are using, use the – –*version* option to *bash* or print the value of the *BASH_VERSION* environment variable.

EXAMPLE 11.1

```
$ bash --version
GNU bash, version 2.03.0(1)-release (sparc-sun-solaris)
Copyright 1998 Free Software Foundation, Inc.

$ echo $BASH_VERSION
2.03.0(1)-release
```

11.1.2 Startup

If the *bash* shell is your login shell, it follows a chain of processes before you see a shell prompt.[2]

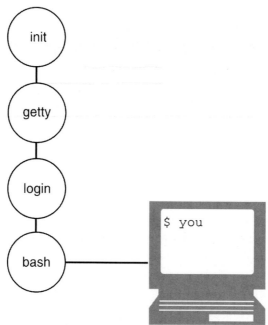

Figure 11.1   Starting the *bash* shell.

---

2. To get the latest version of *bash*, visit *http://www.delorie.com/gnu/*.

When the system boots, the first process to run is called *init*, PID #1. It spawns a *getty* process. This process opens up the terminal ports, providing a place where standard input comes from and a place where standard output and errors go, and puts a login prompt on your screen. The */bin/login* program is then executed. The *login* program prompts for a password, encrypts and verifies the password, sets up an initial environment, and starts up the login shell, */bin/bash*, the last entry in the *passwd* file. The *bash* process looks for the system file, */etc/profile,* and executes its commands. It then looks in the user's home directory for an initialization file called *.bash_profile*. After executing commands from *.bash_profile*,[3] it will execute a command from the user's *ENV* file, usually called *.bashrc*, and finally the default dollar sign ($) prompt appears on your screen and the shell waits for commands. (For more on initialization files, see "The Environment" on page 602.)

Changing the Shell at the Command Line.   If you want to start another shell from the command line temporarily (without changing the */etc/passwd* file), just type the name of the shell. For example, if you are currently using the standard Bourne shell and would rather have *bash* as your shell, you can change the shell at the command line simply by typing *bash*.

EXAMPLE   11.2

```
1    $ ps
     PID    TTY     TIME    CMD
     1574   pts/6   0:00    sh


2    $ bash
     bash-2.03$


3    bash-2.03$ ps
     PID    TTY     TIME    CMD
     1574   pts/6   0:00    sh
     1576   pts/6   0:00    bash
```

EXPLANATION

1   The output of the *ps* command shows what processes are running. Currently, *sh* (the Bourne shell) is running.

2   At the Bourne shell prompt, the user enters *bash* and starts up the Bourne Again shell. A new prompt appears.

3   At the bash prompt, the *ps* command is executed. The output shows that two shells are running and the current shell is now *bash*.

---

3. There are a number of different initialization files used by *bash*; they are discussed on the next pages.

11.1.3 The Environment

The environment of a process consists of variables, open files, the current working directory, functions, resource limits, signals, and so forth. It defines those features that are inherited from one shell to the next and the configuration for the working environment. The configuration for the user's shell is defined in the shell initialization files.

The Initialization Files.   The *bash* shell has a number of startup files that are sourced. Sourcing a file causes all settings in the file to become part of the current shell; i.e., a subshell is not created. (The source command is discussed in "The source or dot Command" on page 621.) The initialization files are sourced depending on the whether the shell is a login shell, an interactive shell (but not the login shell), or a noninteractive shell (a shell script).

When you log on, before the shell prompt appears, the systemwide initialization file, *etc/profile*, is sourced. Next, if it exists, the *.bash_profile* in the user's home directory is sourced. It sets the user's aliases and functions and then sets user-specific environment variables and startup scripts.

If the user doesn't have a *.bash_profile*, but does have a file called *.bash_login*, that file will be sourced, and if he doesn't have a *.bash_login*, but does have a *.profile*, it will be sourced. (The *.bash_login* file is similar to the C shell's *.login* file and the *.profile* is normally sourced by the Bourne shell when it starts up.)

Here is a summary of the order that *bash* processes its initialization files[4] (see Figure 11.2):

```
if /etc/profile exists, source it,
   if ~/.bash_profile exists, source it,
      if  ~/.bashrc exists, source it,
   else if ~/.bash_login exists, source it,
   else if ~/.profile exists, source it.
```

The /etc/profile File.   The */etc/profile* file is a systemwide initialization file set up by the system administrator to perform tasks when the user logs on. It is executed when the *bash* shell starts up. It is also available to all Bourne and Korn shell users on the system and normally performs such tasks as checking the mail spooler for new mail and displaying the message of the day from the */etc/motd* file. (The following examples will make more sense after you have completed this chapter.)

---

4. If the shell is invoked with the *–noprofile* option, none of the initialization files are read.

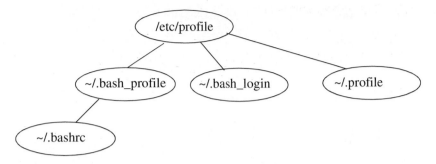

Figure 11.2 Order of processing initialization files.

EXAMPLE 11.3

```
(Sample /etc/profile)
# /etc/profile
# Systemwide environment and startup programs
# Functions and aliases go in /etc/bashrc

1   PATH="$PATH:/usr/X11R6/bin"
2   PS1="[\u@\h \W]\\$ "

3   ulimit -c 1000000    ——— core file limit
4   if [ `id -gn` = `id -un` -a `id -u` -gt 14 ]; then
5       umask 002
    else
        umask 022
    fi

6   USER=`id -un`
7   LOGNAME=$USER
8   MAIL="/var/spool/mail/$USER"

9   HOSTNAME=`/bin/hostname`
10  HISTSIZE=1000
11  HISTFILESIZE=1000
12  export PATH PS1 HOSTNAME HISTSIZE HISTFILESIZE USER LOGNAME MAIL

13  for i in /etc/profile.d/*.sh ; do
14      if [ -x $i ]; then
15          . $i
        fi
16  done

17  unset i #
```

EXPLANATION

1   The *PATH* variable is assigned locations where the shell should search for commands.

2   The primary prompt is assigned. It will be displayed in the shell window as the user's name (\u),the @ symbol, the host machine (\W), and a dollar sign.

3   The *ulimit* command (a shell built-in command) is set to limit the maximum size of core files created to 1,000,000 bytes. Core files are memory dumps of programs that have crashed, and they take up a lot of disk space.

4   This line reads, *if the user's group name is equal to the user's name and the user's ID number is greater than 14... (see 5)*

5   Then set the *umask* to 002. When directories are created they will get 775 permissions and files will get 664 permissions. Otherwise, the *umask* is set to 022, giving 755 to directories and 644 to files.

6   The *USER* variable is assigned the username (*id –un*).

7   The *LOGNAME* variable is set to the value in *$USER*.

8   The *MAIL* variable is assigned the path to the mail spooler where the user's mail is saved.

9   The *HOSTNAME* variable is assigned the name of the user's host machine.

10   The *HISTSIZE* variable is set to *1000*. *HISTSIZE* controls the number of history items that are remembered (from the history list stored in the shell's memory) and saved in the history file after the shell exits.

11   The *HISTFILESIZE* is set to limit the number of commands stored in the history file to *1000*, i.e., the history file is truncated after it reaches 1,000 lines. (See "History" on page 632.)

12   These variables are exported so that they will be available in subshells and child processes.

13   For each file (ending in .*sh*) in the *etc/profile.d* directory... (see 14)

14   Check to see if the file is executable, and if it is... (see 15)

15   Execute (source) the file with the dot command. The files in the */etc/profile.d* directory: *lang.sh* and *mc.sh*, respectively, set the character and font sets and create a function called *mc* that starts up a visual/browser file manager program called *Midnight Commander*. To see how the file manager works, type *mc* at the *bash* prompt.

16   The *done* keyword marks the end of the *for* loop.

17   The variable *i* is *unset*, i.e., removed from shell's name space. The value of *i* is whatever was assigned to it while in the *for* loop, if anything was assigned at all.

The ~/.bash_profile File.   If the ~/.bash_profile is found in the user's home directory, it is sourced after the /etc/profile. If ~/.bash_profile doesn't exist, bash will look for another user-defined file, ~./bash_login, and source it, and if ~./bash_login doesn't exist, it will source the ~/.profile, if it exists. Only one of the three files (~/.bash_profile, ~/.bash_login, or ~/.profile) will be sourced. *Bash* will also check to see if the user has a .bashrc file and then source it.

EXAMPLE 11.4

```
(Sample .bash_profile)

    # .bash_profile
    # The file is sourced by bash only when the user logs on.

    # Get the aliases and functions
1   if [ -f ~/.bashrc ]; then
2           . ~/.bashrc
    fi

    # User-specific environment and startup programs

3   PATH=$PATH:$HOME/bin
4   ENV=$HOME/.bashrc       # or BASH_ENV=$HOME/.bashrc
5   USERNAME="root"

6   export USERNAME ENV PATH
7   mesg n
8   if [ $TERM = linux ]
    then
            startx    # Start the X Window system
    fi
```

EXPLANATION

1   *If* there is a file called *.bashrc* in the user's home directory... (see 2)
2   Execute (source) the *.bashrc* file for the login shell.
3   The *PATH* variable is appended with a path to the user's *bin* directory, normally the place where shell scripts are stored.
4   The *BASH_ENV*[a] (*ENV*) file is set to the pathname for the *.bashrc* file, an initialization file that will be sourced for interactive *bash* shells and scripts only if the *BASH_ENV* (*ENV*) variable is set. The *.bashrc* file contains user-defined aliases and functions.
5   The variable *USERNAME* is set to *root*.
6   The variables are exported so that they are available to subshells and other processes will know about them.
7   The *mesg* command is executed with the *n* option, disallowing others to write to the terminal.
8   If the value of the *TERM* variable is *linux*, then *startx* will start the X window system (the graphical user interface allowing multiple virtual consoles), rather than starting an interactive session in the Linux console window. Because the *~/.bash_profile* is only sourced when you log in, the login shell would be the best place to start up your X windows session.

---

a.   *BASH_ENV* is used by versions of *bash* starting at 2.0.

See p. 453 for aliases↗

The *BASH_ENV* (*ENV*) Variable.   Before *bash* version 2.0, the *BASH_ENV* file was simply called the *ENV* file (same as in Korn shell). The *BASH_ENV* (*ENV*) variable is set in the ~/.*bash_profile*. It is assigned the name of a file that will be executed every time an interactive *bash* shell or *bash* script is started. The *BASH_ENV* (*ENV*) file will contain special *bash* variables and aliases. The name is conventionally .*bashrc*, but you can call it anything you want. The *BASH_ENV* (*ENV*) file is not processed when the privileged option is on (*bash –p* or *set –o privileged*) or the – *–norc* command line option is used (*bash –norc* or *bash – –norc* [*bash 2.x +*]).

The .*bashrc* File.   The *BASH_ENV* (*ENV*) variable is assigned (by convention) the name .*bashrc*. This file is automatically sourced every time a new or interactive *bash* shell or *bash* script starts. It contains settings that pertain only to the *bash* shell.

EXAMPLE   11.5

```
(Sample .bashrc)
# If the .bashrc file exists, it is in the user's home directory.
# It contains aliases (nicknames for commands) and user-defined
# functions.

# .bashrc
# User-specific aliases and functions


1   set -o vi
2   set -o noclobber
3   set -o ignoreeof
4   alias rm='rm -i'
    alias cp='cp -i'
    alias mv='mv -i'
5   stty erase ^h
    # Source global definitions
6   if [ -f /etc/bashrc ]; then
        . /etc/bashrc
    fi
7   case "$-" in
8      *i*) echo This is an interactive bash shell
            ;;
9      *)   echo This shell is noninteractive
            ;;
    esac
10  history_control=ignoredups

11  function cd { builtin cd $1; echo $PWD; }
```

EXPLANATION

1 The *set* command with the *–o* switch turns on or off special built-in options. (See "The set –o Options" on page 610.) If the switch is *–o*, a minus sign, the option is turned on, and if a plus sign, the option is turned off. The *vi* option allows interactive command line editing. For example, *set –o vi* turns on interactive command-line editing, whereas *set vi +o* turns it off. (See Table 11.1 on page 610.)

2 The *noclobber* option is turned on, which prevents the user from overwriting files when using redirection; e.g., *sort filex > filex*. (See "Standard I/O and Redirection" on page 697.)

3 When exiting a shell, normally you can type ^D (Control-D). With *ignoreeof* set, you must type *exit*.

4 The alias for *rm*, *rm –i*, causes *rm* to be interactive (*–i*), i.e., it will ask the user if it's OK to remove files before actually removing them.The alias for the *cp*, *cp –i*, command causes the copy to be interactive.

5 The *stty* command is used to set the terminal backspace key to erase. ^H represents the Backspace key.

6 If a file called */etc/bashrc* exists, source it.

7 If the shell is interactive, the special variable, $–, will contain an *i*. If not, you are probably running a script. The *case* command evaluates $–.

8 If the value returned from $– matches *i*, i.e., any string containing an *i*, then the shell prints *This is an interactive shell.*

9 Otherwise, the shell prints *This shell is noninteractive.* If you start up a script, or a new shell at the prompt, you will be able to tell whether or not your shell is interactive. It is only here to let you test your understanding of the terms "interactive" and "noninteractive" shell.

10 The *history_control* setting is used to control how commands are saved in the history file. This line says, *Don't save commands in the history file if they're already there.*; i.e., ignore duplicates.

11 This is a user-defined function. When the user changes directories, the present working directory, *PWD*, is printed. The function is named *cd* and contains within its definition, the command *cd*. The special built-in command, called *builtin*, precedes the *cd* command within the function definition to prevent the function from going into an infinite recursion; i.e., from calling itself indefinitely.

The */etc/bashrc* File. Systemwide functions and aliases can be set in the */etc/bashrc* file. The primary prompt is often set here.

```
(Sample /etc/bashrc)

    # Systemwide functions and aliases
    # Environment stuff goes in /etc/profile

    # For some unknown reason bash refuses to inherit
    # PS1 in some circumstances that I can't figure out.
    # Putting PS1 here ensures that it gets loaded every time.

1   PS1="[\u@\h \W]\\$ "

2   alias which="type -path"
```

EXPLANATION

1   Systemwide functions and aliases are set here. The primary *bash* prompt is set to the name of the user (\u), and @ symbol, the host machine (\h), the basename of the current working directory, and a dollar sign. (See Table 11.2 on page 616.) This prompt will appear for all interactive shells.

2   Aliases, nicknames for commands, are usually set in the user's *.bashrc* file. The alias was preset and is available when *bash* starts up. You use it when you want to find out where a program resides on disk; i.e., what directory it is found in; e.g., *which ls* will print */bin/ls*.

The ~/.profile File.   The *.profile* file is a user-defined initialization file. It is found in the user's home directory, and sourced once at login if running *sh* (Bourne shell). If running *bash, .profile* will be run if *bash* cannot find any other of the initialization files listed above. It allows a user to customize and modify his shell environment. Environment and terminal settings are normally put here, and if a window application or database application is to be initiated, it is started here.

EXAMPLE 11.7

```
(Sample .profile)
# A login initialization file sourced when running as sh or the
#.bash_profile or .bash_login are not found.
1    TERM=xterm
2    HOSTNAME=`uname -n`
3    EDITOR=/bin/vi
4    PATH=/bin:/usr/ucb:/usr/bin:/usr/local:/etc:/bin:/usr/bin:.
5    PS1="$HOSTNAME $ > "
6    export TERM HOSTNAME EDITOR PATH PS1
7    stty erase ^h
8    go () { cd $1; PS1=`pwd`; PS1=`basename $PS1`; }
9    trap '$HOME/.logout' EXIT
10   clear
```

EXPLANATION

1   The *TERM* variable is assigned the value of the terminal type, *xterm*.

2   Because the *uname –n* command is enclosed in backquotes, the shell will perform command substitution, i.e., the output of the command (the name of the host machine) will be assigned to the variable *HOSTNAME*.

3   The *EDITOR* variable is assigned */bin/vi*. Programs such as *mail* and *history* will now have this variable available when defining an editor.

4   The *PATH* variable is assigned the directory entries that the shell searches in order to find a UNIX program. If, for example, you type *ls*, the shell will search the *PATH* until it finds that program in one of the listed directories. If it never finds the program, the shell will tell you so.

5   The primary prompt is assigned the value of *HOSTNAME*, the machine name, and the $ and > symbols.

6   All of the variables listed are exported. They will be known by child processes started from this shell.

7   The *stty* command sets terminal options. The Erase key is set to ^H, so that when you press the Backspace key, the letter typed preceding the cursor is erased.

8   A function called *go* is defined. The purpose of this function is to take one argument, a directory name, *cd* to that directory, and set the primary prompt to the present working directory. The *basename* command removes all but the last entry of the path. The prompt will show you the current directory.

9   The *trap* command is a signal handling command. When you exit the shell, that is, log out, the *.logout* file will be executed. The *.logout* file is a user-defined file containing commands that will be executed just before logging out, commands that will clean up temp files or log the time of log out, etc.

10 The *clear* command clears the screen.

The ~/.bash–logout File.   When the user logs out (exits the login shell), if a file called ~/.bash_logout exists, it is sourced. This file normally contains commands to clean up temporary files, truncate the history file, record the time of logout, etc.

Options to Prevent Startup Files from Being Executed.   If *bash* is invoked with the − −*noprofile* option (e.g., *bash − −noprofile*), then the */etc/profile, ~/.bash_profile, ~/.bash_login*, or *~/.profile* startup files will not be sourced.

   If invoked with the *–p* option (e.g., *bash –p*), *bash* will not read the user's *~/.profile* file.

   If *bash* is invoked as *sh* (Bourne shell), it tries to mimic the behavior of the Bourne shell as closely as possible. For a login shell, it attempts to source only */etc/profile* and *~/.profile*, in that order. The *–noprofile* option may still be used to disable this behavior. If the shell is invoked as *sh,* it does not attempt to source any other startup files.

The .inputrc File.   Another default initalization file, *.inputrc*, is also read when *bash* starts up. This file, if it exists in the user's home directory, contains variables to custom-ize keystroke behavior and settings that bind strings, macros, and control functions to keys. The names for the key bindings and what they do are found in the Readline library, a library that is used by applications that manipulate text. The bindings are used partic-ularly by the built-in *emacs* and *vi* editors, when performing command line editing. (See "Command Line Editing" on page 641 for more on *readline*.)

11.1.4 Setting *bash* Options with the Built-In *set* and *shopt* Commands

The set –o Options.   The *set* command can take options when the *–o* switch is used. Options allow you to customize the shell environment. They are either on or off, and are normally set in the *BASH_ENV (ENV)* file. Many of the options for the *set* command are set with an abbreviated form. For example, *set –o noclobber* can also be written, *set –C.* (See Table 11.1.)

Table 11.1   The Built-In *set* Command Options

Name of Option	*Shortcut Switch*	*What It Does*
allexport	*–a*	Automatically marks new or modified variables for export from the time the option is set, until unset.
braceexpand	*–B*	Enables brace expansion, and is a default setting.
emacs		For command line editing, uses the *emacs* built-in editor, and is a default setting.
errexit	*–e*	If a command returns a nonzero exit status (fails), exits. Not set when reading initialization files.

Table 11.1 The Built-In *set* Command Options (continued)

Name of Option	*Shortcut Switch*	*What It Does*
histexpand	–H	Enables ! and !! when performing history substitution, and is a default setting.
history		Enables command line history; on by default.
ignoreeof		Disables EOF (Control-D) from exiting a shell; must type exit. Same as setting shell variable, *IGNOREEOF=10*.
keyword	–k	Places keyword arguments in the environment for a command.
interactive-comments		For interactive shells, a leading # is used to comment out any text remaining on the line.
monitor	–m	Allows job control.
noclobber	–C	Protects files from being overwritten when redirection is used.
noexec	–n	Reads commands, but does not execute them. Used to check the syntax of scripts. Not on when running interactively.
noglob	–d	Disables pathname expansion; i.e., turns off wildcards.
notify	–b	Notifies user when background job finishes.
nounset	–u	Displays an error when expanding a variable that has not been set.
onecmd	–t	Exit after reading and executing one command.
physical	–P	If set, does not follow symbolic links when typing *cd* or *pwd*. The physical directory is used instead.
posix		Shell behavior is changed if the default operation doesn't match the POSIX standard.
privileged	–p	When set, the shell does not read the *.profile* or *ENV* file and shell functions are not inherited from the environment; automatically set for *setuid* scripts.
posix		Change the default behavior to POSIX 1003.2.
verbose	–v	Turns on the *verbose* mode for debugging.
vi		For command line editing, uses the *vi* built-in editor.
xtrace	–x	Turns on the echo mode for debugging.

FORMAT

```
set -o option  # Turns on the option.
set +o option  # Turns off the option.
set -[a-z]  # Abbreviation for an option; the minus turns it on.
set +[a-z]  # Abbreviation for an option; the plus turns it off.
```

EXAMPLE 11.8

```
1   set -o allexport
2   set +o allexport
3   set -a
4   set +a
```

EXPLANATION

1   Sets the *allexport* option. This option causes all variables to be automatically exported to subshells.

2   Unsets the *allexport* option. All variables will now be local in the current shell.

3   Sets the *allexport* option. Same as 1. Not every option has an abbreviation. (See Table 11.1.)

4   Unsets the *allexport* option. Same as 2.

EXAMPLE 11.9

```
1 $ set -o
  braceexpand      on
  errexit          off
  hashall          on
  histexpand       on
  keyword          off
  monitor          on
  noclobber        off
  noexec           off
  noglob           off
  notify           off
  nounset          off
  onecmd           off
  physical         off
  privileged       off
  verbose          off
  xtrace           off
```

EXAMPLE 11.9 (CONTINUED)

```
   history         on
   ignoreeof       off
   interactive-comments on
   posix           off
   emacs           off
   vi              on

2  $ set -o noclobber
3  $ date > outfile
4  $ ls > outfile
   bash: outfile: Cannot clobber existing file.
5  $ set +o noclobber
6  $ ls > outfile
7  $ set -C
```

EXPLANATION

1   With the *–o* option, the set command lists all the options currently set or not set.

2   To set an option, the *–o* option is used. The *noclobber* option is set. It protects you from overwriting files when using redirection. Without *noclobber*, the file to the right of the > symbol is truncated if it exists, and created if it doesn't exist.

3   The output of the UNIX *date* command is redirected to a file called *outfile*.

4   This time, the *outfile* exists. By attempting to redirect the output of *ls* to *outfile*, the shell complains that the file already exists. Without *noclobber* set, it would be clobbered.

5   With the *+o* option to the set command, *noclobber* is turned off.

6   This time, trying to overwrite *outfile* is fine because *noclobber* is no longer set.

7   Using the *–C* switch to the *set* command is an alternate way of turning on *noclobber*. *+C* would turn it off.

The *shopt* Built-In (Version 2.x+).   The *shopt* (*shell options*) built-in command is used in newer versions of *bash* as an alternative to the *set* command. In many ways *shopt* duplicates the *set* built-in command, but it adds more options for configuring the shell. See Table 11.27 on page 712 for a list of all the *shopt* options. In the following example, *shopt* with the *–p* option prints all the available options settings. The *–u* switch indicates an unset option and *–s* indicates one that is currently set.

EXAMPLE 11.10

```
1   $ shopt -p
    shopt -u cdable_vars
    shopt -u cdspell
    shopt -u checkhash
    shopt -u checkwinsize
    shopt -s cmdhist
    shopt -u dotglob
    shopt -u execfail
    shopt -s expand_aliases
    shopt -u extglob
    shopt -u histreedit
    shopt -u histappend
    shopt -u histverify
    shopt -s hostcomplete
    shopt -u huponexit
    shopt -s interactive_comments
    shopt -u lithist
    shopt -u mailwarn
    shopt -u nocaseglob
    shopt -u nullglob
    shopt -s promptvars
    shopt -u restricted_shell
    shopt -u shift_verbose
    shopt -s sourcepath

2   $ shopt -s cdspell
3   $ shopt -p cdspell
    shopt -s cdspell
4   $ cd /hame
    /home
5   $ pwd
    /home
6   $ cd /ur/lcal/ban
    /usr/local/man
7   $ shopt -u cdspell
8   $ shopt -p cdspell
    shopt -u cdspell
```

EXPLANATION

1. With the –*p* (print) option, the *shopt* command lists all settable shell options and their current values, either set (–*s*) or unset (–*u*).

2. With the –*s* option, *shopt* sets (or turns on) an option. The *cdspell* option causes the shell to correct minor spelling errors on directory names given as arguments to the *cd* command. It will correct simple typos, insert missing letters, and even transpose letters if it can.

3. With the –*p* option and the name of the option, *shopt* indicates whether the option is set. The option has been set (–*s*).

EXPLANATION (CONTINUED)

4   In this example, the user tries to *cd* to his home directory, but misspells *home*. The shell fixes the spelling; i.e., *hame* becomes *home*. The directory is changed to */home*.

5   The output of the *pwd* command displays the current working directory, showing that the directory was really changed even though the user spelled it wrong.

6   This time the directory name is missing letters and has a misspelling for the last entry, *ban*. The shell makes a pretty good attempt to spell out the correct pathname by inserting the missing letters, and correcting *ban* to *man*. Because the *b* in *ban* is the first misspelled character, the shell searches in the directory for an entry that might end with *a* and *n*. It finds *man*.

7   With the *–u* switch[a], *shopt* unsets (or turns off) the option.

8   With the *–p* switch and the name of the option, *shopt* indicates whether the option is set. The *cdspell* option has been unset (*–u*).

a. The words switch or option are interchangeable. They are arguments to a command that contain a leading dash.

11.1.5 The Prompts

When used interactively, the shell prompts you for input. When you see the prompt, you know that you can start typing commands. The *bash* shell provides four prompts: the primary prompt is a dollar sign ($), and the secondary prompt is a right angle bracket symbol (>). The third and fourth prompts, *PS3* and *PS4* respectively, will be discussed later. The prompts are displayed when the shell is running interactively. You can change these prompts.

The variable *PS1* is set to a string containing the primary prompt. Its value, the dollar sign, appears when you log on and waits for user input, normally a UNIX command. The variable *PS2* is the secondary prompt, initially set to the right angle bracket character (>). It appears if you have partially typed a command and then pressed Enter. You can change the primary and secondary prompts.

The Primary Prompt.   The dollar sign (or *bash* $) is the default primary prompt. You can change your prompt. Normally prompts are defined in */etc/bashrc* or the user initialization file, *.bash_profile*, or *.profile* (Bourne shell).

EXAMPLE 11.11

```
1   $ PS1="$(uname -n) > "
2   chargers >
```

EXPLANATION

1   The default primary prompt is a dollar sign (*bash $*). The *PS1* prompt is being re-set to the name of the machine[a] (*uname –n*) and a > symbol.

2   The new prompt is displayed.

a.   The command, *uname –n*, is executed because it is enclosed in a set of parentheses preceded by a dollar sign. An alternative would be to enclose the command in backquotes. See "Command Substitution" on page 686.)

Setting the Prompt with Special Escape Sequences.   By inserting special backslash/escape sequences into the prompt string, you can customize the prompts. Table 11.2 lists the special sequences.

Table 11.2   Prompt String Settings

Backslash Sequence	What It Evaluates To
\t	The current time in HH:MM:SS format.
\d	The date in "Weekday Month Date" format (e.g., Tue May 26).
\n	Newline.
\s	The name of the shell, the basename of $0 (the portion following the final slash).
\w	The current working directory.
\W	The basename of the current working directory.
\u	The username of the current user.
\h	The hostname.
\#	The command number of this command.
\!	The history number of this command.
\$	If the effective UID is 0, a #, otherwise a $.
\nnn	The character corresponding to the octal number *nnn*.
\\	Backslash.
\[	Begin a sequence of nonprinting characters; could be used to embed a terminal control sequence into the prompt.
\]	End a sequence of nonprinting characters.

Table 11.2 Prompt String Settings (continued)

Backslash Sequence	What It Evaluates To
New in bash Version 2.x+:	
\a	The ASCII bell character.
\@	The current time in 12-hour AM/PM format.
\H	The hostname.
\T	The current time in 12-hour format: HH:MM:SS.
\e	The ASCII escape character (033).
\v	The version of *bash*, e.g., 2.03.
\V	The release and pathlevel of *bash*; e.g., 2.03.0.

EXAMPLE 11.12

```
1   $  PS1="[\u@\h \W]\\$ "
    [ellie@homebound ellie]$

2   $  PS1="\W:\d> "
    ellie:Tue May 18>
```

EXPLANATION

1   You customize the primary *bash* prompt using special backslash/escape sequences. \u evaluates to the user's login name, \h to the host machine, and \W is the basename for the current working directory. There are two backslashes. The first backslash escapes the second backslash, resulting in \$. The dollar sign is protected from shell interpretation and thus printed literally.

2   The primary prompt is assigned \W, the escape sequence evaluating to the basename of the current working directory, and \d, the escape sequence evaluating to today's date.

The Secondary Prompt.   The *PS2* variable is assigned a string called the secondary prompt. Its value is displayed to standard error, which is the screen by default. This prompt appears when you have not completed a command or more input is expected. The default secondary prompt is >.

EXAMPLE 11.13

```
1   $ echo "Hello
2   > there"
3   Hello
    there
4   $


5   $ PS2="----> "
6   $ echo 'Hi
7   ------>
    ------>
    ------> there'
      Hi

    there
      $

8 $ PS2="\s:PS2 > "
  $ echo 'Hello
  bash:PS2 > what are
  bash:PS2 > you
  bash:PS2 > trying to do?
  bash:PS2 > '
  Hello
  what are
  you
  trying to do?
$
```

EXPLANATION

1   The double quotes must be matched after the string "*Hello*.

2   When a newline is entered, the secondary prompt appears. Until the closing double quotes are entered, the secondary prompt will be displayed.

3   The output of the *echo* command is displayed.

4   The primary prompt is displayed.

5   The secondary prompt is reset.

6   The single quote must be matched after the string '*Hi*.

7   When a newline is entered, the new secondary prompt appears. Until the closing single quote is entered, the secondary prompt will be displayed.

8   The *PS2* prompt is set to the name of the shell (\s) followed by a string consisting of a colon, *PS2* and >, followed by a space.

The Search Path. *Bash* uses the *PATH* variable to locate commands typed at the command line. The path is a colon-separated list of directories used by the shell when searching for commands. The default path is system-dependent, and is set by the administrator who installs *bash*. The path is searched from left to right. The dot at the end of the path represents the current working directory. If the command is not found in any of the directories listed in the path, the shell sends to standard error the message *filename: not found*. The path is normally set in the *.bash_profile* if running the *bash shell* or *.profile* file if using *sh,* the Bourne shell.

   If the dot is not included in the path and you are executing a command or script from the current working directory, the name of the script must be preceded with a *./*, such as *./program_name,* so that shell can find the program.

EXAMPLE 11.14

```
(Printing the PATH)
1   $ echo $PATH
    /usr/gnu/bin:/usr/local/bin:/usr/ucb:/bin:/usr/bin:.

(Setting the PATH)
2   $ PATH=$HOME:/usr/ucb:/usr:/usr/bin:/usr/local/bin:
3   $ export PATH
4   $ runit
    bash: runit: command not found
5   $ ./runit
    < program starts running here >
```

EXPLANATION

1   By echoing $PATH, the value of the *PATH* variable is displayed. The path consists of a list of colon-separated elements and is searched from left to right. The dot at the end of the path represents the user's current working directory.

2   To set the path, a list of colon-separated directories are assigned to the *PATH* variable. Note that in this path, the dot is not at the end of the path, perhaps as a security measure.

3   By exporting the path, child processes will have access to it. It is not necessary to export the PATH on a separate line: It could be written as follows: *export PATH=$HOME:/usr/ucb:/bin:.,* etc., on the same line.

4   Because the dot is not in the search path, when the *runit* program is executed in the present working directory, *bash* can't find it.

5   Because the program name is preceded with a dot and a slash (*./*), the shell will be able to find it, and execute it, if it is the current working directory.

The *hash* Command.   The *hash* command controls the internal hash table used by the shell to improve efficiency in searching for commands. Instead of searching the path each time a command is entered, the first time you type a command, the shell uses the search path to find the command, and then stores it in a table in the shell's memory. The next time you use the same command, the shell uses the *hash* table to find it. This makes it much faster to access a command than having to search the complete path. If you know that you will be using a command often, you can add the command to the *hash* table. You can also remove commands from the table. The output of the *hash* command displays the number of times the shell has used the table to find a command (*hits*) and the full pathname of the command. The *hash* command with the *–r* option clears the hash table. An argument of – – disables option checking for the rest of the arguments. Hashing is automatically implemented by *bash*. Although you can turn it off, if there isn't any compelling reason to do so, don't.

LIKE TRACKED ALIASES IN KSH & POSIX

EXAMPLE   11.15

```
(Printing the PATH)

(Command line)
1   hash
    hits     command
    1        /usr/bin/mesg
    4        /usr/bin/man
    2        /bin/ls


2   hash -r
3   hash
    No commands in hash table

4   hash find
    hits     command
    0        /usr/bin/find
```

EXPLANATION

1   The *hash* command displays the full pathname of commands that have been executed in this login session.(Built-in commands are not listed) The number of hits is the number of times the *hash* table has been used to find the command.

2   The *–r* option to the *hash* command erases all remembered locations in the *hash* table.

3   After the *–r* option was used in the last command, the *hash* command reports that there are no commands currently in the table.

4   If you know you are going to use a command often, you can add it to the *hash* table by giving it as an argument to the *hash* command. The *find* command has been added. The table has zero hits because the command hasn't been used yet.

The *source* or *dot* Command. The *source* command (from the C shell) is a built-in *bash* shell command. The *dot* command, simply a period, (from the Bourne shell) is another name for *source*. Both commands take a scriptname as an argument. The script will be executed in the environment of the current shell; that is, a child process will not be started. All variables set in the script will become part of the current shell's environment. Likewise, all variables set in the current shell will become part of the script's environment. The *source* (or *dot*) command is normally used to reexecute any of the initialization files, e.g., *.bash_profile*, *.profile*, etc, if they have been modified. For example, if one of the settings, such as the *EDITOR* or *TERM* variable, has been changed in the *.bash_profile* since you logged on, you can use the *source* command to reexecute commands in the *.bash_profile* without logging out and then logging back on. A file, such as *.bash_profile*, or for that matter any shell script, does not need execute permissions to be sourced with either the *dot* or the *source* commands.

EXAMPLE 11.16

```
$ source .bash_profile
$ . .bash_profile
```

EXPLANATION

The *source or dot* command executes the initialization file, *.bash_profile*, within the context of the current shell. Local and global variables are redefined within this shell. The *dot* command makes it unnecessary to log out and then log back in again after the file has been modified.[a]

---

a. If the *.bash_profile* were executed directly as a script, a child shell would be started. Then the variables would be set in the child shell, and when the child shell exited, the parent shell would not have any of the settings available to it.

11.1.6 The Command Line

After you log on, the *bash* shell displays its primary prompt, a dollar sign by default. The shell is your command interpreter. When the shell is running interactively, it reads commands from the terminal and breaks the command line into words. A command line consists of one or more words (or tokens), separated by whitespace (blanks and/or tabs), and terminated with a newline, generated by pressing the Enter key. The first word is the command, and subsequent words are the command's arguments. The command may be a UNIX executable program such as *ls* or *date*, a user-defined function, a built-in command such as *cd* or *pwd*, or a shell script. The command may contain special characters, called metacharacters, which the shell must interpret while parsing the command line. If a command line is too long, the backslash character, followed by a newline, will allow you to continue typing on the next line. The secondary prompt will appear until the command line is terminated.

The Order of Processing Commands. The first word on the command line is the command to be executed. The command may be a keyword, an alias, a function, a special built-in command or utility, an executable program, or a shell script. The command is executed according to its type in the following order:

1. Aliases

2. Keywords (such as *if, function, while, until*)

3. Functions

4. Built-in commands

5. Executables and scripts

Special built-in commands and functions are defined within the shell, and therefore are executed from within the context of the current shell, making them much faster in execution. Scripts and executable programs such as *ls* and *date* are stored on disk, and the shell, in order to execute them, must first locate them within the directory hierarchy by searching the *PATH* environment variable; the shell then forks a new shell that executes the script. To find out the type of command you are using—i.e., a built-in command, an alias, a function, or an executable, etc.—use the built-in *type* command. (See Example 11.17.)

EXAMPLE 11.17

```
$ type pwd
pwd is a shell builtin
$ type test
test is a shell builtin
$ type clear
clear is /usr/bin/clear
$ type m
m is aliased to 'more'
$ type bc
bc is /usr/bin/bc
$ type if
if is a shell keyword
$ type -path cal
/usr/bin/cal
$ type which
which is aliased to 'type -path'
$ type greetings
greetings is a function
greetings ()
{
        echo "Welcome to my world!";
}
```

Built-In Commands and the *help* Command.   Built-in commands are commands that are part of the internal source code for the shell. They are built-in and readily available to the shell, whereas commands such as *date, cal,* and *finger* are compiled binary programs that reside on the disk. There is less overhead in executing a built-in because it involves no disk operations. Built-in commands are executed by the shell before the programs on disk. *Bash* has added a new online help system so that you can see all the built-ins, or a description for a particular built-in; *help* itself is a built-in command. See Table 11.28 on page 714 for a complete list of built-in commands.

EXAMPLE   11.18

```
1   $ help help
    help: help [pattern ...]
    Display helpful information about built-in commands. if PATTERN
    is specified, gives detailed help on all commands matching
    PATTERN, otherwise a list of the built-ins is printed.


2   $ help pw
    pwd: pwd
        Print the current working directory.
```

Changing the Order of Command Line Processing.   *Bash* provides three built-in commands that can override the order of command line processing: *command, builtin,* and *enable.*

The *command* built-in eliminates aliases and functions from being looked up in the order of processing. Only built-ins and executables, found in the search path, will be processed.

The *builtin* command looks up only built-ins, ignoring functions and executables found in the path.

The *enable* built-in command turns built-ins on and off. By default, built-ins are enabled. Disabling a built-in allows an executable command found on the disk to be to be executed without specifying a full pathname, even if it has the same name as a built-in. (In normal processing, *bash* searches for built-ins before disk executable commands.) Built-ins become disabled by using the *–n* switch. For example, a classic confusion for new shell programmers is naming a script *test.* Because *test* is a built-in command, the shell will try to execute it rather than the user's script (a built-in is normally executed before any executable program). By typing: *enable –n test,* the *test* built-in is disabled, and the user's script will take precedence.

Without options, the *enable* built-in prints a list of all the built-ins. Each of the following built-ins are described in "Shell Built-In Commands" on page 714.

EXAMPLE 11.19

```
1    $ enable
     enable .
     enable :
     enable [
     enable alias
     enable bg
     enable bind
     enable break
     enable builtin
     enable cd
     enable command
     enable continue
     enable declare
     enable dirs
        . . . . .
     enable read
     enable readonly
     enable return
     enable set
     enable shift
     enable shopt
        . . . . .
     enable type
     enable typeset
     enable ulimit
     enable umask
     enable unalias
     enable unset
     enable wait


2    enable -n test

3    function cd { builtin cd; echo $PWD; }
```

EXPLANATION

1 The *enable* built-in, without any options, displays a complete list of all *bash* shell built-in commands. This example shows just part of that list.

2 With the *–n* switch, the *test* built-in command is disabled. Now, you execute your script named *test* without worrying about the built-in *test* being executed instead. It's not good practice to name a script by the same name as an operating system command, because if you try to run the same script in another shell, the disabling of built-ins doesn't exist.

3 The function is called *cd*. The *builtin* command causes the *cd* within the function definition to be called instead of the function *cd*, which would cause an endless recursive loop.

The Exit Status. After a command or program terminates, it returns an exit status to the parent process. The exit status is a number between 0 and 255. By convention, when a program exits, if the status returned is zero, the command was successful in its execution. When the exit status is nonzero, the command failed in some way. If a command is not found by the shell, the exit status returned is 127. If a fatal signal causes the command to terminate, the exit status is 128 plus the value of the signal that caused it to die.

The shell status variable, ?, is set to the value of the exit status of the last command that was executed. Success or failure of a program is determined by the programmer who wrote the program.

EXAMPLE 11.20

```
1   $ grep ellie /etc/passwd
    ellie:MrHJEFd2YpkJY:501:501::/home/ellie:/bin/bash
2   $ echo $?
    0

3   $ grep nicky /etc/passwd
4   $ echo $?
    1

5   $ grep ellie /junk
    grep: /junk: No such file or directory
6   $ echo $?
    2

7   $ grip ellie /etc/passwd
    bash: grip: command not found
8   $ echo $?
    127

9   $ find /  name core 'C     User presses Control-C
10  $ echo $?
    130
```

EXPLANATION

1. The *grep* program searches for the pattern *ellie* in the */etc/passwd* file and is successful. The line from */etc/passwd* is displayed.

2. The *?* variable is set to the exit value of the *grep* command. Zero indicates successful status.

3. The *grep* program cannot find user *nicky* in the */etc/passwd* file.

4. The *grep* program cannot find the pattern; the *?* variable return value is nonzero. An exit status of *1* indicates failure.

5. The *grep* fails because the */junk* file cannot be opened. The *grep* error message is sent to standard error, the screen.

6 If *grep* cannot find the file, it returns an exit status of 2.

7 The *grip* command is not found by the shell.

8 Because the command is not found, the exit status, *127*, is returned.

9 The find command is interrupted when the *SIGINT* signal is sent by pressing Control-C. The signal number for Ctrl-C is 2.

10 The status returned from a process that has been killed is 128 + the number of the signal; i.e., 128 + 2.

Multiple Commands at the Command Line. A command line can consist of multiple commands. Each command is separated by a semicolon, and the command line is terminated with a newline. The exit status is that of the last command in the chain of commands.

EXAMPLE 11.21

```
$ ls; pwd; date
```

EXPLANATION

The commands are executed from left to right, one after the other, until the newline is reached.

Grouping Commands. Commands may also be grouped so that all of the output is either piped to another command or redirected to a file.

EXAMPLE 11.22

```
$ ( ls; pwd; date ) > outputfile
```

EXPLANATION

The output of each of the commands is sent to the file called *outputfile*. The spaces inside the parentheses are necessary.

Conditional Execution of Commands. With conditional execution, two command strings are separated by the special metacharacters, double ampersands (*&&*) and double vertical bars (||). The command on the right of either of these metacharacters will or will not be executed based on the exit condition of the command on the left.

EXAMPLE 11.23

```
$ cc prgm1.c -o prgm1 && prgm1
```

EXPLANATION

If the first command is successful (has a zero exit status), the command after the *&&* is executed; i.e., if the *cc* program can successfully compile *prgm1.c*, the resulting executable program, *prgm1*, will be executed.

EXAMPLE 11.24

```
$ cc prog.c >& err || mail bob < err
```

EXPLANATION

If the first command fails (has a nonzero exit status), the command after the || is executed; i.e., if the *cc* program cannot compile *prog.c*, the errors are sent to a file called *err*, and user *bob* will be mailed the *err* file.

Commands in the Background.   Normally, when you execute a command, it runs in the foreground, and the prompt does not reappear until the command has completed execution. It is not always convenient to wait for the command to complete. When you place an ampersand (*&*) at the end of the command line, the shell will return the shell prompt immediately and execute the command in the background concurrently. You do not have to wait to start up another command. The output from a background job will be sent to the screen as it processes. Therefore, if you intend to run a command in the background, the output of that command might be redirected to a file or piped to another device, such as a printer, so that the output does not interfere with what you are doing.

The *!* variable contains the PID number of the last job put in the background. (See "Job Control" on page 628 for more on background processing.)

EXAMPLE 11.25

```
1   $ man sh | lp&
2   [1] 1557
3   $ kill -9 $!
```

EXPLANATION

1   The output of the *man* command (the manual pages for the UNIX command) is
    piped to the printer. The ampersand at the end of the command line puts the job
    in the background.

2   There are two numbers that appear on the screen: the number in square brackets
    indicates that this is the first job to be placed in the background; the second num-
    ber is the PID, or the process identification number of this job.

3   The shell prompt appears immediately. While your program is running in the
    background, the shell is waiting for another command in the foreground. The *!*
    variable evaluates to the PID of the job most recently put in the background. If
    you get it in time, you will kill this job before it goes to the print queue.

11.1.7 Job Control

Job control is a powerful feature of the *bash* shell that allows you to selectivly run programs, called *jobs*, in the background or foreground. A running program is called a process or a job and each process has a process ID number, called the PID. Normally, a
command typed at the command line is running in the foreground and will continue
until it has finished unless you send a signal by pressing Ctrl-C or Ctrl-\ to terminate it.
With job control you can send a job to the background and let it keep running; you can
stop a job by pressing Ctrl-Z, which sends the job to the background and suspends it;
you can cause a stopped job to run in the background; you can bring a background job
back to the foreground; and you can even kill the jobs you have running in the background or foreground. For a list of job commands, see Table 11.3 on page 630.

By default, job control is already set (some older versions of UNIX do not support this
feature). If disabled, it can be reset by any one of the following commands:

FORMAT

```
set -m            # set job control in the .bashrc file
set -o monitor    # set job control in the .bashrc file
bash -m -i        # set job control when invoking interactive bash
```

EXAMPLE 11.26

```
1   $ vi
    [1]+  Stopped     vi

2   $ sleep 25&
    [2] 4538

3   $ jobs
    [2]+  Running     sleep 25&
    [1]-  Stopped        vi
```

EXAMPLE   11.26 (CONTINUED)

```
4   $ jobs -l
    [2]+ 4538    Running       sleep 25&
    [1]- 4537    Stopped       vi


5   $ jobs %%
    [2]+ 4538    Running       sleep 25&


6   $ fg %1


7   $ jobs -x echo %1
    4537


8   $ kill %1          # or  kill 4537
    [1]+    Stopped      vi
    Vim: Caught deadly signal TERM
    Vim: Finished.
    [1]+    Exit 1       vi
```

EXPLANATION

1   After the vi editor is invoked, you can press ^Z (Control-Z) to suspend the vi session. The editor will be suspended in the background, and after the message *Stopped* appears, the shell prompt will appear immediately.

2   The ampersand at the end of the command causes the *sleep* command, with an argument of 25, to execute in the background. The notation [2] means that this is the second job to be run in the background and the PID of this job is 4538.

3   The *jobs* command displays the jobs currently in the background.

4   The *jobs* command with the –l option displays the processes (jobs) running in the background and the PID numbers of those jobs.

5   The %% argument causes *jobs* to display the most recent command put in the job table.

6   The *fg* command followed by a percent sign and the job number will bring that numbered job into the foreground. Without a number, *fg* brings the most recently backgrounded job back into the foreground.

7   The –x option can be used to print just the PID number of the job. %1 refers to the vi session that was stopped in the first example.

8   The *kill* command sends a *TERM* signal to the process and kills it. The vi program is killed. You can specify either the job number or the PID number as arguments to the *kill* command.

Table 11.3 Job Control Commands

Command	Meaning
jobs	Lists all the jobs running.
^Z (Ctrl-Z)	Stops (suspends) the job; the prompt appears on the screen.
bg	Starts running the stopped job in the background.
fg	Brings a background job to the foreground.
stop	Suspends a background job.
stty tostop	Suspends a background job if it sends output to the terminal.
kill	Sends the *kill* signal to a specified job.
wait [n]	Waits for a specified job and returns its exit status, where *n* is a PID or job number.

Argument to jobs command	Represents
%n	Job number *n*.
%sting	Job name starting with string.
%?string	Job name containing string.
%%	Current job.
%+	Current job.
%−	Previous job, before current job.
−r	Lists all running jobs.
−s	Lists all suspended jobs.

New *jobs* Options.   Two new options were added to the *jobs* command in *bash* versions 2.x. They are the *−r* and *−s* options. The *−r* option lists all running jobs, and the *−s* option lists all stopped jobs.

The *disown* Built-In.   The *disown* built-in command (*bash* 2.x) removes a specified job from the job table. After the job has been removed, the shell will no longer recognize it as a viable job process and it can only be referenced by its process ID number.

11.2 **Command Line Shortcuts**

11.2.1 Command and Filename Completion

To save typing, *bash* implements command and filename completion, a mechanism that allows you to type part of a command or filename, press the Tab key, and the rest of the word will be completed for you.

If you type the first letters in a command and press the Tab key, *bash* will attempt to complete the command and execute it. If *bash* cannot complete the filename or command, because neither exists, the terminal may beep and the cursor will stay at the end of the command. If there is more than one command starting with those characters and you press the Tab key a second time, all commands that start with those characters will be listed.

If there are several files starting with the same letters, *bash* will complete the shortest name that matches, expand out the filename until the characters differ, and then flash the cursor for you to complete the rest.

EXAMPLE 11.27

```
1   $ ls
    file1 file2 foo foobarckle fumble

2   $ ls fu[tab]        # Expands to filename to fumble

3   $ ls fx[tab]        # Terminal beeps, nothing happens

4   $ ls fi[tab]        # Expands to file_  (_ is a cursor)

5   $ ls fi[tab][tab]   # Lists all possibilities
    file1 file2

6   $ ls foob[tab]      # Expands to foobarckle

7   $ da[tab]           # Completes the date command
    date
    Tue Feb 28 18:53:40 PST 2001

8   $ ca[tab][tab]      # Lists all commands starting with ca
    cal    captoinfo  case   cat
```

EXPLANATION

1   All files are listed for the current working directory.
2   After *fu* is typed, the Tab key is pressed, causing the spelling of the filename to be completed to *fumble*, and listed.

EXPLANATION (CONTINUED)

3   Because none of the files start with *fx*, the terminal beeps and the cursor remains but does nothing. (The terminal may not beep if that feature has been disabled.)

4   There are a number of files starting with *fi*; the filenames are completed until the letters are no longer the same. If another Tab key is pressed, all files with that spelling are listed.

5   By pressing two Tab keys, a list of all files beginning with *file* is printed.

6   When the Tab key is pressed, the filename is expanded to *foobarckle*.

7   When the Tab key is pressed after *da*, the only command that begins with *da* is the *date* command. The command name is expanded and executed.

8   When the Tab key is pressed after *ca*, nothing happens because more than one command starts with *ca*. Pressing the Tab key twice lists all commands starting with *ca*.

11.2.2 History

The history mechanism keeps a history list, a numbered record of the commands that you have typed at the command line. During a login session, the commands you type are stored in the the shell's memory in a history *list* and then appended to the history *file* when you exit. You can recall a command from the history list and reexecute it without retyping the command. The *history* built-in command displays the history list. The default name for the history file is *.bash_history,* and it is located in your home directory.

When *bash* starts accessing the history file, the *HISTSIZE* variable specifies how many commands can be copied from the history file into the history list. The default size is 500. The *HISTFILE* variable specifies the name of the command history file (*~/.bash_history* is the default) where commands are stored. If unset, the command history is not saved when an interactive shell exits.

The history file grows from one login session to the next. The *HISTFILESIZE* variable controls the maximum number of lines contained in the history file. When this variable is assigned a value, the history file is truncated when it surpasses that number of lines. The default size is 500.

The *fc −l* command can be used to display or edit commands in the history list.

Table 11.4 History Variables

FCEDIT	The pathname of the UNIX editor that uses the *fc* command.
HISTCMD	The history number, or index in the history list, of the current command. If HISTCMD is unset, it loses its special properties, even if it is subsequently reset.
HISTCONTROL	If set to a value of *ignorespace*, lines that begin with a space character are not entered on the history list. If set to a value of *ignoredups*, lines matching the last history line are not entered. A value of *ignoreboth* combines the two options. If unset, or if set to any other value than those above, all lines read by the parser are saved on the history list.
HISTFILE	Specifies file in which to store command history. The default value is ~/.bash_history. If unset, the command history is not saved when an interactive shell exits.
HISTFILESIZE	The maximum number of lines contained in the history file. When this variable is assigned a value, the history file is truncated, if necessary, to contain no more than that number of lines. The default value is 500.
HISTIGNORE	A colon-separated list of patterns used to decide which command lines should be saved on the history list. Each pattern is anchored to the beginning of the line and consists of normal shell pattern matching characters. An & can be used in the pattern causing the *history* command to ignore duplicates; e.g., *ty??:&* would match for any command line starting with *ty* followed by two characters, and any duplicates of that command. Those commands would not be placed in the history list.
HISTSIZE	The number of commands to remember in the command history. The default value is 500.

11.2.3 Accessing Commands from the History File

The Arrow Keys.   To access commands from the history file, you can use the arrow keys on the keyboard to move up and down through the history file, and from left to right. You can edit any of the lines from the history file by using the standard keys for deleting, updating, backspacing, etc. As soon as you have edited the line, pressing the Enter key will cause the command line to be reexecuted.

Table 11.5 The Arrow Keys

↑	Up arrow moves up the history list.
↓	Down arrow moves down the history list.
→	Right arrow moves cursor to right on *history* command.
‹	Left arrow moves left on *history* command.

The *history* Built-In Command.   The *history* built-in command displays the history of commands typed preceded by an event number.

EXAMPLE   11.28

```
1   $ history
    982   ls
    983   for i in 1 2 3
    984   do
    985   echo $i
    986   done
    987   echo $i
    988   man xterm
    989   adfasdfasdfadfasdfasdfadfasdfasdf
    990   id -gn
    991   id -un
    992   id -u
    993   man id
    994   more /etc/passwd
    995   man ulimit
    996   man bash
    997   man baswh
    998   man bash
    999   history
    1000  history
```

EXPLANATION

1   The built-in *history* command displays a list of numbered commands from the history list. Any lines listed with an * have been modified.

The *fc* Command.   The *fc* command, also called the *fix* command, can be used in two ways: (1) to select commands from the history list, and (2) to edit the commands in either the *vi* or *emacs* editor, or for that matter, any editor on your system.

In the first form, *fc* with the *–l* option can select specific lines or ranges of lines from the history list. When the *–l* switch is on, the output goes to the screen. For example, *fc –l*, the default, prints the last 16 lines from the history list, *fc –l 10* selects lines numbered 10 through the end of the list, and *fc –l –3* selects the last three lines. The *–n* switch turns off the numbering of commands in the history list. With this option on, you could select a range of commands and redirect them to a file, which in turn could be executed as a shell script. The *–r* switch reverses the order of the commands.

The second form of *fc* is described in "Command Line Editing" on page 641.

Table 11.6 The *fc* Command

fc *Argument*	*Meaning*
–e editor	Puts history list into editor.
–l n–m	Lists commands in range from *n* to *m*.
–n	Turns off numbering of history list.
–r	Reverses the order of the history list.
–s string	Accesses command starting with string.

EXAMPLE 11.29

```
1   $ fc -l
    4        ls
    5        history
    6        exit
    7        history
    8        ls
    9        pwd
    10       clear
    11       cal 2000
    12       history
    13       vi file
    14       history
    15       ls -l
    16       date
    17       more file
    18       echo a b c d
    19       cd
    20       history
2   $ fc -l -3
    19       cd
    20       history
    21       fc -l
3   $ fc -ln
             exit
             history
             ls
             pwd
             clear
             cal 2000
             history
             vi file
             history
             ls -l
```

EXAMPLE 11.29 (CONTINUED)

```
            date
            more file
            echo a b c d
            cd
            history
            fc -l
            fc -l -3
```

4 $ **fc -ln -3 > saved**

5 $ **more saved**
```
            fc -l
            fc -l -3
            fc -ln
```
6 $ **fc -l 15**
```
    15          ls -l
    16          date
    17          more file
    18          echo a b c d
    19          cd
    20          history
    21          fc -l
    22          fc -l -3
    23          fc -ln
    24          fc -ln -3 > saved
    25          more saved
    26          history
```
7 $ **fc -l 15 20**
```
    15          ls -l
    16          date
    17          more file
    18          echo a b c d
    19          cd
    20          history
```

EXPLANATION

1   *fc –l* selects the last 16 commands from the history list.

2   *fc –l –3* selects the last three commands from the history list.

3   *fc* with the *–ln* options prints the history list without line numbers.

4   The last three commands, without line numbers, from the history list are redirected to a file called *saved*.

5   The contents of the file *saved* are displayed.

6   Commands from the history list, starting at number 15, are listed.

7   Commands numbered 15 through 20 are displayed.

If *fc* is given the –*s* option, a string pattern can be used to reexecute a previous command; e.g., *fc* –*s rm* will cause the most previous line containing the pattern *rm* to be reexecuted. To emulate the Korn shell's *redo* command, you can create a *bash* alias called *r*, e.g., *alias r='fc –s'* so that if you type *r vi* at the command line, the last history item containing that pattern will be reexecuted; in this case, the *vi* editor will be started just as it was the last time it started, including any arguments passed.

EXAMPLE   11.30

```
1   $ history
    1    ls
    2    pwd
    3    clear
    4    cal 2000
    5    history
    6    ls -l
    7    date
    8    more file
    9    echo a b c d

2   $ fc -s da
    date
    Thu Jul  15 12:33:25 PST 2001

3   $ alias r="fc -s"
4   $ date +%T
    18:12:32

5   $ r d
    date +%T
    18:13:19
```

EXPLANATION

1   The built-in *history* command displays the history list.

2   *fc* with the –*s* option searches for the last command that began with string *da*. The *date* command is found in the history list and is reexecuted.

3   An alias (a user-defined nickname) called *r* is assigned the command *fc* –*s*. This means that any time *r* is typed at the command line, it will be substituted with *fc* –*s*.

4   The *date* command is executed. It will print the current time.

5   The alias is used as a shortcut to the *fs* –*s* command. The last command beginning with a *d* is reexecuted.

Reexecuting History Commands (bang! bang!). To reexecute a command from the history list, the exclamation point (called bang) is used. If you type two exclamation points (*!!*) *bang, bang,* the last command in the history list is reexecuted. If you type an exclamation point, followed by a number, the command listed by that number is reexecuted. If you type an exclamation point and a letter or string, the last command that started with that letter or string is reexecuted. The caret (^) is also used as a shortcut method for editing the previous command. See Table 11.7 for a complete list of history substitution characters.

Table 11.7 Substitution and History

Event Designator	Meaning
!	Indicates the start of history substitution.
!!	Reexecutes the previous command.
!N	Reexecutes the Nth command from the history list.
!–N	Reexecutes the Nth command back from present command.
!string	Reexecutes the last command starting with *string*.
!?string?	Reexecutes the last command containing *string*.
!?string?%	Reexecutes the most recent command line argument from the history list containing *string*.
!$	Uses the last argument from the last history command in the current command line.
!! string	Appends string to the previous command and executes.
!N string	Appends string to Nth command in history list and executes.
!N:s/old/new/	In previous Nth command, substitutes the first occurrence of old string with new string.
!N:gs/old/new/	In previous Nth command, globally substitutes old string with new string.
*^old^new^*	In last *history* command, substitutes old string with new string.
command !N:wn	Executes current command appending an argument (*wn*) from the Nth previous command. *Wn* is a number starting at 0, 1, 2, ... designating the number of the word from the previous command; word *0* is the command itself, and *1* is its first argument, etc. (See Example 11.32.)

EXAMPLE 11.31

```
1   $ date
    Mon Jul  12 12:27:35 PST 2001


2   $ !!
    date
    Mon Jul  12 12:28:25 PST 2001


3   $ !106
    date
    Mon Jul  12 12:29:26 PST 2001


4   $ !d
    date
    Mon Jul  12 12:30:09 PST 2001


5   $ dare
    dare: Command not found.


6   $ ^r^t
    date
    Mon Jul  12 12:33:25 PST 2001
```

EXPLANATION

1   The UNIX *date* command is executed at the command line. The history list is updated. This is the last command on the list.

2   The *!!* (bang bang) gets the last command from the history list; the command is reexecuted.

3   Command number 106 from the history list is reexecuted.

4   The last command on the history list that started with the letter *d* is reexecuted.

5   The command is mistyped. It should be *date*, not *dare*.

6   The carets are used to substitute letters from the last command on the history list. The first occurrence of an *r* is replaced with a *t*; i.e., *dare* becomes *date*.

EXAMPLE 11.32

```
1   $ ls  file1 file2 file3
    file1 file2 file3

    $ vi !:1
    vi file1

2   $ ls file1 file2 file
    file1 file2 file3

    $ ls !:2
    ls file2
    file2

3   $ ls file1 file2 file3
    $ ls  !:3
    ls file3
    file3

4   $ echo a b c
    a b c
    $ echo !$
    echo c
    c

5   $ echo a b c
    a b c
    $ echo !^
    echo a
    a

6   % echo a b c
    a b c
    % echo !*
    echo a b c
    a b c

7   % !!:p
    echo a b c
```

EXPLANATION

1   The *ls* command lists *file1*, *file2*, and *file3*. The history list is updated. The command line is broken into words, starting with word number zero. If the word number is preceded by a colon, that word can be extracted from the history list. The *!:1* notation means, *get the first argument from the last command on the history list and replace it in the command string.* The first argument from the last command is *file1*. (Word *0* is the command itself.)

EXPLANATION (CONTINUED)

2   The *!:2* is replaced with the second argument of the last command, *file2*, and given as an argument to *ls*. *file2* is printed. (*file2* is the third word.)

3   *ls !:3* reads, *go to the last command on the history list and get the fourth word (words start at zero) and pass it to the* ls *command as an argument.* (*file3* is the fourth word.)

4   The bang (*!*) with the dollar sign (*$*) refers to the last argument of the last command on the history list. The last argument is *c*.

5   The caret (*^*) represents the first argument after the command. The bang (*!*) with the *^* refers to the first argument of the last command on the history list. The first argument of the last command is *a*.

6   The asterisk (***) represents all arguments after the command. The *!* with the *** refers to all of the arguments of the last command on the history list.

7   The last command from the history list is printed but not executed. The history list is updated. You could now perform caret substitutions on that line.

Command Line Editing.   The *bash* shell provides two built-in editors, *emacs* and *vi*, that allow you to interactively edit your history list. When you use the editing features at the command line, whether in *vi* or *emacs* mode, the *readline* functions determine which keys will perform certain functions. For example, if using *emacs*, Ctrl-P allows you to scroll upward in the command line history, whereas if using *vi*, the K key moves upward through the history list. *Readline* also controls the arrow keys, cursor movement, changing, deleting, inserting text, and redoing or undoing corrections. Another feature of *readline* is the completion feature previously discussed in "Command and Filename Completion" on page 631. This allows you to type part of a command, filename, or variable, and then, by pressing the Tab key, the rest of the word is completed. There are many more features provided by the Readline library designed to help manipulate text at the command line.

The *emacs* built-in editor is the default built-in editor and is modeless, whereas the *vi* built-in editor works in two modes, one to execute commands on lines and the other to enter text. If you use UNIX, you are probably familiar with at least one of these editors. To enable the *vi* editor, add the *set* command listed below[5] and put this line in your *~/.bashrc* file. To set *vi*, type what's shown in the following example, at either the prompt or in the *~/.bashrc* file.

---

5.   If the set *–o* (editor) has not been set, but the *EDITOR* variable has been set to either *emacs* or *vi*, then bash will use that definition.

EXAMPLE 11.33

```
set -o vi
```

EXPLANATION

Sets the built-in *vi* editor for command line editing of the history list.

To switch to the *emacs* editor, type:

EXAMPLE 11.34

```
set -o emacs
```

EXPLANATION

Sets the built-in *emacs* editor for command line editing of the history list.

The *vi* Built-In Editor.   To edit the history list, go to the command line and press the Esc key. Then press the *K* key if you want to scroll upward in the history list, and the *J* key[6] to move downward, just like standard *vi* motion keys. When you find the command that you want to edit, use the standard keys that you would use in *vi* for moving left and right, deleting, inserting, and changing text. (See Table 11.8.) After making the edit, press the Enter key. The command will be executed and added to the bottom of the history list.

Table 11.8   *vi* Commands

Command	Function
Moving Through the History File:	
Esc k *or* +	Move up the history list.
Esc j *or* –	Move down the history list.
G	Move to first line in history file.
5G	Move to fifth command in history file for *string*.
/string	Search upward through history file.
?	String search downward through history file.

---

6. *vi* is case-sensitive; an uppercase *J* and a lowercase *j* are different commands.

Table 11.8   *vi* Commands (continued)

Command	Function
Moving Around on a Line:	
h	Move left on a line.
l	Move right on a line.
b	Move backward a word.
e *or* w	Move forward a word.
^ *or* 0	Move to beginning of first character on the line.
$	Move to end of line.
Editing with vi:	
a A	Append text.
i I	Insert text.
dd dw x	Delete text into a buffer (line, word, or character).
cc C	Change text.
u U	Undo.
yy Y	Yank (copy a line into buffer).
p P	Put yanked or deleted line down below or above the line.
r R	Replace a letter or any amount of text on a line.

The *emacs* Built-In Editor.   If using the *emacs* built-in editor, like *vi*, start at the command line. To start moving upward through the history file, press ^P. To move down, press ^N. Use *emacs* editing commands to change or correct text, then press Enter and the command will be reexecuted. See Table 11.9.

Table 11.9   *emacs* Commands

Command	Function
Ctrl-P	Move up history file.
Ctrl-N	Move down history file.
Ctrl-B	Move backward one character.
Ctrl-R	Search backward for string.
Esc B	Move backward one word.
Ctrl-F	Move forward one character.

Table 11.9 *emacs* Commands (continued)

Command	Function
Esc F	Move forward one word.
Ctrl-A	Move to the beginning of the line.
Ctrl-E	Move to the end of the line.
Esc <	Move to the first line of the history file.
Esc >	Move to the last line of the history file.

Editing with emacs:

Command	Function
Ctrl-U	Delete the line.
Ctrl-Y	Put the line back.
Ctrl-K	Delete from cursor to the end line.
Ctrl-D	Delete a letter.
Esc D	Delete one word forward.
Esc H	Delete one word backward.
Esc space	Set a mark at cursor position.
Ctrl-X Ctrl-X	Exchange cursor and mark.
Ctrl-P Ctrl-Y	Push region from cursor to mark into a buffer (Ctrl-P) and put it down (Ctrl-Y).

FCEDIT and Editing Commands.   If the *fc* command is given the *−e* option followed by the name of a UNIX editor, that editor is invoked containing history commands selected from the history list; e.g., *fc −e vi −1 −3* will invoke the *vi* editor, create a temporary file in */tmp*, with the last three commands from the history list in the *vi* buffer. The commands can be edited or commented out. (Preceding the command with a # will comment it.) If the user quits the editor, the commands will all be echoed and executed.[7]

If the editor name is not given, the value of the *FCEDIT* variable is used (typically set in the initialization files, either *bash_profile* or *.profile*), and the value of the *EDITOR* variable is used if *FCEDIT* is not set. When editing is complete, and you exit the editor, all of the edited commands are echoed and executed.

---

7. Whether the user saves and quits the editor, or simply quits the editor, the commands will all be executed, unless they are commented or deleted.

EXAMPLE 11.35

```
1   $ FCEDIT=/bin/vi
2   $ pwd
3   $ fc
< Starts up the full screen vi editor with the pwd command on line 1>
```

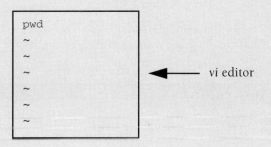

```
4   $ history
    1 date
    2 ls -l
    3 echo "hello"
    4 pwd

5   $ fc -3 -1       # Start vi, edit, write/quit, and execute
                     # last 3 commands.
```

EXPLANATION

1　The *FCEDIT* variable can be assigned the pathname for any of the UNIX text editors you have on your system, such as *vi*, *emacs*, etc. If not set, the *vi* editor is the default.

2　The *pwd* command is typed at the command line. It will be placed in the *history* file.

3　The *fc* command caused the editor (set in *FCEDIT*) to be invoked with the last command typed in the editor window. After the user writes and quits the editor, any commands typed there will be executed.

4　The *history* command lists recently typed commands.

5　The *fc* command is used to start up the editor with the last three commands from the *history* file in the editor's buffer.

11.2.4 Aliases

An *alias* is a *bash* user-defined abbreviation for a command. Aliases are useful if a command has a number of options and arguments or the syntax is difficult to remember. Aliases set at the command line are not inherited by subshells. Aliases are normally set in the *.bashrc* file. Because the *.bashrc* is executed when a new shell is started, any aliases set there will be reset for the new shell. Aliases may also be passed into shell scripts but will cause potential portability problems unless they are set directly within the script.

Listing Aliases. The *alias* built-in command lists all set aliases. The alias is printed first, followed by the real command or commands it represents.

EXAMPLE 11.36

```
$ alias
alias co='compress'
alias cp='cp -i'
alias mroe='more'
alias mv='mv -i'
alias ls='ls --colorztty'
alias uc='uncompress'
```

EXPLANATION

The *alias* command lists the alias (nickname) for the command and the real command the alias represents after the = sign.

Creating Aliases. The *alias* command is used to create an alias. The first argument is the name of the alias, the nickname for the command. The rest of the line consists of the command or commands that will be executed when the alias is executed. *Bash* aliases cannot take arguments (see "Defining Functions" on page 693). Multiple commands are separated by a semicolon, and commands containing spaces and metacharacters are surrounded by single quotes.

EXAMPLE 11.37

```
1   $ alias m=more
2   $ alias mroe=more
3   $ alias lF='ls -alF'
4   $ alias r='fc -s'
```

EXPLANATION

1   The nickname for the *more* command is set to *m*.

2   The alias for the *more* command is set to *mroe*. This is handy if you can't spell.

3   The alias definition is enclosed in quotes because of the whitespace. The alias *lF* is a nickname for the command *ls –alF.*

4   The alias *r* will be used instead of *fc –s* to recall commands from the history list by a specified pattern; e.g., *r vi* will reexecute the last command in the history list containing the pattern *vi*.

Deleting Aliases.   The *unalias* command is used to delete an alias. To temporarily turn off an alias, precede the alias name by a backslash.

EXAMPLE 11.38

```
1   $ unalias mroe
2   $ \ls
```

EXPLANATION

1   The *unalias* command deletes the alias *mroe* from the list of defined aliases.

2   The alias *ls* is temporarily turned off for this execution of the command only.

11.2.5 Manipulating the Directory Stack

If you find that as you work, you *cd* up and down the directory tree into many of the same directories, you can make it easy to access those directories by pushing them onto a directory stack and manipulating the stack. The *pushd* built-in command pushes directories onto a stack and the *popd* command removes them. (See Example 11.39.) The stack is a list of directories with the directory at the left being the most recent directory pushed onto the stack. The directories can be listed with the built-in *dirs* command.

The *dirs* Built-In Command.   The built-in command *dirs*, with a –l option, displays the directory stack with each of its directories in full pathname format; without an option, *dirs* uses a tilde to denote the home directory. With a +n option, *dirs* displays the *nth* directory entry counting from the left in the directory list, starting at 0. With –n option, it does the same thing, but starts at the right-hand side of the directory list with 0.

The *pushd* and *popd* Commands.   The *pushd* command, with a directory as an argument, causes the new directory to be added to the directory stack and, at the same time, changes to that directory. If the argument is a +n where n is a number, *pushd* rotates the stack so that the nth directory from the stack, starting at the left-hand side, is pushed onto the top of the stack. With a –*n* option, it does the same thing but starts at the right-hand side. Without arguments, *pushd* exchanges the top two elements of the directory stack, making it easy to switch back and forth between directories.

   The *popd* command removes a directory from the top of the stack, and changes to that directory. With +*n*, where *n* is a number, *popd* removes the *n*th entry, starting at the left of the list shown by *dirs*.

EXAMPLE   11.39

```
1   $ pwd
    /home/ellie

    $ pushd ..
    /home  ~

    $ pwd
    /home

2   $ pushd          # Swap the two top directories on the stack
    ~  /home

    $ pwd
    /home/ellie

3   $ pushd perlclass
    ~/perlclass   ~   /home

4   $ dirs
    ~/perlclass  ~  /home

5   $ dirs -l
    /home/ellie/perlclass /home/ellie   /home

6   $ popd
    ~/home

    $ pwd
    /home/ellie

7   $ popd
    /home

    $ pwd
    /home

8   $ popd
    bash: popd: Directory stack empty.
```

EXPLANATION

1   First the *pwd* command displays the present working directory, */home/ellie*. Next the *pushd* command with .. as its argument, pushes the parent directory (..) onto the directory stack. The output of *pushd* indicates that */home* is at the top of the directory stack (starting at the left-hand side of the displayed list) and the user's home directory, represented by the tilde character (~) is at the bottom of the stack. *pushd* also changes the directory to the one that was pushed onto the stack; i.e., .. which translates to */home*. The new directory is displayed with the second *pwd* command.

2   *Pushd*, without arguments, exchanges the two top directory entries on the stack and changes to the swapped directory; in this example, the directory is switched back to the user's home directory, */home/ellie*.

3   The *pushd* command will push its argument, *~/perlclass*, onto the stack, and change to that directory.

4   The built-in *dirs* command displays the directory stack, with the top level starting at left-hand side of the listing. The tilde expands to the user's home directory.

5   With the *–l* option, *dirs* list displays the directory stack with full pathnames instead of using tilde expansion.

6   The *popd* command removes a directory from the top of the stack, and changes to that directory.

7   The *popd* command removes another directory from the top of the stack, and changes to that directory.

8   The *popd* command cannot remove any more directory entries because the stack is empty, and issues an error message saying so.

11.2.6   Metacharacters (Wildcards)

Metacharacters are special characters used to represent something other than themselves. Shell metacharacters are called *wildcards*. Table 11.10 lists metacharacters and what they do.

Table 11.10   Metacharacters

Metacharacter	Meaning
\	Literally interprets the following character.
&	Processes in the background.
;	Separates commands.
$	Substitutes variables.
?	Matches for a single character.

Table 11.10   Metacharacters (continued)

Metacharacter	Meaning
[abc]	Matches for one character from a set of characters; e.g., a, b, or c.
[!abc]	Matches for one character *not* from the set of characters; e.g., not a, b, or c.
*	Matches for zero or more characters.
(cmds)	Executes commands in a subshell.
{cmds}	Executes commands in current shell.

11.2.7 Filename Substitution (Globbing)

When evaluating the command line, the shell uses metacharacters to abbreviate filenames or pathnames that match a certain set of characters. The filename substitution metacharacters listed in Table 11.11 are expanded into an alphabetically listed set of filenames. The process of expanding the metacharacter into filenames is also called *filename substitution,* or *globbing.* If a metacharacter is used and there is no filename that matches it, the shell treats the metacharacter as a literal character.

Table 11.11   Shell Metacharacters and Filename Substitution

Metacharacter	Meaning
*	Matches zero or more characters.
?	Matches exactly one character.
[abc]	Matches one character in the set a, b, or c.
[!abc]	Matches one character not in the set, not a, b, or c.
{a,ile,ax}	Matches for a character or set of characters.
[! a–z]	Matches one character *not* in the range from a to z.
\	Escapes or disables the metacharacter.

The Asterisk.   The asterisk is a wildcard that matches for zero or more of any characters in a filename.

EXAMPLE 11.40

```
1   $ ls  *
    abc abc1 abc122 abc123 abc2 file1 file1.bak file2 file2.bak none
    nonsense nobody nothing nowhere one
2   $ ls  *.bak
    file1.bak file2.bak
3   $ echo a*
    ab abc1 abc122 abc123 abc2
```

EXPLANATION

1   The asterisk expands to all of the files in the present working directory. All of the files are passed as arguments to *ls* and displayed.

2   All files starting with zero or more characters and ending with *.bak* are matched and listed.

3   All files starting with *a*, followed by zero or more characters, are matched and passed as arguments to the *echo* command.

The Question Mark.   The question mark represents a single character in a filename. When a filename contains one or more question marks, the shell performs filename substitution by replacing the question mark with the character it matches in the filename.

EXAMPLE 11.41

```
1   $ ls
    abc    abc122   abc2    file1.bak   file2.bak   nonsense   nothing   one
    abc1   abc123   file1   file2   none   noone   nowhere

2   $ ls a?c?
    abc1 abc2

3   $ ls ??
    ls: ??: No such file or directory

4   $ echo  abc???
    abc122 abc123

5   $ echo ??
    ??
```

EXPLANATION

1   The files in the current directory are listed.

2   Filenames starting with *a*, followed by a single character, followed by *c* and a single character, are matched and listed.

3   Filenames containing exactly two characters are listed, if found. Because there are not any two-character files, the question marks are treated as a literal filename. Such a file is not found, and the error message is printed.

4   Filenames starting with *abc* and followed by exactly three characters are expanded and displayed by the *echo* command.

5   There are no files in the directory that contain exactly two characters. The shell treats the question mark as a literal question mark if it cannot find a match.

The Square Brackets.   The brackets are used to match filenames containing *one* character in a set or range of characters.

EXAMPLE 11.42

```
1   $ ls
    abc abc122 abc2 file1.bak file2.bak nonsense nothing
    one abc1 abc123 file1 file2 none noone nowhere

2   $ ls abc[123]
    abc1   abc2

3   $ ls abc[1-3]
    abc1   abc2

4   $ ls [a-z][a-z][a-z]
    abc one

5   $ ls [!f-z]???
    abc1   abc2

6   $ ls abc12[23]
    abc122 abc123
```

EXPLANATION

1   All of the files in the present working directory are listed.

2   All filenames containing four characters are matched and listed if the filename starts with *abc*, followed by *1*, *2*, or *3*. Only one character from the set in the brackets is matched.

EXPLANATION (CONTINUED)

3   All filenames containing four characters are matched and listed, if the filename starts with *abc* and is followed by a number in the range from *1* to *3*.

4   All filenames containing three characters are matched and listed, if the filename contains exactly three lowercase alphabetic characters.

5   All filenames containing four characters are listed if the first character is *not* a letter between *f* and *z* (*[!f–z]*, followed by three of any characters, where *?* represents a single character.

6   Files are listed if the filenames contain *abc12* followed by *2* or *3*.

Brace Expansion. The curly braces match for any of a list of comma-separated strings. Normally the strings are filenames. Any characters prepended to the opening curly brace are called the *preamble*, and any characters appended to the closing curly brace are called the *postamble*. Both the *preamble* and *postamble* are optional. There can be no unquoted whitespace within the braces.

EXAMPLE 11.43

```
1   $ ls
    a.c b.c abc ab3 ab4 ab5 file1 file2 file3 file4 file5 foo
    faa fumble

2   $ ls f{oo,aa,umble}
    foo faa fumble

3   $ ls a{.c,c,b[3-5]}
    a.c ab3 ab4 ab5

4   $ mkdir /usr/local/src/bash/{old,new,dist,bugs}

5   $ chown root /usr/{ucb/{ex,edit},lib/{ex?.?*,how_ex}}

6   $ echo fo{o, um}*
    fo{o, um}*

7   $ echo {mam,pap,ba}a
    mama papa baa

8   $ echo post{script,office,ure}
    postscript postoffice posture
```

EXPLANATION

1   All the files in the current directory are listed.

2   Files starting with *f* and followed by the strings *oo, aa,* or *umble* are listed. Spaces inside the curly braces will cause the error message *Missing }*.

3   Files starting with *a* followed by *.c, c,* or *b3, b4,* or *b5* are listed. (The square brackets can be used inside the curly braces.)

4   Four new directories will be made in */usr/local/src/bash: old, new, dist,* and *bugs*.

5   Root ownership will be given to files, *ex* and *edit,* in directory */usr /ucb* and to files named *ex* followed by one character, a period, and at least one more character, and a file called *how_ex* in directory */usr/lib*.

6   Brace expansion will not occur if there are any unquoted spaces within the braces.

7   Brace expansion does not necessarily always cause expansion of filenames. In this example the postamble *a* is added to each of the strings within the curly braces and echoed back after the expansion.

8   The preamble is the string *post,* followed by a comma-separated list enclosed within braces. Brace expansion is performed and the resulting strings are displayed.

Escaping Metacharacters.   To use a metacharacter as a literal character, use the backslash to prevent the metacharacter from being interpreted.

EXAMPLE 11.44

```
1   $ ls
    abc file1 youx


2   $ echo How are you?
    How are youx


3   $ echo How are you\?
    How are you?


4   $ echo  When does this line \
    > ever end\?
    When does this line ever end?
```

EXPLANATION

1   The files in the present working directory are listed. (Note the file *youx*.)

EXPLANATION (CONTINUED)

2   The shell will perform filename expansion on the *?*. Any files in the current directory starting with *y-o-u* and followed by exactly one character are matched and substituted in the string. The filename *youx* will be substituted in the string to read *How are youx* (probably not what you wanted to happen).

3   By preceding the question mark with a backslash, it is escaped, meaning that the shell will not try to interpret it as a wildcard.

4   The newline is escaped by preceding it with a backslash. The secondary prompt is displayed until the string is terminated with a newline. The question mark (*?*) is escaped to protect it from filename expansion.

Tilde and Hyphen Expansion.   The tilde character was adopted by the *bash* shell (from the C shell) for pathname expansion. The tilde by itself evaluates to the full pathname of the user's home directory.[8] When the tilde is appended with a username, it expands to the full pathname of that user.

When the plus sign follows the tilde, the value of the *PWD* (present working directory) replaces the tilde. The tilde followed by the hyphen character is replaced with the previous working directory; *OLDPWD* also refers to the previous working directory.

EXAMPLE 11.45

```
1   $ echo ~
    /home/jody/ellie

2   $ echo ~joe
    /home/joe

3   $ echo ~+
    /home/jody/ellie/perl

4   $ echo ~-
    /home/jody/ellie/prac

5   $ echo $OLDPWD
    /home/jody/ellie/prac

6   $ cd -
    /home/jody/ellie/prac
```

---

8.   The tilde character will not be expanded if enclosed in either double or single quotes.

EXPLANATION

1   The tilde evaluates to the full pathname of the user's home directory.

2   The tilde preceding the username evaluates to the full pathname of *joe's* home directory.

3   The ~+ notation evaluates to the full pathname of the working directory.

4   The ~– notation evaluates to the previous working directory.

5   The *OLDPWD* variable contains the previous working directory.

6   The hyphen refers to the previous working directory; *cd* to go to the previous working directory and display the directory.

Controlling Wildcards (Globbing).   If the *bash noglob* variable is set or if the *set* command is given a *–f* option, filename substitution, called globbing, is turned off, meaning that all metacharacters represent themselves; they are not used as wildcards. This can be useful when searching for patterns containing metacharacters in programs like *grep, sed*, or *awk*. If globbing is not set, all metacharacters must be escaped with a backslash to turn off wildcard interpretation.

   The built-in *shopt* command (*bash* versions 2.x) also supports options for controlling globbing.

EXAMPLE 11.46

```
1   $ set noglob  or  set -f

2   $ print * ?? [] ~ $LOGNAME
    * ?? [] /home/jody/ellie ellie

3   $ unset noglob  or  set +f

4   $ shopt -s dotglob    # Only available in bash versions 2.x

5   $ echo *bash*
    .bash_history .bash_logout .bash_profile .bashrc bashnote
    bashtest
```

EXPLANATION

1   The *–f* option is given as an argument to the *set* command. It turns off the special meaning of wildcards used for filename expansion.

2   The filename expansion metacharacters are displayed as themselves without any interpretation. Note that the tilde and the dollar sign are still expanded, because they are not used for filename expansion.

3   If either *noglob* is <u>unset</u> or the *+f* option is set, filename metacharacters <u>will be expanded</u>.

EXPLANATION (CONTINUED)

4   The *shopt* built-in allows you to set options for the shell. The *dotglob* option allows filenames to be matched with globbing metacharacters, even if they start with a dot. Normally the files starting with a dot are invisible and not recognized when performing filename expansion.

5   Because the *dotglob* option was set in line 4, when the wildcard * is used for filename expansion, the filenames starting with a dot are also expanded if the filename contains the pattern *bash*.

Extended Filename Globbing (*bash 2.x*).   Derived from Korn shell pattern matching, *bash 2.x* has included this extended functionality, allowing regular expression-type syntax. The regular expression operators are not recognized unless the *extglob* option to the *shopt* command is turned on:

```
shopt -s extglob
```

Table 11.12 Extended Pattern Matching

Regular Expression	Meaning
abc?(2|9)1	? matches zero or one occurrences of any pattern in the parentheses. The vertical bar represents an *or* condition; e.g., either 2 or 9. Matches *abc21*, *abc91*, or *abc1*.
abc*([0–9])	* matches zero or more occurrences of any pattern in the parentheses. Matches *abc* followed by zero or more digits; e.g., *abc*, *abc1234*, *abc3*, *abc2*, etc.
abc+([0–9])	+ matches one or more occurrences of any pattern in the parentheses. Matches *abc* followed by one or more digits; e.g., *abc3*, *abc123*, etc.
no@(one|ne)	@ matches exactly one occurrence of any pattern in the parentheses. Matches *noone* or *none*.
no!(thing|where)	! matches all strings *except* those matched by any of the patterns in the parentheses. Matches *no*, *nobody*, or *noone*, but not *nothing* or *nowhere*.

EXAMPLE 11.47

```
1   $ shopt -s extglob

2   $ ls
    abc        abc122    f1    f3      nonsense    nothing    one
    abc1       abc2      f2    none    noone       nowhere

3   $ ls abc?(1|2)
    abc        abc1      abc2

4   $ ls abc*([1-5])
    abc        abc1      abc122    abc2

5   $ ls abc+([0-5])
    abc1       abc122    abc2

6   $ ls no@(thing|ne)
    none       nothing

7   $ ls no!(thing)
    none       nonsense    noone    nowhere
```

EXPLANATION

1   The *shopt* built-in is used to set the *extglob* (extended globbing) option, allowing *bash* to recognize extended pattern matching characters.

2   All the files in the present working directory are listed.

3   Matches filenames starting with *abc* and followed by *zero characters or one* of either of the patterns in parentheses. Matches *abc*, *abc1*, or *abc2*.

4   Matches filenames starting with *abc* and followed by *zero or more* numbers between *1* and *5*. Matches *abc*, *abc1*, *abc122*, *abc123*, and *abc2*.

5   Matches filenames starting with *abc* and followed by *one or more* numbers between *0* and *5*. Matches *abc1*, *abc122*, *abc123*, and *abc2*.

6   Matches filenames starting with *no* and followed by *exactly thing* or *ne*. Matches *nothing* or *none*.

7   Matches filenames starting with *no* and followed by anything except *thing*. Matches *none*, *nonsense*, *noone*, and *nowhere*. The *!* means *not*.

11.3 Variables

Types of Variables.   There are two types of variables: local and environment. Local variables are known only to the shell in which they were created. Environment variables are available to any child processes spawned from the shell from which they were created. Some variables are created by the user and others are special shell variables.

Naming Conventions.   Variable names must begin with an alphabetic or underscore character. The remaining characters can be alphabetic, decimal digits (0 to 9), or an underscore character. Any other characters mark the termination of the variable name. Names are case-sensitive. When assigning a value to a variable, do not include any whitespace surrounding the equal sign. To set the variable to null, follow the equal sign with a newline. The simplest format for creating a local variable is to assign a value to a variable in the following format.

FORMAT

```
variable=value
```

EXAMPLE 11.48

```
name=Tommy
```

The *declare* Built-In.   There are two built-in commands, *declare* and *typeset*, used to create variables, with options to control the way the variable is set. The *typeset* command (from Korn shell) is exactly the same as the *declare* command (*bash*). The *bash* documentation says, "The *typeset* command is supplied for compatibility with the Korn shell; however, it has been deprecated in favor of the *declare* built-in command."[9] So from this point on we'll use the *declare* built-in (even though we could just as easily have chosen to use *typeset*).

Without arguments, *declare* lists all set variables. Normally read-only variables cannot be reassigned or unset. If read-only variables are created with *declare*, they *cannot* be unset, but they *can* be reassigned. Integer-type variables can also be assigned with *declare*.

FORMAT

```
declare variable=value
```

EXAMPLE 11.49

```
declare name=Tommy
```

---

9.   Bash Reference Manual: *http://www.delorie.com/gnu/docs/bash/bashref_56.html*.

Table 11.13 *declare* Options

Option	Meaning
–*f*	Lists functions names and definitions.
–*r*	Makes variables read-only.
–*x*	Exports variable names to subshells.
–*i*	Makes variables integer types.
–*a*[a]	Treats variable as an array; i.e., assigns elements.
–*F*[a]	Lists just function names.

a. –*a* and –*F* are implemented only on versions of *bash* 2.x.

11.3.1 Local Variables and Scope

The scope of a variable refers to where the variable is visible within a program. For the shell, the scope of local variables is confined to the shell in which the variable is created.

When assigning a value, there can be no whitespace surrounding the equal sign. To set the variable to null, the equal sign is followed by a newline.[10]

A dollar sign is used in front of a variable to extract the value stored there.

The *local* function can be used to create local variables, but this is only used within functions. (See "Defining Functions" on page 693.)

Setting Local Variables.   Local variables can be set by simply assigning a value to a variable name, or by using the *declare* built-in function as shown in Example 11.50.

EXAMPLE 11.50

```
1   $ round=world or declare round=world
    $ echo $round
    world

2   $ name="Peter Piper"
    $ echo $name
    Peter Piper

3   $ x=
    $ echo $x

4   $ file.bak="$HOME/junk"
    bash: file.bak=/home/jody/ellie/junk: not found
```

---

10. A variable set to a value or to null will be displayed by using the *set* command, but an unset variable will not.

EXPLANATION

1   The local variable *round* is assigned the value *world*. When the shell encounters the dollar sign preceding a variable name, it performs variable substitution. The value of the variable is displayed. (Don't confuse the prompt (*$*) with the *$* used to perform variable substitution.)

2   The local variable *name* is assigned the value *"Peter Piper"*. The quotes are needed to hide the whitespace so that the shell will not split the string into separate words when it parses the command line. The value of the variable is displayed.

3   The local variable *x* is not assigned a value. It will be assigned null. The null value, an empty string, is displayed.

4   The period in the variable name is illegal. The only characters allowed in a variable name are numbers, letters, and the underscore. The shell tries to execute the string as a command.

EXAMPLE 11.51

```
1   $ echo $$
    1313
2   $ round=world
    $ echo $round
    world
3   $ bash              # Start a subshell

4   $ echo $$
    1326
5   $ echo $round
6   $ exit              # Exits this shell, returns to parent shell

7   $ echo $$
    1313
8   $ echo $round
    world
```

EXPLANATION

1   The value of the double dollar sign variable evaluates to the PID of the current shell. The PID of this shell is *1313*.

2   The local variable *round* is assigned the string value *world*, and the value of the variable is displayed.

3   A new *bash* shell is started. This is called a *subshell*, or *child shell*.

4   The PID of this shell is *1326*. The parent shell's PID is *1313*.

5   The local variable *round* is not defined in this shell. A blank line is printed.

EXPLANATION (CONTINUED)

6   The *exit* command terminates this shell and returns to the parent shell. (Control-D will also exit this shell.)

7   The parent shell returns. Its PID is displayed.

8   The value of the variable *round* is displayed. It is local to this shell.

Setting Read-Only Variables.   A read-only variable is a special variable that cannot be redefined or unset. If, however, the *declare* function is used, a read-only variable can be redefined, but not unset.

EXAMPLE 11.52

```
1   $ name=Tom
2   $ readonly name
    $ echo $name
    Tom

3   $ unset name
    bash: unset: name: cannot unset: readonly variable
4   $ name=Joe
    bash: name: readonly variable

5   $ declare -r city='Santa Clara'
6   $ unset city
    bash: unset: city: cannot unset: readonly variable

7   $ declare city='San Francisco'      # What happened here?
    $ echo $city
    San Francisco
```

EXPLANATION

1   The local variable *name* is assigned the value *Tom*.

2   The variable is made read-only.

3   A read-only variable cannot be unset.

4   A read-only variable cannot be redefined.

5   The *declare* built-in command assigns a read-only variable, *city*, the value *Santa Clara*. Quotes are necessary when assigning a string containing whitespace.

6   Since it is read-only, the variable cannot be unset.

7   When a read-only variable is created with the *declare* command, it cannot be unset, but it can be reassigned.

11.3.2 Environment Variables

Environment variables are available to the shell in which they are created and any sub-shells or processes spawned from that shell. They are often called global variables to differentiate them from local variables. By convention, environment variables are capitalized. Environment variables are variables that have been exported with the *export* built-in command.

The shell in which a variable is created is called the *parent shell*. If a new shell is started from the parent shell, it is called the *child shell*. Environment variables are passed to any child process started from the shell where the environment variables were created. They are passed from parent to child to grandchild, etc., but not the other direction; i.e., a child process can create an environment variable, but cannot pass it back to its parent, only to its children.[11] Some of the environment variables, such as *HOME, LOGNAME, PATH,* and *SHELL,* are set before you log on by the */bin/login* program. Normally, environment variables are defined and stored in the *.bash_profile* file in the user's home directory. See Table 11.15 for a list of environment variables.

Setting Environment Variables. To set environment variables, the *export* command is used either after assigning a value or when the variable is set. The *declare* built-in, given the *–x* option, will do the same. (Do not use the $ on a variable when exporting it.)

FORMAT
```
export variable=value
variable=value; export variable
declare -x variable=value
```

EXAMPLE 11.53
```
export NAME=john
PS1= '\d:\W:$USER> ' ; export PS1
declare -x TERM=sun
```

Table 11.14 The *export* Command and Its Options

Option	Value
– –	Marks the end of option processing; the remaining parameters are arguments.
–f	Name-value pairs are treated as functions, not variables.
–n	Converts a global (exported) variable to a local variable. The variable will not be exported to child processes.
–p	Displays all the global variables.

11. Like DNA, inheritance goes one direction only, from parent to child.

EXAMPLE 11.54

```
1   $ export TERM=sun      # or declare -x TERM=sun

2   $ NAME="John Smith"
    $ export NAME
    $ echo $NAME
    John Smith

3   $ echo $$
    319              # pid number for parent shell

4   $ bash          # Start a subshell

5   $ echo $$
    340              # pid number for new shell

6   $ echo $NAME
    John Smith

7   $ declare -x NAME="April Jenner"
    $ echo $NAME
    April Jenner

8   $ exit
                    # Exit the subshell and go back to parent shell
9   $ echo $$
    319              # pid number for parent shell
10  $ echo $NAME
    John Smith
```

EXPLANATION

1   The *TERM* variable is assigned *sun*. The variable is exported at the same time. Now, processes started from this shell will inherit the variable. You can use *declare –x* to do the same thing.

2   The variable *NAME* is defined and exported to make it available to subshells started from the shell.

3   The value of this shell's PID is printed.

4   A new *bash* shell is started. The new shell is called the *child*. The original shell is its *parent*.

5   The PID of the new *bash* shell is stored in the $$ variable and its value is echoed.

6   The variable, set in the parent shell, was exported to this new shell and is displayed.

7   The built-in *declare* function is another way to set a variable. With the –x switch, *declare* marks the variable for export. The variable is reset to *April Jenner*. It is exported to all subshells, but will not affect the parent shell. Exported values are not propagated upward to the parent shell.

8　This *bash* child shell is exited.

9　The PID of the parent is displayed again.

10　The variable NAME contains its original value. Variables retain their values when exported from parent to child shell. The child cannot change the value of a variable for its parent.

Table 11.15　*Bash* Environment Variables

Variable Name	Meaning
_ (underscore)	The last argument to the previous command.
BASH	Expands to the full pathname used to invoke this instance of *bash*.
BASH_ENV	Same as *ENV* but set only in *bash* versions 2.0 or above.[a]
BASH_VERSINFO	Version information about this version of *bash* if the version is 2.0 or above.[a]
BASH_VERSION	Expands to the version number of this instance of *bash*.
CDPATH	The search path for the *cd* command. This is a colon-separated list of directories in which the shell looks for destination directories specified by the *cd* command. A sample value is .:~:/usr.
COLUMNS	If set, defines the width of the edit window for shell edit modes and the select command.
DIRSTACK	The current contents of the directory stack if the *bash* version is 2.0 or above.[a]
EDITOR	Pathname for a built-in editor: *emacs*, *gmacs*, or *vi*.
ENV	The environment file that is executed every time a new *bash* shell is started, including a script. Normally the filename assigned to this variable is *.bashrc*. The value of *ENV* is subjected to parameter expansion, command substitution, and arithmetic expansion before being interpreted as a pathname.
EUID	Expands to the effective user ID of the current user, initialized at shell startup.
FCEDIT	Default editor name for the *fc* command.
FIGNORE	A colon-separated list of suffixes to ignore when performing filename completion. A filename whose suffix matches one of the entries in *FIGNORE* is excluded from the list of matched filenames. A sample value is .o:~.
FORMAT	Used to format the output of the *time* reserved word on a command pipeline.
GLOBIGNORE	A list of files that will be ignored during filename expansion (called globbing).[a]

Table 11.15 *Bash* Environment Variables (continued)

Variable Name	Meaning
GROUPS	An array of groups to which the current user belongs.[a]
HISTCMD	The history number, or index in the history list, of the current command. If HISTCMD is unset, it loses its special properties, even if it is subsequently reset.
HISTCONTROL	If set to a value of *ignorespace*, lines that begin with a space character are not entered on the history list. If set to a value of *ignoredups*, lines matching the last history line are not entered. A value of *ignoreboth* combines the two options. If unset, or if set to any other value than those above, all lines read by the parser are saved on the history list.
HISTFILE	Specifies file in which to store command history. The default value is ~/.bash_history. If unset, the command history is not saved when an interactive shell exits.
HISTFILESIZE	The maximum number of lines contained in the history file. When this variable is assigned a value, the history file is truncated, if necessary, to contain no more than that number of lines. The default value is *500*.
HISTSIZE	The number of commands to remember in the command history. The default value is *500*.
HOME	Home directory; used by *cd* when no directory is specified.
HOSTFILE	Contains the name of a file in the same format as in */etc/hosts* that should be read when the shell needs to complete a hostname. The file may be changed interactively; the next time hostname completion is attempted, *bash* adds the contents of the new file to the already existing database.
HOSTTYPE	Automatically set to the type of machine on which *bash* is executing. The default is system-dependent.
IFS	Internal field separators, normally SPACE, TAB, and NEWLINE, used for field splitting of words resulting from command substitution, lists in loop constructs, and reading input.
IGNOREEOF	Controls the action of the shell on receipt of an *EOF* character as the sole input. If set, the value is the number of consecutive *EOF* characters typed as the first characters on an input line before *bash* exits. If the variable exists but does not have a numeric value, or has no value, the default value is *10*. If it does not exist, *EOF* signifies the end of input to the shell. This is only in effect for interactive shells.
INPUTRC	The filename for the *readline* startup file, overriding the default of ~/.inputrc.
LANG	Used to determine the locale category for any category not specifically selected with a variable starting with *LC_*.[a]

Table 11.15 *Bash* Environment Variables (continued)

Variable Name	Meaning
LC_ALL	Overrides the value of *LANG* and any other *LC_* variable.[a]
LC_COLLATE	Determines the collation order used when sorting the results of pathname expansion and the behavior of range expressions, equivalence classes, and collating sequences when matching pathnames and patterns.[a]
LC_MESSAGES	Determines the locale used to translate double-quoted strings preceded by a $.[a]
LINENO	Each time this parameter is referenced, the shell substitutes a decimal number representing the current sequential line number (starting with 1) within a script or function.
MACHTYPE	Contains a string describing the system on which *bash* is executing.[a]
MAIL	If this parameter is set to the name of a mail file and the *MAILPATH* parameter is not set, the shell informs the user of the arrival of mail in the specified file.
MAIL_WARNING	If set, and a file that *bash* is checking for mail has been accessed since the last time it was checked, the message *The mail in [filename where mail is stored] has been read* is printed.
MAILCHECK	This parameter specifies how often (in seconds) the shell will check for the arrival of mail in the files specified by the *MAILPATH* or *MAIL* parameters. The default value is 600 seconds (10 minutes). If set to zero, the shell will check before issuing each primary prompt.
MAILPATH	A colon-separated list of filenames. If this parameter is set, the shell informs the user of the arrival of mail in any of the specified files. Each filename can be followed by a % and a message that will be printed when the modification time changes. The default message is *You have mail*.
OLDPWD	Last working directory.
OPTARG	The value of the last option argument processed by the *getopts* built-in command.
OPTERR	If set to *1*, displays error messages from the *getopts* built-in.
OPTIND	The index of the next argument to be processed by the *getopts* built-in command.
OSTYPE	Automatically set to a string that describes the operating system on which *bash* is executing. The default is system-dependent.
PATH	The search path for commands. It is a colon-separated list of directories in which the shell looks for commands. The default path is system-dependent, and is set by the administrator who installs *bash*. A common value is /usr/gnu/bin:/usr/local/bin:/usr/ucb:/bin:/usr/bin:.

Table 11.15 *Bash* Environment Variables (continued)

Variable Name	Meaning
PIPESTATUS	An array containing a list of exit status values from processes in the most recently executed foreground jobs in a pipeline.
PPID	Process ID of the parent process.
PROMPT_COMMAND	The command assigned to this variable is executed before the primary prompt is displayed.
PS1	Primary prompt string, by default $.
PS2	Secondary prompt string, by default >.
PS3	Selection prompt string used with the *select* command, by default #?.
PS4	Debug prompt string used when tracing is turned on, by default +. Tracing can be turned on with *set –x*.
PWD	Present working directory; set by *cd*.
RANDOM	Each time this parameter is referenced, a random integer is generated. The sequence of random numbers may be initialized by assigning a value to *RANDOM*. If *RANDOM* is unset, it loses its special properties, even if it is subsequently reset.
REPLY	Set when *read* is not supplied arguments.
SECONDS	Each time *SECONDS* is referenced, the number of seconds since shell invocation is returned. If a value is assigned to *SECONDS*, the value returned upon subsequent references is the number of seconds since the assignment plus the value assigned. If *SECONDS* is unset, it loses its special properties, even if it is subsequently reset.
SHELL	When the shell is invoked, it scans the environment for this name. The shell gives default values to *PATH, PS1, PS2, MAILCHECK*, and *IFS. HOME* and *MAIL* are set by *login(1)*.
SHELLOPTS	Contains a list of enabled shell options, such as *braceexpand, hashall, monitor,* etc.
SHLVL	Incremented by one each time an instance of *bash* is started.
TMOUT	Specifies number of seconds to wait for input before exiting.
UID	Expands to the user ID of the current user, initialized at shell startup.

a. Not available in *bash* versions prior to 2.x.

Unsetting Variables. Both local and environment variables can be unset by using the *unset* command, unless the variables are set as read-only.

EXAMPLE 11.55

```
unset name; unset TERM
```

EXPLANATION

The *unset* command removes the variable from the shell's memory.

Printing the Values of Variables: The *echo* Command. The built-in *echo* command prints its arguments to standard output. *Echo*, with the *–e* option, allows the use of numerous escape sequences that control the appearance of the output. Table 11.16 lists the *echo* options and escape sequences.

Table 11.16 *echo* Options and Escape Sequences

Option	Meaning
–e	Allows interpretation of the escape sequences shown below.
–n	Suppresses newline at the end of a line of output.
–E[a]	Disables the interpretation of these escape characters, even on systems where they are interpreted by default (*bash* 2.x).

Escape Sequence	
\a[a]	Alert (bell).
\b	Backspace.
\c	Prints the line without a newline.
\f	Form feed.
\n	Newline.
\r	Return.
\t	Tab.
\v	Vertical tab.
\\	Backslash.
\nnn	The character whose ASCII code is *nnn* (octal).

a. Not available in *bash* versions prior to 2.x.

When using the escape sequences, don't forget to use the *–e* switch!

EXAMPLE 11.56

```
1   $ echo The username is $LOGNAME.
    The username is ellie.

2   $ echo -e "\t\tHello there\c"
              Hello there$

3   $ echo -n "Hello there"
    Hello there$
```

EXPLANATION

1   The *echo* command prints its arguments to the screen. Variable substitution is performed by the shell before the *echo* command is executed.

2   The *echo* command, with the *–e* option, supports escape sequences similar to those of the C programming language. The $ is the shell prompt.

3   When the *–n* option is on, the line is printed without the newline. The escape sequences are not supported by this version of *echo*.

The *printf* Command.   The GNU version of *printf*[12] can be used to format printed output. It prints the formatted string in the same way as the C *printf* function. The format consists of a string that may contain formatting instructions to describe how the printed output will look. The formatting instructions are designated with a % followed by specifiers (*diouxXfeEgGcs*) where *%f* would represent a floating point number and *%d* would represent a whole (decimal) number.

To see a complete listing of *printf* specifiers and how to use them, type at the command line prompt: *printf – –help*. To see what version of *printf* you are using, type: *printf – –version*. If you are using *bash 2.x*, the built-in *printf* command uses the same format as the executable version in */usr/bin*.

FORMAT

```
printf format [argument...]
```

EXAMPLE 11.57

```
printf "%10.2f%5d\n" 10.5   25
```

---

12. On *bash* versions 2.x, *printf* is a built-in command.

Table 11.17 Format Specifiers for the *printf* Command

Format Specifier	Value
\"	Double quote.
\0NNN	An octal character where NNN represents 0 to 3 digits.
\\	Backslash.
\a	Alert or beep.
\b	Backspace.
\c	Produce no further output.
\f	Form feed.
\n	Newline.
\r	Return.
\t	Horizontal tab.
\v	Vertical tab.
\xNNN	Hexadecimal character, where NNN is 1 to 3 digits.
%%	A single %.
%b	Argument as a string with \ escapes interpreted.

EXAMPLE 11.58

```
1   $ printf --version
    printf (GNU sh-utils) 1.16

2   $ type printf
    printf is a shell builtin

3   $ printf "The number is %.2f\n" 100
    The number is 100.00

4   $ printf "%-20s%-15s%10.2f\n" "Jody" "Savage" 28
    Jody                Savage             28.00

5   $ printf "|%-20s|%-15s|%10.2f|\n" "Jody" "Savage" 28
    Jody                |Savage         |     28.00|

6   $ printf "%s's average was %.1f%%.\n" "Jody" $(( (80+70+90)/3 ))
    Jody's average was 80.0%.
```

EXPLANATION

1   The GNU version of the *printf* command is printed.

2   If using *bash2.x*, *printf* is a built-in command.

3   The argument *100* is printed as a floating point number with only 2 places to the right of the decimal point as designated by the specification *%.2f* in the format string. Unlike C, there are no commas separating the arguments.

4   The format string specifies that three conversions will take place: the first one is *%–20s* (a left-justified, 20-character string), next is *%–15s* (a left-justified, 15-character string, and last *%10.2f* (a right-justified, 10-character floating point number, one of whose characters is the period and the last two characters are the two numbers to the right of the decimal point). Each argument is formatted in the order of the corresponding % signs, so that string *Jody* corresponds to first %, string *Savage* corresponds to the second %, and the number 28 to the last % sign.

5   This line is the same as line 4 except vertical bars have been added to demonstrate left- and right-justification of the strings.

6   The *printf* command formats the string *Jody* and formats the result of the arithmetic expansion. (See "Arithmetic Expansion" on page 689.) Two percent (%%) signs are needed to print one percent sign (%).

Variable Expansion Modifiers (Parameter Expansion).   Variables can be tested and modified by using special modifiers. The modifier provides a shortcut conditional test to check if a variable has been set, and then assigns a value to the variable based on the outcome of the test. See Table 11.18 for a list of variable modifiers.

Table 11.18   Variable Modifiers

Modifier	*Value*
${*variable*:–*word*}	If *variable* is set and is non-null, substitute its value; otherwise, substitute *word*.
${*variable*:=*word*}	If *variable* is set or is non-null, substitute its value; otherwise, set it to *word*. The value of *variable* is substituted permanently. Positional parameters may not be assigned in this way.
${*variable*:+*word*}	If variable is set and is non-null, substitute *word*; otherwise, substitute nothing.
${*variable*:?*word*}	If *variable* is set and is non-null, substitute its value; otherwise, print *word* and exit from the shell. If *word* is omitted, the message *parameter null or not set* is printed.
${*variable*:*offset*}	Gets the substring of the value in *variable* starting at *offset*, where *offset* starts at 0 to the end of the string.[a]
${*variable*:*offset*:*length*}	Gets the substring of the value in *variable* starting at *offset*, length characters over.

a. Not available on *bash* versions prior to 2.0.

Using the colon with any of the modifiers (–, =, +, ?) checks whether the variable is not set or is null; without the colon, a variable set to null is considered to be set.

EXAMPLE 11.59

```
(Substitute Temporary Default Values)
1    $ fruit=peach
2    $ echo ${fruit:-plum}
     peach

3    $ echo ${newfruit:-apple}
     apple
4    $ echo $newfruit

5    $ echo $EDITOR        # More realistic example

6    $ echo ${EDITOR:-/bin/vi}
     /bin/vi
7    $ echo $EDITOR

8    $ name=
     $ echo ${name-Joe}
9    $ echo ${name:-Joe}
     Joe
```

EXPLANATION

1   The variable *fruit* is assigned the value *peach*.

2   The special modifier will check to see if the variable *fruit* has been set. If it has, the value is printed; if not, *plum* is substituted for *fruit* and its value is printed.

3   The variable *newfruit* has not been set. The value *apple* will be temporarily substituted for *newfruit*.

4   The setting was only temporary. The variable *newfruit* is not set.

5   The environment variable *EDITOR* has not been set.

6   The :– modifier substitutes *EDITOR* with */bin/vi*.

7   The *EDITOR* was never set. Nothing prints.

8   The variable *name* is set to null. By not prefixing the modifier with a colon, the variable is considered to be set, even if to null, and the new value *Joe* is not assigned to *name*.

9   The colon causes the modifier to check that a variable is either *not* set or is set to null. In either case, the value *Joe* will be substituted for *name*.

EXAMPLE 11.60

(Substitute Permanent Default Values)

```
1   $ name=

2   $ echo  ${name:=Peter}
    Peter

3   $ echo $name
    Peter

4   $ echo ${EDITOR:=/bin/vi}
    /bin/vi

5   $ echo $EDITOR
    /bin/vi
```

EXPLANATION

1   The variable *name* is assigned the null value.
2   The special modifier := will check to see if the variable name has been set. If it has been set, it will not be changed; if it is either null or not set, it will be assigned the value to the right of the equal sign. *Peter* is assigned to *name* since the variable is set to null. The setting is permanent.
3   The variable *name* still contains the value *Peter*.
4   The value of the variable *EDITOR* is set to */bin/vi*.
5   The value of the variable *EDITOR* is displayed.

EXAMPLE 11.61

(Substitute Temporary Alternate Value)

```
1   $ foo=grapes

2   $ echo ${foo:+pears}
    pears

3   $ echo $foo
    grapes
    $
```

EXPLANATION

1   The variable *foo* has been assigned the value *grapes*.
2   The special modifier :+ will check to see if the variable has been set. If it has been set, *pears* will temporarily be substituted for *foo*; if not, null is returned.
3   The variable *foo* now has its original value.

EXAMPLE 11.62

(Creating Error Messages Based On Default Values)

```
1   $ echo ${namex:?"namex is undefined"}
    namex: namex is undefined
```

```
2   $ echo ${y?}
    y: parameter null or not set
```

EXPLANATION

1   The :? modifier will check to see if the variable has been set. If not, the string to the right of the ? is printed to standard error, after the name of the variable. If in a script, the script exits.
2   If a message is not provided after the ?, the shell sends a default message to standard error.

EXAMPLE 11.63

(Creating Substring[a])

```
1   $ var=notebook
```

```
2   $ echo ${var:0:4}
    note
```

```
3   $ echo ${var:4:4}
    book
```

```
4   $ echo ${var:0:2}
    no
```

a. Not available in versions of *bash* prior to 2.x.

EXPLANATION

1   The variable is assigned the value, *notebook*.

2   The substring of *var* starts at offset 0, the *n* in *notebook*, and has a length of 4 characters, ending at the *e*.

3   The substring of *var* starts at offset 4, the *b* in *notebook*, and has a length of 4 characters, ending at the *k*.

4   The substring of *var* starts at offset 0, the *n* in *notebook*, and has a length of 2 characters, ending at the *o*.

Variable Expansion of Substrings.   Pattern-matching arguments are used to strip off certain portions of a string from either the front or end of the string. The most common use for these operators is stripping off pathname elements from the head or tail of the path. See Table 11.19.

Table 11.19   Variable Expansion Substrings^a

Expression	Function
${variable%pattern}	Matches the *smallest trailing portion* of the value of *variable* to *pattern* and removes it.
${variable%%pattern}	Matches the *largest trailing portion* of the value of *variable* to *pattern* and removes it.
${variable#pattern}	Matches the *smallest leading portion* of the value of *variable* to *pattern* and removes it.
${variable##pattern}	Matches the *largest leading portion* of the value of *variable* to *pattern* and removes it.
${#variable}	Substitutes the number of characters in the variable. If * or @, the length is the number of positional parameters.

a. Not available on versions of *bash* prior to 2.x.

EXAMPLE 11.64

```
1   $ pathname="/usr/bin/local/bin"
2   $ echo ${pathname%/bin*}
    /usr/bin/local
```

EXPLANATION

1 The local variable *pathname* is assigned */usr/bin/local/bin*.

2 The *%* removes the *smallest trailing portion* of *pathname* containing the pattern */bin*, followed by zero or more characters; that is, it strips off */bin*.

EXAMPLE 11.65

```
1  $ pathname="usr/bin/local/bin"
2  $ echo ${pathname%%/bin*}
   /usr
```

EXPLANATION

1 The local variable *pathname* is assigned */usr/bin/local/bin*.

2 The *%%* removes the *largest trailing portion* of *pathname* containing the pattern */bin*, followed by zero or more characters; that is, it strips off */bin/local/bin*

EXAMPLE 11.66

```
1  $ pathname=/home/lilliput/jake/.bashrc
2  $ echo ${pathname#/home}
   /lilliput/jake/.bashrc
```

EXPLANATION

1 The local variable *pathname* is assigned */home/lilliput/jake/.bashrc*.

2 The *#* removes the *smallest leading portion* of *pathname* containing the pattern */home*; that is, */home* is stripped from the beginning of the path variable.

EXAMPLE 11.67

```
1  $ pathname=/home/liliput/jake/.bashrc
2  $ echo ${pathname##*/}
   .bashrc
```

EXPLANATION

1   The local variable *pathname* is assigned */home/liliput/jake/.bashrc*.

2   The ## removes the *largest leading portion* of *pathname* containing zero or more characters up to and including the last slash; that is, it strips off */home/lilliput/jake* from the path variable.

EXAMPLE 11.68

```
1   $ name="Ebenezer Scrooge"
2   $ echo  ${#name}
    16
```

EXPLANATION

1   The variable *name* is assigned the string *Ebenezer Scrooge*.

2   The ${#variable} syntax displays the number of characters in the string assigned to the variable *name*. There are 16 characters in *Ebenezer Scrooge*.

Positional Parameters.   Normally, the special built-in variables, often called positional parameters, are used in shell scripts when passing arguments from the command line, or used in functions to hold the value of arguments passed to the function. The variables are called positional parameters because they are referenced by numbers 1, 2, 3, and so on, representing their respective positions in the parameter list. See Table 11.20.

The name of the shell script is stored in the $0 variable. The positional parameters can be set, reset, and unset with the *set* command.

Table 11.20   Positional Parameters

Expression	Function
$0	References the name of the current shell script.
$1–$9	Positional parameters *1–9*.
${10}	Positional parameter *10*.
$#	Evaluates to the number of positional parameters.
$*	Evaluates to all the positional parameters.
$@	Same as $*, except when double quoted.
"$*"	Evaluates to "$1 $2 $3", etc.
"$@"	Evaluates to "$1" "$2" "$3", etc.

EXAMPLE 11.69

```
1   $ set punky tommy bert jody
    $ echo $*              # Prints all the positional parameters
    punky tommy bert jody

2   $ echo $1              # Prints the first position
    punky

3   $ echo $2 $3           # Prints the second and third position
    tommy bert

4   $ echo $#              # Prints the total number of positional
    4                      # parameters

5   $ set a b c d e f g h i j k l m
    $ print $10            # Prints the first positional parameter
    a0                     # followed by a 0.

    $ echo ${10} ${11}     # Prints the 10th and 11th positions
    j k

6   $ echo $#
    13

7   $ echo $*
    a b c d e f g h i j k l m

8   $ set file1 file2 file3
    $ echo \$$#
    $3

9   $ eval echo \$$#
    file3

10  $ set --               # Unsets all positional parameters
```

EXPLANATION

1   The *set* command assigns values to positional parameters. The $* special variable contains all of the parameters set.

2   The value of the first positional parameter, *punky,* is displayed.

3   The value of the second and third parameters, *tommy* and *bert,* are displayed.

4   The $# special variable contains the number of positional parameters currently set.

5   The *set* command resets all of the positional parameters. The original parameter list is cleared. To print any positional parameters beyond 9, use the curly braces to keep the two digits together. Otherwise, the value of the first positional parameter is printed, followed by the number appended to it.

6   The number of positional parameters is now *13.*

7   The values of all the positional parameters are printed.

8   The dollar sign is escaped; $# is the number of arguments. The *echo* command displays $3, a literal dollar sign followed by the number of positional parameters.

9   The *eval* command parses the command line a second time before executing the command. The first time parsed by the shell, the print would display $3; the second time, after *eval*, the *print* displays the value of $3, *file3.*

10 The *set* command with the – – option clears or unsets all positional parameters.

Other Special Variables.   The shell has special variables consisting of a single character. The dollar sign preceding the character allows you to access the value stored in the variable. See Table 11.21.

Table 11.21   Special Variables

Variable	Meaning
$	The PID of the shell.
–	The *sh* options currently set.
?	The exit value of last executed command.
!	The PID of the last job put in the background.

EXAMPLE 11.70

```
1    $ echo The pid of this shell is $$
     The pid of this shell is 4725

2    $ echo The options for this shell are $-
     The options for this shell are imh

3    $ grep dodo /etc/passwd
     $ echo $?
     1

4    $ sleep 25&
     4736
     $ echo $!
     4736
```

EXPLANATION

1   The $ variable holds the value of the PID for this process.

2   The – variable lists all options for this interactive *bash* shell.

3   The *grep* command searches for the string *dodo* in the */etc/passwd* file. The *?* variable holds the exit status of the last command executed. Since the value returned from *grep* is *1*, *grep* is assumed to have failed in its search. An exit status of zero indicates a successful exit.

4   The *!* variable holds the PID number of the last command placed in the background. The *&* appended to the *sleep* command sends the command to the background.

11.3.3 Quoting

Quoting is used to protect special metacharacters from interpretation and prevent parameter expansion. There are three methods of quoting: the backslash, single quotes, and double quotes. The characters listed in Table 11.22 are special to the shell and must be quoted.

Table 11.22 Special Metacharacters Requiring Quotes

Metacharacter	Meaning
;	Command separator.
&	Background processing.
( )	Command grouping; creates a subshell.
{ }	Command grouping; does not create a subshell.
|	Pipe.
<	Input redirection.
>	Output redirection.
newline	Command termination.
space/tab	Word delimiter.
$	Variable substitution character.
* [ ] ?	Shell metacharacters for filename expansion.

Single and double quotes must be matched. Single quotes protect special metacharacters, such as $, *, ?, |, >, and <, from interpretation. Double quotes also protect special metacharacters from being interpreted, but allow variable and command substitution characters (the dollar sign and backquotes) to be processed. Single quotes will protect double quotes and double quotes will protect single quotes.

Unlike the Bourne shell, *bash* tries to let you know if you have mismatched quotes. If running interactively, a secondary prompt appears when quotes are not matched; if in a shell script, the file is scanned and if the quote is not matched, the shell will attempt to match it with the next available quote. If the shell cannot match it with the next available quote, the program aborts and the message *bash:unexpected EOF while looking for* ` " ` appears on the terminal. Quoting can be a real hassle for even the best of shell programmers! See Appendix C for shell quoting rules.

The Backslash.   The backslash is used to quote (or escape) a single character from interpretation. The backslash is not interpreted if placed in single quotes. The backslash will protect the dollar sign ($), backquotes (` `), and the backslash from interpretation if enclosed in double quotes.

EXAMPLE 11.71

```
1   $ echo Where are you going\?
    Where are you going?

2   $ echo Start on this line and \
    >  go to the next line.
    Start on this line and go to the next line.

3   $ echo \\
    \

4   $ echo '\\'
    \\

5   $ echo '\$5.00'
    \$5.00

6   $ echo "\$5.00"
    $5.00

7   $ echo 'Don\'t you need $5.00?'
    >
    >'

    Don\t you need .00?
```

EXPLANATION

1 The backslash prevents the shell from performing filename substitution on the question mark.

2 The backslash escapes the newline, allowing the next line to become part of this line.

3 Because the backslash itself is a special character, it prevents the backslash following it from interpretation.

4 The backslash is not interpreted when enclosed in single quotes.

5 All characters in single quotes are treated literally. The backslash does not serve any purpose here.

6 When enclosed in double quotes, the backslash prevents the dollar sign from being interpreted for variable substitution.

7 The backslash is not interpreted when inside single quotes; therefore, the shell sees three single quotes (the one at the end of the string is not matched). A secondary prompt appears, waiting for a closing single quote. When the shell finally gets the closing quote, it strips out all of the quotes and passes the string on to the *echo* command. Because the first two quotes were matched, the rest of the string *t you need $5.00?* was not enclosed within any quotes. The shell tried to evaluate $5; it was empty and *.00* printed.

Single Quotes.   Single quotes must be matched. They protect all metacharacters from interpretation. To print a single quote, it must be enclosed in double quotes or escaped with a backslash.

EXAMPLE 11.72

```
1  $ echo 'hi there
   > how are you?
   > When will this end?
   > When the quote is matched
   > oh'
```

EXAMPLE 11.72 (CONTINUED)

```
hi there
how are you?
When will this end?
When the quote is matched
oh
```

2   `$ echo Don\'t you need '$5.00?'`
```
Don't you need $5.00?
```

3   `$ echo 'Mother yelled, "Time to eat!"'`
```
Mother yelled, "Time to eat!"
```

EXPLANATION

1   The single quote is not matched on the line. The Bourne shell produces a secondary prompt. It is waiting for the quote to be matched.

2   The single quotes protect all metacharacters from interpretation. The apostrophe in *Don't* is escaped with a backslash (the backslash protects a single character, rather than a string). Otherwise, it would match the single quote before the $. Then the single quote at the end of the string would not have a mate. The $ and the *?* are enclosed in a pair of single quotes, protecting them from shell interpretation; i.e., treating them as literals.

3   The single quotes protect the double quotes in this string.

Double Quotes.   Double quotes must be matched, will allow variable and command substitution, and protect any other special metacharacters from being interpreted by the shell.

EXAMPLE 11.73

1   `$ name=Jody`

2   `$ echo "Hi $name, I'm glad to meet you!"`
```
Hi Jody, I'm glad to meet you!
```

3   `$ echo "Hey $name, the time is $(date)"`
```
Hey Jody, the time is Wed Jul 14 14:04:11 PST 2001
```

EXPLANATION

1   The variable *name* is assigned the string *Jody*.

2   The double quotes surrounding the string will protect all special metacharacters from interpretation, with the exception of $ in *$name*. Variable substitution is performed within double quotes.

3   Variable substitution and command substitution are both performed when enclosed within double quotes. The variable *name* is expanded, and the command in parentheses, *date*, is executed. (See "Command Substitution" below.)

11.3.4 Command Substitution

Command substitution is used when assigning the output of a command to a variable or when substituting the output of a command within a string. All shells use backquotes to perform command substitution.[13] *Bash* allows two forms: the older form, where the command(s) is placed within backquotes, and the new Korn-style form, where the command(s) is placed within a set of parentheses preceded by a dollar sign.

Bash performs the expansion by executing the command and returning the standard output of the command, with any trailing newlines deleted. When the old-style backquote form of substitution is used, the backslash retains its literal meaning except when followed by $, `, or \. When using the $(*command*) form, all characters between the parentheses make up the command; none are treated specially.

Command substitutions may be nested. To nest when using the old form, the inner backquotes must be escaped with backslashes.

FORMAT

```
`UNIX command`    # Old method with backquotes

$(UNIX command)   # New method
```

---

13. The *bash* shell allows backquotes for command substitution for upward-compatibility, but provides an alternate method as well.

EXAMPLE 11.74

```
(The Old Way)
1   $ echo "The hour is `date +%H`"
    The hour is 09

2   $ name=`awk -F: '{print $1}' database`
    $ echo $name
    Ebenezer Scrooge

3   $ ls `ls /etc`
    shutdown

4   $ set `date`
5   $ echo $*
    Wed Jul 14 09:35:21 PDT 2001
6   $ echo $2 $6
    Jul 2001

7   $ echo `basename \`pwd\``
    ellie
```

EXPLANATION

1   The output of the *date* command is substituted into the string.

2   The output of the *awk* command is assigned to the variable *name* and displayed.

3   The output of the *ls* command, enclosed in backquotes, is a list of files from the */etc* directory. The filenames will be arguments to the first *ls* command. All files with the same name in */etc* in the current directory are listed. (The files that are not matches in this directory will cause an error message, such as ls: *termcap: No such file or directory.*)

4   The *set* command assigns the output of the *date* command to positional parameters. Whitespace separates the list of words into its respective parameters.

5   The $* variable holds all of the parameters. The output of the *date* command was stored in the $* variable. Each parameter is separated by whitespace.

6   The second and sixth parameters are printed.

7   To set the variable *dirname* to the name (only) of the present working directory, command substitution is nested. The *pwd* command is executed first, passing the full pathname of the present working directory as an argument to the UNIX command *basename*. The *basename* command strips off all but the last element of a pathname. When nesting commands within backquotes, the backquotes for the inner command must be escaped with a backslash.

The *bash* alternate for using backquotes in command substitution is presented below in Example 11.75.

EXAMPLE 11.75

```
(The New Way)
1   $ d=$(date)
    $ echo $d
    Wed Jul 14 09:35:21 PDT 2001

2   $ lines = $(cat filex)

3   $ echo The time is $(date +%H)
    The time is 09

4   $ machine=$(uname -n)
    $ echo $machine
    jody

5   $ pwd
    /usr/local/bin
    $ dirname="$(basename $(pwd)) "    # Nesting commands
    $ echo $dirname
    bin

6   $ echo $(cal)                           # Newlines are lost
    July 2001 S M Tu W Th F S 1 2 3 4 5 6 7 8 9 10 11 12 13 14 15
    16 17 18 19 20 21 22 23 24 25 26 27 28 29 30 31

7   $ echo "$(cal)"
         July 2001
     S  M  Tu  W  Th  F   S
                 1   2   3
     4  5   6  7   8   9  10
    11 12  13 14  15  16  17
    18 19  20 21  22  23  24
    25 26  27 28  29  30  31
```

EXPLANATION

1   The *date* command is enclosed within parentheses. The output of the command is substituted into the expression, then assigned to the variable *d,* and displayed.

2   The output from the *cat* command is assigned to the variable *lines.*

3   Again the *date* command is enclosed in parentheses. The output of *date +%H,* the current hour, is substituted for the expression and echoed to the screen.

4   The variable *machine* is assigned the output of *uname –n,* the name of the host machine. The value of the *machine* variable is echoed to the screen.

5   The output of the *pwd* command (present working directory) is */usr/local/bin*.The
     variable *dirname* is assigned the output resulting from command substitution
     where the command substitutions are nested. *$(pwd)* is the first command substi-
     tution to be be performed. The output of the *pwd* command is substituted in the
     expression, then the *basename* program will use the results of that substitution,
     /usr/local/bin, as its argument, resulting in *basename /usr/local/bin*.

6   The output of the *cal* (the current month) command is echoed. The trailing new-
     lines are deleted when command substitution is performed.

7   When you put the whole command substitution expression in double quotes, the
     trailing newlines are preserved, and calendar looks like it should.

11.3.5 Arithmetic Expansion

The shell performs arithmetic expansion by evaluating an arithmetic expression and
substituting the result. The expression is treated as if it were in double quotes and the
expressions may be nested. For a complete discussion of arithmetic operations, and
arithmetic evaluations, see "The let Command" on page 732.

There are two formats for evaluating arithmetic expressions:

FORMAT

```
$[ expression ]
$(( expression ))
```

EXAMPLE 11.76

```
echo $[ 5 + 4 - 2 ]
7
echo $[ 5 + 3 * 2]
11
echo $[(5 + 3) * 2]
16
echo $(( 5 + 4 ))
9
echo $(( 5 / 0 ))
bash: 5/0: division by 0 ( error token is "0")
```

11.3.6 Order of Expansion

When you are performing the expansion of variables, commands, arithmetic expressions, and pathnames, the shell is programmed to follow a specific order when scanning the command line. Assuming that the variables are not quoted, the processing is performed in the following order:

1. Brace expansion
2. Tilde expansion
3. Parameter expansion
4. Variable substitution
5. Command substitution
6. Arithmetic expansion
7. Word splitting
8. Pathname expansion

11.3.7 Arrays (Versions 2.x)

Versions of *bash* 2.x, provide for creation of one-dimensional arrays. Arrays allow you to collect a list of words into one variable name, such as a list of numbers, a list of names, or a list of files. Arrays are created with the built-in function *declare –a*, or can be created on the fly by giving a subscript to a variable name, such as *x[0]=5*. The index value is an integer starting at 0. There is no maximum size limit on the array, and indices do not have to be ordered numbers, i.e., *x[0], x[1], x[2]*.... To extract an element of an array, the syntax is *${arrayname[index]}*. If *declare* is given the *–a* and *–r* options, a read-only array is created.

FORMAT

```
declare -a variable_name
variable = ( item1 item2 item3 ... )
```

EXAMPLE 11.77

```
declare -a nums=(45 33 100 65)
declare -ar names      (array is readonly)
names=( Tom  Dick  Harry)
states=( ME  [3]=CA  CT )
x[0]=55
n[4]=100
```

When assigning values to an array, they are automatically started at index 0 and incremented by 1 for each additional element added. You do not have to provide indices in an assignment, and if you do, they do not have to be in order. To unset an array, use the *unset* command followed by the array name, and to unset one element of the array, use *unset* and the arrayname[subscript] syntax.

The *declare*, *local*, and *read-only* built-ins also can take the *–a* option to declare an array. The *read* command with the *–a* option is used to read in a list of words from standard input into array elements.

EXAMPLE 11.78

```
1   $ declare -a friends

2   $ friends=(Sheryl Peter Louise)

3   $ echo ${friends[0]}
    Sheryl

4   $ echo ${friends[1]}
    Peter

5   $ echo ${friends[2]}
    Louise

6   $ echo "All the friends are ${friends[*]}"
    All the friends are Sheryl Peter Louise

7   $ echo "The number of elements in the array is ${#friends[*]}"
    The number of elements in the array is 3

8   $ unset friends   or unset ${friends[*]}
```

EXPLANATION

1   The *declare* built-in command is used to explicitly declare an array, but it is not necessary. Any variable that uses a subscript, such as *variable[0]*, when being assigned a value, will automatically be treated as an array.

2   The array *friends* is assigned a list of values: *Sheryl, Peter,* and *Louise.*

3   The first element of the *friends* array is accessed by enclosing the array name and its subscript in curly braces, with an index of 0 used as the value of the subscript. *Sheryl* is printed.

4   The second element of the *friends* array is accessed by using the index value of 1.

5   The third element of the *friends* array is accessed by using the index value of 2.

6   When you place the asterisk within the subscript, all of the elements of the array can be accessed. This line displays all the elements in the *friends* array.

7   The syntax *${#friends[*]}* produces the size of the array; i.e., the number of elements in the array. On the other hand, *${#friends[0]}* produces the number of characters in the value of the first element of the array. There are six characters in *Sheryl.*

8   The *unset* built-in command deletes the whole array. Just one element of the array can be removed by typing: *unset friends[1]*; this would remove *Sheryl.*

EXAMPLE 11.79

```
1   $ x[3]=100
    $ echo ${x[*]}
    100

2   $ echo ${x[0]}

3   $ echo ${x[3]}
    100

4   $ states=(ME  [3]=CA  [2]=CT)
    $ echo ${states[*]}
    ME CA CT

5   $ echo ${states[0]}
    ME

6   $ echo ${states[1]}

7   $ echo ${states[2]}
    CT

8   $ echo ${states[3]}
    CA
```

EXPLANATION

1. The third element of the array, *x*, is being assigned 100. It doesn't matter if the index number is 3, but because the first two elements do not exist yet, the size of the array is only 1. $\{x[*]\}$ displays the one element of the array, *x*.

2. *x[1]* has no value, and neither do *x[1]* and *x[2]*.

3. *x[3]* has a value of *100*.

4. The *states* array is being assigned *ME* at index *0*, *CA* at index 3, and *CT* at index 2. In this example, you can see that *bash* doesn't care at what index you store values, and that the index numbers do not have to be contiguous.

5. The first element of the *states* array is printed.

6. There is nothing stored in *states[1]*.

7. The third element of the *states* array, *states[2]*, was assigned *CT*.

8. The fourth element of the *states* array, *states[3]*, was assigned *CA*.

11.3.8 An Introduction to Functions

Bash functions are used to execute a group of commands with a name within the context of the current shell (a child process is not forked). They are like scripts, only more efficient. Once defined, functions become part of the shell's memory so that when the function is called, the shell does not have to read it in from the disk as it does with a file. Often functions are used to improve the modularity of a script. Once defined, functions can be used again and again. Although functions can be defined at the prompt when running interactively, they are often defined in the user's initialization file, *.bash_profile*. They must be defined before they are invoked.

Defining Functions. There are two ways to declare a *bash* function. One way, the old Bourne shell way, is to give the function name followed by a set of empty parentheses, followed by the function definition. The new way (Korn shell way) is to use the *function* keyword followed by the function name and then the function definition. If using the new way, the parentheses are optional. The function definition is enclosed in curly braces. It consists of commands separated by semicolons. The last command is terminated with a semicolon. Spaces around the curly braces are required. Any arguments passed to the function are treated as positional parameters within the function. The positional parameters in a function are local to the function. The *local* built-in function allows local variables to be created within the function definition. Functions may also be recursive, i.e., call themselves an unlimited number of times.

FORMAT

```
function_name () { commands ; commands; }
function function_name { commands ; commands; }
function function_name () { commands ; commands; }
```

EXAMPLE 11.80

```
1  $ function greet { echo "Hello $LOGNAME, today is $(date)"; }
2  $ greet
   Hello ellie, today is Wed Jul 14 14:56:31 PDT  2001

3  $ greet () { echo "Hello $LOGNAME, today is $(date)"; }
4  $ greet
   Hello ellie, today is Wed Jul 14 15:16:22 PDT  2001

5  $ declare -f
   declare -f greet()
   {
       echo "Hello $LOGNAME, today is $(date)"
   }


6  $ declare -Fᵃ
   declare -f greet

7  $ export -f greet

8  $ bash                      Start subshell
9  $ greet
   Hello ellie, today is Wed Jul 14 17:59:24 PDT  2001
```

a.   Only on *bash* version 2.x.

EXPLANATION

1   The keyword *function* is followed by the name of the function, *greet*. The function definition is surrounded by curly braces. There must be a space after the opening curly brace. Statements on the same line are terminated with a semicolon.

2   When the *greet* function is invoked, the command(s) enclosed within the curly braces are executed in the context of the current shell.

3   The *greet* function is defined again using the Bourne shell syntax, the name of the function, followed by an empty set of parentheses, and the function definition.

4   The *greet* function is invoked again.

5   The *declare* command with the *–f* switch lists all functions defined in this shell and their definitions.

6   The *declare* command with the *–F* switch lists only function names.

7   The *export* command with the *–f* switch makes the function global, i.e., available to subshells.

8   A new *bash* shell is started.

9   The function is defined for this child shell because it was exported.

EXAMPLE 11.81

```
1   $ function fun {
        echo "The current working directory is $PWD."
        echo "Here is a list of your files: "
        ls
        echo "Today is $(date +%A).";
    }
2   $ fun
    The current working directory is /home.
    Here is a list of your files:
    abc       abc123    file1.bak   none      nothing    tmp
    abc1      abc2      file2       nonsense  nowhere    touch
    abc122    file1     file2.bak   noone     one
    Today is Wednesday.

3   $ function welcome { echo "Hi $1 and $2"; }
4   $ welcome tom joe
    Hi tom and joe

5   $ set jane anna lizzy
6   $ echo $*
    jane anna lizzy
```

EXAMPLE 11.81 (CONTINUED)

```
7   $ welcome johan joe
    hi johan and joe

8   $ echo  $1 $2
    johan joe

9   $ unset -f welcome        # unsets the function
```

EXPLANATION

1   The function *fun* is named and defined. The keyword *function* is followed by the function's name and a list of commands enclosed in curly braces. Commands are listed on separate line; if they are listed on the same line, they must be separated by semicolons. A space is required after the first curly brace or you will get a syntax error. A function must be defined before it can be used.

2   The function behaves just like a script when invoked. Each of the commands in the function definition are executed in turn.

3   There are two positional parameters used in the function *welcome*. When arguments are given to the function, the positional parameters are assigned those values.

4   The arguments to the function, *tom* and *joe*, are assigned to $1 and $2, respectively. The positional parameters in a function are private to the function and will not interfere with any used outside the function.

5   The positional parameters are set at the command line. These variables have nothing to do with the ones set in the function.

6   $* displays the values of the currently set positional parameters.

7   The function *welcome* is called. *Johan* and *joe* are the values assigned to the positional parameters.

8   The positional variables assigned at the command line are unaffected by those set in the function.

9   The *unset* built-in command with the –*f* switch unsets the function. It is no longer defined.

Listing and Unsetting Functions. To list functions and their definitions, use the *declare* command. In *bash* versions 2.x and above, *declare –F* lists just function names. The function and its definition will appear in the output, along with the exported and local variables. Functions and their definitions are unset with the *unset –f* command.

11.3.9 Standard I/O and Redirection

When the shell starts up, it inherits three files: *stdin*, *stdout*, and *stderr*. Standard input normally comes from the keyboard. Standard output and standard error normally go to the screen. There are times when you want to read input from a file or send output or errors to a file. This can be accomplished by using I/O redirection. See Table 11.23 for a list of redirection operators.

Table 11.23 Redirection

Redirection Operator	What It Does
<	Redirects input.
>	Redirects output.
>>	Appends output.
2>	Redirects error.
&>	Redirects output and error.
>&	Redirects output and error (preferred way).
2>&1	Redirects error to where output is going.
1>&2	Redirects output to where error is going.
>|	Overrides *noclobber* when redirecting output.
<> filename	Uses file as both standard input and output if a device file (from */dev*).

EXAMPLE 11.82

```
1   $ tr '[A-Z]'  '[a-z]' < myfile     # Redirect  input

2   $ ls > lsfile                      # Redirect output
    $ cat lsfile
    dir1
    dir2
    file1
    file2
    file3

3   $ date >> lsfile                   # Redirect and append otuput
    $ cat lsfile
    dir1
    dir2
    file1
    file2
    file3
    Sun Sept 17 12:57:22 PDT 2001


4   $ cc prog.c 2> errfile             # Redirect error

5   $ find . -name \*.c -print > foundit 2> /dev/null
    # Redirect output to foundit and errors to /dev/null,
    # respectively.

6   $ find . -name \*.c -print >& foundit
    # Redirect both output and errors to foundit.

7   $ find . -name \*.c -print > foundit 2>&1
    # Redirect output to foundit and send errors to where output
    # is going; i.e. foundit

8   $ echo "File needs an argument" 1>&2
    # Send standard output to error
```

EXPLANATION

1 Instead of getting input from the keyboard, standard input is redirected from the file *myfile* to the UNIX *tr* command. All uppercase letters are converted to lowercase.

2 Instead of sending output to the screen, the *ls* command redirects its output to the file *lsfile*.

3 The output of the *date* command is redirected and appended to *lsfile*.

4 The C program source file *prog.c* is compiled. If the compile fails, the standard error is redirected to the file *errfile*. Now you can take your error file to the local guru for an explanation (of sorts)!

5 The *find* command starts searching in the current working directory for filenames ending in *.c*, and prints the filenames to a file named *foundit*. Errors from the *find* command are sent to */dev/null*.

6 The *find* command starts searching in the current working directory for filenames ending in *.c*, and prints the filenames to a file named *foundit*. The errors are also sent to *foundit*.

7 Same as 6.

8 The *echo* command sends its message to standard error. Its standard output is merged with standard error.

The *exec* Command and Redirection. The *exec* command can be used to replace the current program with a new one without starting a new process. Standard output or input can be changed with the *exec* command without creating a subshell. (See Table 11.24.) If a file is opened with *exec*, subsequent *read* commands will move the file pointer down the file a line at a time until the end of the file. The file must be closed to start reading from the beginning again. However, if using UNIX utilities such as *cat* and *sort*, the operating system closes the file after each command has completed.

Table 11.24 The *exec* Command

exec *Command*	*What It Does*
exec ls	*ls* executes in place of the shell. When *ls* is finished, the shell in which it was started does not return.
exec < filea	Opens *filea* for reading standard input.
exec > filex	Opens *filex* for writing standard output.
exec 3< datfile	Opens *datfile* as file descriptor 3 for reading input.
sort <&3	*Datfile* is sorted.
exec 4>newfile	Opens *newfile* as file descriptor (fd) 4 for writing.
ls >&4	Output of *ls* is redirected to *newfile*.
exec 5<&4	Makes fd 5 a copy of fd 4.
exec 3<&–	Closes fd 3.

EXAMPLE 11.83

```
1   $ exec date
    Thu Oct 14 10:07:34  PDT 2001
     <Login prompt appears if you are in your login shell >

2   $ exec > temp
    $ ls
    $ pwd
    $ echo Hello
3   $ exec > /dev/tty
4   $ echo Hello
    Hello
```

EXPLANATION

1   The *exec* command executes the *date* command in the current shell (does not fork a child shell). Because the *date* command is executed in place of the current shell, when the *date* command exits, the shell terminates. If a *bash* shell had been started from the TC shell, the *bash* shell would exit and the TC shell prompt would appear. If you are in your login shell when you try this, you will be logged out. If you are working interactively in a shell window, the window exits.

2   The *exec* command opens standard output for the current shell to the *temp* file. Output from *ls, pwd,* and *echo* will no longer go to the screen, but to *temp*. (See Figure 11.3.)

3   The *exec* command reopens standard output to the terminal. Now, output will go to the screen as shown in line 4.

4   Standard output has been directed back to the terminal (*/dev/tty*).

Figure 11.3 The *exec* command and file descriptors.

EXAMPLE 11.84

```
1   > bash
2   $ cat doit
    pwd
    echo hello
    date
3   $ exec < doit
    /home/homebound/ellie/shell
    hello
    Thu Oct 14 10:07:34  PDT 2001
4   >
```

EXPLANATION

1   From a TC shell prompt, *bash* is started up. (This is done so that when the *exec* command exits, the user will not be logged out.)

2   The contents of a file called *doit* are displayed.

3   The *exec* command opens standard input to the file called *doit*. Input is read from the file instead of from the keyboard. The commands from the file *doit* are executed in place of the current shell. When the last command exits, so does the shell.

4   The *bash* shell exited when the *exec* command completed. The TC shell prompt appeared. It was the parent shell. If you had been in your login shell when the *exec* finished, you would be logged out; if in a window, the window would have disappeared.

EXAMPLE 11.85

```
1   $ exec 3> filex
2   $ who >& 3
3   $ date >& 3
4   $ exec 3>&-
5   $ exec 3<filex
6   $ cat <&3
    ellie   tty1    Jul 21 09:50
    ellie   ttyp1   Jul 21 11:16   (:0.0)
    ellie   ttyp0   Jul 21 16:49   (:0.0)
    Wed Jul 21 17:15:18 PDT 2001
7   $ exec 3<&-
8   $ date >& 3
    date: write error: Bad file descriptor
```

EXPLANATION

1 File descriptor 3 (fd 3) is assigned to *filex* and opened for redirection of output. See Figure 11.4(a).

2 The output of the *who* command is sent to fd 3, *filex*.

3 The output of the *date* command is sent to fd 3; *filex* is already opened, so the output is appended to *filex*.

4 Fd 3 is closed.

5 The *exec* command opens fd 3 for reading input. Input will be redirected from *filex*. See Figure 11.4(b).

6 The *cat* program reads from fd 3, assigned to *filex*.

7 The *exec* command closes fd 3. (Actually, the operating system will close the file once end of file is reached.)

8 When attempting to send the output of the *date* command to fd 3, *bash* reports an error condition, because *fd* 3 was previously closed.

```
exec 3>filex                    exec 3<filex

┌─────────────────┐            ┌─────────────────┐
│101│             │            │102│             │
│   └─────────────│            │   └─────────────│
│                 │            │                 │
│   /bin/bash     │            │   /bin/bash     │
│                 │            │                 │
├───┬─────────────┤            ├───┬─────────────┤
│ 0 │ stdin       │            │ 0 │ stdin       │
├───┼─────────────┤            ├───┼─────────────┤
│ 1 │ stdout      │            │ 1 │ stdout      │
├───┼─────────────┤            ├───┼─────────────┤
│ 2 │ stderr      │            │ 2 │ stderr      │
├───┼─────────────┤            ├───┼─────────────┤
│ 3 │ filex       │            │ 3 │ filex       │
└───┴─────────────┘            └───┴─────────────┘
  a. opened for writing          b. opened for reading
```

Figure 11.4 *exec* and file descriptors.

11.3.10 Pipes

A *pipe* takes the output from the command on the left-hand side of the pipe symbol and
sends it to the input of the command on the right-hand side of the pipe symbol. A pipeline can consist of more than one pipe.

The purpose of the commands in Example 11.86 is to count the number of people
logged on (*who*), save the output of the command in a file (*tmp*), use the *wc –l* to count
the number of lines in the *tmp* file (*wc –l*), and then remove the *tmp* file (i.e., find the
number of people logged on).

EXAMPLE 11.86

```
1   $ who > tmp
2   $ wc -1 tmp
    4 tmp
3   $ rm tmp

# Using a pipe saves disk space and time.

4   $ who | wc -1
    4

5   $ du .. | sort -n | sed -n '$p'
    1980    ..

6   $ ( du / | sort -n | sed -n '$p' ) 2> /dev/null
    1057747   /
```

EXPLANATION

1   The output of the *who* command is redirected to the *tmp* file.
2   The *wc –l* command displays the number of lines in *tmp*.
3   The *tmp* file is removed.
4   With the pipe facility, you can perform all three of the preceding steps in one step.
    The output of the *who* command is sent to an anonymous kernel buffer; the *wc -l*
    command reads from the buffer and sends its output to the screen. See Figure
    11.5.
5   The output of the *du* command, the number of disk blocks used per directory,
    starting in the parent directory (..), is piped to the *sort* command and sorted nu-
    merically. It is then piped to the *sed* command, which prints the last line of the
    output it receives. See Figure 11.6.

6   The *du* command (starting in the root directory) will send error messages to *stderr* (the screen) if it is unable to get into a directory because the permissions have been turned off. When you put the whole command line in a set of parentheses, all the output is sent to the screen, and all the errors are directed to the UNIX bit bucket, */dev/null*.

Figure 11.5   The pipe.

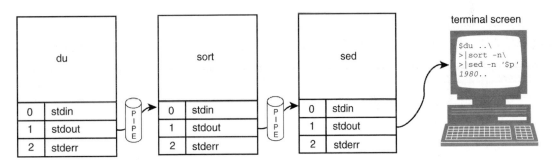

Figure 11.6   Multiple pipes (filter).

11.3.11 The *here document* and Redirecting Input

The *here document* is a special form of quoting. It accepts inline text for a program expecting input, such as *mail, sort,* or *cat,* until a user-defined terminator is reached. It is often used in shell scripts for creating menus. The command receiving the input is appended with a << symbol, followed by a user-defined word or symbol, and a newline. The next lines of text will be the lines of input to be sent to the command. The input is terminated when the user-defined word or symbol is then placed on a line by itself in the leftmost column (it cannot have spaces surrounding it). The word is used in place of Control-D to stop the program from reading input.

If the terminator is preceded by the <<– operator, leading tabs, and only tabs, may precede the final terminator. The user-defined terminating word or symbol must match exactly from "here" to "here." The following examples illustrate the use of the *here document* at the command line to demonstrate the syntax. It is much more practical to use them in scripts.

EXAMPLE 11.87

```
1   $ cat << FINISH                  ◀─┐  # FINISH is a user-defined
2   > Hello there $LOGNAME             │  # terminator
3   > The time is $(date +%T).         │
    > I can't wait to see you!!!       │
4   > FINISH                         ◀─┘  # terminator matches first

5   Hello there ellie                     # FINISH on line 1.
    The time is 19:42:12.
    I can't wait to see you!!!
6   $
```

EXPLANATION

1   The UNIX *cat* program will accept input until the word *FINISH* appears on a line by itself.

2   A secondary prompt appears. The following text is input for the *cat* command. Variable substitution is performed within the *here document.*

3   Command substitution, $(*date +%T*), is performed within the *here document.* Could have also used the older form of command substitution: `date +T`.

4   The user-defined terminator *FINISH* marks the end of input for the *cat* program. It cannot have any spaces before or after it and is on a line by itself.

5   The output from the *cat* program is displayed.

6   The shell prompt reappears.

EXAMPLE 11.88

```
1   $ cat <<- DONE
    >   Hello there
    >       What's up?
    >Bye now The time is `date`.
2   >   DONE
      Hello there
          What's up?
      Bye now The time is Sun Feb 819:48:23 PST 2001.
    $
```

EXPLANATION

1   The *cat* program accepts input until *DONE* appears on a line by itself. The <<– operator allows the input and final terminator to be preceded by one or more tabs. Typing this example at the command line may cause problems with the Tab key; the example will work fine, if run from a script.

2   The final matching terminator, *DONE*, is preceded by a tab. The output of the *cat* program is displayed on the screen.

11.3.12 Shell Invocation Options

When the shell is started using the *bash* command, it can take options to modify its behavior. There are two types of options: single-character options and multicharacter options. The single-character options consist of a single leading dash followed by a single character. The multicharacter options consist of two leading dashes and any number of characters. Multicharacter options must appear before single-character options. An interactive login shell normally starts up with –*i* (starts an interactive shell) , –*s* (reads from standard input), and –*m* (enables job control). See Table 11.25.

Table 11.25   *Bash 2.x Shell Invocation Options*

Option	Meaning
–c string	Commands are read from *string*. Any arguments after *string* are assigned to positional parameters, starting at $0.
–D	A list of double quoted strings, preceded by a $, are printed to standard output. These strings are subject to language translation when the current locale is not C or POSIX. The *–n* option is implied; no commands will be executed.
–i	Shell is in the interactive mode. *TERM, QUIT,* and *INTERRUPT* are ignored.
–s	Commands are read from standard input and allows the setting of positional parameters.
–r	Starts a restricted shell.
– –	Signals the end of options and disables further option processing. Any arguments after *– –* or *–* are treated as filenames and arguments.
– –dump–strings	Same as *–D*.
– –help	Displays a usage message for a built-in command and exits.
– –login	Causes *bash* to be invoked as a *login* shell.
– –noediting	When *bash* is running interactively, does not use the Readline library.
– –noprofile	When starting up, *bash* does not read the initialization files: */etc/profile, ~/.bash_profile, ~/.bash_login,* or *~/.profile.*
– –norc	For interactive shells, *bash* will not read the *~/.bashrc* file. Turned on by default, if running shell as *sh*.
– –posix	Changes the behavior of *bash* to match the POSIX 1003.2 standard, if otherwise it wouldn't.
– –quiet	Displays no information at shell startup, the default.
– –rcfile file	If *bash* is interactive, uses this intialization file instead of *~/.bashrc*.

Table 11.25 *Bash* 2.x Shell Invocation Options (continued)

Option	Meaning
– –*restricted*	Starts a restricted shell.
– –*verbose*	Turns on verbose; same as *–v*.
– –*version*	Displays version information about this *bash* shell and exits.

11.3.13 The *set* Command and Options

The *set* command can be used to turn shell options on and off, as well as for handling command line arguments. To turn an option on, the dash (–) is prepended to the option; to turn an option off, the plus sign (+) is prepended to the option. See Table 11.26 for a list of *set* options.

EXAMPLE 11.89

```
1   $ set -f

2   $ echo *
    *

3   $ echo ??
    ??

4   $ set +f
```

EXPLANATION

1   The *f* option is turned on, disabling filename expansion.
2   The asterisk is not expanded.
3   The question marks are not expanded.
4   The *f* is turned off; filename expansion is enabled.

Table 11.26 The Built-In *set* Command Options

Name of Option	Shortcut Switch	What It Does
allexport	*–a*	Automatically marks new or modified variables for export from the time the option is set, until unset.
braceexpand	*–B*	Enables brace expansion, and is a default setting.
emacs		For command line editing, uses the *emacs* built-in editor, and is a default setting.
errexit	*–e*	If a command returns a nonzero exit status (fails), exits. Not set when reading initialization files.
histexpand	*–H*	Enables *!* and *!!* when performing history substitution, and is a default setting.
history		Enables command line history; on by default.
ignoreeof		Disables EOF (Control-D) from exiting a shell; must type *exit*. Same as setting shell variable, *IGNOREEOF=10*.
keyword	*–k*	Places keyword arguments in the environment for a command.
interactive_comments		For interactive shells, a leading # is used to comment out any text remaining on the line.
monitor	*–m*	Allows job control.
noclobber	*–C*	Protects files from being overwritten when redirection is used.
noexec	*–n*	Reads commands, but does not execute them. Used to check the syntax of scripts. Not on when running interactively.
noglob	*–d*	Disables pathname expansion; i.e., turns off wildcards.
notify	*–b*	Notifies user when background job finishes.

Table 11.26   The Built-In *set* Command Options (continued)

Name of Option	Shortcut Switch	What It Does
nounset	–u	Displays an error when expanding a variable that has not been set.
onecmd	–t	Exits after reading and executing one command.
physical	–P	If set, does not follow symbolic links when typing *cd* or *pwd*. The physical directory is used instead.
posix		Shell behavior is changed if the default operation doesn't match the POSIX standard.
privileged	–p	When set, the shell does not read the *.profile* or ENV file and shell functions are not inherited from the environment; automatically set for *setuid* scripts.
verbose	–v	Turns on the *verbose* mode for debugging.
vi		For command line editing, uses the vi built-in editor.
xtrace	x	Turns on the echo mode for debugging.

11.3.14   The *shopt* Command and Options

The *shopt* (*bash* 2.x) command can also be used to turn shell options on and off.

Table 11.27 The *shopt* Command Options

Option	Meaning
cdable_vars	If an argument to the *cd* built-in command is not a directory, it is assumed to be the name of a variable whose value is the directory to change to.
cdspell	Corrects minor errors in the spelling of a directory name in a *cd* command. The errors checked for are transposed characters, a missing character, and a character too many. If a correction is found, the corrected path is printed, and the command proceeds. Only used by interactive shells.
checkhash	*Bash* checks that a command found in the hash table exists before trying to execute it. If a hashed command no longer exists, a normal path search is performed.
checkwinsize	*Bash* checks the window size after each command and, if necessary, updates the values of *LINES* and *COLUMNS*.
cmdhist	*Bash* attempts to save all lines of a multiple-line command in the same history entry. This allows easy re-editing of multiline commands.
dotglob	*Bash* includes filenames beginning with a dot (.) in the results of filename expansion.
execfail	A noninteractive shell will not exit if it cannot execute the file specified as an argument to the *exec* built-in command. An interactive shell does not exit if *exec* fails.
expand_aliases	Aliases are expanded. Enabled by default.
extglob	The extended pattern matching features (regular expression metacharacters derived from Korn shell for filename expansion) are enabled.
histappend	The history list is appended to the file named by the value of the HISTFILE variable when the shell exits, rather than overwriting the file.
histreedit	If *readline* is being used, a user is given the opportunity to re-edit a failed history substitution.
histverify	If set, and *readline* is being used, the results of history substitution are not immediately passed to the shell parser. Instead, the resulting line is loaded into the *readline* editing buffer, allowing further modification.

Table 11.27 The *shopt* Command Options (continued)

Option	*Meaning*
hostcomplete	If set, and *readline* is being used, *bash* will attempt to perform hostname completion when a word containing @ is being completed. Enabled by default.
huponexit	If set, *bash* will send *SIGHUP* (hangup signal) to all jobs when an interactive login shell exits.
interactive_comments	Allows a word beginning with # to cause that word and all remaining characters on that line to be ignored in an interactive shell. Enabled by default.
lithist	If enabled, and the *cmdhist* option is enabled, multiline commands are saved to the history with embedded newlines rather than using semicolon separators where possible.
mailwarn	If set, and a file that *bash* is checking for mail has been accessed since the last time it was checked, the message *The mail in mailfile has been read* is displayed.
nocaseglob	If set, *bash* matches filenames in a case-insensitive fashion when performing filename expansion.
nullglob	If set, *bash* allows filename patterns that match no files to expand to a null string, rather than themselves.
promptvars	If set, prompt strings undergo variable and parameter expansion after being expanded. Enabled by default.
restricted_shell	The shell sets this option if it is started in restricted mode. The value may not be changed. This is not reset when the startup files are executed, allowing the startup files to discover whether or not a shell is restricted.
shift_verbose	If this is set, the *shift* built-in prints an error message when the shift count exceeds the number of positional parameters.
sourcepath	If set, the *source* built-in uses the value of *PATH* to find the directory containing the file supplied as an argument. Enabled by default.
source	A synonym for dot (.).

11.3.15 Shell Built-In Commands

The shell has a number of commands that are built-in to its source code. Because the commands are built-in, the shell doesn't have to locate them on disk, making execution much faster. The *help* feature provided with *bash* gives you online help for any built-in command. The built-in commands are listed in Table 11.28.

Table 11.28   Built-In Commands

Command	What It Does
:	Do-nothing command; returns exit status zero.
. file	The *dot* command reads and executes command from file.
break [n]	See "Loop Control" on page 778.
.	Executes program in context of current process; same as *source*.
alias	Lists and creates "nicknames" for existing commands.
bg	Puts a job in the background.
bind	Display current key and function bindings, or binds keys to a *readline* function or macro.
break	Breaks out of the innermost loop.
builtin [sh–builtin [args]]	Runs a shell built-in, passing it args and returning 0 exit status. Useful if a function and built-in have the same name.
cd [arg]	Changes the directory to home if no *arg* or to value of *arg*.
command command [arg]	Runs a command even if a function has the same name; i.e., bypasses function lookup.
continue [n]	See "Loop Control" on page 778.
declare [var]	Displays all variables or declares variables with optional attributes.
dirs	Displays a list of currently remembered directories resulting from *pushd*.
disown	Removes an active job from the job table.
echo [args]	Displays args terminated with a newline.

Table 11.28 Built-In Commands (continued)

Command	What It Does
enable	Enables and disables shell built-in commands.
eval [args]	Reads args as input to the shell and executes the resulting command(s).
exec command	Runs command in place of this shell.
exit [n]	Exits the shell with status *n*.
export [var]	Makes *var* known to subshells.
fc	*History's* fix command for editing history commands.
fg	Puts background job into foreground.
getopts	Parses and processes command line options.
hash	Controls the internal hash table for quicker searches for commands.
help [command]	Displays helpful info about built-in commands and, if command is specified, detailed help about that built-in command.
history	Displays the *history* list with line numbers.
jobs	Lists jobs put in the background.
kill [–signal process]	Sends the signal to the PID number or job number of the process. Type at the prompt: *kill –l.*
getopts	Used in shell scripts to parse command line and check for legal options.
let	Used for evaluating arithmetic expressions and assigning results of arithmetic calculations to variables.
local	Used in functions to restrict the scope of variables to the function.
logout	Exits the login shell.
popd	Removes entries from the directory stack.
pushd	Adds entries to the directory stack.
pwd	Prints present working directory.

Table 11.28   Built-In Commands (continued)

Command	What It Does
read [var]	Reads line from standard input into variable var.
readonly [var]	Makes variable var read-only. Cannot be reset.
return [n]	Returns from a function where n is the exit value given to the return.
set	Sets options and positional parameters. See "The set Command and Positional Parameters" on page 735.
shift [n]	Shifts positional parameters to the left n times.
stop pid	Halts execution of the process number PID.
suspend	Stops execution of the current shell (but not if a login shell).
test	Checks file types and evaluates conditional expressions.
times	Prints accumulated user and system times for processes run from this shell.
trap [arg] [n]	When shell receives signal n (0, 1, 2, or 15), executes arg.
type [command]	Prints the type of command; e.g., pwd is a built-in shell command.
typeset	Same as declare. Sets variables and gives them attributes.
ulimit	Diplays and sets process resource limits.
umask [octal digits]	Sets user file creation mode mask for owner, group, and others.
unalias	Unsets aliases.
unset [name]	Unset value of variable or function.
wait [pid#n]	Waits for background process with PID number n and reports termination status.

BASH SHELL LAB EXERCISES

Lab 43: Getting Started

1. What process puts the login prompt on your screen?

2. What process assigns values to *HOME*, *LOGNAME*, and *PATH*?

3. How do you know what shell you are using?

4. What command will allow you to change your login shell?

5. Where is your login shell assigned? (What file?)

6. Explain the difference between the */etc/profile* and *~/.bash_profile* file. Which one is executed first?

7. Edit your *.bash_profile* file as follows:

    a. Welcome the user.

    b. Add your home directory to the path if it is not there.

    c. Set erase to the Backspace key using *stty*.

    d. Type *source.bash_profile*. What is the function of the *source* command?

8. What is the *BASH_ENV* file? When is it executed?

9. What is the default primary prompt?

    a. Change the prompt to include the time of day and your home directory.

    b. What is the default secondary prompt? What is its function?

10. Explain the function of each of the following settings:

    a. set *–o ignoreeof*

    b. set *–o noclobber*

    c. set *–o emacs*

    d. set *–o vi*

11. In what file are the settings in the previous example stored? Why are they stored there?

12. What does *shopt –p* do? Why use *shopt* instead of *set*?

13. What is a built-in command? How can you tell if a command is a built-in or an executable? What is the purpose of the *builtin* command? The *enable* command?

14. What would cause the shell to return an exit status of *127*?

Lab 44: Job Control

1. What is the difference between a program and a process? What is a job?

2. What is the PID of your shell?

3. How do you stop a job?

4. What command brings a background job into the foreground?

5. How do you list all running jobs? All stopped jobs?

6. What is the purpose of the *kill* command?

7. What does *jobs –l* display? What does *kill –l* display?

Lab 45: Command Completion, History, and Aliases

1. What is filename completion?

2. What is the name of the file that stores a history of commands entered at the command line?

3. What does the *HISTSIZE* variable control? What does *HISTFILESIZE* control?

4. What does bang, bang mean?

5. How would you reexecute the last command that started with a *v*?

6. How would you reexecute the 125th command? How would you print the history list in reverse?

7. How do you set interactive editing to use the *vi* editor? In what initialization file would you put this setting?

8. What is the *fc* command?

9. What is the purpose of the Readline library? From what initialization file does it read instructions?

10. What is key binding? How do you find out what keys are bound?

11. What is the universal argument?

12. Create an alias for the following commands:

    a. *clear*

    b. *fc –s*

    c. *ls – –color=tty*

    d. *kill –l*

Lab 46: Shell Metacharacters

1. Make a directory called *wildcards*. *Cd* to that directory and type at the prompt:

```
touch ab abc a1 a2 a3 a11 a12 ba ba.1 ba.2 filex filey AbC ABC
ABc2 abc
```

2. Write and test the command that will do the following:

   a. List all files starting with *a*.

   b. List all files ending in at least one digit.

   c. List all files starting with *a* or *A*.

   d. List all files ending in a period, followed by a digit.

   e. List all files containing just two alphabetic characters.

   f. List three character files where all letters are uppercase.

   g. List files ending in *10*, *11*, or *12*.

   h. List files ending in *x* or *y*.

   i. List all files ending in a digit, an uppercase letter, or a lowercase letter.

   j. List all files *not* starting with a *b* or *B*.

   k. Remove two character files starting with *a* or *A*.

Lab 47: Redirection

1. What are the names of the three file streams associated with your terminal?

2. What is a file descriptor?

3. What command would you use to do the following:

    a. Redirect the output of the *ls* command to a file called *lsfile*?

    b. Redirect and append the output of the *date* command to *lsfile*?

    c. Redirect the output of the *who* command to *lsfile*? What happened?

4. What happens when you type *cp* all by itself?

5. How do you save the error message from the above example to a file?

6. Use the *find* command to find all files, starting from the parent directory, of type *directory*. Save the standard output in a file called *found* and any errors in a file called *found.errs*.

7. Take the output of three commands and redirect the output to a file called *gottem_all*?

8. Use a pipe(s) with the *ps* and *wc* commands to find out how many processes you are currently running.

Lab 48: Variables

1. What is a positional parameter? Type at the command line:

   set dogs cats birds fish

   a. How do you list all of the positional parameters?

   b. Which positional parameter is assigned *birds*?

   c. How do you print the number of positional parameters?

   d. How do you remove all the positional parameters from the shell's memory?

2. What is an environment variable? What is the command used to list them? Create an environment variable called *CITY* and assign it the value of your home town. How do you export it?

3. What is a local variable? Set a local variable to your name. Print its value. Unset it.

4. What is the function of *declare –i*?

5. What does the $$ variable display? What does the $! display?

chapter
12

Programming
with the *bash* Shell

12.1 Introduction

When commands are executed from within a file, instead of from the command line, the file is called a shell script and the shell is running noninteractively. When the *bash* shell starts running noninteractively, it looks for the environment variable, BASH_ENV (ENV) and starts up the file (normally .*bashrc*) assigned as its value. After the BASH_ENV file has been read, the shell will start executing commands in the script.[1]

12.1.1 The Steps in Creating a Shell Script

A shell script is normally written in an editor and consists of commands interspersed with comments. Comments are preceded by a pound sign and consist of text used to document what is going on.

The First Line. The first line at the top left corner of the script will indicate the program that will be executing the lines in the script. This line, commonly called the *shbang* line, is written as

```
#!/bin/bash
```

The *#!* is called a magic number and is used by the kernel to identify the program that should be interpreting the lines in the script. This line must be the top line of your script. The *bash* program can also accept arguments to modify its behavior. See Table 12.8 on page 813 for a list of *bash* options.

---

1. When *bash* starts interactively, if the *–norc* or *– –norc* option is given, the BASH_ENV or ENV file will not be read.

Comments. *Comments* are lines preceded by a pound sign (#) and can be on a line by themselves or on a line following a script command. They are used to document your script. It is sometimes difficult to understand what the script is supposed to do if it is not commented. Although comments are important, they are often too sparse or not used at all. Try to get used to commenting what you are doing not only for someone else, but also for yourself. Two days from now you may not recall exactly what you were trying to do.

Executable Statements and *bash* Shell Constructs. A *bash* shell program consists of a combination of UNIX commands, *bash* shell commands, programming constructs, and comments.

Making the Script Executable. When you create a file, it is not given the execute permission. You need this permission to run your script. Use the *chmod* command to turn on the execute permission.

EXAMPLE 12.1

```
1   $ chmod +x myscript
2   $ ls -lF  myscript
    -rwxr-xr-x    1 ellie   0 Jul  13:00 myscript*
```

EXPLANATION

1　The *chmod* command is used to turn on the execute permission for the user, group, and others.
2　The output of the *ls* command indicates that all users have execute permission on the *myscript* file. The asterisk at the end of the filename also indicates that this is an executable program.

A Scripting Session. In the following example, the user will create a script in the editor. After the user saves the file, the execute permissions are turned on, and the script is executed. If there are errors in the program, the shell will respond immediately.

EXAMPLE 12.2

```
(The Script)
1   #!/bin/bash
2   # This is the first Bash shell program of the day.
    # Scriptname: greetings
    # Written by:  Barbara Bashful
3   echo "Hello $LOGNAME, it's nice talking to you."
4   echo "Your present working directory is `pwd`."
    echo "You are working on a machine called `uname -n`."
    echo "Here is a list of your files."
5   ls    # List files in the present working directory
6   echo  "Bye for now $LOGNAME. The time is `date +%T`!"
```

(The Command Line)
```
    $ greetings      # Don't forget to turn turn on x permission!
    bash: ./greetings: Permission denied.

    $ chmod +x greetings
    $ greetings  or  ./greetings
3   Hello barbara, it's nice talking to you.
4   Your present working directory is /home/lion/barbara/prog
    You are working on a machine called lion.
    Here is a list of your files.

5   Afile        cplus      letter      prac
    Answerbook    cprog      library     prac1
    bourne        joke       notes       perl5
6   Bye for now barbara. The time is 18:05:07!
```

EXPLANATION

1   The first line of the script, #!/bin/bash, lets the kernel know what interpreter will execute the lines in this program, in this case the *bash* (Bourne Again shell) interpreter.

2   The comments are nonexecutable lines preceded by a pound sign. They can be on a line by themselves or appended to a line after a command.

3   After variable substitution is performed by the shell, the *echo* command displays the line on the screen.

4   After command substitution is performed by the shell, the *echo* command displays the line on the screen.

5   The *ls* command is executed. The comment will be ignored by the shell.

6   The *echo* command displays the string enclosed within double quotes. Variables and command substitution (backquotes) are expanded when placed within double quotes. In this case, the quotes were really not necessary.

12.2 Reading User Input

12.2.1 Variables (Review)

In the last chapter we talked about declaring and unsetting variables. Variables are set local to the current shell or as environment variables. Unless your shell script will invoke another script, variables are normally set as local variables within a script. (See "Variables" on page 659.)

To extract the value from a variable, precede the variable with a dollar sign. You can enclose the variable within double quotes and the dollar sign will be interpreted by the shell for variable expansion. Variable expansion is not performed if the variable is enclosed in single quotes.

EXAMPLE 12.3

```
1   name="John Doe"  or declare name="John Doe"    # local variable
2   export NAME="John Doe"      # global variable
3   echo "$name" "$NAME"        # extract the value
```

12.2.2 The *read* Command

The *read* command is a built-in command used to read input from the terminal or from a file (see Table 12.1). The *read* command takes a line of input until a newline is reached. The newline at the end of a line will be translated into a null byte when read. If no names are supplied, the line read is assigned to the special built-in variable, *REPLY*. You can also use the *read* command to cause a program to stop until the user hits Enter. To see how the *read* command is most effectively used for reading lines of input from a file, see "Looping Commands" on page 763. The –r option to *read* causes the backslash/newline pair to be ignored; the backslash is treated as part of the line. The *read* command has four options to control its behavior:–a, –e, –p, and –r.[2]

Table 12.1 The *read* Command

Format	Meaning
read answer	Reads a line from standard input and assigns it to the variable *answer*.
read first last	Reads a line from standard input to the first whitespace or newline, putting the first word typed into the variable *first* and the rest of the line into the variable *last*.
read	Reads a line from standard input and assigns it to the built-in variable, *REPLY*.

---

2. Options –a, –e, and –p are available only in *bash* versions 2.x.

Table 12.1   The *read* Command (continued)

Format	Meaning
read –a arrayname	Reads a list of words into an array called *arrayname*.[a]
read –e	Used in interactive shells with command line editing in effect; e.g., if editor is *vi*, *vi* commands can be used on the input line.[a]
read –p prompt	Prints a prompt, waits for input, and stores input in *REPLY* variable.[a]
read –r line	Allows the input to contain a backslash.[a]

a. Not implemented on versions of *bash* prior to 2.0.

EXAMPLE 12.4

```
(The Script)
    #!/bin/bash
    # Scriptname: nosy
    echo -e "Are you happy? \c"
1   read answer
    echo "$answer is the right response."
    echo -e "What is your full name? \c"
2   read first middle last
    echo "Hello  $first"

    echo -n "Where do you work? "
3   read
4   echo I guess $REPLY keeps you busy!
---------------------------------------------------------ᵃ
5   read -p "Enter your job title: "
6   echo "I thought you might be an $REPLY."

7   echo -n "Who are your best friends? "
8   read -a friends
9   echo "Say hi to ${friends[2]}."
---------------------------------------------------------
(The Output)
    $ nosy
    Are you happy? Yes
1   Yes is the right response.
2   What is your full name? Jon Jake Jones
    Hello Jon
3   Where do you work? the Chico Nut Factory
4   I guess the Chico Nut Factory keeps you busy!
5   Enter your job title: Accountant
6   I thought you might be an Accountant.
7,8 Who are your best friends?  Melvin Tim Ernesto
9   Say hi to Ernesto.
```

a. The commands listed below this line are not implemented on versions of *bash* prior to 2.x.

EXPLANATION

1   The *read* command accepts a line of user input and assigns the input to the variable *answer*.

2   The *read* command accepts input from the user and assigns the first word of input to the variable *first*, the second word of input to the variable *middle*, and all the rest of the words up to the end of the line to the variable *last*.

3   A line is read from standard input and stored in the built-in *REPLY* variable.

4   The value of the *REPLY* variable is printed.

5   With the *–p* option, the *read* command produces a prompt, *Enter your job title:* and stores the line of input in the special built-in *REPLY* variable.

6   The value of the *REPLY* variable is displayed in the string.

7   The user is asked to enter input.

8   With the *–a* option, the *read* command takes input as an array of words. The array is called *friends*. The elements read into the array are *Melvin, Tim,* and *Ernesto*.

9   The third element of the *friends* array, *Ernesto*, is printed. Array indices start at 0.

EXAMPLE 12.5

```
(The Script)
    #!/bin/bash
    # Scriptname: printer_check
    # Script to clear a hung-up printer
1   if [ $LOGNAME != root ]
    then
        echo "Must have root privileges to run this program"
        exit 1
    fi
2   cat << EOF
    Warning: All jobs in the printer queue will be removed.
    Please turn off the printer now. Press return when you
    are ready to continue. Otherwise press Control C.
    EOF
3   read JUNK        # Wait until the user turns off the printer
    echo
4   /etc/rc.d/init.d/lpd stop        # Stop the printer
5   echo -e "\nPlease turn the printer on now."
6   echo "Press Enter to continue"
```

EXAMPLE 12.5 (CONTINUED)

```
7   read JUNK                     # Stall until the user turns the printer
                                  # back on
    echo                          # A blank line is printed
8   /etc/rc.d/init.d/lpd start    # Start the printer
```

EXPLANATION

1   Checks to see if user is *root*. If not, sends an error and exits.

2   Creates a *here document*. Warning message is displayed on the screen.

3   The *read* command waits for user input. When the user presses Enter, the variable *JUNK* accepts whatever is typed. The variable is not used for anything. The *read* in this case is used to wait until the user turns off the printer, comes back, and presses Enter.

4   The *lpd* program stops the printer daemon.

5   Now it's time to turn the printer back on!

6   The user is asked to press Enter when ready.

7   Whatever the user types is read into the variable *JUNK*, and when Enter is pressed, the program will resume execution.

8   The *lpd* program starts the print daemons.

12.3 Arithmetic

12.3.1 Integers (*declare* and *let* Commands)

The *declare* Command.   Variables can be declared as integers with the *declare –i* command. If you attempt to assign any string value, *bash* assigns *0* to the variable. Arithmetic can be performed on variables that have been declared as integers. (If the variable has not been declared as an integer, the built-in *let* command allows arithmetic operations. See "The let Command" on page 732.) If you attempt to assign a floating point number, *bash* reports a syntax error. Numbers can also be represented in different bases such as *binary*, *octal*, and *hex*.

EXAMPLE 12.6

```
1   $ declare -i num

2   $ num=hello
    $ echo $num
    0

3   $ num=5 + 5
    bash: +: command not found

4   $ num=5+5
    $ echo $num
    10

5   $ num=4*6
    $ echo $num
    24

6   $ num="4 * 6"
    $ echo $num
    24

7   $ num=6.5
    bash: num: 6.5: sytax error in expression (remainder of
    expression is ".5")
```

EXPLANATION

1   The *declare* command with the *–i* option creates an integer variable *num*.
2   Trying to assign the string *hello* to the integer variable *num* causes the string to be stored as zero.
3   The whitespace must be quoted or removed unless the *let* command is used.
4   The whitespace is removed and arithmetic is performed.
5   Multiplication is performed and the result assigned to *num*.
6   The whitespace is quoted so that the multiplication can be performed and to keep the shell from expanding the wildcard (*).
7   Because the variable is set to integer, adding a fractional part causes a *bash* syntax error.

Listing Integers.   The *declare* command with only the *–i* argument will list all preset integers and their values, as shown in the following display.

```
$ declare -i
declare -ir EUID="15"          # effective user id
declare -ir PPID="235"         # parent process id
declare -ir UID="15"           # user id
```

Representing and Using Different Bases. Numbers can be represented in decimal (base 10, the default), octal (base 8), hexadecimal (base 16), and a range from base 2 to 36.

FORMAT

```
variable=base#number-in-that-base
```

EXAMPLE 12.7

```
n=2#101     Base is 2; number 101 is in base 2
```

EXAMPLE 12.8

```
(The Command Line)
1   $ declare -i x=017
    $ echo $x
    15
2   $ x=2#101
    $ echo $x
    5
3   $ x=8#17
    $ echo $x
    15
4   $ x=16#b
    $ echo $x
    11
```

EXPLANATION

1   The *declare* function is used to assign an integer variable x the octal value *017*. Octal numbers must start with a leading zero. *15*, the decimal value of *017*, is printed.

2   The variable, x, is assigned the value of *101* (binary). 2 represents the base, separated by a #, and the number in that base, *101*. The value of x is printed as decimal, *5*.

3   The variable *x* is assigned the value of *17* (octal). The value of *x* is printed as decimal, *15*.

4   The variable *x* is assigned the value of *b* (hexadecimal). The value of *x* is decimal *11*.

The *let* Command.   The *let* command is a *bash* shell built-in command that is used to perform integer arithmetic and numeric expression testing. To see what *let* operators your version of *bash* supports, type at the prompt:

```
help let
```

A list of the operators is also found in Table 12.4 on page 745.

EXAMPLE 12.9

```
1    $ i=5   or let i=5

2    $ let i=i+1
     $ echo $i
     6

3    $ let "i = i + 2"
     $ echo $i
     8

4    $ let "i+=1"
     $ echo $i
     9

5    $ i=3

6    $ (( i+=4))
     $ echo $i
     7

7    $ (( i=i-2 ))
     $ echo $i
     5
```

EXPLANATION

1   The variable *i* is assigned the value 5.

2   The *let* command will add *1* to the value of *i*. The $ (dollar sign) is not required for variable substitution when performing arithmetic.

3   The quotes are needed if the arguments contain whitespace.

EXPLANATION (CONTINUED)

4   The shortcut operator, +=, is used to add *1* to the value of *i*.

5   The variable *i* is assigned the value 5.

6   The double parentheses can be used to replace *let*.[a]
    4 is added and assigned to *i*.

7   2 is subtracted from *i*. We could have also written *i−=2*

a. Double parentheses (( )) are used to replace *let* on versions of *bash* 2.x.

12.3.2 Floating Point Arithmetic

Bash supports only integer arithmetic, but the *bc*, *awk*, and *nawk* utilities are useful if you need to perform more complex calculations.

EXAMPLE   12.10

```
(The Command Line)
1   $ n=`echo "scale=3; 13 / 2" | bc`
    $ echo $n
    6.500

2   product=`gawk -v x=2.45 -v y=3.123 'BEGIN{printf "%.2f\n",x*y}'`
    $ echo $product
    7.65
```

EXPLANATION

1   The output of the *echo* command is piped to the *bc* program. The scale is set to 3, which is the number of significant digits to the right of the decimal point that will be printed. The calculation is to divide *13* by *2*. The entire pipeline is enclosed in backquotes. Command substitution will be performed and the output assigned to the variable *n*.

2   The *gawk* program gets its values from the argument list passed in at the command line, *x=2.45 y=3.123*. After the numbers are multiplied, the *printf* function formats and prints the result with a precision of two places to the right of the decimal point. The output is assigned to the variable *product*.

12.4 Positional Parameters and Command Line Arguments

12.4.1 Positional Parameters

Information can be passed into a script via the command line. Each word (separated by whitespace) following the scriptname is called an argument.

Command line arguments can be referenced in scripts with positional parameters; for example, *$1* for the first argument, *$2* for the second argument, *$3* for the third argument, and so on. After *$9*, curly braces are used to keep the number as one number. For example, positional parameter *10* is referenced as *${10}*. The *$#* variable is used to test for the number of parameters, and *$** is used to display all of them. Positional parameters can be set or reset with the *set* command. When the *set* command is used, any positional parameters previously set are cleared out. See Table 12.2.

Table 12.2 Positional Parameters

Positional Parameter	What It References
$0	References the name of the script.
$#	Holds the value of the number of positional parameters.
*$**	Lists all of the positional parameters.
$@	Means the same as *$**, except when enclosed in double quotes.
"*$**"	Expands to a single argument (e.g., "*$1 $2 $3*").
"*$@*"	Expands to separate arguments (e.g., "*$1*" "*$2*" "*$3*").
$1 ... ${10}	References individual positional parameters.

EXAMPLE 12.11

```
(The Script)
    #!/bin/bash
    # Scriptname: greetings2
    echo "This script is called $0."
1   echo  "$0  $1 and $2"
    echo "The number of positional parameters is $#"
    -------------------------------------------------------------
```

EXAMPLE 12.11 (CONTINUED)

```
(The Command Line)
      $ chmod +x greetings2
2     $ greetings2
      This script is called  greetings2.
      greetings  and
      The number of positional paramters is

3     $ greetings2 Tommy
      This script is called greetings2.
      greetings Tommy and
      The number of positional parameters is 1

4     $ greetings2 Tommy Kimberly
      This script is called greetings2.
      greetings Tommy and Kimberly
      The number of positional parameters is 2
```

EXPLANATION

1   In the script *greetings2*, positional parameter *$0* references the scriptname, *$1* the first command line agreement, and *$2* the second command line agreement.

2   The *greetings2* script is executed without any arguments passed. The output illustrates that the script is called *greetings2* (*$0* in the script) and that *$1* and *$2* were never assigned anything; therefore, their values are null and nothing is printed.

3   This time, one argument is passed, *Tommy*. *Tommy* is assigned to positional parameter *1*.

4   Two arguments are entered, *Tommy* and *Kimberly*. *Tommy* is assigned to *$1* and *Kimberly* is assigned to *$2*.

12.4.2 The *set* Command and Positional Parameters

The *set* command with arguments resets the positional parameters.[3] Once reset, the old parameter list is lost. To unset all of the positional parameters, use *set − −*. *$0* is always the name of the script.

---

3. Remember, without arguments, the *set* command displays all the variables that have been set for this shell, local and exported. With options, the *set* command turns on and off shell control options such as *−x* and *−v*.

EXAMPLE 12.12

```
(The Script)
    #!/bin/bash
    # Scriptname: args
    # Script to test command line arguments
1   echo The name of this script is $0.
2   echo The arguments are $*.
3   echo The first argument is $1.
4   echo The second argument is $2.
5   echo The number of arguments is $#.
6   oldargs=$*
7   set Jake Nicky Scott      # Reset the positional parameters
8   echo All the positional parameters are $*.
9   echo The number of postional parameters is $#.
10  echo "Good-bye for now, $1."
11  set $(date)               # Reset the positional parameters
12  echo The date is $2 $3, $6.
13  echo "The value of \$oldargs is $oldargs."
14  set $oldargs
15  echo $1 $2 $3

(The Output)
    $ args a b c d
1   The name of this script is args.
2   The arguments are a b c d.
3   The first argument is a.
4   The second argument is b.
5   The number of arguments is 4.
8   All the positional parameters are Jake Nicky Scott.
9   The number of positional parameters is 3.
10  Good-bye for now, Jake.
12  The date is Mar 25, 2001.
13  The value of $oldargs is a b c d.
15  Wed Mar 25
```

EXPLANATION

1 The name of the script is stored in the $0 variable.

2 $* represents all of the positional parameters.

3 $1 represents the first positional parameter (command line argument).

4 $2 represents the second positional parameter.

5 $# is the total number of positional parameters (command line arguments).

6 All positional parameters are saved in a variable called *oldargs*.

7 The *set* command allows you to reset the positional parameters, clearing out the old list. Now, $1 is *Jake,* $2 is *Nicky,* and $3 is *Scott.*

EXPLANATION (CONTINUED)

8 $* represents all of the parameters, *Jake, Nicky*, and *Scott*.

9 $# represents the number of parameters, *3*.

10 *$1* is *Jake*.

11 After command substitution is performed, i.e., *date* is executed, the positional parameters are reset to the output of the *date* command.

12 The new values of *$2, $3*, and *$6* are displayed.

13 The values saved in *oldargs* are printed.

14 The *set* command creates positional parameters from the values stored in *oldargs*.

15 The first three positional parameters are displayed.

EXAMPLE 12.13

```
(The Script)
    #!/bin/bash
    # Scriptname: checker
    # Script to demonstrate the use of special variable
    # modifiers and arguments
1   name=${1:?"requires an argument" }
    echo Hello $name

(The Command Line)
2   $ checker
    checker: 1: requires an argument
3   $ checker Sue
    Hello Sue
```

EXPLANATION

1 The special variable modifier *:?* will check whether *$1* has a value. If not, the script exits and the message is printed.

2 The program is executed without an argument. *$1* is not assigned a value; an error is displayed.

3 The *checker* program is given a command line argument, *Sue*. In the script, *$1* is assigned *Sue*. The program continues.

How $* and $@ Differ.   The $* and $@ differ only when enclosed in double quotes. When $* is enclosed within double quotes, the parameter list becomes a single string. When $@ is enclosed within double quotes, each of the parameters is quoted; that is, each word is treated as a separate string.

EXAMPLE 12.14

```
1   $ set 'apple pie' pears peaches
2   $ for i in $*
    > do
    > echo $i
    > done
    apple
    pie
    pears
    peaches


3   $ set 'apple pie' pears peaches
4   $ for i in "$*"
    > do
    > echo $i
    > done
    apple pie pears peaches


5   $ set 'apple pie' pears peaches
6   $ for i in $@
    > do
    > echo $i
    > done
    apple
    pie
    pears
    peaches


7   $ set 'apple pie' pears peaches
8   $ for i in "$@"                  # At last!!
    > do
    > echo $i
    > done
    apple pie
    pears
    peaches
```

EXPLANATION

1   The positional parameters are set.

2   When $* is expanded, the quotes surrounding *apple pie* are stripped; *apple* and *pie* become two separate words. The *for* loop assigns each of the words, in turn, to the variable *i*, and then prints the value of *i*. Each time through the loop, the word on the left is shifted off, and the next word is assigned to the variable *i*.

3   The positional parameters are set.

4   By enclosing $* in double quotes, the entire parameter list becomes one string, *apple pie pears peaches*. The entire list is assigned to *i* as a single word. The loop makes one iteration.

5   The positional parameters are set.

6   Unquoted, $@ and $* behave the same way (see entry 2 of this explanation).

7   The positional parameters are set.

8   By surrounding $@ with double quotes, each of the positional parameters is treated as a quoted string. The list would be *apple pie*, *pears*, and *peaches*. The desired result is finally achieved.

12.5 Conditional Constructs and Flow Control

12.5.1 Exit Status

Conditional commands allow you to perform some task(s) based on whether a condition succeeds or fails. The *if* command is the simplest form of decision-making; the *if/else* commands allow a two-way decision; and the *if/elif/else* commands allow a multiway decision.

   Bash allows you to test two types of conditions: the success or failure of commands or whether an expression is true or false. In either case, the exit status is always used. An exit status of zero indicates success or true, and an exit status that is nonzero indicates failure or false. The *?* status variable contains a numeric value representing the exit status. To refresh your memory on how exit status works, look at Example 12.15.

```
    (At the Command Line)

1   $ name=Tom
2   $ grep "$name"  /etc/passwd
    Tom:8ZKX2F:5102:40:Tom Savage:/home/tom:/bin/sh
3   $ echo $?
    0               # Success!
4   $ name=Fred
5   $ grep "$name" /etc/passwd
    $ echo $?
    1               # Failure
```

EXPLANATION

1   The variable *name* is assigned the string *Tom*.

2   The *grep* command will search for string *Tom* in the *passwd* file.

3   The *?* variable contains the exit status of the last command executed; in this case, the exit status of *grep*. If *grep* is successful in finding the string *Tom*, it will return an exit status of zero. The *grep* command was successful.

4   The variable *name* is assigned *Fred*.

5   The *grep* command searches for Fred in the *passwd* file and is unable to find him. The *?* variable has a value of 1, indicating that *grep* failed.

12.5.2 The Built-In *test* Command

To evaluate an expression, the built-in *test* command is commonly used. This command is also linked to the bracket symbol. Either the *test* command itself can be used, or the expression can be enclosed in set of single brackets. Shell metacharacter expansion is not performed on expressions evaluated with the simple *test* command or when square brackets are used. Since word splitting is performed on variables, strings containing whitespace must be quoted. (See Example 12.16.)

On versions of *bash* 2.x, double brackets *[[ ]]* (the built-in compound *test* command) can be used to evaluate expressions. Word splitting is not performed on variables and pattern matching is done, allowing the expansion of metacharacters. A literal string containing whitespace must be quoted and if a string (with or without whitespace) is to be evaluated as an exact string, rather than part of a pattern, it too must be enclosed in quotes. The logical operators *&&* (*and*) and *||* (*or*) replace the *–a* and *–o* operators used with the simple *test* command. (See Example 12.17.)

Although the *test* command can evaluate arithmetic expressions, you may prefer to use the *let* command with its rich set of C-like operators (*bash* 2.x). The *let* command can be represented alternatively by enclosing its expression in a set of double parentheses. (See Example 12.18.)

Whether you are using the *test* command, compound command, or *let* command, the result of an expression is tested, with zero status indicating success and nonzero status indicating failure. (See Table 11.10 on page 649.)

The following examples illustrate how the exit status is tested with the built-in *test* command and the alternate form of *test*, a set of single brackets *[ ]*; the compound command, a set of double brackets *[[ ]]*; and the *let* command, a set of double parentheses *(( ))*.

EXAMPLE 12.16

```
(The test Command)
(At the Command Line)

1  $ name=Tom
2  $ grep "$name" /etc/passwd
3  $ echo $?
4  $ test $name != Tom
5  $ echo $?
   1              # Failure
6  $ [ $name = Tom ]
       # Brackets replace the test command
7  $ echo $?
   0
8  $ [ $name = [Tt]?? ]
   $ echo $?
   1
9  $ x=5
   $ y=20
10 $ [ $x -gt $y ]
   $ echo $?
   1
11 $ [ $x -le $y ]
   $ echo $?
   0
```

EXPLANATION

1   The variable *name* is assigned the string *Tom*.

2   The *grep* command will search for string *Tom* in the *passwd* file.

3   The *?* variable contains the exit status of the last command executed, in this case, the exit status of *grep*. If *grep* is successful in finding the string *Tom*, it will return an exit status of zero. The *grep* command was successful.

4   The *test* command is used to evaluate strings, numbers, and perform file testing. Like all commands, it returns an exit status. If the exit status is zero, the expression is true; if the exit status is one, the expression evaluates to false. There *must* be spaces surrounding the equal sign. The value of *name* is tested to see if it is not equal to *Tom*.

5   The test fails and returns an exit status of one.

6   The brackets are an alternate notation for the *test* command. There must be spaces after the first bracket. The expression is tested to see if *name* evaluates to the string *Tom*. *Bash* allows either a single or double equal sign to be used to test for equality of strings.

7   The exit status of the test is *0*. The test was successful because *$name* is equal to *Tom*.

8 The *test* command does not allow wildcard expansion. Because the question mark is treated as a literal character, the test fails. *Tom* and *[Tt]??* are not equal. The exit status is *1*, indicating that the text in line 8 failed.

9 *x* and *y* are given numeric values.

10 The *test* command uses numeric relational operators to test its operands; in this example it tests if $x is greater than (–gt) $y, and returns *0* exit status if true, *1* if false. (See Table 12.3 on page 744.)

11 Tests if $x less than or equal to (–le) $y, returning *0* exit status if true,*1* if false.

EXAMPLE 12.17

```
(The compound test command)(bash 2.x)
    $ name=Tom; friend=Joseph
1   $ [[ $name == [Tt]om ]]          # Wildcards allowed
    $ echo $?
    0
2   $ [[ $name == [Tt]om && $friend == "Jose" ]]
    $ echo $?
    1
3   $ shopt -s extglob              # Turns on extended pattern matching
4   $ name=Tommy
5   $ [[ $name == [Tt]o+(m)y ]]
    $ echo $?
    0
```

EXPLANATION

1 If using the compound *test* command, shell metacharacters can be used in string tests. In this example, the expression is tested for string equality where *name* can match either *Tom* or *tom* or *tommy*, etc. If the expression is true, the exit status (?) is *0*.

2 The logical operators *&&* (*and*) and *||* (*or*) can be used with the compound test. If *&&* is used, both expressions must be true, and if the first expression evaluates as false, no further checking is done. With the *||* logical operator, only one of the expressions must be true. If the first expression evaluates true, no further checking is done. Note that *"Jose"* is quoted. If not quoted, the *friend* variable would be checked to see if it contained the pattern *Jose*. *Jose* would match, and so would *Joseph*. The expression evaluates to false because the second condition is not true. The exit status is *1*.

3 Extended pattern matching is turned on with the built-in *shopt* command.

4 The variable is assigned the value *Tommy*.

5 In this test, the expression is tested for string equality using the new pattern-matching metacharacters. It tests if *name* matches a string starting with *T* or *t*, followed by an *o*, one or more *m* characters, and a *y*.

EXAMPLE 12.18

```
      (The let Command) (bash 2.x)
      (At the Command Line)
  1   $ x=2
      $ y=3

  2   (( x > 2 ))
      echo $?
      1

  3   (( x < 2 ))
      echo $?
      0

  4   (( x == 2 && y == 3 ))
      echo $?
      0

  5   (( x > 2 || y < 3 ))
      echo $?
      1
```

EXPLANATION

1 *x* and *y* are assigned numeric values.

2 The double parentheses replace the *let* command to evaluate the numeric expression. If *x* is greater than *y*, the exit status is *0*. Because the condition is not true, the exit status is *1*. The *?* variable holds the exit status of the last command executed; i.e., the (( )) command. Note: To evaluate a variable, the dollar sign is not necessary when the variable is enclosed in (( )).

3 The double parentheses evaluate the expression. If *x* is less than 2, and exit status of *0* is returned; otherwise, *1* is returned.

4 The compound expression is evaluated. The expression is tested as follows: if *x* is equal to *2* *and* *y* is equal to *3* (i.e., *both* expressions are true), then an exit status of *0* is returned; otherwise, *1* is returned.

5 The compound expression is evaluated. The expression is tested as follows: if *x* is greater than *2* *or* *y* is less than *3* (i.e., *one* of the expressions is true), then an exit status of *0* is returned; otherwise, *1* is returned.

Table 12.3 The *test* Command Operators

Test Operator	Tests True If
String Test	
[string1 = string2] [string1==string2]	*String1* is equal to *String2* (*space surrounding* = *required*). (Can be used instead of the single = sign on *bash* versions 2.x.)
[string1 != string2]	*String1* is not equal to *String2* (*space surrounding* != *required*).
[string]	*String* is not null.
[−z string]	Length of *string* is zero.
[−n string]	Length of *string* is nonzero.
[−l string]	Length of *string* (number of characters).
Examples:	*test −n $word* or *[−n $word]* *test tom = sue* or *[tom = sue]*
Logical Test	
[string1 −a string1]	Both *string1* **and** *string2* are true.
[string1 −o string2]	Either *string1* **or** *string2* is true.
[! string1]	**Not** a *string1* match.
Logical Test (Compound Test)[a]	
[[pattern1 && pattern2]]	Both *pattern1* **and** *pattern2* are true.
[[pattern1 || pattern2]]	Either *pattern1* **or** *pattern2* is true.
[[! pattern]]	**Not** a *pattern* match.
Integer Test	
[int1 −eq int2]	*Int1* is equal to *int2*.
[int1 −ne int2]	*Int1* is not equal to *int2*.
[int1 −gt int2]	*Int1* is greater than *int2*.
[int1 −ge int2]	*Int1* is greater than or equal to *int2*.
[int1 −lt int2]	*Int1* is less than *int2*.
[int1 −le int2]	*Int1* is less than or equal to *int2*.
Binary Operators for File Testing	
[file1 −nt file2]	True if *file1* is newer than *file2* (according to modification date).
[file1 −ot file2]	True if *file1* is older than *file2*.
[file1 −ef file2]	True if *file1* and *file2* have the same device or inode numbers.

a. With the compound test, *pattern* can contain pattern matching metacharacters; for exact string testing, *pattern2* must be enclosed in quotes.

Table 12.4 The *let* Command Operators

Operator	Meaning
− +	Unary minus and plus.
! ~	Logical and bitwise not (negation).
* / %	Multiply, divide, remainder.
+ −	Add, subtract.

let Operators Not Implemented Prior to *bash* 2.x

<< >>	Bitwise left shift, right shift.
<= >= < >	Comparison operators.
=_ !=	Equal to and not equal to.
&	Bitwise *and*.
^	Bitwise exclusive *or.*
|	Bitwise *or.*
&&	Logical *and.*
||	Logical *or.*
= *= /= %= += −= <<_ >>= &= ^= |=	Assignment and shortcut assignment.

12.5.3 The *if* Command

The simplest form of conditional is the *if* command. The command (a *bash* built-in or executable) following the *if* construct is executed and its exit status is returned. The exit status is usually determined by the programmer who wrote the utility. If the exit status is zero, the command succeeded and the statement(s) after the *then* keyword are executed. In the C shell, the expression following the *if* command is a Boolean-type expression as in C. But in the Bash, Bourne, and Korn shells, the statement following the *if* is a command or group of commands. If the exit status of the command being evaluated is zero, the block of statements after the *then* is executed until *fi* is reached. The *fi* terminates the *if* block. If the exit status is nonzero, meaning that the command failed in some way, the statement(s) after the *then* keyword are ignored and control goes to the line directly after the *fi* statement.

It is important that you know the exit status of the commands being tested. For example, the exit status of *grep* is reliable in letting you know whether *grep* found the pattern it was searching for in a file. If *grep* is successful in its search, it returns a zero exit status; if not, it returns one. The *sed* and *gawk* programs also search for patterns, but they will report a successful exit status regardless of whether they find the pattern. The criterion for success with *sed* and *gawk* is correct syntax, not functionality.

```
    if command
    then
        command
        command
    fi
------------------------------------
```

(Using **test** for numbers and strings -- old format)

```
    if test expression
    then
        command
    fi
            or

    if [ string/numeric expression ] then
            command
    fi
------------------------------------
```

(Using **test** for strings -- new formst)

```
    if [[ string expression ]] then
            command
    fi
```

(Using **let** for numbers -- new format)

```
    if (( numeric expression ))

------------------------------------
```

EXAMPLE 12.19

```
1  if grep "$name" /etc/passwd > /dev/null 2>&1
2  then
        echo Found $name!
3  fi
```

EXPLANATION

1   The *grep* command searches for its argument, *name*, in the */etc/passwd* database. Standard output and standard error are redirected to */dev/null*, the UNIX bit bucket.

2   If the exit status of the *grep* command is zero, the program goes to the *then* statement and executes commands until *fi* is reached. Indentation of commands between the *then* and *fi* keywords is a convention used to make the program more readable, and hence, easier to debug.

3   The *fi* terminates the list of commands following the *then* statement.

EXAMPLE 12.20

```
1   echo  "Are you o.k. (y/n) ?"
    read answer
2   if [ "$answer" = Y -o "$answer" = y ]
    then
          echo  "Glad to hear it."
3   fi


4   if [ $answer = Y -o "$answer" = y ]
    [: too many arguments


    ------------------------------------------------
5   if [[ $answer == [Yy]* || $answer == Maybe ]]ª
    then
          echo  "Glad to hear it."
    fi


6   shopt -s extglob


7   answer="not really"


8   if [[ $answer = [Nn]o?( way|t really) ]]
    then
          echo "So sorry. "
    fi
```

a.   Lines 5 through 8 are only implemented on versions of *bash* 2.x.

EXPLANATION

1   The user is asked the question and told to respond. The *read* command waits for a response.

2   The *test* command, represented by square brackets, is used to test expressions. It returns an exit status of zero if the expression is true and nonzero if the expression is false. If the variable *answer* evaluates to *Y* or *y*, the commands after the *then* statement are executed. (The *test* command does not allow the use of wildcards when testing expressions, and spaces must surround the square brackets, as well as the = operators. See Table 12.3.) *$answer* is double quoted to hold it together as a single string. Otherwise the *test* command will fail.

3   The *fi* terminates the *if* on line 2.

4   The *test* command fails if more than one word appears before the = operator. For example, if the user entered *yes, you betcha*, the *answer* variable would evaluate to three words, causing the *test* to fail, *unless $answer* is enclosed in double quotes. The resulting error message is shown here.

5   The compound command operators *[[ ]]* allow the expansion of shell metacharacters in a string expression. The variable does not need quotes surrounding it, even if it contains more than one word, as it did with the old *test* command.

6   The *shopt* built-in, if set to *extglob*, allows expanded parameter expansion. See Table 11.12 on page 657.

7   The *answer* variable is set to the string *"not really"*.

8   Extended pattern matching is used here. The expression reads, *if the value of the answer variable matches a string starting with* no *or* No *and if followed by zero or one occurrences of the expression in the parentheses, the expression is true.* The expression could be evaluated to *no, No, no way, No way, not really,* or *Not really.*

The *exit* Command and the *?* Variable.   The *exit* command is used to terminate the script and return to the command line. You may want the script to exit if some condition occurs. The argument given to the *exit* command is a number ranging from 0 to 255. If the program exits with zero as an argument, the program exited with success. A nonzero argument indicates some kind of failure. The argument given to the *exit* command is stored in the shell's *?* variable.

EXAMPLE 12.21

```
(The Script)
$ cat bigfiles
    # Name: bigfiles
    # Purpose: Use the find command to find any files in the root
    # partition that have not been modified within the past n (any
    # number within 30 days) days and are larger than 20 blocks
    # (512-byte blocks)
```

EXAMPLE 12.21 (CONTINUED)

```
1   if (( $# != 2 ))ᵃ              # [ $# -ne 2 ]
    then
        echo  "Usage:    $0 mdays size " 1>&2
        exit 1
2   fi
3   if (( $1 <  0 || $1 > 30 ))ᵇ     # [ $1 -lt 0 -o $1 -gt 30 ]
    then

        echo "mdays is out of range"
        exit 2
4   fi
5   if (( $2 <= 20 ))        # [ $2 -le 20 ]
    then
        echo "size is out of range"
        exit 3
6   fi

7   find / -xdev -mtime $1 -size +$2


(The Command Line)
$ bigfiles
Usage: bigfiles mdays size

$ echo $?
1

$ bigfiles 400 80
mdays is out of range

$ echo $?
2

$ bigfiles 25 2
size is out of range

$ echo $?
3

$ bigfiles 2 25
(Output of find prints here)
```

a.   Not implemented on versions prior to *bash* 2.x. On older versions could also be written `if let $(( $# != 2 ))`.
b.   Same as above. On older versions could also be written `if let $(( $1 <  0 || $1 > 30 )`.

EXPLANATION

1 The statement reads: *If the number of arguments is not equal to 2, print the error message and send it to standard error, then exit the script with an exit status of 1.* Either the built-in *test* command or the *let* command can be used to test numeric expressions.

2 The *fi* marks the end of the block of statements after *then*.

3 The statement reads: *If the value of the first positional parameter passed in from the command line is less than 0 or greater than 30, then print the message and exit with a status of 2.* See Table 12.4 on page 745 for numeric operators.

4 The *fi* ends the *if* block.

5 The statement reads: *If the value of the second positional parameter passed in at the command line is less than or equal to 20 (512-byte blocks), then print the message and exit with a status of 3.*

6 The *fi* ends the *if* block.

7 The *find* command starts its search in the root directory. The *–xdev* option prevents *find* from searching other partitions. The *–mtime* option takes a number argument, which is the number of days since the file was modified, and the *–size* option takes a number argument, which is the size of the file in 512-byte blocks.

Checking for Null Values.   When checking for null values in a variable, use double quotes to hold the null value or the *test* command will fail.

EXAMPLE 12.22

```
(The Script)
1   if [ "$name" = "" ]        # Alternative to  [ ! "$name" ]
                               # or [ -z "$name" ]

    then
        echo The name variable is null
    fi

(From System showmount program, which displays all remotely mounted
systems)
    remotes=$(/usr/sbin/showmount)
2   if [ "X${remotes}" != "X" ]
    then
        /usr/sbin/wall ${remotes}
                   . . .
3   fi
```

1 If the *name* variable evaluates to null, the test is true. The double quotes are used to represent null.

2 The *showmount* command lists all clients remotely mounted from a host machine. The command will list either one or more clients, or nothing. The variable *remotes* will either have a value assigned or will be null. The letter *X* precedes the variable *remotes* when being tested. If *remotes* evaluates to null, no clients are remotely logged on and *X* will be equal to *X*, causing the program to start execution again on line 3. If the variable has a value, for example, the hostname *pluto*, the expression would read *if Xpluto != X*, and the *wall* command would be executed. (All users on remote machines will be sent a message.) The purpose of using *X* in the expression is to guarantee that even if the value of *remotes* is null, there will always be a placeholder on either side of the *!=* operator in the expression.

3 The *fi* terminates the *if*.

Nested *if* Commands.   When *if* statements are nested, the *fi* statement always goes with the nearest *if* statement. Indenting the nested *ifs* makes it easier to see which *if* statement goes with which *fi* statement.

12.5.4 The *if/else* Command

The *if/else* commands allow a two-way decision-making process. If the command after the *if* fails, the commands after the *else* are executed.

```
if  command
then
    command(s)
else
    command(s)
fi
```

```
(The Script)
    #!/bin/bash
    # Scriptname: grepit
1   if grep "$name" /etc/passwd >& /dev/null; then
        echo Found $name!
3   else
4       echo "Can't find $name."
        exit 1
5   fi
```

EXPLANATION

1   The *grep* command searches for its argument, *name*, in the NIS *passwd* database. Because the user does not need to see the output, standard output and standard error are redirected to */dev/null*, the UNIX bit bucket.

2   If the exit status of the *ypmatch* command is zero, program control goes to the *then* statement and executes commands until *else* is reached.

3   The commands under the *else* statement are executed if the *ypmatch* command fails to find $name in the *passwd* database; that is, the exit status of *ypmatch* must be nonzero for the commands in the *else* block to be executed.

4   If the value in $name is not found in the *passwd* database, this *echo* statement is executed and the program exits with a value of *1*, indicating failure.

5   The *fi* terminates the *if*.

EXAMPLE 12.24

```
(The Script)
#!/bin/bash
# Scriptname: idcheck
# purpose:check user id to see if user is root.
# Only root has a uid of 0.
# Format for id output:uid=9496(ellie) gid=40 groups=40
# root's uid=0

1   id=`id | gawk -F'[=()' '{print $2}'`        # get user id
    echo your user id is: $id
2   if  (( id == 0 ))ᵃ    # [ $id -eq 0 ] (See cd file: idcheck2)
    then
3       echo "you are superuser."
4   else
        echo "you are not superuser."
5   fi


(The Command Line)
6   $ idcheck
    your user id is: 9496
    you are not superuser.
7   $ su
    Password:
8   # idcheck
    your user id is: 0
    you are superuser
```

a.   Not implemented on versions of *bash* prior to 2.x.

EXPLANATION

1   The *id* command is piped to the *gawk* command. *Nawk* uses an equal sign and open parenthesis as field separators, extracts the user ID from the output, and assigns the output to the variable *id*.

2,3,4   If the value of *id* is equal to zero, then line 3 is executed. If *id* is not equal to zero, the *else* statements are executed.

5   The *fi* marks the end of the *if* command.

6   The *idcheck* script is executed by the current user, whose UID is 9496.

7   The *su* command switches the user to *root*.

8   The # prompt indicates that the superuser (root) is the new user. The UID for root is *0*.

12.5.5 The *if/elif/else* Command

The *if/elif/else* commands allow a multiway decision-making process. If the command following the *if* fails, the command following the *elif* is tested. If that command succeeds, the commands under its *then* statement are executed. If the command after the *elif* fails, the next *elif* command is checked. If none of the commands succeeds, the *else* commands are executed. The *else* block is called the default.

FORMAT

```
if  command
then
    command(s)
elif command
then
    commands(s)
elif command
then
    command(s)
else
    command(s)
fi
```

EXAMPLE 12.25

```
(The Script)
    #!/bin/bash
    # Scriptname: tellme
    # Using the old-style test command

1   echo -n "How old are you? "
    read age
2   if [ $age -lt 0 -o $age -gt 120 ]
    then
        echo  "Welcome to our planet! "
        exit 1
    fi
3   if  [ $age -ge 0 -a $age -le 12 ]
    then
        echo "A child is a garden of verses"
    elif [ $age -ge 12 -a $age -le 19 ]
    then
        echo "Rebel without a cause"
    elif [ $age -ge 20 -a  $age -le 29 ]
    then
        echo "You got the world by the tail!!"
    elif [ $age -ge  30 -a  $age -le 39 ]
    then
        echo "Thirty something..."
4   else
        echo "Sorry I asked"
5   fi


(The Output)
$ tellme
How old are you? 200
Welcome to our planet!

$ tellme
How old are you? 13
Rebel without a cause

$ tellme
How old are you? 55
Sorry I asked
```

EXAMPLE 12.25 (CONTINUED)

```
-----------------------------------------------------------
    #!/bin/bash
    # Using the new (( )) compound let command
    # Scriptname: tellme2

1   echo -n "How old are you? "
    read age
2   if (( age < 0 || age > 120 ))
    then
        echo "Welcome to our planet! "
        exit 1
    fi
3   if ((age >= 0 && age <= 12))
    then
        echo "A child is a garden of verses"
    elif ((age >= 13 && age <= 19 ))
    then
        echo "Rebel without a cause"
    elif (( age >= 19 &&  age <= 29 ))
    then
        echo "You got the world by the tail!!"
    elif  (( age >=  30 &&  age <= 39 ))
    then
        echo "Thirty something..."
4   else
        echo "Sorry I asked"
5   fi
```

EXPLANATION

1   The user is asked for input. The input is assigned to the variable *age*.

2   A numeric test is performed by the *test* command. If *age* is less than *0* or greater than *120*, the *echo* command is executed and the program terminates with an exit status of one. The interactive shell prompt will appear.

3   A numeric test is performed by the *test* command. If *age* is greater than or equal to *0* and less than or equal to *12*, the *test* command returns exit status zero, true, and the statement after the *then* is executed. Otherwise, program control goes to the *elif*. If that test is false, the next *elif* is tested.

4   The *else* construct is the default. If none of the above statements are true, the *else* commands will be executed.

5   The *fi* terminates the initial *if* statement.

12.5.6 File Testing

Often when you are writing scripts, your script will require that there are certain files available and that those files have specific permissions, are of a certain type, or have other attributes. You will find file testing a necessary part of writing dependable scripts.

Table 12.5 File Test Operators

Test Operator	Tests True If
–b *filename*	Block special file.
–c *filename*	Character special file.
–d *filename*	Directory existence.
–e *filename*	File existence.
–f *filename*	Regular file existence and not a directory.
–G *filename*	True if file exists and is owned by the effective group ID.
–g *filename*	Set-group-ID is set.
–k *filename*	Sticky bit is set.
–L *filename*	File is a symbolic link.
–p *filename*	File is a named pipe.
–O *filename*	File exists and is owned by the effective user ID.
–r *filename*	File is readable.
–S *filename*	File is a socket.
–s *filename*	File is nonzero size.
–t *fd*	True if *fd* (file descriptor) is opened on a terminal.
–u *filename*	Set-user-ID bit is set.
–w *filename*	File is writeable.
–x *filename*	File is executable.

EXAMPLE 12.26

```
(The Script)
    #!/bin/bash
    # Using the old style test command
    # filename: perm_check
    file=./testing


1   if [ -d $file ]
    then
         echo "$file is a directory"
2   elif [ -f $file ]
    then
3        if [ -r $file -a -w $file -a -x $file ]
         then    # nested if command
              echo "You have read,write,and execute \
              permission on $file."
4        fi
5   else
         echo "$file is neither a file nor a directory. "
6   fi


------------------------------------------------

    #!/bin/bash
    # Using the new compound operator for test (( ))ᵃ
    # filename: perm_check2
    file=./testing


1   if [[ -d $file ]]
    then
         echo "$file is a directory"
2   elif [[ -f $file ]]
    then
3        if [[ -r $file && -w $file && -x $file ]]
         then    # nested if command
              echo "You have read,write,and execute \
              permission on $file."
4        fi
5   else
         echo "$file is neither a file nor a directory. "
6   fi
```

a.   New-style test with compound operators not implemented before *bash* 2.x.

EXPLANATION

1   If the file *testing* is a directory, print *testing is a directory.*
2   If the file *testing* is not a directory, *else if* the file is a plain file, then...
3   If the file *testing* is readable and writeable, and executable, then...
4   The *fi* terminates the innermost *if* command.
5   The *else* commands are executed *if* lines 1 and 2 are not true.
6   This *fi* goes with the first *if*.

12.5.7 The *null* Command

The *null* command, represented by a colon, is a built-in, do-nothing command that returns an exit status of zero. It is used as a placeholder after an *if* command when you have nothing to say, but need a command or the program will produce an error message because it requires something after the *then* statement. Often the null command is used as an argument to the *loop* command to make the loop a forever loop.

EXAMPLE 12.27

```
(The Script)
    #!/bin/bash
    # filename: name_grep
1   name=Tom
2   if grep "$name" databasefile >& /dev/null
    then
3       :
4   else
        echo "$1 not found in databasefile"
        exit 1
    fi
```

EXPLANATION

1   The variable *name* is assigned the string *Tom.*
2   The *if* command tests the exit status of the *grep* command. If *Tom* is found in the database file, the *null* command, a colon, is executed and does nothing. Both output and errors are redirected to */dev/null.*
3   The colon is the *null* command. It does nothing other than returning a *0* exit status.
4   What we really want to do is print an error message and exit if *Tom* is *not found.* The commands after the *else* will be executed if the *grep* command fails.

EXAMPLE 12.28

```
(The Command Line)
1   $ DATAFILE=
2   $ : ${DATAFILE:=$HOME/db/datafile}
    $ echo $DATAFILE
    /home/jody/ellie/db/datafile
3   $ : ${DATAFILE:=$HOME/junk}
    $ echo $DATAFILE
    /home/jody/ellie/db/datafile
```

EXPLANATION

1   The variable *DATAFILE* is assigned null.

2   The colon command is a do-nothing command. The modifier (:=) returns a value that can be assigned to a variable or used in a test. In this example, the expression is passed as an argument to the do-nothing command. The shell will perform variable substitution; that is, assign the pathname to *DATAFILE* if *DATAFILE* does not already have a value. The variable *DATAFILE* is permanently set.

3   Because the variable has already been set, it will not be reset with the default value provided on the right of the modifier.

EXAMPLE 12.29

```
(The Script)
    #!/bin/bash
1   # Scriptname: wholenum
    # Purpose:The expr command tests that the user enters an
    # integer
    #
    echo "Enter an integer."
    read number
2   if expr "$number" + 0 >& /dev/null
    then
3       :
    else
4       echo "You did not enter an integer value."
        exit 1
5   fi
```

EXPLANATION

1   The user is asked to enter an integer. The number is assigned to the variable *number*.

2   The *expr* command evaluates the expression. If addition can be performed, the number is a whole number and *expr* returns a successful exit status. All output is redirected to the bit bucket */dev/null*.

3   If *expr* is successful, it returns a zero exit status, and the colon command does nothing.

4   If the *expr* command fails, it returns a nonzero exit status, the *echo* command displays the message, and the program exits.

5   The *fi* ends the *if* block.

12.5.8 The *case* Command

The *case* command is a multiway branching command used as an alternative to *if/elif* commands. The value of the *case* variable is matched against *value1, value2*, and so forth, until a match is found. When a value matches the *case* variable, the commands following the value are executed until the double semicolons are reached. Then execution starts after the word *esac* (*case* spelled backward).

   If the *case* variable is not matched, the program executes the commands after the **)*, the default value, until *;;* or *esac* is reached. The **)* value functions the same as the *else* statement in *if/else* conditionals. The *case* values allow the use of shell wildcards and the vertical bar (pipe symbol) for *or*ing two values.

FORMAT

```
case variable in
value1)
   command(s)
   ;;
value2)
   command(s)
   ;;
*)
command(s)
   ;;
esac
```

EXAMPLE 12.30

```
(The Script)
    #!/bin/bash
    # Scriptname: xcolors
1   echo -n "Choose a foreground color for your xterm window: "
    read color
2   case "$color" in
3   [Bb]l??)
4       xterm -fg blue -fn terminal &
5       ;;
6   [Gg]ree*)
        xterm -fg darkgreen -fn terminal &
        ;;
7   red | orange)                 # The vertical bar means "or"
        xterm -fg "$color"  -fn terminal &
        ;;
8   *)
        xterm -fn terminal
        ;;
9   esac
10  echo  "Out of case command"
```

EXPLANATION

1   The user is asked for input. The input is assigned to the variable *color*.

2   The *case* command evaluates the expression *$color*.

3   If the color begins with a *B* or *b*, followed by the letter *l* and any two characters, the *case* expression matches the first value. The value is terminated with a single closed parenthesis. The wildcards are shell metacharacters used for filename expansion. The *xterm* command sets the foreground color to blue.

4   The statement is executed if the value in line number 3 matches the *case* expression.

5   The double semicolons are required after the last command in this block of commands. Control branches to line 10 when the semicolons are reached. The script is easier to debug if the semicolons are on their own line.

6   If the *case* expression matches a *G* or *g*, followed by the letters *ree* and ending in zero or more of any other characters, the *xterm* command is executed. The double semicolons terminate the block of statements and control branches to line 10.

7   The vertical bar is used as an *or* conditional operator. If the *case* expression matches either *red* or *orange*, the *xterm* command is executed.

8   This is the default value. If none of the above values match the *case* expression, the commands after the **)* are executed.

9   The *esac* statement terminates the *case* command.

10 After one of the *case* values are matched, execution continues here.

Creating Menus with the *here document* and *case* Command.   The *here document* and *case* command are often used together. The *here document* is used to create a menu of choices that will be displayed to the screen. The user will be asked to select one of the menu items, and the *case* command will test against the set of choices to execute the appropriate command.

EXAMPLE 12.31

```
(From the .bash_profile File)
    echo "Select a terminal type:  "
1   cat <<- ENDIT
        1) unix
        2) xterm
        3) sun
2   ENDIT
3   read choice
4   case "$choice" in
5   1)  TERM=unix
        export TERM
        ;;
    2)   TERM=xterm
        export TERM
        ;;
6   3)  TERM=sun
        export TERM
        ;;
7   esac
8   echo "TERM is $TERM."

(The Output)
$ . .bash_profile
    Select a terminal type:
    1) unix
    2) xterm
    3) sun
    2                 <-- User input
    TERM is xterm.
```

EXPLANATION

1   If this segment of script is put in the *.bash_profile*, when you log on, you will be given a chance to select the proper terminal type. The *here document* is used to display a menu of choices.

2   The user-defined *ENDIT* terminator marks the end of the *here document*.

3   The *read* command stores the user input in the variable *TERM*.

4   The *case* command evaluates the variable *TERM* and compares that value with one of the values preceding the closing parenthesis: *1, 2,* or ***.

5   The first value tested is *1*. If there is a match, the terminal is set to a *unix*. The
    TERM variable is exported so that subshells will inherit it.

6   A default value is not required. The *TERM* variable is normally assigned in
    /etc/profile at login time. If the choice is *3*, the terminal is set to a *sun*.

7   The *esac* terminates the *case* command.

8   After the *case* command has finished, this line is executed.

12.6 Looping Commands

Looping commands are used to execute a command or group of commands a set number
of times or until a certain condition is met. The *bash* shell has three types of loops: the
for loop, the *while* loop, and the *until* loop.

12.6.1 The *for* Command

The *for* looping command is used to execute commands a finite number of times on a
list of items. For example, you might use this loop to execute the same commands on a
list of files or usernames. The *for* command is followed by a user-defined variable, the
keyword *in*, and a list of words. The first time in the loop, the first word from the
wordlist is assigned to the variable, and then shifted off the list. Once the word is
assigned to the variable, the body of the loop is entered, and commands between the *do*
and *done* keywords are executed. The next time around the loop, the second word is
assigned to the variable, and so on. The body of the loop starts at the *do* keyword and
ends at the *done* keyword. When all of the words in the list have been shifted off, the
loop ends and program control continues after the *done* keyword.

FORMAT

```
for variable in word_list
do
    command(s)
done
```

EXAMPLE 12.32

```
(The Script)
    #!/bin/bash
    # Scriptname: forloop
1   for pal in Tom Dick Harry Joe
2   do
3       echo "Hi $pal"
4   done
5   echo "Out of loop"

(The Output)
$ forloop
Hi Tom
Hi Dick
Hi Harry
Hi Joe
Out of loop
```

EXPLANATION

1 This *for* loop will iterate through the list of names, *Tom, Dick, Harry,* and *Joe,* shifting each one off (to the left and assigning its value to the user-defined variable, *pal*) after it is used. As soon as all of the words are shifted and the wordlist is empty, the loop ends and execution starts after the *done* keyword. The first time in the loop, the variable *pal* will be assigned the word *Tom.* The second time through the loop, *pal* will be assigned *Dick,* the next time *pal* will be assigned *Harry,* and the last time *pal* will be assigned *Joe.*

2 The *do* keyword is required after the wordlist. If it is used on the same line, the list must be terminated with a semicolon. Example:

```
for pal in Tom Dick Harry Joe; do
```

3 This is the body of the loop. After *Tom* is assigned to the variable *pal,* the commands in the body of the loop (i.e., all commands between the *do* and *done* keywords) are executed.

4 The *done* keyword ends the loop. Once the last word in the list (*Joe*) has been assigned and shifted off, the loop exits, and execution starts at line 2.

5 Control resumes here when the loop exits.

EXAMPLE   12.33

```
(The Command Line)
1   $ cat mylist
    tom
    patty
    ann
    jake

(The Script)
    #!/bin/bash
    # Scriptname: mailer
2   for person in $(cat mylist)
    do
3       mail $person < letter
        echo $person was sent a letter.
4   done
5   echo "The letter has been sent."
```

EXPLANATION

1   The contents of a file called *mylist* are displayed.

2   Command substitution is performed and the contents of *mylist* becomes the wordlist. The first time in the loop, *tom* is assigned to the variable *person*, then it is shifted off to be replaced with *patty,* and so forth.

3   In the body of the loop, each user is mailed a copy of a file called *letter.*

4   The *done* keyword marks the end of this loop iteration.

5   When all of the users in the list have been sent mail and the loop has exited, this line is executed.

EXAMPLE   12.34

```
(The Script)
    #!/bin/bash
    # Scriptname: backup
    # Purpose: Create backup files and store
    # them in a backup directory.
    #
1   dir=/home/jody/ellie/backupscripts
```

EXAMPLE 12.34 (CONTINUED)

```
2   for file in memo[1-5]
    do
3       if [ -f $file ]
        then
            cp $file $dir/$file.bak
            echo "$file is backed up in $dir"
        fi
4   done
```

```
(The Output)
memo1 is backed up in /home/jody/ellie/backupscripts
memo2 is backed up in /home/jody/ellie/backupscripts
memo3 is backed up in /home/jody/ellie/backupscripts
memo4 is backed up in /home/jody/ellie/backupscripts
memo5 is backed up in /home/jody/ellie/backupscripts
```

EXPLANATION

1   The variable *dir* is assigned the directory where the backup scripts are to be stored.

2   The wordlist will consist of all files in the current working directory with names starting with *memo* and ending with numbers between *1* and *5*. Each filename will be assigned, one at time, to the variable *file* for each iteration of the loop.

3   When the body of the loop is entered, the file will be tested to make sure it exists and is a real file. If so, it will be copied into the directory */home/jody/ellie/backupscripts* with the *.bak* extension appended to its name.

4   The *done* marks the end of the loop.

The $* and $@ Variables in Wordlists.   When expanded, the $* and $@ are the same unless enclosed in double quotes. $* evaluates to one string, whereas $@ evaluates to a list of separate words.

EXAMPLE 12.35

```
(The Script)
    #!/bin/bash
    # Scriptname: greet
1   for name in $*            # same as for name in $@
2   do
        echo Hi $name
3   done
```

EXAMPLE 12.35 (CONTINUED)

(The Command Line)
$ **greet Dee Bert Lizzy Tommy**
Hi Dee
Hi Bert
Hi Lizzy
Hi Tommy

EXPLANATION

1   $* and $@ expand to a list of all the positional parameters, in this case, the arguments passed in from the command line: *Dee*, *Bert*, *Lizzy*, and *Tommy*. Each name in the list will be assigned, in turn, to the variable *name* in the *for* loop.

2   The commands in the body of the loop are executed until the list is empty.

3   The *done* keyword marks the end of the loop body.

EXAMPLE 12.36

(The Script)
    #!/bin/bash
    # Scriptname: permx

1   **for file**   # Empty wordlist
    do

2   if [-f $file -a ! -x $file] or if [[-f $file && ! -x $file]]ᵃ
        then

3   chmod +x $file
            echo $file now has execute permission
        fi
    done

(The Command Line)
4   $ **permx ***
    addon now has execute permission
    checkon now has execute permission
    doit now has execute permission

---

a. *Bash 2.x only.*

1   If the *for* loop is not provided with a wordlist, it iterates through the positional parameters. This is the same as *for file* in $*.

2   The filenames are coming in from the command line. The shell expands the asterisk (*) to all filenames in the current working directory. If the file is a plain file and does not have execute permission, line 3 is executed.

3   Execute permission is added for each file being processed.

4   At the command line, the asterisk will be evaluated by the shell as a wildcard and all files in the current directory will be replaced for the *. The files will be passed as arguments to the *permx* script.

12.6.2 The *while* Command

The *while* command evaluates the command following it and, if its exit status is zero, the commands in the body of the loop (commands between *do* and *done*) are executed. When the *done* keyword is reached, control is returned to the top of the loop and the *while* command checks the exit status of the command again. Until the exit status of the command being evaluated by the *while* becomes nonzero, the loop continues. When the exit status reaches nonzero, program execution starts after the *done* keyword.

FORMAT

```
while command
do
    command(s)
done
```

EXAMPLE 12.37

```
(The Script)
    #!/bin/bash
    # Scriptname: num
1   num=0        # Initialize num
2   while (( $num < 10 ))ᵃ    # or  while [ num -lt 10 ]
    do
        echo  -n "$num "
3       let num+=1            # Increment num
    done
4   echo -e "\nAfter loop exits, continue running here"

(The Output)
    0 1 2 3 4 5 6 7 8 9
4   After loop exits, continue running here
```

a. Versions of *bash* 2.x use this form.

EXPLANATION

1 This is the initialization step. The variable *num* is assigned *0*.

2 The *while* command is followed by the *let* command. The *let* command evaluates the arithmetic expression, returning an exit status of *0* (true) if the condition is true; i.e., if the value of *num* is less than *10*, the body of the loop is entered.

3 In the body of the loop, the value of *num* is incremented by one. If the value of *num* never changes, the loop would iterate infinitely or until the process is killed.

4 After the loop exits, the *echo* command (with the *–e* option) prints a newline and the string.

EXAMPLE 12.38

```
(The Script)
    #!/bin/bash
    # Scriptname: quiz
1   echo "Who was the 2nd U.S. president to be impeached?"
    read answer
2   while [[ "$answer" != "Bill Clinton" ]]
3   do
        echo "Wrong try again!"
4       read answer
5   done
6   echo You got it!

(The Output)
$ quiz
Who was the 2nd U.S. president to be impeached? Ronald Reagan
Wrong try again!
Who was the 2nd U.S. president to be impeached?  I give up
Wrong try again!
Who was the 2nd U.S. president to be impeached?  Bill Clinton
You got it!
```

EXPLANATION

1 The *echo* command prompts the user, *Who was the 2nd U.S. president to be impeached?* The *read* command waits for input from the user. The input will be stored in the variable *answer*.

2 The *while* loop is entered and the *test* command, the bracket, tests the expression. If the variable *answer* does not exactly equal the string *Bill Clinton*, the body of the loop is entered and commands between the *do* and *done* are executed.

3 The *do* keyword is the start of the loop body.

EXPLANATION (CONTINUED)

4   The user is asked to re-enter input.

5   The *done* keyword marks the end of the loop body. Control is returned to the top of the *while* loop, and the expression is tested again. As long as *answer* does not evaluate to *Bill Clinton*, the loop will continue to iterate. When the user enters *Bill Clinton*, the loop ends. Program control goes to line 6.

6   When the body of the loop ends, control starts here.

EXAMPLE 12.39

```
(The Script)
$ cat sayit
    #!/bin/bash
    # Scriptname: sayit
    echo   Type q to quit.
    go=start
1   while [ -n "$go" ]     # Make sure to double quote the variable
    do
2       echo -n I love you.
3       read word
4       if [[ $word == [Qq] ]]
        then         # [ "$word" = q -o "$word" = Q ]   Old style
            echo "I'll always love you!"
            go=
        fi
    done


(The Output)
$ sayit
Type q to quit.
I love you.          <-- When user presses Enter, the program continues
I love you.
I love you.
I love you.
I love you.q
I'll always love you!
$
```

1   The command after the *while* is executed and its exit status tested. The *–n* option
     to the *test* command tests for a non-null string. Because *go* initially has a value,
     the test is successful, producing a zero exit status. If the variable *go* is not enclosed
     in double quotes and the variable is null, the *test* command would complain

```
go: test: argument expected
```

2   The loop is entered. The string *I love you* is echoed to the screen.

3   The *read* command waits for user input.

4   The expresson is tested. If the user enters a *q* or *Q*, the string *I'll always love you!*
     is displayed, and the variable *go* is set to null. When the *while* loop is re-entered,
     the test is unsuccessful because the variable is null. The loop terminates. Control
     goes to the line after the *done* statement. In this example, the script will terminate
     because there are no more lines to execute.

12.6.3 The *until* Command

The *until* command is used like the *while* command, but executes the loop statements
only if the command after *until* fails, i.e., if the command returns an exit status of nonzero. When the *done* keyword is reached, control is returned to the top of the loop and
the *until* command checks the exit status of the command again. Until the exit status of
the command being evaluated by *until* becomes zero, the loop continues. When the exit
status reaches zero, the loop exits, and program execution starts after the *done* keyword.

FORMAT

```
until command
do
      command(s)
done
```

EXAMPLE 12.40

```
      #!/bin/bash
1     until who | grep linda
2     do
          sleep 5
3     done
      talk linda@dragonwings
```

EXPLANATION

1   The *until* loop tests the exit status of the last command in the pipeline, *grep*. The *who* command lists who is logged on this machine and pipes its output to *grep*. The *grep* command will return a zero exit status (success) only when it finds user *linda*.

2   If user *linda* has not logged on, the body of the loop is entered and the program sleeps for five seconds.

3   When *linda* logs on, the exit status of the *grep* command will be zero and control will go to the statements following the *done* keyword.

EXAMPLE 12.41

```
(The Script)
$ cat hour
   #!/bin/bash
   # Scriptname: hour
1  let hour=0
2  until (( hour > 24 ))a # or [ $hour -gt 24 ]
   do
3      case "$hour" in
       [0-9]|1[0-1])echo "Good morning!"
           ;;
       12) echo "Lunch time."

           ;;
       1[3-7])echo "Siesta time."
           ;;
       *)  echo "Good night."
           ;;
       esac
4      let hour+=1     # Don't forget to increment the hour
5  done

(The Output)
$ hour
Good morning!
Good morning!
   ...
Lunch time.
Siesta time.
   ...
Good night.
   ...
```

---

a. Versions of *bash* 2.x use this form.

1   The variable *hour* is initialized to *0*.

2   The *let* command tests the arithmetic expression to test for an hour greater than or equal to *24*. If the hour is not greater than or equal to *24*, the body of the loop is entered. The *until* loop is entered if the command following it returns a nonzero exit status. Until the condition is true, the loop continues to iterate.

3   The *case* command evaluates the *hour* variable and tests each of the *case* statements for a match.

4   The *hour* variable is incremented with the *let* command before control returns to the top of the loop.

5   The *done* command marks the end of the loop body.

12.6.4 The *select* Command and Menus

The *here document* is an easy method for creating menus, but *bash* introduces another looping mechanism, called the *select* loop, used primarily for creating menus. A menu of numerically listed items is displayed to standard error. The *PS3* prompt is used to prompt the user for input; by default, *PS3* is #?. After the *PS3* prompt is displayed, the shell waits for user input. The input should be one of the numbers in the menu list. The input is stored in the special shell *REPLY* variable. The number in the *REPLY* variable is associated with the string to the right of the parentheses in the list of selections.

The *case* command is used with the *select* command to allow the user to make a selection from the menu and, based on that selection, execute commands. The *LINES* and *COLUMNS* variables can be used to determine the layout of the menu items displayed on the terminal. (These variables are built in to versions of *bash* 2.x, but are not built in to earlier versions; if they have not been defined, you can define and export them in the *.bash_profile*.) The output is displayed to standard error, each item preceded by a number and closing parenthesis, and the *PS3* prompt is displayed at the bottom of the menu. Because the *select* command is a looping command, it is important to remember to use either the *break* command to get out of the loop, or the *exit* command to exit the script.

```
select var in wordlist
do
    command(s)
done
```

EXAMPLE 12.42

```
(The Script)
    #!/bin/bash
    # Scriptname: runit
1   PS3="Select a program to execute: "
2   select program  in 'ls -F' pwd date
3   do
4       $program
5   done
```

```
(The Command Line)
Select a program to execute: 2
1) ls -F
2) pwd
3) date
/home/ellie
Select a program to execute: 1
1) ls -F
2) pwd
3) date
12abcrty abc12  doit* progs/  xyz
Select a program to execute: 3
1) ls -F
2) pwd
3) date
Sun Mar 12 13:28:25 PST 2001
```

EXPLANATION

1   The *PS3* prompt is assigned the string that will appear below the menu that the *select* loop displays. This prompt is $# by default and is sent to standard error, the screen.

2   The *select* loop consists of a variable called *program* and the three-word list that will be displayed in the menu: *ls –F, pwd,* and *date*. The words in this list are UNIX commands, but they could be any words, e.g., *red, green, yellow,* or *cheese, bread, milk, crackers*. If the word has a space, it must be quoted; e.g., ' *ls –F* '

3   The *do* keyword starts the body of the *select* loop.

4   When the user selects numbers in the menu, that number will be equated with the word value to the right of the number after the parentheses. For example, if he selects number 2, that is associated with *pwd* and *pwd* is stored in the *program* variable. $*program* evaluates to the executable command, *pwd*; the command is executed.

5   The *done* keyword marks the end of the body of statements in the *select* loop. Control will return to the top of the loop. This loop will continue to execute until the user presses ^C.

EXAMPLE   12.43

```
(The Script)
    #!/bin/bash
    # Scriptname name: goodboys
1   PS3="Please choose one of the three boys : "
2   select choice in tom dan guy
3   do
4       case $choice in
        tom)
            echo Tom is a cool dude!
5           break;;             # break out of the select loop
6       dan | guy )
            echo Dan and Guy are both wonderful.
            break;;
        *)
7           echo "$REPLY is not one of your choices" 1>&2
            echo "Try again."
            ;;
8       esac
9   done

(The Command Line)
$ goodboys
1) tom
2) dan
3) guy
Please choose one of the three boys : 2
Dan and Guy are both wonderful.

$ goodboys
1) tom
2) dan
3) guy
Please choose one of the three boys : 4
4 is not one of your choices
Try again.
Please choose one of the three boys : 1
Tom is a cool dude!
$
```

EXPLANATION

1   The *PS3* prompt will be printed above the menu created by the *select* loop on line
    2.
2   The *select* loop is entered. It causes the words in its list to be displayed as a num-
    bered menu.
3   The loop body starts here.

EXPLANATION (CONTINUED)

4   The variable choice is assigned the first value on the list, after which the value is shifted off the list and the next item will be first.

5   The *break* statement sends loop control after line 9.

6   If either *dan* or *guy* are selected, the following *echo* command is executed, followed by the *break* command, sending control after line 9.

7   The built-in *REPLY* variable contains the number of the current list item; i.e., *1*, *2*, or *3*.

8   This marks the end of the *case* command.

9   The *done* marks the end of the *select* loop.

EXAMPLE 12.44

```
(The Script)
    #!/bin/bash
    # Scriptname: ttype
    # Purpose: set the terminal type
    # Author: Andy Admin
1   COLUMNS=60
2   LINES=1
3   PS3="Please enter the terminal type: "
4   select choice in wyse50 vt200 xterm sun
    do
5       case $REPLY in
        1)
6           export TERM=$choice
            echo "TERM=$choice"
            break;;              # break out of the select loop
        2 | 3 )
            export TERM=$choice

            echo "TERM=$choice"
            break;;
        4)
            export TERM=$choice
            echo "TERM=$choice"
            break;;
        *)
7           echo -e "$REPLY is not a valid choice. Try again\n" 1>&2
8           REPLY=    # Causes the menu to be redisplayed
                ;;
        esac
9   done
```

EXAMPLE 12.44 (CONTINUED)

```
(The Command Line)
$ ttype
1) wyse50    2) vt200    3) xterm    4) sun
Please enter the terminal type : 4
TERM=sun


$ ttype
1) wyse50    2) vt200    3) xterm    4) sun
Please enter the terminal type : 3
TERM=xterm


$ ttype
1) wyse50    2) vt200    3) xterm    4) sun
Please enter the terminal type : 7
7 is not a valid choice. Try again.


1) wyse50    2) vt200    3) xterm    4) sun
Please enter the terminal type: 2
TERM=vt200
```

EXPLANATION

1   The *COLUMNS* variable is set to the width of the terminal display in columns for menus created with the *select* loop. The default is 80.

2   The *LINES* variable controls the vertical display of the *select* menu on the terminal. The default is 24 lines. When you change the *LINES* value to *1*, the menu items will be printed on one line, instead of vertically as in the last example.

3   The *PS3* prompt is set and will appear under the menu choices.

4   The *select* loop will print a menu with four selections: *wyse50*, *vt200*, *xterm*, and *sun*. The variable *choice* will be assigned one of these values based on the user's response held in the *REPLY* variable. If *REPLY* is 1, *wyse50* is assigned to *choice*; if *REPLY* is 2, *vt200* is assigned to *choice*; if *REPLY* is 3, *xterm* is assigned to *choice*; and if *REPLY* is 4, *sun* is assigned to *choice*.

5   The *REPLY* variable evaluates to the user's input selection.

6   The terminal type is assigned, exported, and printed.

7   If the user does not enter a number between 1 and 4, he or she will be prompted again. Note that the menu does not appear, just the *PS3* prompt.

8   If the *REPLY* variable is set to null, *e.g.*, *REPLY=*, the menu will be redisplayed.

9   The end of the *select* loop.

12.6.5 Loop Control

If some condition occurs, you may want to break out of a loop, return to the top of the loop, or provide a way to stop an infinite loop. The *bash* shell provides loop control commands to handle these kinds of situations.

The *shift* Command. The *shift* command shifts the parameter list to the left a specified number of times. The *shift* command without an argument shifts the parameter list once to the left. Once the list is shifted, the parameter is removed permanently. Often, the *shift* command is used in a *while* loop when iterating through a list of positional parameters.

FORMAT

```
shift [n]
```

EXAMPLE 12.45

```
(Without a Loop)
(The Script)
    #!/bin/bash
    # Scriptname: shifter
1   set joe mary tom sam
2   shift
3   echo $*
4   set $(date)
5   echo  $*
6   shift 5
7   echo  $*
8   shift 2

(The Output)
3   mary tom sam
5   Thu Mar 16 10:00:12 PST 2001
7   2001
8   shift: shift count must be <= $#
```

EXPLANATION

1   The *set* command sets the positional parameters. $1 is assigned *joe*, $2 is assigned *mary*, $3 is assigned *tom*, and $4 is assigned *sam*. $* represents all of the parameters.

2   The *shift* command shifts the positional parameters to the left; *joe* is shifted off.

3   The parameter list is printed after the shift.

4   The *set* command resets the positional parameters to the output of the UNIX *date* command.

5   The new parameter list is printed.

EXPLANATION (CONTINUED)

6   This time the list is shifted 5 times to the left.

7   The new parameter list is printed.

8   By attempting to shift more times than there are parameters, the shell sends a message to standard error stating that the *shift* command cannot shift more off more parameters that it has. $# is the total number of positional parameters. On versions of *bash* 2.x, no error message occurs.

EXAMPLE 12.46

```
(With a Loop)
(The Script)
    #!/bin/bash
    # Name: doit
    # Purpose: shift through command line arguments
    # Usage: doit [args]
1   while (( $# > 0 ))ᵃ   # or [ $# -gt 0 ]
    do
2       echo $*
3       shift
4   done


(The Command Line)
$ doit a b c d e
a b c d e
b c d e
c d e
d e
e
```

a.   Not implemented of versions of *bash* prior to 2.x.

EXPLANATION

1   The *let* command tests the numeric expression. If the number of positional parameters ($#) is greater than 0, the body of the loop is entered. The positional parameters are coming from the command line as arguments. There are five.

2   All positional parameters are printed.

3   The parameter list is shifted once to the left.

4   The body of the loop ends here; control returns to the top of the loop. Each time the loop is entered, the *shift* command causes the parameter list to be decreased by one. After the first shift, $# (number of positional parameters) is four. When $# has been decreased to zero, the loop ends.

EXAMPLE 12.47

```
(The Script)
    #!/bin/bash
    # Scriptname: dater
    # Purpose: set positional parameters with the set command
    # and shift through the parameters.

1   set $(date)
2   while (( $# > 0 )) # or  [ $# -gt 0 ]   Old style
    do
3       echo $1
4       shift
    done


(The Output)
$ dater
Wed
Mar
15
19:25:00
PST
2001
```

EXPLANATION

1 The *set* command takes the output of the *date* command and assigns the output to positional parameters *$1* through *$6*.

2 The *while* command tests whether the number of positional parameters (*$#*) is greater than *0*. If true, the body of the loop is entered.

3 The *echo* command displays the value of *$1*, the first positional parameter.

4 The *shift* command shifts the parameter list once to the left. Each time through the loop, the list is shifted until the list is empty. At that time, *$#* will be zero and the loop terminates.

The *break* Command.   The built-in *break* command is used to force immediate exit from a loop, but not from a program. (To leave a program, the *exit* command is used.) After the *break* command is executed, control starts after the *done* keyword. The *break* command causes an exit from the innermost loop, so if you have nested loops, the *break* command takes a number as an argument, allowing you to break out of a specific outer loop. If you are nested in three loops, the outermost loop is loop number 3, the next nested loop is loop number 2, and the innermost nested loop is loop number 1. The *break* is useful for exiting from an infinite loop.

FORMAT

```
break [n]
```

EXAMPLE 12.48

```
    #!/bin/bash
    # Scriptname: loopbreak
1   while true; do
2       echo Are you ready to move on\?
        read answer
3       if [[  "$answer"  ==  [Yy] ]]
        then
4           break
5       else
               ....commands...
        fi
6   done
7   print "Here we are"
```

EXPLANATION

1   The *true* command is a UNIX command that always exits with zero status. It is
    often used to start an infinite loop. It is okay to put the *do* statement on the same
    line as the *while* command, as long as a semicolon separates them. The body of
    the loop is entered.

2   The user is asked for input. The user's input is assigned to the variable *answer.*

3   If *$answer* evaluates to Y or y, control goes to line 4.

4   The *break* command is executed, the loop is exited, and control goes to line 7. The
    line *Here we are* is printed. Until the user answers with a Y or y, the program will
    continue to ask for input. This could go on forever!

5   If the test fails in line 3, the *else* commands are executed. When the body of the
    loop ends at the *done* keyword, control starts again at the top of the *while* at line 1.

6   This is the end of the loop body.

7   Control starts here after the *break* command is executed.

The *continue* Command.   The *continue* command returns control to the top of the
loop if some condition becomes true. All commands below the *continue* will be ignored.
If nested within a number of loops, the *continue* command returns control to the innermost loop. If a number is given as its argument, control can then be started at the top of
any loop. If you are nested in three loops, the outermost loop is loop number 3, the next
nested loop is loop number 2, and the innermost nested loop is loop number 1.[4]

---

4. If the *continue* command is given a number higher than the number of loops, the loop exits.

FORMAT

```
continue [n]
```

EXAMPLE 12.49

```
(The mailing List)
    $ cat mail_list
    ernie
    john
    richard
    melanie
    greg
    robin

(The Script)
    #!/bin/bash
    # Scriptname: mailem
    # Purpose: To send a list
1   for name in $(cat  mail_list)
    do
2       if [[ $name == richard ]] ; then
3           continue
        else
4           mail $name < memo
        fi
5   done
```

EXPLANATION

1   After command substitution, $(cat mail_list) or `cat mail_list`, the *for* loop will iterate through the list of names from the file called *mail_list*.

2   If the name matches *richard*, the *continue* command is executed and control goes back to top of the loop where the loop expression is evaluated. Because *richard* has already been shifted off the list, the next user, *melanie*, will be assigned to the variable *name*. Old style: *if ["$name" = richard] ; then*

3   The *continue* command returns control to the top of the loop, skipping any commands in the rest of the loop body.

4   All users in the list, except *richard*, will be mailed a copy of the file *memo*.

5   This is the end of the loop body.

Nested Loops and Loop Control.   When you are using nested loops, the *break* and *continue* commands can be given a numeric, integer argument so that control can go from the inner loop to an outer loop.

EXAMPLE 12.50

(The Script)
```
    #!/bin/bash
    # Scriptname: months
1   for month in Jan Feb Mar Apr May Jun Jul Aug Sep Oct Nov Dec
    do
2       for week in  1 2 3 4
        do
            echo -n "Processing the month of $month. OK? "
            read ans
3           if [ "$ans" = n  -o -z "$ans" ]
            then
4               continue 2
            else
                echo -n "Process week $week of $month? "
                read ans
                if [ "$ans" = n  o -z "$ans"  ]
                then
5                   continue
                else
                    echo "Now processing week $week of $month."
                    sleep 1
                        # Commands go here
                    echo  "Done processing..."
                fi
            fi
6       done
7   done
```

(The Output)
```
$ months
Processing the month of Jan. OK?
Processing the month of Feb. OK? y
Process week 1 of Feb? y
Now processing  week 1 of Feb.
Done processing...
Processing the month of Feb. OK? y
Process week 2 of Feb? y
Now processing week 2 of Feb.
Done processing...
Processing the month of Feb. OK? n
Processing the month of Mar. OK? n
Processing the month of Apr. OK? n
Processing the month of May. OK? n
```

EXPLANATION

1   The outer *for* loop is started. The first time in the loop, *Jan* is assigned to *month*.

2   The inner *for* loop starts. The first time in this loop, *1* is assigned to *week*. The inner loop iterates completely before going back to the outer loop.

3   If the user enters either an *n* or presses Enter, line 4 is executed.

4   The *continue* command with an argument of 2 starts control at the top of the second outermost loop. The *continue* without an argument returns control to the top of the innermost loop.

5   Control is returned to the innermost *for* loop.

6   This *done* terminates the innermost loop.

7   This *done* terminates the outermost loop.

12.6.6 I/O Redirection and Subshells

Input can be piped or redirected to a loop from a file. Output can also be piped or redirected to a file from a loop. The shell starts a subshell to handle I/O redirection and pipes. Any variables defined within the loop will not be known to the rest of the script when the loop terminates.

Redirecting the Output of the Loop to a File.   Output from a *bash* loop can be sent to a file rather than to the screen. See Example 12.51.

EXAMPLE   12.51

```
(The Command Line)
1   $ cat memo
    abc
    def
    ghi

(The Script)
    #!/bin/bash
    # Program name: numberit
    # Put line numbers on all lines of memo
2   if let $(( $# < 1 ))
    then
3       echo "Usage: $0 filename " >&2
        exit 1
    fi
4   count=1                              # Initialize count
```

EXAMPLE 12.51 (CONTINUED)

```
5   cat $1 | while read line
    # Input is coming from file provided at command line
    do
6      let $((count == 1)) && echo "Processing file $1..." > /dev/tty
7      echo -e "$count\t$line"
8      let count+=1
9   done > tmp$$                    # Output is going to a temporary file
10  mv tmp$$ $1


(The Command Line)
11  $ numberit memo
    Processing file memo...


12  $ cat memo
    1   abc
    2   def
    3   ghi
```

EXPLANATION

1 The contents of file *memo* are displayed.

2 If the user did not provide a command line argument when running this script, the number of arguments ($#) will be less than one and the error message appears.

3 The usage message is sent to *stderr* (>&2) if the number of arguments is less than *1*.

4 The *count* variable is assigned the value *1*.

5 The UNIX *cat* command displays the contents of the filename stored in *$1*, and the output is piped to the *while* loop. The *read* command is assigned the first line of the file the first time in the loop, the second line of the file the next time through the loop, and so forth. The *read* command returns a zero exit status if it is successful in reading input and one if it fails.

6 If the value of *count* is *1*, the *echo* command is executed and its output is sent to */dev/tty*, the screen.

7 The *echo* command prints the value of *count*, followed by the line in the file.

8 The *count* is incremented by one.

9 The output of this entire loop, each line of the file in *$1*, is redirected to the file *tmp$$*, with the exception of the first line of the file, which is redirected to the terminal, */dev/tty*.[a]

10 The *tmp* file is renamed to the filename assigned to *$1*.

11 The program is executed. The file to be processed is called *memo*.

12 The file *memo* is displayed after the script has finished, demonstrating that line numbers have been prepended to each line.

a. $$ expands to the PID number of the current shell. By appending this number to the filename, the filename is made unique.

Piping the Output of a Loop to a UNIX Command.   Output can be either piped to another command(s) or redirected to a file.

EXAMPLE 12.52

```
(The Script)
    #!/bin/bash
1   for i in 7 9 2 3 4   5
2   do
        echo  $i
3   done | sort -n

(The Output)
2
3
4
5
7
9
```

EXPLANATION

1   The *for* loop iterates through a list of unsorted numbers.

2   In the body of the loop, the numbers are printed. This output will be piped into the UNIX *sort* command, a numerical sort.

3   The pipe is created after the *done* keyword. The loop is run in a subshell.

Running Loops in the Background.   Loops can be executed to run in the background. The program can continue without waiting for the loop to finish processing.

EXAMPLE 12.53

```
(The Script)
    #!/bin/bash
1   for person in bob jim joe sam
    do
2       mail $person < memo
3   done &
```

EXPLANATION

1   The *for* loop shifts through each of the names in the wordlist: *bob, jim, joe,* and *sam.* Each of the names is assigned to the variable *person*, in turn.

2   In the body of the loop, each person is sent the contents of the *memo* file.

3   The ampersand at the end of the *done* keyword causes the loop to be executed in the background. The program will continue to run while the loop is executing.

12.6.7 *IFS* and Loops

The shell's internal field separator (*IFS*) evaluates to spaces, tabs, and the newline character. It is used as a word (token) separator for commands that parse lists of words, such
as *read, set,* and *for.* It can be reset by the user if a different separator will be used in a
list. Before changing its value, it is a good idea to save the original value of the *IFS* in
another variable. Then it is easy to return to its default value, if needed.

EXAMPLE   12.54

```
(The Script )
$ cat runit2
    #/bin/bash
    # Script is called runit.
    # IFS is the internal field separator and defaults to
    # spaces, tabs, and newlines.
    # In this script it is changed to a colon.
1   names=Tom:Dick:Harry:John
2   oldifs="$IFS"              # Save the original value of IFS
3   IFS=":"
4   for persons in $names
    do
5       echo  Hi $persons
    done
6   IFS="$oldifs"             # Reset the IFS to old value
7   set Jill Jane Jolene      # Set positional parameters
8   for girl in $*
    do
9       echo Howdy $girl
    done


(The Output)
    $ runit2
5   Hi Tom
    Hi Dick
    Hi Harry
    Hi John
9   Howdy Jill
    Howdy Jane
    Howdy Jolene
```

EXPLANATION

1   The *names* variable is set to the string *Tom:Dick:Harry:John.* Each of the words is
    separated by a colon.

2   The value of *IFS*, whitespace, is assigned to another variable, *oldifs.* Since the val-
    ue of the *IFS* is whitespace, it must be quoted to preserve it.

3   The *IFS* is assigned a colon. Now the colon is used to separate words.

EXPLANATION (CONTINUED)

4   After variable substitution, the *for* loop will iterate through each of the names, us-
     ing the colon as the internal field separator between the words.

5   Each of the names in the wordlist are displayed.

6   The *IFS* is reassigned its original value stored in *oldifs*.

7   The positional parameters are set. *$1* is assigned *Jill*, *$2* is assigned *Jane*, and *$3* is
     assigned *Jolene*.

8   *$** evaluates to all the positional parameters, *Jill, Jane,* and *Jolene.* The *for* loop as-
     signs each of the names to the *girl* variable, in turn, through each iteration of the
     loop.

9   Each of the names in the parameter list is displayed.

12.7 Functions

Functions were introduced to the Bourne shell in AT&T's UNIX SystemVR2 and have
been enhanced in the Bourne Again shell. A function is a name for a command or group
of commands. Functions are used to modularize your program and make it more efficient. They are executed in context of the current shell. In other words, a child process
is not spawned as it is when running an executable program such as *ls*. You may even
store functions in another file and load them into your script when you are ready to use
them.

Here is a review of some of the important rules about using functions.

1. The shell determines whether you are using an alias, a function, a built-in com-
    mand, or an executable program (or script) found on the disk. It looks for
    aliases first, then functions, built-in commands, and last, executables.

2. A function must be defined before it is used.

3. The function runs in the current environment; it shares variables with the script
    that invoked it, and lets you pass arguments by assigning them as positional
    parameters. Local variables can be created within a function by using the *local*
    function.

4. If you use the *exit* command in a function, you exit the entire script. If you exit
    the function, you return to where the script left off when the function was
    invoked.

5. The *return* statement in a function returns the exit status of the last command
    executed within the function or the value of the argument given.

6. Functions can be exported to subshells with the *export –f* built-in command.

7. To list functions and definitions, use the *declare –f* command. To list just func-
    tion names, use *declare –F*.[5]

---

5. Only on *bash* versions 2.x.

8. Traps, like variables, are global within functions. They are shared by both the script and the functions invoked in the script. If a trap is defined in a function, it is also shared by the script. This could have unwanted side effects.

9. If functions are stored in another file, they can be loaded into the current script with the *source* or *dot* command.

10. Functions can be recursive; i.e., they can call themselves. There is no limit imposed for the number of recursive calls.

FORMAT

```
function function_name { commands ; commands; }
```

EXAMPLE 12.55

```
function dir { echo "Directories: ";ls -l|awk '/^d/ {print $NF}'; }
```

EXPLANATION

The keyword *function* is followed by the name of the function *dir*. (Sometimes empty parentheses follow the function name, but they are not necessary.) The commands within the curly braces will be executed when *dir* is typed. The purpose of the function is to list only the subdirectories below the present working directory. The spaces surrounding the first curly brace are required.

To Unset a Function.   To remove a function from memory, use the *unset* command.

FORMAT

```
unset -f function_name
```

Exporting Functions.   Functions may be exported so that subshells know about them.

FORMAT

```
export -f function_name
```

12.7.1 Function Arguments and the Return Value

Because the function is executed within the current shell, the variables will be known to both the function and the shell. Any changes made to your environment in the function will also be made to the shell.

Arguments.   Arguments can be passed to functions by using positional parameters. The positional parameters are private to the function; that is, arguments to the function will not affect any positional parameters used outside the function. See Example 12.56.

The Built-In *local* Function.   To create local variables that are private to the function and will disappear after the function exits, use the built-in *local* function. See Example 12.57.

The Built-In *return* Function.   The *return* command can be used to exit the function and return control to the program at the place where the function was invoked. (Remember, if you use *exit* anywhere in your script, including within a function, the script terminates.) The return value of a function is really just the value of the exit status of the last command in the script, unless you give a specific argument to the *return* command. If a value is assigned to the *return* command, that value is stored in the ? variable and can hold an integer value between zero and 256. Because the *return* command is limited to returning only an integer between zero and 256, you can use command substitution to capture the output of a function. Place the entire function in parentheses preceded by a $, e.g., $(*function_name*), or traditional backquotes to capture and assign the output to a variable just as you would if getting the output of a UNIX command.

EXAMPLE 12.56

```
(Passing Arguments)
(The Script)
    #!/bin/bash
    # Scriptname: checker
    # Purpose: Demonstrate function and arguments

1   function Usage { echo "error: $*" 2>&1; exit 1; }

2   if (( $# != 2 ))
    then
3       Usage "$0: requires two arguments"
    fi
4   if [[ ! ( -r $1 && -w $1 ) ]]
    then
5       Usage "$1: not readable and writeable"
    fi
```

EXAMPLE   12.56 (CONTINUED)

```
6    echo The arguments are: $*
 <  Program continues here >
```

```
(Output)
$ checker
error: checker: requires two arguments

$ checker file1 file2
error: file1: not readable and writeable

$ checker filex file2
The arguments are filex file2
```

EXPLANATION

1   The function called *Usage* is defined. It will be used to send an error message to standard error (the screen). Its arguments consist of any string of characters sent when the function is called. The arguments are stored in $*, the special variable that contains all positional parameters. Within a function, positional parameters are local and have no effect on those positional parameters used outside the function.

2   If the number of arguments begin passed into the script from the command line does not equal 2, the program branches to line 3.

3   When the *Usage* function is called, the string *$0: requires two arguments* is passed to the function and stored in the $* varable. The *echo* statement will then send the message to standard error and the script will exit with an exit status of 1 to indicate that something went wrong.[a]

4, 5 If the first argument coming into the program from the command line is not the name of a readable and writeable file, the *Usage* function will be called with *$1: not readable and writeable* as its argument.

6   The arguments coming into the script from the command line are stored in $*. This has no effect on the $* in the function.

a. With the old *test* form, the expression is written `if [ ! \( -r $1 -a -w $1 \) ]`.

EXAMPLE 12.57

```
(Using the return Command)
(The Script)
$ cat do_increment
  #!/bin/bash
  # Scriptname: do_increment
1   increment () {
2     local sum;      # sum is known only in this function
3     let "sum=$1 + 1"
4     return $sum     # Return the value of sum to the script.
  }
5   echo  -n "The sum is "
6   increment 5     # Call function increment; pass 5 as a
                    # parameter. 5 becomes $1 for the increment
                    # function.
7   echo $?         # The return value is stored in $?
8   echo  $sum      # The variable "sum" is not known here

(The Output)
  $ do_increment
4,6 The sum is 6
8
```

EXPLANATION

1   The function called *increment* is defined.

2   The built-in *local* function makes variable *sum* local (private) to this function. It will not exist outside the function. When the function exits, it will be removed.

3   When the function is called, the value of the first argument, $1, will be incremented by one and the result assigned to *sum*.

4   The *return* built-in command, when given an argument, returns to the main script after the line where the function was invoked. It stores its argument in the *?* variable.

5   The string is echoed to the screen.

6   The *increment* function is called with an argument of 5.

7   When the function returns, its exit status is stored in the *?* variable. The exit status is the exit value of the last command executed in the function unless an explicit argument is used in the *return* statement. The argument for *return* must be an integer between 0 and 255.

8   Although the *sum* was defined in the function *increment*, it is local in scope, and therefore also not known outside the function. Nothing is printed.

EXAMPLE 12.58

```
(Using Command Substitution)
(The Script)
$ cat do_square
    #!/bin/bash
    # Scriptname: do_square
1   function square {
       local sq      # sq is local to the function
       let "sq=$1 * $1"
       echo "Number to be squared is $1."
2      echo "The result is $sq "
    }
3   echo "Give me a number to square. "
    read number
4   value_returned=$(square $number) # Command substitution
5   echo   "$value_returned"

(The Output)
    $ do_square
3   Give me a number to square.
    10
5   Number to be squared is 10.
    The result is 100
```

EXPLANATION

1   The function called *square* is defined. Its purpose, when called, is to multiply its argument, *$1*, times itself.

2   The result of squaring the number is printed.

3   The user is asked for input. This is the line where the program starts executing.

4   The function *square* is called with a number (input from the user) as its argument. Command substitution is performed because the function is enclosed in parentheses preceded by a $. The output of the function, both of its *echo* statements, is assigned to the variable *value_returned*.

5   The value returned from the command substitution is printed.

12.7.2 Functions and the *source* (or *dot*) Command

Storing Functions.   Functions are often defined in the *.profile* file so that when you log in, they will be defined. Functions can be exported, and they can be stored in a file. Then when you need the function, the *source* or *dot* command is used with the name of the file to activate the definitions of the functions within it.

EXAMPLE 12.59

```
1   $ cat myfunctions
2   function go() {
        cd $HOME/bin/prog
        PS1=''pwd' > '
        ls
    }
3   function greetings() { echo "Hi $1! Welcome to my world." ; }

4   $ source myfunctions
5   $ greetings george
    Hi george! Welcome to my world.
```

EXPLANATION

1   The file *myfunctions* is displayed. It contains two function definitions.

2   The first function defined is called *go*. It sets the primary prompt to the present working directory.

3   The second function defined is called *greetings*. It will greet the name of the user passed in as an argument.

4   The *source or dot* command loads the contents of the file *myfunctions* into the shell's memory. Now both functions are defined for this shell.

5   The *greetings* function is invoked and executed.

EXAMPLE 12.60

```
(The dbfunctions file shown below contains functions to be used by the
main program.  See cd for complete script.)
1   $ cat dbfunctions
2   function addon () {         # Function defined in file dbfunctions
3       while true
        do
            echo "Adding information "
            echo "Type the full name of employee "
            read name
            echo "Type address for employee "
            read address
            echo "Type start date for employee (4/10/88 ) :"
            read startdate
```

EXAMPLE 12.60 (CONTINUED)

```
            echo $name:$address:$startdate
            echo -n "Is this correct? "
            read ans
            case "$ans"  in
            [Yy]*)
                    echo "Adding info..."
                    echo $name:$address:$startdate>>datafile
                    sort -u datafile -o datafile
                    echo -n "Do you want to go back to the main menu? "
                read ans
                if [[ $ans == [Yy] ]]
                then
4                       return      # Return to calling program
                else
5                       continue    # Go to the top of the loop
                fi
                ;;
            *)
            echo "Do you want to try again? "
            read answer
            case "$answer" in
            [Yy]*) continue;;
            *) exit;;
            esac
                ;;
        esac
    done
6   }    # End of function definition


--------------------------------------------------------------
(The Command Line)
7   $ more mainprog
    #!/bin/bash
    # Scriptname: mainprog
    # This is the main script that will call the function, addon

    datafile=$HOME/bourne/datafile
8   source dbfunctions   # The file is loaded into memory
        if [ ! -e $datafile ]
    then
        echo "$(basename $datafile) does not exist" >&2
        exit 1
    fi
```

EXAMPLE 12.60 (CONTINUED)

```
9        echo "Select one: "
         cat <<EOF
             [1] Add info
             [2] Delete info
             [3] Update info
             [4] Exit
         EOF
         read choice
         case $choice in
10          1) addon          # Calling the addon function
                   ;;
             2) delete         # Calling the delete function
                   ;;
             3) update
                   ;;
             4)
                echo Bye
                exit 0
                   ;;
             *) echo Bad choice
                exit 2
                   ;;
         esac
         echo Returned from function call
         echo The name is $name
         # Variable set in the function are known in this shell.
      done
```

EXPLANATION

1   The *dbfunctions* file is displayed.

2   The *addon* function is defined. Its function is to add new information to the *data-file*.

3   A *while* loop is entered. It will loop forever unless a loop control statement such as *break* or *continue* is included in the body of the loop.

4   The *return* command sends control back to the calling program where the function was called.

5   Control is returned to the top of the *while* loop.

6   The closing curly brace ends the function definition.

7   This is the main script. The function *addon* will be used in this script.

8   The *source* command loads the file *dbfunctions* into the program's memory. Now the function *addon* is defined for this script and available for use. It is as though you had just defined the function right here in the script.

9   A menu is displayed with the *here document*. The user is asked to select a menu item.

10   The *addon* function is invoked.

12.8 Trapping Signals

While your program is running, if you press Control-C or Control-\, your program terminates as soon as the signal arrives. There are times when you would rather not have the program terminate immediately after the signal arrives. You could arrange to ignore the signal and keep running or perform some sort of cleanup operation before actually exiting the script. The *trap* command allows you to control the way a program behaves when it receives a signal.

A *signal* is defined as an asynchronous message that consists of a number that can be sent from one process to another, or by the operating system to a process if certain keys are pressed or if something exceptional happens.[6] The *trap* command tells the shell to terminate the command currently in execution upon the receipt of a signal. If the *trap* command is followed by commands within quotes, the command string will be executed upon receipt of a specified signal. The shell reads the command string twice, once when the trap is set, and again when the signal arrives. If the command string is surrounded by double quotes, all variable and command substitution will be performed when the trap is set the first time. If single quotes enclose the command string, variable and command substitution do not take place until the signal is detected and the trap is executed.

Use the command *kill –l* or *trap –l* to get a list of all signals. Table 12.6 on page 798 provides a list of signal numbers and their corresponding names.

FORMAT

```
trap 'command; command' signal-number
trap 'command; command' signal-name
```

EXAMPLE 12.61

```
trap 'rm tmp*; exit 1'  0 1 2 15
trap 'rm tmp*; exit 1'  EXIT HUP INT TERM
```

EXPLANATION

When any of the signals *1* (hangup), *2* (interrupt), or *15* (software termination) arrives, remove all the *tmp* files and exit.

If an interrupt comes in while the script is running, the *trap* command lets you handle the interrupt signal in several ways. You can let the signal behave normally (default), ignore the signal, or create a handler function to be called when the signal arrives.

Signal names such as *HUP* and *INT* are normally prefixed with *SIG*, for example, *SIGHUP*, *SIGINT*, and so forth.[7] The *bash* shell allows you to use symbolic names for the

---

6. Bolsky, Morris I. and Korn, David G., *The New KornShell Command and Programming Language* (Englewood Cliffs, NJ: Prentice Hall PTR, 1995), p. 327.

7. *SIGKILL*, number 9, often called a "sure kill," is not trapable.

signals, which are the signal names without the *SIG* prefix, or you can use the numeric value for the signal. See Table 12.6. A pseudo signal name *EXIT*, or the number 0, will cause the trap to be executed when the shell exits.

Table 12.6   Signal Numbers and Signals (*kill –l*)

1) *SIGHUP*	9) *SIGKILL*	18) *SIGCONT*	26) *SIGVTALRM*
2) *SIGINT*	10) *SIGUSR1*	19) *SIGSTOP*	27) *SIGPROF*
3) *SIGQUIT*	11) *SIGSEGV*	20) *SIGTSTP*	28) *SIGWINCH*
4) *SIGILL*	12) *SIGUSR2*	21) *SIGTTIN*	29) *SIGIO*
5) *SIGTRAP*	13) *SIGPIPE*	22) *SIGTTOU*	30) *SIGPWR*
6) *SIGABRT*	14) *SIGALRM*	23) *SIGURG*	
7) *SIGBUS*	15) *SIGTERM*	24) *SIGXCPU*	
8) *SIGFPE*	17) *SIGCHLD*	25) *SIGXFSZ*	

Resetting Signals.   To reset a signal to its default behavior, the *trap* command is followed by the signal name or number. *Traps* set in functions are recognized by the shell that invoked the function, once the function has been called. Any traps set outside the function are also recognized with the function.

EXAMPLE 12.62

```
trap 2   or   trap INT
```

EXPLANATION

Resets the default action for signal 2, *SIGINT*. The default action is to kill the process when the interrupt key (Control-C) is pressed.

Ignoring Signals.   If the *trap* command is followed by a pair of empty quotes, the signals listed will be ignored by the process.

EXAMPLE 12.63

```
trap " " 1 2   or    trap "" HUP INT
```

EXPLANATION

Signals 1 (*SIGHUP*) and 2 (*SIGINT*) will be ignored by the shell process.

Listing Traps. To list all traps and the commands assigned to them, type *trap*.

EXAMPLE 12.64

```
(At the command line)
1   $ trap 'echo "Caught ya!; exit"' 2
2   $ trap
    trap -- 'echo "Caught ya!; exit 1"' SIGINT
3   $ trap -
```

EXPLANATION

1   The *trap* command is set to exit on signal 2 (Control-C).

2   The *trap* command without an argument lists all set traps.

3   If the argument is a dash, all signals are reset to their original values, i.e., whatever they were when the shell started up.

EXAMPLE 12.65

```
(The Script)
    #!/bin/bash
    # Scriptname: trapping
    # Script to illustrate the trap command and signals
    # Can use the signal numbers or bash abbreviations seen
    # below. Cannot use SIGINT, SIGQUIT, etc.
1   trap 'echo "Control-C will not terminate $0."'  INT
2   trap 'echo "Control-\ will not terminate $0."'  QUIT
3   trap 'echo "Control-Z will not terminate $0."'  TSTP
4   echo  "Enter any string after the prompt.
    When you are ready to exit, type \"stop\"."
5   while true
    do
6       echo -n "Go ahead...> "
7       read
8       if [[ $REPLY == [Ss]top ]]
        then
9           break
        fi
10  done
```

EXAMPLE 12.65

```
(The Output)
    $ trapping
4   Enter any string after the prompt.
    When you are ready to exit, type "stop".
6   Go ahead...> this is it^C
1   Control-C will not terminate trapping.
6   Go ahead...> this is it again^Z
3   Control-Z will not terminate trapping.
6   Go ahead...> this is never it|^\
2   Control-\ will not terminate trapping.
6   Go ahead...> stop
    $
```

EXPLANATION

1   The first *trap* catches the *INT* signal, Control-C. If Control-C is pressed while the program is running, the command enclosed in quotes will be executed. Instead of aborting, the program will print *Control-C will not terminate trapping* and continue to prompt the user for input.

2   The second *trap* command will be executed when the user presses Control-\, the *QUIT* signal. The string *Control-\ will not terminate trapping* will be displayed and the program will continue to run. This signal, *SIGQUIT* by default, kills the process and produces a core file.

3   The third *trap* command will be executed when the user presses Control-Z, the *TSTP* signal. The string *Control-Z will not terminate trapping* will be displayed, and the program will continue to run. This signal normally causes the program to be suspended in the background if job control is implemented.

4   The user is prompted for input.

5   The *while* loop is entered.

6   The string *Go ahead...>* is printed and the program waits for input (see *read* on the next line).

7   The *read* command assigns user input to the built-in *REPLY* variable.

8   If the value of *REPLY* matches *Stop* or *stop*, the *break* command causes the loop to exit and the program will terminate. Entering *Stop* or *stop* is the only way we will get out of this program unless it is killed with the *kill* command.

9   The *break* command causes the body of the loop to be exited.

10 The *done* keyword marks the end of the loop.

Resetting Signals.   To reset a signal to its default behavior, the *trap* command is followed by the signal name or number.

EXAMPLE 12.66

```
trap 2
```

EXPLANATION

Resets the default action for signal 2, *SIGINT*, which is used to kill a process, i.e., Control-C.

EXAMPLE 12.67

```
trap 'trap 2' 2
```

EXPLANATION

Sets the default action for signal 2 (*SIGINT*) to execute the command string within quotes when the signal arrives. The user must press Control-C twice to terminate the program. The first *trap* catches the signal, the second *trap* resets the trap back to its default action, which is to kill the process.

Traps in Functions. If you use a trap to handle a signal in a function, it will affect the entire script, once the function is called. The trap is global to the script. In the following example, the trap is set to ignore the interrupt key, ^C. This script had to be killed with the *kill* command to stop the looping. It demonstrates potential undesirable side effects when using traps in functions.

EXAMPLE 12.68

```
(The Script)
    #!/bin/bash
1   function trapper () {
        echo "In trapper"
2       trap 'echo "Caught in a trap!"' INT
        # Once set, this trap affects the entire script. Anytime
        # ^C is entered, the script will ignore it.
    }
3   while :
    do
        echo "In the main script"
4       trapper
5       echo "Still in main"
        sleep 5
    done
```

EXAMPLE 12.68 (CONTINUED)

```
(The Output)
$ trapper
In the main script
In trapper
Still in main
^CCaught in a trap!
In the main script
In trapper
Still in main
^CCaught in a trap!
In the main script
```

EXPLANATION

1   The *trapper* function is defined. All variables and traps set in the function are global to the script.

2   The *trap* command will ignore *INT*, signal 2, the interrupt key (^C). If ^C is pressed, the message *Caught in a trap* is printed, and the script continues forever. The script can be killed with the *kill* command or Ctrl-\.

3   The main script starts a forever loop.

4   The function *trapper* is called.

5   When the function returns, execution starts here.

12.9 Debugging

By using the *–n* option to the *bash* command, you can check the syntax of your scripts without really executing any of the commands. If there is a syntax error in the script, the shell will report the error. If there are no errors, nothing is displayed.

The most commonly used method for debugging scripts is the *set* command with the *–x* option, or *bash* invoked with the *–x* option and the scriptname. See Table 12.7 on page 803 for a list of debugging options. These options allow an execution trace of your script. Each command from your script is displayed after substitution has been performed, and then the command is executed. When a line from your script is displayed, it is preceded with a plus (+) sign.

With the verbose option turned on, or by invoking the shell with the *–v* option (*bash –v* scriptname), each line of the script will be displayed just as it was typed in the script, and then executed.

Table 12.7 Debugging Options

Command	Option	What It Does
bash –x scriptname	Echo option	Displays each line of script after variable substitutions and before execution.
bash –v scriptname	Verbose option	Displays each line of script before execution, just as you typed it.
bash –n scriptname	Noexec option	Interprets but does not execute commands.
set –x	Turns on echo	Traces execution in a script.
set +x	Turns off echo	Turns off tracing.

EXAMPLE 12.69

```
(The Script)
$ cat todebug
    #!/bin/bash
    # Scriptname: todebug

1   name="Joe Shmoe"
    if [[ $name == "Joe Blow" ]]
    then
         printf "Hello $name\n"
    fi

    declare -i num=1
    while (( num < 5 ))
    do
         let num+=1
    done
    printf "The total is %d\n", $num

(The Output)
2 bash -x todebug
+ name=Joe Shmoe
+ [[ Joe Shmoe == \J\o\e\ \B\l\o\w ]]
+ declare -i num=1
+ (( num < 5 ))
+ let num+=1
+ (( num < 5 ))
+ let num+=1
+ (( num < 5 ))
+ let num+=1
+ (( num < 5 ))
+ let num+=1
+ (( num < 5 ))
+ printf 'The total is %d\n,' 5
The total is 5
```

EXPLANATION

1   The script is called *todebug*. You can watch the script run with the *–x* switch turned on. Each iteration of the loop is displayed and the values of variables are printed as they are set and when they change.

2   *Bash* is invoked with the *–x* option. Echoing is turned on. Each line of the script will be displayed to the screen prepended with a plus sign (+). Variable substitution is performed before the line is displayed. The result of the execution of the command appears after the line has been displayed.

12.10 Processing Command Line Options with *getopts*

If you are writing scripts that require a number of command line options, positional parameters are not always the most efficient. For example, the UNIX *ls* command takes a number of command line options and arguments. (An option requires a leading dash; an argument does not.) Options can be passed to the program in several ways: *ls –laFi, ls –i –a –l –F, ls –ia –F,* and so forth. If you have a script that requires arguments, positional parameters might be used to process the arguments individually, such as *ls –l –i – F* . Each dash option would be stored in *$1, $2,* and *$3,* respectively. But, what if the user listed all of the options as one dash option, as in *ls –liF*? Now the *–liF* would all be assigned to *$1* in the script. The *getopts* function makes it possible to process command line options and arguments in the same way they are processed by the *ls* program.[8] The *getopts* function will allow the *runit* program to process its arguments using any variety of combinations.

EXAMPLE 12.70

```
(The Command Line )
1   $ runit -x -n  200 filex

2   $ runit -xn200 filex

3   $ runit -xy

4   $ runit -yx -n 30

5   $ runit -n250 -xy filey

( any other combination of these arguments )
```

---

8. See the UNIX manual pages (Section 3) for the C library function *getopt*.

EXPLANATION

1   The program *runit* takes four arguments: *x* is an option, *n* is an option requiring a number argument after it, and *filex* is an argument that stands alone.

2   The program *runit* combines the options *x* and *n* and the number argument *200*; *filex* is also an argument.

3   The program *runit* is invoked with the *x* and *y* options combined.

4   The program *runit* is invoked with the *y* and *x* options combined; the *n* option is passed separately, as is the number argument, *30*.

5   The program *runit* is invoked with the *n* option combined with the number argument, the *x* and *y* options are combined, and the *filey* is separate.

Before getting into all the details of the *runit* program, we examine the line from the program where *getopts* is used to see how it processes the arguments.

EXAMPLE   12.71

```
(A Line from the Script Called "runit")

while getopts :xyn: name
```

EXPLANATION

1   *x*, *y*, and *n* are the options. In this example the first option is preceded by a colon. This tells *getopts* to use silent error reporting. If there is a colon after one of the options, the option expects an argument separated from it by whitespace. An argument is a word that does not begin with a dash. *–n* requires an argument.

2   Any options typed at the command line must begin with a dash.

3   Any options that do not contain a dash tell *getopts* that the option list has ended.

4   Each time *getopts* is called, it places the next option value it finds in the variable *name*. (You can use any variable name here.) If an illegal argument is given, *name* is assigned a question mark.

***getopts* Scripts.**   The following examples illustrate how *getopts* processes arguments.

EXAMPLE 12.72

```
(The Script)
$ cat opts1
    #!/bin/bash
    # Program: opts1
    # Using getopts -- First try --
1   while getopts xy options
    do
2      case $options in
3      x) echo "you entered -x as an option";;
       y) echo "you entered -y as an option";;
       esac
    done


(The Command Line)
4   $ opts1 -x
    you entered -x as an option
5   $ opts1 -xy
    you entered -x as an option
    you entered -y as an option
6   $ opts1 -y
    you entered -y as an option
7   $ opts1 -b
    opts1:   illegal option --  b
8   $ opts1 b
```

EXPLANATION

1   The *getopts* command is used as a condition for the *while* command. The valid options for this program are listed after the *getopts* command; they are *x* and *y*. Each option is tested in the body of the loop, one after the other. Each option will be assigned to the variable *options*, without the leading dash. When there are no longer any arguments to process, *getopts* will exit with a nonzero status, causing the *while* loop to terminate.

2   The *case* command is used to test each of the possible options found in the *options* variable, either *x* or *y*.

3   If *x* was an option, the string *you entered x as an option* is displayed.

4   At the command line, the *opts1* script is given an *x* option, a legal option to be processed by *getopts*.

5   At the command line, the *opts1* script is given an *xy* option; *x* and *y* are legal options to be processed by *getopts*.

6   At the command line, the *opts1* script is given a *y* option, a legal option to be processed by *getopts*.

7   The *opts1* script is given a *b* option, an illegal option. *Getopts* sends an error message to *stderr*.

8   An option without a dash prepended to it is not an option and causes *getopts* to stop processing arguments.

EXAMPLE   12.73

```
(The Script)
$ cat opts2
    #!/bin/bash
    # Program: opts2
    # Using getopts -- Second try --
1   while getopts xy options 2> /dev/null
    do
2     case $options in
      x) echo "you entered -x as an option";;
      y) echo "you entered -y as an option";;
3     \?) echo "Only -x and -y are valid options"  1>&2;;
      esac
    done

(The Command Line)
    $ opts2 -x
    you entered -x as an option

    $ opts2 -y
    you entered -y as an option

    $ opts2 xy

    $ opts2 -xy
    you entered -x as an option
    you entered -y as an option

4   $ opts2 -g
    Only -x and -y are valid options

5   $ opts2 -c
    Only -x and -y are valid options
```

EXPLANATION

1   If there is an error message from *getopts*, it is redirected to */dev/null*.

2   If the option is a bad option, a question mark will be assigned to the *options* variable. The *case* command can be used to test for the question mark, allowing you to print your own error message to standard error.

3   If the *options* variable is assigned the question mark, the *case* statement is executed. The question mark is protected with the backslash so that the shell does not see it as a wildcard and try to perform filename substitution.

4   *g* is not a legal option. A question mark is assigned to the variable *options* and the error message is displayed.

5   *c* is not a legal option. A question mark is assigned to the variable *options* and the error message is displayed.

Special *getopts* Variables. The *getopts* function provides two variables to help keep track of arguments: *OPTIND* and *OPTARG*. *OPTIND* is a special variable that is initialized to one and is incremented each time *getopts* completes processing a command line argument to the number of the next argument *getopts* will process. The *OPTARG* variable contains the value of a legal argument. See Examples 12.74 and 12.75.

EXAMPLE 12.74

```
(The Script)
$ cat opts3
    #!/bin/bash
    # Program: opts3
    # Using getopts -- Third try --
1   while getopts dq: options
    do
        case $options in
2           d) echo "-d is a valid switch ";;
3           q) echo "The argument for -q is $OPTARG";;
            \?) echo "Usage:opts3 -dq filename ... " 1>&2;;
        esac
    done

(The Command Line)
4   $ opts3 -d
    -d is a valid switch

5   $ opts3 -q  foo
    The argument for -q is foo

6   $ opts3 -q
    Usage:opts3 -dq filename ...

7   $ opts3 -e
    Usage:opts3 -dq filename ...

8   $ opts3 e
```

EXPLANATION

1   The *while* command tests the exit status of *getopts*; if *getopts* can successfully process an argument, it returns zero exit status, and the body of the *while* loop is entered. The colon appended to the argument list means that the *q* option requires an argument. The argument will be stored in the special variable, *OPTARG*.

2   One of the legal options is *d*. If *d* is entered as an option, the *d* (without the dash) is stored in the *options* variable.

EXPLANATION (CONTINUED)

3   One of the legal options is *q*. The *q* option requires an argument. There must be a space between the *q* option and its argument. If *q* is entered as an option followed by an argument, the *q*, without the dash, is stored in the *options* variable and the argument is stored in the *OPTARG* variable. If an argument does not follow the *q* option, the question mark is stored in the variable *options*.

4   The *d* option is a legal option to *opts3*.

5   The *q* option with an argument is also a legal option to *opts3*.

6   The *q* option without an argument is an error.

7   The *e* option is invalid. A question mark is stored in the *options* variable if the option is illegal.

8   The option is prepended with neither a dash nor a plus sign. The *getopts* command will not process it as an option and returns a nonzero exit status. The *while* loop is terminated.

EXAMPLE 12.75

```
$ cat opts4
    #!/bin/bash
    # Program: opts4
    # Using getopts -- Fourth try --
1   while getopts xyz: arguments 2>/dev/null
    do
        case $arguments  in
2       x) echo "you entered -x as an option .";;
        y) echo "you entered -y as an option." ;;
3       z) echo "you entered -z as an option."
           echo "\$OPTARG is $OPTARG.";;
4       \?) echo "Usage opts4 [-xy] [-z  argument]"
           exit 1;;
        esac
    done
5   echo "The number of arguments passed was $(( $OPTIND - 1 ))"

(The Command Line)
$ opts4 -xyz foo
You entered -x as an option.
You entered -y as an option.
You entered -z as an option.
$OPTARG is foo.
The number of arguments passed was 2.
```

EXAMPLE   12.75 (CONTINUED)

```
$ opts4 -x -y -z  boo
You entered -x as an option.
You entered -y as an option.
You entered -z as an option.
$OPTARG is boo.
The number of arguments passed was 4.

$ opts4 -d
Usage: opts4  [-xy] [-z argument]
```

EXPLANATION

1   The *while* command tests the exit status of *getopts*; if *getopts* can successfully pro-
    cess an argument, it returns zero exit status, and the body of the *while* loop is en-
    tered. The colon appended to the *z* option tells *getopts* that an argument must fol-
    low the *−z* option. If the option takes an argument, the argument is stored in the
    getopts built-in variable *OPTARG*.

2   If *x* is given as an option, it is stored in the variable *arguments*.

3   If *z* is given as an option with an argument, the argument is stored in the built-in
    variable *OPTARG*.

4   If an invalid option is entered, the question mark is stored in the variable *argu-
    ments* and an error message is displayed.

5   The special *getopts* variable *OPTIND* holds the number of the next option to be
    processed. Its value is always one more than the actual number of command line
    arguments.

12.11 The *eval* Command and Parsing the Command Line

The *eval* command evaluates a command line, performs all shell substitutions, and then
executes the command line. It is used when normal parsing of the command line is not
flexible enough for what we want to do.

EXAMPLE 12.76

```
1   $ set a b c d
2   $ echo The last argument is \$$#
3   The last argument is $4

4   $ eval echo The last argument is \$$#
    The last argument is d

5   $ set -x
    $ eval echo The last argument is \$$#
    + eval echo the last argument is '$4'
    ++ echo the last argument is d
    The last argument is d
```

EXPLANATION

1   Four positional parameters are set.

2   The desired result is to print the value of the last positional parameter. The \$ will print a literal dollar sign. The $# evaluates to 4, the number of positional parameters. After the shell evaluates the $#, it does not parse the line again to get the value of $4.

3   $4 is printed instead of the last argument.

4   After the shell performs variable substitution, the *eval* command performs the variable substitution and then executes the *echo* command.

5   Turn on the echoing to watch the order of parsing.

EXAMPLE 12.77

```
    (From Shutdown Program)
1   eval `/usr/bin/id | /usr/bin/sed 's/[^a-z0-9=].*//'`
2   if [ "${uid:=0}" -ne 0 ]
    then
3       echo $0: Only root can run $0
        exit 2
    fi
```

EXPLANATION

1   This is a tricky one. The *id* program's output is sent to *sed* to extract the *uid* part of the string. The output for *id* is

uid=9496(ellie) gid=40 groups=40
uid=0(root) gid=1(daemon) groups=1(daemon)

The *sed* regular expression reads: *Starting at the beginning of the string, find any character that is not a letter, number, or an equal sign and remove that character and all characters following it.* The result is to substitute everything from the first opening parenthesis to the end of the line with nothing. What is left is either: *uid=9496* or *uid=0*.

After *eval* evaluates the command line, it then executes the resulting command:

uid=9496
or
uid=0

For example, if the user's ID is *root*, the command executed would be *uid=0*. This creates a local variable in the shell called *uid* and assigns zero to it.

2   The value of the *uid* variable is tested for zero, using command modifiers.

3   If the *uid* is not zero, the *echo* command displays the scriptname (*$0*) and the message.

12.12 *bash* Options

12.12.1 Shell Invocation Options

When the shell is started using the *bash* command, it can take options to modify its behavior. There are two types of options: single-character options and multicharacter options. The single-character options consist of a single leading dash followed by a single character. The multicharacter options consist of two leading dashes and any number of characters. Multicharacter options must appear before single-character options. An interactive login shell normally starts up with –*i* (start an interactive shell), –*s* (read from standard input), and –*m* (enable job control). See Table 12.8 on page 813.

Table 12.8 *bash* 2.x Shell Invocation Options

Option	Meaning
−*c string*	Commands are read from *string*. Any arguments after *string* are assigned to positional parameters, starting at *$0*.
−*D*	A list of double quoted strings, preceded by a $, are printed to standard output. These strings are subject to language translation when the current locale is not C or POSIX. The −*n* option is implied; no commands will be executed.
−*i*	Shell is in the interactive mode. *TERM, QUIT,* and *INTERRUPT* are ignored.
−*s*	Commands are read from standard input and allow the setting of positional parameters.
−*r*	Starts a restricted shell.
− −	Signals the end of options and disables further option processing. Any arguments after − − or − are treated as filenames and arguments.
− −*dump−strings*	Same as −*D*.
− −*help*	Displays a usage message for a built-in command and exits.
− −*login*	Causes *bash* to be invoked as a login shell.
− −*noediting*	When *bash* is running interactively, does not use the Readline library.
− −*noprofile*	When starting up, *bash* does not read the initialization files: */etc/profile, ~/.bash_profile, ~/.bash_login,* or *~/.profile*.
− −*norc*	For interactive shells, *bash* will not read the *~/.bashrc* file. Turned on by default, if running shell as *sh*.
− −*posix*	Changes the behavior of *bash* to match the POSIX 1003.2 standard, if otherwise it wouldn't.
− −*quiet*	Displays no information at shell startup, the default.
− −*rcfile file*	If *bash* is interactive, uses this intialization file instead of *~/.bashrc*.
− −*restricted*	Starts a restricted shell.
− −*verbose*	Turns on verbose; same as −*v*.
− −*version*	Displays version information about this *bash* shell and exit.

Table 12.9 *bash* (Versions Prior to 2.x) Shell Invocation Options

−c string	Commands are read from *string*. Any arguments after *string* are assigned to positional parameters, starting at *$0*.
−D	A list of double quoted strings, preceded by a $, are printed to standard output. These strings are subject to language translation when the current locale is not C or POSIX. The *−n* option is implied; no commands will be executed.
−i	Shell is in the interactive mode. *TERM, QUIT,* and *INTERRUPT* are ignored.
−s	Commands are read from standard input and allows the setting of positional parameters.
−r	Starts a restricted shell.
−	Signals the end of options and disables further option processing. Any arguments after − − or − are treated as filenames and arguments.
−login	Causes *bash* to be invoked as a login shell.
−nobraceexpansion	Curly brace expansion is turned off.
−nolineediting	When *bash* is running interactively, does not use the Readline library.
−noprofile	When starting up, *bash* does not read the initialization files: */etc/profile, ~/.bash_profile, ~/.bash_login,* or *~/.profile.*
−posix	Changes the behavior of *bash* to match the POSIX standard, if otherwise it wouldn't.
−quiet	Displays no information at shell startup, the default.
−rcfile file	If *bash* is interactive, uses this intialization file instead of *~/.bashrc.*
−verbose	Turns on verbose; same as *−v.*
−version	Displays version information about this *bash* shell and exit.

12.12.2 The *set* Command and Options

The *set* command can be used to turn shell options on and off, as well as for handling command line arguments. To turn an option on, the dash (−) is prepended to the option; to turn an option off, the plus sign (+) is prepended to the option. See Table 12.10 on page 815 for a list of *set* options.

EXAMPLE 12.78

```
1  $ set -f

2  $ echo *
   *

3  $ echo ??
   ??

4  $ set +f
```

EXPLANATION

1   The *f* option is turned on, disabling filename expansion.
2   The asterisk is not expanded.
3   The question marks are not expanded.
4   The *f* is turned off; filename expansion is enabled.

Table 12.10   The Built-In *set* Command Options

Name of Option	Shortcut Switch	What It Does
allexport	–a	Automatically marks new or modified variables for export from the time the option is set, until unset.
braceexpand	–B	Enables brace expansion, and is a default setting.[a]
emacs		For command line editing, uses the *emacs* built-in editor, and is a default setting.
errexit	–e	If a command returns a nonzero exit status (fails), exits. Not set when reading initialization files.
histexpand	–H	Enables *!* and *!!* when performing history substitution, and is a default setting.[a]
history		Enables command line history; on by default.[a]
ignoreeof		Disables EOF (Control-D) from exiting a shell; must type exit. Same as setting shell variable, *IGNOREEOF=10*.
keyword	–k	Places keyword arguments in the environment for a command.[a]

Table 12.10   The Built-In *set* Command Options (continued)

Name of Option	Shortcut Switch	What It Does
interactive-comments		For interactive shells, a leading # is used to comment out any text remaining on the line.
monitor	−m	Allows job control.
noclobber	−C	Protects files from being overwritten when redirection is used.
noexec	−n	Reads commands, but does not execute them. Used to check the syntax of scripts. Not on when running interactively.
noglob	−d	Disables pathname expansion; i.e., turns off wildcards.
notify	−b	Notifies user when background job finishes
nounset	−u	Displays an error when expanding a variable that has not been set.
onecmd	−t	Exits after reading and executing one command.[a]
physical	−P	If set, does not follow symbolic links when typing *cd* or *pwd*. The physical directory is used instead.
posix		Shell behavior is changed if the default operation doesn't match the POSIX standard.
privileged	−p	When set, the shell does not read the *.profile* or *ENV* file and shell functions are not inherited from the environment; automatically set for *setuid* scripts.
posix		Changes the default behavior to POSIX 1003.2.
verbose	−v	Turns on the *verbose* mode for debugging.
vi		For command line editing, uses the *vi* built-in editor.
xtrace	−x	Turns on the echo mode for debugging.

a. Option applies only to versions of *bash* 2.x.

12.12.3 The *shopt* Command and Options

The *shopt* (*bash* 2.x) command can also be used to turn shell options on and off.

Table 12.11   The *shopt* Command Options

Option	Meaning
cdable_vars	If an argument to the *cd* built-in command is not a directory, it is assumed to be the name of a variable whose value is the directory to change to.
cdspell	Corrects minor errors in the spelling of a directory name in a *cd* command. The errors checked for are transposed characters, a missing character, and a character too many. If a correction is found, the corrected path is printed, and the command proceeds. Only used by interactive shells.
checkhash	*Bash* checks that a command found in the hash table exists before trying to execute it. If a hashed command no longer exists, a normal path search is performed.
checkwinsize	*Bash* checks the window size after each command and, if necessary, updates the values of *LINES* and *COLUMNS*.
cmdhist	*Bash* attempts to save all lines of a multiple-line command in the same history entry. This allows easy re-editing of multiline commands.
dotglob	*Bash* includes filenames beginning with a dot (.) in the results of filename expansion.
execfail	A noninteractive shell will not exit if it cannot execute the file specified as an argument to the *exec* built-in command. An interactive shell does not exit if *exec* fails.
expand_aliases	Aliases are expanded. Enabled by default.
extglob	The extended pattern matching features (regular expression metacharacters derived from Korn shell for filename expansion) are enabled.
histappend	The history list is appended to the file named by the value of the *HISTFILE* variable when the shell exits, rather than overwriting the file.
histreedit	If *readline* is being used, a user is given the opportunity to re-edit a failed history substitution.
histverify	If set, and *readline* is being used, the results of history substitution are not immediately passed to the shell parser. Instead, the resulting line is loaded into the *readline* editing buffer, allowing further modification.
hostcomplete	If set, and *readline* is being used, *bash* will attempt to perform hostname completion when a word containing an @ is being completed. Enabled by default.

Table 12.11 The *shopt* Command Options (continued)

Option	Meaning
huponexit	If set, *bash* will send *SIGHUP* (hangup signal) to all jobs when an interactive login shell exits.
interactive_comments	Allows a word beginning with # to cause that word and all remaining characters on that line to be ignored in an interactive shell. Enabled by default.
lithist	If enabled, and the *cmdhist* option is enabled, multiline commands are saved to the history with embedded newlines rather than using semicolon separators where possible.
mailwarn	If set, and a file that *bash* is checking for mail has been accessed since the last time it was checked, the message *The mail in mailfile has been read* is displayed.
nocaseglob	If set, *bash* matches filenames in a case-insensitive fashion when performing filename expansion.
nullglob	If set, *bash* allows filename patterns that match no files to expand to a null string, rather than themselves.
promptvars	If set, prompt strings undergo variable and parameter expansion after being expanded. Enabled by default.
restricted_shell	The shell sets this option if it is started in restricted mode. The value may not be changed. This is not reset when the startup files are executed, allowing the startup files to discover whether or not a shell is restricted.
shift_verbose	If this is set, the *shift* built-in prints an error message when the shift count exceeds the number of positional parameters.
sourcepath	If set, the *source* built-in uses the value of *PATH* to find the directory containing the file supplied as an argument. Enabled by default.
source	A synonym for dot (.).

12.13 Shell Built-In Commands

The shell has a number of commands that are built-in to its source code. Because the commands are built-in, the shell doesn't have to locate them on disk, making execution much faster. The *help* feature provided with bash give you online help for any built-in command. The built-in commands are listed in Table 12.12 on page 819.

Table 12.12 Built-In Commands

Command	What It Does
.	Executes program in context of current process; same as *source*.
. *file*	The *dot* command reads and executes command from file.
:	Do-nothing command; returns *0* exit status.
alias	Lists and creates "nicknames" for existing commands.
bg	Puts a job in the background.
bind	Displays current key and function bindings, or binds keys to a *readline* function or macro.[a]
break	Breaks out of the innermost loop.
break [n]	See "The break Command" on page 780.
builtin [sh–builtin [args]]	Runs a shell built-in, passing it args, and returning 0 exit status. Useful if a function and built-in have the same name.[a]
cd [arg]	Changes the directory to home if no arg or to value of arg.
command command [arg]	Runs a command even if a function has the same name; i.e., bypasses function lookup.[a]
continue [n]	See "The continue Command" on page 781.
declare [var]	Displays all variables or declares variables with optional attributes.[a]
dirs	Displays a list of currently remembered directories resulting from *pushd*.
disown	Removes an active job from the job table.
echo [args]	Displays *args* terminated with a newline.
enable	Enables and disables shell built-in commands.[a]
eval [args]	Reads *args* as input to the shell and executes the resulting command(s).
exec command	Runs command in place of this shell.
exit [n]	Exits the shell with status *n*.
export [var]	Makes *var* known to subshells.
fc	*History*'s fix command for editing history commands.
fg	Puts background job into foreground.

Table 12.12 Built-In Commands (continued)

Command	What It Does
getopts	Parses and processes command line options.
hash	Controls the internal hash table for quicker searches for commands.
help [command]	Displays helpful info about built-in commands and, if command is specified, detailed help about that built-in command.[a]
history	Displays the *history* list with line numbers.
jobs	Lists jobs put in the background.
kill [–signal process]	Sends the signal to the PID number or job number of the process. Type *kill –l* for a list of signals.
let	Used for evaluating arithmetic expressions and assigning results of arithmetic calculations to variables.
local	Used in functions to restrict the scope of variables to the function.
logout	Exits the login shell.
popd	Removes entries from the directory stack.
pushd	Adds entries to the directory stack.
pwd	Prints present working directory.
read [var]	Reads line from standard input into variable *var*.
readonly [var]	Makes variable *var* read-only. Cannot be reset.
return [n]	Returns from a function where *n* is the exit value given to the return.
set	Sets options and positional parameters. See Table 12.2 on page 734.
shift [n]	Shifts positional parameters to the left *n* times.
stop pid	Halts execution of the process number PID.
suspend	Stops execution of the current shell (but not if a login shell).
test	Checks file types and evaluates conditional expressions.
times	Prints accumulated user and system *times* for processes run from this shell.
trap [arg] [n]	When shell receives signal *n* (0, 1, 2, or 15), executes *arg*.

Table 12.12   Built-In Commands (continued)

Command	What It Does
type [command]	Prints the type of command; e.g., *pwd* is a built-in shell command.
typeset	Same as *declare*. Sets variables and gives them attributes.
ulimit	Diplays and sets process resource limits.
umask [octal digits]	Sets user file creation mode mask for owner, group, and others.
unalias	Unsets aliases.
unset [name]	*Unset* value of variable or function.
wait [pid#n]	Waits for background process with PID number *n* and reports termination status.

a. Option applies to *bash* 2.x and later.

BASH SHELL LAB EXERCISES

Lab 49: First Script

1. Write a script called *greetme* that will do the following:
   a. Contain a comment section with your name, the name of this script, and the purpose of this script.
   b. Greet the user.
   c. Print the date and the time.
   d. Print a calendar for this month.
   e. Print the name of your machine.
   f. Print the name and release of this operating system, (*cat /etc/motd*).
   g. Print a list of all files in your parent directory.
   h. Print all the processes *root* is running.
   i. Print the value of the *TERM, PATH,* and *HOME* variables.
   j. Print your disk usage (*du*).
   k. Use the *id* command to print your group ID.
   l. Print *Please couldn't you loan me $50.00?*
   m. Tell the user *Good bye* and the current hour (see *man* pages for the *date* command).

2. Make sure your script is executable.

   ```
   chmod +x greetme
   ```

3. What was the first line of your script? Why do you need this line?

Lab 50: Command Line Arguments

1. Write a script called *rename* that will take two arguments: the first argument is the name of the original file and the second argument is the new name for the file.

   If the user does not provide two arguments, a usage message will appear on the screen and the script will exit. Here is an example of how the script works:

   ```
   $ rename
   Usage: rename oldfilename newfilename
   $


   $ rename file1 file2
   file1 has been renamed file2
   Here is a listing of the directory:
   a file2
   b file.bak
   ```

2. The following *find* command (SunOS) will list all files in the *root* partition that are larger than 100K and that have been modified in the last week. (Check your *man* pages for the correct *find* syntax on your system.)

   ```
   find / -xdev -mtime -7 -size +200 -print
   ```

3. Write a script called *bigfiles* that will take two arguments: one will be the *mtime* and one the *size* value. An appropriate error message will be sent to *stderr* if the user does not provide two arguments.

4. If you have time, write a script called *vib* that creates backup files for *vi*. The backup files will have the extension *.bak* appended to the original name.

Lab 51: Getting User Input

1. Write a script called *nosy* that will do the following:
   a. Ask the user's full name—first, last, and middle name.
   b. Greet the user by his or her first name.
   c. Ask the user's year of birth and calculate his or her age (use *expr*).
   d. Ask the user's login name and print his or her user ID (*from /etc/passwd*).
   e. Tell the user his or her home directory.
   f. Show the user the processes he or she is running.
   g. Tell the user the day of the week, and the current time in nonmilitary time. The output should resemble

      The day of the week is Tuesday and the current time is 04:07:38 PM.

2. Create a text file called *datafile* (unless this file has already been provided for you). Each entry consists of fields separated by colons. The fields are as follows:
   a. First and last name
   b. Phone number
   c. Address
   d. Birth date
   e. Salary

3. Create a script called *lookup* that will do the following:
   a. Contain a comment section with the scriptname, your name, the date, and the reason for writing this script. The reason for writing this script is to display the datafile in sorted order.
   b. Sort the *datafile* by last names.
   c. Show the user the contents of the *datafile*.
   d. Tell the user the number of entries in the file.
4. Try the *–x* and *–v* options for debugging your script. How did you use these commands? How do they differ?

Lab 52: Conditional Statements

1. Write a script called *checking* that will do the following:
   a. Take a command line argument, a user's login name.
   b. Test to see if a command line argument was provided.
   c. Check to see if the user is in the */etc/passwd* file. If so, will print

      Found <user> in the /etc/passwd file.

      Otherwise, will print

      No such user on our system.

2. In the *lookup* script, ask the user if he or she would like to add an entry to the *datafile*. If the answer is *yes* or *y*:
   a. Prompt the user for a new name, phone, address, birth date, and salary. Each item will be stored in a separate variable. You will provide the colons between the fields and append the information to the *datafile*.
   b. Sort the file by last names. Tell the user you added the entry, and show him or her the line preceded by the line number.

Lab 53: Conditionals and File Testing

1. Rewrite *checking*. After checking whether the named user is in the */etc/passwd* file, the program will check to see if the user is logged on. If so, the program will print all the processes that are running; otherwise it will tell the user

   <user> is not logged on.

2. Use the *let* command to evaluate a set of grades. The script will ask the user for his or her numeric grade on an examination. (Use *declare –i*). The script will test that the grade is within the allowable range between 0 and 100. If not, the program will exit. If the grade is within the range, the user's letter grade will be displayed, e.g., *You received an A. Excellent!* The range is as follows:

   A (90–100)   B (80–89)   C (70–79)   D (60–69)   F (Below 60)

3. The *lookup* script depends on the *datafile* in order to run. In the *lookup* script, check to see if the *datafile* exists and if it is readable and writeable. Add a menu to the *lookup* script to resemble the following:

[1] Add entry.
[2] Delete entry.
[3] View entry.
[4] Exit.

You already have the *Add entry* part of the script written. The *Add entry* routine should now include code that will check to see if the name is already in the *datafile* and if it is, tell the user so. If the name is not there, add the new entry.

Now write the code for the *Delete entry*, *View entry*, and *Exit* functions.

The *Delete* part of the script should first check to see if the entry exists before trying to remove it. If it does, notify the user; otherwise, remove the entry and tell the user you removed it. On exit, make sure that you use a digit to represent the appropriate exit status.

How do you check the exit status from the command line?

Lab 54: The *case* Statement

1. The *ps* command is different on BSD (Berkeley UNIX) and System 5 (AT&T UNIX). UNIX uses the BSD options to *ps*. On System 5, the command to list all processes is

```
ps -ef
```

On UNIX, the command is

```
ps aux
```

Write a program called *systype* that will check for a number of different system types. The cases to test for will be

AIX
UNIX
HP–UX
SCO
OSF1
ULTRIX
SunOS (Solaris / SunOs)
OS

Solaris, HP–UX, SCO, and IRIX are AT&T-type systems. The rest are BSDish.

The version of UNIX you are using will be printed to *stdout*. The system name can be found with the *uname –s* command or from the */etc/motd* file.

2. Write a script called *timegreet* that will do the following:

   a. Provide a comment section at the top of the script, with your name, the date, and the purpose of the program.

   b. Convert the following program to use the *case* command rather than *if/elif*.

```
#!/bin/bash
# Comment section
you=$LOGNAME
hour=$( date +%H )
echo "The time is: $( date +%T )"
if (( hour > 0 && hour < 12 ))
then
    echo "Good morning, $you!"
elif (( hour == 12 ))
then
    echo "Lunch time!"
elif (( hour > 12 && hour < 16 ))
then
    echo "Good afternoon, $you!"
else
    echo "Good night, $you. Sweet dreams."
fi
```

Lab 55: Loops

Select one of the following:

1. Write a program called *mchecker* to check for new mail and write a message to the screen if new mail has arrived.

   a. The program will get the size of the mail spool file for the user. (The spool files are found in */usr/mail/$LOGNAME* on AT&T systems and */usr/spool/mail/$USER* on UNIX and UCB systems. Use the *find* command if you cannot locate the file.) The script will execute in a continuous loop, once every 30 seconds. Each time the loop executes, it will compare the size of the mail spool file with its size from the previous loop. If the new size is greater than the old size, a message will be printed on your screen, saying *Username, You have new mail.*

   The size of a file can be found by looking at the output from *ls –l, wc –c or* from the *find* command.

2. Write a script that will do the following:

   a. Provide a comment section at the top of the script, with your name, the date, and the purpose of the program.

   b. Use the *select* loop to produce a menu of foods.

c. Produce output to resemble the following:

1) steak and potatoes

2) fish and chips

3) soup and salad

Please make a selection. 1

Stick to your ribs.

Watch your cholesterol.

Enjoy your meal.

1) steak and potatoes

2) fish and chips

3) soup and salad

Please make a selection. 2

British are coming!

Enjoy your meal.

1) steak and potatoes

2) fish and chips

3) soup and salad

Please make a selection. 3

Health foods...

Dieting is so boring.

Enjoy your meal.

3. Write a program called *dusage* that will mail a list of users, one at a time, a listing of the number of blocks they are currently using. The list of users will be in a file called *potential_hogs*. One of the users listed in the *potential_hogs* file will be *admin*.

a. Use file testing to check that *potential_hogs* file exists and is readable.

b. A loop will be used to iterate through the list of users. Only those users who are using over 500 blocks will be sent mail. The user *admin* will be skipped over (i.e., he or she does not get a mail message). The mail message will be stored in a *here document* in your *dusage* script.

c. Keep a list of the names of each person who received mail. Do this by creating a log file. After everyone on the list has been sent mail, print the number of people who received mail and a list of their names.

Lab 56: Functions

1. Rewrite the *systype* program as a function that returns the name of the system. Use this function to determine what options you will use with the *ps* command in the *checking* program.

2. The *ps* command to list all processes on AT&T UNIX is

   ```
   ps -ef
   ```

3. On UNIX/BSD UNIX, the command is

   ```
   ps -aux   or ps aux⁹
   ```

4. Write a function called *cleanup* that will remove all temporary files and exit the script. If the interrupt or hangup signal is sent while the program is running, the *trap* command will call the *cleanup* function.

5. Use a *here document* to add a new menu item to the *lookup* script to resemble the following:

   [1] Add entry
   [2] Delete entry
   [3] Change entry
   [4] View entry
   [5] Exit

   Write a function to handle each of the items in the menu. After the user has selected a valid entry, and the function has completed, ask if the user would like to see the menu again. If an invalid entry is entered, the program should print

   Invalid entry, try again.

   and the menu will be redisplayed.

6. Create a submenu under *View entry* in the *lookup* script. The user will be asked if he or she would like to view specific information for a selected individual:

   a) Phone
   b) Address
   c) Birth date
   d) Salary

7. Use the *trap* command in a script to perform a cleanup operation if the interrupt signal is sent while the program is running.

---

9. Using the leading dash with UNIX will produce a warning. See the man page.

chapter

13

The Interactive
TC Shell

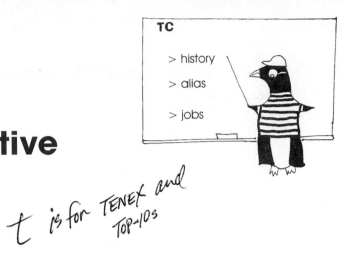

t is for TENEX and TOP-10s

13.1 Introduction

An interactive shell is one in which the standard input, output, and errors are connected to a terminal. When using the TC[1] shell (*tcsh*) interactively, you will type commands at the *tcsh* prompt and wait for a response. The TC shell is a program that starts up at login and interprets commands. It is a public domain enhanced version of its predecessor, the Berkeley UNIX C shell. Added features include command line editing, fancy prompts, programmable completions (filenames, commands, and variables), spelling correction, etc.

The primary *tcsh* source distribution is at *ftp.astron.com,* also *ftp.gw.com,* and *ftp.primate.wisc.edu.*[2] Although *tcsh* is included in most Linux distributions, it can be ported to a number of operating systems, including Solaris, Windows NT, HP-UX, QNX, etc.

This chapter focuses on how to use the TC shell interactively and how to set up your initial working environment. The enhancements over the Berkeley C shell are extensive when working with the shell interactively, as you will see in this chapter. However, when used as a programming language, *tcsh* and *csh* are practically identical. Please refer to Chapter 10 for script writing with *tcsh*. The only change will be that where you see */bin/csh,* you will use */bin/tcsh.*

13.1.1 Versions of *tcsh*

To find out what version of *tcsh* you are using, type at the shell prompt:

```
which tcsh
```

To tell you in what directory *tcsh* is installed (normally */bin*), and to print the version information, type the following:

```
/directory_path/tcsh -c 'echo $version'
```

---

1. The T in *tcsh* has origins dating back to the TENEX and TOP-10s operating systems used by DEC for its PDP-10 computer. These systems had a form of command completion for the monitor. The creator of the *tcsh* admired features of these systems, and hence, added the T to the C shell.

2. See tutorial at *www.tac.nyc.ny.us/mirrors/tcsh-book.*

829

EXAMPLE 13.1

```
1   which tcsh
    /bin/tcsh

2   /bin/tcsh -c 'echo $version'
    tcsh 6.09.09 (Astron) 1998-08-16 (sparc-sun-solaris) options
    8b,nls,dl,al,rh,color
```

13.1.2 Startup

Before the TC shell displays a prompt, it is preceded by a number of processes. See Figure 13.1.

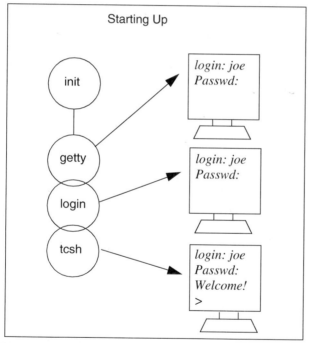

Figure 13.1 System startup and the TC shell.

After the system boots, the first process to run is called *init*, process identification number (PID) 1. It spawns a *getty* process. These processes are responsible for opening up the terminal ports, for providing a place where input comes from (*stdin*) and where standard output (*stdout*) and error (*stderr*) go, and for putting a login prompt on your screen. After the user types his user name, the */bin/login* program is executed. The login program prompts for a password, encrypts and verifies your password, sets up an initial working environment, and then initiates the shell, */bin/tcsh*. The TC shell looks in the

/etc directory for a system startup file called /etc/csh.cshrc and /etc/csh.login (if it exists). It then looks in the user's home directory for a file called ~/.tcshrc, another initialization file used to customize the *tcsh* environment. If that file is not found, it will look for another file that does the same job, called ~/.cshrc (normally invoked when running *csh*). After executing commands in the .tcshrc file (or .cshrc), it will execute the history file, commonly called .history. Then commands in the ~/.login file are executed, and finally the .cshdirs file is executed. Each of these files will be explained in "The TC Shell Environment" on page 832.[3]

   The /etc/csh.cshrc and ~/.tcshrc files will be executed every time a new TC shell is started. The .login file is executed only once when the user logs on, and also contains commands and variables to initialize the user's environment. After executing commands from all the startup files, the prompt (> is the default) appears on your screen and the *tcsh* awaits commands. See Figure 13.2.

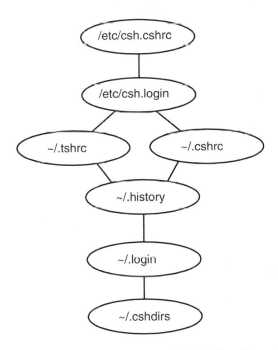

Figure 13.2   If any of these initialization files exist, they are sourced in this sequence.

   When logging out, the user presses Control-D or will be automatically logged out if the *autologout* shell variable has been set. Before logging off, the shell looks for a file called /etc/csh.logout or ~/.logout in the home directory and if either is located, its commands will be executed. The .logout file normally contains commands to clean up temporary files, append data to logfiles, wish the user a good day, etc.

---

3. The order in which these files are read can be changed when *tcsh* is compiled.

13.2 The TC Shell Environment

13.2.1 Initialization Files

After the *tcsh* program starts, it is programmed to execute a systemwide startup file, */etc/csh.cshrc*, and then two shell initialization files in the user's home directory: the *.tcshrc* file and then the *.login* file. These files allow users to initialize their own environment.

EXAMPLE 13.2

```
# /etc/csh.cshrc
# Systemwide environment and startup programs for csh users

1   if ($?PATH) then
2       setenv PATH "${PATH}:/usr/X11R6/bin"
    else
3        setenv PATH "/bin:/usr/bin:/usr/local/bin:/usr/X11R6/bin"
    endif

4   if ($?prompt) then
5       [ "$SHELL" = /bin/tcsh ]
6       if ($status == 0) then
7           set prompt='[%n@%m %c]$ '
8       else
9           set prompt=\['id -nu'@'hostname -s'\]\$\
10      endif
    endif
11  limit coredumpsize 1000000

12  [ 'id -gn' = 'id -un' -a 'id -u' -gt 14 ]
13  if $status then
14      umask 022
    else
15      umask 002
    endif

16  setenv HOSTNAME '/bin/hostname'
17  set history=1000

18  test -d /etc/profile.d
19    if ($status == 0) then
20      set nonomatch
21        foreach i ( /etc/profile.d/*.csh )
22            test -f $i
              if ($status == 0) then
23                    source $i
              endif
          end
24      unset nonomatch
      endif
```

EXPLANATION

1   $?PATH is a test to see if the PATH variable has been set; it returns 1 if true.

2   If the PATH variable has been set, /usr/X11R6/bin is appended to it. This is a directory that contains the X windows files.

3   If the PATH variable has not been previously set, this line sets it to /bin:/usr/bin:/usr/local/bin:/usr/X11R6/bin

4   This line checks to see if the prompt has been set.

5   When you place the expression in square brackets, the expression will be tested and if the result of the expression is true, a zero exit status is returned; otherwise a nonzero exit status is returned. If the value of the SHELL environment variable is /bin/tcsh, the exit status will be 0.

6   The status variable contains the exit status of the last command executed, which in this example, is the previous test on line 5.

7   If the status from the last command was zero, the prompt for the /bin/tcsh is set. The prompt will be set to the user's name followed by an @ symbol, the hostname, and the current working directory (all enclosed in [ ]), followed by a dollar sign; e.g., [ellie@homebound ~]$

8   If the status was nonzero, the else branches program control to line 9.

9   This line sets the prompt for the standard csh program. It will print the user's name (id –un), an @ symbol, and the short name for his host machine, i.e., the hostname cut at the first dot, and a $.

10   The endif terminates the inner if block.

11   The size of core files (usually created when a program crashes for some illegal system operation) is limited to 1,000,000 bytes. Core files are created if you abort a running program with Control-\.

12   If the group ID number and the user ID number are the same, and the user ID number is greater than 14, then the next line will be executed; otherwise, the line under the else will be executed. Typically, user IDs below 14 are for special users, such as root, daemon, adm, lp, etc. (See /etc/passwd. The user ID is in field number 3.)

13   If the test in the previous line returned a nonzero exit status, line 14 is executed, else line 15 is executed.

14   The umask command sets the file creation mask; i.e., the initial permissions for files and directories when created. Directories will get 755 (rwxr-xr-x) and files will get 644 (rw-r--r--) when they are created.

15   Umask is set so that when a directory is created, its permissions will be 775 (rwxrwxr-x) and files will get 664 (rw-rw-r--).

16   The environment variable HOSTNAME is assigned the output of the /bin/hostname command.

EXPLANATION (CONTINUED)

17   The *history* variable is set to *1000*. When commands are typed at the command line, they are saved in a history list. When you set the history variable to *1000*, no more than 1,000 commands will be displayed when the *history* command is typed.

18   The *test* command returns zero exit status if the */etc/profile.d* directory exists, and nonzero if it doesn't.

19   If the status is *0*, the directory exists, and the program branches to line 20.

20   The *nonomatch* variable is set to prevent the shell from sending an error message if any of its special metacharacters (*, ?, []) cannot be matched.

21   The *foreach* loop assigns each file with a *.csh* extension (*.csh) in the */etc/profile.d* directory to the variable *i*, in turn, looping until each file has been tested (lines 22–24).

22   If the filename assigned to variable *i* is a regular file (–*f*), then go to the next line.

23   If the test returned a *0* status (true), then source the file; i.e., execute it in the context of the current environment.

24   The *end* keyword marks the end of the loop body.

The ~/.tcshrc File.   The *.tcshrc* file contains *tcsh* variable settings and is executed every time a *tcsh* subshell is started. Aliases and history are normally set here.

EXAMPLE 13.3

```
(The .tcshrc File)
1  if ( $?prompt ) then
2      set prompt = "\! stardust > "
3      set history = 100
4      set savehist = 5
5      set noclobber
6      set rmstar

7      set cdpath = ( /home/jody/ellie/bin /usr/local/bin /usr/bin )
8      set ignoreeof
9      alias m more
       alias status 'date;du -s'
       alias cd 'cd \!*;set prompt = "\! <$cwd> "'
10 endif
```

EXPLANATION

1   If the prompt has been set (*$?prompt*), the shell is running interactively; i.e., it is not running in a script. Prompts are set only for interactive shells.

2   The primary prompt is set to the number of the current history event, the name *stardust*, and a > character. This will change the > prompt, the default.

3   The *history* variable is set to *100*. This controls the number of history events that will appear on the screen. The last 100 commands you entered will be displayed when you type *history*. (See "History" on page 846.)

4   Normally, when you log out, the history list is cleared. The *savehist* variable allows you to save a specified number of commands from the end of the history list. In this example, the last five commands will be saved in a file in your home directory, the *.history* file, so that when you log in again, the shell can check to see if that file exists and put the history lines saved at the top of the new history list.

5   The *noclobber* variable is set to protect the user from inadvertently removing files when using redirection. For example, *sort myfile > myfile* will destroy *myfile* With *noclobber* set, the message *file exists* will appear on the screen if you attempt to re- direct output to an existing file.

6   If the *tcsh* variable *rmstar* is set, the user will be asked if he really wants to remove all his files after entering *rm *; i.e., he is given a chance to save himself from re- moving all files in his current working directory.

7   The *cdpath* variable is assigned a list of path elements. When changing directories, if you specify just the directory name, and that directory is not a subdirectory di- rectly below the current working directory, the shell will search the *cdpath* direc- tory entries to see if it can find the directory in any of those locations and then will change the directory.

8   The *ignoreeof* variable prevents you from logging out with ^D (Control-D). UNIX utilities that accept input from the keyboard, such as the *mail* program, are termi- nated by pressing ^D. Often, on a slow system, the user will be tempted to press ^D more than once. The first time, the *mail* program would be terminated; the second time, the user is logged out. By setting *ignoreeof*, you are required to type *logout* to log out.

9   The *aliases* are set to give a shorthand notation for a single command or group of commands. Now when you type the alias, the command(s) assigned to it will be executed. The alias for the *more* command is *m*. Every time you type *m*, the *more* command is executed. The *status* alias prints the date and a summary of the user's disk usage. The *cd* alias creates a new prompt every time the user changes direc- tories. The new prompt will contain the number of the current history event (\!*) and the current working directory (*$cwd*) surrounded by < >. (See "Aliases" on page 875.)

10 The *endif* marks the end of the block of statements following the *if* construct on line 1.

The ~/.login File.   The *.login* file is executed one time when you first log in. It normally contains environment variables and terminal settings. It is the file where window applications are usually started. Because environment variables are inherited by processes spawned from this shell and only need to be set once, and terminal settings do not have to be reset for every process, those settings belong in the *.login* file.

EXAMPLE 13.4

```
(The .login File)
1   stty -istrip
2   stty erase ^h
3   stty kill ^u
    #
    # If possible start the windows system.
    # Give a user a chance to bail out
    #
4   if ( $TERM == "linux" ) then
5           echo "Starting X windows.  Press control C \
                to exit within the next 5 seconds "
            sleep 5
6           startx
7   endif
8   set autologout=60
```

EXPLANATION

1 The *stty* command sets options for the terminal. Input characters will not be stripped to seven bits if *–istrip* is used.

2 The *stty* command sets Control-H, the Backspace key, to erase.

3 Any line beginning with # is a comment. It is not an executable statement.

4 If the current terminal window (*tty*) is the console (*linux*), the next line is executed; otherwise, program control goes to the last *endif*.

5 This line is echoed to the screen, and if the user does not press Control-C to kill the process, the program will sleep (pause) for five seconds, and then the *X* windows program will start.

6 The *startx* program launches *X* windows.

7 The *endif* marks the end of the innermost *if* construct.

8 The *autologout* variable is set to 60 so that after 60 minutes of inactivity, the user will automatically be logged out (from the login shell).

13.2.2 The Search Path

The *path* variable is used by the shell to locate commands typed at the command line. The search is from left to right. The dot (.) represents the current working directory. If the command is not found in any of the directories listed in the path, or in the present working directory, the shell sends the message *Command not found.* to standard error. It is recommended that the path be set in the *.login* file.[4] The search path is set differently in the TC shell than it is in the Bash and Korn shells. Each element is separated by whitespace in the TC shell, but separated by colons in the other shells.

The TC shell internally updates the environment variable for *PATH* to maintain compatibility with other programs, such as the Bash, Bourne, or Korn shells, that may be started from this shell and will need to use the *path* variable.

EXAMPLE 13.5

```
# Path is set in the ~/.tcshrc file.

1   set path = (/usr/bin /bin /usr/bsd /usr/local/bin  .)

2   echo $path
    /usr/bin /bin /usr/bsd /usr/local/bin .

# The environment variable PATH will display as a colon-separated list

3   echo $PATH
    /usr/bin:/bin:/usr/bsd:/usr/local/bin:.
```

EXPLANATION

1 The search path is set for *tcsh*. It consists of a space-separated list of directories searched from left to right by *tcsh* when a command is entered at the command line. The search path is local to the current shell. (See "Setting Local Variables" on page 905.)

2 The value of the *path* variable is displayed

3 The value of the environment variable, *PATH*, is displayed. It is a colon-separated list of the same directories as listed in the *path* variable, and is passed to other programs or applications invoked from the current shell. (*Bash*, *sh*, and *ksh* set the path as a colon-separated list.)

The *rehash* Command.   The shell builds an internal hash table consisting of the contents of the directories listed in the search path. (If the dot is in the search path, the files in the dot directory, the current working directory, are not put in the hash table.) For efficiency, the shell uses the hash table to find commands that are typed at the command line, rather than searching the path each time. If a new command is added to one of the directories already listed in the search path, the internal hash table must be recomputed. You do this by typing the following:

```
rehash
```

---

4. Do not confuse the search path variable with the *cdpath* variable set in the *.cshrc* file.

The hash table is also automatically recomputed when you change your path or start another shell.

The *hashstat* Command.   The *hashstat* command displays performance statistics to show the effectiveness of its search for commands from the hash table. The statistics are in terms of "hits" and "misses." If the shell finds most of its commands you used at the end of your path, it has to work harder than if they were at the front of the path, resulting in a higher number of misses than hits. In such cases, you can put the most heavily hit directory toward the front of the path to improve performance.[5] The *unhash* built-in command disables the use of the internal hash table.

```
> hashstat
1024 hash buckets of 16 bits each
```

The *source* Command.   The *source* command is a built-in shell command, that is, part of the shell's internal code. It is used to execute a command or set of commands from a file. Normally, when a command is executed, the shell forks a child process to execute the command, so that any changes made will not affect the original shell, called the parent shell. The *source* command causes the program to be executed in the current shell, so that any variables set within the file will become part of the environment of the current shell. The *source* command is normally used to reexecute the *.tcshrc*, *.cshrc* or *.login* if either has been modified. For example, if the *path* is changed after logging in, type

```
> source .login or source .tcshrc
```

13.2.3 The Shell Prompts

The TC shell has three prompts: the *primary* prompt (a > symbol), the *secondary* prompt (a question mark [?] followed by a *tcsh* command such as *while, foreach,* or *if)*, and a third prompt used for the spelling correction feature. The primary prompt is the prompt that is displayed on the terminal after you have logged in. It can be reset. If you are writing scripts at the prompt that require *tcsh* programming constructs, for example, decision-making or looping, the secondary prompt will appear so that you can continue on to the next line. It will continue to appear after each newline until the construct has been properly terminated. The third prompt appears to confirm automatic spelling correction if spelling correction is turned on. (See "Spelling Correction" on page 874.) It contains the string *CORRECT > corrected command (y|n|e|a)?*. The prompts can be customized by adding special formatting sequences to the prompt string. See Table 13.1.

---

5. On machines without *vfork*(2), prints the number and size of hash buckets.

Table 13.1   Prompt Strings

String	What It Sets
%/	The current working directory.
%~	The current working directory, where ~ represents the user's home directory and other users' home directories are represented by ~*user*.
%c[[0]n], %.[[0]n]	The trailing component of the current working directory, or if *n* (a digit) is given, *n* trailing components.
%C	Like %c, but without ~ substitution.
%h, %!, !	The current history event number.
%M	The full hostname.
%m	The hostname up to the first ".".
%S (%s)	Start (stop) standout mode.
%B (%b)	Start (stop) boldfacing mode.
%U (%u)	Start (stop) underline mode.
%t, %@	The time of day in 12-hour AM/PM format.
%T	Like %t, but in 24-hour format.
%p	The "precise" time of day in 12-hour AM/PM format, with seconds.
%P	Like %p, but in 24-hour format.
^c	*c* is parsed as in bindkey.
\c	*c* is parsed as in bindkey.
%%	A single %.
%n	The user name.
%d	The weekday in *Day* format.
%D	The day in *dd* format.
%w	The month in *Mon* format.
%W	The month in *mm* format.
%y	The year in *yy* format.
%Y	The year in *yyyy* format.
%l	The shell's *tty*.

Table 13.1   Prompt Strings (continued)

String	What It Sets
%L	Clears from the end of the prompt to the end of the display or the end of the line.
%$	Expands the shell or environment variable name immediately after the $.
%#	> (or the first character of the *promptchars* shell variable) for normal users, # (or the second character of *promptchars*) for the superuser.
%{string%}	Includes string as a literal escape sequence. It should be used only to change terminal attributes and should not move the cursor location. This cannot be the last sequence in *prompt*.
%?	The return code of the command executed just before the prompt.
%R	In *prompt2*, the status of the parser. In *prompt3*, the corrected string. In *history*, the history string.

The Primary Prompt.   When running interactively, the prompt waits for you to type a command and press the Enter key. If you do not want to use the default prompt, reset it in the *.tcshrc* file and it will be set for this and all TC shells subsequently started. If you only want it set for this login session, set it at the shell prompt.

EXAMPLE 13.6

```
1   > set prompt = '[ %n@%m %c]# '
2   [ ellie@homebound ~]#  cd ..
3   [ ellie@homebound /home]#  cd ..
```

EXPLANATION

1   The primary prompt is assigned the user's login name (*%n*), followed by the hostname (*%m*), a space, and the current working directory. The string is enclosed in square brackets, followed by a #.

2   The new prompt is displayed. The ~ appearing in the prompt represents the user's home directory. The *cd* command changes directory to the parent directory.

3   The new prompt indicates the current working directory, */home*. In this way the user always know what directory he is in.

The Secondary Prompt.   The secondary prompt appears when you are writing online scripts at the prompt. The secondary prompt can be changed. Whenever shell programming constructs are entered, followed by a newline, the secondary prompt appears and continues to appear until the construct is properly terminated. Writing scripts correctly at the prompt takes practice. Once the command is entered and you press Enter, you cannot back up, and the *tcsh* history mechanism does not save commands typed at the secondary prompt.

EXAMPLE 13.7

```
1    > foreach pal (joe tom ann)
2    foreach? echo Hi $pal
3    foreach? end
     Hi joe
     Hi tom
     Ili ann
4    >
```

EXPLANATION

1   This is an example of online scripting. Because the TC shell is expecting further input after the *foreach* loop is entered, the secondary prompt appears. The *foreach* loop processes each word in the parenthesized list.

2   The first time in the loop, *joe* is assigned to the variable *pal*, and the string *Hi joe* is displayed. The next time through the loop, *tom* is assigned to the variable *pal*, and so on.

3   The *end* statement marks the end of the loop. When all of the items in the parenthesized list have been processed, the loop ends and the primary prompt is displayed.

4   The primary prompt is displayed.

EXAMPLE 13.8

```
1    > set prompt2='%R %% '
2    > foreach name ( joe tom ann )
3    foreach % echo Hi $name
4    foreach % end
     Hi joe
     Hi tom
     Hi ann
5    >
```

EXPLANATION

1   The secondary prompt, *prompt2*, is reset to the formatted string where *%R* is the name of the conditional or looping construct entered in line 2 at the primary prompt. The two percent signs will evaluate to one percent sign.

2   The *foreach* command has been started. This is a looping construct that must end with the keyword *end*. The secondary prompt will continue to appear until the loop is properly terminated.

3   The secondary prompt is *foreach %*.

4   After the *end* keyword is typed, the loop executes.

5   The primary prompt reappears, awaiting user input.

13.2.4 The Command Line

After logging in, the TC shell displays its primary prompt, by default a > symbol. The shell is your command interpreter. When the shell is running interactively, it reads commands from the terminal and breaks the command line into words. A command line consists of one or more words (or tokens) separated by whitespace (blanks and/or tabs) and terminated by a newline, generated by pressing the Enter key. The first word is the command, and subsequent words are the command's options and/or arguments. The command may be a UNIX executable program such as *ls* or *pwd*, an alias, a built-in command such as *cd* or *jobs*, or a shell script. The command may contain special characters, called *metacharacters,* that the shell must interpret while parsing the command line. If the last character in the command line is a backslash, followed by a newline, the line can be continued to the next line.[6]

Exit Status and the *printexitvalue* Variable.   After a command or program terminates, it returns an *exit status* to the parent process. The exit status is a number between 0 and 255. By convention, when a program exits, if the status returned is zero, the program was successful in its execution. When the exit status is nonzero, then it failed in some way. If the program terminated abnormally, then 0200 is added to the status. Built-in commands that fail return an exit status of *1*; otherwise, they return a status of *0*.

   The *tcsh status* variable or *?* variable is set to the value of the exit status of the last command that was executed. Success or failure of a program is determined by the programmer who wrote the program. By setting the *tcsh* variable *printexitvalue*, any time a program exits with a value other than zero, its status will automatically be printed.

---

6. The length of the command line can be 256 characters or more.

EXAMPLE 13.9

```
1   > grep "ellie" /etc/passwd
    ellie:GgMyBsSJavd16s:501:40:E Quigley:/home/jody/ellie:/bin/tcsh
2   > echo $status  or echo $?
    0
3   > grep "nicky" /etc/passwd
4   > echo $status
    1
5   > grep "scott" /etc/passssswd
    grep: /etc/passssswd: No such file or directory
6   > echo $status
    2
7   > set printexitvalue
    > grep "XXX" /etc/passwd
    Exit 1
    >
```

EXPLANATION

1 The *grep* program searches for the pattern *ellie* in the */etc/passwd* file and is successful. The line from */etc/passwd* is displayed.

2 The *status* variable is set to the exit value of the *grep* command; *0* indicates success. The *?* variable also holds the exit status. This is also the variable used by the *bash* and *ksh* shells for checking exit status. (It is not used by *csh*.)

3 The *grep* program cannot find user *nicky* in the */etc/passwd* file.

4 The *grep* program cannot find the pattern, so it returns an exit status of *1*.

5 The *grep* fails because the file */etc/passssswd* cannot be opened.

6 *Grep* cannot find the file, so it returns an exit status of *2*.

7 The special *tcsh* variable *printexitvalue* is set. It will automatically print the exit value of any command that exits with a nonzero value.

Command Grouping. A command line can consist of multiple commands. Each command is separated by a semicolon and the command line is terminated with a newline.

EXAMPLE 13.10

```
> ls; pwd; cal 2001
```

EXPLANATION

The commands are executed from left to right until the newline is reached.

Commands may also be grouped so that all of the output is either piped to another command or redirected to a file. The shell executes commands in a subshell.

EXAMPLE 13.11

```
1  > ( ls ; pwd; cal 2001 ) > outputfile
2  > pwd; ( cd / ; pwd ) ; pwd
   /home/jody/ellie
   /
   /home/jody/ellie
```

EXPLANATION

1   The output of each of the commands is sent to the file called *outputfile*. Without the parentheses, the output of the first two commands would go to the screen, and only the output of the *cal* command would be redirected to the output file.

2   The *pwd* command displays the present working directory. The parentheses cause the commands enclosed within them to be processed by a subshell. The *cd* command is built into the shell. While in the subshell, the directory is changed to *root* and the present working directory is displayed. When out of the subshell, the present working directory of the original shell is displayed.

Conditional Execution of Commands.   With conditional execution, two command strings are separated by two special metacharacters: two ampersands (*&&*), or double vertical lines (||). The command on the right of either of these metacharacters will or will not be executed based on the exit condition of the command on the left.

EXAMPLE 13.12

```
> grep '^tom:' /etc/passwd && mail tom < letter
```

EXPLANATION

If the first command is successful (has a zero exit status), the second command after the *&&* is executed. If the *grep* command successfully finds *tom* in the *passwd* file, the command on the right will be executed: The *mail* program will send *tom* the contents of the *letter* file.

EXAMPLE 13.13

```
> grep '^tom:' /etc/passwd || echo "tom is not a user here."
```

EXPLANATION

If the first command fails (has a nonzero exit status), the second command after the ||
is executed. If the *grep* command does not find *tom* in the *passwd* file, the command
on the right will be executed: The *echo* program will print *tom is not a user here* to the
screen.

Commands in the Background.   Normally, when you execute a command, it runs
in the foreground, and the prompt does not reappear until the command has completed
execution. It is not always convenient to wait for the command to complete. When you
place an ampersand at the end of the command line, the shell prompt will return immediately so that you do not have to wait for the last command to complete before starting
another one. The command running in the background is called a *background job* and
its output will be sent to the screen as it processes. It can be confusing if two commands
are sending output to the screen concurrently. To avoid confusion, you can send the output of the job running in the background to a file or pipe it to another device such as a
printer. It is often handy to start a new shell window in the background. Then you will
have access to both the window from which you started and the new shell window.

EXAMPLE 13.14

```
1   > man tcsh | lpr &
2   [1] 4664
3   >
```

EXPLANATION

1   The output from the *man* pages for the *tcsh* program is piped to the printer. The
    ampersand at the end of the command line puts the job in the background.

2   There are two numbers that appear on the screen: the number in square brackets
    indicates that this is the first job to be placed in the background; the second num-
    ber is the PID of this job.

3   The shell prompt appears immediately. While your program is running in the
    background, the shell is prompting you for another command in the foreground.

13.3 Command Line Shortcuts

13.3.1 History

The *history* mechanism is built into the TC shell. It keeps in memory a sequentially numbered list of the commands, called *events*, that you have typed at the command line. In addition to the number of the history event, it also keeps track of the time the event was entered at the terminal. When the shell reads a command from the terminal, it breaks the command line into words (using whitespace to designate a word break), saves the line to the history list, parses it, and then executes it. The previous command typed is always saved. You can recall a command at any time from the history list and reexecute it without retyping the command. During a login session, the commands you type are appended to the history list until you exit, at which time they can be saved in a file in your home directory, called *.history*[7]. The terms history list and history file can be somewhat confusing. The history list consists of the command lines currently held in the shell's memory. The history file, normally called *.history*, is the text file where those commands are saved for future use. The built-in variable, *savehist*, saves the history list to the *.history* file when you log out and loads its contents into memory when you start up. (See *–S* and *–L* options to the *history* command in Table 13.2.) The *history* built-in command displays the history list. It supports a number of arguments to control how the history is displayed.

Table 13.2 The *history* Command and Options

Option	Meaning
–h	Prints history list without numbers.
–T	Prints timestamps in comment form.
–r	Prints history list in reverse.
–S [filename]	Saves history list to *.history or filename* if given.
–L [filename]	Appends history file (*.history* or *filename*) to the history list.
–M [filename]	Like *–L*, except merges contents of history file with current history list.
–c	Clears the history list in memory, not the history file.
n	*n* is a number, e.g., *history 5*, controlling the number of lines displayed.

---

7. The name of the *.history* file can be changed by assigning the new name to the *histfile* shell variable.

Although the default name for the history file is *.history,* its name can be changed by assigning an alternative name to the built-in shell variable, *histfile.* The *history* shell variable is set to a number specifying how many commands to display and the *histdup* variable can be set so that duplicate entries are not added to the history file.

EXAMPLE 13.15

```
(The Command Line)
> history
1 17:12   cd
2 17:13   ls
3 17:13   more /etc/fstab
4 17:24   /etc/mount
5 17:54   sort index
6 17:56   vi index
```

EXPLANATION

The history list displays the last commands that were typed at the command line. Each event in the list is preceded with a number (called an event number) and the time that it was entered at the command line.

The *history* Variable.   The TC shell *history* variable can be set to the number of events from the history list that will be displayed on the terminal. Normally, this is set in the */etc/.cshrc* or *~/.tcshrc* file, the user's initialization file. It is set to 100 by default. You can also provide an optional second value for the history variable to control the way the history is formatted. This value uses the same formatting sequences as the prompt variable. (See Table 13.1.) The default format string for history is: *%h\t%T\t%R\n.*

EXAMPLE 13.16

```
1   set history=1000

2   set history= ( 1000 '%B%h %R\n' )

3   history
    136 history
    137 set history = ( 1000 '%B%h %R\n' )
    138 history
    139 ls
    140 pwd
    141 cal
    141 pwd
    142 cd
```

EXPLANATION

1   The last 1,000 commands typed at the terminal can be displayed on the screen by typing the *history* command.

2   The last 1,000 commands typed at the terminal are displayed. The format string causes the history list to be displayed in bold text (%B) first with the event number (%h), then a space, and finally the command that was typed (%R) at the command line followed by a newline (\n).

3   When you type *history*, the new format is shown. This is only a selected section of the real history list.

Saving History and the *savehist* Variable.   To save history events across logins, set the *savehist* variable. This variable is normally set in the *.tcshrc* file, the user's initialization file. If the first value assigned to *savehist* is a number, it cannot exceed the number set in the *history* variable, if the *history* variable is set. If the second value is set to *merge*, the history list is merged with the existing history file instead of replacing it. It is sorted by timestamp, and the most recent events saved.

EXAMPLE 13.17

```
1   set savehist
2   set savehist = 1000
3   set savehist = 1000 merge
```

EXPLANATION

1   The commands from the history list are saved in the history file and will be at the top of the history list the next time you log in.

2   The history file is replaced with the last 1,000 commands from the history list, and saved. It will be displayed when you next log in.

3   Rather than replacing the existing history file, the current history list will be merged with the existing history file when you log out and loaded into memory after you log in.

Displaying History.   The *history* command displays the events in the history list. The *history* command also has options that control the number of events and the format of the events that will be displayed. The numbering of events does not necessarily start at one. If you have 100 commands on the history list, and you have set the history variable to 25, you will only see the last 25 commands saved.

EXAMPLE 13.18

```
1   > set history = 10
2   > history
    1 ls
    2 vi file1
    3 df
    4 ps -eaf
    5 history
    6 more /etc/passwd
    7 cd
    8 echo $USER
    9 set
    10 ls
```

EXPLANATION

1   The history variable is set to 10. Only the last 10 lines of the history list will be displayed, even if there may be many more.

2   The last 10 events from the history are displayed. Each command is numbered.

EXAMPLE 13.19

```
1   > history -h        # Print without line numbers
    ls
    vi file1
    df
    ps -eaf
    history
    more /etc/passwd
    cd
    echo $USER
    set
    history -n

2   > history -c
```

EXPLANATION

1   With the *h* option, the history list is displayed without line numbers.

2   With the *c* option, the history list is cleared.

EXAMPLE 13.20

```
   > history -r         # Print the history list in reverse
   11 history -r
   10 history -h
    9 set
    8 echo $USER
    7 cd
    6 more /etc/passwd
    5 history
    4 ps -eaf
    3 df
    2 vi file1
    1 ls
```

EXPLANATION

The history list is displayed in reverse order.

EXAMPLE 13.21

```
   > history 5         # Print the last 5 events on the history list
    7   echo $USER
    8   cd
    9   set
   10   history -n
   11   history 5
```

EXPLANATION

The last five commands on the history list are executed.

Accessing Commands from the History File.   There are several ways to access and repeat commands from the history list. You can use the arrow keys to scroll up and down the history list, and to move left and right across lines, editing as you go; you can use a mechanism called history substitution to reexecute and fix spelling mistakes; or you can use the built-in *emacs* or *vi* editors to retrieve, edit, and execute previous commands. We'll step through each of these procedures and then you can choose whatever way works best for you.

1. **The Arrow Keys**
   To access commands from the history list, you can use the arrow keys on the keyboard to move up and down through the history list, and from left to right. You can edit any of the lines in the history list by using the standard keys for deleting, backspacing, etc. As soon as you have edited the line, pressing the carriage return (Enter key) will cause the command line to be reexecute. You can also use standard *emacs* or *vi* commands to edit the history list. (See Table 13.5

on page 856 and Table 13.6 on page 857). The arrow keys behave the same way for both the *vi* and *emacs* key bindings. (See Table 13.3.)

Table 13.3 The Arrow Keys

↑	Up arrow moves up the history list.
↓	Down arrow moves down the history list.
→	Right arrow moves cursor to right on *history* command.
←	Left arrow moves cursor to left on *history* command.

2. **Reexecuting and Bang! Bang!**

   To reexecute a command from the history list, use the exclamation point (bang) to start history substitution. The exclamation point can begin anywhere on the line and can be escaped with a backslash. If the *!* is followed by a space, tab, or newline, it will not be interpreted. There are a number of ways to use history substitution to designate what part of the history list you want to redo. (See Table 13.4 on page 854.) If you type two exclamation points (*!!*), the last command is reexecuted. If you type the exclamation point followed by a number, the number is associated with the command from the history list and the command is executed. If you type an exclamation point and a letter, the last command that started with that letter is executed. The caret (^) is also used as a shortcut method for editing the previous command.

   After history substitution is performed, the history list is updated with the results of the substitution shown in the command. For example, if you type *!!*, the last command will be reexecuted and saved in the history list in its expanded form. If you want the last command to be added to the history list in its literal form; i.e., *!!*, then set the *histlit* shell variable.

EXAMPLE 13.22

```
1   > date
    Mon Feb  8 12:27:35 PST 2001

2   > !!
    date
    Mon Aug 10 12:28:25 PST 2001

3   > !3
    date
    Mon Aug 10 12:29:26 PST 2001

4   > !d
    date
    Mon Aug 10 12:30:09 PST 2001
```

EXAMPLE 13.22 (CONTINUED)

```
5   > dare
    dare: Command not found.


6   > ^r^t
    date
    Mon Apr  10 16:15:25 PDT 2001


7   > history
    1 16:16  ls
    2 16:16  date
    3 16:17  date
    4 16:18  date
    5 16:18  dare
    6 16:18  date


8   > set histlit


9   > history
    1 16:18  ls
    2 16:19  date
    3 16:19  !!
    4 16:20  !3
    5 16:21  dare
    6 16:21  ^r^t
```

EXPLANATION

1   The UNIX *date* command is executed at the command line. The history list is updated. This is the last command on the list.

2   The *!!* (bang bang) gets the last command from the history list; the command is reexecuted.

3   The third command on the history list is reexecuted.

4   The last command on the history list that started with the letter *d* is reexecuted.

5   The command is mistyped.

6   The carets are used to substitute letters from the last command on the history list. The first occurrence of an *r* is replaced with a *t*.

7   The *history* command displays the history list, after history substitution has been performed.

8   By setting *histlit,* the shell will perform history substitution, but will put the literal command typed, on the history list; i.e., just as it was typed.

9   When *histlit* is set, the output of the *history* command shows what commands were literally typed before history substitution took place. (This is just a demo; the history numbers are not accurate.)

EXAMPLE 13.23

1   > **cat file1 file2 file3**

      <Contents of files displayed here>

    > **vi !:1**
    vi file1

2   > **cat file1 file2 file3**

    <Contents of file, file2, and file3 are displayed here>

    > **ls !:2**
    ls file2
    file2

3   > **cat file1 file2 file3**
    > **ls !:3**
    ls file3
    file3

4   > **echo a b c**
    a b c
    > **echo !$**
    echo c
    c

5   > **echo a b c**
    a b c
    > **echo !^**
    echo a
    a

6   > **echo a b c**
    a b c
    > **echo !***
    echo a b c
    a b c

7   > **!!:p**
    echo a b c

EXPLANATION

1   The *cat* command displays the contents of *file1, file2,* and *file3* to the screen. The history list is updated. The command line is broken into words, starting with word number zero. If the word number is preceded by a colon, that word can be extracted from the history list. The *!:1* notation means, *get the first argument from the last command on the history list and replace it in the command string.* The first argument from the last command is *file1.* (Word *0* is the command itself.)

2   The *!:2* is replaced with the second argument of the last command, *file2,* and given as an argument to *ls. file2* is printed. (*file2* is the third word.)

3   *ls !:3* reads, *go to the last command on the history list and get the fourth word (words start at zero) and pass it to the* ls *command as an argument.* (*file3* is the fourth word.)

4   The bang (*!*) with the dollar sign (*$*) refers to the last argument of the last command on the history list. The last argument is *c.*

5   The caret (*^*) represents the first argument after the command. The bang (*!*) with the *^* refers to the first argument of the last command on the history list. The first argument of the last command is *a.*

6   The asterisk (***) represents all arguments after the command. The bang (*!*) with the *** refers to all of the arguments of the last command on the history list.

7   The last command from the history list is printed but not executed. The history list is updated. You could now perform caret substitutions on that line.

Table 13.4   Substitution and History

Event Designators	Meaning
!	Indicates the start of history substitution.
!!	Reexecutes the previous command.
!N	Reexecutes the Nth command from the history list.
!–N	Reexecutes the Nth command back from present command.
!string	Reexecutes the last command starting with *string.*
!?string?	Reexecutes the last command containing *string.*
!?string?%	Reexecutes the most recent command line argument from the history list containing *string.*
*!^*	Uses the first argument of the last history command in the current command line.
!*	Uses all of the arguments from the last history command in the current command line.

Table 13.4   Substitution and History (continued)

Event Designators	Meaning
!$	Uses the last argument from the last history command in the current command line.
!! string	Appends string to the previous command and executes.
!N string	Appends string to Nth command in history list and executes.
!N:s/old/new/	In previous Nth command, substitutes the first occurrence of old string with new string.
!N:gs/old/new/	In previous Nth command, globally substitutes old string with new string.
*^old^new^*	In last history command, substitutes old string with new string.
command !N:wn	Executes current command appending an argument (*wn*) from the Nth previous command. *wn* is a number starting at 0, 1, 2, ... designating the number of the word from the previous command; word 0 is the command itself, and 1 is its first argument, etc.
!N:p	Puts the command at the bottom of the history list and prints it, but doesn't execute it.

13.3.2   The Built-In Command Line Editors

The command line can be edited by using the same type of key sequences that you use in either the *emacs* or *vi* editors. You can use editor commands to scroll up and down the history list. Once the command is found, it can be edited, and by pressing the Enter key, reexecuted. When the shell was compiled, it was given a default set of key bindings for the *emacs* editor.

The *bindkey* Built-In Command.   The built-in *bindkey* command is used to select either *vi* or *emacs* for command line editing and to list and set key bindings for the respective editors. To use *vi* as your command line editor, use *bindkey* with the –*v* option:

```
bindkey -v
```

and to go back to *emacs*:

```
bindkey -e
```

To see a list of editor commands and a short description of what each does, type

```
bindkey -l
```

And to see the actual keys and how they are bound, type

```
bindkey
```

To actually bind keys to commands, see "Binding Keys" on page 858.

The *vi* Built-In Editor.   To edit the history list, go to the command line and press the Esc key. Then press the K key if you want to scroll upward in the history list, and the J key to move downward, just like standard *vi* motion keys. When you find the command that you want to edit, use the standard keys that you would use in *vi* for moving left and right, deleting, inserting, and changing text. See Table 13.5. After making the edit, press the Enter key. The command will be executed and added to the bottom of the history list. If you want to add or insert text, then use any of the insertion commands (*i, e, o, O*, etc.). Remember, *vi* has two modes: the command mode and the insert mode. You are always in the insert mode when you are actually typing text. To get back to the command mode, press the Escape key (Esc).

Table 13.5   *vi* Commands

Command	Function
Moving Through the History File	
Esc k *or* +	Move up the history list.
Esc j *or* –	Move down the history list.
G	Move to first line in history file.
5G	Move to fifth command in history file.
/string	Search upward through history file.
?	String search downward through history file.
Moving Around on a Line	
h	Move left on a line.
l	Move right on a line.
b	Move backward a word.
e *or* w	Move forward a word.
^ *or* 0	Move to beginning of first character on the line.
$	Move to end of line.
Editing with vi	
a A	Append text.
i I	Insert text.
dd dw x	Delete text into a buffer (line, word, or character).
cc C	Change text.
u U	Undo.
yy Y	Yank (copy a line into buffer).
p P	Put yanked or deleted line down below or above the line.
r R	Replace a letter or any amount of text on a line.

The *emacs* Built-In Editor.   If you are using the *emacs* built-in editor, like vi, start at the command line. To start moving upward through the history file, press ^P. To move down, press ^N . Use *emacs* editing commands to change or correct text, then press Enter, and the command will be reexecuted. See Table 13.6.

Table 13.6   *emacs* Commands

Command	Function
Ctrl-P	Move up history file.
Ctrl-N	Move down history file.
Ctrl-B	Move backward one character.
Ctrl-R	Search backward for string.
Esc B	Move back one word.
Ctrl-F	Move forward one character.
Esc F	Move forward one word.
Ctrl-A	Move to the beginning of the line.
Ctrl-E	Move to the end of the line.
Esc <	Move to the first line of the history file.
Esc >	Move to the last line of the history file.
Editing with emacs	
Ctrl-U	Delete the line.
Ctrl-Y	Put the line back.
Ctrl-K	Delete from cursor to the end line.
Ctrl-D	Delete a letter.
Esc D	Delete one word forward.
Esc H	Delete one word backward.
Esc space	Set a mark at cursor position.
Ctrl-X Ctrl-X	Exchange cursor and mark.
Ctrl-P Ctrl-Y	Push region from cursor to mark into a buffer (Ctrl-P) and put it down (Ctrl-Y).

Binding Keys.   The *bindkey* built-in command lists all the standard key bindings including key bindings for *emacs* and *vi*. The key bindings are divided up into four groups: the standard key bindings, alternative key bindings, multicharacter key bindings, and the arrow key bindings. The *bindkey* command also allows you to change the current bindings of keys.

EXAMPLE 13.24

```
1   > bindkey
    Standard key bindings
    "^@"              ->   is undefined
    "^A"              ->   beginning-of-line
    "^B"              ->   backward-char
    "^C"              ->   tty-sigintr
    "^D"              ->   list-or-eof
    "^E"              ->   end-of-line
    "^F"              ->   forward-char
    "^L"              ->   clear-screen
    "^M"              ->   newline
         ...    ....
    Alternative key bindings
    "^@"              ->   is undefined
    "^A"              ->   beginning-of-line
    "^B"              ->   is undefined
    "^C"              ->   tty-sigintr
    "^D"              ->   list-choices
    "^E"              ->   end-of-line
    "^F"              ->   is undefined
       ......  .....
    Multi-character bindings
    "^[[A"            -> up-history
    "^[[B"            -> down-history
    "^[[C"            -> forward-char
    "^[[D"            -> backward-char
    "^[OA"            -> up-history
    "^[OB"            -> down-history
        ...   ....
    Arrow key bindings
    down              -> down-history
    up                -> up-history
    left              -> backward-char
    right             -> forward-char
```

The *–l* option to *bindkey* lists the editor commands and what they do. See Example 13.25.

EXAMPLE 13.25

```
> bindkey -l

backward-char
    Move back a character
backward-delete-char
    Delete the character behind cursor
backward-delete-word
    Cut from beginning of current word to cursor - saved in cut buffer
backward-kill-line
    Cut from beginning of line to cursor - save in cut buffer
backward-word
    Move to beginning of current word
beginning-of-line
    Move to beginning of line
capitalize-word
    Capitalize the characters from cursor to end of current word
change-case
    Vi change case of character under cursor and advance one character
change-till-end-of-line
    Vi change to end of line
clear-screen
Standard key bindings
    ..... ...
```

The *bindkey* command can also display the values for individual key bindings, as shown in Example 13.26. The *emacs* mappings are shown by default, but with the *–a* option to *bindkey*, the alternate mappings for *vi* keys are displayed. The arguments to *bindkey* are specified as a sequence of special characters to represent the key sequences followed by the editing command key to which the key will be bound. You can bind keys not only to *emacs* or *vi* editor commands, but also to UNIX commands and strings.

Table 13.7 Key Binding Characters

Characters	*Meaning*
^C	Control-C.
^[	Esc.
^?	Del.
\a	Control-G (bell).
\b	Control-H (backspace).

Table 13.7   Key Binding Characters (continued)

Characters	Meaning
\e	Esc (escape).
\f	Formfeed.
\n	Newline.
\r	Return.
\t	Tab.
\v	Control-K (vertical tab).
\nnn	ASCII octal number.

EXAMPLE 13.26

```
1  > bindkey ^L
   "^L"       ->      clear-screen

2  > bindkey ^C
   "^C"       ->      tty-sigintr

3  > bindkey "j"
   "j"        ->      self-insert-command

4  > bindkey -v

5  > bindkey -a "j"
   "j"        ->      down-history
```

EXPLANATION

1 The *bindkey* command with a Control key (^L) displays to what command the control key is bound. ^L causes the screen to be cleared.

2 Control-C (^C) is bound to the interrupt signal, which normally terminates a process.

3 Lowercase j is an *emacs* self-insert-command that does nothing but insert that letter into the buffer.

4 In order to see the alternate *vi* key bindings, be sure you have set the *vi* command line editor with *bindkey –v*, as shown here.

5 With the *–a* option, *bindkey* displays the alternate key mapping for j; i.e., the *vi* key for moving down the history list.

EXAMPLE 13.27

```
1   > bindkey "^T" clear-screen

2   > bindkey "^T"
    "^T"      ->      clear-screen

3   > bindkey -a "^T"
    "^T"      ->      undefined-key

4   > bindkey -a  [Control-v Control t] clear-screen
        Press keys one after the other

5   > bindkey -a [Control-v Control t]
    "^T"       ->       clear-screen

6   > bindkey -s '\ehi'  'Hello to you!\n'
    > echo [Esc]hi    Press escape followed by 'h' and 'i'
      Hello to you!
    >
7   > bindkey '^[hi'
    "^[hi"    ->    "Hello to you!"

8   > bindkey -r '\[hi'

9   > bindkey '\ehi'
    Unbound extended key "^[hi"

10  > bindkey -c '\ex' 'ls | more'
```

EXPLANATION

1 Control-T is bound to the command to clear the screen, a default *emacs* key mapping. This key sequence was not originally bound to anything. Now when the Control and T keys are pressed together, the screen will be cleared.

2 The *bindkey* command, with the key sequence as an argument, will display the mapping for that sequence, if there is one.

3 With the *–a* option and a key sequence, *bindkey* displays the value of the alternate key map, *vi*. In this example, *bindkey* with the *–a* option and the key sequence shows that the alternate mapping (*vi*) does not have this sequence bound to anything.

4 With the *–a* option, *bindkey* can bind keys to the alternate key map, *vi*. By pressing Control-V followed by Control-T, the key sequence is created and assigned the value *clear-screen*. Control-V/Control-T can also be represented as "^T", as shown in the previous example.

5 The *bindkey* function displays the alternate mapping for ^T and its command.

EXPLANATION (CONTINUED)

6 With the *–s* command, *bindkey* will bind a literal string to a key sequence. Here the string *Hello to you!\n* is bound to the escape sequence *hi*. By pressing the Esc key and then an *h* and an *i*, the string will be sent to standard output.

7 The *bindkey* command displays the binding for the escape sequence *hi*. The ^[is another way to represent Esc (escape).

8 With the *–r* option, *bindkey* removes a key binding.

9 Because the key binding was removed, the output says that this extended key sequence is not bound.

10 With the *–c* option, *bindkey* can bind a key sequence to a UNIX command. In this example, pressing the Escape key followed by the X key will cause the command *ls* to be piped to *more*.

Table 13.8   *bindkey* Options

bindkey	*Lists All Key Bindings*
bindkey –a	Allow alternate key mapping.
bindkey –d	Restore default bindings.
bindkey –e	Use *emacs* bindings.
bindkey –l	Display all editing commands and what they mean.
bindkey –u	Display usage message.
bindkey –v	Use *vi* key bindings.
bindkey key	Display binding for key.
bindkey key command	Bind key to *emacs* or *vi* command.
bindkey –c key command	Bind key to UNIX command.
bindkey –s key string	Bind key to string.
bindkey –r key	Remove key binding.

13.3.3 Command, Filename, and Variable Completion

To save typing, *tcsh* has a mechanism called *completion* that allows you to type part of a command, filename, or variable, and then, by pressing the Tab key, have the rest of the word completed for you.

   If you type the first few letters of a command and press the Tab key, *tcsh* will attempt to complete the command name. If *tcsh* cannot complete the command because it doesn't exist, the terminal will beep and the cursor will stay at the end of the command.

If there is more than one command starting with those characters, by pressing Control-D, all commands that start with those characters will be listed.

Filename and variable completion work the same as command completion. With filename completion, if there are several files starting with the same letters, *tcsh* will complete the shortest name that matches, expand out the filename until the characters differ, and then flash the cursor for you to complete the rest. See Example 13.28.

The *autolist* Variable.   If the *autolist* variable is set, and there are a number of possible completions, all of the possible commands, variables, or filenames will be listed depending on what type of completion is being performed when the Tab key is pressed.

EXAMPLE   13.28

```
1    > ls
     file1 file2 foo foobarckle fumble

2    > ls fu[tab]        # eExpands to filename to fumble

3    > ls fx[tab]        # Terminal beeps, nothing happens

4    > ls fi[tab]        # Expands to file_   (_ is a cursor)

5    > set autolist

6    > ls f[tab]         # Lists all possibilities
     file1 file2 foo foobarckle fumble

7    > ls foob[tab]      # Expands to foobarckle

8    > da[tab]           # Completes the date command
     date
     Fri Aug 9 21:15:38 PDT 2001

9    > ca[tab]           # Lists all commands starting with ca
     cal    captoinfo  case    cat

10   > echo $ho[tab]me   # Expands shell variables
     /home/ellie/

11   > echo $h[tab]
     history home
```

EXPLANATION

1   All files are listed for the current working directory.
2   After *fu* is typed, the Tab key is pressed, causing the filename to be completed to *fumble*, and listed.
3   Because none of the files start with *fx*, the terminal beeps and the cursor remains but does nothing.

EXPLANATION (CONTINUED)

4   There are a number of files starting with *fi*; the filenames are completed until the letters are no longer the same. When you press Control-D, all files with that spelling are listed.

5   The *autolist* variable is set. If there are a number of choices when you press the Tab key, *autolist* displays all the possibilities.

6   After you press the Tab key, a list of all files beginning with *f* are printed.

7   When the Tab key is pressed, the filename is expanded to *foobarckle*.

8   When the Tab key is pressed after *da*, the only command that begins with *da* is the *date* command. The command name is expanded and executed.

9   Because *autolist* is set, when the Tab key is pressed after *ca*, all commands starting with *ca* are listed. If *autolist* is not set, type Control-D to get a list.

10 The leading $ on a word indicates that the shell should perform variable expansion when the Tab key is pressed to complete the word. The variable *home* is completed.

11 Variable completion is ambiguous in this example. When completion is attempted by pressing the Tab key, all possible shell variables are listed.

The *fignore* Variable.   The shell variable, *fignore*, can be set to ignore certain filename extensions when filename completion is in use. For example, you may not want to expand files that end in *.o* because they are unreadable object files. Or maybe you don't want the *.gif* files to be accidently removed when filenames are expanded. For whatever reason, the *fignore* variable can be assigned a list of extensions for files that will be excluded from filename expansion.

EXAMPLE 13.29

```
1   > ls
    baby        box.gif     file2       prog.c
    baby.gif    file1       file3       prog.o

2   > set fignore = (.o .gif )

3   > echo ba[tab]     # Completes baby but ignores baby.gif
    baby

4   > echo box[tab].gif    # fignore is ignored if only one completion
    box.gif                # is possible

5   > vi prog[tab]         # Expands to prog.c
    Starts vi with prog.c as its argument
```

EXPLANATION

1   The files in the current working directory are listed. Note that some of the files have extensions on their names.

2   The *fignore* variable allows you to list those filename extensions that should be ignored when filename completion is performed. All filenames ending in either *.o* or *.gif* will be ignored.

3   By pressing the Tab key, only the file *baby* is listed, not *baby.gif*. The *.gif* files are ignored.

4   Even though *.gif* is listed as a suffix to be ignored, *fignore* will not take effect when there are no other possible completions, such as the same filename without the *.gif* extension as in line 3.

5   When the *vi* editor is invoked, *prog* is expanded to *prog.c*.

The *complete* Shell Variable.   This is a variable that does a lot! It is a little tricky trying to decipher all it can do from the *tcsh* man page, but you may find some of these examples helpful for a start. You can control what kind of completion you are doing. For example maybe you only want completion to expand directory names, or a filename depending on its position in the command line, or maybe you would like certain commands to be expanded and others excluded, or even create a list of possible words that can be expanded. Whatever it is you want to do with completion, no doubt, the *complete* shell variable will accommodate you.

Filename completion can be even more sophisticated if the *complete* shell variable is set to *enchance*. This causes tab completion to ignore case; to treat hyphens, periods, and underscores as word separators; and to consider hyphens and underscores as equivalent.

EXAMPLE 13.30

```
1   > set complete=enchance

2   > ls g..[tab]     expands to gawk-3.0.3
    gawk-3.0.3

3   > ls GAW[tab]     expands to gawk-3.0.3
    gawk-3.0.3
```

EXPLANATION

1   By setting the *complete* shell variable to *enchance*, Tab completion will ignore case; will treat hyphens, periods, and underscores as word separators; and will consider hyphens and underscores as equivalent.

   2   With *enchance* set, filename completion expands *g..* to any files starting with a *g*, followed by any two characters (*..*), and any characters to complete the filename, including hyphens, periods, etc.

   3   With *enchance* set, filename completion expands *GAW* to any files starting with *GAW*, where *GAW* can be any combination of upper and lowercase letters, and the remaining characters can be any characters even if they contain hyphens, periods, and underscores.

Programming Completions.   To customize completions to a more specific functionality, you can program the completions, and then store them in the *~/.tcshrc* file, making them part of your *tcsh* environment each time you start a new TC shell. The purpose of programming completions is to improve efficiency and select types of commands and arguments that will be affected. (The Tab key for word completion and Control-D to list possible completions still work the same way as they did for simple completions.)

Types of Completions.   There three types of completions: *p*, *n*, and *c*. A *p*-type completion is position-dependent. It rules the way a completion is performed based on the *position* of a word in the command line, where position *0* is the command, position *1* is the first argument, position *2* is the second argument, etc. Suppose, for example, you wanted to guarantee that any time a completion is performed for the built-in *cd* command, the first (and only) argument to *cd* is completed only if it is a directory name, nothing else; then you can program the completion as shown in the following example:

```
complete  cd   'p/1/d/'
```

The *complete* command is followed by the *cd* command and what is called the completion *rule*. The *p* stands for the word position in the command line. The *cd* command is position *0* and its first argument is position *1*. The pattern part of the rule is enclosed in slashes (*p/1/* means position *1*, the first argument to *cd*), and will be affected by the completion rule. The *d* part of the pattern is called a *word type*. See Table 13.9 on page 868 for a complete list of word types. The *d* word type means that only directories are to be affected by the completion. A filename or alias, for example, would not be completed if given as the first argument to *cd*. The rule states that whenever tab completion is performed on the *cd* command, it will only take place if the first argument is a directory, and Control-D will only list directories if the match is ambiguous; i.e., there is more than one possible completion. See Example 13.31 for *p*-type completions.

EXAMPLE 13.31

```
# p-type completions (positional completion)

1   > complete
    alias       'p/1/a/'
    cd          'p/1/d/'
    ftp         'p/1/( owl ftp.funet.fi prep.ai.mit.edu )'
    man         'p/*/c/'

2   > complete  vi  'p/*/t/'

3   > complete vi
    vi  'p/*/t/'

4   > set autolist

5   > man fin[tab]    # Completes command names
    find      find2perl   findaffix   findsmb  finger

6   > vi b[tab]        # Completes only filenames, not directories
    bashtest binded bindings bindit

7   > vi na[tab]mes

8   > cd sh[tab]ellsolutions/

9   > set hosts = ( netcom.com 192.100.1.10 192.0.0.200 )

10  > complete telnet 'p/1/$hosts/'

11  > telnet net[tab]com.com
    telnet netcom.com

12  > alias m[tab]    # Completes alias names
    mc mroe mv

13  > ftp prep[tab]
```

EXPLANATION

1   The *complete* built-in command, without arguments, lists all programmed completions. The following examples (lines 2 through 11) use these completion rules.

2   This rule states that if Tab completion is used when typing arguments to the vi command, that all arguments (*), must be of type *t* (i.e., plain text files) for completion to performed.

3   The *complete* command, with the name of a command as its argument, displays the completion rule for that command. The completion rule for vi is displayed.

EXPLANATION (CONTINUED)

4   By setting the *autolist* built-in command all possible Tab completions will automatically be printed. (You don't have to press Control-D.)

5   The *man* command has a programmed completion: *complete man 'p/1/c/'*. This rule states that the first argument given to the *man* command must be a command, because *c* is defined as a command word type. In this example, completion is attempted with the letters *fin* as the argument to *man*. All manual commands starting with *fin* will be displayed.

6   Only filenames will be completed, because the *vi* editor completion was programmed to complete only text files, not directories.

7   According to the *vi* completion rule, only text filenames will be completed, no matter how many arguments are passed.

8   When filename completion is performed on the first argument to the built-in *cd* command, the only word that will be completed must be the name of a directory as stated in the completion rule. The argument in this example will expand to a directory called *shellsolutions*.

9   The variable *hosts* is set to a list of IP addresses or hostnames.

10 The completion rule for *telnet* states that completion will be performed if position 1 contains one of the hostnames set in the *hosts* variable. This is a list word type completion.

11 The *telnet* command is executed and the word beginning with *net,* followed by pressing the Tab key, is completed to *netcom.com*, which is one of the hostnames in the *hosts* variable, previously set.

12 The *alias* completion is performed if the user types the word *alias* followed by a word that will be expanded to all aliases that contain that word. Word type *a* means only aliases are expanded for *p*, postition 1.

Table 13.9   Completion Word Types

Word	Type
a	Alias.
b	Editor key-binding commands.
c	Commands (built-in or external).
C	External commands that begin with the supplied path prefix.
d	Directory.
D	Directories that begin with the supplied path prefix.
e	Environment variables.

Table 13.9 Completion Word Types (continued)

Word	Type
f	Filenames (not directory).
F	Filenames that begin with the supplied path prefix.
g	Groupnames.
j	Jobs.
l	Limits.
n	Nothing.
s	Shell variables.
S	Signals.
t	Plain (text) files.
T	Plain (text) files beginning with the supplied path prefix.
v	Any variables.
u	Usernames.
X	Command names for which completions have been defined.
x	Like *n*, but prints a message if ^D is typed.
C, D, F, T	Like *c, d, f, t*, but selects completions from a given directory.
(list)	Selects completions from words in a list

A *c*-type completion is used to complete a pattern in the current word. The current word refers to the pattern enclosed in forward slashes. It rules that if the pattern is matched, any completion performed will finish the pattern.

EXAMPLE 13.32

```
# c-type completions

1   > complete
    stty      'c/-/(raw xcase noflsh)/'
    bash      'c/-no/(profile rc braceexpansion)/'
    find      'c/ /(user name type exec)/'
    man       'c/perl/(delta faq toc data modlib locale)/'

2   > stty -r[tab]aw
    stty -raw
```

EXAMPLE 13.32 (CONTINUED)

```
3  > bash -nop[tab]rofile
   bash -noprofile


4  > find / -n[tab]ame .tcshrc -p[tab]rint
   find / -name .tcshrc -print


5  > man perlde[tab]lta
   man perldelta


6  > uncomplete stty
   > complete
   bash      'c/-no/(profile rc braceexpansion)/'
   find      'c/-/(user name type exec)/'
   man       'c/perl/(delta faq toc data modlib locale)/'


7  > uncomplete *
```

EXPLANATION

1 These examples demonstrate a *c*-type completion. If the pattern in the first set of forward slashes is typed, that pattern will be completed by one of the words listed in the parentheses when a character(s) from that list is typed, followed by the Tab key.

2 When the *stty* command is typed, followed by a dash (–) character, the word will be completed to –*raw*, if a dash, an *r*, and the Tab key are entered. One of the words from the rule list in parentheses (*raw xcase noflsh*) can be completed.

3 When the *bash* command is typed, followed by the pattern, –*no*, that pattern will be completed to –*noprofile*, if the pattern –*no* is followed by a *p* and the Tab key. Completion is performed from one of the words in the rule list (*profile rc braceexpansion*); in this example, resulting in –*noprofile*.

4 Arguments to the *find* command are completed if the dash (–) character is completed by typing significant characters from any of the words in the *find* rule list (*user name type exec*).

5 When the *man* command is typed, the pattern *perl* is completed to *perldelta* since the pattern is followed by one of the words from the list (*delta faq toc data modlib locale*).

6 The *uncomplete* built-in command removes the completion rule for *stty*. The other completion rules remain.

7 The *uncomplete* built-in command, with the asterisk as its argument, removes all completion rules.

An *n*-type completion matches the first word and completes the second one.

EXAMPLE 13.33

```
# n-type completions (next word completion)

1   > complete
    rm   'n/-r/d/'
    find 'n/-exec/c/'

2   > ls -ld testing
    drwxr-sr-x  2  ellie  root   1024 Aug 29 11:02 testing

3   > rm -r te[tab]sting
```

EXPLANATION

1. These examples demonstrate an *n*-type completion. If the word in the first set of forward slashes is typed (the current word) and matched, the next word (in the second set of forward slashes) will be completed according to the word type. The *complete* command lists two *n*-type completions, one for the *rm* command and one for the *find* command. When the *rm* command is executed with the –*r* switch, the word following –*r* must be of type directory if completion is to be performed. The rule for the *find* command is: if the –*exec* option is given, any words following it must be commands if completion is to be performed.
2. The output of the *ls* command shows that *testing* is a directory.
3. Filename completion is successful for the *rm* command because word completion is attempted for a directory named *testing*. If *testing* were a plain file, the completion would not have been performed.

13.3.4 Manipulating the Directory Stack

If you find that as you work, you *cd* up and down the directory tree into many of the same directories, you can make it easy to access those directories by pushing them onto a directory stack and manipulating the stack. The directory stack is often compared to stacking trays in a cafeteria where the trays are stacked on top of each other, the first one being at the bottom of the stack. The *pushd* built-in command pushes directories onto a stack and the *popd* command removes them. (See following Examples.) The stack is a numbered list of directories with the top directory being the most recent directory pushed onto the stack. The directories are numbered starting with the top directory at 0, the next one numbered 1, etc. The *dirs* built-in command, with a –*v* option, displays the numbered directory stack.

The *pushd* and *popd* Commands. The *pushd* command with a directory as an argument causes the new directory to be added to the directory stack and, at the same time, changes to that directory. If the argument is a dash (–), the dash refers to the previous working directory. If the argument is a + and a number (*n*), *pushd* extracts the *n*th directory from the stack and pushes it onto the top, then changes to that directory. Without arguments, *pushd* exchanges the top two elements of the directory stack, making it easy to switch back and forth between directories. There are a number of shell variables that control the way *pushd* works. (See "Setting Local Variables" on page 905.)

To save a directory stack across login sessions, you must set the *savedirs* variable in one of the *tcsh* initialization files (e.g., ~/.tcshrc). The directory stack will be stored in a file called ~/.cshdirs and will be automatically sourced when the shell starts up.

The *popd* command removes a directory from the top of the stack, and changes to that directory.

Table 13.10 Directory Stack Variables

pushdtohome	If set, *pushd* without arguments is same as *pushd* ~ or *cd*.
dunique	Before pushing a directory onto the stack, removes any directories with the same name.
pushdsilent	Doesn't print the directory stack when *pushd* is executed.
deextract	If set, *pushd* +n extracts the nth directory from the directory stack before pushing it onto the stack.
pushtohome	Without arguments, pushes to ~, the user's home directory.
dirsfile	Can be assigned a filename where the directory stack can be saved across logins.
savedirs	Saves the directory stack across logins.
dirstack	Used to display the stack or assign directories to it.

EXAMPLE 13.34

```
1  > pwd
   /home/ellie

   > pushd ..
   /home ~

   > pwd
   /home

2  > pushd          # Swap the two top directories on the stack
   ~ /home

   > pwd
   /home/ellie
```

EXAMPLE 13.34 (CONTINUED)

```
3   > pushd perlclass
    ~/perlclass  ~  /home
```

```
4   > dirs -v
    0        ~/perlclass
    1        ~
    2        /home
```

Directory stack

0	~/perlclass
1	~
2	/home

```
5   > popd
    ~        /home
    > pwd
    /home/ellie
```

```
6   > popd
    /home
```

```
    > pwd
    /home
```

```
7   > popd
    popd: Directory stack empty.
```

EXPLANATION

1 First the *pwd* command displays the present working directory, */home/ellie*. Next the *pushd* command, with .. as its argument, pushes the parent directory (..) onto the directory stack. The output of *pushd* indicates that */home* is at the top of the directory stack and the user's home directory (~), */home/ellie*, is at the bottom of the stack. *pushd* also changes the directory to the one that was pushed onto the stack; i.e., .. , which translates to */home*. The new directory is displayed with the second *pwd* command.

2 *pushd*, without arguments, exchanges the two top directory entries on the stack and changes to the swapped directory; in this example, the directory is switched back to the user's home directory, */home/ellie*.

3 The *pushd* command will push its argument, *~/perlclass*, onto the stack, and change to that directory.

4 The built-in *dirs* command displays the numbered directory stack, with 0 being the top level. See the directory stack chart on the right side of this Example.

5 The *popd* command removes a directory from the top of the stack and changes to that directory.

6 The *popd* command removes another directory from the top of the stack and changes to that directory.

7 The *popd* command cannot remove any more directory entries because the stack is empty, and issues an error message saying so.

13.3.5 Spelling Correction

Spelling correction, a feature added to the TC shell, is the ability to correct spelling errors in filenames, commands, and variables. If using the *emacs* built-in editor, the spelling error can be corrected by using the spelling correction keys, bound to the *Meta-s* or *Meta-S* keys (use the Alt or Esc key if you don't have Meta) and *Meta-$* to correct an entire line. The value of the prompt, *prompt3*, displays the spelling correction prompt.[8]

If you are using the *vi* built-in editor, set the built-in variable *correct*, and the shell will prompt you to fix the spelling.

EXAMPLE 13.35

```
1   > fimger[Alt-s]      # Replaces fimger with finger

2   > set correct=all

3   > dite

    CORRECT>date (y|n|e|a)? yes
    Wed Aug 11 19:26:27 PDT 2001

4   > dite

    CORRECT>date (y|n|e|a)? no
    dite: Command not found.
    >

5   > dite

    CORRECT>date (y|n|e|a)? edit
    > dite█         # Waits for user to edit and then executes command

6   > dite

    CORRECT>date (y|n|e|a)? abort
    >
```

EXPLANATION

1   By pressing the *Meta* (or Alt or Esc) key together with an *s*, the spelling of a command, filename, or variable can be corrected. This does not work if you are using the built-in *vi* editor.

---

8. The *tcsh* man page warns that spelling correction is not guaranteed to work the way you may intend and is provided as an experimental feature.

2   By setting *correct* to *all*, *tcsh* will attempt to correct all spelling errors in the command line. This feature is available for both *emacs* and *vi* key bindings.

3   Because the command was incorrectly spelled, the third prompt, *prompt3, COR-RECT>date (y|n|e|a)?* appears on the screen, and the user is supposed to type the letter *y* if he wants the spelling corrected, an *n* if he doesn't, an *e* if he wants to edit the line himself, or an *a* if he wants to abort the whole operation.

4   If the user wants the command to be unchanged, he types an *n* for no.

5   If the user wants to edit the correction, he types an *e*, and he will be prompted to fix or enhance the command himself.

6   If the correction is incorrect or not wanted, the user types an *a*, and the spelling correction is aborted.

Table 13.11 The *correct* Variable Arguments

Argument	*What It Does*
cmd	Spell-corrects commands.
complete	Completes commands.
all	Spell-corrects entire command line.

13.3.6 Aliases

An *alias* is a TC shell user-defined abbreviation for a command. Aliases are useful if a command has a number of options and arguments or the syntax is difficult to remember. Aliases set at the command line are not inherited by subshells. Aliases are normally set in the *.tcshrc* file. Because the *.tcshrc* is executed when a new shell is started, any aliases set there will get reset for the new shell. Aliases may also be passed into shell scripts but will cause potential portability problems, unless they are directly set within the script.

The TC shell has some additional preset aliases, which remain undefined until you define them. They are: *beepcmd, cwdcmd, periodic,* and *precomd*. These aliases are listed and defined in "Special Aliases" on page 940.

Listing Aliases.   The *alias* built-in command lists all set aliases. The alias is printed first, followed by the real command or commands it represents.

EXAMPLE 13.36

```
> alias
apache  $HOME/apache/httpd -f $HOME/apache/conf/httpd.conf
co      compress
cp      cp -i
ls1     enscript -B -r -Porange -f Courier8 !* &
mailq   /usr/lib/sendmail -bp
mc      setenv MC '/usr/bin/mc -P !*'; cd $MC; unsetenv MC
mroe    more
mv      mv -i
uc      uncompress
uu      uudecode
vg      vgrind -t -s11 !:1 | lpr -t
weekly  (cd /home/jody/ellie/activity; ./weekly_report; echo
Done)
```

EXPLANATION

The *alias* command lists the alias (nickname) for the command in the first column and the real command the alias represents in the second column.

Creating Aliases.   The *alias* command is used to create an alias. The first argument is the name of the alias, the nickname for the command. The rest of the line consists of the command or commands that will be executed when the alias is executed. Multiple commands are separated by a semicolon, and commands containing spaces and meta-characters are surrounded by single quotes.

FORMAT

```
alias
alias aliasname command
alias aliasname 'command command(s)'
unalias aliasname
```

EXAMPLE 13.37

```
1  > alias m more
2  > alias mroe more
3  > alias lf ls-F
4  > alias cd 'cd \!*; set prompt = "%/ > "'
```

EXAMPLE 13.37 (CONTINUED)

```
5   > cd ..
6   /home/jody > cd /          # New prompt displayed
    / >

7   > set tperiod = 60
    > alias periodic 'echo You have worked an hour, nonstop'
8   > alias Usage 'echo "Error: \!* " ; exit 1'
```

EXPLANATION

1   The nickname for the *more* command is set to *m*.

2   The alias for the *more* command is set to *mroe*. This is handy if you can't spell.

3   The alias *lf* is a nickname for the *tcsh* built-in command *ls –F.* It lists files like *ls – F*, but is faster.

4   When *cd* is executed, the alias for *cd* will cause *cd* to go to the directory named as an argument and will then reset the prompt to the current working directory (%/) followed by the string >. The *!** is used by the alias in the same way it is used by the *history* mechanism. The backslash prevents the *history* mechanism from evaluating the *!** first before the alias has a chance to use it. The *\!** represents the arguments from the most recent command on the history list. The alias definition is enclosed in quotes because of the whitespace.

5   After the *cd* command changes to the parent directory, the prompt is expanded to the current working directory (%/) and a > symbol.[a]

6   The new directory is */home/jody*, which is reflected in the prompt; after changing directory to root (/), the prompt again reflects the change.

7   The *tperiod* variable is set to 60 minutes. The alias, *periodic*, is a preset alias. Every 60 minutes, the echo statement will be displayed.

8   This alias is useful in scripts to produce a diagnostic message and to then exit the script.

a. If using */bin/csh* as your shell, replace *%/* with *$cwd* when setting the prompt.

Deleting Aliases.   The *unalias* command is used to delete an alias. To temporarily turn off an alias, precede the alias name by a backslash.

EXAMPLE 13.38

```
1   > unalias mroe
2   > \cd ..
```

EXPLANATION

1   The *unalias* command deletes the alias *mroe* from the list of defined aliases.

2   The alias *cd* is temporarily turned off for this execution of the command only.

Alias Loop.   An alias loop occurs when an alias definition references another alias that references back to the original alias.

EXAMPLE 13.39

```
1   > alias m more
2   > alias mroe m
3   > alias m mroe          # Causes a loop
4   > m datafile
    Alias loop.
```

EXPLANATION

1   The alias is *m*. The alias definition is *more*. Every time *m* is used, the *more* command is executed.

2   The alias is *mroe*. The alias definition is *m*. If *mroe* is typed, the alias *m* is invoked and the *more* command is executed.

3   This is the culprit. If alias *m* is used, it invokes alias *mroe*, and alias *mroe* references back to *m*, causing an alias loop. Nothing bad happens. You just get an error message.

4   Alias *m* is used. It is circular. *M* calls *mroe* and *mroe* calls *m*, then *m* calls *mroe*, etc. Rather than looping forever, the TC shell catches the problem and displays an error message.

13.4 Job Control

Job control is a powerful feature of the TC shell that allows you to run programs, called *jobs*, in the background or foreground. Normally, a command typed at the command line is running in the foreground and will continue until it has finished. If you have a windowing program, job control may not be necessary because you can simply open another window to start a new task. On the other hand, with a single terminal, job control is a very useful feature. For a list of job commands, see Table 13.12.

Table 13.12 Job Control Commands

Command	Meaning
jobs	Lists all the jobs running.
^Z (Ctrl-Z)	Stops (suspends) the job; the prompt appears on the screen.
bg	Starts running the stopped job in the background.
fg	Brings a background job to the foreground.
kill	Sends the *kill* signal to a specified job.

Argument to Jobs Command	Represents
%n	Job number *n*.
%string	Job name starting with *string*.
%?string	Job name containing *string*.
%%	Current job.
%+	Current job.
%–	Previous job, before current job.

13.4.1 Background Jobs

The Ampersand.   If a command takes a long time to complete, you can append the command with an ampersand and the job will execute in the background. The *tcsh* prompt returns immediately and now you can type another command. Now the two commands are running concurrently, one in the background and one in the foreground. They both send their standard output to the screen. If you place a job in the background, it is a good idea to redirect its output either to a file or pipe it to a device such as a printer.

EXAMPLE 13.40

```
1   > find . -name core -exec rm {} \; &
2   [1]  543
3   >
```

EXPLANATION

1   The *find* command runs in the background. (Without the *–print* option, the *find* command does not send any output to the screen).[a]

2   The number in square brackets indicates this is the first job to be run in the background and the PID for this process is *543*.

3   The prompt returns immediately. The shell waits for user input.

a. The *find* syntax requires a semicolon at the end of an *exec* statement. The semicolon is preceded by a backslash to prevent the shell from interpreting it.

The Suspend Key Sequence.   To suspend a program, the suspend key sequence, ^Z, is issued. The job is now suspended (stopped), the shell prompt is displayed, and the program will not resume until the *fg* or *bg* commands are issued. (When using the *vi* editor, the *ZZ* command writes and saves a file. Do not confuse this with ^Z, which would suspend the *vi* session.) If you try to log out when a job is suspended, the message *There are suspended jobs* appears on the screen.

The *jobs* Command and the *listjobs* Variable.   The *tcsh* built-in command *jobs* displays the programs that are currently active and either running or suspended in the background. *Running* means the job is executing in the background. When a job is *suspended*, it is stopped; it is not in execution. In both cases, the terminal is free to accept other commands. If you attempt to exit the shell while jobs are stopped, the warning, *There are suspended jobs* will appear on the screen. When you attempt to exit immediately a second time, the shell will go ahead and terminate the suspended jobs. You set the *tcsh* built-in *listjobs* variable if you want to automatically print a message when you suspend a job.

EXAMPLE 13.41

```
(The Command Line)

1   > jobs
2   [1]   +               Suspended     vi filex
    [2]   -               Running       sleep 25

3   > jobs -l
    [1]   +     355       Suspended     vi filex
    [2]   -     356       Running       sleep 25

4   [2] Done                            sleep 25
```

EXAMPLE 13.41 (CONTINUED)

```
5  > set listjobs = long
   > sleep 1000
   Press Control-Z to suspend job

   [1]  +  3337 Suspended            sleep 1000
   >

6  > set notify
```

EXPLANATION

1   The *jobs* command lists the currently active jobs.

2   The notation *[1]* is the number of the first job; the plus sign indicates that the job is not the most recent job to be placed in the background; the dash indicates that this is the most recent job put in the background; *Suspended* means that this job was stopped with ^Z and is not currently active.

3   The *–l* option (long listing) displays the number of the job as well as the PID of the job. The notation *[2]* is the number of the second job, in this case, the last job placed in the background. The dash indicates that this is the most recent job. The *sleep* command is running in the background.

4   After *sleep* has been running for 25 seconds, the job will complete and a message saying that it has finished appears on the screen.

5   The *tcsh listjobs* variable, when set to *long*, will print the number of a job as well as its process ID number when it is suspended. (See Table 13.25 on page 941 for a list of built-in *tcsh* variables.).

6   Normally the shell notifies you if a job is stopped just before it prints a prompt, but if the shell variable *notify* is set, the shell will notify you immediately if there is any change in the status of a background job. For example, if you are working in the *vi* editor, and a background job is terminated, a message will appear immediately in your *vi* window like this:
    [1]   Terminated   sleep 20

13.4.2 Foreground and Background Commands

The *fg* command brings a background job into the foreground. The *bg* command starts a suspended job running in the background. A percent sign and the number of a job can be used as arguments to *fg* and *bg* if you want to select a particular job for job control.

EXAMPLE 13.42

```
1   > jobs
2   [1] + Suspended              vi filex
    [2] - Running                cc prog.c -o prog

3   > fg %1
    vi filex
    (vi session starts)

4   > kill %2
    [2] Terminated               c prog.c -o prog

5   > sleep 15
    (Press ^z)


    Suspended
6   > bg
    [1] sleep 15 &
    [1] Done    sleep 15
```

EXPLANATION

1   The *jobs* command lists currently running processes, called jobs.

2   The first job is the *vi* session (suspended), the second job is the *cc* command (running).

3   The job numbered *[1]* is brought to the foreground. The number is preceded with a percent sign.

4   The *kill* command is built-in. It sends the *TERM* (terminate) signal, by default, to a process. The argument is either the number or the PID of the process.

5   The *sleep* command is stopped by pressing ^Z. The *sleep* command is not using the CPU and is suspended in the background.

6   The *bg* command causes the last background job to start executing in the background. The *sleep* program will start the countdown in seconds before execution resumes.[a]

a. Programs such as *grep*, *sed*, and *awk* have a set of metacharacters, called regular expression metacharacters, for pattern matching. These should not be confused with shell metacharacters.

13.4.3 Scheduling Jobs

The *sched* built-in command allows you to create a list of jobs that will be scheduled to run at some specific time. The *sched* command, without arguments, displays a numbered list of all the scheduled events. It sets times in the form *hh:mm* (hour:minute) where hour can be in military or 12-hour AM/PM format. Time can also be specified as a relative time with a + sign; i.e., relative to the current time, and with a – sign, the event is removed from the list.[9]

FORMAT

```
sched
sched [+]hh:mm  command
sched -n
```

EXAMPLE 13.43

```
1   > sched 14:30  echo '^G Time to start your lecture!'

2   > sched 5PM  echo Time to go home.

3   > sched +1:30 /home/ellie/scripts/logfile.sc

4   > sched
    1     17:47 /home/scripts/logfile.sc
    2     5PM  echo Time to go home.
    3     14:30  echo '^G Time to start your lecture!'

5   > sched -2
    > sched
    1     17:47 /home/scripts/logfile.sc
    2     14:30  echo '^G Time to start your lecture!'
```

EXPLANATION

1   The *sched* command schedules the echo command to be executed at 14:30. At that time a beep will sound (Control-G)[a] and the message will be displayed.

2   The *sched* command will schedule the echo command to be executed at 5 PM.

3   The script, *logfile.sc*, is scheduled to be executed 1 hour and 30 minutes from now.

4   The *sched* command displays the scheduled events, in numeric order, the last one first.

5   With a numeric argument, *sched* will remove the numbered job from the scheduled list. Job number 2 was removed, as shown in the output of *sched*.

a. To get the ^G into the echo statement, type Ctrl-M followed by Ctrl-V, followed by Ctrl-G.

9. The *tcsh* man page says that a command in the scheduled-event list is executed just before the first prompt is printed after the time when the command is scheduled. If it so happens that the exact time when the command is to be run is missed, an overdue command will execute at the next prompt.

13.5 Metacharacters

Metacharacters are special characters that are used to represent something other than themselves. As a rule of thumb, characters that are neither letters nor numbers may be metacharacters. The shell has its own set of metacharacters, often called *shell wildcards*. Shell metacharacters can be used to group commands together, to abbreviate filenames and pathnames, to redirect and pipe input/output, to place commands in the background, and so forth. Table 13.13 presents a partial list of shell metacharacters.

Table 13.13 Shell Metacharacters

Metacharacter	Purpose	Example	Meaning
$	Variable substitution	*set name=Tom echo $name Tom*	Sets the variable *name* to *Tom*; displays the value stored there.
!	History substitution	*!3*	Reexecutes the third event from the history list.
*	Filename substitution	*rm **	Removes all files.
?	Filename substitution	*ls ??*	Lists all two-character files.
[ ]	Filename substitution	*cat f[123]*	Displays contents of *f1, f2, f3*.
;	Command separator	*ls;date;pwd*	Each command is executed in turn.
&	Background processing	*lp mbox&*	Printing is done in the background. Prompt returns immediately.
>	Redirection of output	*ls > file*	Redirects standard output to *file*.
<	Redirection of input	*ls < file*	Redirects standard input from *file*.
>&	Redirection of output and error	*ls >& file*	Redirects both output and errors to *file*.
>!	If *noclobber* is set, override it	*ls >! file*	If *file* exists, truncate and overwrite it, even if *noclobber* is set.
>>!	If *noclobber* is set, override it	*ls >>! file*	If *file* does not exist, create it, even if *noclobber* is set.
( )	Groups commands to be executed in a subshell	*(ls ; pwd) >tmp*	Executes commands and sends output to *tmp* file.
{ }	Groups commands to be executed in this shell	*{ cd /; echo $cwd }*	Changes to root directory and displays current working directory.

13.5.1 Filename Substitution

When evaluating the command line, the shell uses metacharacters to abbreviate filenames or pathnames that match a certain set of characters. The filename substitution metacharacters listed in Table 13.14 are expanded into an alphabetically listed set of filenames. The process of expanding a metacharacter into filenames is also called *globbing*. Unlike the other shells, when the C shell cannot substitute a filename for the metacharacter it is supposed to represent, the shell reports *No match*.

Table 13.14 Shell Metacharacters and Filename Substitution

Metacharacter	Meaning
*	Matches zero or more characters.
?	Matches exactly one character.
[abc]	Matches one character in the set *a*, *b*, or *c*.
[a–z]	Matches one character in the range *a* to *z*.
[^abc]	Matches any character that is not *a*, *b*, or *c*.
{a, ile, ax}	Matches for a character or set of characters.
~	Substitutes the user's home directory for tilde.
\	Escapes or disables the metacharacter.

Expanding the Metacharacters. The shell performs filename substitution by evaluating its metacharacters and replacing them with the appropriate letters or digits in a filename.

The Asterisk. The asterisk matches zero or more characters in a filename.

```
EXAMPLE   13.44
1    > ls
     a.c b.c abc ab3 file1 file2 file3 file4 file5

2    > echo *
     a.c b.c abc ab3 file1 file2 file3 file4 file5

3    > ls  *.c
     a.c b.c

4    > ls ^*.c
     abc ab3 file1 file2 file3 file4 file5

5    > rm  z*p
     No match.
```

EXPLANATION

1   All the files in the current directory are listed.

2   The *echo* program prints all its arguments to the screen. The asterisk (also called a *splat*) is a wildcard that means, *match for zero or more of any characters found in a filename*. All the files in the directory are matched and echoed to the screen.

3   Filenames ending in *.c* are listed.

4   All files not ending in *.c* are listed.

5   Because none of the files in the directory start with *z*, the shell reports *No match*.

The Question Mark.   The question mark matches exactly one character in a filename.

EXAMPLE 13.45

```
1   > ls
    a.c b.c abc ab3 file1 file2 file3 file4 file5

2   > ls ???
    abc ab3

3   > echo How are you?
    No match.

4   > echo How are you\?
    How are you?
```

EXPLANATION

1   All the files in the current directory are listed.

2   The question mark matches for a single-character filename. Any filenames consisting of three characters are listed.

3   The shell looks for a filename spelled *y-o-u* followed by one character. There is not a file in the directory that matches these characters. The shell prints *No match*.

4   The backslash preceding the question mark is used to turn off the special meaning of the question mark. Now the shell treats the question mark as a literal character.

The Square Brackets.   The square brackets (*[]*)match a filename for one character from a set or range of characters.

EXAMPLE 13.46

```
1   > ls
    a.c b.c abc ab3 file1 file2 file3 file4 file5 file10
    file11  file12


2   > ls file[123]
    file1 file2 file3


3   > ls file[^123]
    file4 file5


4   > ls [A-Za-z][a-z][1-5]
    ab3


5   > ls file1[0-2]
    file10 file11 file12
```

EXPLANATION

1   All the files in the current directory are listed.
2   Filenames starting with *file* followed by *1*, *2*, or *3* are matched and listed.
3   Filenames starting with *file* followed by a single character other than *1*, *2*, or *3* are matched and listed.
4   Filenames starting with one letter (uppercase or lowercase), followed by one lowercase letter, and followed by a number between *1* and *5* are matched and listed.
5   Filenames starting with *file1* and followed by a *0*, *1*, or *2* are listed.

The Curly Braces.   The curly braces (*{}*) match for a character or string of characters in a filename that may or may not already exist.

EXAMPLE 13.47

```
1   > ls
    a.c b.c abc ab3 ab4 ab5 file1 file2 file3 file4 file5 foo
    faa fumble


2   > ls f{oo,aa,umble}
    foo faa fumble


3   > ls a{.c,c,b[3-5]}
    a.c ab3 ab4 ab5


4   > mkdir prog{1,2,3}


5   > echo tweedle{dee,dum}, {l,cl,m}ove{r}
    tweedledee tweedledum, lover clover mover
```

EXPLANATION

1   All the files in the current directory are listed.

2   Files starting with *f* and followed by the strings *oo, aa,* or *umble* are listed. Spaces inside the curly braces will cause the error message *Missing }*.

3   Files starting with *a* followed by *.c, c,* or *b3, b4,* or *b5* are listed. (The square brackets can be used inside the curly braces.)

4   Rather than typing *prog1, prog2,* and *prog3* and separate arguments to the *mkdir* command, you can use the braces to generate the new directory names.

5   Each of the words is expanded using the braced portions either as prefixes or suffixes. It is important that the words in braces contain no whitespace.

Escaping Metacharacters and *nonomatch*.   The backslash is used to escape the special meaning of a single character. The escaped character will represent itself.

EXAMPLE 13.48

```
1    > got milk?
     got: No match.

2    > got milk\?
     got: Command not found.

3    > set nonomatch
     > got milk?
     got: Command not found.
```

EXPLANATION

1   The question mark is a file substitution metacharacter and evaluates to a single character. The shell looks for a file in the present working directory that contains the characters *m-i-l-k*, followed by a single character. If the shell cannot find the file, it reports *No match*. This shows you something about the order in which the shell parses the command line. The metacharacters are evaluated before the shell tries to locate the *got* command.

2   The backslash protects the metacharacter from interpretation, often called escaping the metacharacter. Now the shell does not complain about a *No match,* but searches the path for the *got* command, which is not found.

3   The built-in *nonomatch* variable, when set, turns off error reporting when a metacharacter is not matched. Instead of reporting *No match,* UNIX reports that *got* is not a command.

Tilde Expansion. The tilde character (~) by itself expands to the full pathname of the user's home directory. When the tilde is prepended to a username, it expands to the full pathname of that user's home directory. When prepended to a path, it expands to the home directory and the rest of the pathname.

EXAMPLE 13.49

```
1   > echo ~
    /home/jody/ellie

2   > cd ~/desktop/perlstuff
    > pwd
    /home/jody/ellie/desktop/perlstuff

3   > cd ~joe
    > pwd
    /home/bambi/joe
```

EXPLANATION

1   The tilde expands to the user's home directory.
2   The tilde followed by a pathname expands to the user's home directory, followed by */desktop/perlstuff*.
3   The tilde followed by a username expands to the home directory of the user. In this example, the directory is changed to that user's home directory.

Turning Off Metacharacters with *noglob*. If the *noglob* variable is set, filename substitution is turned off, meaning that all metacharacters represent themselves; they are not used as wildcards. This can be useful when searching for patterns in programs like *grep*, *sed*, or *awk*, which may contain metacharacters that the shell may try to expand.

EXAMPLE 13.50

```
1   > set noglob
2   > echo * ?? [] ~
    * ?? [] ~
```

EXPLANATION

1   The variable *noglob* is set. It turns off the special meaning of the wildcards.
2   The metacharacters are displayed as themselves without any interpretation.

13.6 Redirection and Pipes

Normally, standard output (*stdout*) from a command goes to the screen, standard input (*stdin*) comes from the keyboard, and error messages (*stderr*) go to the screen. The shell allows you to use the special redirection metacharacters to redirect the input/output to or from a file. The redirection operators (<, >, >>, >&) are followed by a filename. This file is opened by the shell before the command on the left-hand side is executed.

Pipes, represented by a vertical bar (|) symbol, allow the output of one command to be sent to the input of another command. The command on the left-hand side of the pipe is called the *writer* because it writes to the pipe. The command on the right-hand side of the pipe is the *reader* because it reads from the pipe. See Table 13.15 for a list of redirection and pipe metacharacters.

Table 13.15   Redirection Metacharacters

Metacharacter	*Meaning*
command < file	Redirects input from *file* to *command*.
command > file	Redirects output from *command* to *file*.
command >& file	Redirects output and errors to *file*.
command >> file	Redirects output of *command* and appends it to *file*.
command >>& file	Redirects and appends output and errors of *command* to *file*.
command << WORD	Redirects input from first *WORD* to terminating *WORD* to *command*.
<input>	User input goes here. It will be treated as a doubly quoted string of text.
WORD	*WORD* marks the termination of input to *command*.
*command	command*	Pipes output of first *command* to input of second *command*.
command |& command	Pipes output and errors of first *command* to input of second *command*.
command >! file	If the *noclobber* variable is set, overrides its effects for this command and either open or overwrite *file*.
command >>! file	Overrides *noclobber* variable; if *file* does not exist, it is created and output from *command* is appended to it.
command >>&! file	Overrides *noclobber* variable; if *file* does not exist, it is created and both output and errors are appended to it.

13.6.1 Redirecting Input

Instead of the input coming from the terminal keyboard, it can be redirected from a file. The shell will open the file on the right-hand side of the < symbol and the program on the left will read from the file. If the file does not exist, the error *No such file or directory* will be reported by the shell.

FORMAT

```
command < file
```

EXAMPLE 13.51

```
mail bob < memo
```

EXPLANATION

The file *memo* is opened by the shell, and the input is redirected to the *mail* program. Simply, the user *bob* is sent a file called *memo* by the *mail* program.

13.6.2 The *here document*

The *here document* is another way to redirect input to a command in the form of a quoted block of text. It is used in shell scripts for creating menus and processing input from other programs. Normally, programs that accept input from the keyboard are terminated with Control-D (^D). The *here document* provides an alternate way of sending input to a program and terminating the input without typing ^D. The << symbol is followed by a user-defined word, often called a *terminator*. Input will be directed to the command on the left-hand side of the << symbol until the user-defined terminator is reached. The final terminator is on a line by itself, and *cannot* be surrounded by any spaces. Variable and command substitution are performed within the *here document*. Normally, *here documents* are used in shell scripts to create menus and provide input to commands such as *mail, bc, ex, ftp*, etc.

FORMAT

```
command << MARK
        ... input ...
MARK
```

EXAMPLE 13.52

```
(Without the here document)

(The Command Line)
1   > cat
2   Hello There.
    How are you?
    I'm tired of this.
3   ^d

(The Output)
4   Hello There.
    How are you?
    I'm tired of this.
```

EXPLANATION

1   The *cat* program, without arguments, waits for keyboard input.

2   The user types input at the keyboard.

3   The user types ^D to terminate input to the *cat* program.

4   The *cat* program sends its output to the screen.

EXAMPLE 13.53

```
(With the here document)

(The Command Line)
1   > cat << DONE
2   ? Hello There.
    ? How are you?
    ? I'm tired of this.
3   ? DONE
4   Hello There.    <----The output from the here document
    How are you?
    I'm tired of this.
```

EXPLANATION

1   The *cat* program will receive input from the first *DONE* to the terminating *DONE*. The words are user-defined terminators.

EXPLANATION (CONTINUED)

2   The question mark (?) is the secondary prompt, *prompt2*. It will appear until the *here document* is terminated with the user-defined terminator, *DONE*. These lines are input. When the word *DONE* is reached, no more input is accepted.

3   The final terminator marks the end of input. There cannot be any spaces on either side of this word.

4   The text between the first word *DONE* and the final word *DONE* is the output of the *cat* command (from *here* to *here*) and is sent to the screen. The final *DONE* must be against the left margin with no space or other text to the right of it.

EXAMPLE 13.54

```
(The Command Line)
1   > set name = steve
2   > mail $name << EOF
3   ? Hello there, $name
4   ? The hour is now `date +%H`
5   ? EOF
6   >
```

EXPLANATION

1   The shell variable *name* is assigned the username *steve*. (Normally, this example would be included in a shell script.)

2   The variable *name* is expanded within the *here document*.

3   The question mark (?) is the secondary prompt, *prompt2*. It will appear until the *here document* is terminated with the user-defined terminator, *EOF*. The *mail* program will receive input until the terminator *EOF* is reached.

4   Command substitution is performed within the *here document*; that is, the command within the backquotes is executed and the output of the command is replaced within the string.

5   The terminator *EOF* is reached, and input to the *mail* program is stopped.

13.6.3 Redirecting Output

By default, the standard output of a command or commands goes to the terminal screen. To redirect standard output from the screen to a file, use the > symbol. The command is on the left-hand side of the > symbol, and a filename is on the right-hand side. The shell will open the file on the right-hand side of the > symbol. If the file does not exist, the shell will create it; if it does exist, the shell will open the file and truncate it. Often files are inadvertently removed when using redirection. (A special *tcsh* variable, called *noclobber*, can be set to prevent redirection from clobbering an existing file. See Table 13.16 on page 898.)

FORMAT

```
command > file
```

EXAMPLE 13.55

```
cat file1 file2 > file3
```

EXPLANATION

The contents of *file1* and *file2* are concatenated and the output is sent to *file3*. Remember that the shell opens *file3* before it attempts to execute the *cat* command. If *file3* already exists and contains data, the data will be lost. If *file3* does not exist, it will be created.

Appending Output to an Existing File.   To append output to an existing file, use the >> symbol. If the file on the right-hand side of the >> symbol does not exist, it is created; if it does exist, the file is opened and output is appended to the end of the file.

FORMAT

```
command >> file
```

EXAMPLE 13.56

```
date >> outfile
```

EXPLANATION

The standard output of the *date* command is redirected and appended to *outfile*.

Redirecting Output and Error.   The >& symbol is used to redirect both standard output and standard error to a file. Normally, a command is either successful and sends its output to *stdout*, or fails and sends its error messages to *stderr*. Some recursive programs, such as *find* and *du*, send both standard output and errors to the screen as they move through the directory tree. When you use the >& symbol, both standard output and standard error can be saved in a file and examined. The TC shell does not provide a symbol for redirection of only standard error, but it is possible to get just the standard error by executing the command in a subshell. See Figure 13.3.

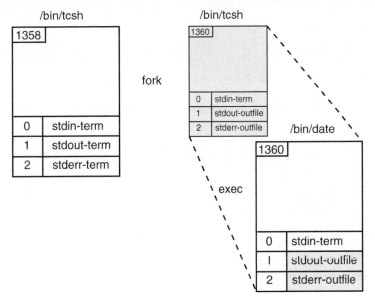

Figure 13.3   Redirecting *stdout* and *stderr*. See Example 13.57.

```
1   > date
    Tue Aug 3 10:31:56  PDT  2001
2   > date >& outfile
3   > cat outfile
    Tue Aug 3 10:31:56  PDT  2001
```

EXPLANATION

1   The output of the *date* command is sent to standard output, the screen.

2   The output and errors are sent to *outfile*.

3   Because there were no errors, the standard output is sent to *outfile* and the contents of the file are displayed.

EXAMPLE 13.58

```
1  > cp file1 file2
2  > cp file1
   cp: missing destination file
   Try 'cp --help' for more information
3  > cp file1 >& errorfile
4  > cat errorfile
   cp: missing destination file
   Try 'cp --help' for more information
```

EXPLANATION

1 To copy a file, the *cp* command requires both a source file and a destination file. The *cp* command makes a copy of *file1* and puts the copy in *file2*. Because the *cp* command is given the correct syntax, nothing is displayed to the screen. The copy was successful.

2 This time the destination file is missing and the *cp* command fails, sending an error to *stderr*, the terminal.

3 The *>&* symbol is used to send both *stdout* and *stderr* to *errorfile*. Because the only output from the command is the error message, that is what is saved in *errorfile*.

4 The contents of *errorfile* are displayed, showing that it contains the error message produced by the *cp* command.

Separating Output and Errors.   Standard output and standard error can be separated by enclosing the command in parentheses. When a command is enclosed in parentheses, the TC shell starts up a subshell, handles redirection from within the subshell, and then executes the command. By using the technique shown in Example 13.59, you can separate the standard output from the errors.

EXAMPLE 13.59

```
(The Command Line)
1  > find . -name '*.c' >& outputfile
2  > (find . -name '*.c' > goodstuff) >& badstuff
```

EXPLANATION

1 The *find* command will start at the current directory, searching for all files ending in *.c*, and will print the output to *outputfile*. If an error occurs, that will also go into *outputfile*.

2 The *find* command is enclosed within parentheses. The shell will create a subshell to handle the command. Before creating the subshell, the words outside the parentheses will be processed; that is, the *badstuff* file will be opened for both standard output and error. When the subshell is started, it inherits the standard input, output, and errors from its parent. The subshell then has standard input coming from the keyboard, and both standard output and standard error going to the *badstuff* file. Now the subshell will handle the > operator. The *stdout* will be assigned the file *goodstuff*. The output is going to *goodstuff*, and the errors are going to *badstuff*. See Figure 13.4.

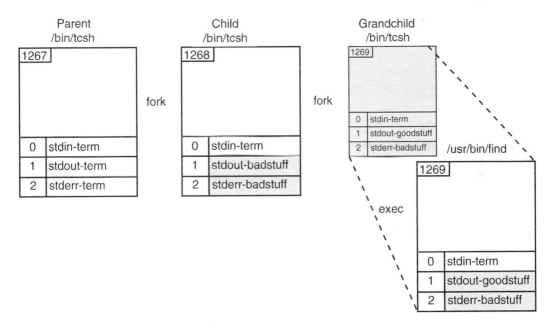

Figure 13.4 Separating *stdout* and *stderr*.

The *noclobber* Variable. The special TC shell built-in variable *noclobber*, when set, protects you from clobbering files with redirection. See Table 13.16.

Table 13.16 The *noclobber* Variable

noclobber *Is Not Set*	File Exists	File Does Not Exist
command > file	*file* is overwritten.	*file* is created.
command >> file	*file* is appended to.	*file* is created.
noclobber *Is Set*		
command > file	Error message.	*file* is created.
command >> file	File is appended to.	Error message.
***Overwriting* noclobber**		
command >! file	If the *noclobber* variable is set, override its effects for this *command* and either open or truncate *file*, redirecting output of *command* to *file*.
command >>! file	Override *noclobber* variable; if *file* does not exist, it is created and output from *command* is appended to it.

EXAMPLE 13.60

```
1   > cat filex
    abc
    123

2   > date > filex
3   > cat filex
    Tue Mar 18 11:51:04  PST 2001

4   > set noclobber
5   > date > filex
    filex: File exists.

6   > ls >! filex      # Override noclobber for this command only
    > cat filex
    abc
    ab1
    dir
    filex
    plan.c

7   > ls > filex
    filex:  File exists.

8   > date >> XXX
    XXX: No such file or directory.

9   > date >>! XXX         # Override noclobber for this command only

10  > unset noclobber      # Turn off noclobber permanently
```

EXPLANATION

1 The contents of *filex* are displayed on the screen.

2 The output of the *date* command is redirected to *filex*. The file is truncated and its original contents overwritten.

3 The contents of *filex* are displayed.

4 The *noclobber* variable is set.

5 Because *filex* already exists and *noclobber* is set, the shell reports that the file exists and will not allow it to be overwritten.

6 The output of *ls* is redirected to *filex* because the >! operator overrides the effects of *noclobber*.

7 The effects of the >! symbol were temporary. It does not turn off *noclobber*. It simply overrides *noclobber* for the command where it is implemented.

8 Attempting to redirect and append the output of the *date* command to a nonexistent file causes an error message when *noclobber* is set.

9 The *noclobber* variable is overridden with the exclamation mark attached to the >> redirection symbol.

10 The *noclobber* variable is unset.

13.7 Variables

Tcsh variables hold only strings or a set of strings. Some variables are built into the shell and can be set either by turning them on or off, such as the *noclobber* or *filec* variable. Others are assigned a string value, such as the *path* variable. You can create your own variables and assign them to strings or the output of commands. Variable names are case-sensitive and may contain up to 20 characters consisting of numbers, letters, and the underscore.

There are two types of variables: local and environment. The scope of a variable is its visibility. A local variable is visible to the shell where it is defined. The scope of environment variables is often called *global*. Their scope is for this shell and all processes spawned (started) from this shell. If a local variable is created with *set −r*, it will be *read-only*, meaning that it cannot be changed or unset.

The dollar sign ($) is a special metacharacter that, when preceding a variable name, tells the shell to extract the value of that variable. The *echo* command, when given the variable as an argument, will display the value of the variable after the shell has processed the command line and performed variable substitution.

The special notation $?, when prepended to the variable name, lets you know whether the variable has been set. If a one is returned, it means true, the variable has been set. If a zero is returned, it means false, the variable has not been set.

EXAMPLE 13.61

```
1   > set autologout
2   > set history = 50
3   > set name = George
4   > set machine = `uname -n`
5   > echo $?machine
    1
6   echo  $?blah
    0
```

EXPLANATION

1   Sets the *tcsh* built-in variable *autologout* variable to cause automatic logout after a specified time of inactivity has passed.

2   Sets the built-in variable *history* to *50* to control the number of events displayed.

3   Sets the user-defined variable *name* to *George*.

4   Sets the user-defined variable *machine* to the output of the UNIX command. The command is in backquotes, telling the shell to perform command substitution.

5   The *$?* is prepended to the variable name to test whether the variable has been set. Because the test yields a *1* (true), the variable has been set.

6   The *$?* yields *0* (false). The variable has not been set.

13.7.1 Printing the Values of Variables

The *echo* Command.   The built-in *echo* command prints its arguments to standard output. The *echo* allows the use of numerous escape sequences, which are interpreted and displayed as tabs, newlines, form feed, etc. Table 13.17 lists the *echo* options and escape sequences.

The TC shell uses the style of both BSD and SVR4, but allows you to modify the behavior of the *echo* command by using the built-in *echo_style* variable; e.g., *set echo_style=bsd*. See Table 13.18. See the manual page for *echo*.

Table 13.17 *echo* Options and Escape Sequences

Option	Meaning
–n	Suppresses newline at the end of a line of output.

Escape Sequence

\a	Alert (bell).
\b	Backspace.
\c	Print the line without a newline.
\f	Form feed.
\n	Newline.
\r	Return.
\t	Tab.
\v	Vertical tab.
\\	Backslash.
\nnn	The character whose ASCII code is *nnn* (octal).

Table 13.18 The *echo_style* Variable

bsd	If the first argument is –n, the newline is suppressed.
sysv	Expands escape sequences in echo strings.
both	Both –n and escape sequences are in effect (the default).
none	Recognizes neither *sysv* or *bsd*.

EXAMPLE 13.62

```
1   > echo The username is $LOGNAME.
    The username is ellie.

2   > echo "\t\tHello there\c"
                Hello there>

3   > echo -n "Hello there"
    Hello there$

4   > set echo_style=none

5   > echo  "\t\tHello there\c"
    -n \t\tHello there\c
```

EXPLANATION

1   The *echo* command prints its arguments to the screen. Variable substitution is performed by the shell before the *echo* command is executed.

2   The *echo* command, by default, supports escape sequences similar to those of the C programming language and used in the SVR4 version of *echo*. The > is the shell prompt.

3   With the *–n* option, echo displays the string without the newline.

4   The *echo_style* variable is assigned the value *none*. Neither the BSD *–n* switch nor the SVR4 escape sequences are in effect.

5   With the new *echo* style, the string is displayed.

The *printf* Command.   The GNU version of *printf* can be used to format printed output. It prints the formatted string in the same way as the C *printf* function. The format consists of a string that may contain formatting instructions to describe how the printed output will look. The formatting instructions are designated with a % followed by specifiers (*diouxXfeEgGcs*), where %*f* would represent a floating point number and %*d* would represent a whole (decimal) number.

To see a complete listing of *printf* specifiers and how to use them, type at the command line prompt: *printf – –help.* To see what version of *printf* you are using, type *printf – –version.* If using *bash* 2.x, the built-in *printf* command uses the same format as the executable version in */usr/bin*.

FORMAT

```
printf format [argument...]
```

EXAMPLE 13.63

```
printf "%10.2f%5d\n" 10.5   25
```

Table 13.19 Format Specifiers for the *printf* Command

Format Specifier	Value
\"	Double quote.
\0NNN	An octal character in which NNN represents 0 to 3 digits.
\\	Backslash.
\a	Alert or beep.
\b	Backspace.
\c	Produce no further output.
\f	Form feed.
\n	Newline.
\r	Carriage return.
\t	Horizontal tab.
\v	Vertical tab.
\xNNN	Hexadecimal character in which NNN is 1 to 3 digits.
%%	Single %.
%b	ARGUMENT as a string with \ escapes interpreted.

EXAMPLE 13.64

```
1   > printf --version
    printf (GNU sh-utils) 1.16


2   > printf "The number is %.2f\n" 100
    The number is 100.00


3   > printf "%-20s%-15s%10.2f\n" "Jody" "Savage" 28
    Jody                Savage              28.00


4   > printf "|%-20s|%-15s|%10.2f|\n" "Jody" "Savage" 28
    |Jody                |Savage         |     28.00|


5   > printf "%s's average was %.1f%%.\n" "Jody" $(( (80+70+90)/3 ))
    Jody's average was 80.0%.
```

EXPLANATION

1   The GNU version of the *printf* command is printed. It is found in */usr/bin*.

2   The argument *100* is printed as a floating point number with only two places to the right of the decimal point printing, designated by the format specification *%.2f* in the format string. Note that unlike C, there are no commas separating the arguments.

3, 4 This time the format string specifies that three conversions will take place: the first one is *%–20s* (a left-justified, 20-character string), next is *%–15s* (a left-justified, 15-character string), and last *%10.2f* (a right-justified 10-character floating point number, one of those characters is the period and the last two characters are the two numbers to the right of the decimal point). Each argument is formatted in the order of the corresponding % signs, so that string *Jody* corresponds to first %, string *Savage* corresponds to the second %, and the number *28* to the last % sign. The vertical bars are used to demonstrate the width of the fields.

5   The *printf* command formats the string *Jody* and the result of the arithmetic expansion. (Refer to "Arithmetic Expansion" on page 689.) Two percent (%%) signs are needed to print one percent sign (%).

Curly Braces and Variables.   Curly braces insulate a variable from any characters that may follow it. They can be used to concatenate a string to the end of the variable.

EXAMPLE 13.65

```
1   > set var = net
    > echo $var
net

2   > echo $varwork
varwork: Undefined variable.

3   > echo ${var}work
network
```

EXPLANATION

1   The curly braces surrounding the variable name insulate the variable from characters that follow it.
2   A variable called *varwork* has not been defined. The shell prints an error message.
3   The curly braces shield the variable from characters appended to it. $var is expanded and the string *work* is appended.

13.7.2 Local Variables (Visibility and Naming)

Local variables are known only in the shell where they were created. If a local variable is set in the *.tcshrc* file, the variable will be reset every time a new TC shell is started. By convention, local variables are named with lowercase letters.

Setting Local Variables.   If the string being assigned contains more than one word, it must be quoted; otherwise, only the first word will be assigned to the variable. It does not matter if there are spaces around the equal sign, but if there is a space on one side of the equal sign, there must be one on the other side.

EXAMPLE 13.66

```
1   > set round = world
2   > set name = "Santa Claus"

3   > echo $round
 world

4   > echo $name
Santa Claus

5   > tcsh              # Start a subshell
6   > echo $name
name: Undefined variable.
```

EXPLANATION

1   The local variable *round* is assigned the value *world*.

2   The local variable *name* is assigned the value *Santa Claus*. The double quotes keep the shell from evaluating the whitespace between *Santa* and *Claus*.

3   The dollar sign prepended to the variable allows the shell to perform variable substitution, that is, to extract the value stored in the variable.

4   Variable substitution is performed.

5   A new TC shell (called a subshell) process is started.

6   In the subshell, the variable *name* has not been defined. It was defined in the parent shell as a local variable.

Read-Only Variables.   Read-only variables are local variables that, once set, cannot be changed or unset or an error message will result. Environment variables cannot be made read-only.

EXAMPLE 13.67

```
1   > set -r name = Tommy

2   > unset name
    unset: $name is read-only.

3   > set name = Danny
    set: $name is read-only
```

The *set* Command.   The *set* command prints all local variables set for this shell.

EXAMPLE 13.68

```
(The Command Line)
> set
addsuffix
argv          ()
cwd           /home/jody/meta
dirstack      /home/ellie/meta
echo_style both
edit
```

EXAMPLE   13.68 (CONTINUED)

```
gid       501
group     ellie
history   500
home      /home/ellie
i         /etc/profile.d/mc.csh
owd       /home/ellie
noclobber
path  (/usr/sbin /sbin /usr/local/bin /bin  /usr/bin /usr/X11R6/bin )

prompt    [%n@%m  %c]#
prompt2   %R?
prompt3   CORRECT>%R  (y|n|e|a)?
savedirs
shell     /bin/tcsh
shlvl     2
status    0
tcsh      6.07.09
term      xterm
user      ellie
version tcsh 6.09.09 (Astron) 1998-08-16 (sparc-sun-solaris)
options 8b,nls,dl,al,rh,color
```

EXPLANATION

All of the local variables set for this shell are printed. Many of these variables, such as *history, dirstack,* and *noclobber*, are set in the *.tcshrc* file. Others, such as *argv, cwd, shell, term, user, version,* and *status* variables are preset, built-in variables.

Built-In Local Variables.   The shell has a number of predefined variables with their own definitions. Some of the variables are either on or off. For example, if you set *noclobber*, the variable is on and effective, and when you unset *noclobber*, it is turned off. Some variables require a definition when set. Built-in variables are usually set in the *.tcshrc* file if they are to be effective for all interactive TC shells and *tcsh* scripts. Some of the built-in variables already discussed include *noclobber, cdpath, history, rmstar,* and *noglob*. For a complete list, see Table 13.24 on page 929.

13.7.3 Environment Variables

Environment variables are often called *global* variables. They are defined in the shell where they were created and inherited by all shells spawned from that shell. Although environment variables are inherited by subshells, those defined in subshells are not passed back to parent shells. Inheritance is from parent to child, not the other way around (like real life). By convention, environment variables are named with capital letters.

EXAMPLE 13.69

```
(The Command Line)
1   > setenv TERM wyse
2   > setenv PERSON "Joe Jr."
3   > echo $TERM
    wyse
4   > echo $PERSON
    Joe Jr.
5   > echo $$          # $$ evaluates to the PID of the current shell
    206

6   > tcsh             # Start a subshell
7   > echo $$
    211
8   > echo $PERSON
    Joe Jr.

9   > setenv PERSON "Nelly Nerd"
10  > echo $PERSON
    Nelly Nerd
11  > exit             # Exit the subshell

12  > echo $$
    206
13  > echo $PERSON     # Back in parent shell
    Joe Jr.
```

EXPLANATION

1   The shell environment variable *TERM* is set to a *wyse* terminal.

2   The user-defined variable *PERSON* is set to *Joe Jr.* The quotes are used to protect the space.

3   The dollar sign ($) prepended to the variable name allows the shell to evaluate the contents of the variable, called variable substitution.

4   The value of the environment variable *PERSON* is printed.

5   The $$ variable contains the PID of the current shell. The PID is *206*.

6   The *tcsh* command starts a new TC shell, called a subshell.

7   The PID of the current shell is printed. Because this is a new TC shell, it has a different PID number. The PID is *211*.

8   The environment variable *PERSON* was inherited by the new shell.

9   The *PERSON* variable is reset to *Nelly Nerd*. This variable will be inherited by any shells spawned from this shell.

10 The new value of the *PERSON* variable is printed.

EXPLANATION (CONTINUED)

11 This shell is exited.

12 The original shell is running; to attest to that, the PID *206* is printed. It is the same as it was before the subshell was started.

13 The *PERSON* variable contains its original value.

Displaying Environment Variables.   The *printenv* (BSD) and *env* (SVR4) commands print all the environment variables set for this shell and its subshells. The *setenv* command prints variables and their values on both the UCB and SVR4 versions of TC shell.

EXAMPLE 13.70

```
> env  or  printenv  or  setenv
USERNAME=root
COLORTERM=rxvt-xpm
HISTSIZE=1000
HOSTNAME=homebound
LOGNAME=ellie
HISTFILESIZE=1000
MAIL=/var/spool/mail/ellie
MACHTYPE=i386
COLORFGBG=0;default;15
TERM=xterm
HOSTTYPE=i386-unix
PATH=/usr/sbin:/sbin:/usr/local/bin:/bin:/usr/bin:usr/X11R6/bin:/home
/ellie/bin;/root/bash-2.03/:/usr/X11R6/bin:/home/ellie/bin;/root/bash-
2.03/:/usr/X11R6/bin
HOME=/root
SHELL=/bin/bash
PS1=[\u@\h \W]\$
USER=ellie
VENDOR=intel
GROUP=ellie
HOSTDISPLAY=homebound:0.0
DISPLAY=:0.0
HOST=homebound
OSTYPE=unix
WINDOWID=37748738
PWD=/home/ellie
SHLVL=6
_=/usr/bin/env
```

EXPLANATION

The environment variables are set for this session and all processes that are started from this shell are displayed by using either one of the built-in commands: *env* or *printenv*. Many applications require the setting of environment variables. For example, the *mail* command has a *MAIL* variable set to the location of the user's mail spooler and the *xterm* program has a *DISPLAY* variable that determines which bit map display terminal to use. When any of these programs are executed, the values in their respective variables are passed on to them.

13.8 Arrays

13.8.1 What Is an Array?

In the TC shell, an array is simply a list of words, separated by spaces or tabs, and enclosed in parentheses. The elements of the array are numbered by subscripts starting at one. If there is not an array element for a subscript, the message *Subscript out of range* is displayed. Command substitution will also create an array. If the $# notation precedes an array name, the number of elements in the array is displayed.

EXAMPLE 13.71

```
1   > set fruit = ( apples pears peaches plums )
2   > echo $fruit
    apples pears peaches plums

3   > echo $fruit[1]        # Subscripts start at 1
    apples

4   > echo $fruit[2-4]      # Prints the 2nd, 3rd, and 4th elements
    pears peaches plums

5   > echo $fruit[6]
    Subscript out of range.

6   > echo $fruit[*]        # Prints all elements of the array
    apples pears peaches plums

7   > echo $#fruit          # Prints the number of elements
    4

8   > echo $%fruit          # Prints the number of characters in the list
    23
```

EXAMPLE 13.71 (CONTINUED)

```
9   > echo $fruit[$#fruit]        # Prints the last element
    plums

10  > set fruit[2] = bananas      # Reassigns the second element
    > echo $fruit
    apples bananas peaches plums

11  > set path = ( ~ /usr/bin /usr /usr/local/bin . )
    > echo $path
    /home/jody/ellie /usr/bin /usr /usr/local/bin .

12  > echo $path[1]
    /home/jody/ellie
```

EXPLANATION

1   The wordlist is enclosed within parentheses. Each word is separated by whitespace. The array is called *fruit*.

2   The words in the *fruit* array are printed.

3   The first element of the *fruit* array is printed. The subscripts start at one.

4   The second, third, and fourth elements of the wordlist are printed. The dash allows you to specify a range.

5   The array does not have six elements. The subscript is out of range.

6   All elements of the *fruit* array are printed.

7   The $# preceding the array is used to obtain the number of elements in the array. There are four elements in the *fruit* array.

8   The $% preceding a variable or an array prints the number of characters in the word(s).

9   Because the subscript $#fruit evaluates to the total number of elements in the array, if that value is used as an index value of the array, i.e., [$#fruit], the last element of the *fruit* array is printed.

10 The second element of the array is assigned a new value. The array is printed with its replaced value, *bananas*.

11 The *path* variable is a special TC shell array of directories used to search for commands. When you create an array, the individual elements of the path can be accessed or changed.

12 The first element of *path* is printed.

The *shift* Command and Arrays.   If the built-in *shift* command takes an array name as its argument, it shifts off (to the left) the first element of the array. The length of the array is decreased by one. Without an argument, the *shift* command shifts off the first element of the built-in *argv* array.

Table 13.20   Variable Modifiers

Special Modifier	Example	What It Means
$?	$?var	Returns *1* if *var* is set; *0* if not.
$#	$#var	Returns the number of words in *var*.
$%	$%var	Returns the number of characters in *var*.

EXAMPLE 13.72

```
1   > set names = ( Mark Tom Liz Dan Jody )

2   > echo $names
    Mark Tom Liz Dan Jody

3   > echo $names[1]
    Mark

4   > shift  names

5   > echo $names
    Tom Liz Dan Jody

6   > echo $names[1]
    Tom

7   > set days = ( Monday Tuesday )

8   > shift days

9   > echo $days
    Tuesday

10  > shift days

11  > echo $days

12  > shift days
    shift: no more words.
```

EXPLANATION

1 The array is called *names*. It is assigned the list of words in parentheses. Each word is separated by whitespace.

2 The array is printed.

3 The first element of the array is printed.

4 The array is shifted to the left by one element. The word *Mark* is shifted off.

5 The array was decreased by one element after the *shift*.

6 The first element of the array, after the *shift*, is *Tom*.

7 An array called *days* is created. It has two elements, *Monday* and *Tuesday*.

8 The *days* array is shifted one to the left.

9 The array is printed. *Tuesday* is the only element left.

10 The *days* array is shifted again. The array is empty.

11 The *days* array is empty.

12 This time, attempting to shift causes the shell to send an error message indicating that it cannot shift elements from an empty array.

Creating an Array from a String. You may want to create a wordlist out of a quoted string. This is accomplished by placing the string variable within a set of parentheses.

EXAMPLE 13.73

```
1   > set name = "Thomas Ben Savage"
    > echo $name[1]
    Thomas Ben Savage

2   > echo $name[2]
    Subscript out of range.

3   > set name = ( $name )

4   > echo $name[1] $name[2] $name[3]
    Thomas Ben Savage
```

EXPLANATION

1 The variable *name* is assigned the string *Thomas Ben Savage*.
2 When treated as an array, there is only one element, the entire string.
3 The variable is enclosed in parentheses, creating an array of words, called *name*.
4 The three elements of the new array are displayed.

13.9 Special Variables and Modifiers

Built into the TC shell are several variables consisting of one character. The $ preceding the character allows variable interpretation. See Table 13.21.

Table 13.21 Variables and Their Meanings

Variable	Example	Meaning
$?var	echo $?name	Returns *1* if variable has been set, *0* if not.
$#var	echo $#fruit	Prints the number of elements in an array.
$%var	echo $%name	Prints number of characters in a variable or array.
$$	echo $$	Prints the PID of the current shell.
$<	set name = $<	Accepts a line of input from user up to newline.
$?	echo $?	Same as *$status*. Contains the exit status of the last command.
$!	kill $!	Contains the process ID number of the last job put in the background.

EXAMPLE 13.74

```
1   > set num
    > echo $?num
    1

2   > echo $path
    /home/jody/ellie   /usr  /bin   /usr/local/bin
    > echo $#path
    3

3   > echo $$
    245

    > tcsh                  # Start a subshell
    > echo $$
    248

4   > set name = $<
    Christy Campbell
    > echo $name
    Christy

5   > set name = "$<"
    Christy Campbell
    > echo $name
    Christy Campbell
```

EXPLANATION

1   The variable *num* is set to null. The $? preceding the variable evaluates to one if the variable has been set (either to null or some value), and to zero if the variable has not been set.

2   The *path* variable is printed. It is an array of three elements. The $# preceding the variable extracts and prints the number of elements in the array.

3   The $$ is the PID of the current process, in this case, the C shell.

4   The $< variable accepts a word of input from the user up to the first space or new-line, whichever comes first, and stores the word in the *name* variable. The value of the *name* variable is displayed.

5   The $< variable, when quoted (double quotes) accepts a line of input from the user up to, but not including, the newline, and stores the line in the *name* variable. The value of the *name* variable is displayed.

13.9.1 Pathname Variable Modifiers

If a pathname is assigned to a variable, it is possible to manipulate the pathname variable by appending special TC shell extensions to it. The pathname is divided into four parts: *head*, *tail*, *root*, and *extension*. See Table 13.22 for examples of pathname modifiers and what they do.

Table 13.22 Pathname Modifiers

`set pn = /home/ellie/prog/check.c`

Modifier	Meaning	Example	Result
:r	root	echo $pn:r	/home/ellie/prog/check
:h	head	echo $pn:h	/home/ellie/prog
:t	tail	echo $pn:t	check.c
:e	extension	echo $pn:e	c
:g	global	echo $p:gt	(See Example 13.75)

EXAMPLE 13.75

```
1   > set pathvar = /home/danny/program.c

2   > echo $pathvar:r
    /home/danny/program

3   > echo $pathvar:h
    /home/danny

4   > echo $pathvar:t
    program.c

5   > echo $pathvar:e
    c

6   > set pathvar = ( /home/* )
    echo $pathvar
    /home/jody /home/local /home/lost+found /home/perl /home/tmp

7   > echo $pathvar:gt
    jody  local  lost+found  perl tmp
```

EXPLANATION

1   The variable *pathvar* is set to */home/danny/program.c*.

2   When *:r* is appended to the variable, the extension is removed when displayed.

3   When *:h* is appended to the variable, the head of the path is displayed; that is, the last element of the path is removed.

4   When *:t* is appended to the variable, the tail end of the path (the last element) is displayed.

5   When *:e* is appended to the variable, the extension is displayed.

6   The variable is set to */home/**. The asterisk expands to all the pathnames in the current directory starting in */home/*.

7   When *:gt* is appended to the variable, the tail end of each (global) of the path elements is displayed.

13.9.2   Upper- and Lowercase Modifiers

A special history modifier can be used to change the case of letters in a variable.

Table 13.23   Case Modifiers

Modifier	Effect
:u	Uppercase the first lowercase letter in a word.
:l	Lowercase the first uppercase letter in a word.
:g	Apply a modifier once to each word.
:a	Apply a modifier as many times as possible to a single word.

EXAMPLE   13.76

```
1   > set name = nicky
    > echo $name:u
    Nicky

2   > set name = ( nicky jake )
    > echo $name:gu
    Nicky Jake

3   > echo $name:agu
    NICKY JAKE
```

EXAMPLE 13.76 (CONTINUED)

```
4   > set name = ( TOMMY DANNY )
    > echo $name:ag1
    tommy danny

5   > set name = "$name:agu"
    > echo $name
    TOMMY DANNY
```

EXPLANATION

1 When *:u* is appended to the variable, the first letter in its value is uppercased.
2 When *:gu* is appended to the variable, the first letter in each word in the list of values is uppercased.
3 When *:agu* is appended to the variable, all letters in its value are uppercased.
4 When *:agl* is appended to the variable, all letters in its value are lowercased.
5 The variable is reset with all letters in its list uppercased.

13.10 Command Substitution

13.10.1 Backquotes

A string or variable can be assigned the output of a UNIX command by placing the command in backquotes. This is called *command substitution*. (On the keyboard, the backquotes are normally below the tilde character.) If the output of a command is assigned to a variable, it is stored as a wordlist or array. (See "Wordlists and Command Substitution" on page 919.)

EXAMPLE 13.77

```
1   > echo The name of my machine is `uname -n`.
    The name of my machine is stardust.

2   > echo The present working directory is `pwd`.
    The present working directory is /home/stardust/john.

3   > set d = `date`
    > echo $d
    Tue Mar 28 14:24:21 PDT 2001
```

1   The UNIX command *uname –n* is enclosed in backquotes. When the shell encounters the backquotes, it will execute the enclosed command, *uname –n*, and substitute the output of the command, *stardust*, into the string. When the *echo* command prints its arguments to standard output, the name of the machine will be one of its arguments.

2   The UNIX command *pwd* is executed by the shell and the output is substituted in place within the string.

3   The local variable *d* is assigned the output of the *date* command. The output is stored as a list of words (an array).

Wordlists and Command Substitution.   When a command is enclosed in backquotes and assigned to a variable, the resulting value is an array (wordlist). Each element of the array can be accessed by appending a subscript to the array name. The subscripts start at one. If a subscript that is greater than the number of words in the array is used, the TC shell prints *Subscript out of range*. If the output of a command consists of more than one line, the newlines are stripped from each line and replaced with a single space.

After an array is created, the built-in *shift* command can be used to remove words starting at word number one. Once a word is shifted off, it cannot be retrieved.

EXAMPLE   13.78

```
1   > set d = `date`
    > echo $d
    Tue Mar 28 14:04:49 PST 2001

2   > echo $d[1-3]
    Tue Mar 28

3   > echo $d[6]
    2001

4   > echo $d[7]
    Subscript out of range.

5   > echo "The calendar for the month of March is `cal 3 2000`"
    The calendar for month of March is March 2001 S M Tu W
    Th F S 1 2 3 4 5 6 7 8 9 10 11 12 13 14 15 16 17 18 19 20 21
    22 23 24 25 26 27 28 29 30 31
```

EXPLANATION

1   The variable *d* is assigned the output of the UNIX *date* command. The output is stored as an array. The value of the variable is displayed.

2   The first three elements of the array are displayed.

3   The sixth element of the array is displayed.

4   There are not seven elements in the array. The shell reports that the subscript is out of range.

5   The output spans more than one line. Each newline is replaced with a space. This may not be the output you expected.

EXAMPLE 13.79

```
1   > set machine = `rusers | awk '/tom/{print $1}'`

2   > echo $machine
    dumbo bambi dolphin

3   > echo $#machine
    3

4   > echo $machine[$#machine]
    dolphin

5   > echo $machine
    dumbo bambi dolphin

6   > shift $machine
    > echo $machine
    bambi dolphin

7   > echo $machine[1]
    bambi

8   > echo $#machine
    2
```

EXPLANATION

1   The output of the *rusers* command is piped to *awk*. If the regular expression *tom* is found, *awk* prints the first field. The first field, in this case, is the name of the machine(s) where user *tom* is logged on.

2   User *tom* is logged on three machines. The names of the machines are displayed.

3   The number of elements in the array is accessed by preceding the array name with $#. There are three elements in the array.

4   The last element of the array is displayed. The number of elements in the array ($#*machine*) is used as a subscript.

EXPLANATION (CONTINUED)

5   The array is displayed.

6   The *shift* command shifts the array to the left. The first element of the array is dropped and the subscripts are renumbered, starting at one.

7   The first element of the array after the *shift* is displayed.

8   After the *shift*, the length of the array has decreased by one.

13.11 Quoting

The TC shell has a whole set of metacharacters that have some special meaning. In fact, almost any character on your keyboard that is not a letter or a number has some special meaning for the shell. Here is a partial list:

* ? [ ] $ ~ ! ^ & { } ( ) > < | ; : %

The backslash and quotes are used to escape the interpretation of metacharacters by the shell. Whereas the backslash is used to escape a single character, the quotes can be used to protect a string of characters. There are some general rules for using quotes:

1. Quotes are paired and must be matched on a line. The backslash character can be used to escape a newline so that a quote can be matched on the next line.
2. Single quotes will protect double quotes, and double quotes will protect single quotes.
3. Single quotes protect all metacharacters from interpretation, with the exception of the history character (*!*).
4. Double quotes protect all metacharacters from interpretation, with the exception of the history character (*!*), the variable substitution character (*$*), and the backquotes (used for command substitution).

13.11.1 The Backslash

The backslash is used to quote a single character and is the only character that can be used to escape a history character sequence (such as *!!* or *!string* or *!5*). Often the backslash is used to escape the newline character. The special *tcsh* variable *backslash_quote* can be used for quoting quotes and backslashes, but will not work in *csh* scripts. (See Example 13.80.)

EXAMPLE 13.80

```
1   > echo Who are you?
    echo: No match.

2   > echo Who are you\?
    Who are you?

3   > echo This is a very,very long line and this is where\
    ? I break the line.
    This is a very, very long line and this is where I break the
    line.

4   > echo "\abc"
    \abc
    > echo '\abc'
    \abc
    > echo \\abc
    \abc

5   > echo 'I can\'t help it!'
    Unmatched `.

6   > set backslash_quote
    > echo 'I can't help it!'
    I can't help it!
```

EXPLANATION

1   The question mark is used for filename expansion. It matches for a single character. The shell is looking for a file in the current directory that is spelled *y-o-u*, followed by a single character. Because there is not a file by that name in the directory, the shell complains that it could not find a match with *No match*.

2   The shell will not try to interpret the question mark because it is escaped with the backslash.

3   The string is continued to the next line by escaping the newline with a backslash. (The *?* is the secondary prompt, *prompt2*.)

4   If the backslash is enclosed in either single or double quotes, it is printed. When not enclosed in quotes, the backslash escapes itself.

5   When enclosed in single quotes the backslash is ignored as a quoting character; i.e., it will not protect the single apostrophe in *can't*. The shell sees three single quotes and reports an unmatched quote.

6   The *tcsh* variable *backslash_quote*, if set, causes backslashes to always quote backslashes, single quotes, and double quotes.

13.11.2 Single Quotes

Single quotes must be matched on the same line and will escape all metacharacters with the exception of the history (bang) character (*!*), which is not protected because the shell evaluates history before it does quotes (but not before backslashes).

EXAMPLE 13.81

```
1   > echo 'I need $5.00'
    I need $5.00


2   > cp file1 file2
    > echo 'I need $500.00 now!!'
    echo 'I need $500.00 nowcp file1 file2'


3   > echo 'I need $500.00 now\!\!'
    I need $500.00 now!!


4   > echo 'This is going to be a long line so
    Unmatched '.


5   > echo 'This is going to be a long line so \
    ? I used the backslash to suppress the newline'
    This is going to be a long line so
    I used the backslash to suppress the newline
```

EXPLANATION

1   The string is enclosed in single quotes. All characters, except the history (bang) character (*!*), are protected from shell interpretation.

2   After you use the *cp* command, the *echo* program is executed. Because the *!!* was not protected from shell interpretation by using the backslash character, the last command on the history list is reexecuted and the *cp* command becomes part of the string.

3   By quoting the history characters (*!!*) with backslashes, they are protected from history substitution.

4   The quotes must be matched on the same line, or the shell reports *Unmatched*.

5   If the line is to be continued, the backslash character is used to escape the newline character. The quote is matched at the end of the next line. Even though the shell ignored the newline, the *echo* command did not. (The *?* is the secondary prompt, *prompt2*.)

13.11.3 Double Quotes

Double quotes must be matched, will allow variable and command substitution, and hide everything else except the history (bang (*!*)). The backslash will not escape the dollar sign when enclosed in double quotes.

EXAMPLE 13.82

```
1   > set name = Bob
    > echo "Hi $name"
    Hi Bob

2   > echo "I don't have time."
    I don't have time.

3   > echo "WOW!!"        # Watch the history metacharacter!
    echo "Wowecho "Wow!!""

4   > echo "WOW\!\!"
    Wow!!

5   > echo "I need \$5.00"
    I need \.00
```

EXPLANATION

1 The local variable *name* is assigned the value *Bob*. The double quotes allow the dollar sign to be used for variable substitution.

2 The single quote is protected within double quotes.

3 Double or single quotes will not protect the exclamation point from shell interpretation. The built-in *history* command is looking for the last command that began with a double quote and that event was not found.

4 The backslash is used to protect the exclamation point.

5 The backslash does not escape the dollar sign when used within double quotes.

13.11.4 Combining Double and Single Quotes

As long as the quoting rules are adhered to, double quotes and single quotes can be used in a variety of combinations in a single command.

EXAMPLE 13.83

```
1   > set name = Tom

2   > echo "I can't give $name" ' $5.00\!\!'
    I can't give Tom $5.00!!

3   > echo She cried, \"Oh help me\!\!'" ', $name.
    She cried, "Oh help me!!", Tom.
```

EXPLANATION

1   The local variable *name* is assigned *Tom*.

2   The single quote in the word *can't* is protected when enclosed within double quotes. The shell would try to perform variable substitution if the dollar sign in *$5.00* were within double quotes. Therefore, the string *$5.00* is enclosed in single quotes so that the dollar sign will be a literal. The exclamation point is protected with a backslash because neither double nor single quotes can protect it from shell interpretation.

3   The first conversational quotes are protected by the backslash. The exclamation point is also protected with a backslash. The last conversational quotes are enclosed in a set of single quotes. Single quotes will protect double quotes.

13.11.5 Steps to Successful Quoting

In a more complex command, it is often difficult to match quotes properly unless you follow the steps listed here. (See Appendix C.)

1. Know the UNIX command and its syntax. Before variable substitution, hard code the values into the command line to see if you get the expected results.

```
> awk -F: '/^Zippy Pinhead/{print "Phone is  " $2}' datafile
Phone is 408-123-4563
```

2. If the UNIX command worked correctly, then plug in the variables. At this point, do not remove or change any quotes. Simply put the variables in place of the words they represent. In this example, replace *Zippy Pinhead* with *$name*.

```
> set name = "Zippy Pinhead"
> awk -F: '/^$name/{print "Phone is " $2}' datafile
```

3. Play the quoting game as follows: Starting at the left-hand side with the first single quote, insert a matching single quote just before the dollar sign in *$name*. Now you have a set of matched quotes.

```
awk -F: '/^'$name/{print "Phone is " $2}' datafile
```

Now, right after the last letter, *e* in *$name*, place another single quote. (Believe me, this works.) This quote matches the quote after the closing curly brace.

```
> awk -F: '/^'$name'/{print "Phone is  " $2}' datafile
```

Count the number of single quotes, starting at the left-hand side. You have four, a nice even number. Everything within each set of single quotes is ignored by the shell. The quotes are matched as follows:

```
> nawk -F: '$1 ~ /'$name'/{print $2}' filename
```

4. Last step: Double quote the variables. Surround each variable very snugly within a set of double quotes. The double quotes protect the whitespace in the expanded variable; for example, the space in *Zippy Pinhead* is protected.

```
> nawk -F: '$1 ~ /'"$name"'/{print $2}' filename
```

13.11.6 Quoting Variables

The *:x* and *:q* modifiers are used when it's necessary to quote variables.

Quoting with the *:q* Modifier.   The *:q* modifier is used to replace double quotes.

EXAMPLE 13.84

```
1   > set name = "Daniel Savage"

2   > grep $name:q database
    same as

3   > grep "$name" database

4   > set food = "apple pie"

5   > set dessert = ( $food "ice cream")

6   > echo $#dessert
    3

7   > echo $dessert[1]
    apple

8   > echo $dessert[2]
    pie
```

EXAMPLE 13.84 (CONTINUED)

```
 9   > echo $dessert[3]
     ice cream

10   > set dessert = ($food:q "ice cream")

11   > echo $#dessert
     2

12   > echo $dessert[1]
     apple pie

13   > echo $dessert[2]
     ice cream
```

EXPLANATION

1   The variable is assigned the string *Daniel Savage.*

2   When *:q* is appended to the variable, the variable is quoted. This is the same as enclosing the variable in double quotes.

3   The double quotes surrounding the variable *$name* allow variable substitution to take place, but protect any whitespace characters. Without the double quotes, the *grep* program will search for *Daniel* in a file called *Savage* and a file called *database.*

4   The variable *food* is assigned the string *apple pie.*

5   The variable *dessert* is assigned an array (wordlist) consisting of *apple pie* and *ice cream.*

6   The number of elements in the *dessert* array is three. When the *food* variable was expanded, the quotes were removed. There are three elements, *apple, pie,* and *ice cream.*

7   The first element of the array is printed. The variable expands to separated words if not quoted.

8   The second element of the array is printed.

9   Since *"ice cream"* is quoted, it is treated as one word.

10 The *dessert* array is assigned *apple pie* and *ice cream.* The *:q* can be used to quote the variable in the same way double quotes quote the variable; i.e., *$food:q* is the same as *"$food".*

11 The array consists of two strings, *apple pie* and *ice cream.*

12 The first element of the array, *apple pie,* is printed.

13 The second element of the array, *ice cream,* is printed.

Quoting with the :x Modifier.   If you are creating an array and any of the words in the list contain metacharacters, :x prevents the shell from interpreting the metacharacters when performing variable substitution.

EXAMPLE   13.85

```
1   > set  things = "*.c  a??  file[1-5]"
    > echo $#things
    1

2   > set newthings = ( $things )
    set: No match.

3   > set newthings = ( $things:x )

4   > echo $#newthings
    3

5   > echo "$newthings[1] $newthings[2] $newthings[3] "
    *.c  a??    file[1-5]

6   >  grep $newthings[2]:q filex
```

EXPLANATION

1   The variable *things* is assigned a string. Each string contains a wildcard. The number of elements in the variable is one, one string.

2   When attempting to create an array out of the string *things*, the TC shell tries to expand the wildcard characters to perform filename substitution within *things* and produces a *No match*.

3   The :x extension prevents the shell from expanding the wildcards in the *things* variable.

4   The array *newthings* consists of three elements.

5   To print the elements of the array, they must be quoted or, again, the shell will try to expand the wildcards.

6   The :q quotes the variable just as though the variable were surrounded by double quotes. The *grep* program will print any lines containing the pattern *a??* in file *filex*.

13.12 Built-In Commands

Rather than residing on disk like UNIX executable commands, built-in commands are part of the TC shell's internal code and are executed from within the shell. If a built-in command occurs as any component of a pipeline except the last, it is executed in a subshell. The *tcsh* command, aptly called *builtins*, lists all the built-in commands:

EXAMPLE   13.86

```
1   > builtins
:            @            alias      alloc      bg         bindkey    break
breaksw      builtins     case       cd         chdir      complete   continue
default      dirs         echo       echotc     else       end        endif
endsw        eval         exec       exit       fg         filetest   foreach
glob         goto         hashstat   history    hup        if         jobs
kill         limit        log        login      logout     ls-F       nice
nohup        notify       onintr     popd       printenv   pushd      rehash
repeat       sched        set        setenv     settc      setty      shift
source       stop         suspend    switch     telltc     time       umask
unalias      uncomplete   unhash     unlimit    unset      unsetenv   wait
where        which        while
```

See Table 13.24 for a list of built-in commands.

Table 13.24   Built-In Commands and Their Meanings

Built-In Command	Meaning
:	Interprets null command, but performs no action
alias [name [wordlist]]	A nickname for a command. Without arguments, prints all aliases, with a name, prints the name for the alias; with a name and wordlist, sets the alias.
alloc	Displays amount of dynamic memory acquired, broken down into used and free memory. Varies across systems.
bg [%job] %job &	Runs the current or specified jobs in the background. A synonym for the bg built-in command.

Table 13.24 Built-In Commands and Their Meanings (continued)

Built-In Command	*Meaning*
bindkey [–l|–d|–e|–v|–u] (+) *bindkey [–a] [–b] [–k] [–r] [– –] key* *bindkey [–a] [–b] [–k] [–c|–s] [– –]* *key command*	Without options, the first form lists all bound keys and the editor command to which each is bound, the second form lists the editor command to which key is bound, and the third form binds the editor command command to key. Options include:

–l   Lists all editor commands and a short description of each.

–d   Binds all keys to the standard bindings for the default editor.

–e   Binds all keys to the standard GNU *emacs*-like bindings.

–v   Binds all keys to the standard *vi*-like bindings.

–a   Lists or changes key-bindings in the alternative key map. This is the key map used in *vi* command mode.

–b   This key is interpreted as a control character written as ^character (e.g., *^A*) or C-character (e.g., *C-A*), a meta-character written M-character (e.g., *M-A*), a function key written F-string (e.g., *F-string*), or an extended prefix key written X-character (e.g., *X-A*).

–k   This key is interpreted as a symbolic arrow key name, which may be one of down, up, left, or right.

–r   Removes key's binding. Be careful: *bindkey–r* does not bind key to self-insert-command (q.v.), it unbinds key completely.

–c   This command is interpreted as a built-in or external command, instead of an editor command.

–s   This command is taken as a literal string and treated as terminal input when key is typed. Bound keys in commands are themselves reinterpreted, and this continues for 10 levels of interpretation.

– – Forces a break from option processing, so the next word is taken as a key even if it begins with a hyphen (–).

–u   (or any invalid option) Prints a usage message.

This key may be a single character or a string. If a command is bound to a string, the first character of the string is bound to sequence-lead-in and the entire string is bound to the command.

Control characters in key can be literal (they can be typed by preceding them with the editor command quoted-insert, normally bound to ^V) or written caret-character style, e.g., ^A. Delete is written ^? (caret-question mark). Key and command can contain backslashed escape sequences (in the style of System V *echo*) as follows:

\a Bell	\f Form feed	\t Horizontal tab	\b Backspace
\n Newline	\v Vertical tab	\e Escape	\r Carriage return

\nnn The ASCII character corresponding to the octal number *nnn*.
\ nullifies the special meaning of the following character, if it has any, notably backslash (\) and caret (^).

Table 13.24   Built-In Commands and Their Meanings (continued)

Built-In Command	*Meaning*
break	Breaks out of the innermost *foreach* or *while* loop.
breaksw	Breaks from a *switch*, resuming after the *endsw*.
builtins	Prints the names of all built-in commands.
bye	A synonym for the logout built-in command. Available only if the shell was so compiled; see the version shell variable.
case label:	A label in a *switch* statement.
cd [dir]	Changes the shell's working directory to *dir*. If no argument is given, changes to the home directory of the user.

cd [–p] [–l] [–n|–v] [name]	If a directory name is given, changes the shell's working directory to name. If not, changes to home. If *name* is – it is interpreted as the previous working directory.
	    –p, prints the final directory stack, just like *dirs*.
	    –l, *–n*, and *–v* flags have the same effect on *cd* as on *dirs*, and they imply *–p*.

chdir	A synonym for the *cd* built-in command.
complete [command [word/pattern/list[:select]/[[suffix]/] ...]]	Without arguments, lists all completions. With *command*, lists completions for *command*. With *command* and *word* etc., defines completions. (See "Programming Completions" on page 866.)
continue	Continues execution of the nearest enclosing *while* or *foreach*
default:	Labels the *default* case in a switch statement. The *default* should come after all case labels.

dirs [–l] [–n|–v]
dirs –S|–L [filename]
dirs –c
	The first form prints the directory stack. The top of the stack is at the left and the first directory in the stack is the current directory. *–l*, ~ or ~*name* in the output is expanded explicitly to home or the pathname of the home directory for user name.
	    (+) *–n*, entries are wrapped before they reach the edge of the screen.
	    (+) *–v*, entries are printed one per line preceded by their stack postions.
	    –S, the second form saves the directory stack to filename as a series of *cd* and *pushd* commands.
	    –L, the shell source's filename, which is presumably a directory stack file saved.
	In either case, *dirsfile* is used if filename is not given and ~/.cshdirs is used if *dirsfile* is unset.
	    With *–c*, form clears the directory stack.

Table 13.24   Built-In Commands and Their Meanings (continued)

Built-In Command	Meaning
echo [–n] list	Writes the words in *list* to the shell's standard output, separated by SPACE characters. The output is terminated with a NEWLINE unless the *–n* option is used.
echo [–n] word ...	Writes each word to the shell's standard output, separated by spaces and terminated with a newline. The *echo_style* shell variable may be set to emulate (or not) the flags and escape sequences of the BSD and/or System V versions of *echo*.
echotc [–sv] arg ...	Exercises the terminal capabilities in *args*. For example, *echotc home* sends the cursor to the home position. If arg is *baud*, *cols*, *lines*, *meta*, or *tabs*, prints the value of that capability. With *–s*, nonexistent capabilities return the empty string rather than causing an error. With *–v*, messages are verbose.
else if (expr2) then	See "The if/else if Statements" on page 401.

else
end
endif
endsw
	See the description of the *foreach*, *if*, *switch*, and *while* statements below.

end	Executes the commands between the *while* and the matching *end* while *expr* evaluates nonzero. *while* and *end* must appear alone on their input lines. *break* and *continue* may be used to terminate or continue the loop prematurely. If the input is a terminal, the user is prompted the first time through the loop as with *foreach*.
eval arg ...	Treats the arguments as input to the shell and executes the resulting command(s) in the context of the current shell. This is usually used to execute commands generated as the result of command or variable substitution, since parsing occurs before these substitutions.
eval command	Runs *command* as standard input to the shell and executes the resulting commands. This is usually used to execute commands generated as the result of command or variable substitution, since parsing occurs before these substitutions (e.g., *eval tset –s options*).
exec command	Executes *command* in place of the current shell, which terminates.
exit [(expr)]	Exits the shell, either with the value of the status variable or with the value specified by *expr*.
fg [% job] %job	Brings the current or specified *job* into the foreground. A synonym for the *fg* built-in command.

Table 13.24 Built-In Commands and Their Meanings (continued)

Built-In Command	Meaning
filetest –op file ...	Applies *op* (which is a file inquiry operator) to each file and returns the results as a space-separated list.
foreach name (wordlist) *...* *end*	See "The foreach Loop" on page 412.
foreach var (wordlist)	See "The foreach Loop" on page 412.
getspath	Prints the system execution path. (TCF only) (*tcsh* only)
getxvers	Prints the experimental version prefix. (TCF only) (*tcsh* only)
glob wordlist	Performs filename expansion on wordlist. Like *echo*, but no *escapes* (\) are recognized. Words are delimited by null characters in the output.
goto label	See "The goto" on page 405.
goto word	*word* is filename and command-substituted to yield a string of the form *label*. The shell rewinds its input as much as possible, searches for a line of the form *label:*, possibly preceded by blanks or tabs, and continues execution after that line.
hashstat	Prints a statistics line indicating how effective the internal hash table has been at locating commands (and avoiding *execs*). An *exec* is attempted for each component of the path where the *hash* function indicates a possible hit, and in each component that does not begin with a backslash.
history [–hTr] [n] *history –S|–L|–M [filename]* *history –c*	The first form prints the history event list. If *n* is given, only the *n* most recent events are printed or saved. With *–h*, the history list is printed without leading numbers. If *–T* is specified, timestamps are printed in comment form. (This can be used to produce files suitable for loading with *history –L* or *source –h*.) With *–r*, the order of printing is most recent first rather than oldest first. (See "History" on page 846.) With *–c*, clears the history list.
hup [command]	With *command*, runs *command* such that it will exit on a hangup signal and arranges for the shell to send it a hangup signal when the shell exits. Note that commands may set their own response to hangups, overriding *hup*. Without an argument (allowed only in a shell script), causes the shell to exit on a hangup for the remainder of the script.

Table 13.24 Built-In Commands and Their Meanings (continued)

Built-In Command	*Meaning*
if (expr) command	If *expr* evaluates true, then *command* is executed. Variable substitution on *command* happens early, at the same time it does for the rest of the *if command. Command* must be a simple command, not an alias, a pipeline, a command list or a parenthesized command list, but it may have arguments. Input/output redirection occurs even if *expr* is false and *command* is thus not executed; this is a bug.

if (expr) then
...
else if (expr2) then
...
else
...
endif
	If the specified *expr* is true then the commands to the first else are executed; otherwise if *expr2* is true then the commands to the second else are executed, etc. Any number of *else if* pairs are possible; only one *endif* is needed. The *else* part is likewise optional. (The words *else* and *endif* must appear at the beginning of input lines; the *if* must appear alone on its input line or after an *else*.)

inlib shared-library ...	Adds each *shared-library* to the current environment. There is no way to remove a shared library. (Domain/OS only)
jobs [–l]	Lists the active *jobs* under job control. With *–l*, lists IDs in addition to the normal information.
kill [–sig] [pid] [%job] ... *kill –l*	Sends the *TERM* (terminate) signal, by default or by the signal specified, to the specified ID, the job indicated, or the current job. Signals are given either by number or name. There is no default. Typing *kill* does not send a signal to the current job. If the signal being sent is *TERM* (terminate) or *HUP* (hangup), then the job or process is sent a *CONT* (continue) signal as well. With *–l*, lists the signal names that can be sent.
limit [–h] [resource [max-use]]	Limits the consumption by the current process or any process it spawns, each not to exceed *max-use* on the specified *resource*. If *max-use* is omitted, print the current *limit*; if *resource* is omitted, display all *limit*s. With *–h*, uses hard limits instead of the current limits. Hard limits impose a ceiling on the values of the current limits. Only the superuser may raise the hard limits. Resource is one of: *cputime,* maximum CPU seconds per process; *filesize,* largest single file allowed; *datasize,* maximum data size (including stack) for the process; *stacksize,* maximum stack size for the process; *coredump,* maximum size of a core dump; and *descriptors,* maximum value for a file descriptor.
log	Prints the *watch* shell variable and reports on each user indicated in watch who is logged in, regardless of when they last logged in. See also *watchlog*.
login	Terminates a login shell, replacing it with an instance of */bin/login*.

Table 13.24   Built-In Commands and Their Meanings (continued)

Built-In Command	*Meaning*
login [username|–p]	Terminates a *login* shell and invokes *login*. The *.logout* file is not processed. If *username* is omitted, *login* prompts for the name of a user. With *–p*, preserves the current environment (variables).
logout	Terminates a login shell.
ls –F [–switch ...] [file ...]	Lists files like *ls –F*, but much faster. It identifies each type of special file in the listing with a special character: / Directory * Executable # Block device % Character device | Named pipe (systems with named pipes only) = Socket (systems with sockets only) @ Symbolic link (systems with symbolic links only) + Hidden directory (AIX only) or context-dependent (HP/UX only) : Network special (HP/UX only) If the *listlinks* shell variable is set, symbolic links are identified in more detail (only, of course, on systems which have them): @ Symbolic link to a nondirectory > Symbolic link to a directory & Symbolic link to nowhere The *ls –F* built-in can list files using different colors depending on the filetype or extension.
migrate [–site] pid|%jobid ... *migrate –site*	The first form migrates the process or job to the site specified or the default site determined by the system path. The second form is equivalent to *migrate –site $$*. It migrates the current process to the specified site. Migrating the shell itself can cause unexpected behavior, since the shell does not like to lose its *tty*. (TCF only)
@ *@ name = expr* *@ name[index] = expr* *@ name++|– –* *@ name[index]++|– –*	The first form prints the values of all shell variables. The second form assigns the value of *expr* to name. The third form assigns the value of *expr* to the indexth component of name; both name and its indexth component must already exist. The fourth and fifth forms increment (++) or decrement (– –) name or its indexth component.
newgrp [–] group	Equivalent to *exec newgrp*. Available only if the shell was so compiled; see the version shell variable.

Table 13.24   Built-In Commands and Their Meanings (continued)

Built-In Command	Meaning
nice [+number][command]	Sets the scheduling priority for the shell to number, or, without number, to 4. With *command*, runs *command* at the appropriate priority. The greater the number, the less CPU the process gets. The superuser may specify negative priority by using *nice –number* .... Command is always executed in a subshell, and the restrictions placed on commands in simple if statements apply.
nohup [command]	Runs *command* with *HUPs* (hangups) ignored. With no arguments, ignores *HUPs* throughout the remainder of a script.
notify [%job]	Notifies the user asynchronously when the status of the current or of a specified *job* changes.
onintr [– | label]	Controls the action of the shell on interrupts. With no arguments, *onintr* restores the default action of the shell on interrupts. (The shell terminates shell scripts and returns to the terminal command input level.) With the minus sign argument, the shell ignores all interrupts. With a *label* argument, the shell executes a *goto label* when an interrupt is received or a child process terminates because it was interrupted.
popd [+n]	Pops the directory stack and *cd* to the new top directory. The elements of the directory stack are numbered from zero, starting at the top. With +n, discard the *n*th entry in the stack.
printenv [name]	Prints the names and values of all environment variables or, with name, the value of the environment variable name.
pushd [+n | dir]	Pushes a directory onto the directory stack. With no arguments, exchanges the top two elements. With +n, rotates the *n*th entry to the top of the stack and *cd* to it. With *dir*, pushes the current working directory onto the stack and changes to *dir*.
rehash	Recomputes the internal hash table of the contents of directories listed in the *path* variable to account for new commands added.
repeat count command	Repeats command *count* times.
rootnode //nodename	Changes the rootnode to *//nodename*, so that / will be interpreted as *//nodename*. (Domain/OS only)
sched *sched [+]hh:mm command* *sched –n*	The first form prints the scheduled-event list. The *sched* shell variable may be set to define the format in which the scheduled-event list is printed. The second form adds command to the scheduled-event list.

Table 13.24 Built-In Commands and Their Meanings (continued)

Built-In Command	Meaning
set *set name ...* *set name=word ...* *set [–r] [–f|–l] name=(wordlist) ...* *(+)* *set name[index]=word ...* *set –r* *set –r name ...* *set –r name=word ...*	The first form of the command prints the value of all shell variables. Variables which contain more than a single word print as a parenthesized word list. The second form sets name to the null string. The third form sets name to the single word. The fourth form sets name to the list of words in wordlist. In all cases the value is command and filename expanded. If *–r* is specified, the value is set read-only. If *–f* or *–l* are specified, set only unique words keeping their order. *–f* prefers the first occurrence of a word, and *–l* the last occurrence of the word. The fifth form sets the index'th component of name to word; this component must already exist. The sixth form lists the names (only) of all shell variables which are read-only (*tcsh* only). The seventh form makes name read-only, whether or not it has a value (*tcsh* only). The eighth form is the same as the third form, but makes name read-only at the same time (*tcsh* only).
set [var [= value]]	See "Variables" on page 899.
setenv [VAR [word]]	See "Variables" on page 899. The most commonly used environment variables, *USER, TERM,* and *PATH*, are automatically imported to and exported from the *csh* variables *user, term,* and *path*; there is no need to use *setenv* for these. In addition, the shell sets the *PWD* environment variable from the *csh* variable *cwd* whenever the latter changes.
setenv [name [value]]	Without arguments, prints the names and values of all environment variables. Given name, sets the environment variable name to value or, without value, to the null string.
setpath path	Equivalent to *setpath*. (Mach only)
setspath LOCAL|site|cpu ...	Sets the system execution path. (TCF only)
settc cap value	Tells the shell to believe that the terminal capability cap has the value *value*. No sanity checking is done. Concept terminal users may have to *settc xn no* to get proper wrapping at the rightmost column.
setty [–d|–q|–x] [–a] [[+|–]mode]	Controls which tty modes the shell does not allow to change. *–d, –q,* or *–x* tells *setty* to act on the *edit, quote,* or *execute* set of *tty* modes, respectively; without *–d, –q,* or *–x, execute* is used. Without other arguments, *setty* lists the modes in the chosen set which are fixed on (*+mode*) or off (*–mode*). The available modes, and thus the display, vary from system to system. With *–a*, lists all *tty* modes in the chosen set whether or not they are fixed. With *+mode, –mode,* or *mode,* fixes mode on or off or removes control from mode in the chosen set. For example, *setty +echok echoe* fixes *echok* mode on and allows commands to turn *echoe* mode on or off, both when the shell is executing commands.

Table 13.24 Built-In Commands and Their Meanings (continued)

Built-In Command	Meaning
setxvers [string]	Sets the experimental version prefix to string, or removes it if string is omitted. (TCF only)
shift [variable]	The components of *argv*, or *variable*, if supplied, are shifted to the left, discarding the first component. It is an error for *variable* not to be set, or to have a null value.
source [–h] name	Reads commands from *name*. *Source* commands may be nested, but if they are nested too deeply, the shell may run out of file descriptors. An error in a sourced file at any level terminates all nested *source* commands. Used commonly to reexecute the *.login* or *.cshrc* files to ensure variable settings are handled within the current shell, i.e., shell does not create a child shell (fork). With *–h*, places commands from the filename on the history list without executing them.
stop [%job] ...	Stops the current or specified background *job*.
suspend	Stops the shell in its tracks, much as if it had been sent a stop signal with ^Z. This is most often used to stop shells started by *su*.
switch (string)	See "The switch Command" on page 409.
telltc	Lists the values of all terminal capabilities.
time [command]	With no argument, prints a summary of *time* used by this shell and its children. With an optional *command*, executes *command* and print a summary of the *time* it uses.
umask [value]	Displays the file creation mask. With *value*, sets the file creation mask. *Value*, given in octal, is *xored* with the permissions of 666 for files and 777 for directories to arrive at the permissions for new files. Permissions cannot be added via *umask*.
unalias pattern	Removes all aliases whose names match pattern. *unalias* * thus removes all aliases. It is not an error for nothing to be unaliased.
uncomplete pattern	Removes all completions whose names match pattern. *uncomplete* * thus removes all completions.
unhash	Disables the internal hash table.
universe universe	Sets the universe to universe. (Masscomp/RTU only)
unlimit [–h] [resource]	Removes the limitation on resource or, if no resource is specified, all resource limitations. With *–h*, the corresponding hard limits are removed. Only the superuser may do this.

Table 13.24 Built-In Commands and Their Meanings (continued)

Built-In Command	*Meaning*
unsetenv pattern	Removes all environment variables whose names match pattern. *unsetenv* * thus removes all environment variables; this is a bad idea. If there is no pattern to be *unsetenv*ed, no error will result from this built-in.
unsetenv variable	Removes *variable* from the environment. Pattern matching, as with *unset*, is not performed.
@ [var =expr] *@ [var[n] =expr]*	With no arguments, displays the values for all shell variables. With arguments, the variable *var*, or the *n*th word in the value of *var*, is set to the value that *expr* evaluates to.
ver [systype [command]]	Without arguments, prints *SYSTYPE*. With *systype*, sets *SYSTYPE* to *systype*. With *systype* and *command*, executes *command* under *systype. systype* may be *bsd4.3* or *sys5.3*. (Domain/OS only)
wait	Waits for background jobs to finish (or for an interrupt) before prompting.
warp universe	Sets the universe to universe. (Convex/OS only)
watchlog	An alternate name for the log built-in command (q.v.). Available only if the shell was so compiled; see the version shell variable.
where command	Reports all known instances of command, including aliases, built-ins, and executables in path.
which command	Displays the command that will be executed by the shell after substitutions, path searching, etc. The built-in command is just like *which*, but it correctly reports *tcsh* aliases and built-ins and is 10 to 100 times faster.
while (expr)	See "The while Loop" on page 415.

13.12.1 Special Aliases

If set, each of the TC shell aliases executes automatically at the indicated time. They are all initially undefined.

beepcmd	Runs when the shell wants to ring the terminal bell.
cwdcmd	Runs after every change of working directory.
periodic	Runs every *tperiod* minutes; e.g., > *set tperiod = 30* > *alias periodic date*
precmd	Runs just before each prompt is printed; e.g., *alias precmd date.*

13.12.2 Special Built-In Shell Variables

The built-in shell variables have special meaning to the shell and are used to modify and control the way many of the shell commmands behave. They are local variables and therefore most of them are set in the *.tcshrc* file if they are to be passed on to and affect child TC shells.

When the shell starts up, it automatically sets the following variables: *addsuffix, argv, autologout, command, echo_style, edit, gid, group, home, loginsh, oid, path, prompt, prompt2, prompt3, shell, shlvl, tcsh, term, tty, uid, user,* and *version.* Unless the user decides to change them, these variables will remain fixed. The shell also keeps track of and changes special variables that may need periodic updates, such as, *cwd, dirstack, owd,* and *status,* and when the user logs out, the shell sets the *logout* variable.

Some of the local variables have a corresponding environment variable of the same name. If one of the environment or local variables are affected by a change in the user's environment, the shell will synchronize the local and environment variables[10] so that their values always match. Examples of cross-matched variables are *afuser, group, home, path, shlvl, term,* and *user.* (Although *cwd* and *PWD* have the same meaning, they are not cross-matched. Even though the syntax is different for the *path* and *PATH* variables, they are automatically crossed-matched if either one is changed.)

---

10. This is true unless the variable is a read-only variable, and then there will be no synchronization.

Table 13.25 Special Shell Variables*

Variable	Effect
addsufix	For filename completion, adds slashes at the end of directories and space to the end of normal files if they are matched. Set by default.
afsuser	If set, *autologout*'s autolock feature uses its value instead of the local username for kerberos authentication.
ampm	If set, all times are shown in 12-hour AM/PM format.
argv	An array of command line arguments to the shell; also represented as $1, $2, etc.
autocorrect	Invokes the spell checker before each attempt at filename, command, or variable completion.
autoexpand	If set, the expand-history editor command is invoked automatically before each completion attempt.
autolist	If set, possibilities are listed after an ambiguous completion. If set to *ambiguous*, possibilities are listed only when no new characters are added by completion.
autologout	Its argument is the number of minutes of inactivity before automatic logout; the second optional argument is the number of minutes before automatic locking causes the screen to lock.
backslash quote	If set, a backslash will always quote itself, a single quote, or a double quote.
cdpath	A list of directories in which *cd* should search for subdirectories if they aren't found in the current directory.
color	Enables color display for the built-in command, *ls –F* and passes – –*color=auto* to *ls*
complete	If set to *enhance*, completion ignores case, considers periods, hyphens, and underscores to be word separators, and hyphens and underscores to be equivalent.
correct	If set to *cmd*, commands are automatically spelling-corrected. If set to *complete*, commands are automatically completed. If set to *all*, the entire command line is corrected.
cwd	The full pathname of the current working directory.
dextract	If set, *pushd +n* extracts the nth directory from the directory stack rather than rotating it to the top.
dirsfile	The default location in which *dirs –S* and *dirs –L* look for a history file. If unset, ~/.cshdirs is used.

Table 13.25 Special Shell Variables* (continued)

Variable	Effect
dirstack	A list of all directories on the directory stack.
dunique	Will not allow *pushd* to keep duplicate directory entries on the stack.
echo	If set, each command with its arguments is echoed just before it is executed. Set by the −*x* command line option.
echo-style	Sets the style for *echo*. If set to *bsd* will not echo a newline if the first argument is −*n*; if set to *sysv*, recognizes backslashed escape sequences in echo strings; if set to *both*, recognizes both the −*n* flag and backslashed escape sequences; the default, and if set to none, recognizes neither.
edit	Sets the command-line editor for interactive shells; set by default.
ellipsis	If set, the %c/%. and %C prompt sequences (see the "The Shell Prompts" on page 838) indicate skipped directories with an ellipsis (...) instead of /<skipped>.
fignore	Lists filename suffixes to be ignored by completion.
filec	In *tcsh*, completion is always used and this variable is ignored. If set in *csh*, filename completion is used.
gid	The user's read group ID number.
group	The user's group name.
histchars	A string value determining the characters used in history substitution. The first character of its value is used as the history substitution character to replace the default character, *!*. The second character of its value replaces the character ^ in quick substitutions.
histdup	Controls handling of duplicate entries in the history list. Can be set to *all* (removes all duplicates) , *prev* (removes the current command if it duplicates the previous command), or *erase* (inserts the current event for an older duplicate event).
histfile	The default location in which *history* −*S* and *history* −*L* look for a history file. If unset, ~/.history is used.
histlit	Enters events on the history list literally; i.e., unexpanded by history substitution.
history	The first word indicates the number of history events to save. The optional second word (+) indicates the format in which history is printed.
home	The home directory of the user; same as ~.

Table 13.25   Special Shell Variables* (continued)

Variable	Effect
ignoreeof	If logging out by pressing Control-D, prints *Use exit* to leave *tcsh*. Prevents inadvertently logging out.
implicitcd	If set, the shell treats a directory name typed as a command as though it were a request to change to that directory and changes to it.
inputmode	If set to *insert* or *overwrite*, puts the editor into that input mode at the beginning of each line.
listflags	If set to *x*, *a*, or *A*, or any combination (e.g., *xA*), values are used as flags to *ls –F*, making it act like *ls –xF*, *ls –Fa*, *ls –FA*, or any combination of those flags.
listjobs	If set, all jobs are listed when a job is suspended. If set to *long*, the listing is in long format.
listlinks	If set, the *ls –F* built-in command shows the type of file to which each symbolic link points.
listmax	The maximum number of items that the *list-choices* editor command will list without asking first.
listmaxrows	The maximum number of rows of items which the *list-choices* editor command will list without asking first.
loginsh	Set by the shell if it is a login shell. Setting or unsetting it within a shell has no effect. See also *shlvl* later in this table.
logout	Set by the shell to *normal* before a normal logout, *automatic* before an automatic logout, and *hangup* if the shell was killed by a hangup signal.
mail	The names of the files or directories to check for incoming mail. After 10 minutes if new mail has come in, will print *You have new mail*.
matchbeep	If set to *never*, completion never beeps; if set to *nomatch*, completion beeps only when there is no match; and when set to *ambiguous*, beeps when there are multiple matches.
nobeep	Disables all beeping.
noclobber	Safeguards against the accidental removal of existing files when redirection is used; e.g., *ls > file*.
noglob	If set, inhibits filename and directory stack substitutions when using wildcards.
nokanji	If set and the shell supports Kanji (see the version shell variable), it is disabled so that the Meta key can be used.

Table 13.25 Special Shell Variables* (continued)

Variable	Effect
nonomatch	If set, a filename substitution or directory stack substitution that does not match any existing files is left untouched rather than causing an error.
nostat	A list of directories (or glob patterns that match directories) that should not be *stated* during a completion operation. This is usually used to exclude directories which take too much time to *stat*.
notify	If set, the shell announces job completions asynchronously instead of waiting until just before the prompt appears.
oid	The user's real organization ID. (Domain/OS only)
owd	The old or previous working directory.
path	A list of directories in which to look for executable commands. *path* is set by the shell at startup from the *PATH* environment variable or, if *PATH* does not exist, to a system-dependent default something like */usr/local/bin /usr/bsd/bin /usr/bin*.
printexitvalue	If set and an interactive program exits with a nonzero status, the shell prints *Exit status*.
prompt	The string printed before reading each command from the terminal; may include special formatting sequences (See "The Shell Prompts" on page 838).
prompt2	The string with which to prompt in *while* and *foreach* loops and after lines ending in \. The same format sequences may be used as in *prompt*; note the variable meaning of %R. Set by default to %R? in interactive shells.
prompt3	The string with which to prompt when confirming automatic spelling correction. The same format sequences may be used as in prompt; note the variable meaning of %R. Set by default to *CORRECT>%R (y|n|e|a)?* in interactive shells.
promptchars	If set (to a two-character string), the %# formatting sequence in the prompt shell variable is replaced with the first character for normal users and the second character for the superuser.
pushtohome	If set, *pushd* without arguments does *pushd ~*, like *cd*.
pushdsilent	If set, *pushd* and *popd* do not print the directory stack.
recexact	If set, completion completes on an exact match even if a longer match is possible.
recognize_only_ executables	If set, command listing displays only files in the path that are executable.

Table 13.25 Special Shell Variables* (continued)

Variable	Effect
rmstar	If set, the user is prompted before *rm* * is executed.
rprompt	The string to print on the right-hand side of the screen (after the command input) when the prompt is being displayed on the left. It recognises the same formatting characters as prompt. It will automatically disappear and reappear as necessary, to ensure that command input isn't obscured, and will only appear if the prompt, command input, and itself will fit together on the first line. If edit isn't set, then *rprompt* will be printed after the prompt and before the command input.
savedirs	If set, the shell does *dirs –S* before exiting.
savehist	If set, the shell does *history –S* before exiting. If the first word is set to a number, at most that many lines are saved. (The number must be less than or equal to history.) If the second word is set to *merge*, the history list is merged with the existing history file instead of replacing it (if there is one) and sorted by timestamp and the most recent events are retained.
sched	The format in which the *sched* built-in command prints scheduled events; if not given, %h\t%T\t%R\n is used. The format sequences are described above under prompt; note the variable meaning of %R.
shell	The file in which the shell resides. This is used in forking shells to interpret files that have execute bits set, but that are not executable by the system. (See the description of built-in and nonbuilt-in command execution.) Initialized to the (system-dependent) home of the shell.
shlvl	The number of nested shells. Reset to *1* in login shells. See also *loginsh*.
status	The status returned by the last command. If it terminated abnormally, then 0200 is added to the status. Built-in commands that fail return exit status *1*, all other built-in commands return status *0*.
symlinks	Can be set to several different values to control symbolic link (*symlink*) resolution. (See *tcsh* man page for examples.)
tcsh	The version number of the shell in the format *R.VV.PP*, where *R* is the major release number, *VV* the current version, and *PP* the patch level.
term	The terminal type. Usually set in *~/.login* as described under "Startup" on page 830.

Table 13.25   Special Shell Variables* (continued)

Variable	Effect
time	If set to a number, then the *time* built-in executes automatically after each command which takes more than that many CPU seconds. If there is a second word, it is used as a format string for the output of the *time* built-in. The following sequences may be used in the format string:

%U	The time the process spent in user mode in CPU seconds.
%S	The time the process spent in kernel mode in CPU seconds.
%E	The elapsed (wall clock) time in seconds.
%P	The CPU percentage computed as (%U + %S) / %E.
%W	Number of times the process was swapped.
%X	The average amount in (shared) text space used in KB.
%D	The average amount in (unshared) data/stack space used in KB.
%K	The total space used (%X + %D) in KB.
%M	The maximum memory the process had in use at any time in KB.
%F	The number of major page faults (page needed to be brought from disk).
%R	The number of minor page faults.
%I	The number of input operations.
%O	The number of output operations.
%r	The number of socket messages received.
%s	The number of socket messages sent.
%k	The number of signals received.
%w	The number of voluntary context switches (waits).
%c	The number of involuntary context switches.

Only the first four sequences are supported on systems without BSD resource limit functions. The default time format is *%Uu %Ss %E %P %X+%Dk %I+%Oio %Fpf+%Ww* for systems that support resource usage reporting and *%Uu %Ss %E %P* for systems that do not.

Under Sequent's DYNIX/ptx, %X, %D, %K, %r, and %s are not available, but the following additional sequences are:

%Y	The number of system calls performed.
%Z	The number of pages that are zero-filled on demand.
%i	The number of times a process' resident set size was increased by the kernel.
%d	The number of times a process' resident set size was decreased by the kernel.
%l	The number of read system calls performed.
%m	The number of write system calls performed.
%p	The number of reads from raw disk devices.
%q	The number of writes to raw disk devices.

The default time format is *%Uu %Ss $E %P %I+%Oio %Fpf+%Ww*. Note that the CPU percentage can be higher than 100 percent on multiprocessors.

Table 13.25   Special Shell Variables* (continued)

Variable	Effect
tperiod	The period, in minutes, between executions of the *periodic* special alias.
tty	The name of the *tty*, or empty if not attached to one.
uid	The user's real user ID.
user	The user's login name.
verbose	If set, causes the words of each command to be printed, after history substitution (if any). Set by the *−v* command line option.
version	The version ID stamp. It contains the shell's version number (see *tcsh*), origin, release date, vendor, operating system, etc.

* Adapted from the *tcsh* manual pages.

Shell Command Line Switches.   The TC shell can take a number of command line switches (also called flag arguments) to control or modify its behavior. The command line switches are listed in Table 13.26.

Table 13.26   Shell Command Line Switches*

Switch	Meaning
−	Specifies the shell is a login shell.
−b	Forces a "break" from option processing. Any shell arguments thereafter, will not be treated as options. The remaining arguments will not be interpreted as shell options. Must include this option if shell is set-user-ID.
−c	If a single argument follows the *−c*, commands are read from the argument (a filename). Remaining arguments are placed in the *argv* shell variable.
−d	The shell loads the directory stack from ~/.cshdirs.
−Dname[=value]	Sets the environment variable name to value.
−e	The shell exits if any invoked command terminates abnormally or yields a nonzero exit status.
−f	Called the fast startup because the shell ignores ~/.tcshrc when starting a new TC shell.
−F	The shell uses *fork* instead of *vfork* to spawn processes. (Convex/OS only)

Table 13.26 *Shell Command Line Switches* (continued)*

Switch	Meaning
−*i*	The shell is interactive and prompts input, even if it appears to not be a terminal. This option isn't necessary if input and output are connected to a terminal.
−*l*	The shell is a login shell if −*l* is the only flag specified.
−*m*	The shell loads ~/.tcshrc even if it does not belong to the effective user.
−*n*	Used for debugging scripts. The shell parses commands but does not execute them.
−*q*	The shell accepts the *SIGQUIT* signal and behaves when it is used under a debugger. Job control is disabled.
−*s*	Command input is taken from the standard input.
−*t*	The shell reads and executes a single line of input. A backslash (\) may be used to escape the newline at the end of this line and continue on to another line.
−*v*	Sets the *verbose* shell variable so that command input is echoed after history substitution. Used to debug shell scripts.
−*x*	Sets the *echo* shell variable so that commands are echoed before execution and after history and variable substitution. Used to debug shell scripts.
−*V*	Sets the *verbose* shell variable before executing the ~/.tcshrc file.
−*X*	Sets the *echo* shell variable before executing the ~/.tcshrc file.

* Adapted from the *tcsh* manual pages.

TC SHELL LAB EXERCISES

Lab 57: Getting Started

1. What does the *init* process do?
2. What is the function of the *login* process?
3. How do you know what shell you are using?
4. How can you change your login shell?
5. Explain the difference between the *.tcshrc*, *.cshrc*, and *.login* files. Which one is executed first?

6. Edit your *.tcshrc* file as follows:

   a. Create three of your own aliases.

   b. Reset your prompt with the host machine name, time, and username.

   c. Set the following variables and put a comment after each variable explaining what it does.

7. Type the following:

   ```
   source .tcshrc
   ```

   What does the *source* command do?

8. Edit your *.login* file as follows:

   a. Welcome the user.

   b. Add your home directory to the path if it is not there.

   c. Source the *.login* file.

9. What is the difference between *path* and *PATH*?

Lab 58: History

1. In what file are history events stored when you log out? What variable controls the number of history events to be displayed? What is the purpose of the *savehist* variable?

2. Print your history list in reverse.

3. Print your history list without line numbers.

4. Type the following commands:

   a. *ls −a*

   b. *date '+%T'*

   c. *cal 2000*

   d. *cat /etc/passwd*

   e. *cd*

5. Type *history.* What is the output?

   a. How do you reexecute the last command?

   b. Now type *echo a b c.*

   Use the *history* command to reexecute the *echo* command with only its last argument, *c.*

6. Use history to print and execute the last command in your history list that started with the letter *d.*

7. Execute the last command that started with *c.*

8. Execute the *echo* command and the last argument from the previous command.

9. Use the history substitution command to replace the *T* in the *date* command with an *H.*

10. How do you use the *bindkey* command to start the *vi* editor for command line editing?

11. How do you list the editor commands and what they do?

12. How do you see how the editing keys are actually bound?

13. Describe what the *fignore* variable does.

Lab 59: Shell Metacharacters

1. Type at the prompt:

```
touch ab abc a1 a2 a3 all a12 ba ba.1 ba.2 filex filey AbC ABC
ABc2 abc
```

2. Write and test the command that will do the following:
   a. List all files starting with *a*.
   b. List all files ending in at least one digit.
   c. List all files not starting with an *a* or *A*.
   d. List all files ending in a period, followed by a digit.
   e. List all files containing just two letters.
   f. List three-character files where all letters are uppercase.
   g. List files ending in *11* or *12*.
   h. List files ending in *x* or *y*.
   i. List all files ending in a digit, an uppercase letter, or a lowercase letter.
   j. List all files containing a *b*.
   k. Remove two-character files starting with *a*.

Lab 60: Redirection

1. What are the names of the three file streams associated with your terminal?
2. What is a file descriptor?
3. What command would you use to do the following:
   a. Redirect the output of the *ls* command to a file called *lsfile*?
   b. Redirect and append the output of the *date* command to *lsfile*?
   c. Redirect the output of the *who* command to *lsfile*? What happened?
4. What happens when you type *cp* all by itself?
   a. How do you save the error message from the above example to a file?
5. Use the *find* command to find all files, starting from the parent directory, and of type *directory*. Save the standard output in a file called *found* and any errors in a file called *found.errs*.
6. What is *noclobber*? How do you override it?
7. Take the output of three commands and redirect the output to a file called *gottemall*.
8. Use a pipe(s) with the *ps* and *wc* commands to find out how many processes you are currently running.

Lab 61: Variables and Arrays

1. What is the difference between a local variable and an environment variable?
2. How do you list all local variables? Environmental variables?

3. In what initialization file would you store local variables? Why?

4. Create an array called *fruit*. Put five kinds of fruit in the array.

    a. Print the array.

    b. Print the last element of the array.

    c. Print the number of elements in the array.

    d. Remove the first element from the array.

    e. If you store an item that isn't fruit in the array, is it OK?

5. Describe the difference between a wordlist and a string.

appendix

A

Useful UNIX Utilities
for Shell Programmers

at—at, batch—execute commands at a later time

at [−csm] [−f script] [−qqueue] time [date] [+ increment]
at −l [job...]
at −r job...
batch

at and *batch* read commands from standard input to be executed at a later time. *at* allows you to specify when the commands should be executed, while jobs queued with *batch* will execute when system load level permits. Executes commands read from *stdin* or a file at some later time. Unless redirected, the output is mailed to the user.

EXAMPLE A.1

```
1    at 6:30am Dec 12 < program
2    at noon tomorrow < program
3    at 1945 pm August 9 < program
4    at now + 3 hours < program
5    at 8:30am Jan 4 < program
6    at -r 83883555320.a
```

EXPLANATION

1   At 6:30 in the morning on December 12th, start the job.

2   At noon tomorrow start the job.

3   At 7:45 in the evening on August 9th, start the job.

4   In three hours start the job.

5   At 8:30 in the morning of January 4th, start the job.

6   Removes previously scheduled job *83883555320.a.*

awk—pattern scanning and processing language

awk [–fprogram–file] [–Fc] [prog] [parameters]
[filename...]

awk scans each input filename for lines that match any of a set of patterns specified in *prog*.

EXAMPLE A.2

```
1   awk '{print $1, $2}' file
2   awk '/John/{print $3, $4}' file
3   awk -F: '{print $3}' /etc/passwd
4   date | awk '{print $6}'
```

EXPLANATION

1   Prints the first two fields of *file* where fields are separated by whitespace.
2   Prints fields 3 and 4 if the pattern *John* is found.
3   Using a colon as the field separator, prints the third field of the */etc/passwd* file.
4   Sends the output of the *date* command to *awk* and prints the sixth field.

banner—make posters

banner prints its arguments (each up to 10 characters long) in large letters on the standard output.

EXAMPLE A.3

```
banner Happy Birthday
```

EXPLANATION

Displays in banner format the string *Happy Birthday*.

basename—with a directory name delivers portions of the pathname

basename string [suffix]
dirname string

basename deletes any prefix ending in / (forward slash) and the suffix (if present in string) from string, and prints the result on the standard output.

EXAMPLE A.4

```
1   basename /usr/local/bin
2   scriptname="`basename $0`"
```

EXPLANATION

1   Strips off the prefix */usr/local/* and displays *bin*.

2   Assigns just the name of the script, $0, to the variable *scriptname*.

bc—processes precision arithmetic

> bc [–c] [–l] [filename...]

bc is an interactive processor for a language that resembles C but provides unlimited precision arithmetic. It takes input from any files given, then reads the standard input.

EXAMPLE A.5

```
1   bc << EOF
    scale=3
    4.5 + 5.6 / 3
    EOF
    Output : 6.366
    ------------------------------
2   bc
    ibase=2
    5
    101 (Output)
    20
    10100 (Output
    ^D
```

EXPLANATION

1   This is a *here document*. From the first EOF to the last EOF input is given to the *bc* command. The scale specifies the number of digits to the right of the decimal point. The result of the calculation is displayed on the screen.

2   The number base is two. The number is converted to binary (AT&T only).

bdiff—compares two big files

bdiff compares two files that are too large for *diff*.

cal—displays a calendar

> cal [[month] year]

cal prints a calendar for the specified year. If a month is also specified, a calendar just for that month is printed. If neither is specified, a calendar for the present month is printed.

EXAMPLE A.6

```
1   cal 1997
2   cal 5 1978
```

EXPLANATION

1   Prints the calendar year 1997.
2   Prints the month of May for 1978.

cat—concatenates and displays files

cat [–bnsuvet] filename...

cat reads each filename in sequence and writes it on the standard output. If no input file is given, or if the argument – is encountered, *cat* reads from the standard input file.

EXAMPLE A.7

```
1   cat /etc/passwd
2   cat -n file1 file2 >> file3
```

EXPLANATION

1   Displays the contents of the */etc/passwd* file.
2   Concatenates *file1* and *file2* and appends output to *file3*. The *–n* switch causes each line to be numbered.

chmod—change the permissions mode of a file

chmod [–fR] mode filename...
chmod [ugoa]{ + | – | = }[rwxlsStTugo] filename...

chmod changes or assigns the mode of a file. The mode of a file specifies its permissions and other attributes. The mode may be absolute or symbolic.

EXAMPLE A.8

```
1   chmod +x script.file
2   chmod u+x,g-x file
3   chmod 755 *
```

EXPLANATION

1   Turns on execute permission for user, group, and others on *script.file*.
2   Turns on execute permission for user, and removes it from group on *file*.

EXPLANATION (CONTINUED)

3   Turns on read, write, and execute for the user, read and execute for the group, and read and execute for others on all files in the current working directory. The value is octal (111 101 101).

```
rwxxr-xr-x
```

chown—changes owner of file

chown [–fhR] owner filename ...

chown changes the owner of the files to owner. The owner may be either a decimal user ID or a login name found in */etc/passwd* file. Only the owner of a file (or the super-user) may change the owner of that file.

EXAMPLE   A.9

```
1    chown john filex
2    chown -R ellie ellie
```

EXPLANATION

1   Changes the user ID of *filex* to *john.*
2   Recursively changes the ownership to *ellie* for all files in *ellie* directory.

clear—clears the terminal screen

cmp—compares two files

cmp [–l] [–s] filename1 filename2

The two files are compared. *cmp* makes no comment if the files are the same; if they differ, it announces the byte and line numbers at which the first difference occurred.

EXAMPLE   A.10

```
cmp file.new file.old
```

EXPLANATION

If the files differ, the character number and the line number are displayed.

compress—compress, uncompress, zcat compress, uncompress files, or display expanded files

compress [–cfv] [–b bits] [filename...]
uncompress [–cv] [filename...]
zcat [filename...]

compress reduces the size of the named files using adaptive Lempel-Ziv coding. Whenever possible, each file is replaced by one with a .Z extension. The ownership modes, access time, and modification time will stay the same. If no files are specified, the standard input is compressed to the standard output.

EXAMPLE A.11

```
1   compress -v book
    book:Compression:35.07% -- replaced with book.Z
2   ls
    book.Z
```

EXPLANATION

1   Compresses the book into a file called *book.Z* and displays the percentage that the file was compressed and its new name.

cp—copies files

cp [–i] [–p] [–r] [filename ...] target

The *cp* command copies *filename* to another target, which is either a file or directory. The filename and target cannot have the same name. If the target is not a directory, only one file may be specified before it; if it is a directory, more than one file may be specified. If target does not exist, *cp* creates a file named *target*. If target exists and is not a directory, its contents are overwritten. If target is a directory, the file(s) are copied to that directory.

EXAMPLE A.12

```
1   cp file1 file2
2   cp chapter1 book
3   cp -r desktop /usr/bin/tester
```

EXPLANATION

1   Copies the contents of *file1* to *file2*.

2   Copies the contents of *chapter1* to the *book* directory. In the *book* directory, *chapter1* has its original name.

3   Recursively copies the entire *desktop* directory into */usr/bin/tester*.

cpio—copy file archives in and out

cpio –i [bBcdfkmrsStuvV6] [–C bufsize] [–E filename]
[–H header] [–I filename [–M message]] [–R id]
[pattern ...]
cpio –o [aABcLvV] [–C bufsize] [–H header]
[–O filename [–M message]]
cpio –p [adlLmuvV] [–R id] directory

Copies file archives according to the modifiers given, usually for backup to a tape or directory.

EXAMPLE A.13

```
find . -depth -print | cpio -pdmv /home/john/tmp
```

EXPLANATION

Starting at the current directory, *find* descends the directory hierarchy, printing each entries of the directory even if the directory does not have write permission, and sends the filenames to *cpio* to be copied into the *john/tmp* directory in the */home* partition.

cron—the clock daemon

cron executes commands at specified dates and times. Regularly scheduled jobs can be specified in the */etc/crontab* file. In order to use *cron*, one of the following must be true: (1) you are superuser, (2) you are regular user, but your user ID is listed in the */etc/cron.allow* file; (3) you are regular user, but your system contains a file */etc/cron.deny*, which is empty.

crypt—encodes or decodes a file

crypt [password]

crypt encrypts and decrypts the contents of a file. The password is a key that selects a type of transformation.

cut—removes selected fields or characters from each line of a file

cut –clist [filename ...]
cut –flist [–dc] [–s] [filename ...]

The *cut* command cuts out columns or characters from a line of a file; if no files are given, uses standard input. The *–d* option specifies the field delimiter. The default delimiter is a tab.

EXAMPLE A.14

```
1   cut -d: -f1,3 /etc/passwd
2   cut -d: -f1-5 /etc/passwd
3   cut -c1-3,8-12 /etc/passwd
4   date | cut -c1-3
```

EXPLANATION

1   Using the colon as a field delimiter, displays fields 1 and 3 of the */etc/passwd* file.

2   Using the colon as a field separator, displays fields 1 through 5 of the *etc/passwd* file.

EXPLANATION (CONTINUED)

3   Cuts and displays characters 1 through 3 and 8 through 12 of each line from the */etc/passwd* file.

4   Sends the output of the *date* command as input to *cut*. The first three characters are printed.

date—displays the date and time or sets the date

```
[ –u ] [ –a [ – ] sss.fff ] [ yymmddhhmm [ .ss ] ]
[+format ]
```

Without arguments, the *date* command displays the date and time. If the command line argument starts with a plus sign, the rest of the argument is used to format the output. If a percent sign is used, the next character is a formatting character to extract a particular part of the date, such as just the year or weekday. To set the date. the command line argument is expressed in digits representing the year, month, day, hours, and minutes.

EXAMPLE A.15

```
1    date +%T
2    date +20%y
3    date "+It is now %m/%d /%y"
```

EXPLANATION

1   Displays the time as *20:25:51*

2   Displays *2096*.

3   Displays *It is now 07/25/96*.

diff—compares two files for differences diff [–bitw] [–c | –Cn

Compares two files and displays the differences on a line-by-line basis. Also displays commands that you would use with the *ed* editor to make changes.

EXAMPLE A.16

```
diff file1 file2
1c1
< hello there
---
> Hello there.
2a3
> I'm fine.
```

EXPLANATION

Shows how each line of *file1* and *file2* differs. The first file is represented by the < symbol, and the second file by the > symbol. Each line is preceded by an *ed* command indicating the editing command that would be used to make the files the same.

du—summarizes disk usage

du [–arskod] [name ...]

The *du* command reports the number of 512-byte blocks contained in all files and (recursively) directories within each directory and file specified.

EXAMPLE A.17

```
1   du -s /desktop
2   du -a
```

EXPLANATION

1   Displays a summary of the block usage for all the files in */desktop* and its subdirectories.

2   Displays block usage for each file in this directory and subdirectories.

echo—echoes arguments

echo [argument] ...
echo [–n] [argument]

echo writes its arguments separated by blanks and terminated by a newline on the standard output.

System V echo options:
\b	backspace
\c	suppress newline
\f	form feed
\n	newline
\r	return
\t	tab
\v	vertical tab
\\	backslash
\0*n*	*n* is a 1, 2, or 3, octal value

egrep—searches a file for a pattern using full regular expressions

egrep [–bchilnsv] [–e special–expression][–f filename]
[strings] [filename ...]

egrep (expression grep) searches files for a pattern of characters and prints all lines that contain that pattern. *egrep* uses full regular expressions (expressions with string values that use the full set of alphanumeric and special characters) to match the patterns.

EXAMPLE A.18

```
1    egrep 'Tom|John' datafile
2    egrep '^ [A-Z]+' file
```

EXPLANATION

1   Display all lines in *datafile* containing the pattern either *Tom* or *John*.

2   Display al lines starting with one or more uppercase letters.

expr—evaluates arguments as an expression

> expr arguments

The arguments are taken as an expression. After evaluation, the result is written to the standard output. The terms of the expression must be separated by blanks. Characters special to the shell must be escaped. Used in Bourne shell scripts for performing simple arithmetic operations.

EXAMPLE A.19

```
1    expr 5 + 4
2    expr 5 \* 3
3    num=0
     num=`expr $num + 1`
```

EXPLANATION

1   Prints the sum of *5 + 4*

2   Prints of result of *5 * 3*. The asterisk is protected from shell expansion.

3   After assigning *0* to variable *num*, the expr command adds 1 to *num* and result is assigned to *num*.

fgrep—search a file for a character string

> fgrep [–bchilnsvx] [–e special string]
> [–f filename] [strings] [filename ...]

fgrep (fast grep) searches files for a character string and prints all lines that contain that string. *fgrep* is different from *grep* and *egrep* because it interprets regular expression metacharacters as literals.

EXAMPLE A.20

```
1    fgrep '***' *
2    fgrep '[ ] * ? $' filex
```

EXPLANATION

1   Displays any line containing three asterisks from each file in the present directory. All characters are treated as themselves; i.e., metacharacters are not special.

2   Displays any lines in *filex* containing the string enclosed in quotes.

file—determines the type of a file by looking at its contents

file [[–f ffile] [–cl] [–m mfile] filename...

file performs a series of tests on each filename in an attempt to determine what it contains. If the contents of the file appear to be ASCII text, *file* examines the first 512 bytes and tries to guess its language.

EXAMPLE A.21

```
1   file bin/ls
    /bin/ls:sparc pure dynamically linked executable
2   file go
    go:    executable shell script
3   file junk
    junk:   English text
```

EXPLANATION

1   *ls* is a binary file dynamically linked when executed.

2   *go* is an executable shell script.

3   *junk* is a file containing ASCII text.

find—finds files

find path–name–list expression

find recursively descends the directory hierarchy for each pathname in the pathname list (i.e., one or more pathnames) seeking files that match options. First argument is the path where the search starts. The rest of the arguments specify some criteria by which to find the files, such as name, size, owner, permissions, etc. Check the UNIX manual pages for different syntax.

EXAMPLE A.22

```
1   find . -name \*.c -print
2   find .. -type f -print
3   find . -type d -print
4   find / -size 0 - exec rm "{}" \;
5   find ~ -perm 644 -print
6   find . -type f -size +500c -atime +21 -ok rm -f "{}" \;
```

EXAMPLE A.22 (CONTINUED)

```
7   find . -name core -print 2> /dev/null (Bourne and Korn Shells)
    ( find . -name core -print > /dev/tty ) >& /dev/null ( C shell)
8   find / -user ellie xdev -print
9   find ~ -atime +31 -exec mv {} /old/{} \; -print
```

EXPLANATION

1   Starting at the present working directory (dot), finds all files ending in *.c* and prints the full pathname of the file.

2   Starting at the parent directory (dot dot), finds all files of type *file*; i.e., files that are not directories.

3   Starting at the present directory (dot), finds all directory files.

4   Starting at the root directory, finds all files of size zero and removes them. The {} are used as a place holder for the name of each file as it is found.

5   Starting at the user's home directory ~ (Korn and C shells), finds all files that have permissions 644 (read and write for the owner, and read permission for the group and others).

6   Starting at the present working directory, finds files that are over 500 bytes and have not been accessed in the last 21 days and asks if it is okay to remove them.

7   Starting at the present working directory, finds and displays all files named *core* and sends errors to */dev/null*, the UNIX bit bucket.

8   Prints all files on the *root* partition that belong to user *ellie*.

9   Moves files that are older than 31 days into a directory, */old*, and prints the files as it moves them.

finger—displays information about local and remote users

> finger [–bfhilmpqsw] [username...]
> finger [–l] username@hostname...

By default, the *finger* command displays information about each logged-in user, including login name, full name, terminal name (prepended with a * if write permission is denied), idle time, login time, and location if known.

fmt—simple text formatters

> fmt [–c] [–s] [–w width | –width] [inputfile...]

fmt is a simple text formatter that fills and joins lines to produce output lines of (up to) the number of characters specified in the –w width option. The default width is 72. *fmt* concatenates the input files listed as arguments. If none are given, *fmt* formats text from the standard input.

```
fmt -c -w45 letter
```

EXPLANATION

Formats *letter*. The *–c* switch preserves the indentation of the first two lines within the paragraph and aligns the left margin of each subsequent line with that of the second line. The *–w* switch fills the output line of up to 45 columns.

fold—folds long lines

fold [–w width | –width] [filename ...]

Fold the contents of the specified filenames, or the standard input if no files are specified, breaking the lines to have maximum width. The default for width is 80. Width should be a multiple of 8 if tabs are present, or the tabs should be expanded.

ftp—file transfer program

ftp [–dgintv] [hostname]

The *ftp* command is the user interface to the Internet standard File Transfer Protocol (FTP). *ftp* transfers files to and from a remote network site. The file transfer program is not limited to UNIX machines.

EXAMPLE A.24

```
1   ftp ftp.uu.net
2   ftp -n 127.150.28.56
```

EXPLANATION

1   *ftp* to the machine *ftp.uu.net*, a large repository run by the UUNET service that handles e-mail and net news for UNIX systems.

2   Opens a connection to the machine at 127.45.4.1 and does not attempt to auto-login.

getopt(s)—parses command line options

The *getopts* command supersedes *getopt*. *getopts* is used to break up options in command lines for easy parsing by shell procedures and to check for legal options.

grep—searches a file for a pattern

grep [–bchilnsvw] limited–regular–expression
  [filename ...]

grep searches files for a pattern and prints all lines that contain that pattern. Uses regular expressions metacharacters to match the patterns. *egrep* has an extended set of metacharacters.

EXAMPLE A.25

```
1   grep Tom file1 file2 file3
2   grep -in '^tom savage' *
```

EXPLANATION

1   *Grep* displays all lines in *file1*, *file2*, and *file3* that contain the pattern *Tom*.

2   *Grep* displays all lines with line numbers from the files in the current working directory that contain *tom savage* if *tom savage* is at the beginning of the line, ignoring case.

groups—prints group membership of user

groups [user...]

The command *groups* prints on standard output the groups to which you or the optionally specified user belong.

id—prints the username, user ID, group name and group ID

/usr/bin/id [–a]

id displays your user ID, username, group ID, and group name. If your real ID and your effective ID's do not match, both are printed.

jsh—the standard, job control shell

jsh [–acefhiknprstuvx] [argument...]

The command *jsh* is an interface to the standard Bourne shell which provides all of the functionality of the Bourne shell and enables job control.

line—reads one line

line copies one line (up to a newline) from the standard input and writes it on the standard output. It returns an exit code of one on EOF and always prints at least a newline. It is often used within shell files to read from the user's terminal.

logname—gets the name of the user running the process

lp—sends output to a printer (AT&T)

lp [–cmsw] [–ddest] [–number] [–ooption] [–ttitle] filename ...
cancel [ids] [printers]

lp, cancel sends or cancels requests to a lineprinter.

EXAMPLE A.26

```
1   lp -n5 filea fileb
2   lp -dShakespeare filex
```

EXPLANATION

1   Send five copies of *filea* and *fileb* to the printer.

2   Specify *Shakespeare* as the printer where *filex* will be printed.

lpr—sends output to a printer (UCB)

lpr [–Pprinter] [–#copies] [–Cclass] [–Jjob]
[–Ttitle] [–i [indent]] [–1234font] [–wcols]
[–r] [–m] [–h] [–s] [filter–option]
[filename ...]

lpr creates a printer job in a spooling area for subsequent printing as facilities become available. Each printer job consists of a control job and one or more data files.

EXAMPLE A.27

```
1   lpr -#5 filea fileb
2   lpr -PShakespeare filex
```

EXPLANATION

1   Send five copies of *filea* and *fileb* to the printer.

2   Specify Shakespeare as the printer where *filex* will be printed.

lpstat—print information about the status of the LP print service (AT&T)

lpq—print information about the status of the printer (UCB)

ls—lists contents of directory

ls [–abcCdfFgilLmnopqrRstux1] [names]

For each directory argument, *ls* lists the contents of the directory; for each file argument, *ls* repeats its name and any other information requested. The output is sorted alphabetically by default. When no argument is given, the current directory is listed.

EXAMPLE A.28

```
1   ls -alF
2   ls -d a*
3   ls -i
```

EXPLANATION

1   The *−a* lists invisible files (those files beginning with a dot), the *−l* is a long listing showing attributes of the file, the *−F* puts a slash at the end of directory filenames, a * at the end of executable scriptnames, and an @ symbol at the end of symbolically linked files.

2   If the argument to the *−d* switch is a directory, only the name of the directory is displayed, not its contents.

3   The *−i* switch causes each filename to be preceded by its inode number.

mail—mail, rmail—read mail or send mail to users

```
Sending mail
  mail [ –tw ] [ –m message_type ] recipient...
  rmail [ –tw ] [ –m message_type ] recipient...
Reading mail
  mail [ –ehpPqr ] [ –f filename ]
Forwarding mail
  mail –F recipient...
Debugging
  mail [ –x debug_level ] [ other_mail_options ] recipient...
  mail [ –T mailsurr_file ] recipient...
```

A recipient is usually a username recognized by *login*. When recipients are named, mail assumes a message is being sent. It reads from the standard input up to an end-of-file (Ctrl-D), or if reading from a terminal, until it reads a line consisting of just a period. When either of those indicators is received, *mail* adds the letter to the mailfile for each recipient.

mailx—interactive message processing system

```
mailx [ –deHiInNUvV ] [ –f [ filename|+folder ]]
  [ –T filename ] [ –u user ] [ recipient... ]
mailx [ –dFinUv ] [ –h number ] [ –r address ][ –s subject ] recipient...
```

The mail utilities listed above provide an interactive interface for sending, receiving, and manipulating mail messages. Basic Networking Utilities must be installed for some of the features to work. Incoming mail is stored in a file called *mailbox*, and after it is read, is sent to a file called *mbox*.

make—maintains, updates, and regenerates groups of related programs and files

```
make [ –f makefile ] ... [ –d ] [ –dd ] [ –D ]
[ –DD ] [ –e ] [ –i ] [ –k ] [ –n ] [ –p ] [ –P ]
[ –q ] [ –r ] [ –s ] [ –S ] [ –t ] [ target ... ]
[ macro=value ... ]
```

make updates files according to commands listed in a description file, and if the target file is newer than the dependency file of the same name, *make* will update the target file.

mesg—permits or denies messages resulting from the write command

mesg [–n] [–y]

mesg with argument –*n* forbids messages via *write* by revoking nonuser write permission on the user's terminal. *mesg* with argument –*y* reinstates permission. All by itself, *mesg* reports the current state without changing it.

mkdir—creates a directory

mkdir [–p] dirname ...

more—browse or page through a text file

more [–cdflrsuw] [–lines] [+linenumber] [+/pattern]
  [filename ...]
page [–cdflrsuw] [–lines] [+linenumber] [+/pattern]
  [filename ...]

more is a filter that displays the contents of a text file on the terminal, one screenful at a time. It normally pauses after each screenful, and prints —*More*— at the bottom of the screen.

mv—move or rename files

mv [–f] [–i] filename1 [filename2 ...] target

The *mv* command moves a source filename to a target filename. The filename and the target may not have the same name. If *target* is not a directory, only one file may be specified before it; if it is a directory, more than one file may be specified. If *target* does not exist, *mv* creates a file named *target*. If *target* exists and is not a directory, its contents are overwritten. If *target* is a directory the file(s) are moved to that directory.

EXAMPLE A.29

```
1   mv file1 newname
2   mv -i test1 test2 train
```

EXPLANATION

1   Renames *file1* to *newname*. If *newname* exists its contents are overwritten.
2   Moves files *test1* and *test2* to the *train* directory. The –*i* switch is for interactive mode, meaning it asks before moving the files.

nawk—pattern scanning and processing language

nawk [–F re] [–v var=value] ['prog'] [filename ...]
nawk [–F re] [–v var=value] [–f progfile][filename ...]

nawk scans each input filename for lines that match any of a set of patterns. The command string must be enclosed in single quotes (') to protect it from the shell. *Awk* programs consist of a set of pattern/action statements used to filter specific information from a file, pipe, or *stdin*.

newgrp—log in to a new group

newgrp [–] [group]

newgrp logs a user into a new group by changing a user's real and effective group ID. The user remains logged in and the current directory is unchanged. The execution of *newgrp* always replaces the current shell with a new shell, even if the command terminates with an error (unknown group).

news—prints news items

news [–a] [–n] [–s] [items]

news is used to keep the user informed of current events. By convention, these events are described by files in the directory */var/news*. When invoked without arguments, *news* prints the contents of all current files in */var/news*, most recent first, with each preceded by an appropriate header.

nice—runs a command at low priority

nice [–increment] command [arguments]

/usr/bin/nice executes a command with a lower CPU scheduling priority. The invoking process (generally the user's shell) must be in the time-sharing scheduling class. The command is executed in the time-sharing class. An increment of 10 is the default. The increment value must be in a range between 1 and 19, unless you are the superuser. Also a *csh* built-in.

nohup—makes commands immune to hangups and quits

/usr/bin/nohup command [arguments]

There are three distinct versions of *nohup*. *nohup* is built in to the C shell and is an executable program available in */usr/bin/nohup* when using the Bourne shell. The Bourne shell version of *nohup* executes commands such that they are immune to *HUP* (hangup) and *TERM* (terminate) signals. If the standard output is a terminal, it is redirected to the file *nohup.out*. The standard error is redirected to follow the standard output. The priority is incremented by five. *nohup* should be invoked from the shell with & in order to prevent it from responding to interrupts or input from the next user.

EXAMPLE A.30

```
nohup lookup &
```

EXPLANATION

The *lookup* program will run in the background and continue to run until it has completed, even if a the user logs off. Any output generated goes to a file in the current directory called *nohup.out*.

---

od—octal dump

od [–bcCDdFfOoSsvXx] [filename] [[+] offset [.] [b]]

od displays filename in one or more formats, as selected by the first argument. If the first argument is missing, –*o* is default; e.g., the file can be displayed in bytes octal, ASCII, decimal, hex, etc.

pack—pack, pcat, unpack—compresses and expands files

pack [–] [–f] name ...
pcat name ...
unpack name ...

pack compresses files. Wherever possible (and useful), each input file *name* is replaced by a packed file *name.z* with the same access modes, access and modified dates, and owner as those of *name*. Typically, text files are reduced to 60–75% of their original size. *pcat* does for packed files what *cat* does for ordinary files, except that *pcat* cannot be used as a filter. The specified files are unpacked and written to the standard output. Thus, to view a packed file named *name.z*, use *pcat name.z* or just *pcat name. Unpack* expands files created by *pack*.

passwd—changes the login password and password attributes

passwd [name]
passwd [–d | –l] [–f] [–n min] [–w warn][–x max] name
passwd –s [–a]
passwd –s [name]

The *passwd* command changes the password or lists password attributes associated with the user's login name. Additionally, privileged users may use *passwd* to install or change passwords and attributes associated with any login name.

paste—merges same lines of several files or subsequent lines of one file

paste filename1 filename2...
paste –d list filename1 filename2...
paste –s [–d list] filename1 filename2...

paste concatenates corresponding lines of the given input files *filename1*, *filename2*, etc. It treats each file as a column or columns of a table and pastes them together horizontally (see *cut*).

EXAMPLE A.31

```
1   ls | paste - - -
2   paste -s -d"\t\n" testfile1 testfile2
3   paste file1 file2
```

EXPLANATION

1   Files are listed in three columns and glued together with a Tab.

2   Combines a pair of lines into a single line using a Tab and newline as the delimiter, i.e., the first pair of lines are glued with a Tab; the next pair are glued by a newline, the next pair by a Tab, etc. The *–s* switch causes subsequent lines from *testfile1* to be pasted first and then subsequent lines from *testfile2*.

3   A line from *file1* is pasted to a line from *file2*, glued together by a Tab so that the file lines appear as two columns.

pcat—(see *pack*)

pg—displays files a page at a time

pg [–number] [–p string] [–cefnrs] [+linenumber]
  [+/pattern/] [filename ...]

The *pg* command is a filter that allows you to page through filenames one screenful at a time on a terminal. If no filename is specified or if it encounters the file name –, *pg* reads from standard input. Each screenful is followed by a prompt. If the user types a Return, another page is displayed. It allows you to back up and review something that has already passed. (See *more*.)

pr—prints files

pr [[–columns] [–wwidth] [–a]] [–eck] [–ick] [–drtfp]
  [+page] [–nck] [–ooffset] [–llength] [–sseparator]
  [–   hheader] [–F] [filename ...]
pr [[–m] [–wwidth]] [–eck] [–ick] [–drtfp] [+page] [–nck]
  [–ooffset] [–llength] [–sseparator] [–hheader] [–F]
  [filename1 filename2 ...]

The *pr* command formats and prints the contents of a file according to different format options. By default, the listing is sent to *stdout* and is separated into pages, each headed by the page number, the date and time that the file was last modified, and the name of the file. If no options are specified, the default file format is 66 lines with a five-line header and five-line trailer.

EXAMPLE A.32

```
pr -2dh "TITLE" file1 file2
```

EXPLANATION

Prints two columns double sided with header "TITLE" for *file1* and *file2*.

ps—reports process status

> ps [–acdefjl] [–g grplist] [–p proclist]
>   [–s sidlist] [–t term] [–u uidlist]

ps prints information about active processes. Without options, *ps* prints information about processes associated with the controlling terminal. The output contains only the process ID, terminal identifier, cumulative execution time, and the command name. Otherwise, the information that is displayed is controlled by the options. The *ps* options are not the same for AT&T and Berkeley type versions of UNIX.

EXAMPLE A.33

```
1   ps -aux | grep '^linda'        # ucb
2   ps -ef | grep '^ *linda'       # at&t
```

EXPLANATION

1   Prints all processes running and pipes the output to the *grep* program, and print-
    ing only those processes owned by user *linda*, where *linda* is at the beginning of
    each line. (UCB version).

2   Same as the first example, only the AT&T version.

pwd—displays the present working directory name

rcp—remote file copy

> rcp [–p] filename1 filename2
> rcp [–pr] filename...directory

The *rcp* command copies files between machines in the following form:

> remothostname:path
> user@hostname:file
> user@hostname.domainname:file

EXAMPLE A.34

```
1   rcp dolphin:filename /tmp/newfilename
2   rcp filename broncos:newfilename
```

    1   Copy *filename* from remote machine *dolphin* to */tmp/newfilename* on this machine.

    2   Copy *filename* from this machine to remote machine *broncos* and name it *newfilename*.

rlogin—remote login

    rlogin [–L] [–8] [–ec] [–l username] hostname

rlogin establishes a remote login session from your terminal to the remote machine named *hostname*. Hostnames are listed in the host's database, which may be contained in the */etc/hosts* file, the Network Information Service (NIS) hosts map, the Internet domain name server, or a combination of these. Each host has one official name (the first name in the database entry), and optionally one or more nicknames. Either official hostnames or nicknames may be specified in *hostname*. A list of trusted hostnames can be stored in the machine's file */etc/hosts.equiv*.

rm—removes files from directories

    rm [–f] [–i] filename...
    rm –r [–f] [–i] dirname...[filename...]

rm removes the entries for one or more files from a directory if the file has write permission. If filename is a symbolic link, the link will be removed, but the file or directory to which it refers will not be deleted. A user does not need write permission on a symbolic link to remove it, provided they have write permissions in the directory.

```
1   rm file1 file2
2   rm -i *
3   rm -rf dir
```

    1   Removes *file1* and *file2* from the directory.

    2   Removes all files in the present working directory, but asks first if it is okay.

    3   Recursively removes all files and directories below *dir* and ignores error messages.

rmdir—removes a directory

    rmdir [–p] [–s] dirname...

Removes a directory if it is empty. With *–p*, parent directories are also removed.

rsh—starts a remote shell

rsh [–n] [–l username] hostname command
rsh hostname [–n] [–l username] command

rsh connects to the specified hostname and executes the specified command. *rsh* copies its standard input to the remote command, the standard output of the remote command to its standard output, and the standard error of the remote command to its standard error. Interrupt, quit, and terminate signals are propagated to the remote command; *rsh* normally terminates when the remote command does. If a command is not given, then *rsh* logs you on to the remote host using *rlogin*.

EXAMPLE A.36

```
1   rsh bluebird ps -ef
2   rsh -l john owl ls; echo $PATH;cat .profile
```

EXPLANATION

1   Connect to machine *bluebird* and display all processes running on that machine.

2   Go to the remote machine *owl* as user *john* and execute all three commands.

ruptime—shows the host status of local machines

ruptime [–alrtu]

ruptime gives a status line like *uptime* for each machine on the local network; these are formed from packets broadcast by each host on the network once a minute. Machines for which no status report has been received for five minutes are shown as being down. Normally, the listing is sorted by host name, but this order can be changed by specifying one of *ruptime*'s options.

rwho—who is logged in on local machines

rwho [–a]

The *rwho* command produces output similar to *who*, but for all machines on your network. However, it does not work through gateways and host must have the directory */var/spool/rwho* as well as the *rwho* daemon running. If no report has been received from a machine for five minutes, *rwho* assumes the machine is down, and does not report users last known to be logged into that machine. If a user has not typed to the system for a minute or more, *rwho* reports this idle time. If a user has not typed to the system for an hour or more, the user is omitted from the output of *rwho*, unless the *–a* flag is given.

script—creates a typescript of a terminal session

script [–a] [filename]

script makes a typescript of everything printed on your terminal. The typescript is written to a filename. If no filename is given, the typescript is saved in the file called *typescript*. The script ends when the shell exits or when Ctrl-D is typed.

EXAMPLE A.37

```
1   script
2   script myfile
```

EXPLANATION

1   Starts up a script session in a new shell. Everything displayed on the terminal is stored in a file called *typescript*. Must press ^d or exit to end the session.

2   Starts up a script session in a new shell, storing everything displayed on the terminal in *myfile*. Must press ^d or exit to end the session.

sed—streamlined editor

sed [–n] [–e script] [–f sfilename] [filename ...]

sed copies the named *filename* (standard input default) to the standard output, edited according to a script of command. Does not change the original file.

EXAMPLE A.38

```
1   sed 's/Elizabeth/Lizzy/g' file
2   sed '/Dork/d' file
3   sed -n '15,20p' file
```

EXPLANATION

1   Substitute all occurrences of *Elizabeth* with *Lizzy* in file and display on the terminal screen.

2   Remove all lines containing *Dork* and print the remaining lines on the screen.

3   Print only lines 15 through 20.

size—prints section sizes in bytes of object files

size [–f] [–F] [–n] [–o] [–V] [–x] filename...

The *size* command produces segment or section size information in bytes for each loaded section in *ELF* or *COFF* object files. *size* prints out the size of the text, data, and *bss* (uninitialized data) segments (or sections) and their total.

sleep—suspends execution for some number of seconds

sleep time

sleep suspends execution for time seconds. It is used to execute a command after a certain amount of time.

EXAMPLE A.39

```
1    (sleep 105; command)&
2    (In Script)
     while true
     do
         command
         sleep 60
     done
```

EXPLANATION

1   After 105 seconds, command is executed. Prompt returns immediately.

2   Enters loop; executes command and sleeps for a minute before entering the loop again.

sort—sort and/or merge files

sort [–cmu] [–ooutput] [–T directory] [–ykmem]
    [–dfiMnr] [–btx] [+pos1 [–pos2]] [filename...]

The *sort* command sorts (ASCII) lines of all the named files together and writes the result on the standard output. Comparisons are based on one or more sort keys extracted from each line of input. By default, there is one sort key, the entire input line, and ordering is lexicographic by bytes in machine collating sequence.

EXAMPLE A.40

```
1    sort filename
2    sort -u filename
3    sort -r filename
4    sort +1 -2 filename
5    sort -2n filename
6    sort -t: +2n -3 filename
7    sort -f filename
8    sort -b +1 filename
```

EXPLANATION

1   Sorts the lines alphabetically.

2   Sorts out duplicate entries.

3   Sorts in reverse.

4   Sorts starting on field 1 (fields are separated by whitespace and start at field 0), stopping at field 2 rather than sorting to the end of the line.

5   Sorts the third field numerically.

EXPLANATION (CONTINUED)

6   Sorts numercially starting at field 2 and stopping at field 3, with the colon designated as the field separator (−t:).

7   Sorts folding in upper and lowercase letters.

8   Sorts starting at field 1, removing leading blanks.

spell—finds spelling errors

spell [−blvx] [−d hlist] [−s hstop] [+local_file] [filename]...

spell collects words from the named filenames and looks them up in a spelling list. Words that neither occur among nor are derivable from (by applying certain inflections, prefixes, and/or suffixes) words in the spelling list are printed on the standard output. If no filenames are named, words are collected from the standard input.

split—splits a file into pieces

split [−n] [filename [name]]

split reads *filename* and writes it in *n* line pieces into a set of output files. The first output file is named with *aa* appended, and so on lexicographically, up to *zz* (a maximum of 676 files). The maximum length of *name* is 2 characters less than the maximum filename length allowed by the filesystem. See *statvfs*. If no output name is given, *x* is used as the default (output files will be called *xaa*, *xab*, and so forth).

EXAMPLE A.41

```
1   split -500 filea
2   split -1000 fileb out
```

EXPLANATION

1   Splits *filea* into 500 line files. Files are named *xaa*, *xab*, *xac*, etc.

2   Splits *fileb* into 1000 line files named *out.aa*, *out.ab*, etc.

strings—finds any printable strings in an object or binary file

strings [−a] [−o] [−number] [filename...]

The *strings* command looks for ASCII strings in a binary file. A string is any sequence of four or more printing characters ending with a newline or a null character. *strings* is useful for identifying random object files and many other things.

EXAMPLE A.42

```
strings /bin/nawk | head -2
```

EXPLANATION

Prints any ASCII text in the first two lines of the binary executable */bin/nawk*.

stty—sets the options for a terminal

stty [–a] [–g] [modes]

stty sets certain terminal I/O options for the device that is the current standard input; without arguments, it reports the settings of certain options.

EXAMPLE A.43

```
1   stty erase <Press backspace key> or ^h
2   stty -echo; read secretword; stty echo
3   stty -a (AT&T) or stty -everything (BSD)
```

EXPLANATION

1   Sets the backspace key to erase.

2   Turns off echoing; waits for user input; turns echoing back on.

3   Lists all possible options to *stty*.

su—become superuser or another user

su [–] [username [arg ...]]

su allows one to become another user without logging off. The default username is *root* (superuser). To use *su*, the appropriate password must be supplied (unless the invoker is already root). If the password is correct, *su* creates a new shell process that has the real and effective user ID, group IDs, and supplementary group list set to those of the specified username. The new shell will be the shell specified in the shell field of username's password file entry. If no shell is specified, *sh* (Bourne shell) is used. To return to normal user ID privileges, type Ctrl-D to exit the new shell. The – option specifies a complete login.

sum—calculates a checksum for a file

sync—updates the superblock and sends changed blocks to disk

tabs—set tab stops on a terminal

tail—displays the tail end of a file.

tail +[–number [lbc] [f] [filename]
tail +[–number [l] [rf] [filename]

When a plus sign precedes the number, *tail* displays blocks, characters, or lines counting from the beginning of the file. If a hyphen precedes the number, *tail* counts from the end of the file.

EXAMPLE A.44

```
1   tail +50 filex
2   tail -20 filex
3   tail filex
```

EXPLANATION

1   Displays contents of *filex* starting at line 50.
2   Displays the last 20 lines of *filex*.
3   Displays the last 10 lines of *filex*.

talk—allows you to talk to another user

talk username [ttyname]

talk is a visual communications program that copies lines from your terminal to that of another user.

EXAMPLE A.45

```
talk joe@cowboys
```

EXPLANATION

Opens a request to talk to user *joe* on a machine called *cowboys*.

tar—stores and retrieves files from an archive file, normally a tape device

tar [−] c|r|t|u|x [bBefFhilmopvwX0134778] [tarfile]
[blocksize] [exclude–file] [–I include–file]
filename1 filename2 … –C directory filenameN …

EXAMPLE A.46

```
1   tar cvf /dev/diskette
2   tar tvf /dev/fd0
3   tar xvf /dev/fd0
```

EXPLANATION

1   Sends all files under the present working directory to tape at device */dev/diskette*, and prints the files that are being sent.
2   Displays the table of contents of what is on tape device */dev/fd0*.
3   Extracts all files from tape and prints which files were extracted.

tee—replicates the standard output

> tee [–ai] [filename]

tee copies the standard input to the standard output and one or more files, as in *ls|tee outfile*. Output goes to screen and to *outfile*.

EXAMPLE A.47

```
date | tee nowfile
```

EXPLANATION

The output of the *date* command is displayed on the screen and also stored in *nowfile*.

telnet— communicates with a remote host

EXAMPLE A.48

```
telnet necom.com
```

EXPLANATION

Opens a session with the remote host *necom.com*

test—evaluates an expression

test evaluates an expression and returns an exit status indicating that the expression is either true (zero) or false (not zero). Used primarily by Bourne and Korn shell for string, numeric, and file testing. The C shell has most of the tests built-in.

EXAMPLE A.49

```
1   test 5 gt 6
2   echo $? ( Bourne and Korn Shells)
    (Output is 1, meaning the result of the test is not true.)
```

EXPLANATION

1   The *test* command performs an integer test to see if 5 is greater than 6.

2   The $? variable contains the exit status of the last command. If a nonzero status is reported, the test results are not true; if the return status is zero, the the test result is true.

time—displays a summary of time used by this shell and its children

timex—times a command; reports process data and system activity

> timex [–o] [–p [–fhkmrt]] [–s] command

The given command is executed; the elapsed time, user time, and system time spent in execution are reported in seconds. Optionally, process accounting data for the command and all its children can be listed or summarized, and total system activity during the execution interval can be reported. The output of *timex* is written on standard error.

touch—updates access time and/or modification time of a file

> touch [–amc] [mmddhhmm [yy]] filename...

touch causes the access and modification times of each argument to be updated. The filename is created if it does not exist. If no time is specified the current time is used.

EXAMPLE A.50

```
touch a b c
```

EXPLANATION

Three files, *a*, *b*, and *c* are created. If any of them already exist, the modification timestamp on the files is updated.

tput—initializes a terminal or queries the *terminfo* database

> tput [–Ttype] capname [parms...]
> tput [–Ttype] init
> tput [–Ttype] reset
> tput [–Ttype] longname
> tput –S <<

tput uses the *terminfo* database to make the values of terminal-dependent capabilities and information available to the shell (see *sh*), to initialize or reset the terminal, or return the long name of the requested terminal type.

EXAMPLE A.51

```
1   tput longname
2   bold='tput smso'
    unbold='tput rmso'
    echo "${bold}Enter your id: ${offbold}\c"
```

EXPLANATION

1   Displays a long name for the terminal from the *terminfo* database.
2   Sets the shell variable *bold* to turn on the highlighting of displayed text. Then sets the shell variable *unbold* to return to normal text display. The line *Enter your id:* is highlighted in black with white letters. Further text is displayed normally.

tr—translates characters

tr [−cds] [string1 [string2]]

tr copies the standard input to the standard output with substitution or deletion of selected characters. Input characters found in *string1* are mapped into the corresponding characters of *string2*. The forward slash can be used with an octal digit to represent the ASCII code. When *string2* (with any repetitions of characters) contains fewer characters than *string1*, characters in *string1* with no corresponding character in *string2* are not translated. Octal values for characters may be used when preceded with a backslash:

\11	Tab
\12	Newline
\042	Single quote
\047	Double quote

EXAMPLE A.52

```
1   tr 'A' 'B' < filex
2   tr '[A-Z]' [a-z]' < filex
3   tr -d ' ' < filex
4   tr c '\11' '\11' < filex
5   tr -s ':' ' ' < filex
6   tr '\047' '\042'
```

EXPLANATION

1   Translates *As* to *Bs* in *filex*.

2   Translates all uppercase letters to lowercase letters.

3   Deletes all spaces from *filex*.

4   Replaces (squeezes) multiple tabs with single tabs in *filex*.

5   Squeezes multiple colons into single spaces in *filex*.

6   Translates double quotes to single quotes in text coming from standard input.

true—provide successful exit status

true does nothing, successfully, meaning that it always returns a zero exit status, indicating success. Used in Bourne and Korn shell programs as a command to start an infinite loop.

```
while true
do
  command
done
```

tsort —topological sort

/usr/ccs/bin/tsort [filename]

The *tsort* command produces, on the standard output, an ordered list of items consistent with a partial ordering of items mentioned in the input filename. If no filename is specified, the standard input is understood. The input consists of pairs of items (nonempty strings) separated by blanks. Pairs of different items indicate ordering. Pairs of identical items indicate presence, but not ordering.

tty—gets the name of the terminal

tty [–l] [–s]

tty prints the path name of the user's terminal.

umask—sets file-creation mode mask for permissions

umask [ooo]

The user file-creation mode mask is set to *000*. The three octal digits refer to read/write/execute permissions for owner, group, and other, respectively. The value of each specified digit is subtracted from the corresponding "digit" specified by the system for the creation of a file. For example, *umask 022* removes write permission for group and other (files normally created with mode 777 become mode 755; files created with mode 666 become mode 644). If *000* is omitted, the current value of the mask is printed. *umask* is recognized and executed by the shell.

EXAMPLE A.53

```
1   umask
2   umask 027
```

EXPLANATION

1   Displays the current file permission mask.
2   The directory permissions, 777, minus the *umask* 027 is 750. The file permissions, 666, minus the *umask* 027 is 640. When created, directories and files will be assigned the permissions created by *umask*.

---

uname—prints name of current machine

uname [–amnprsv]
uname [–S system_name]

uname prints information about the current system on the standard output. If no options are specified, *uname* prints the current operating system's name. The options print selected information returned by *uname* and/or *sysinfo*.

EXAMPLE A.54

```
1   uname -n
2   uname -a
```

EXPLANATION

1   Prints the name of the host machine.
2   Prints the machine hardware name, network nodename, operating system release number, the operating system name, and the operating system version—same as *–m, –n, –r, –s,* and *–v.*

uncompress—restores files to their original state after they have been compressed using the compress command

uncompress [–cFv] [file . . .]

EXAMPLE A.55

```
uncompress file.Z
```

EXPLANATION

Restore *file.Z* back to its original state; i.e., what it was before being compressed.

uniq—reports on duplicate lines in a file

uniq [[–u] [–d] [–c] [+n] [–n]] [input [output]]

uniq reads the input file, comparing adjacent lines. In the normal case, the second and succeeding copies of repeated lines are removed; the remainder is written on the output file. Input and output should always be different.

EXAMPLE A.56

```
1   uniq file1 file2
2   uniq -d -2 file3
```

EXPLANATION

1   Removes duplicate adjacent lines from *file1* and puts output in *file2*.
2   Displays the duplicate lines where the duplicate starts at third field.

units—converts quantities expressed in standard scales to other scales

units converts quantities expressed in various standard scales to their equivalents in other scales. It works interactively in this fashion:

```
You have: inch
You want: cm
    * 2.540000e+00
    / 3.937008e–01
```

unpack—expands files created by *pack*

unpack expands files created by *pack*. For each filename specified in the command, a search is made for a file called *name.z* (or just *name*, if *name* ends in *.z*). If this file appears to be a packed file, it is replaced by its expanded version. The new file has the *.z* suffix stripped from its name, and has the same access modes, access and modification dates, and owner as those of the packed file.

uucp—copy files to another system, UNIX-to-UNIX system copy

```
uucp [ –c | –C ] [ –d | –f ] [ –ggrade ] [ –j ] [ –m ] [ –nuser ] [ –r ] [ –sfile ] [ –
xdebug_level ]
    source–file destination–file
```

uucp copies files named by the source-file arguments to the destination-file argument.

uuencode—uuencode, uudecode—encode a binary file into ASCII text in order to send it through e-mail, or convert it back into its original form

```
uuencode [ source–file ] file–label
uudecode [ encoded–file ]
```

uuencode converts a binary file into an ASCII-encoded representation that can be sent using mail. The label argument specifies the output filename to use when decoding. If no file is given, *stdin* is encoded. *uudecode* reads an encoded file, strips off any leading and trailing lines added by mailer programs, and recreates the original binary data with the filename and the mode and owner specified in the header. The encoded file is an ordinary ASCII text file; it can be edited by any text editor. But it is best only to change the mode or file-label in the header to avoid corrupting the decoded binary.

EXAMPLE A.57

```
1    uuencode mybinfile decodedname > uumybinfile.tosend
2    uudecode uumybinfile.tosend
```

EXPLANATION

1   The first argument, *mybinfile,* is the existing file to be encoded. The second argument is the name to be used for the *uudecoded* file, after mailing the file, and *uumybinfile.tosend* is the file that is sent through the mail.

2   This decodes the *uuencoded* file and creates a filename as given as the second argument to *uuencode.*

wc—counts lines, words, and characters

> wc [–lwc] [filename ...]

wc counts lines, words, and characters in a file or in the standard input if no filename is given. A word is a string of characters delimited by a space, tab, or newline.

EXAMPLE A.58

```
1   wc filex
2   who | wc -l
3   wc -l filex
```

EXPLANATION

1 Prints the number of lines, words, and characters in *filex*.
2 The output of the *who* command is piped to *wc*, displaying the number of lines counted.
3 Prints the number of lines in *filex*.

---

what—extracts SCCS version information from a file by printing information found after the @(#) pattern

> what [–s] filename

what searches each filename for the occurrence of the pattern @(#), which the SCCS *get* command substitutes for the %Z% keyword, and prints what follows up to a " >, newline, \, or null character.

which—locates a command and displays its pathname or alias (UCB)

> which [filename]

which takes a list of names and looks for the files that would be executed had the names been given as commands. Each argument is expanded if it is aliased, and searched for along the user's path. Both aliases and path are taken from the user's *.cshrc* file. Only .cshrc file is used.

whereis—locates the binary, source, and manual page files for a command (UCB)

> whereis [–bmsu] [–BMS directory ... –f] filename

who—displays who is logged on the system

write—writes a message to another user

> write username [ttyname]

write copies lines from your terminal to another user's terminal.

xargs—constructs an argument list(s) and executes a command

xargs [flags] [command [initial–arguments]]

xargs allows you to transfer contents of files into a command line and dynamically build command lines.

EXAMPLE A.59

```
1   ls $1 | xargs -i -t mv $1/{} $2/{}
2   ls | xargs -p -l rm -rf
```

EXPLANATION

1   Moves all files from directory $1 to directory $2, and echos each *mv* command just before executing.
2   Prompts (*-p*) the user which files are to be removed one at a time and removes each one.

zcat—uncompress a compressed file to standard output. Same as *uncompress –c*

zcat [file . . .]

EXAMPLE A.60

```
zcat book.doc.Z | more
```

EXPLANATION

Uncompresses *book.doc.Z* and pipes the output to *more*.

B

Comparison of the Shells

B.1 The Shells Compared

Feature	Bourne	C	TC	Korn	Bash
Aliases	no	yes	yes	yes	yes
Advanced Pattern Matching	no	no	no	yes	yes
Command Line Editing	no	no	yes	yes*	yes
Directory Stacks (*pushd, popd*)	no	yes	yes	no	yes
Filename Completion	no	yes*	yes	yes	yes
Functions	yes	no	no	yes	yes
History	no	yes	yes	yes	yes
Job Control	no	yes	yes	yes	yes
Key Binding	no	no	yes	no	yes
Prompt Formatting	no	no	yes	no	yes
Spelling Correction	no	no	yes*	no	yes[†]

* not a default setting; must be set by the user.

[†] *cdspell* is a *shopt* option set to correct minor spelling errors in directory names when *cd* is used.

B.2 *tcsh* versus *csh*

The TC shell (*tcsh*) is an enhanced version of the Berkeley C shell (*csh*). Listed here are some of the new features.

- An enhanced history mechanism
- A built-in command line editor (*emacs* or *vi*) for editing the command line
- Formatting the prompts
- A spelling correction facility and special prompts for spelling correction and looping
- Enhanced and programmed word completion for completing commands, filenames, variables, usernames, etc.
- Ability to create and modify key bindings
- Automatic, periodic, and timed events (scheduled events, special aliases, automatic logout, terminal locking, etc.)
- New built-in commands (*hup, ls –F, newgrp, printenv, which, where,* etc.)
- New built-in variables (*gid, loginsh, oid, shlvl, tty, uid, version, HOST, REMOTEHOST, VENDOR, OSTYPE, MACHTYPE*)
- Read-only variables
- Better bug reporting facility

B.3 *bash* versus *sh*

The Bourne Again (*bash*) shell has the following features not found in the traditional Bourne shell (*sh*).

- Formatting the prompts
- History (*csh* style)
- Aliases
- A built-in command line editor (emacs or vi) for editing the command line
- Directory manipulation with *pushd* and *popd*
- *Csh*-type job control to stop or run jobs in the background, bring them to the foreground, etc. with command such as *bg, fg,* Ctrl-Z, etc.
- Tilde, brace, and parameter expansion
- Key bindings to customize key sequences
- Advanced pattern matching
- Arrays
- The *select* loop (from Korn shell)
- Many new built-in commands

Feature	csh/tcsh	Bourne	Bash	Korn
Variables:				
Assigning values to local variables	`set x = 5`	`x=5`	`x=5`	`x=5`
Assigning variable attributes			`declare or typeset`	`typeset`
Assigning values to environment variables	`setenv NAME Bob`	`NAME='Bob' ; export NAME`	`export NAME='Bob'`	`export NAME='Bob'`
Read-Only Variables:				

Accessing variables	`echo $NAME`
	`set var = net`
	`echo ${var}work`
	`network`
		`echo $NAME`
		`var=net`
		`echo ${var}work`
		`network`
			`echo $NAME`
			`var=net`
			`echo ${var}work`
			`network`
				`echo $NAME or print $NAME`
				`var=net`
				`print ${var}work`
				`network`

Number of characters	`echo $%var` (tcsh only)	N/A	`${#var}`	`${#var}`
Special Variables:				
PID of the process	`$$`	`$$`	`$$`	`$$`
Exit status	`$status, $?`	`$?`	`$?`	`$?`
Last background job	`$!` (tcsh only)	`$!`	`$!`	`$!`
Arrays:				

Assigning arrays	`set x = ( a b c )`	N/A	`y[0]='a'; y[2]='b';`
			`y[2]='c'`
			`fruit=(apples pears`
			`peaches plums)`
				`y[0]='a'; y[1]='b';`
				`y[2]='c'`
				`set -A fruit apples`
				`pears plums`

Accessing array elements	`echo $x[1] $x[2]`	N/A	`echo ${y[0]} ${y[1]}`	`print ${y[0]} ${y[1]}`
All elements	`echo $x or $x[*]`	N/A	`echo ${y[*]}, ${fruit[0]}`	`print ${y[*]}, ${fruit[0]}`
No. of elements	`echo $#x`	N/A	`echo ${#y[*]}`	`print ${#y[*]}`

Feature	csh/tcsh	Bourne	Bash	Korn
Command Substitution:				
Assigning output of command to variable	set d = `date`	d=`date`	d=$(date) or d=`date`	d=$(date) or d=`date`
Accessing values	echo $d echo $d[1], $d[2], ... echo $#d	echo $d	echo $d	print $d
Command Line Arguments (Positional Parameters):				
Accessing	$argv[1], $argv[2] or $1, $2 ...	$1, $2 ... $9	$1, $2, ... ${10} ...	$1, $2, ... ${10} ...
Setting positional parameters	N/A	set a b c set `date` echo $1 $2 ...	set a b c set `date` or set $(date) echo $1 $2 ...	set a b c set `date` or set $(date) print $1 $2 ...
No. of command line arguments	$#argv $# (tcsh)	$#	$#	$#
No. of characters in $arg[number]	$%1, $%2, (tcsh)	N/A	N/A	N/A
Metacharacters for Filename Expansion:				
Matches for:				
Single character	?	?	?	?
Zero or more characters	*	*	*	*
One character from a set	[abc]	[abc]	[abc]	[abc]
One character from a range of characters in a set	[a-c]	[a-c]	[a-c]	[a-c]

Metacharacters for Filename Expansion (continued):

Feature	csh/tcsh	Bourne	Bash	Korn
One character not in the set	`N/A` (csh) `[^abc]` (tcsh)	`[!abc]`	`[!abc]`	`[!abc]`
? matches zero or one occurrences of any pattern in the parentheses. The vertical bar represents an *or* condition; e.g., either 2 or 9. Matches *abc21*, *abc91*, or *abc1*.			`abc?(2|9)1`	`abc?(2|9)1`
Filenames not matching a pattern	`^pattern` (tcsh)			

I/O Redirection and Pipes:

Feature	csh/tcsh	Bourne	Bash	Korn
Command output redirected to a file	`cmd > file`	`cmd > file`	`cmd > file`	`cmd > file`
Command output redirected and appended to a file	`cmd >> file`	`cmd >> file`	`cmd >> file`	`cmd >> file`
Command input redirected from a file	`cmd < file`	`cmd < file`	`cmd < file`	`cmd < file`
Command errors redirected to a file	`(cmd > /dev/tty) >&errors`	`cmd 2>errors`	`cmd 2> file`	`cmd 2> errors`
Output and errors redirected to a file	`cmd >& file`	`cmd > file 2>&1`	`cmd >& file` or `cmd &> file` or `cmd > file 2>&1`	`cmd > file 2>&1`

Feature	csh/tcsh	Bourne	Bash	Korn
I/O Redirection and Pipes (continued):				
Assign output and ignore noclobber	`cmd >| file`	N/A	`cmd >| file`	`cmd >| file`

here document	`cmd << EOF`
	`input`
	`EOF`
		`cmd << EOF`
		`input`
		`EOF`
			`cmd << EOF`
			`input`
			`EOF`
				`cmd << EOF`
				`input`
				`EOF`

Pipe output of one command to input of another command	`cmd	cmd`	`cmd	cmd`	`cmd	cmd`	`cmd	cmd`
Pipe output and error to a command	`cmd |& cmd`	N/A	N/A	(See coprocesses)
Coprocess	N/A	N/A	N/A	`command |&`
Conditional statement	`cmd && cmd` `cmd || cmd`	`cmd && cmd` `cmd || cmd`	`cmd && cmd` `cmd || cmd`	`cmd && cmd` `cmd || cmd`
Reading from the Keyboard:				

Read a line of input and store into variable(s)	`set var = $<`
	`set var = 'line'`
		`read var`
		`read var1 var2...`
			`read var`
			`read var1 var2...`
			`read`
			`read -p prompt`
			`read -a arrayname`
				`read var`
				`read var1 var2...`
				`read`
				`read var?"Enter value"`

Arithmetic:				
Perform calculation	`@ var = 5 + 1`	``var=`expr 5 + 1` ``	`(( var = 5 + 1 ))` `let var=5+1`	`(( var = 5 + 1 ))` `let var=5+1`

Feature	csh/tcsh	Bourne	Bash	Korn
Tilde Expansion:				
Represent home directory of user	~username	N/A	~username	~username
Represent home directory	~	N/A	~	~
Represent present working directory	N/A	N/A	~+	~+
Represent previous working directory	N/A	N/A	~-	~-
Aliases:				
Create an alias	alias m more	N/A	alias m=more	alias m=more
List aliases	alias	N/A	alias, alias -p	alias, alias -t
Remove an alias	unalias m	N/A	unalias m	unalias m
History:				
Set history	set history = 25	N/A	automatic or HISTSIZE=25	automatic or HISTSIZE=25
Display numbered history list	history		history, fc -l	history, fc -l
Display portion of list selected by number	history 5		history 5	history 5 10 history -5
Reexecute a command	!! (last command) !5 (5th command) !v (last command starting with v)		!! (last command) !5 (5th command) !v (last command starting with v)	r (last command) r5 (5th command) r v (last command starting with v)
Set interactive editor	N/A (csh) bindkey -v or bindkey -e (tcsh)	N/A	set -o vi set -o emacs	set -o vi set -o emacs

Feature	csh/tcsh	Bourne	Bash	Korn
Signals:				
Command	`onintr`	`trap`	`trap`	`trap`
Initialization Files:				
Executed at login	`.login`	`.profile`	`.bash_profile`	`.profile`
Executed every time the shell is invoked	`.cshrc`	N/A	`BASH_ENV=.bashrc` (or other filename) (bash 2.x) `ENV=.bashrc`	`ENV=.kshrc` (or other filename)
Functions:				
Define a function	N/A	`fun() { commands; }`	`function fun { commands; }`	`function fun { commands; }`
Call a function	N/A	`fun` `fun param1 param2 ...`	`fun` `fun param1 param2 ...`	`fun` `fun param1 param2 ...`

Programming Constructs:

if conditional:

csh/tcsh:
```
if ( expression )
then
    commands
endif

if { ( command ) }
then
    commands
endif
```

Bourne:
```
if [ expression ]
then
    commands
fi

if command
then
    commands
fi
```

Bash:
```
if [[ string expression ]]
then
    commands
fi

if (( numeric expression ))
then
    commands
fi
```

Korn:
```
if [[ string expression ]]
then
    commands
fi

if (( numeric expression ))
then
    commands
fi
```

if/else conditional:

csh/tcsh:
```
if ( expression )
then
    commands
else
    commands
endif
```

Bourne:
```
if command
then
    commands
else
    commands
fi
```

Bash:
```
if command
then
    commands
else
    ...
fi
```

Korn:
```
if command
then
    commands
else
    ...
fi
```

Programming Constructs (continued):

Feature	csh/tcsh	Bourne	Bash	Korn
if/else/elseif conditional	```if (expression) then
commands
else if (expression) then
commands
else
commands
endif```	```if command
then
commands
elif command
then
commands
else
commands
fi```	```if command
then
commands
elif command
then
commands
else
commands
fi```	```if command
then
commands
elif command
then
commands
else
commands
fi```
goto	```goto label
...
label:```	N/A	N/A	N/A
switch and *case*	```switch ("$value")
case pattern1:
commands
breaksw
case pattern2:
commands
breaksw
default:
commands
breaksw
endsw```	```case "$value" in
pattern1) commands
;;
pattern2) commands
;;
*) commands
;;
esac```	```case "$value" in
pattern1) commands
;;
pattern2) commands
;;
*) commands
;;
esac```	```case "$value" in
pattern1) commands
;;
pattern2) commands
;;
*) commands
;;
esac```

Loops:

Feature	csh/tcsh	Bourne	Bash	Korn
while loops	```while (expression)
commands
end```	```while command
do
command
done```	```while command
do
command
done```	```while command
do
commands
done```
for/foreach	```foreach var (wordlist)
commands
end```	```for var in wordlist
do
commands
done```	```for var in wordlist
do
commands
done```	```for var in wordlist
do
commands
done```

Feature	csh/tcsh	Bourne	Bash	Korn
Loops (continued):				

until		`until command`
		`do`
		`    commands`
		`done`
			`until command`
			`do`
			`    commands`
			`done`
				`until command`
				`do`
				`    commands`
				`done`

repeat	`repeat 3 "echo hello"`
	`hello`
	`hello`
	`hello`
		N/A	N/A	N/A

select	N/A	N/A	`PS3="Please select a menu item"`
			`select var in wordlist`
			`do`
			`    commands`
			`done`
				`PS3="Please select a menu item"`
				`select var in wordlist`
				`do`
				`    commands`
				`done`

appendix

C

Steps for Using Quoting Correctly

C.1 Backslash

1. Precedes a character and escapes that character.
2. Same as putting single quotes around one character.

C.2 Single Quotes

1. Must be matched.
2. Protect all metacharacters from interpretation except the following:
     a. Itself.
     b. Exclamation point (*csh* only).
     c. Backslash.

Examples:

C Shell	Bourne Shell	Korn Shell
echo '$><%^&*'	echo '$*&!><?'	echo '$*&!><?'
echo 'I need $5.00\!'	echo 'I need \$5.00!'	echo 'I need \$5.00!'
echo 'She cried, "Help"'	echo 'She cried, "Help"'	echo 'She cried, "Help"'
echo '\\\\'	echo '\\\\'	print '\\\\'
\\\\	\\	\\

C.3 Double Quotes

1. Must be matched.
2. Protect all metacharacters from interpretation except the following:
   a. Itself.
   b. Exclamation point (*csh* only).
   c. $ used for variable substitution.
   d. ` ` Backquotes for command substitution.

Examples:

C Shell	Bourne Shell	Korn Shell
echo "Hello $LOGNAME\!"	echo "Hello $LOGNAME!"	print "Hello $LOGNAME!"
echo "I don't care"	echo "I don't care"	print "I don't care"
echo "The date is `date`"	echo "The date is `date`"	print "The date is $(date)"
echo "\\\\"	echo "\\\\"	print "\\\\"
\\\\	\	\

C.4 Combining Quotes

The end result is to be able to embed the shell variable in the *awk* command line and have the shell expand the variable without interfering with *nawk*'s field designators, $1 and $2.

C.5 Setting the Shell Variable

```
name="Jacob Savage"     (Bourne and Korn Shell)
set name = "Jacob Savage"  ( C Shell )
```

(The line from the datafile)
Jacob Savage:408-298-7732:934 La Barbara Dr. , San Jose, CA:02/27/78:500000

(The *nawk* command line)
nawk -F: '$1 ~ /^' "$name" '/{print $2}' datafile

(Output)
408-298-7732

Step 1:

Test your knowledge of the UNIX command at the command line before plugging in any shell variables.

> **nawk -F: '$1 ~ /^Jacob Savage/{print $2}' filename**

(Output)
408-298-7732

Step 2:

Plug in the shell variable without changing anything else. Leave all quotes as they were.

> **nawk -F: '$1 ~ /^$name/{print $2}' datafile**

Starting at the left-hand side of the *awk* command leave the first quote as is; right before the shell dollar sign in *$name*, place another single quote. Now the first quote is matched and all text within these two quotes is protected from shell interference. The variable is exposed. Now put another single quote right after the *e* in *$name*. This starts another matched set of single quotes ending after *awk*'s closing curly brace. Everything within this set of quotes is also protected from shell interpretation.

> **nawk -F: '$1 ~ /^'$name'/{print $2}' datafile**

Step 3:

Enclose the shell variable in a set of double quotes. This allows the variable to be expanded but the value of the variable will be treated as single string if it contains whitespace. The whitespace must be protected so that the command line is parsed properly.

> **nawk -F: '$1 ~ /^' "$name" '/{print $2}' datafile**

Count the number of quotes. There should be an even number of single quotes and an even number of double quotes.

Example:

> **oldname="Ellie Main"**
> **newname="Eleanor Quigley"**

1. Make sure the command works.

> **nawk -F: '/^Ellie Main/{$1="Eleanor Quigley"; print $0}' datafile**

2. Plug in the variables.

> **nawk -F: '/^$oldname/{$1="$newname"; print $0}' datafile**

3.   Play the quoting game. Starting at the first single quote at the left, move across the line until you come to the variable $oldname and place another single quote just before the dollar sign. Put another single quote right after the last letter in the variable name.

Now move to the right and place another single quote right before the dollar sign in $newname. Put another single quote after the last character in $newname.

nawk -F: '/^'$oldname'/{$1=" '$newname' "; print $0}' datafile

4.   Count the number of single quotes. If the number of single quotes is an even number, each quote has a matching quote. If not, you have forgotten a step.

5.   Enclose each of the shell variables in double quotes. The double quotes are placed snugly around the shell variable.

nawk -F: '/^' "$oldname"'/{$1=" ' "$newname" ' "; print $0}' datafile

INDEX

About the Author

Ellie Quigley is the author of *Perl by Example*, *UNIX Shells by Example*, and *Linux Shells by Example*. She is also the creator of the world's number one interactive Perl course, *Perl Multimedia Cyber Classroom*. A leading instructor and trainer, her courses in Perl and UNIX shell programming at the University of California Santa Cruz Extension Program and at Sun Microsystems have become legendary throughout Silicon Valley.

About the CD-ROM

Script files and datafiles are contained in separate directories for each chapter, chap01 through chap13.

The script names and datafile names are the same as in the book.

NOTE: Some of the early scripts send mail to a specified list of persons, so you may choose not to run these scripts (or you may want to change the list to just include your own e-mail address to ensure it works okay).

For example, to run Example 1.6, just change directory to chap01 and run "ex_1.6" from the command line. (You may need to run "chmod +x ex_1.6" first to ensure that it has execute permission. If so, you'll have to do this for every script file.) The script "ex_1.6" requires a datafile named "guests" which is provided in the same chap01 directory.

CHAPTERS 7 THROUGH 10:

Chapters 7 through 10 have many examples, so the example files are separated into subdirectories by example number. For example, Chapter 7 contains subdirectories named:

    Ex_7.05-7.40
    Ex_7.49-7.60
    Ex_7.74-7.80
    Ex_7.81-7.105

For example, to run Example 7.5 requires the datafile named "employees" which is contained in directory chap07/Ex_7.05-7.40. You can change to that directory and run the command line shown in the book for Example 7.5.

MINOR SCRIPT CHANGES:

Lastly, a few of the scripts in the book ask for a datafile to be in a certain directory. The CD version of each of these scripts has been changed to look for the datafile in the same directory as the script. This minor change was made to enable each script to run immediately without further modification.

For instance, Example 1.6 in the book has a line:
    set guestfile = ~/shell/guests

The CD version of the script has been changed to:
    set guestfile = ./guests

HAPPY SHELLING!!